ROUTLEDGE INTERNATI(
HANDBOOK OF GOLF SCI

Golf is one of the world's major sports and consequently the focus of world-class scientific research. This landmark publication is the most comprehensive book ever published on the science of golf, covering every sub-discipline from physiology, biomechanics and psychology to strength and conditioning, youth development and equipment design.

Showcasing original research from leading golf scientists across the globe, it examines the fundamental science underpinning the game and demonstrates how it can be applied in practice to improve and develop players. Each chapter provides a definitive account of the current state of knowledge in a particular area of golf science, addressing the limitations of existing research, presenting new areas for development and discussing the implications for coaches, players, scientists and the wider golfing public. Truly international in scope, the variety of topics explored include:

- biomechanics and equipment
- skill learning and technology
- performance development
- psychological techniques for success
- the golfing body.

This is an essential reference for any student or researcher with an interest in the game, or any coach or professional looking to improve their knowledge.

Martin Toms is a senior lecturer in the School of Sport, Exercise and Rehabilitation at the University of Birmingham, UK. He has a PhD in Youth Sport and Developmental Socialisation from Loughborough University and focuses upon the youth sport and talent experience. In golf, he has worked across the world in golf education and has been involved in European projects exploring occupational standards within the golf industry, as well as teaching and researching talent development in the game. He has been working with the PGA (GB&I) since 2000 on their education programmes, and currently has over a dozen postgraduate students researching social scientific aspects of golf. Martin is a board member of the World Scientific Congress of Golf and a regular speaker at academic and golf-related conferences. He is also involved with universities across the world in the development of academic content and golf-related courses linked to PGA programmes. He is currently Editor-in-Chief of *The International Journal of Golf Science*. His PhD (Loughborough University) is in the field of youth sport.

Section Editors:

Sasho MacKenzie is an associate professor in the Department of Human Kinetics at St. Francis Xavier University, Canada. He holds a PhD in biomechanics from the University of Saskatchewan, which focused on 3D forward dynamics simulation of the golf swing. His research focuses on golf biomechanics, equipment optimisation and the most advantageous training techniques. He consults for several entities in the golf industry, including Ping and FootJoy.

Sam Robertson is head of research and innovation for the Western Bulldogs Australian Football Club and an associate professor in sport science at Victoria University in Melbourne, Australia. He is also the leader of the Analytics and Technology research group within the Institute of Sport, Exercise and Active Living.

Marc Lochbaum is a professor of sport and exercise psychology at Texas Tech University, USA, and studies elementary school physical activity programming, achievement goals in sport and physical activity, and meta-analyses in sport and exercise psychology. He maintains a visiting position at the Olympic Research Institute in Jyväskylä, Finland. To date, his research funding totals over four million USD. He is an avid golfer.

Kieran Kingston is a senior lecturer in sport psychology and research methods in the Cardiff School of Sport at Cardiff Metropolitan University, UK. His interests in teaching and research are in the development and maintenance of confidence and motivation in sport and their links with psychological well-being and performance. He has worked as a consultant with team and individual athletes; and as a category 1 golfer for the past 30 years, he has a particular interest in the psychology of golf.

Andrea Fradkin is an associate professor at Bloomsburg University, USA, and has been researching golf for 18 years. She received her PhD in epidemiology and preventive medicine at Monash University in Melbourne, Australia, and completed a post-doctoral fellowship at the University of Pittsburgh. Her research is an amalgamation of epidemiology, injury prevention, performance improvement and biomechanics.

'Over the last 20 years, golf at the highest level has moved from a game to a sport. The highest standards of preparation and the professionalism of the athlete have become increasingly important determinants of success. Today you hear far more emphasis on preparing to succeed and performance development than technical coaching. This is more apparent now than at any time in the history of the sport. The margins between success and failure are becoming finer and so understanding the "science" of golf is key to anyone involved in playing or developing players — as this outstanding book explains.' – *Martin Slumbers, Chief Executive, The R&A*

'The *Routledge International Handbook of Golf Science* provides an extraordinary perspective on our sport through 39 separate research papers. By covering biomechanics, participation, skill acquisition, performance and the health benefits of golf, this is a valuable, data-driven resource.' – *Steve Mona, CEO, World Golf Foundation*

ROUTLEDGE INTERNATIONAL HANDBOOK OF GOLF SCIENCE

Edited by Martin Toms

Part editors:
Sasho MacKenzie
Sam Robertson
Marc Lochbaum
Kieran Kingston
Andrea Fradkin

Routledge
Taylor & Francis Group

LONDON AND NEW YORK

First published 2018 by Routledge

2 Park Square, Milton Park, Abingdon, Oxfordshire OX14 4RN
52 Vanderbilt Avenue, New York, NY 10017

Routledge is an imprint of the Taylor & Francis Group, an informa business

First issued in paperback 2020

British Library Cataloguing-in-Publication Data
A catalogue record for this book is available from the British Library

Library of Congress Cataloging-in-Publication Data
A catalog record for this book has been requested

ISBN: 978-1-138-18912-6 (hbk)
ISBN: 978-0-367-89688-1 (pbk)

Typeset in Bembo and Minion
by Book Now Ltd, London

CONTENTS

Contents

Contents

FIGURES

TABLES

CONTRIBUTORS

Landry Actkinson, Dallas, USA

Charles H. Adler, Mayo Clinic Arizona, USA

Max Adler, Golf Digest, USA

Eric Alpenfels, Pinehurst Resort & Country Club, USA

Christopher P. Bertram, University of Fraser Valley, USA

Matthew W. Bridge, University of Birmingham, UK

Laura M. Carey, SportUK Institute of Sport, UK

David Carless, Leeds Beckett University, UK

Howie J. Carson, University of Central Lancashire, UK

Joe Causer, Liverpool John Moores University, UK

Guillaume Chauvel, Université de Bourgogne Franche-Comté, France

Amanda Cheetham, University of Arizona, USA

Bob Christina, University of North Carolina-Greensboro, USA

Graeme L. Close, Liverpool John Moores University, UK

Dave Collins, University of Central Lancashire, UK

Debbie J. Crews, Arizona State University, USA

Jennifer Cumming, University of Birmingham, UK

Kitrina Douglas, Leeds Beckett University, UK

Kerrie Evans, Griffith University, Australia

Malcolm M. Fairweather, SportUK Institute of Sport, UK

Damian Farrow, Victoria University, Australia

Charles Fitzsimmons, Western University, Canada

Gerard J. Fogarty, University of Southern Queensland, Australia

Andrea Fradkin, Bloomsburg University, USA

Andrea J. Furst, Mental Notes Consulting, UK

Paul S. Glazier, National Sports Institute of Malaysia, Malaysia

Sandy Gordon, The University of Western Australia, Australia

Mark A. Guadagnoli, University of Nevada, USA

Amy Harris, Minnesota State University, USA

Roger Hawkes, European Tour Golf, UK

John Hellström, Swedish Golf Federation, Sweden

Sean A. Horan, Griffith University, Australia

Robin C. Jackson, Loughborough University, UK

Evan Jenkins, University of Edinburgh, UK

Zişan Kazak Çetinkalp, Ege University, Turkey

Kieran Kingston, Cardiff Metropolitan University, UK

Niamh Kitching, Limerick Institute of Technology, Ireland

Peter F. Lamb, University of Otago, New Zealand

David M. Lindsay, University of Calgary, Canada

Marc Lochbaum, Texas Tech University, USA

Scott K. Lynn, California State University at Fullerton, USA

Bryan A. McCullick, University of Georgia, USA

Sasho MacKenzie, St. Francis Xavier University, Canada

Ronald G. Marteniuk, Simon Fraser University, USA

Rich Masters, University of Waikato, New Zealand

Nicholas Middleton, Zen Golf, UK

Andrew Morrison, Edinburgh Napier University, UK

James P. Morton, Liverpool John Moores University, UK

Andrew Murray, University of Edinburgh, UK

Jay-Lee Nair, Mental Notes Consulting, Singapore

Robert J. Neal, Golf BioDymanics Inc., USA

Elliott Newell, University of Birmingham, UK

Steven Orr, University of Central Lancashire, UK

Aaron L. Pauls, University of Nevada, USA

Jamie Poolton, Leeds Beckett University, UK

Jamie Pugh, Liverpool John Moores University, UK

Richard J. Rendleman, Jr., University of North Carolina at Chapel Hill, USA

Sam Robertson, Victoria University, Australia

Warren Ryan, Minnesota Golf Association, USA

Daniel Sachau, Minnesota State University, USA

Paul G. Schempp, University of Georgia, USA

Luke Simmering, Legasus Group, USA

Patrick R. Thomas, Griffith University, Australia

Martin Toms, University of Birmingham, UK

Anthony A. Vandervoort, University of Western Ontario, Canada

Sam Vine, University of Exeter, UK

Eric S. Wallace, Ulster University, UK

Colin A. Webster, University of South Carolina, USA

Fredrik Weibull, University of Birmingham, UK

Robert E. Wharen, Jr., Mayo Clinic, Florida, USA

A. Mark Williams, University of Utah, USA

Mark Wilson, University of Exeter, UK

Jonathan Wright, Professional Golfers' Association of Great Britain & Ireland, UK

Will Wu, Long Beach State University, USA

Gabriele Wulf, University of Nevada, Las Vegas, USA

EDITOR'S INTRODUCTION

The study of golf as an academic discipline is one that has emerged and developed significantly over the past two decades. Through the development of the field of sports science, kinesiology, biomechanics, physiology, psychology, coaching, engineering and also medicine, the interest and focus upon golf has grown rapidly. The growth of the game across the world has also raised the profile of the sport and its associated research interest and the wider industry. It is not just a sport however, but a vehicle for physical activity, social engagement, health (both physical and mental) and rehabilitation. The multi-billion-dollar industry engages researchers, academics, policy-makers and coaches from across many disciplines as the game develops, with mega-events such as the games (re)inclusion in the Olympics in 2016 continuing to increase this interest.

Away from the playing of the game, golf itself has become a programme of study within university education, with specific golf science/business programmes having been established in universities across the world at both undergraduate and postgraduate levels. With the development and engagement of the key organisations involved in golf (such as the national Professional Golfers' Associations) forming relationships with universities, this has also ensured that golf training at all levels now includes and involves cutting-edge research and academic knowledge as part of its core. As such, there is now a plethora of undergraduate and postgraduate students (at masters and doctoral levels) now exploring the game from multidisciplinary and interdisciplinary angles. This is an essential part of the modern game and highlights how it has developed from the early days of (mainly) engineering and equipment technology perspectives (as can be seen in the early 'Science and Golf' textbooks from the 1990s).

The aim of the *Routledge International Handbook of Golf Science* is to bring in key academics in the field to produce summaries of the existing research (i.e. not simply provide an inclusion of empirical papers) in such a way that it can be used by students, researchers and practitioners (e.g. those involved in coaching, management, sports science and other golf support roles) to help develop the game at both applied and theoretical levels. The chapters herein provide a flavour of the key topics currently under examination in the sport. The chapters are by no means exhaustive and do not claim to cover all areas of the game that are being investigated at the moment. Rather, they provide the reader with an idea of the current breadth of research and topics under investigation at the time of publication. I certainly welcome future proposals for reviews of literature for the next edition of the book from those involved in the academic study of the game.

The handbook intends to provide a crucial and timely contribution to the essential research and student-focused literature in the area of golf. It features chapters written by leading scholars and experts from across the world. The handbook examines the most important areas within golf research and development as defined by some of the experts in their fields. Each chapter provides a definitive account of the state of knowledge on their individual subject area and provides a synopsis of existing research as well as suggests areas where this can be developed, considering the implications for coaches, players, scientists and the wider golfing public. This is very deliberately a multidisciplinary (and interdisciplinary) handbook and will not only fill the void of the 'Science and Golf' texts (from the proceedings of the World Scientific Congress of Golf from 1990), but also extends its remit beyond pure science to incorporate other key areas of the game that have so far been exempt from these publications. The book deliberately does not extend into the area of the business of golf, course management, the environment or course design, but does acknowledge that these are key aspects of the game in themselves but can be found in other publications. It is, as already stated, rather an exploration of some of the areas of the game that have developed over the past few decades.

The prospective audience for this text includes students undertaking golf-related training programmes across the world (including those undertaking PGA qualifications within their own country); students studying sports science and associated degree programmes; policy-makers; sports scientists; coaches; golf federations; governing bodies; performance directors; academy managers – and interested golfers themselves.

The book has been divided into six parts and the chapters presented in a way to balance the contributions. That is not to say that the contents, chapters and topic areas do not overlap between parts/authors, but that these were an appropriate way to structure the book for the reader. Each part has a detailed introduction to it written by the part editors, and these act as an initial summary of the chapters. Part I highlights some of the key issues regarding the development and importance of the use of *Biomechanics and Equipment* and their impact upon the performance of technique for the golfer. Part II explores some of the research linked to SL and T in the game and also the role these have played in the game. Part III looks at a number of areas of research and knowledge around PD and how this can be developed further. Part IV looks at the pivotal role of PT for S in the game and also the importance of mental health. Part V identifies the growing area of the physiology on TGB and its impact upon the game. Lastly, Part VI explores the developing work of social science in the game, and in particular how this has an impact upon understanding the GiT. There are clearly links between and within each part, as there are other areas of research that could have been included in this book. However, as stated earlier, the areas missing in this edition are certainly ones that could be considered in the next edition.

It has been a pleasure to work with so many colleagues to put this book together – in particular, the chance to produce an inter- and multidisciplinary text with so many experts providing a review of the current research in the field. I suspect that over the next decade, research will become even more focused upon particular areas of the game as national and international agendas change and develop, not to mention the inclusion of the game in the Olympic cycle. However things develop, the role of the individual player will be central within the research that takes place, and I welcome the increasing volume of empirical work in all areas of the game. I hope that those of you reading this book will find answers, but also raise additional questions that can challenge the researchers, academics, policy-makers and players themselves. It is that endeavour that has created the quarter of a million words in this (first) edition of the golf science book. May that develop more extensively in the future!

Martin Toms
University of Birmingham, UK

ACKNOWLEDGEMENTS

It is important to note our thanks to the chapter authors of this book, and to those involved in the process of editing, reviewing and supporting the production process. More specifically, we cannot forget those who have developed the science of the game through study, research and participation over the past decades. This book acknowledges the work of those involved in all aspects of the game, both now and in the future.

PART I

Biomechanics and equipment

Introduction

Helping golfers play better is a goal for everyone in the golf industry. This is true for coaches, equipment companies, and organizations focused on growing the game. The movements a golfer makes to advance the ball and the equipment used in that effort are two crucial pieces of a complex puzzle that represents golf performance. This part of the book will focus on selected topics within the biomechanics and equipment technology aspects of golf performance.

This part opens with a chapter by Morrison and Wallace on the connection between golf coaches and golf biomechanics research. The study of biomechanics has certainly resulted in knowledge generation, which has translated into improved performance across a wide spectrum of sporting skills. However, knowledge generation is not sufficient if it sits on the shelf in a researcher's office. This knowledge must be clearly relayed to coaches who can put it into practice with the athlete. It is probably unrealistic to expect the average golf instructor to be able to access and understand research disseminated in a scientific journal format. However, even if research findings on golf biomechanics are made more accessible and digestible (perhaps this part is a small step in that direction), the obligation still exists for the golf instructor to have sufficient knowledge of the underlying biomechanical principles (e.g., Newton's laws). Unfortunately, a clear educational path currently does not exist in this regard. A further issue is the type of research questions that are being addressed. Are golf biomechanics researchers attempting to answer questions that are deemed relevant by the practitioner? Are the practitioners focused on the most relevant questions?

Lynn and Wu focus their contribution on one particular area of biomechanics research. They argue that the application of ground reaction force and pressure information in golf swing instruction has recently become popular. The ground reaction forces acting at the golfer's feet – along with gravity and air resistance, which are secondary – determine the linear and angular momentum of the golfer + club system, which will govern how the clubhead is delivered to the ball. The use of pressure- and force-recording devices to quantify a golfer's kinetic interaction with the ground has become commonplace among golf instructors. A clear indication of this is that the terms 'pressure shift' and 'weight shift' are now clearly delineated in most popular golf instructor education platforms. Previously, the concept of weight shift was an ambiguous mix of centre of mass motion and foot pressure. These devices are typically used to provide feedback during a golf lesson.

For example, an instructor may explain to a golfer how they should push into the ground to change their ground reaction force pattern, which will subsequently alter their body movement and club delivery. However, while it can be helpful for the golfer to think of the ground reaction forces as external forces they can manipulate to achieve a desired movement pattern, an argument can also be made for a contradictory view. The forces the ground applies to the feet are merely a 'reaction' to the forces generated by the body's muscles. If the golfer makes the 'correct' pattern of movement, as a result of the proper sequence and magnitude of muscle contractions, then the ground reaction forces will simply be an inevitable byproduct of the process. As such, an equally viable focus of instruction can be centred on communicating how the golfer should move his/her body, which is the focus of subsequent chapters in this part.

Certainly, much of the golf instruction literature is focussed on executing the correct sequence of movements and, in particular, has the golfer think about generating specific kinematic patterns. Two chapters in this part take a critical look at the kinematic patterns of the golf swing from different perspectives. In the first of these parts, Neal lays the framework for the terminology and fundamentals of the concept. An in-depth comparison of the kinematic sequence graphs of an expert and novice golfer provides the reader with a solid foundation to explore the concept further. Neal demonstrates the pervasiveness of a proximal-to-distal sequence of movement across many sports and with many methods of measurement and analysis, which speaks to the robustness of the phenomenon as principal for increasing the speed of a distal segment or implement. Lamb and Glazier offer a thorough treatment of the theory of the proximal-to-distal movement pattern, as well as a critical look at the experimental and computer simulation research that has led to the continued discussion of the topic in the golf instruction industry. Importantly, both chapters clearly imply that a perfect proximal-to-distal kinematic sequence is not a requirement to play golf at the highest level. There are a couple of factors that can help explain the discrepancy between computer simulation findings, which seem to unequivocally support the theory, and the measured movement patterns of the world's best golfers. The first is that, until recently, forward dynamics models of the golf swing (capable of undergoing optimization) have not included a 'trail' side in the model. MacKenzie and Normore (2015) used a 12-segment golfer-club model with 34 degrees of freedom to demonstrate that a forward dynamics model – with a trailside connection to the club – still generates a proximal-to-distal sequence when optimized for clubhead speed. However, it was also shown that a clubhead speed within 2 mph of the optimal could be attained with a disruption to the proximal-to-distal peaking order. The disruption was similar in extent to that of PGA Tour players who do not portray an 'ideal' sequence. The second is that, inherently, forward dynamic models have no regard for the trade-off between actions that maximize clubhead speed and actions that maximize the delivery of the clubhead in the intended manner. The longest drivers on the PGA Tour use swing techniques with the driver that generate clubhead speeds less than 130 mph. By comparison, any reasonably talented long drive competitor would have a clubhead speed well in excess of this mark with the same club. While the physical characteristics of the individual athletes certainly play a large role, differences in swing technique and effort level can be clearly observed. A technique and an effort level that heavily optimize for clubhead speed will likely be associated with an increase in clubhead delivery variability, which outweighs the benefit of the increased clubhead speed on an actual golf course. The more encompassing concept of swing variability is explored by Lamb and Glazier in their second contribution to this part.

Golf performance is strongly associated with the ability to strike the ball with the required clubhead kinematics (e.g., velocity, impact location on face, and orientation) to produce the intended ball trajectory. An increase in the variability in delivered clubhead kinematics, relative to that required, will result in more strokes to complete a round of golf. It seems intuitive that minimizing the swing-to-swing variability in biomechanical variables that comprise a stroke (e.g., center of pressure trace, amount of forearm supination, and force applied to the grip) would be associated with delivering the clubhead closer to the required manner. However, Glazier and Lamb effectively argue that, while relatively high levels of variability in swing mechanics are likely detrimental, working towards a swing void of mechanical variability is at odds with our current understanding of how humans organize their actions to generate a repeatable outcome (e.g., ball trajectory). Consider the example of two golfers, Alan and Bob, who have differing amounts of variability in lead forearm supination and lead upper arm external rotation at impact. For simplicity, assume that both golfers have *average* supination and external rotation angles of 0° at impact and that when both angles are 0°, the clubface is orientated as intended. Let us further assume that a change in either angle will influence the clubface angle in the same manner. Alan has a variability of ±2° for both angles, and Bob has a variability of ±4°. It seems logical to assume that Alan would have less variability in the delivered face angle. However, it is quite possible that the opposite is true if Bob functionally 'cancels out' deviations in these 2 degrees of freedom, while Alan does not. For example, perhaps Alan always has forearm and upper arm angles that match in sign (e.g., +1° supination and +1° external rotation), which would meaningfully change the face angle from that intended. Conversely, Bob always has forearm and upper arm angles that are opposite in sign ((e.g., −3° supination and +3° external rotation), which would result in delivering the clubhead as intended. As espoused by Glazier and Lamb, scenarios such as this suggest that more emphasis should be placed on understanding the role of variability in the execution of a golf swing. Recent advances in the precision of golf swing measurement technologies, coupled with a simultaneous increase in their availability, have made this type of research more tenable.

The routine use of ball flight monitors, in particular, has allowed coaches and club fitters to tweak golf club components, such as the shaft, to fit the individual golfer. Without being able to precisely quantify how relatively small changes to shaft parameters can have meaningful improvements in ball flight, club fitting would be much less commonplace. The golf shaft is the mediator between the golfer and the clubhead during the swing, and the final chapter of this part, written by me, explores the numerous shaft parameters that can be manipulated to influence ball flight and ball flight repeatability.

Sasho MacKenzie
St. Francis Xavier University, Canada

Reference

MacKenzie, S. & Normore, R. (2015) How the Golfer Transfers Energy to the Club, *International Journal of Golf Science*, 3 (Supplemental), S57–S58.

1

THE GOLF COACHING–BIOMECHANICS INTERFACE

Andrew Morrison and Eric S. Wallace

Introduction

The fundamental goal of golf coaching is to improve the performance of the player. The successful translation of sports science knowledge to golf coaching is dependent on the coach's level of understanding of sports science, the perceived relevance of the specific sports science discipline, and the communication process between research findings and golf coaching practice. A biomechanical understanding of a skill is often deemed essential for a coach, where the technical execution of the skill, such as in golf, is the key determinant of success. However, it is acknowledged (Coleman, 1999) that existing biomechanics knowledge has not yet been fully integrated into golf coaching practice. The problem arises from the need for researchers to exchange ideas and findings via accepted scientific methods that result in peer-reviewed publications that are neither readily accessible to nor understandable by coaches. Furthermore, questions arising from coaches' field experiences are not usually formulated into research studies by researchers. Bridging the gap between sports science research and the coaching process that integrates biomechanics knowledge in technique analysis is an ongoing challenge. This chapter explores the knowledge levels and opinions of coaches on the role of sports science, with a focus on biomechanics, the barriers to the application of biomechanics in golf coaching, and the communication process among coach, player, and biomechanist. Key features of technique analysis, including biomechanical qualitative and quantitative methods, and a range of researched outcome variables are contextualised in relation to coaching practice. Available models and guidelines for the successful application of biomechanics in golf coaching are presented, leading to implications for the game.

Theory–practice divide

A theory–practice divide is perceived to exist between sport science, in general, and coaching. Coleman (1999) suggests that there are two major issues in the application of biomechanics to coaching. Firstly, he suggests that the understanding of Newton's laws is poor, a contention that more recently has also been observed among college students (Yılmaz & Yalçın, 2012). This inhibits the understanding of what is actually happening in a biomechanical system. Secondly, a sound mathematical knowledge base is required to understand quantitative analysis.

While physiological and psychological studies might be intuitively understood by coaches, mathematically based biomechanics papers can often be incomprehensible (Coleman, 1999). Research carried out to investigate this issue can be summarised into three approaches: the sources of coaching knowledge, the differences in goals between coaching and sports science, and models to bridge the resultant gap. The following section is not an exhaustive review of the literature, but it does give examples of relevant pieces of research.

Coaches' knowledge of the sports sciences

The majority of studies on golf coaching have been more concerned with the coaching process (e.g., Schempp et al., 2007), characteristics of golf coaches (Schempp et al., 1998), and the coach–athlete relationship (Jowett & Nezlek, 2011; Toner et al., 2012) than with the application of sports science to coaching per se. Nevertheless, several studies have investigated the preferred sources of coaches' knowledge of the sports sciences across a range of sports, which provide useful background and context to the topic of interfacing biomechanics and golf coaching. Schempp et al. (1998) found that the predominant source of coaching knowledge came from other teachers and teaching experience. More recently, informal sources such as other coaches, along with self-reflection and experience, were cited as the preferred sources (Erickson et al., 2008). In comparison, the perceived role of sports science as a source of knowledge has been extremely limited. Gould et al. (1990) administered a questionnaire to 130 US elite coaches from predominantly Olympic sports on their educational needs. Of the eight bodies of knowledge identified within sport (skills of the sport, strategies of the sport, sport pedagogy, sport psychology, sport physiology, sport medicine, sport biomechanics, and sport law), the coaches ranked sports biomechanics seventh in their understanding of the topics. The only subject that ranked lower was sport law. It is then unsurprising that the coaches also ranked sports biomechanics seventh among the areas they most actively studied, just ahead of sports medicine. These findings were corroborated by Abrahams et al. (2006) in their development of a coaching schematic. By interviewing 16 coaches about their coaching process, they were able to ascertain what coaches deemed to be 'required knowledge'. The main categories were defined in order of the frequency that they were mentioned: sport-specific knowledge, communication, skill acquisition, and the 'ologies' – referring to sports science (psychology, physiology, and biomechanics). Biomechanics was the least referenced within the 'ologies' category. The coaches in this study were from a range of sports, some of which could be considered high in technical analysis, such as athletics and cycling. More recently, Mooney et al. (2015) found similar results with US swimming coaches. Surveying 298 Level 3 Swimming coaches, Mooney et al. (2015) found that biomechanics ranked last among sports science provision for perceived importance for inclusion in a training programme. Although qualitative analysis of 2D video was used regularly by the coaches, all other forms of biomechanical analysis were not routinely used.

These studies appear to suggest that biomechanics was not highly valued as a source of knowledge in coaching compared to the other sports science disciplines. Moreover, little appears to have changed over the past 25 years.

Other studies have approached the problem from a different perspective, with a comparison of views between coaches and sports scientists. Williams and Kendall (2007) compared how elite Australian coaches and sports science researchers from a variety of sports perceived the research needs of elite coaching practice. There appeared to be some similarities in opinions between the two groups. For instance, both coaches and sports scientists believed research questions should be devised together, although in reality, it was usually the researcher alone who devised the research question. There were differences in how they believed the research findings should be disseminated. While researchers prioritised scientific journals and sports science conferences, coaches prioritised coaching conferences. The sources from which they kept their knowledge up-to-date were also different in all categories between the two groups. Thus, while there is some agreement on how research should be conducted, the dissemination of the research does not appear to meet the perceived needs of the coaches.

In another comparative analysis, Thompson et al. (2009) performed an in-depth assessment of the technical knowledge of sprinting coaches compared to the sprinting bio-mechanics literature. They found that while in some cases there was agreement between the two sources, there were also some gaps. These gaps came in the form of not only conflict between the research findings and the coaches' knowledge, but also by the finding that some areas that the coaches deemed to be important had no scientific literature base to support them. The reasons for the differences between the biomechanics research and the coaches' knowledge are unclear. Whether the coaches were aware of the contradictory research in relation to their practices but disagreed with it, or whether the issue was related to dissemination of the research needs to be clarified. Furthermore, the results of this study appear to suggest that there are areas deemed important to coaches that deserve further biomechanical investigation.

The origins of elite coaching knowledge in gymnastics and why some sources were pre-ferred have been investigated by Irwin et al. (2004). The coaches suggested that given a specific problem, they would first try to solve it themselves through watching videos or using coaching manuals. They would then approach other coaches. Finally, if they needed to do so, they would consult a biomechanist. However, this was not always the case, as one coach suggested that they would not ask a 'theorist', rather they would prefer to find someone who also had 'done the skill' or coached it. This view that the biomechanist needed to have coached or played the sport was backed up in a later study by Williams and Kendall (2007). Experience of the practitioner in the sport being analysed appears to be important to some coaches when determining the weight they give to the information provided. Although this was only voiced by a minority of coaches in the study by Irwin et al. (2004), perceived relevance of the information being provided may be a major barrier to coaches using sports science in general.

Studies that are more recent have addressed this topic of coaches' views on the application and value of sports science at a national level across a variety of sports. Martindale and Nash (2013) investigated the perceptions of 58 UK coaches across four sports (football, rugby league, curling, and judo). They found three main barriers to the transfer of knowledge between sports science and coaching. First, some of the coaches perceived that the practical application and relevance of sports science was lacking, particularly in relation to non-elite players. Second, the integration of and access to sports science were also seen as barriers. Good working relation-ships were seen as important in the use of sports science. Some suggested that sports science was not accessible across skill levels, and at lower levels, they would be lucky to receive any support in this area. Third, as with the previous studies, dissemination of the research was also regarded as an issue, with access to the academic literature and the jargon it contained both being seen as barriers to its use. Similar findings were reported with Turkish coaches across a variety of sports (Kilic & Ince, 2015), who found lack of access to research and the applicabil-ity of the research as barriers to its use. However, they also compared the educational level of the coaches and found that those with graduate degrees perceived that research that is more relevant was being done in their area. Therefore, while the relevance of research and access to research findings constitute important barriers to coaches' utilisation of research, these barriers may be linked to coaches' educational backgrounds.

Technique analysis and biomechanics

The biomechanical analysis of movement has been depicted to exist on a continuum from quantitative to qualitative (Knudson & Morrison, 2002). Qualitative technique analysis has been defined as "the systematic observation and introspective judgement of the quality of human movement for the purposes of providing the most appropriate remediation to improve performance" (Knudson & Morrison, 1996, p. 31). Technique analysis in coaching is still dominated by a qualitative approach (Mooney et al., 2015), and this is said to have been derived from a need for the coach to rationalise the advice given to players (Lees, 2002). While it is established that the role of a golf coach incorporates a variety of disciplines, it is still technique analysis that receives the most attention (Wiren, 1991). Even prior to the creation of the PGA (GB&I) in 1901 and the PGA of America in 1916, forms of golf coaching had been around for long enough for books to be published on the topic (Taylor, 1903). In contrast, biomechanics as a discipline only emerged in the late 1960s in an attempt to apply physics to sporting movements (Lees, 2002; Knudson, 2007). The British Association of Sport and Exercise Sciences defines biomechanics as "an examination of the causes and consequences of human movement and the interaction of the body with apparatus or equipment through the application of mechanical principles" (BASES, 2016). Contrary to the performance setting in which coaches perform qualitative analysis, quantitative biomechanical analysis has been predominantly performed in laboratory situations by sports scientists. Due to the cost and complexity of much of the hardware and software used in biomechanics, its use in more applied settings has been hindered (Lees, 2002). With qualitative and quantitative analysis occurring in largely different settings and performed by different professions (coaches and sports scientists respectively), the two discipline approaches are inherently at risk of drifting apart.

The gap between the analysis methods of coaches and biomechanists in golf can be best demonstrated with a comparison between biomechanics research and golf coaching literature. Some key examples of this disparity in the two approaches are outlined below.

Sequencing is often used to describe a movement in qualitative analysis (Lees, 2002). One of the most commonly referenced sequences in the golf swing is the transition sequence from the backswing to the downswing (e.g., Neal et al., 2007). Many coaches have suggested that the sequence of transition from backswing to downswing should be sequenced as follows – pelvis, upper torso, arms, and then club (Hogan, 1957; Harmon & Andrisani, 1998; Suttie, 2005). Hogan (1957) contended that if the downswing starts with the hands, the rotation of the hips stops early, the club is forced out from the proper line and is swung across the ball-to-target line, causing a slice (a shot that starts left and curves right). In the biomechanics literature, the sequence in which the pelvis and torso rotate back towards the target from the top of the backswing has been investigated. The difference in axial rotation between the pelvis and upper torso at the top of the backswing has been termed the X-factor (McLean, 1992). Subsequently, the amount by which this angle increases to its maximum value in the downswing has been termed the X-factor stretch (Cheetham et al., 2001). Although the X-factor stretch does not directly measure the sequence in which the pelvis and upper torso change direction at the top of the swing, an increase in this angle from the top of the backswing would suggest that the pelvis initiates the downswing. The value for the X-factor stretch has been shown to be greater in higher-skilled golfers (Cheetham et al., 2001) and to be positively correlated with clubhead speed (Myers et al., 2008).

The combined role that the arms and wrist joint complex play in the transition sequence has not been adequately researched in biomechanics research, but the timing of release of the wrist angle (referred to as wrist uncocking) has been investigated by many authors (e.g., Milburn,

1982; Sprigings & MacKenzie, 2002). The results of these studies have been consistent in their claim that the release of the angle between the club shaft and forearm should be delayed until the later stages of the golf swing to take advantage of the summation of angular velocity from the proximal to the distal segment. However, the outcome variable used has been predominantly the clubhead speed at impact. Although this is clearly a highly important relationship, the reference to wrist release in the coaching literature also includes effects on the direction of the shot (e.g., Hogan, 1957). Therefore, while both 'wrist release' and X-factor have been much researched from the point of view of clubhead speed, gaps still remain in the literature regarding shot direction and the role of the wrist complex in the transition phase.

A common approach to identify key successful performance variables in golf has been to compare two or more ability groups (Cheetham et al., 2001; Fradkin et al., 2004; Bradshaw et al., 2009; Fedorcik et al., 2012). Apart from skill level being variably defined in these studies, the comparative use of skill level in golf research may be misplaced. To compare skill levels in golf would suggest that the technique of the higher-skilled individual is optimal or, at least, desirable. In motor learning, many authors have discouraged the use of technique templates (Hay & Reid, 1988; Knudson & Morrison, 2002; Lees, 2002; Bartlett, 2007). The idea that there might be an optimum swing technique in golf is contrary to concepts such as the motor abundance theory, which suggests that there are multiple movement strategies that can satisfy equivalent outcomes (Latash, 2010; Morrison et al., 2016). While ability level comparisons may be a popular method of analysis, it may not yield as useful results in golf as in other sports (Knight, 2004; Glazier, 2011; Langdown et al., 2012). From a golf coaching perspective, the PGA (2012) advocates the use of the 'laws, principles and preference' deterministic model espoused by Wiren (1991). Regarding this model, Wiren (1991, p. 3) states that:

> Although a model can be constructed which exemplifies sound principles, there is no perfect swing. Rather, there are a variety of possibilities that are functional and can be considered correct as long as they do not violate physical law.

Overall, it can be stated that initial descriptive research is a fundamental step in the research process (Bishop, 2008), and comparison of skill levels may yield important insights on which to base further research.

Bridging the gap between coaching and biomechanics

Notwithstanding the issues around coaches' knowledge and coach–biomechanist communication, the main gap between biomechanics research and coaching appears, until recently, to have been the outcome variables selected for swing technique analysis. Clubhead speed and velocity have dominated as outcome variables used in scientific regression and correlation analysis (Keogh & Hume, 2012). However, there are a number of principle-based factors, as depicted by Wiren (1991), which have also recently been shown to be the focus of empirical research (Morrison, 2016). The technology exists today to accurately measure a wide range of biomechanical and shot outcome variables, including the recent advances in determining clubface and path orientations at impact (Betzler et al., 2012; Sweeney et al., 2013), along with modern and commercially available devices to measure or predict initial ball launch conditions and ball flight parameters. The transfer of these quantitative findings to coaching practice is now much more readily accessible; however, the interpretation of the many variables to understand their relevance to technique analysis, and ultimately performance, needs to be done systematically.

A structured process of developing relevant sports science research was developed by Bishop (2008): the 'Applied Research Model for the Sports Sciences' (ARMSS). The model follows three broad steps: description, experimentation, and implementation. This model describes a logical progression through different types of research that ultimately lead to implementation in a sports setting. He indicated the need for consultation with coaches and sports science staff in the first stage: 'defining the problem'. The implementation step also includes a consideration of the barriers to uptake of the research findings by coaches and sports science staff. More specific to biomechanics, though applied to gymnastics, Irwin and Kerwin (2008) developed the concept they referred to as the 'Coaching–Biomechanics Interface'. The term refers to a process that is intended to bridge any practice–theory gap that may exist between coaches and biomechanists. Although the bulk of their text describes five areas in which coaches can benefit from biomechanics, their description of the communication between coach and biomechanist is what appears to underpin the model –

> The process is based on a coach's tacit knowledge in relation to the practices that are routinely used to develop athletes' skills. This information, through systematic conversation with a biomechanist, is then turned into biomechanical variables that can either be measured or analysed theoretically.
>
> (Irwin et al., 2013, p. 148)

By definition, tacit knowledge in coaching is gained implicitly through experience and is therefore not often articulated by the coach (Nash & Collins, 2006). This may be the reason that Irwin et al. (2013) imply this information is transferred in a structured process. Irwin et al. (2013, p. 148) go on to emphasise that "this cycle of extracting, processing and imparting new scientifically grounded knowledge or understanding represents the whole or the actuality of the Coaching–Biomechanics Interface". This cyclic communication with coaches suggests a similar process to that outlined in the model by Bishop (2008). Irwin et al. (2013) later devised a depiction of the model illustrating these inter-relationships and how the Coaching–Biomechanics Interface forms a bridge between the *technical understanding of the skill* supplied by the coach and the *biomechanical determinants of performance* derived by the biomechanist. On the basis of this coach–biomechanist communication, they recommend five coaching benefits that may be derived from biomechanics: 1) enhance coaches' technical understanding of skills; 2) evaluation of coaching practices in enhancing skills; 3) evaluation of training practices to enhance skills; 4) facilitating the evolution of technique within the sport; and 5) assisting in optimising performance (i.e., by theoretically justifying the modification of a skill).

Some researchers have started to implement these models in golf. A study by Smith et al. (2012) investigated golf coaches' perceptions of the key technical parameters in a successful golf swing with the intention to highlight some of the key parameters for future relevant biomechanical research. Their findings identified three main elements of the golf swing: ball flight, club motion, and body motion. They also reported the descriptors that coaches used regarding the swing, such as powerful, accurate, consistent, repeatable, controlled, and simple. There is a suggestion that the ball flight was a result of the club and body motion; however, the relationships that coaches perceived to exist between the club and body motion were not fully addressed. Later, Smith et al. (2015) conducted an observational and semi-structured interview study to identify the key technical parameters that high-level golf coaches associate with a successful golf swing. Five intrinsically linked key technical parameters were identified: 'Posture', 'Body Rotation', 'Arm and Wrist Action', 'Sequential Movement and Body Segments', and 'Club Motion'. The parameters Posture and Body Rotation were further subcategorised and compared to the existing biomechanical literature, with proposals made to guide future golf biomechanics research and coaching technologies.

On the theme of the golf coaching–biomechanics interface, Morrison (2016) undertook a qualitative inquiry to determine the analysis and decision-making processes that coaches used when making technical changes to a golf swing and also to obtain their opinions on biomechanics research and consultancy services. Purposeful sampling was undertaken with 18 PGA (GB&I) professionals who had at least 10 years' coaching experience at the regional level or above or had coached at least one international amateur or professional golfer. Coaches based swing changes at one end of a continuum on observations obtained solely from ball flight and considered there to be no 'perfect swing', while at the other end of the continuum, a swing technique model was used, with others operating a mixed approach. Coaches generally displayed negative views about biomechanics, believing that biomechanists only use swing models and that the ensuing information they provide is often too complex, although they acknowledged a lack of understanding on their part of biomechanical principles.

Implications for the game

While there are a myriad of interacting factors that determine the successful execution of a given golf stroke, a sound understanding of the role of biomechanics and its application to technique analysis by the golf coach are yet to be fully realised. In order to improve the transfer of existing and future knowledge to coaching practice, several important and linked steps need to occur.

According to the Coaching–Biomechanics Interface Model, a combination of the coaches' technical understanding of the skill and the biomechanical determinants of performance can be used to generate meaningful information that can be fed back to the player (Irwin et al., 2013). In order to achieve this, biomechanists must continue to conduct relevant research to provide an evidence base on which to base these biomechanical determinants of performance. The process by which this evidence base is developed could well follow Bishop's (2008) eight-stage applied research model, whereby the biomechanist and golf professional work closely together to define the research question, followed by experimentation by the biomechanist, leading to implementation by the golf professional. It is imperative that the biomechanics research community continues to undertake rigorous scientific research that leads to peer-reviewed outputs, while at the same time ensuring that the knowledge is translated and disseminated in a meaningful way to the coach. In terms of current knowledge, performance analysis literature has given insights into the importance of key measures identified by coaches, such as shot accuracy and the trade-off between shot accuracy and distance (Alexander & Kern, 2005; James & Rees, 2008; Pelz et al., 2008; Hellström et al., 2013); however, less research has addressed the causes of particular types of shots, such as draw, fade, and high and low trajectories. Research also exists on the relationship between biomechanics and injury prevention in golf (Marshall & McNair, 2013); however, there is much scope for further research in this area, as well as in post-injury rehabilitation, which involves close collaboration with health professionals at all stages of the research process, leading to evidence-based implementation. Increasingly, the importance of a holistic approach to golf coaching (especially at the elite levels) involving the full range of sports scientists, strength and conditioning experts, and health professionals is being realised; however, the linkages between them need to be professionally managed.

There is an onus on all PGAs to provide education programmes at both trainee and continued professional development levels, which include biomechanical principles and findings related to swing movement analysis. These syllabi should be presented in such a way that the laws and principles that underpin biomechanics are not abstract but are clearly relevant and directly related to technique analysis. Provided this condition is met, golf trainee and qualified coaches need to be open to accept the challenges faced by studying the biomechanics discipline.

Summary and future directions

It is thus contended that biomechanics is central to swing analysis, yet the biomechanics discipline is neither well understood nor applied by the golf professional. The many reasons for this observation have been outlined, including the current biomechanics knowledge levels of coaches, the barriers to the use of biomechanics in golf coaching, the nature and the relevance of the information provided, as well as the communication process between coach and biomechanist. In this chapter, specific areas of biomechanical research that are not well aligned with golf coaching practice have been identified. Recommendations have been proposed to bridge the gap between biomechanics theory and practice. The similar approaches of Bishop (2008) and Irwin et al. (2013) provide the basis for these recommendations, and early examples of their use are reported here. By facilitating conversations among coaches, sports scientists, strength and conditioning experts, and health professionals, it is hoped that the game of golf can be enhanced for its many participants and, indeed, potentially grown.

References

Abraham, A.; Collins, D. & Martindale, R. (2006) The Coaching Schematic: Validation Through Expert Coach Consensus, *Journal of Sports Sciences*, 24 (6), 549–564.

Alexander, D. & Kern, W. (2005) Drive for Show and Putt for Dough? An Analysis of the Earnings of PGA Tour Golfers, *Journal of Sports Economics*, 6 (1), 46–60.

Bartlett, R. (2007) *Introduction to Sports Biomechanics: Analysing Human Movement Patterns*, London: Routledge.

BASES (2016) *About BASES*, Available at www.Bases.Org.Uk/About (Accessed April 6, 2016).

Betzler, N.; Monk, S.; Wallace, E. & Otto, S. (2012) Effects of Golf Shaft Stiffness on Strain, Clubhead Presentation and Wrist Kinematics, *Sports Biomechanics*, 11 (2), 223–238.

Bishop, D. (2008) An Applied Research Model for the Sport Sciences, *Sports Medicine*, 38 (3), 253–263.

Bradshaw, E.; Keogh, J.; Hume, P.; Maulder, P.; Nortje, J. & Marnewick, M. (2009) The Effect of Biological Movement Variability on the Performance of the Golf Swing in High- and Low-Handicapped Players, *Research Quarterly for Exercise and Sport*, 80, 185–196.

Cheetham, P.; Martin, P.; Mottram, R. & St Laurent, B. (2001) The Importance of Stretching the 'X-Factor' in the Downswing of Golf: The 'X-Factor Stretch', In: P. Thomas (Ed.) *Optimising Performance in Golf*, Queensland, Australia: Australian Academic Press, pp. 192–199.

Coleman, S. (1999) Biomechanics and Its Application to Coaching Practice, In: N. Cross & J. Lyle (Eds.) *The Coaching Process: Principles and Practice for Sport*, Oxford, UK: Butterworth-Heinemann, pp. 130–151.

Erickson, K.; Bruner, M.; Macdonald, D. & Côté, J. (2008) Gaining Insight into Actual and Preferred Sources of Coaching Knowledge, *International Journal of Sports Science and Coaching*, 3 (4), 527–538.

Fedorcik, G.; Queen, R.; Abbey, A.; Moorman, C. & Ruch, D. (2012) Differences in Wrist Mechanics During the Golf Swing Based on Golf Handicap, *Journal of Science and Medicine in Sport*, 15 (3), 250–254.

Fradkin, A.; Sherman, C. & Finch, C. (2004) How Well Does Club Head Speed Correlate With Golf Handicaps? *Journal of Science and Medicine in Sport*, 7 (4), 465–472.

Glazier, P. (2011) Movement Variability in the Golf Swing: Theoretical Methodological and Practical Issues, *Research Quarterly for Exercise and Sport*, 82 (2), 157–161.

Gould, D.; Giannini, S.; Krane, V. & Hodge, K. (1990) Educational Needs of Elite US National Team, Pan American and Olympic Coaches, *Journal of Teaching and Physical Education*, 9 (4), 332–344.

Harmon, B. & Andrisani, J. (1998) *The Four Cornerstones of Winning Golf* (Fireside Ed.), New York, NY: Simon & Schuster.

Hay, J. & Reid, G. (1988) *Anatomy, Mechanics and Human Motion* (2nd Ed.), London: Prentice Hall.

Hellström, J.; Nilsson, J. & Isberg, L. (2013) Drive for Dough. PGA Tour Golfers' Tee Shot Functional Accuracy, Distance and Hole Score, *Journal of Sports Sciences*, 32 (5), 462–469.

Hogan, B. (1957) *Ben Hogan's Five Lessons: The Modern Fundamentals of Golf*, New York, NY: Simon & Schuster.

Irwin, G. & Kerwin, D. (2008) Biomechanics for coaches, In: R. L. Jones, M. Hughes & K. Kingston (Eds.) *Introduction to Sports Coaching: Connecting Theory to Practice*, Abingdon, UK: Routledge, pp. 87–100.

Irwin, G., Bezodis, I. & Kerwin, D. (2013) Biomechanics for Coaches, In: R. L. Jones & K. Kingston (Eds.) *Introduction to Sports Coaching: Connecting Theory to Practice* (2nd Ed.), Abingdon, UK: Routledge, pp. 145–160.

Irwin, G.; Hanton, S. & Kerwin, D. (2004) Reflective Practice and the Origins of Elite Coaching Knowledge, *Reflective Practice*, 5 (3), 425–442.

James, N. & Rees, G. (2008) Approach Shot Accuracy as a Performance Indicator for US PGA Tour Golf Professionals, *International Journal of Sports Science and Coaching*, 3 (1 Supplement), 145–160.

Jowett, S. & Nezlek, J. (2011) Relationship Interdependence and Satisfaction with Important Outcomes in Coach-Athlete Dyads, *Journal of Social and Personal Relationships*, 29 (3), 287–301.

Keogh, J. & Hume, P. A. (2012) Evidence for Biomechanics and Motor Learning Research Improving Golf Performance, *Sports Biomechanics*, 11 (2), 288–309.

Kilic, K. & Ince, M. (2015) Use of Sports Science Knowledge by Turkish Coaches, *International Journal of Exercise Science*, 8 (1), 21–37.

Knight, C. (2004) Neuromotor Issues in the Learning and Control of Golf Skill, *Research Quarterly for Exercise and Sport*, 75 (1), 9–15.

Knudson, D. (2007) Qualitative Biomechanical Principles for Application in Coaching, *Sports Biomechanics*, 6 (1), 109–118.

Knudson, D. & Morrison, C. (1996) An Integrated Qualitative Analysis of Overarm Throwing, *Journal of Physical Education, Recreation & Dance*, 67 (6), 31–36.

Knudson, D. & Morrison, C. (2002) *Qualitative Analysis of Human Movement* (2nd Ed.), Champaign, IL: Human Kinetics.

Langdown, B.; Bridge, M. & Li, F.-X. (2012) Movement Variability in the Golf Swing, *Sports Biomechanics*, 11 (2), 273–287.

Latash, M. (2010) Motor Synergies and the Equilibrium-Point Hypothesis, *Motor Control*, 14 (3), 294–322.

Lees, A. (2002) Technique Analysis in Sports: A Critical Review, *Journal of Sports Sciences*, 20 (10), 813–828.

Marshall, R. & Mcnair, P. (2013) Biomechanical Risk Factors and Mechanisms of Knee Injury in Golfers, *Sports Biomechanics*, 12 (3), 221–230.

Martindale, R. & Nash, C. (2013) Sports Science Relevance and Application: Perceptions of UK Coaches, *Journal of Sports Sciences*, 31 (8), 807–819.

McLean, J. (1992) Widen the Gap, *Golf Magazine*, 34 (12), 49–53.

Milburn, P. (1982) Summation of Segmental Velocities in the Golf Swing, *Medicine and Science in Sports and Exercise*, 14 (1), 60–64.

Mooney, R.; Corley, G.; Godfrey, A.; Osborough, C.; Newell, J.; Quinlan, L. & Ólaighin, G. (2015) Analysis of Swimming Performance: Perceptions and Practices of US-Based Swimming Coaches, *Journal of Sports Sciences*, 34 (11), 997–1005.

Morrison, A. (2016) *Golf Coaching-Biomechanics Interface*, Unpublished Doctoral Thesis, Northern Ireland: University of Ulster.

Morrison, A.; Mcgrath, D. & Wallace, E. (2016) Motor Abundance and Control Structure in the Golf Swing, *Human Movement Science*, 46, 129–147.

Myers, J.; Lephart, S.; Tsai, Y.-S.; Sell, T.; Smoliga, J. & Jolly, J. (2008) The Role of Upper Torso and Pelvis Rotation in Driving Performance During the Golf Swing, *Journal of Sports Sciences*, 26 (2), 181–188.

Nash, C. & Collins, D. (2006) Tacit Knowledge in Expert Coaching: Science or Art? *Quest*, 58 (4), 465–477.

Neal, R.; Lumsden, R.; Holland, M. & Mason, B. (2007) Body Segment Sequencing and Timing in Golf, *International Journal of Sports Science and Coaching*, 2 (1 Supplement), 25–36.

Pelz, D.; Pelz, E.; Evans, K. & Bracey, D. (2008) Golfer Performance: Amateurs vs. Pros, In: D. Crews & R. Lutz (Eds.) *Science and Golf V: Proceedings of the Wold Scientific Congress of Golf*, Mesa, AZ: Energy in Motion Inc., pp. 146–153.

PGA (2012) *PGA Study Guide: Introduction to Golf Coaching*, Sutton Coldfield, UK: Professional Golfers Association Ltd.

Schempp, P.; Webster, C.; Mccullick, B.; Busch, C. & Sannen-Mason, I. (2007) How the Best Get Better: An Analysis of the Self-Monitoring Strategies Used by Expert Golf Instructors, *Sport, Education and Society*, 12 (2), 175–192.

Schempp, P.; You, J. & Clark, B. (1998) The Antecedents of Expertise in Golf Instruction, In: M. Farrally & A. Cochran (Eds.) *Science and Golf III*. London: Human Kinetics, pp. 283–293.

Smith, A.; Roberts, J.; Wallace, E. & Forrester, S. (2012) Professional Golf Coaches' Perceptions of the Key Technical Parameters in the Golf Swing, *Procedia Engineering*, 34, 224–229.

Smith, A.; Roberts, J.; Wallace, E.; Kong, P.; Forrester, S.; MacKenzie, S. & Robertson, S. (2015) Golf Coaches' Perceptions of Key Technical Swing Parameters Compared to Biomechanical Literature, *International Journal of Sports Science and Coaching*, 10 (4), 739–756.

Sprigings, E. & Mackenzie, S. (2002) Examining the Delayed Release in the Golf Swing Using Computer Simulation, *Sports Engineering*, 5, 23–32.

Suttie, J. K. (2005) *Your Perfect Swing*. Leeds, UK: Human Kinetics Publishers.

Sweeney, M.; Mills, P.; Alderson, J. & Elliott, B. (2013) The Influence of Club-Head Kinematics on Early Ball Flight Characteristics in the Golf Drive, *Sports Biomechanics*, 12 (3), 247–258.

Taylor, J. H. (1903) *Taylor on Golf*, London: Hutchinson & Co.

Thompson, A.; Bezodis, I. & Jones, R. (2009) An in-Depth Assessment of Expert Sprint Coaches' Technical Knowledge, *Journal of Sports Sciences*, 27 (8), 855–861.

Toner, J.; Nelson, L.; Potrac, P.; Gilbourne, D. & Marshall, P. (2012) From 'Blame' to 'Shame' in a Coach-Athlete Relationship in Golf: A Tale of Shared Critical Reflection and the Re-Storying of Narrative Experience, *Sports Coaching Review*, 1 (1), 67–78.

Williams, S. & Kendall, L. (2007) Perceptions of Elite Coaches and Sports Scientists of the Research Needs for Elite Coaching Practice, *Journal of Sports Sciences*, 25 (14), 1577–1586.

Wiren, G. (1991) *The PGA Manual of Golf: The Professional's Way to Play Better Golf*, New York, NY: Hungry Minds Inc.

Yılmaz, İ. & Yalçın, N. (2012) The Relationship of Procedural and Declarative Knowledge of Science Teacher Candidates in Newton's Laws of Motion to Understanding, *American International Journal of Contemporary Research*, 2 (3), 50–56.

2

THE USE OF GROUND REACTION FORCES AND PRESSURES IN GOLF SWING INSTRUCTION

Scott K. Lynn and Will Wu

Introduction

An important first step for golf instructors in improving the performance of any golfer is the analysis of their current techniques and swing patterns (Sherman et al., 2001). Traditional golf instruction has mainly relied on collecting swing kinematics in order to analyze swing movements/positions and provide feedback to the golfer. This is mainly because golf coaches have had the ability to record and measure the kinematics of the golf swing for many years. This began with simple single-plane qualitative analyses of still images of the golf swing (Rehling, 1955), then progressed to combining multiple two-dimensional images to produce three-dimensional (3D) data (Neal & Wilson, 1985), and we now have more complex quantitative analyses using modern 3D motion capture systems (Cheetham et al., 2008; Lynn et al., 2013). Using kinematic feedback in golf instruction has proven to be an effective instructional technique (Guadagnoli et al., 2002); however, new technology now gives the golf teacher the ability to measure the forces that go into producing these motions of the golf swing.

Newton's First Law tells us that in order to change the motion state of an object (speed it up or slow it down), we need external forces/torques. The external forces/torques needed to produce or stop motion require that we have something to push off of in order to create them; and in golf, the only thing we can push off of is the ground. How we push into the ground with our feet will help determine the resulting motions of our body; therefore, controlling these forces is essential in producing efficient and effective golf swings.

The forces coming from the connection between the golfer's feet and the ground are called ground reaction forces (GRFs). Technologies that can measure these GRFs have been in wide use in biomechanics laboratories for many years, but they have just recently been made readily available to the golf instructor. There are two forms of technology that provide different types of information about the GRFs occurring during the golf swing: (i) a pressure plate/mat and (ii) a force plate.

Review of current research

(i)   Pressure plate/mat

Pressure is defined as the amount of force per unit area and is measured only perpendicular or normal to the surface. In golf, this can help us to determine how much vertical force is under different parts of both feet during the swing and how these move during the swing. Note that in Figure 2.1(a), the pressure is mainly on the toes of this golfer at set-up, while in Figure 2.1(b), this golfer has a lot of pressure concentrated on the right toe (75%) during the downswing. This could be potentially useful information for the golf instructor as having a record of the athlete's pressure profiles during the swing when he/she is hitting the ball well could allow the former to identify what patterns have changed much more quickly if they begin to struggle with their ball striking. For example, if the golfer in Figure 2.1(a) had more balanced pressures between heels and toes when they were hitting the ball well, this could be an easy fix in set-up pressure that may help get them back on track quickly.

These technologies use a certain number of capacitance or conductance sensors that are embedded into the pressure plate or mat. Both of these types of sensors increase the magnitude of the output electric current as a greater normal or perpendicular force is applied to the sensor; therefore, both have to be calibrated so that the measured voltage is accurately converted into a magnitude of force (Caldwell et al., 2014). The resolution of the pressure distribution is primarily determined by the size of the individual cells, so a greater number of smaller cells will give pressure data with a higher resolution than a smaller number of bigger cells (Caldwell et al., 2014). This pressure data can then be used to calculate the location of the centre of pressure (COP), which is the average location of all the measured pressures in each cell. The total COP will be within the area outlined by both feet if they are both in contact with the ground (Caldwell et al., 2014); however, the COP can also be calculated within each foot so it can be determined if the pressure is focused on the toe, heel, inside, or outside part of the foot (Cavanagh, 1978). In Figure 2.1(a) and 2.1(b), the larger dot represents the total COP, while the smaller dots represent the COP within each individual foot. Many of the technologies that measure pressure distribution during the golf swing also include the path of the total COP during the golf swing, and these have created much interest recently with the establishment of two main companies who have begun marketing these products to golf instructors: Swing Catalyst/ Initial Force AS in 2006 and Boditrak Golf LLC in 2014. The path of the COP is represented as the thick line in Figures 2.1(a) and 2.1(b). Note that in Figure 2.1(a), the golfer is at set–up, so the COP is at the beginning of its path, while in Figure 2.1(b), the golfer is just starting the transition from backswing to downswing. It should be noted that the COP can move in two directions during the swing. It can move towards or away from the target (for the purposes of this chapter, this will be called the COP_y direction and is shown as right/left motion of the COP in Figure 2.1. Note: Both of the golfers tested in Figure 2.1 were right-handed golfers, so motion to the left is towards the target; while movement to the right is away from the target). The COP can also move towards the toes or towards the heels (for the purposes of this chapter, this will be called the COP_x direction and is shown as up/down motion of the COP in Figure 2.1. Note: The upward motion of the COP means it moves towards the toes or closer to the golf ball, while the downward motion of the COP means it moves towards the heels or away from the golf ball).

Ball and Best (2007a, 2007b, 2012) have done much work examining the path of the COP in the golf swing and have discovered great variability among individuals. Their original work simply examined the movement in the COP_y direction (right/left or towards/away from the target), and they identified two basic swing styles that they termed 'Front foot' and 'Reverse' style swings (Ball & Best, 2007a). Both swing styles began with the pressure slightly shifted towards the front foot (55%) at set-up, both then had the COP move to the right or away from the target during the backswing, and to the left or towards the target during the early downswing (Ball & Best, 2007a). It was in the late downswing that these two groups differed in terms of the path of the COP. The 'Front foot' group continued to move the COP_y to the left, or towards the target, during the entire downswing, while the 'Reverse' style swing had the COP_y turn around and move towards the back foot or away from the target during the late downswing and into the follow-through (Ball & Best, 2007a). Figure 2.1(c) and 2.1(d) show examples of typical COP patterns that fit into these two swing styles: Figure 2.1(c) is an example of a 'Front foot' style swing, and Figure 2.1(d) is an example of a 'Reverse' style swing. It should be noted that the position of the COP for both golfers in Figure 2.1(c) and 2.1(d) are shown at impact and both athletes are extremely skilled PGA Tour professionals, who were both ranked within the Top 25 in the world when their driver swings were tested. This is confirmed by the research of Ball and Best who showed that skill level could not distinguish between 'Front foot' and 'Reverse' style swings, as these swing styles were present in both extremely skilled professional golfers and in high handicaps (Ball & Best, 2007a). Ball and Best (2007b) also found that both groups achieved higher clubhead speeds in different ways. The 'Front foot' group achieved faster clubhead speeds, with larger and faster movements of the COP_y towards the target. This means those 'Front foot' golfers who transferred more pressure from the back to the front foot at higher speeds also achieved higher clubhead speeds. For the 'Reverse' golfers, those who positioned the COP_y further back towards their back foot during the late downswing as the club approached ball contact and those who reversed the movement of the COP_y more quickly achieved higher clubhead speeds (Ball & Best, 2007b). Further work by Ball and Best (2011) revealed that the 'Reverse' style swings also tended to have their COP_x shifted more towards

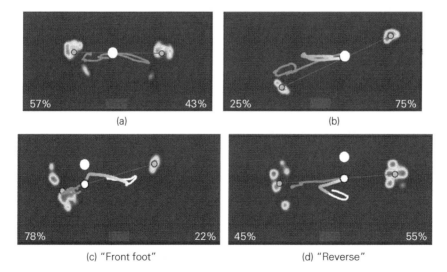

Figure 2.1 Pressure plates showing the pressures within each foot and the path of the centre of pressure (COP) for (a) a golfer at address, (b) a golfer during the downswing, (c) a 'front foot' golfer at impact, and (d) a 'reverse' golfer at impact.

Note: All images are shown from above for right-handed golfers, with the ball above each figure and the target to the left.

the toes as they approached ball contact than the movements in the 'Front Foot' group. This is also displayed in the example swings shown in Figure 2.1(c), as the 'Front Foot' style swing has much more pressure on the front/left heel than the 'Reverse' style swing at impact. A more recent study also found that loading more pressure onto the lateral aspect of the target side foot at impact correlated with higher clubhead speeds (Pataky, 2015). However, the limited research performed on pressure transfers during the golf swing must be interpreted with caution as all of these studies were based on a relatively small number of golfers. It has also been suggested that attempting to achieve the same COP pattern with every golfer would not be ideal, and golf instructors need to account for the variability in each golfer in order to achieve the optimal COP path for each individual (Ball & Best, 2012). It should also be noted that the current literature has also not yet examined how certain COP paths help to determine other measures known to affect the flight of the golf ball, i.e., club path, angle of attack, dynamic loft, smash factor, and so on. None of the studies cited herein included any information on these ball flight determinants, and this needs to be clarified in the literature.

(ii) Force plate

Since pressure plates/mats only give you information about the forces that are perpendicular/normal to the surface, a different technology is needed to measure all the 3D GRFs that produce and control the motions of the golf swing. These 3D GRFs can be measured with force plate technology. There are two types of force plates that are commercially available: (1) strain gauges – are less expensive, have good static capabilities, but do not have a large range or good sensitivity; (2) piezoelectric – allow for high-frequency measurements with good sensitivity but must have special electronics to measure static force (Caldwell et al., 2014). Current force plate models have four instrumented pedestals under each corner of the force plate and can measure forces in 3D – vertical (Z), towards and away from the target or right/left (Y), towards and away from the ball or towards the toes/heels (X). It also must be understood that no matter how many objects are applying force to different locations on a force plate (i.e., both feet independently applying forces to the ground in golf), it can only measure one resultant GRF vector, which is the sum of all the forces acting on it (Caldwell et al., 2014). This is different from pressure plates where we can see what each foot is doing independent of the other and is also the reason many biomechanics laboratories specializing in golf analysis have each foot on a separate force plate. Another important quantity for golf professionals that is measured by a force plate is the torque or twisting force about the vertical axis of the plate (Z) – this is called the free moment on the plate (Caldwell et al., 2014). Force plates are the current golf standard in the measurement of GRFs; however, they are currently significantly more expensive then pressure measurement devices.

The largest magnitudes of GRFs that are measured during the golf swing are in the vertical (Z) direction. The magnitudes of the forces in this direction can be extremely large for those who produce extremely fast clubhead speeds. For example, the golfer shown in Figure 2.2(a) competes in long drive contests and was tested on a two-force plate system (AMTI, Newton, MA, USA) in the California State University, Fullerton Biomechanics Laboratory, in 2015. During this testing session, he was able to achieve a peak vertical force on his front/left leg of 1788 N (which equates to approximately 182 kg or 400 lbs of force on just one leg) during the downswing. The golfer shown in Figure 2.2(b) has consistently been ranked among the longest drivers on the PGA Tour between 2006 and 2016 and was tested on a one-force plate system in 2014. He was able to achieve a peak vertical force of 251% of his bodyweight (which would equate to approximately 215 kg or 475 lbs shared between both legs) during the downswing, which resulted in a drive that carried 313 yards or approximately 286 m. This could be useful

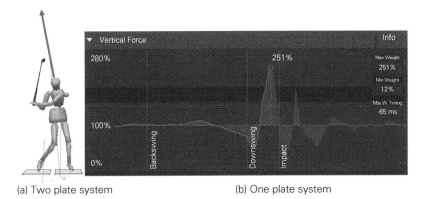

(a) Two plate system   (b) One plate system

Figure 2.2   Two displays of vertical forces measured during the golf swing with (a) a two-force plate system, and (b) a one-force plate system.

anecdotal information for those working in the golf fitness industry, as it can be hypothesized that increasing the amount of vertical force a golfer can produce/handle may help in producing faster clubhead speeds and longer drives. Research also has shown that the magnitude and timing of this vertical force can help distinguish between skilled golfers and those who are less skilled (Barrentine et al., 1994; Lynn et al., 2012). Barrentine et al. (1994) discovered differences in the timing of the peak vertical forces in the lead foot relative to when these forces peaked in the trail foot among two groups of golfers: PGA professionals (n = 20 teaching and tour professionals, mean = 0.55 ± 0.18 seconds between peaks) and high-handicap golfers (n = 20 golfers with handicaps ≥ 16, mean = 0.63 ± 0.18 seconds between peaks) (Barrentine et al., 1994). Another study compared collegiate golfers (n = 18) to beginner golfers (n = 23) hitting a five-iron (Lynn et al., 2012), and it was discovered that the collegiate golfers transferred vertical force to their lead foot earlier on during the downswing.

The shearing forces that are created in the Y-direction (towards/away from the target or right/left forces) appear to be important in producing and decelerating or stopping the linear or translational motions of the golfer during the swing (Lynn et al., 2012). These forces produced the most differences between collegiate golfers and beginners (Lynn et al., 2012). There were several differences in these forces between the groups in this study: (1) the collegiate golfers produced more GRF towards the target with their trail foot and had this force peak much earlier in the swing; (2) the beginner golfers tended to have a small amount of GRF directed towards the target and this force turned around and was directed away from the target early in the downswing; and (3) the collegiate athletes did not produce this braking or decelerating GRF that is directed away from the target until just before ball contact (Lynn et al., 2012). These shearing forces have also been found to be important in regulating the distance that a shot travels with a given club or hitting shots of 'in-between' yardages (McNitt-Gray et al., 2013). Skilled athletes generally tend to produce forces that are directed towards the target during the transition/early downswing in order to generate some momentum going towards the target. This is shown in a two-force plate system in Figure 2.3(a), where the forces produced in the Y-direction are both pointed towards the target and would be creating momentum in that direction. Later on in the downswing, it is important that this forward momentum is decelerated so that the golfer avoids a common swing fault of too much lateral slide of the body towards the target or 'swaying' (Leadbetter, 1990). These decelerating forces are shown in Figure 2.3(b), where the golfer is producing forces with both feet that are directed away from the target in the Y-direction in the late downswing as they approach impact.

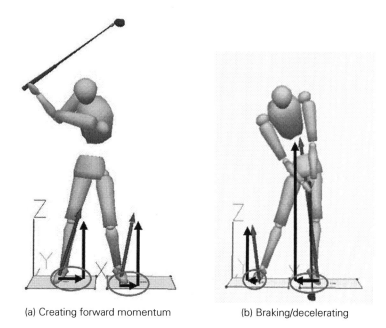

(a) Creating forward momentum   (b) Braking/decelerating

Figure 2.3 Forces collected on a two-force plate system showing (a) the early downswing when Y-directed forces both point towards the target and (b) the late downswing when both Y-directed forces point away from the target.

Source: Figures from (Lynn et al., 2012).

Finally, the shearing forces that are created in the X-direction (towards/away from the ball or towards the toes/heels) appear to be important in producing the angular or rotational movements that are produced during the swing (Lynn et al., 2012). These forces produced in the lead and trail feet act in opposite directions from each other during both the backswing and the downswing. These forces act in opposite directions on either side of the body's axis of rotation in the transverse plane, creating force couples (Hellström, 2009; Lynn et al., 2012). Figure 2.4(a) shows these forces created during the backswing, where the GRF is anteriorly directed in the lead foot and posteriorly directed in the trail foot, while Figure 2.4(b) shows these forces during the downswing, where the GRF is posteriorly directed in the lead foot and anteriorly directed in the trail foot. It is common that some golfers have their trail foot slip backwards (or away from the ball) during the downswing at some point. This is a result of a lack of friction between the trail foot and the ground when they are producing the action force of pushing posteriorly into the ground during the downswing. With appropriate normal force (or pressure), and hence friction between the foot and the ground, this action force produces the measured anteriorly directed reaction force acting on the trail foot in Figure 2.4(b). Research has shown differences in both magnitude and timing of these X-directed forces as higher-skilled athletes have been shown to produce this shear force with their trail foot earlier in the downswing (Barrentine et al., 1994) and collegiate athletes produce much greater magnitudes of these shear forces in their trail foot as compared with beginner golfers (Lynn et al., 2012). Producing these rotational forces early in the downswing would be essential to ensuring that there is enough time to accomplish the proximal-to-distal sequencing of body rotations, which has been identified as a critical component in producing an effective golf swing (Cheetham et al., 2008; Tinmark et al., 2010). With a single-force plate system, these X-directed forces are difficult to interpret,

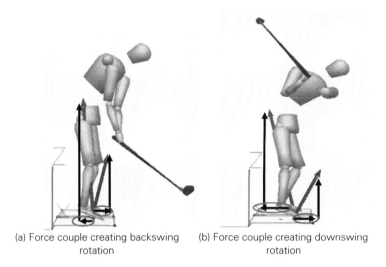

(a) Force couple creating backswing   (b) Force couple creating downswing
rotation   rotation

Figure 2.4   X-directed forces collected on a two-plate system showing (a) the backswing force couple, and
(b) the downswing force couple.

Source: Reproduced with permission from Lynn et al. 2012.

as the opposite direction of the forces produced by each foot causes them to cancel one another, so they do not show up in the net Fx signal. However, the force couple they produce will still contribute to the free moment reading on the single-plate system.

(iii) Combining 3D kinematics and force data (joint moments)

The combination of 3D kinematic data, 3D GRF data, and some golfer-specific anthropo-metrics data allows for the calculations of the external joint forces and moments that go into producing any movement (Selbie et al., 2014). This process uses an inverse dynamics-linked segment model and has been employed in the biomechanics literature to answer many ques-tions, such as the mechanical determinants of knee osteoarthritis (Deluzio & Astephen, 2007; Lynn et al., 2007), the efficiency of different exercises and movement patterns (Butler et al., 2010; Lynn & Noffal, 2010b, 2012), how alterations in running style affect joint loading and the development of running injuries (Willy et al., 2012; Valenzuela et al., 2015), as well as the propensity for anterior cruciate ligament (ACL) injury when landing from a jump (Bates et al., 2013; Myer et al., 2015). This technique gives great insight into the patterns of movement employed by the individual as well as the mechanics of the golf swing. Currently, only a few studies have used inverse dynamics in the evaluation of lower body kinetics during the golf swing (Gatt et al., 1998; Lynn & Noffal, 2010a; Noffal et al., 2014; Ward et al., 2014). These studies help estimate the external load that is placed on a joint during any movement. Lynn and Noffal (2010a) found that placing the target side foot in an externally rotated position at the start of the swing could help to relieve some of the stress on the medial compartment of the knee joint, while shifting that load onto the lateral compartment. This shift of load onto the lateral compartment of the knee also produces a large torque on the knee joint, which is known to be related to the development of various knee pathologies (Hewett et al., 2005). Future research using inverse dynamics to calculate the loading of the joints during the golf swing has great potential in helping to understand how to make the golf swing safer and more efficient.

Implications for the game

Technology, data, and instruction

The advancement in golf technology has provided athletes, instructors, and scientists an enormous amount of information related to the golf swing, which has provided new insights into optimizing swing mechanics for a given athlete – this now includes those forces between the golfer and the ground that create the motions of the golf swing. While technology has provided a new level of information, instructors must remember that this detailed information is analysis rather than instruction. In other words, there is a distinct difference between identifying characteristics of the swing and providing instruction to refine movement and outcome – analysis describes what is occurring with the swing, while instruction is a form of 'communication' that enables the athlete to incorporate the swing as part of a repeatable and adaptable movement pattern. The accessibility of force/pressure data may cause instructors to fall into the trap of using technology as a primary learning tool. Rather than using kinetic information as a primary learning tool, instructors and athletes would be better served to use the information as a new avenue to drive learning strategies. Often, instructors fall into the trap of overusing technologies by giving their athletes too much information (refer Chapter 1 in this book by Morrison & Wallace). These issues are related to a concept termed 'augmented feedback' within the Motor Control and Learning literature.

The field of Motor Control and Learning can provide specific insights into utilizing technology within a teaching or learning environment. In short, Motor Control and Learning is the scientific pursuit that studies how humans control and acquire movements. As such, there are specific evidence-based principles that can aid golf practitioners in fully maximizing the information provided by feedback systems (Magill, 2006; Schmidt & Lee, 2014). A feedback system consists of any external sources that provide information that the golfer cannot obtain by one's self. For the sake of this chapter, this will be data from a pressure or force plate. This information, which the golfer cannot obtain alone, is termed augmented feedback. The goal of using augmented feedback effectively is to structure the allocation of information in such a manner that the athlete uses the augmented information to enhance the information he/she obtains independently from their sensory system by what they see, hear, feel, taste, or smell; this type of information is known as task-intrinsic feedback. The improper use of feedback systems occurs when feedback is provided in a manner in which the athlete relies too heavily on the feedback source. Winstein and Schmidt (1990) nicely demonstrated how the heavy use or high frequency of feedback hindered learning. In their study, participants who received half the amount of feedback, compared to a high-frequency feedback group, performed better when tested after 24 hours of no practice.

So, what do these types of learning situations look like? When feedback is used properly, it is used less rather than more. Magill (2006) shows that overuse of augmented feedback will cause the athlete to be overreliant or dependent on the augmented information; when the feedback source is removed (i.e., in competition), the student will be unable to successfully use or interpret their task-intrinsic information because the abundance of information did not allow them to use the augmented feedback to enhance the use and interpretation of their task-intrinsic feedback. Utilizing feedback sparingly forces the student to explore and use the extra information in relation to their task-intrinsic feedback, causing them to explore and discover the desired swing characteristic(s).

What are specific strategies for using feedback properly? For beginners, a systematic approach of distributing information is recommended. Some evidence-based strategies include faded feedback and/or bandwidth feedback. Supported by Winstein and Schmidt (1990), a faded schedule of feedback consists of systematically reducing the amount of augmented feedback over the course of the learning session. This systematic approach can be used from a time or number-of-shots perspective. For a time-based example, using a 60-minute period, the first 15 minutes of practice consist of providing force/pressure feedback after every swing. For the next 15 minutes, force/pressure data is provided every other swing. After 30 minutes, the coach would then provide force/pressure data every third trial, and for the final 15 minutes, the coach switches from every third swing to every fourth swing. The rate of 'fading' can be determined by the coach and may be based on the stage of learning of the golfer. Less-skilled beginners may have a slightly slow rate of fading, whereas those with more skill may have a faster rate of fading.

Like the fading technique, the bandwidth technique also reduces augmented feedback over the course of the practice session. The bandwidth technique is much more user-friendly for the instructor because the instructor does not have to monitor the schedule of feedback on a swing-by-swing basis. Instead, the instructor sets a limitation or criteria of acceptable performance (perhaps using a launch monitor). If anything is outside the limit, feedback is provided, but if the performance is in the acceptable range, the instructor does not provide augmented feedback. These methods that reduce the amount of augmented feedback in practice are good for the athlete as they prevent them from receiving too much information and allow them to utilize their task-intrinsic feedback. Then, the augmented information from the force/pressure data becomes a reference to compare and calibrate what they are seeing, hearing, or feeling. Numerous studies demonstrate the beneficial learning effects of a performance bandwidth approach to feedback (Lee et al., 1990; Goodwin & Meeuwsen, 1995; Lai & Shea, 1999). While these studies manipulate the bandwidth of feedback in different ways, they draw the same conclusion in which reduction of feedback over the practice sessions enhances learning.

For advanced athletes, a method of reducing feedback is called self-controlled feedback. Using this method, coaches provide the athletes with the control to ask for when they want augmented feedback from the pressure/force plate. In other words, the athlete is in charge of the amount of information they receive on a swing-by-swing basis. Based on studies involving self-controlled learning (Chiviacowsky & Wulf, 2002; Wu & Magill, 2011), athletes will start out requesting high amounts of feedback and slowly fade or reduce the amount of feedback on their own. The reduction in feedback over the course of the practice session is not random. Instead, athletes will ask for feedback on a systematic basis, whereby they ask for feedback mainly of the 'good' swings. In the meantime, or between feedback requests, athletes will be actively engaged in trying to find a movement solution to the force/pressure variable they are trying to improve upon. It is important that they do not rely on the feedback to provide them an answer after every swing but use it more as a reference to check if what they 'feel' or have observed was correct. This method is better suited for experienced athletes because they have an existing knowledge set about their good and bad swings, as well as the ability to adapt to swing changes. Therefore, the force/pressure plate can be used mainly to confirm the golfer's own task-intrinsic information.

Summary and future directions

There is great potential in using new technology that can measure pressures and GRFs in golf instruction. Research has begun to determine how these forces at the ground can affect the resultant motions of the body and the club during the golf swing. Although this is the case, it must be recognized that there is great variability in effective golf swing techniques and, therefore, ideal pressures and GRF patterns will vary between individuals. It is also important that practitioners are aware that they must use pressure and ground force technology in proper ways in order to optimize learning. Pressure and GRF information should be provided in a way that athletes do not rely on this technology, but they use it to better understand their own intrinsic information provided from all their senses.

References

Ball, K. & Best, R. (2007a) Different Centre of Pressure Patterns Within the Golf Stroke I: Cluster Analysis, *Journal of Sports Sciences*, 25 (7), 757–770.

Ball, K. & Best, R. (2007b) Different Centre of Pressure Patterns Within the Golf Stroke II: Group-Based Analysis, *Journal of Sports Sciences*, 25 (7), 771–779.

Ball, K. & Best, R. (2011) Golf Styles and Centre of Pressure Patterns When Using Different Golf Clubs, *Journal of Sports Sciences*, 29 (6), 587–590.

Ball, K. & Best, R. (2012) Centre of Pressure Patterns in the Golf Swing: Individual-Based Analysis, *Sports Biomechanics*, 11 (2), 175–189.

Barrentine, S.; Fleisig, G. & Johnson, H. (1994) Ground Reaction Forces and Torques of Professional and Amateur Golfers, In: A. Cochran & M. Farrally (Eds.) *Science and Golf II: Proceedings of the World Scientific Congress of Golf*, London: E & FN Spon, pp. 33–39.

Bates, N.; Ford, K.; Myer, G. & Hewett, T. (2013) Kinetic and Kinematic Differences Between First and Second Landings of a Drop Vertical Jump Task: Implications for Injury Risk Assessments, *Clinical Biomechanics*, 28 (4), 459–466.

Butler, R.; Plisky, P.; Southers, C.; Scoma, C. & Kiesel, K. (2010) Biomechanical Analysis of the Different Classifications of the Functional Movement Screen Deep Squat Test, *Sports Biomechanics*, 9 (4), 270–279.

Caldwell, G.; Robertson, D. & Whittlesey, S. (2014) Forces and Their Measurement, In: D. Robertson; G. Caldwell; J. Hamill; G. Kamen, & S. Whittlesey (Eds.) *Research Methods in Biomechanics*, Champaign, IL: Human Kinetics, pp. 79–108.

Cavanagh, P. (1978) A Technique for Averaging Center of Pressure Paths From a Force Platform, *Journal of Biomechanics*, 11 (10–12), 487–491.

Cheetham, P.; Rose, G.; Hinrichs, R.; Neal, R.; Mottram, R.; Hurrion, P. & Vint, P. (2008) Comparison of Kinematic Sequence Parameters Between Amateur and Professional Golfers, In: D. Crews & R. Lutz (Eds.) *Science and Golf V: Proceedings of the World Scientific Congress of Golf*, Mesa, AZ: Energy in Motion, pp. 30–36.

Chiviacowsky, S. & Wulf, G. (2002) Self-Controlled Feedback: Does It Enhance Learning Because Performers Get Feedback When They Need It? *Research Quarterly for Exercise and Sport*, 73 (4), 408–415.

Deluzio, K. & Astephen, J. (2007) Biomechanical Features of Gait Waveform Data Associated with Knee Osteoarthritis: An Application of Principal Component Analysis, *Gait & Posture*, 25 (1), 86–93.

Gatt, C.; Pavol, M.; Parker, R. & Grabiner, M. (1998) Three-Dimensional Knee Joint Kinetics During a Golf Swing: Influences of Skill Level and Footwear, *American Journal of Sports Medicine*, 26 (2), 285–294.

Goodwin, J.E. & Meeuwsen, H.J. (1995) Using Bandwidth Knowledge of Results to Alter Relative Frequencies During Motor Skill Acquisition, *Research Quarterly for Exercise and Sport*, 66 (2), 99–104.

Guadagnoli, M.; Holcomb, W. & Davis, M. (2002) The Efficacy of Video Feedback for Learning the Golf Swing, *Journal of Sports Sciences*, 20 (8), 615–622.

Hellström, J. (2009) Competitive Elite Golf a Review of the Relationships Between Playing Results, Technique and Physique, *Sports Medicine*, 39 (9), 723–741.

Hewett, T.; Myer, G.; Ford, K.; Heidt, R.; Colosimo, A. & Mclean, S. (2005) Biomechanical Measures of Neuromuscular Control and Valgus Loading of the Knee Predict Anterior Cruciate Ligament Injury Risk in Female Athletes, *American Journal of Sports Medicine*, 33 (4), 492–501.

Lai, Q. & Shea, C. (1999) The Role of Reduced Frequency of Knowledge of Results During Practice, *Research Quarterly for Exercise and Sport*, 70 (1), 33–40.

Leadbetter, D. (1990) *The Golf Swing*, London: Harper Colling Publishers.

Lee, T.; White, M. & Carnahan, H. (1990) On the Role of Knowledge of Results in Motor Learning: Exploring the Guidance Hypothesis, *Journal of Motor Behavior*, 22 (2), 191–208.

Lynn, S. & Noffal, G. (2010a) Frontal Plane Knee Moments in Golf: Effect of Target Side Foot Position at Address, *Journal of Sports Science and Medicine*, 9 (2), 275 281.

Lynn, S. & Noffal, G. (2010b) Hip and Knee Moment Differences Between High and Low Rated Functional Movement Screen (FMS) Squats, *Medicine and Science in Sports and Exercise*, 42 (5 Supplement 1), 402.

Lynn, S. & Noffal, G. (2012) Lower Extremity Biomechanics During a Regular and Counterbalanced Squat, *Journal of Strength and Conditioning Research*, 26 (9), 2417–2425.

Lynn, S.; Frazier, B.; New, W.; Wu, W.; Cheetham, P. & Noffal, G. (2013) Rotational Kinematics of the Pelvis During the Golf Swing: Skill Level Differences and Relationship to Club and Ball Impact Conditions, *International Journal of Golf Science*, 2 (2), 116–125.

Lynn, S.; Noffal, G.; Wu, W. & Vandervoort, A. (2012) Using Principal Components Analysis to Determine Differences in 3D Loading Patterns Between Beginner and Collegiate Level Golfers, *International Journal of Golf Science*, 1 (1), 25–41.

Lynn, S.; Reid, S. & Costigan, P. (2007) The Influence of Gait Pattern on Signs of Knee Osteoarthritis in Older Adults Over A 5–11 Year Follow-Up Period: A Case Study Analysis, *The Knee*, 14 (1), 22–28.

Magill, R. (2006) *Motor Learning and Control* (8th Ed.), Boston, MA: Mcgraw-Hill.

McNitt-Gray, J.; Munaretto, J.; Zaferiou, A.; Requejo, P. & Flashner, H. (2013) Regulation of Reaction Forces During the Golf Swing, *Sports Biomechanics*, 12 (2), 121–131.

Myer, G.; Ford, K.; Di Stasi, S.; Foss, K.; Micheli, L. & Hewett, T. (2015) High Knee Abduction Moments Are Common Risk Factors for Patellofemoral Pain (PFP) and Anterior Cruciate Ligament (ACL) Injury in Girls: Is PFP Itself a Predictor for Subsequent ACL Injury? *British Journal of Sports Medicine*, 49 (2), 118–122.

Neal, R. & Wilson, B. (1985) 3D Kinematics and Kinetics of the Golf Swing, *International Journal of Sport Biomechanics*, 1 (3), 221–232.

Noffal, G.; Lynn, S.; Bradburn, H.; New, K. & Frazier, B. (2014) Differences in Frontal Plane Knee Moments Between Elite and Recreational Golfers, *Medicine and Science in Sports and Exercise*, 46 (5 Supplement 1), 411–412.

Pataky, T. (2015) Correlation Between Maximum In-Shoe Pressures and Club Head Speed in Amateur Golfers, *Journal of Sports Sciences*, 33 (2), 192–197.

Rehling, C. (1955) Analysis of Techniques of the Golf Drive, *Research Quarterly. American Association for Health, Physical Education and Recreation*, 26 (1), 80–81.

Schmidt, R. & Lee, T. (2014) *Motor Learning and Performance: From Principles to Application*, Champaign, IL: Human Kinetics.

Selbie, W.; Hamill, J. & Kepple, T. (2014) Three-Dimensional Kinetics, In: D. Robertson; G. Caldwell; J. Hamill; G. Kamen, & S. Whittlesey (Eds.) *Research Methods in Biomechanics*, Champaign, IL: Human Kinetics, pp. 151–176.

Sherman, C.; Sparrow, W.; Jolley, D. & Eldering, J. (2001) Coaches' Perceptions of Golf Swing Kinematics, *International Journal of Sport Psychology*, 32 (3), 257–270.

Tinmark, F.; Hellström, J.; Halvorsen, K. & Thorstensson, A. (2010) Elite Golfers' Kinematic Sequence in Full-Swing and Partial-Swing Shots, *Sports Biomechanics*, 9 (4), 236–244.

Valenzuela, K.; Lynn, S.; Mikelson, L.; Noffal, G. & Judelson, D. (2015) Effect of Acute Alterations in Foot Strike Patterns During Running on Sagittal Plane Lower Limb Kinematics and Kinetics, *Journal of Sports Science and Medicine*, 14 (1), 225–232.

Ward, C.; Charles, J.; Lynn, S.; Frazier, B.; New, K. & Noffal, G. (2014) Differences in Hip Moments in the Downswing Between Skill Levels and Relationship to Pelvic Kinematics, *International Journal of Golf Science*, 3 (Supplement), S110–S112.

Willy, R.; Manal, K.; Witvrouw, E. & Davis, I. (2012) Are Mechanics Different Between Male and Female Runners with Patellofemoral Pain? *Medicine and Science in Sports and Exercise*, 44 (11), 2165–2171.

Winstein, C. & Schmidt, R. (1990) Reduced Frequency of Knowledge of Results Enhances Motor Skill Learning, *Journal of Experimental Psychology: Learning, Memory, and Cognition*, 16 (4), 677–691.

Wu, W. & Magill, R. (2011) Allowing Learners to Choose: Self-Controlled Practice Schedules for Learning Multiple Movement Patterns, *Research Quarterly in Exercise and Sport*, 82 (3), 449–457.

3

THE SEQUENCE OF BODY SEGMENT INTERACTIONS IN THE GOLF SWING

Peter F. Lamb and Paul S. Glazier

Introduction

Golf is widely regarded to be a challenging game to master. The difficulty of the sport becomes clear when we consider that a large component of the game relies on a full swing that requires the club to be swung by the body not only at high speed but also with great precision. In fact, the higher the speed of the club, the more critical the precision becomes; this presents a conundrum for the golfer who recognises that high clubhead speed can be advantageous if controlled, as it may lead to longer drives (Hume et al., 2005). Fortunately, an effective swing increases both clubhead speed and accuracy. The exact recipe, however, varies between golfers and situations because of differences in physical characteristics, histories, and demands of the shot (refer Chapter 5: Inter- and Intra-individual Movement Variability in the Golf Swing). Instead, we can present general biomechanical principles that golfers should be aware of, so that they can explore swing techniques that improve performance, constrained or guided by those principles.

Although each golfer's body is unique, in general, our bodies possess many common characteristics. Our bodies have evolved to fulfil certain purposes that aided our survival, such as long distance running (Bramble & Lieberman, 2004) and throwing (Roach et al., 2013), which have been vital for successful hunting. Mass is concentrated at our core, meaning proximal muscles (e.g., pectoralis major and gluteus maximus) tend to be wider, stronger, and heavier than muscles that move our most distal body segments. This structure gave us our advantage when hunting; swinging our legs underneath our body during running allowed us to run long distances while expending relatively little energy. For example, the tibia is shorter compared to the more proximal femur; this decrease in distal bone length helps decrease the moment of inertia of the lower extremity and subsequently aids running economy. The diameter of long bones also tapers off in a proximal-to-distal fashion, further helping to reduce moment of inertia. Examining effective running biomechanics also reveals the importance of reducing the moment of inertia, as can be seen by the flexed knee bringing the mass of the leg close to the body during the forward swing – another step in decreasing the energy demand (Novacheck, 1998). Similarly, the need to execute a powerful throwing motion led to the development of long-bone length and diameter, as well as tendon insertion points, well suited for generating high rotational speeds (Roach et al., 2013). This meant that the upper extremity is much more capable of high-speed movements compared to the moderate-speed, endurance movements of the lower extremity. These biomechanical characteristics remain with us and have important implications for the golf swing, in particular, the sequence of body segment movements, which is the focus of the remainder of this chapter.

Review of current research

Early work on proximal-to-distal sequencing

The book *The Search for the Perfect Swing* by Alastair Cochran and John Stobbs (1968) constituted a ground-breaking contribution to our understanding of their golf swing. This achievement is even more impressive when considering the limitations in the technology for measurement and computation nearly half a century ago. Much of this chapter refers back to the original models and reasoning of Cochran and Stobbs, as their work has influenced many researchers of golf biomechanics, and much of their work remains relevant today.

Cochran and Stobbs (1968) modelled the swing as three cylinders of decreasing diameter stacked on top of each other and free to rotate about a common vertical axis (Figure 3.1). Each successive cylinder, which represented different components of the golfer's core, was connected to the lower one by a spring, which could inhibit rotation when being stretched but also, and more importantly, could store elastic energy. Representing the lead arm and the club in this model were two levers constituting a double pendulum. The proximal end of the lead arm lever was connected to the top cylinder and the distal end was joined by a free hinge to the proximal end of the club lever. If the cylinders in Figure 3.1 were rotated clockwise until the springs were stretched to their limit, it would be advantageous in terms of clubhead speed to release the

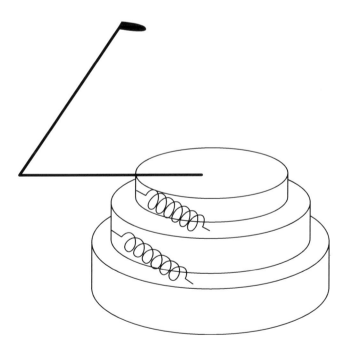

Figure 3.1   Mechanical model of the golf swing proposed by Cochran and Stobbs.

Source: Adapted from Cochran and Stobbs, 1968, p. 51.

springs sequentially from bottom to top. In other words, once the bottom spring has done all the work it can on the system, the top spring could be released in order to continue accelerating the top cylinder. Following this sequence, therefore, allows the springs at the bottom to transfer energy more efficiently to the club. This was one of the first accounts of the proximal-to-distal sequence of segmental motion in the golf swing.

Additionally, the contraction of the releasing springs not only accelerates the higher cylinder, but also, as a consequence, decelerates the lower cylinder. Verifying this unstated behaviour of Cochran and Stobbs's model, Bunn (1972) argued that, to maximise the linear speed of the last segment in a kinematic chain, each segment should reach its respective maximum velocity in a proximal-to-distal sequence. This meant that a segment should reach its maximum velocity after its proximal neighbour has begun decelerating. Bunn's reasoning was based on the components of the system's angular momentum: if distal segments could be tucked in close to the body until late in the movement, the moment of inertia could be minimised and the angular velocity maximised – a movement principle well built into our anatomy, as discussed at the beginning of the chapter. At impact, if the segments were released away from the body, the radius of rotation of the lead arm and club could be increased, thereby increasing the linear velocity of the club. The summation of speed principle was not originally crafted with the golf swing in mind, but it was rather a more general principle applicable to many sporting actions; however, the implications for golf are clear. Putnam (1993) later substantiated these claims with mathematical equations of motion. Putnam also showed that distal segments were accelerated by not only muscle torques at the proximal joint but also interaction torques that were dependent on inertial forces and contact forces between neighbouring segments. Thus, each segment will influence the motion of its neighbouring segment, by joint forces, in a way dependent on its state (position and rate of change of that position). The proximal-to-distal sequencing of distal segments arises because of the mechanical behaviour of linked systems.

Cochran and Stobbs (1968, p. 50) stated that the double pendulum had to be driven "smoothly and strongly" and that the angle of wrist cock should be maintained until "the time that uncocking will take place of its own accord". In other words, the swinging lead arm and club experience a centrifugal force that, in the club's case, will want it to continue moving in a straight line away from the arc of the swing. This will serve to uncock the wrists on the downswing, bringing the lead arm and club into a straight line, with no need for wrist torque. Jorgensen (1970) showed mathematically that, to maximise clubhead speed at impact, a negative wrist torque "hindering" the wrist angle uncocking is necessary.

The core of the golfer in Figure 3.1 is represented by stacked cylinders decreasing in size from bottom to top. This configuration reflects a key difference in proximal core segments compared to distal limb segments. While distal limb segments are connected end-to-end and rotate around a more horizontally oriented axis (i.e., upper arm ad/abduction), proximal core segments tend to rotate around a more vertically oriented axis running through the middle of the stacked segments. These differences relate to how energy and momentum are transferred between them. Empirical evidence for proximal-to-distal sequencing between core segments is discussed next, followed by the addition of distal limbs and the club in later parts.

Core rotation sequence and the X-factor

In a 1992 article for the *Golf Magazine*, golf instructor, Jim McLean, observed that long drivers on the PGA TOUR seemed to have a greater difference in shoulder and hip turn compared to the shortest drivers on tour (McLean, 1992). McLean called this swing feature the "X-Factor" because of how imaginary lines connecting the hip joint centres and shoulder joint centres crossed and resembled an "X" when viewed from above. We should note that "hip" and "shoulder" turn, as they are often called in popular golf publications, are not meant to represent rotation of the femur in the hip socket and rotation of the humerus in the shoulder girdle, respectively. Rather, these terms are intended to indicate rotation of the pelvis and rotation of the upper ribcage, or thorax, respectively. We will use the terms *pelvis* and *thorax* rotation in place of the golf terms hip and shoulder turn for the rest of the chapter.

Subsequent research has shown the relative angular displacement between the pelvis and thorax about an axis oriented approximately normal to the swing plane at the transition from backswing to downswing, which roughly corresponds to McLean's conception of the X-Factor, to have a strong relationship with clubhead speed (Myers et al., 2008; Chu et al., 2010; Brown et al., 2011). Unfortunately, variations in coordinate system, segment, angle, and transition timing definitions complicate comparisons between studies. Surprisingly, even though clubhead speed and handicap are strongly related (Fradkin et al., 2004), the X-Factor has not been shown to discriminate between skill levels (McTeigue et al., 1994; Cheetham et al., 2001; Egret et al., 2004; Cole & Grimshaw, 2009), with the exception of the study by Zheng et al. (2008), which found a significant difference only in the two extreme skill groups. The X-Factor is related to swing speed but does not seem to be acquired; instead, it appears to be individual specific and likely related to body anthropometrics as well as joint mobility and flexibility. Accordingly, discussion may be necessary to determine whether coaches should encourage golfers to increase their X-Factor. Notably, McLean's article had a marked impact on how the golf world thought about coordination between the core segments of the golfer.

By starting the downswing with pelvis rotation towards the target, followed by the thorax, Burden et al. (1998) suggested that low-handicap golfers could increase clubhead speed and that this pattern adhered to the summation-of-speed principle. Cheetham et al. (2001) found similar results and introduced a discrete variable called "X-Factor Stretch", which is the amount by which the X-Factor was increased as a result of delaying thorax rotation early in the downswing. Cheetham et al. found that highly skilled golfers increased the angular separation of the pelvis and thorax during the downswing more than less-skilled golfers did. Although small groups were compared, it is worth noting that there was no difference in the X-Factor between the groups, only the amount by which the X-Factor *stretched*, or increased, during the downswing. The effect of X-Factor Stretch could be explained by its initiation of the stretch-shortening cycle. Although it is not understood completely, the stretch-shortening cycle is thought to invoke several mechanisms important for generating speed:

a) By effectively increasing the range of motion, the distance over which the distal segment is able to accelerate is increased, which increases the amount of work done and, therefore, the kinetic energy and speed of the distal segment.

b) Pre-stretching the muscle enables it to begin the concentric contraction phase with a higher active state and force value (van Ingen Schenau et al., 1997).

c) Stretching muscles can also trigger the stretch reflex, which increases neural activity within the muscle, initiating a contraction to resist the stretch. The force–velocity relationship for skeletal muscle also indicates that stronger responses can be achieved if the muscle is stretched quickly (Komi, 2000).

Incidentally, Roach et al. (2013) pointed out that decoupling the pelvis and thorax was an important adaptation that allowed increased torque production in the core, critical for throwing actions. X-Factor Stretch seems to be what Cochran and Stobbs had in mind when they created their model consisting of the cylinders stacked on top of each other connected by springs. During the downswing, if the pelvis starts rotating towards the target earlier than the thorax, then the oblique abdominals would be put on stretch – the same way as the spring connecting the cylinders can be stretched by increasing the angular displacement between them. For golfers to increase their X-Factor Stretch, many exercises are available to increase thorax mobility and pelvis stability (refer to Chapter 30: Strength and Conditioning for Golf).

The contribution of the stretched core muscles associated with the X-Factor Stretch to club-head speed has been disputed by Kwon et al. (2012). In a sample of 14 elite-level golfers, the authors showed that the "swing plane" is only close to planar during the execution phase of the swing (from shaft horizontal on the downswing to shaft horizontal on the follow-through). Kwon et al. defined a "functional swing plane", which was a minimisation of trajectory errors for different phases of the swing. During the early downswing, the hands and club drop from a more upright plane onto a shallower plane for the execution phase, which is consistent with the findings of Vaughan (1981). The thorax was shown to rotate on a more horizontal plane, which led the authors to suggest that torque supplied to the arms from the thorax would consequently act to pull the club below the functional swing plane as impact approached. This deviation from the functional swing plane at impact would either cause a mishit with suboptimal clubhead speed or a compensation to get the moving distal segments back on plane, which would be inefficient, be difficult to control, and result in suboptimal clubhead speed. It is not clear, however, whether the authors considered a brief contribution of the thorax and its subsequent deceleration, as with the proximal-to-distal sequencing discussed thus far, or whether they considered the thorax to be doing work on the arms for the entire swing, which would most likely act to pull the club away from the swing plane. Furthermore, they did not explain why they thought segments rotating in slightly different planes would not meaningfully exchange energy. We suggest research needs to be conducted to determine the mechanism linking the X-Factor Stretch to clubhead speed, if any.

Adding the upper extremity

If we add the upper extremity to the core segments discussed so far, we may expect that:

a) Maximum speeds are reached in a proximal-to-distal sequence; and
b) The magnitude of those maximum speeds increases in the proximal to distal direction.

Cheetham et al. (2008) reported the maximum speeds and timings of the pelvis, thorax, arms, and club. They found that PGA professionals achieved higher peak segment speeds than a group of amateur golfers, and that the magnitudes of those peak segment speeds followed the familiar proximal-to-distal order. The timing between the peak speeds of successive segments, on average, followed the proximal-to-distal sequence for the professionals, but not for the amateurs. The comparison of timing between groups, however, did not reach statistical significance. The authors noted the high timing variability for the amateurs, which is an important finding on its own and likely contributed to the unclear distinction between groups. Neal et al. (2008) looked more closely at sequencing between "well-timed" shots and "poorly timed" shots, which were self-identified by the study participants. Their study design added to that of Cheetham et al., who may have unintentionally included poor shots in a study of optimal sequencing and timing. However, Neal et al. (2008) found no differences between well-timed and poorly timed shots. They explained that golfers tend to attribute high quality to a shot when contact is good and are relatively insensitive to timing differences.

If we reconsider the throwing example in the Introduction, if the implement being thrown were a spear, one of the keys to success is to maintain its orientation so that its long axis is close to parallel with its velocity vector – this prevents an end-over-end torque from ruining the throw. Swinging a golf club, on the other hand, is much different as the club rotates roughly around its long axis but also substantially around axes orthogonal to the long axis. Indeed, Anderson (2007) postulated that adding a golf club to the open link system might interfere with the proximal-to-distal sequencing shown for other "evolved" sports, such as throwing, discussed at the start of this chapter. Accordingly, the club – as an extension to the distal-most segment of our body – does not follow the natural tapering of volume, mass, and length found in body segments and likely requires an adaptation of coordination in the golf swing to achieve optimal speeds and control. Analysis of a dataset consisting of nearly 500 low-handicap and scratch golfers showed that the angular velocities of the pelvis, thorax, and arms peaked at about the same time in the swing, while the clubhead velocity peaked later and very close to impact. Anderson (2007) noted that *body* segments peaked at around the same time and the *non-body* segment – the club – peaked later, which could be considered evidence counter to the principle of proximal-to-distal sequencing along the segments mentioned. Anderson's findings are in contrast to the findings of others (Cheetham et al., 2008; Neal et al., 2008; MacKenzie and Sprigings, 2009). Furthermore, Anderson (2007) found that several kinetic quantities, such as angular momentum and kinetic energy, did not follow a proximal-to-distal sequence. Similar to angular velocity, distal segments showed higher peak total kinetic energy, but the timings of peak energies were approximately the same for the body segments and later for the club. It is difficult to explain the differences reported by Anderson (2007) relative to the rest of the literature; the movement model used and the kinematics calculations, although seemingly valid, make comparisons between studies difficult. In support of Anderson's findings, Nesbit and Serrano (2005) found that work was mainly done by the lumbar region; however, the timing of peak work found by Nesbit and Serrano generally followed the proximal-to-distal sequence.

The aforementioned empirical studies made inferences from groups, or large samples, of golfers (Anderson, 2007; Cheetham et al., 2008; Neal et al., 2008), as is common in sports biomechanics research. However, Ball and Best (2007) showed that different swing styles exist among low-handicap golfers, and that the specific style does not relate to playing ability. The fact that several swing styles may exist in Anderson's (2007) large dataset may explain the discrepancy between his results and those of other researchers. Representing a group of golfers by a mean value and simple measure of dispersion around the mean, such as standard deviation, may mask individuals within the group who exhibit common timing profiles and are sensitive to timing differences. As laid out by Button et al. (2006), coordination profiling may be the path to understanding nuance in movement patterning wherein individual variability is sufficiently large, which appears to be the case in the golf swing. Additionally, it is possible that smaller sample studies were prone to sampling bias, which could have the effect of magnifying the presence of proximal-to-distal sequencing.

Work by Kenny et al. (2008) also showed evidence against the proximal-to-distal sequencing principle in the golf swing. The authors created a forward dynamics model and set the muscle torques using the 3D kinematics of an elite-level golfer. The authors found that the kinetic energy for the arms peaked before those of the pelvis and thorax segments and suggested that the proximal-to-distal sequence may not be optimal. However, as MacKenzie and Sprigings (2009) point out, Kenny et al. (2008) did not actually investigate "optimal" sequencing; rather, they studied the sequencing of one elite-level golfer and assumed that the golfer's movement pattern was optimal. In Kenny et al.'s (2008) forward dynamics model, they could have manipulated muscle torque sequencing to find an optimal sequence, which has been done by others, particularly when looking at wrist torque.

Many mathematical and simulation studies have been conducted to test what Cochran and Stobbs originally suggested (i.e., that the end element in the model, the wrist hinge, should uncock by forces extending it on its own accord). In order for this to occur, a negative torque needs to be applied to maintain an acute wrist angle and to keep the club as close as possible to the swing hub (Neal & Wilson, 1985; Sprigings & Mackenzie, 2002; Coleman & Rankin, 2005). Keeping the club close reduces the moment of inertia while the more proximal segments build up angular velocity. It is now generally accepted that wrist torque through ulnar deviation has relatively little effect on increasing clubhead speed and, in fact, is more likely to negatively affect the timing of the swing for all but the best golfers. MacKenzie and Sprigings (2009) built on past simulation studies by looking at the optimal muscle activation sequence across the proximal and distal segments in the golf swing. The authors found that, for the most part, the optimal sequence followed a proximal-to-distal pattern. The muscle torque initiating the thorax rotation was the first to become active in their model, followed by the abduction torque at the shoulder and the wrist ulnar deviation shortly after. There was, however, one exception: an additional element in the upper extremity – forearm rotation – was activated last, which constituted a deviation from a proximal-to-distal sequence. MacKenzie and Sprigings explained that ulnar deviation contributed very little to accelerating the golf club because close to impact ulnar deviation is perpendicular to the direction of the golf club's movement. Forearm rotation is the final element in the sequence and, assuming that the golf club shaft and lead forearm were not parallel, contributes substantially to clubhead speed at impact. This pattern of activation fits with the findings of Marshall and Elliot (2000), who have looked mainly at throwing and tennis ground strokes. More specifically, long axis rotation of the upper arm is important for generating linear speed at the endpoint and occurs later than the proximal-to-distal sequence suggests.

Implications for the game

Findings in the literature on the importance of proximal-to-distal sequencing in the golf swing remain equivocal and have not reached a consensus. Simulation studies have shown that proximal-to-distal sequencing is consistent with optimality (MacKenzie & Sprigings, 2009), although with a slightly modified set of segments than originally proposed by Cochran and Stobbs (1968). To summarise, the pelvis should reach its maximum angular velocity first, followed by the thorax and the lead arm, at which point only negative torque should be applied at the wrist to maintain its acute angle until late in the downswing; the wrists should either uncock naturally due to centrifugal force or, if the golfer's skill level permits, a well-timed positive wrist torque can be applied, and finally forearm rotation tops up the clubhead speed and squares the face for impact.

Many empirical studies have shown that this sequence is not present, even in elite-level golfers. This can be explained in a number of ways:

- Many studies have used different models and calculations for various reasons. Although these discrepancies do not necessarily invalidate the findings of these investigations, they do make comparisons between studies difficult.
- The game of golf consists of more than hitting a ball with a full swing under laboratory conditions. Many players may be able to achieve low handicap or even professional status because of outstanding performance in other areas of the game, such as short game, putting, and a strong psychological component.
- Golfers are all constrained in different ways by their physical strengths and weaknesses, as well as strengths and weaknesses that have crept in over years of training, practice, and development in varying environments. These constraints may lead golfers to discover swings that work well, although not optimally (refer Chapter 5: Inter- and Intra-individual Movement Variability in the Golf Swing).

With these considerations in mind, golfers and practitioners should consider whether instilling a proximal-to-distal sequence might be beneficial. If a golfer who is free of major physical limitations struggles to achieve satisfactory distance, the timing of the swing may be at fault. Similarly, symptomatic shot patterns (e.g., high weak fade) are often consistent with poor timing or sequencing. In these situations, 3D systems, such as AMM3D and Golf Biodynamics, offer practical solutions for analysing the sequencing of the swing and for intervening to improve. As with most aspects of the golf swing, one solution does not fit all. Elite-level golfers looking to fine-tune their performance may not find it worthwhile to rebuild their swings to follow the proximal-to-distal sequence. Similarly, it may not be safe for golfers with physical constraints to try to achieve the sequence swing outlined in this chapter. The X-Factor Stretch in particular needs further research to determine possible links with and mechanisms of lower back injury, which is already a large and growing problem in golf.

Summary and future directions

We have identified support in the literature as well as counterexamples for a particular proximal-to-distal sequence of segment interactions in the golf swing. Although the movements of the golfer's segments can be measured with great precision, and scientific understanding of their role in the swing has reached great heights, "combining the movements is where the art begins" (Cochran & Stobbs, 1968, p. 47). There will always be examples of golfers with idiosyncratic swings who outperform those with simple, rhythmic, and well-timed swings. Rather than prescribing to-the-millimetre specifications of how the body should move in this chapter, we have offered guiding principles that golfers and practitioners should be aware of, and carefully consider, when technically inspecting their own or others' swings.

In a paradox whereby empirical studies may not be able to find what is optimal and simulation studies may not be able to find what is practical, we urge both sides to work to narrow these limitations. Empirical studies should focus on individual movement and coordination patterns or groups based on a common profile so that important findings are not covered up by group means. Simulation studies should continue to expand their models not just to represent a single golfer but a population of golfers with varying constraints.

References

Anderson, B. (2007) *Speed Generation in the Golf Swing: An Analysis of Angular Kinematics, Kinetic Energy and Angular Momentum in Player Body Segments*, Unpublished Msc Thesis, Canada: University of Calgary.

Ball, K. & Best, R. (2007) Different Centre of Pressure Patterns Within the Golf Stroke I: Cluster Analysis, *Journal of Sports Sciences*, 25 (7), 757–770.

Bramble, D. & Lieberman, D. (2004) Endurance Running and the Evolution of Homo, *Nature*, 432(7015), 345–352.

Brown, S.; Nevill, A.; Monk, S.; Otto, S.; Selbie, W. & Wallace, E. (2011) Determination of the Swing Technique Characteristics and Performance Outcome Relationship in Golf Driving for Low Handicap Female Golfers, *Journal of Sports Sciences*, 29 (14), 1483–1491.

Bunn, J. (1972) *Scientific Principles of Coaching* (2nd Ed.), Englewood Cliffs, NJ: Prentice Hall.

Burden, A.; Grimshaw, P. & Wallace, E. (1998) Hip and Shoulder Rotations During the Golf Swing of Sub-10 Handicap Players, *Journal of Sports Sciences*, 16 (2), 165–176.

Button, C.; Davids, K. & Schöllhorn, W. (2006) Coordination Profiling of Movement Systems, In: K. Davids; S. Bennett, & K. Newell (Eds.) *Movement System Variability*, Champaign, IL: Human Kinetics, pp. 133–152.

Cheetham, P.; Martin, P.; Mottram, R. & St. Laurent, B. (2001) The Importance of Stretching the "X-Factor" in the Downswing of Golf: The "X-Factor stretch", In: P. Thomas (Ed.) *Optimising Performance in Golf*, Brisbane, Australia: Australian Academic Press, pp. 192–199.

Cheetham, P.; Rose, G.; Hinrichs, R.; Neal, R.; Mottram, R.; Hurrion, P. & Vint, P. (2008) Comparison of Kinematic Sequence Parameters Between Amateur and Professional Golfers, In: D. Crews & R. Lutz (Eds.) *Science and Golf V: Proceedings of the World Scientific Congress of Golf*, Phoenix, AZ: Energy in Motion Inc., pp. 30–36.

Chu, Y.; Sell, T. & Lephart, S. (2010) The Relationship Between Biomechanical Variables and Driving Performance During the Golf Swing, *Journal of Sports Sciences*, 28 (11), 1251–1259.

Cochran, A. & Stobbs, J. (1968) *The Search for the Perfect Swing*, London: Heinemann.

Cole, M. & Grimshaw, P. (2009) The X-Factor and its Relationship to Golfing Performance, *Journal of Quantitative Analysis in Sports*, 5 (1), 1–19.

Coleman, S. & Rankin, A. (2005) A Three-Dimensional Examination of the Planar Nature of the Golf Swing, *Journal of Sports Sciences*, 23 (3), 227–234.

Egret, C.; Weber, J.; Dujardin, F. & Chollet, D. (2004) The Effect of Electromyographic Equipment on Golf Swing Kinematics, *Isokinetics and Exercise Science*, 12, 199–202.

Fradkin, A.; Sherman, C. & Finch, C. (2004) How Well Does Club Head Speed Correlate With Golf Handicaps? *Journal of Science and Medicine in Sport*, 7 (4), 465–472.

Hume, P.; Keogh, J. & Reid, D. (2005) The Role of Biomechanics in Maximising Distance and Accuracy of Golf Shots, *Sports Medicine*, 35 (5), 429–449.

Jorgensen, T. (1970) On the Dynamics of the Swing of a Golf Club, *American Journal of Physics*, 38 (5), 644–651.

Kenny, I.; McCloy, A.; Wallace, E. & Otto, S. (2008) Segmental Sequencing of Kinetic Energy in a Computer-Simulated Golf Swing, *Sports Engineering*, 11 (1), 37–45.

Komi, P. (2000) Stretch-Shortening Cycle: A Powerful Model to Study Normal and Fatigued Muscle, *Journal of Biomechanics*, 33 (10), 1197–1206.

Kwon, Y.-H.; Como, C.; Singhal, K.; Lee, S. & Han, K. (2012) Assessment of Planarity of the Golf Swing Based on the Functional Swing Plane of the Clubhead and Motion Planes of the Body Points, *Sports Biomechanics*, 11 (2), 127–148.

MacKenzie, S. & Sprigings, E. (2009) A Three-Dimensional Forward Dynamics Model of the Golf Swing, *Sports Engineering*, 11 (4), 165–175.

Marshall, R. & Elliott, B. (2000) Long-Axis Rotation: The Missing Link in Proximal-to-Distal Segmental Sequencing, *Journal of Sports Sciences*, 18 (4), 247–254.

McLean, J. (1992) Widen the Gap, *Golf Magazine*, 12, 49–53.

McTeigue, M.; Lamb, S.; Mottram, R. & Pirozzolo, F. (1994) Spine and Hip Motion Analysis During the Golf Swing, In: A. Cochran & M. Farrally (Eds.) *Science and Golf II: Proceedings of the World Scientific Congress of Golf*, London: E & FN Spon, pp. 50–58.

Myers, J.; Lephart, S.; Tsai, Y.-S.; Sell, T.; Smoliga, J. & Jolly, J. (2008) The Role of Upper Torso and Pelvis Rotation in Driving Performance During the Golf Swing, *Journal of Sports Sciences*, 26 (2), 181–188.

Neal, R. & Wilson, B. (1985) 3D Kinematics and Kinetics of the Golf Swing, *International Journal of Sport Biomechanics*, 1 (3), 221–232.

Neal, R.; Lumsden, R.; Holland, M. & Mason, B. (2008) Segment Interactions: Sequencing and Timing in the Downswing, In: D. Crews & R. Lutz (Eds.) *World Scientific Congress of Golf V*, Phoenix, AZ: Energy In Motion Inc., pp. 21–29.

Nesbit, S. & Serrano, M. (2005) Work and Power Analysis of the Golf Swing, *Journal of Sports Science and Medicine*, 4 (4), 520–533.

Novacheck, T. (1998) The Biomechanics of Running, *Gait and Posture*, 7 (1), 77–95.

Putnam, C. (1993) Sequential Motions of Body Segments in Striking and Throwing Skills: Descriptions and Explanations, *Journal of Biomechanics*, 26 (Supplement 1), 125–135.

Roach, N.; Venkadesan, M.; Rainbow, M. & Lieberman, D. (2013) Elastic Energy Storage in the Shoulder and the Evolution of High-Speed Throwing in Homo, *Nature*, 498 (7455), 483–486.

Sprigings, E. & MacKenzie, S. (2002) Examining the Delayed Release in the Golf Swing Using Computer Simulation, *Sports Engineering*, 5 (1), 23–32.

van Ingen Schenau, G.; Bobbert, M. & de Haan, A. (1997) Does Elastic Energy Enhance Work and Efficiency in the Stretch-Shortening Cycle? *Journal of Applied Biomechanics*, 13 (4), 389–415.

Vaughan, C. L. (1981) A Three-Dimensional Analysis of the Forces and Torques Applied by a Golfer During the Downswing, In: A. Morecki; K. Fidelus; K. Kedzior, & A. Wit (Eds.) *Biomechanics VII-B*, Baltimore, MA: University Park Press, pp. 325–331.

Zheng, N.; Barrentine, S.; Fleisig, G. & Andrews, J. (2008) Kinematic Analysis of Swing in Pro and Amateur Golfers, *International Journal of Sports Medicine*, 29 (6), 487–493.

4

THE KINEMATIC SEQUENCE

Achieving an efficient downswing

Robert J. Neal

Introduction

Since the research by Broadie (2015), which showed how important driving distance is to success in golf, it is clear that golfers need to understand how to drive the ball further. While there are a number of factors that affect how far the ball will travel, clubhead speed is by far the most important. Generating clubhead speed at impact is a function of how much energy can be generated by the body and how that energy can be transferred across joints to arrive at the clubhead at impact. This chapter initially describes the phenomenon of the kinematic sequence, followed by reference to the scientific work that underpins the idea.

A golfer's ability to create energy and transfer it effectively to the clubhead is a hallmark of high-level performance. One of the measures that have been used to illuminate this ability is the 'kinematic sequence'; a graphical representation of the angular velocity components of selected body segments during the downswing. In the scientific literature, proximal-to-distal patterns of motion are those movements of a linked kinematic chain in which the movement commences with the proximal link, by the onset of torques that cross the appropriate joints, and continue distally along the chain. The way in which the sequence of segment motions evolves and the way in which the movement is organized is dependent on the initial conditions and the requirements of the task (Chapman & Sanderson, 1993). Thus, in golf one hears a discussion of the kinematic sequence in relation to swing efficiency. The use of the word 'efficiency', in the layman's world and as used by golf coaches and commentators, is not consistent with those of classical mechanics (i.e., the ratio of energy output to energy input). Instead, it refers to the ability to generate clubhead speed at the appropriate time during the swing using a pattern of movement that 'looks' effortless to the casual observer.

The topic of segment interactions during proximal-to-distal patterns of motion has been the focus of attention of much research. Putnam (1983) developed a new and interesting framework to study segment interactions and formulated the equations of motion to investigate planar motion of a two-segment system. These concepts were developed further to include a third segment (Hoy & Zernicke, 1985) and the three-dimensional (3D) motion of two segments (Feltner & Dapena, 1989). Burko et al. (1999) increased the complexity of the model allowing three-segment motion to be analyzed in 3D.

The most common tasks that have been investigated by researchers working in this field have been throwing (various forms), hitting (golf, hockey, baseball) and kicking. The three most common classifications of throwing include underarm, sidearm and overarm. Javelin throwing or baseball pitching are good examples of overarm throwing, and while the motion of the torso segments is probably similar to that in golf, the motion at the joints of the upper limbs is quite different. Fast-pitch softball and 10-pin bowling are activities that would be classified as underarm actions. The movement of the body and limbs during these activities has a lot in common with the golf swing, which is a very specialized underarm throw. Sequencing in golf has received increased attention, at least in the popular press, over the past decade.

The notions of summation of speed and summation of energy, along with summation of force, have been used in biomechanics as 'principles' to understand movement qualitatively. When these concepts are studied quantitatively, there is little research evidence in support of these ideas. The first attempts at showing the summation of speed principle were for throwing activities. The challenge (and it remains challenging) is to choose which axes, planes and directions of movement are most representative of the movement outcome as well as the human body's ability to create such movement.

In the following sections, some different ways of representing the phenomena are described and discussed. Strengths and weaknesses of each approach are identified. However, before embarking on a description of the sequencing and timing approaches used in golf, it is imperative that the phases of the motion be defined.

Swing phases

For the purposes of this book chapter, only the downswing phase will be considered and it is defined as the epoch from the point in time when all segments have changed direction after the backswing until the clubhead contacts the ball (or ground). While there is some logic to the argument that many coaches contend that a good set-up and takeaway sequence are important to achieve a good golf swing, there have been no systematic studies that have correlated takeaway sequence to transition, downswing sequence and 'efficiency'. Thus, for this chapter, the focus is on the ensuing kinematics during the downswing rather than during transition or backswing.

Efficiency of effectiveness

In the context of this chapter, efficiency (the common term used by golfers and their coaches) does not carry the same meaning that it would do in physiology (e.g., McKardle et al., 2010) or traditional mechanics, wherein efficiency is the quotient of work output and energy input. Efficiency is about maximizing the output (e.g., energy) and minimizing the effort required to create the output. It is the ratio of energy in to energy out. In golf, it would be difficult to argue that the body would be trying to create maximum efficiency during the downswing. Rather, the objective, in full swings, is about creating optimal energy of the clubhead at impact rather than trying to minimize the physiological energy cost. It would probably be better for the golf industry to use the term 'effective' downswing kinematic sequence to describe the energy creation and transfer that highly skilled golfers display – rather than 'efficient sequence' – since it is highly unlikely that minimizing energy cost is the objective function in the golf swing. Furthermore, golfers are not always trying to maximize clubhead speed. In fact, highly skilled players are attempting to optimize clubhead speed at impact to create the exact carry distance needed for the shot. For example, with pitch and chip shots as well as putts, creating the appropriate amount of energy at impact is the desired goal.

Describing the kinematic sequence

Numerous features can be gleaned from careful interpretation of a kinematic sequence graph (Figure 4.1). These features are described below so that the reader can comprehend the types of approaches, as well as the strengths and weaknesses of each approach. The x-axis of each graph is time, with the start of transition denoted at $t_0 = 0$ and calculated as the point in time where the axial rotational velocity of the pelvis changes from negative to positive. Plotted on the ordinate is the component of the angular velocity that appears to be most related to the activity of generating rotational speed of the club. Of course, the requirement of playing good golf is that this plane (i.e., the plane fitted to the clubhead as it moves from pelvis height on either side of impact) must be oriented correctly relative to the target.

Just as Feltner and Dapena (1989) developed a procedure to describe the dominant movements of the upper limb in throwing, Neal's (2012) method selects the predominant rotational velocity components of the torso and upper limb segments in golf. The underpinning logic of this approach was to create a method that best described the appropriate angular velocity component of the involved segments in creating a golf swing. An assumption of this method is that as the speed of the clubhead increases, the motion of the arms, hands and club become planar. Specifically, each segment has its own plane of motion.

Firstly, it is evident that while the linear velocity of the clubhead at impact is the variable that is of most interest, since it largely determines the trajectory of the golf ball, it is the angular movements of the body segments and joints that create the clubhead velocity. Thus, the variables that are typically used to describe a kinematic sequence are angular velocities. Selected components of the angular velocity vector of the different body segments used to quantify the sequence are described below. The pelvis and upper torso (UT) components are located about an axis running through the centre of each segment, which is parallel to the spine (in the appropriate section of the spine). Thus, for the pelvis, the line of the posterior surface of the sacrum would be a close approximation to this axis, whereas for the UT, a line through the midline of the torso between T1 and T12 (thoracic spine) would represent this axis. The angular velocity components that are plotted for the other three segments (lead arm, lead hand and club) were calculated as follows. A plane of best fit was determined for each segment as it moved during the downswing. Rather than fit a plane for the entire swing, only those samples in the epoch from the point where the lead arm was parallel with the ground through to impact were used. The scalar product of the segment's total angular velocity and the unit vector that was normal to this plane gave the component of the angular velocity that is 'in plane'. These are the components that are plotted in the graph.

Figure 4.1 shows the kinematic sequence of a highly skilled, professional golfer. This sequence would be described as ideal because of the following characteristics. The peak angular speeds of the segments appear in time order from proximal to distal end. In other words, the pelvis reaches its peak first, followed by the UT, then the lead arm and lastly the hands and club. The peak angular speed of the most distal segment, the club (within its plane of motion), appears at or just prior to impact. The time lags between the peaks are of similar magnitudes and are of the order of 30 ms. The peak speed of each successive distal segment is higher than the contiguous proximal one, and these speed 'jumps' are of the order of 250°/s.

A number of authors (e.g., Cheetham et al., 2001) have discussed the possibility of stretch-shortening cycles (SSCs) being present in the golf swing, and there is some evidence for that phenomenon within the kinematic sequence graph. For example, when the proximal segment is rotating more rapidly than the distal segment, the relative angular displacement between the two segments is increasing. Thus, the structures in the body (i.e., muscles, tendons and fascia) on one side of the joint are lengthening, while the ones on the other side are shortening.

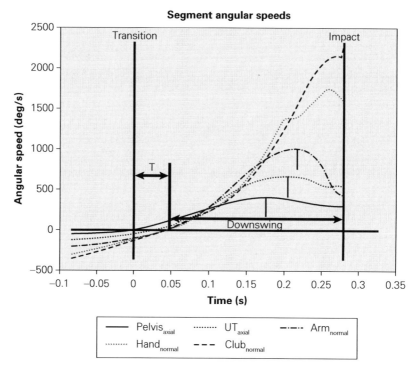

Figure 4.1 Kinematic sequence during the downswing of a professional golfer using a six-iron.

Note: **T** indicates the transition phase.

This phenomenon occurs due to the positive work done by the muscles that accelerate the proximal segment. Of course, it is not known whether those muscles that are lengthening are also trying to contract at this point in time, so it is not clear whether an SSC is present. Using horizontal flexion–extension at the lead shoulder joint as an example should help to clarify this idea. In the backswing, the lead shoulder is undergoing horizontal flexion, primarily through the action of the pectoralis muscles. To stop this movement and then create horizontal extension, the muscles on the posterior side of the shoulder (e.g., posterior deltoids, latissimus dorsi and lower trapezius) would contract. Initially, it is theorized that they would contract eccentrically, but once sufficient force is applied, they would begin to shorten (contract concentrically). This series of events could be considered an SSC at the lead shoulder and would be a great topic for further study using modelling techniques and electromyography (EMG).

Upon close examination of the graph in Figure 4.1, there are four instances in which the proximal segment is rotating faster than the distal one.

1   Early in the transition phase (T) through to time $t = 0.09$, the pelvis (solid line) is rotating faster than the UT (black dotted line).
2   From the point just prior to the transition phase end ($t = 0.04$), the UT is rotating faster than the arm (dash-dot line).
3   For almost half of the downswing phase ($t = 0.07$ to $t = 0.16$), the arm is rotating faster than the hand (grey dotted line).
4   During the middle half of the downswing ($t = 0.11$ to $t = 0.19$), the hand is rotating faster than the club (dashed line).

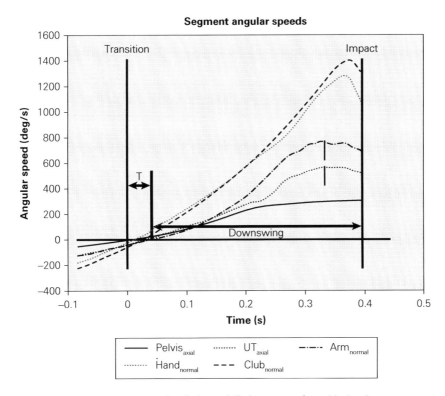

Figure 4.2 Kinematic sequence example of a lesser skilled, amateur player (six-iron).

It would be interesting to find out, using muscle modelling techniques in conjunction with empirical data, whether the muscles that cross these different joints do at any stage display eccentric, followed immediately by concentric muscle, action.

By way of comparison, a graph of an amateur golfer is included as Figure 4.2. The main differences that can be noted with this player compared to the highly skilled player are that the transition phase is much shorter, the peak speeds are much lower, the order of the peak speeds is different and the evidence for SSC use is weak (at best). The reader can also note that the acceleration–deceleration profile is much different from that of the professional player who has both greater positive and negative accelerations of the proximal segments (pelvis, UT and arm) during the downswing phase than the amateur player. The implication of the high decelerations is that energy is flowing from the proximal to the distal segment. The data in Figure 4.2 are consistent with the results presented by Cheetham et al. (2008), who examined differences between amateur and professional golfers. They reported that almost all of the 18 discrete variables that they chose to describe a kinematic sequence were different between the two groups.

Sequencing versus timing

In the common literature, there appears to be ambiguity when referring to timing (and perhaps to sequencing). In fact, many television commentators and golf coaches will describe a well-hit shot that looks effortless on the part of the player, as being 'well-timed'. The quantification of this phenomenon is neither well described nor well understood. It appears (Neal et al., 2007) that from a player's perspective, the notion of being well timed has more to do with where on the clubhead the ball makes contact and less to do with feelings of lag by the player. No other published studies have investigated this phenomenon.

Qualitative observations in the field indicate that small time lags between the peak angular velocities of the adjoining segments is a variable that is sensitive to shot-to-shot differences. Thus, the peaking order and the times between peaks seem to be reasonable candidates at this stage to quantify shots that are well timed versus those that are mistimed. This idea also challenges the common practice in golf of using only one trial (usually a good shot!) as the swing on which an analysis is completed. Shot-to-shot variability in timing and sequencing are likely to be related to differences in shot quality and ball contact efficacy. Thus, investigations of these notions would seem to be a very useful addition to the research.

Sequencing, on the other hand, seems to be a simple way of classifying the order in which the peak angular velocities occur. The sequence for the professional golfer is often described as 1, 2, 3, 4 and 5 (pelvis, UT, arm, hand and club), whereas the pattern for the lesser-skilled player would be 5, 1, 1, 3 and 4 (pelvis, UT, arm, hand and club; see the example graph) or typically 5, 1, 3, 2 and 4 (pelvis, UT, arm, hand and club). This simple method of classifying the peaking order gives golfers and their coaches something that they can easily understand.

Robustness of phenomenon (use of different 'methods' to calculate and then graph the data)

One of the most important aspects to understand when evaluating the notion of summation of speed (or energy or force) is how persistent the phenomenon is with different methods used to display or calculate the data. In Figure 4.3, the same swing as displayed in Figure 4.1 was used but instead of looking at selected components of the angular velocity vector, the total angular speed (the square root of the sum of the squared components) of each segment is plotted. The same conclusions for both can be drawn (peaking order is the same, evidence for SSC is present, timing lags are very similar, velocity increases as time progresses and the speeds of the distal contiguous segment are greater than those of the proximal ones). One subtle difference is that both the hand and club reach maximum angular velocity at impact.

A second method, suggested by Kwon et al. (2012, 2013), uses the angular velocity component for each segment that is normal to the functional swing plane (FSP). The FSP is described as the plane of best fit of the trajectory of the golf club during the time when the shaft is parallel with the ground prior to and after impact. The data in Figure 4.4 represent this treatment of the same data depicted in Figures 4.1 and 4.3. One can notice that while four of the segments maintain their same relative orders and illustrate increasing angular velocity as a function of time, the peak speed of the pelvis occurs much later in the downswing. The timing lags and the speed gains are very similar despite the different ways in which the data are treated. Thus, proximal-to-distal sequencing is present and robust in that it can be quantitatively described using a variety of methods.

Pitching downswing sequence

Recently, there has been much conjecture about the nature of the kinematic sequence for short pitch and wedge shots. Some golf instructors (Sieckmann & Denunzio, 2015) have claimed that the transition sequence for pitching is the reverse of the full swing sequence;

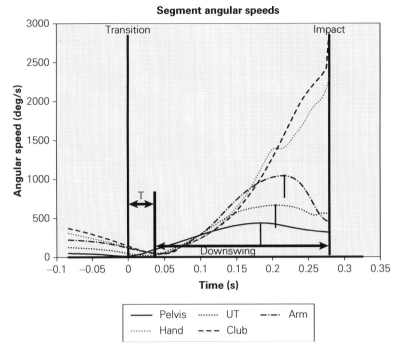

Figure 4.3 Total segment angular speeds for the five segments plotted as a function of time.

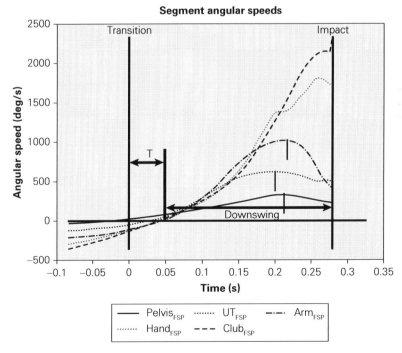

Figure 4.4 Kinematic sequence of the highly skilled professional player using the methods described by Kwon et al. (2012, 2013).

(a)

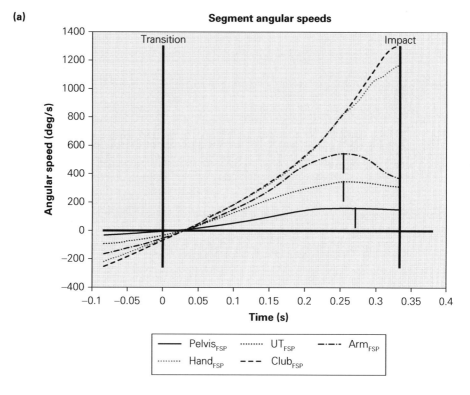

(b)

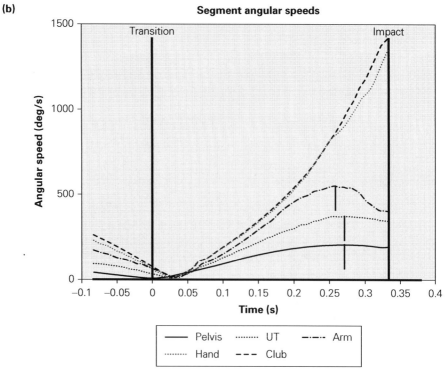

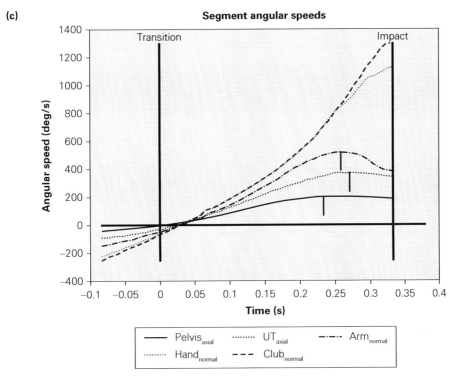

Figure 4.5 Kinematic sequence graphs for a 40 yard pitch shot of a professional golfer. Kwon et al.'s (2012, 2013) FSP method is shown in panel (a), total angular speed is shown in panel (b) and the axial velocity components of the pelvis and UT, as well as the normals to the planes, are shown in panel (c).

the order in which the segments change direction is exactly the opposite of the full shot (i.e., club first, then hands, arms, UT and pelvis). Others (e.g., Neal, 2013; Sinclair, 2016) believe that the sequence in transition is almost identical to full shots, but the patterns of acceleration–deceleration vary. In order for the reader to get a picture of the sequencing for a small pitch shot, the graphs displayed in Figure 4.5 represent the patterns displayed by the same touring professional (who also happens to be an incredibly good wedge player!) hitting a 40-yard wedge shot.

Perusal of the data in Figure 4.5 leads one to conclude that the pattern is different from a full swing but not 'opposite', as Sieckmann and Denunzio (2015) claim. Once again, as with full-speed shots, the different methods used to calculate the velocities show different peaking orders but the shapes of the lines in the graphs are quite similar. Note also how 'flat' the angular velocity curves for the pelvis and UT are around the times that peak speed is attained. The selection of a 'peak' of a line whose slope is zero (or close to zero) is ill defined, and the selected points could well be a reflection of the noise in the signal rather than the signal itself! Thus, although technically the methods illustrate different peaking orders, it could be cogently and logically argued that because the speeds are almost constant around the peaks, the peaking order is unimportant in this skill and is highly dependent on the quality of the data and not necessarily the method selected to calculate and then display the data.

Review of current research

While sequencing, timing and segment interactions in a variety of activities have seen research interest dating back to the 1930s (Bunn, 1930), followed by a surge in the 1970s (Plagenhoef 1971; Bunn, 1972), the phenomena did not really capture the interest of researchers until the past 30 years. The technological tools to measure segment motion saw rapid development over these years, allowing people to quickly calculate the kinematics of human movement. Even back in the 1980s, research was painstaking and time consuming compared to today, when these data are calculated almost in real time! Putnam (1983) provided insights that spawned renewed interest in segment interactions and that led to a relatively large body of biomechanical work that has investigated sequencing and timing in activities as different as throwing, walking, running and kicking. Rather than provide a comprehensive review of that early work, this review of current research is based on studies that have been conducted on throwing and golf over the past 20 years (approximately). By including throwing and golf swing (really a modified form of throwing), one can get a better sense of how important the notion of sequencing and timing is, and that scientists across a whole range of activities feel that this phenomenon is a hallmark of expertise and can be used to help understand human movement and control.

It appears as though the concept of proximal-to-distal sequencing is reasonably well accepted within the biomechanics literature, although there is ambiguity in the way in which it is measured and defined. The phenomenon is discussed in numerous activities, including tennis (Marshall & Elliott, 2000), handball (van den Tillar & Ettema, 2011), throwing (Feltner & Dapena, 1989; Escamilla et al., 2002), field hockey (Bretigny et al., 2008) and golf (Meister et al., 2011). The precise way in which people have attempted to describe proximal-to-distal sequencing is where the research seems clouded. The illustrations earlier in this paper were an effort to show that if different data analytics are applied to the same data, differing conclusions about sequencing and timing arise. The challenge is to come up with a process that is widely accepted to describe the phenomenon, allowing clarity within the research.

Another example of how operational definitions constrain conclusions is the work on throwing conducted by van den Tillar and Ettema (2009). Their conclusions were that temporal proximal-to-distal sequencing was found only for the initiation of the joint movements but no such sequence was found for the maximal velocity of the joints and distal endpoints of segments. Southard (2009), on the other hand, noted that timing lags were present in throwing at sub-maximal speeds and that they could be used to differentiate between throwing skill levels. Furthermore, Southard claimed that wrist lag was the best discriminator of young (child-like) and adult throwing patterns. In golf, Zheng et al. (2008) examined differences among golfers of four different skill levels (pro, low-handicap, mid-handicap and high–handicap levels). The higher angular velocities generated by the professionals appeared to be related to the ability to maintain separation between the UT and pelvis segments, as well as in maintaining an extended left elbow and a flexed wrist position later into the downswing.

In a study of field hockey drive shots (a similar action to the golf swing), Bretigny et al. (2008) showed a proximal-to-distal sequence of motion for both types of shots studied, as well as evidence of lag (inter-limb disassociation) of the lead upper limb. Findings by Tinmark et al. (2010) showed a significant proximal-to-distal temporal relationship and a concomitant successive increase in maximum (peak) segment angular speed in every shot condition (pitch shots, five-iron and driver) for both genders and levels of expertise.

An additional study by Lorson et al. (2013) showed that patterns of throwing (qualitatively assessed) improved through adolescence, peaked at adulthood and then declined. It would be interesting to know whether this pattern exists quantitatively and in golf. Furthermore, if this phenomenon is evident in golf, what are the implications for older-aged participants?

Theory on feedback and the humans' ability to modify sequence in the last few milliseconds of the downswing suggest that it is not possible for the body to alter the movement based on feedback because the loop times are too long to effect change. Osis and Stefanyshyn's (2012) work challenged this view using a research protocol that changed the stiffness of the system (club shaft and vibration interference with little motors) late in the downswing. They demonstrated significant slowing of the club grip during club release for a high-stiffness shaft with vibration. This finding suggests that proprioceptive feedback, if available to players, allows adaptation to changes in club stiffness by modifying the release dynamics of the club late in the downswing.

The research cited above focused on kinematic measures of movement. Putnam (1991) concluded that the motion-dependent torques (i.e., the part of the resultant joint torque that is dependent on either the angular velocity or acceleration of the adjoining, distal segment) help to explain proximal-to-distal sequencing and that the summation of speed principle appears to provide a sound explanation of the proximal-to-distal phenomenon. The summation of force and 'general' statements concerning the effect of decelerations of contiguous segments do not seem to hold water. Primarily, the notion of summing forces across segments (as opposed, e.g., to summing energy) does not have a good theoretical basis. Perhaps total impulse applied to segments might be a better set of variables to describe the proximal-to-distal phenomenon or sequencing and timing than peak forces. Peak forces are more likely to be predictors of injury or failure than of efficiency of movement.

It is evident from numerous simulation studies that the timing of active/passive torques influences clubhead speed (Kojima & Chapman, 1992; Neal et al., 1999; Sprigings & Neal, 2000; Sprigings & Mackenzie, 2002; Chen et al., 2007). These studies show strong evidence for timing and sequencing in the application of the forces and torques that create movement of the body segments and the club. Thus, although the summation of force principle does not hold (Putnam, 1991), the timing of the application of the forces and torques does show a proximal-to-distal pattern.

As suggested earlier in this paper, the kinetic energy (KE) of the clubhead at impact is probably a better choice of mechanical variable to describe the 'effectiveness' of the swing than clubhead speed. This variable includes both the mass and speed of the segment (including the club) and is a direct result of the work done by the forces and torques created by the muscles. Kenny et al. (2008) showed a high level of correlation between driver and iron peak KE, as well as timing of peak KE relative to impact. In addition, peak KE magnitudes increased sequentially from the proximal to the distal segments during swing simulations for both the driver and seven-iron, supporting the principle of the summation of speed. However, timing of peak KE was not sequential from the proximal to the distal segments, nor did segments peak simultaneously. Rather, arms peaked first, followed by hips, torso and club. This seems to indicate a subjective optimal coordination of sequencing. Clearly, greater research effort needs to be directed towards understanding the work/energy relationship in golf and whether it would be better for players and coaches to understand energy flow through the system rather than describing angular velocity.

Implications for the game

Knowledge of kinematic sequencing is crucial in coaching, but of equal importance to coaches is the ability to use this information to build a system of coaching that includes proximal-to-distal patterns of movements as a foundational element of a sound golf swing. Furthermore, a good coach must have a systematic approach to teaching these foundations (not just proximal-to-distal patterns but other movement skills that are the foundations of success). Included in this system would be the ability to break down the golf swing into a number of smaller movement skills that can be taught and then 'chunked' together to form a full swing. Implicit in this coaching process is the development of drills, the use of teaching aids and biofeedback, to enhance the quality of the learning process to ensure that the student learns to move correctly.

Getting all coaches and biomechanists to use the same or similar approaches for presenting data will be important to ensure that miscommunication is minimized and factions do not develop among golf coaches. Already, it is evident that if different analytical techniques are used to manipulate data and those data are presented in varying ways, there is opportunity for a multitude of interpretations of the same movement phenomenon! It behoves the biomechanists and golf coaches who are involved in golf swing mechanics at an advanced level to meet and decide on principles and systems of producing and presenting biomechanical data.

An important message to get out to golfers themselves is that sequencing of the movement of the segments of the body is not an inherent (genetically determined) skill. Movement patterns change over time and with experience. As an example, the throwing pattern adopted by a 3-year-old kid is hardly representative of the pattern used by a major league baseball pitcher. The coordination and sub-skills possessed by both people in this example are wildly different.

Golfers should also be informed that having a perfect sequence is not the 'only' thing that is important in their swings. If you cannot match the correct kinematic sequence with the combination of correct position and orientation of the body and club, then the effectiveness of your swing is very low. In fact, you could have a perfect sequence but miss the ball! It is fair to say, however, that an ideal transition sequence goes a long way to creating good downswing dynamics and sequencing.

Summary and future directions

The following points are suggestions made with both a research cap and a practitioner's hat on! To understand proximal-to-distal patterns of movement across a wide variety of golf skills/shots would be a worthy objective. To reach that goal, I have suggested a couple of directions for future work (applied research).

Instead of using speed or angular velocity, we should use segment KE (KE is a scalar variable and therefore obviates the problems associated with the different methods that are used to display angular velocities of the segments). It is also indicative of the mechanical work (both angular and linear) that the golfer does during the downswing, giving insight into the muscular forces and torques applied across the joints. If KE turns out to be the best candidate for describing proximal-to-distal sequencing and timing for all types of shots (e.g., small pitch and wedge shots, with bunker shots and perhaps even putts), then a universally accepted practice would help golfers and their coaches understand swing inadequacies.

Research investigating the notion of SSC using appropriate modelling methods is needed. It is important to understand why this pattern of proximal-to-distal sequencing is evident in many activities. While it is likely to be related to the properties of the muscular–skeletal system (e.g., force–velocity relationship for human muscle and length–tension relationships in muscle), those relationships have not been established. It would also be great to see research on the roles of different types of muscles (mono- versus bi-articular) in creating and transferring energy throughout the body.

Research investigating the following small, but different ways in which data are collected on golfers must be done. Does hitting real golf balls (i.e., not just a 'whiffle' ball) make a difference to the movements of a golfer? Does hitting indoors, into a net, versus outdoors to a real target make a difference to the kinematics and, therefore, the sequencing and timing patterns that golfers adopt? How consistent are the shot-to-shot sequencing and timing and how many shots need to be struck and analyzed before you could be sure that you are describing the patterns of movement that a golfer uses (generally) as opposed to an outlier?

Efforts should be made to extend the qualitative work of Langendorfer and Roberton (2002), which showed, for children, that throwing movement patterns changed within filming sessions and longitudinally. This work has major implications for instructors/coaches who are trying to improve the swings of their clients. How best to make these changes and then getting them to 'stick' (be retained) is of paramount importance.

Lastly, a very important message to get out to the golf community is that while the holy grail of movement may be a perfect kinematic sequence, many successful professional players do not use this pattern when executing their golf swings. Cheetham and Mackenzie (2016) noted that only 42% of tour professionals display the ideal peaking order. Thus, you can be successful at the highest levels of golf without an ideal kinematic sequence!

References

Bretigny, P.; Seifert, L.; Leroy, D. & Chollet, D. (2008) Upper-Limb Kinematics and Coordination of Short Grip and Classic Drives in Field Hockey, *Journal of Applied Biomechanics*, 24 (3), 215–223.

Broadie, M.N. (2015) *Every Shot Counts*, New York, NY: Penguin Books.

Bunn, J. (1972) *Scientific Principles of Coaching*, Englewood Cliffs, NJ: Prentice-Hall.

Burko, D.; Neal, R. & Sprigings, E. (1999) Three-Dimensional Segment Interactions in a Three-Segment Model, In: W. Herzog & A. Jinha (Eds.) *Proceedings of the 1999 International Society of Biomechanics Congress*, Calgary, Canada: University of Calgary, p. 354.

Chapman, A. & Sanderson, G. (1993) Analysis of Muscular Work in Multisegmental Movements, In: J. Winters & S. Woo (Eds.) *Multiple Muscle Systems: Biomechanics and Movement Organization*, New York: Springer-Verlag, pp. 608–619.

Cheetham, P. & Mackenzie, S. (2016) Forces and Motion – Kinetics and Kinematics, *Workshop Presented at Sinclair's Golf Training Center*, Dallax, TX, April 14, 2016.

Cheetham, P.; Martin, P.; Mottram, R. & St Laurent, B. (2001) The Importance of Stretching the "X-Factor" in the Downswing of Golf: The "X-Factor" Stretch, In: P. Thomas (Ed.) *Optimising Performance in Golf*, Brisbane, Australia: Australian Academic Press, pp. 192–199.

Cheetham, P.; Rose, G.; Hinrichs, R.; Neal, R.; Mottram, R.; Hurrion, P. & Vint, P. (2008) Comparison of Kinematic Sequence Parameters Between Amateur and Professional Golfers, In: D. Crews & R. Lutz (Eds.) *Science and Golf V: Proceedings of the World Scientific Congress of Golf*, Mesa, AZ: Energy in Motion, pp. 30–36.

Chen, C.; Inoue, Y. & Shibara, K. (2007) Numerical Study on the Wrist Action During the Golf Downswing, *Sports Engineering*, 10 (1), 23–31.

Escamilla, R.; Fleisig, G.; Barrentine, S.; Andrews, J. & Moorman, C. (2002) Kinematic and Kinetic Comparison of American and Korean Professional Baseball Pitchers, *Sports Biomechanics*, 1 (2), 213–228.

Feltner, M. & Dapena, J. (1989) Three-Dimensional Interactions in a Two-Segment Kinetic Chain. Part I: General Model, *International Journal of Sports Biomechanics*, 5 (4), 403–419.

Hoy, M. & Zernicke, R. (1985) Modulation of Limb Dynamics During the Swing Phase of Locomotion, *Journal of Biomechanics*, 18 (1), 49–60.

Kenny, I.; Mccloy, A.; Wallace, E. & Otto, S. (2008) Segmental Sequencing of Kinetic Energy in a Computer-Simulated Golf Swing, *Sports Engineering*, 11 (1), 37–45.

Kojima, T. & Chapman, A. (1992) Is the Proximal to Distal Sequence of Torque Onset a Common Feature of All Types of Simulated Throws and Puts? *Journal of Biomechanics*, 25 (7), 710.

Kwon, Y.; Como, C.; Han, K.; Lee, S. & Singhal, K. (2012) Assessment of Planarity of the Golf Swing Based on the Functional Swing Plane of the Clubhead and Motion Planes of the Body Points, *Sports Biomechanics*, 11 (2), 127–148.

Kwon, Y.; Han, K.; Como, C.; Lee, S. & Singhal, K. (2013) Validity of the X-Factor Computation Methods and Relationship Between the X-Factor Parameters and Clubhead Velocity in Skilled Golfers, *Sports Biomechanics*, 12 (1), 231–246.

Langendorfer, S. & Roberton, M. (2002) Individual Pathways in the Development of Forceful Throwing, *Research Quarterly for Exercise and Sport*, 76 (3), 245–256.

Lorson, K.; Stodden, D.; Langenorfer, S. & Goodway, J. (2013) Age and Gender Differences in Adolescent and Adult Overarm Throwing, *Research Quarterly for Exercise and Sport*, 84 (2) 239–244.

Marshall, R. & Elliott, B. (2000) Long Axis Rotation: The Missing Link in Proximal-to-Distal Segmental Sequencing, *Journal of Sports Sciences*, 18 (4), 247–254.

McCardle, W.D.; Katch, F.I. & Katch, V. (2010) *Essentials of Exercise Physiology* (4th Ed.), Philadelphia, PA: Lippincott Williams & Wilkins.

Meister, D.; Ladd, A.; Butler, E.; Zhao, B.; Rogers, A.; Ray, C. & Rose, J. (2011) Rotational Biomechanics of the Elite Golf Swing: Benchmarks for Amateurs, *Journal of Applied Biomechanics*, 27 (3), 242–251.

Neal, R. (2013) *The 3D Biomechanics of Pitching: How Do Highly Skilled Players Control Distance?* Presentation to the Professional Golfers' Association (GB&I), Harrogate, October 6–8, 2013.

Neal, R.; Burko, D.; Sprigings, E. & Landeo, R. (1999) Segment Interactions During the Golf Swing: 3 Segments in 3D, In: W. Herzog & A. Jinha (Eds.) *Proceedings of the 1999 International Society of Biomechanics Congress*, Calgary, Canada: University of Calgary, P. 690.

Neal, R.; Lumsden, R.; Holland, M. & Mason, B. (2007) Body Segment Sequencing and Timing in Golf, In: S. Jenkins (Ed.) *Annual Review of Golf Coaching*, London: Multi-Science Co., pp. 25–36.

Neal, R.J. (2012) Amplifying Body Speed: Stretch-shortening At the Lead Shoulder, In: D. Crews (Ed.) *Science and Golf VI: Proceedings of the World Scientific Congress of Golf*, London: E & FN Spon.

Osis, S. & Stefanyshyn, D. (2012) Golf Players Exhibit Changes to Grip Speed Parameters During Club Release in Response to Changes in Club Stiffness, *Human Movement Science*, 31 (1), 91–100.

Plagenhoef, S. (1971) *Patterns of Human Motion*, Englewood Cliffs, NJ: Prentice-Hall.

Putnam, C. (1983) Interaction Between Segments During a Kicking Motion, In: K. Matsui & K. Kobayashi (Eds.) *Biomechanics VIII-B*, Champaign, IL: Human Kinetics, pp. 688–694.

Putnam, C. (1991) A Segment Interaction Analysis of Proximal-to-Distal Sequential Segment Motions, *Medicine and Science in Sport and Exercise*, 23 (1), 130–144.

Sieckmann, J. & Denunzio, D. (2015) *Your Short Game Solution: Mastering the Finesse Game From 120 Yards and In*, New York, NY: Penguin Random House LLC.

Sinclair, J. (2016) Discovering the Differences Between 2D Video and 3D Motion Capture, *Presentation to the Proponent Group*, Orlando, January 26, 2016.

Southard, D. (2009) Throwing Pattern: Changes in Timing of Joint Lag According to Age Between and Within Skill, *Research Quarterly for Exercise and Sport*, 80 (2), 213–222.

Sprigings, E. & Mackenzie, S. (2002) Examining the Delayed Release in the Golf Swing Using Computer Simulation, *Sports Engineering*, 5 (1), 23–32.

Sprigings, E. & Neal, R. (2000) An Insight into the Importance of Wrist Torque in Driving the Golf Ball: A Simulation Study, *Journal of Applied Biomechanics*, 16 (4), 356–366.

Tinmark, F.; Hellström, J.; Halvorsen, K. & Thorstensson, A. (2010) Elite Golfers' Kinematic Sequence in Fullswing and Partial-Swing Shots, *Sports Biomechanics*, 9 (4), 236–244.

van den Tillar, R. & Ettema, G. (2009) Is There a Proximal-to-Distal Sequence in Overarm Throwing in Team Handball? *Journal of Sports Sciences*, 27 (9), 949–955.

van den Tillar, R. & Ettema, G. (2011) A Comparison of Kinematics Between Overarm Throwing with 20% Underweight, Regular, and 20% Overweight Balls, *Journal of Applied Biomechanics*, 27 (4), 252–257.

Zheng, N.; Barrentine, S.; Fleisig, G. & Andrews, J. (2008) Kinematic Analysis of Swing in Pro and Amateur Golfers, *International Journal of Sports Medicine*, 29 (6), 487–493.

5

INTER-AND INTRA-INDIVIDUAL MOVEMENT VARIABILITY IN THE GOLF SWING

Paul S. Glazier and Peter F. Lamb

Introduction

The golf swing has come under more scrutiny than perhaps any other sports technique, if not in the scientific literature, certainly in the sports coaching literature, popular press, and television coverage. The exact reason for this attention is unclear but it is likely to be related to the unique task constraints of golf (i.e., the spatial and temporal certainty of hitting a stationary ball to a stationary target often several hundred metres away) and the general perception that technique and performance in golf, perhaps more so than in any other sport, are inimitably linked (i.e., a better technique leads to better performance). Most coaching manuals, magazine articles, and instructional videos on golf advocate that the key to improving a golfer's game and lowering his or her score is the development of a simple, consistent, and repeatable golf swing (e.g., Leadbetter & Huggan, 1990). A set grip, stance, backswing, downswing, and follow-through have typically been promoted, which are presumed to represent a 'perfect' or 'ideal' golf swing that every aspiring golfer wishing to improve his or her game should aim to achieve and golf-coaching practitioners can use as a template to compare their students' techniques against to identify faults, prescribe fixes, and evaluate injury risk (e.g., Sherman & Finch, 1999; Sherman et al., 2001; Smith et al., 2015). The general consensus of opinion, therefore, appears to be that inter- and intra-individual movement variability[1] in the golf swing is detrimental to performance and should be eliminated or coached out.

Although there has been some conflicting evidence, these coaching philosophies have provided the basis for, and have received some support in, scientific investigations published on the biomechanics of the golf swing (e.g., Richards et al., 1985; Sanders & Owen, 1992). The motor learning and control literatures, too, have traditionally emphasised invariant movement patterns as a hallmark feature of expert motor performance (e.g., Schmidt, 1985). Typically, any inter-individual variability has been viewed as deviations from a putative common optimal movement pattern (e.g., Brisson & Alain, 1996) and, thus, deemed to be error, and any intra-individual variability has typically been seen as corruptive noise, either in the neural signals or in the hierarchical control structure (i.e., motor program) that specifies them (e.g., Faisal et al., 2008). More recently, however, theoretical and empirical investigations in human movement science, based on the principles and concepts of dynamical systems theory, have suggested that movement variability may both afford, and be a reflection of, great flexibility and adaptability in the movement system[2] (refer to excellent texts by Newell & Corcos, 1993; Davids et al., 2006; Smith et al., 2014; Stergiou, 2016). Although invariance of impact location is highly desirable (Figure 5.1), there is growing evidence that variance in the underlying movement patterns, which is largely attributable to internal and external constraints imposed on the golfer (Newell, 1986) as well as nonlinearities introduced by the physical self-organisation of system degrees of freedom (Kelso, 1995), is likely to be integral to consistent ball striking and adept golf performance (refer to Newell & James, 2008, for a more general discussion about the inverse relationship between process and outcome variability).

Considering these recent theoretical and empirical developments, the purpose of this chapter is to provide readers with a review of the existing literature that has examined inter- and intra-individual movement variability in the golf swing. A thorough examination of the nature and role of movement variability in the golf swing is long overdue (refer to Langdown et al., 2012, for an initial attempt), particularly considering the ubiquity of this aspect of motor performance and the fact that it has been a recurring topic of debate in the sport and human movement sciences for some time (e.g., Hatze, 1986; Slifkin & Newell, 1998; Bartlett et al., 2007), but seldom has it been given due consideration in the golf literature. Furthermore, in a status report on golf science that appeared in the *Journal of Sports Sciences* in 2003, Farrally et al. (2003) targeted the resolution of variability and consistency issues, especially those related to the ageing population of golfers, as a priority for future golf research agendas (refer to Wallace et al., 2008, and Evans & Tuttle, 2015, for similar recommendations). Apart from a few notable recent exceptions (Horan et al., 2011; Morrison et al., 2016), there has been a paucity of high-quality, systematic investigations into the nature and role of movement variability in the golf swing. In addition to being informative for the golfer and golf coaching practitioner, we anticipate that this chapter will spur interest and provide the much-needed impetus for further scientific endeavour in this important area of study.

We begin by surveying and critically reviewing the golf-related scientific literature that has considered, either implicitly or explicitly, inter- and intra-individual movement variability in the golf swing before discussing the practical relevance of movement variability, specifically its

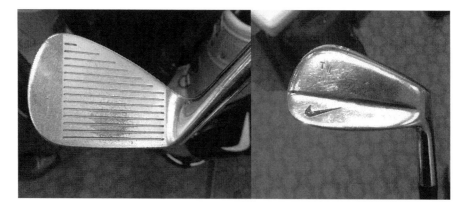

Figure 5.1   An iron used by Tiger Woods showing a distinctive ball wear mark approximating the centre of percussion or 'sweet spot' (Wicks et al., 1998). Although this wear mark is a consequence of highly consistent ball striking during repetitive practice and competition play, research suggests that the movement patterns and golf club trajectories used to produce these consistent impacts were likely to be far less consistent (i.e., more variable).

implications for golf biomechanics research, golf club design, development, and fitting, as well as golf coaching practice.

Movement variability in the golf swing: a review of the literature

Inter- and intra-individual movement variability in the golf swing has received some coverage in the scientific literature since biomechanical investigations into this sport technique commenced midway through the past century. However, movement variability has largely been subordinate, and studied as an adjunct, to more conventional quasi-experimental analyses seeking to establish relationships between technique characteristics and performance outcomes (e.g., Chu et al., 2010) or differences in these technique characteristics among groups of golfers of different playing abilities (e.g., Zheng et al., 2008). Accordingly, movement variability has typically been indexed as the standard deviation of a given biomechanical parameter and largely treated as an operational measure that compromises the statistical power of an investigation rather than a theoretical construct worthy of empirical investigation in its own right (Glazier, 2011).

Inter-individual movement variability in the golf swing

Early, predominantly observational, analyses based on high-speed cinematography showed large differences in the techniques adopted by golfers of similar playing ability. For example, Plagenhoef (1971) reported substantial variation in various aspects of the swings of 20 touring professionals, including Arnold Palmer, Tom Weiskopf, Raymond Floyd and Doug Sanders, among others. The length of the backswing, as denoted by the angle of the golf shaft when viewed from the front, varied considerably from 40° above to 40° below the horizontal. Similarly, when viewed down the line, the angle of the lead arm varied from 35° to 60° above the horizontal, although most golfers were between 45° and 55°. The angle between the left forearm and the shaft of the golf club at the top of the backswing varied from 42° to 80°, with the majority of golfers ranging from 62° to 68°. Further joint moment analyses were conducted by Gearon (1970, cited in Plagenhoef, 1971) on Sanders and Weiskopf because of their markedly contrasting styles. Weiskopf was found to be upper body dominant (i.e., muscular action of his arms and torso contributed more to clubhead speed than that of his lower extremities), whereas Sanders tended to be lower extremity dominant. In summarising this early work, Plagenhoef (1983, p. 189) concluded: "The variations in technique are extreme due to anatomical and ability differences and no personal conclusions should be made based on the swing pattern of others. There is no one perfect technique for everyone."

More recent biomechanical investigations have broadly corroborated the findings of earlier, less-sophisticated analyses and have generally demonstrated moderate-to-large amounts of inter-individual movement variability in the golf swing. Most studies that have reported inter-individual variability have used external force measurements, particularly ground reaction forces. For example, Williams and Cavanagh (1983) found that force–time and centre of pressure (COP) patterns exhibited as much variation among golfers within their respective expertise group (0–7, 8–14, and >15 handicaps) as there was between groups. As each group comprised only three, four, and five golfers, respectively, these results should be treated with caution, although a similar, more recent, study by Williams (2004) using a larger sample ($n = 28$) reported comparable findings. Wallace et al. (1994) also reported large variations in the magnitude and timing of pressures underneath different regions of the feet among a group ($n = 6$) of <10 handicap golfers performing a series of drives. In contrast to these results, however, Richards et al. (1985) reported less inter-individual variability of COP patterns in a group of <10 handicap golfers ($n = 10$) than in a group of >20 handicap golfers ($n = 10$). This finding prompted the authors to suggest that expertise in golf may be typified by progression towards a common weight transfer pattern, although subsequent research by Ball and Best (2007) has shown that golfers of similar expertise can adopt different styles of weight transfer (e.g., 'front foot' or 'reverse') and still produce effective performance outcomes.

Owing perhaps to the computational complexity and well-documented methodological challenges posed by inverse dynamics analyses (e.g., Hatze, 2002), the number of investigations that have examined the variability of internal forces has been more limited. Hosea et al. (1990) examined lumbar spine loads in amateur ($n = 4$) and professional ($n = 4$) golfers and reported that the variability of shear loads was almost four times greater in the former compared to that in the latter. The authors speculated that this was due to the greater variability of swing mechanics in the amateurs, although movement kinematics were not reported. Gatt et al. (1998) also reported large amounts of inter-individual variability, both in the mean peak forces and moments of the knees, as well as in their spatial orientations at the instant of peak loading, in a group of healthy 4–18 handicap golfers ($n = 13$). The inter-individual variability of peak knee forces and moments in this study were calculated to be, on average, almost three times greater than the amount of intra-individual variability in this group of golfers. Based on these findings, it was concluded that there is no 'normal' pattern of knee loading during the golf swing and that predicting the likelihood of a particular golfer sustaining injury is not possible with any degree of certainty.

Large amounts of inter-individual variability have also been reported in grip forces. Komi et al. (2008) found that each of the golfers they analysed exhibited their own unique, highly consistent, 'signature' grip force, although certain features, such as impact occurring near a local minimum and between local maxima, were common across some or all golfers (Figure 5.2). Langlais and Broker (2014) also reported signature grip forces across a small ($n = 8$) group of 0–7 handicap golfers even when using different clubs (driver and seven-iron), although inter-individual variability reduced markedly at impact. These findings collectively appear to support the results of an earlier study by Nesbit (2005), which showed that each golfer analysed produced his or her own unique signature alpha torque (i.e., torque acting in the plane of the swing responsible for the dominant angular motion of the club) at the handle of the golf club. Although grip forces were not directly measured in that study (load forces were only estimated based on the results of an inverse dynamics model of the golfer), grip forces and load forces have been shown to be tightly coupled when wielding handheld sports implements (refer to Li & Turrell, 2002, for a review). Nesbit (2005) also noted that golfers typically adopted one of two styles of swing. Some golfers ('hitters') tended to rapidly increase alpha torque during the first half of the downswing before maintaining clubhead speed thereafter until impact, whereas others ('swingers') tended to gradually increase alpha torque over the entire duration of the downswing.

Far fewer studies have considered inter-individual variability in golf swing kinematics. Despite reporting comparable average pelvis and thorax rotations and orientations at key moments during the swing, McTeigue et al. (1994) observed considerable inter-individual variability among tournament professional golfers on the regular ($n = 51$) and senior ($n = 46$) PGA tours. Similarly, Burden et al. (1998) reported large amounts of inter-individual variability in pelvis and thorax rotations during the backswing and downswing phases of the golf swing in a group ($n = 8$) of <10 handicap golfers. Interestingly, Sanders and Owen (1992) also reported some inter-individual variability in the hub movement (defined as the focal point of the clubhead path) of expert golfers ($n = 6$), but not as much as exemplified by novice golfers ($n = 6$). In terms of impact kinematics, Williams and Sih (2002) reported wide variations in clubhead path and clubface orientation at impact in a group ($n = 24$) of golfers of varying expertise (handicaps ranging from 0 to 36). It was suggested that, for some golfers, the variability in path and orientation may compensate for idiosyncrasies in their individual swings.

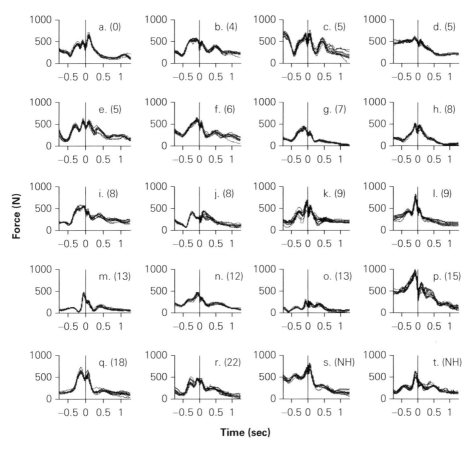

Figure 5.2 Total grip force from 10 shots of 20 golfers ('a.' to 't.') with varying expertise levels (handicaps shown in parentheses) synchronised to impact.

Source: Reproduced from Komi et al. 2008, with permission.

Electromyographic analyses reporting inter-individual variability have also been scarce. Abernethy et al. (1990) found that inter-individual variability in muscle activity was high in the lead upper limb during the golf swing, even among the expert golfers, which may indicate that each of these golfers was using a different movement strategy (no kinematics were reported). These findings corroborated with those of an earlier study by Slater-Hammel (1948), which also showed large variations in the timing and general coordination of upper extremity muscle activity in a small ($n = 4$) group of recreational golfers. In contrast, Barclay and McIlroy (1990) noted a general pattern of upper extremity muscle activity that was identifiable in most of the golfers analysed, although differences were observed in the magnitude and duration of muscle bursts, particularly when comparing certain high- and low-handicap golfers.

Intra-individual movement variability in the golf swing

Many empirical studies that have considered intra-individual movement variability have consistently found, somewhat unsurprisingly, that expert golfers exhibit high consistency (i.e., low intra-individual movement variability) over repeated shots under approximately the same environmental and task constraints. For example, Carlsöö (1967) found that intra-individual variability in ground reaction forces for a champion golfer were "extraordinarily small" (p. 77) despite data being collected over multiple sessions during the off-season. However, there is some conjecture about whether more-skilled golfers exhibit less intra-individual variability (i.e., are more consistent) than less skilled golfers. McTeigue et al. (1994), for example, reported considerably less variability in the amount of pelvis and thorax rotation over repeated trials for PGA tour professionals compared to amateurs. Barclay and McIlroy (1990) also reported that low-handicap golfers exhibited less variability in upper extremity muscle activity and swing duration than high-handicap golfers. Similarly, Neal et al. (1990) found that expert golfers exhibited less temporal (backswing, early downswing, and late downswing phase durations) and spatial (shoulder and wrist joint kinematics) variability than novice golfers performing different shots. In contrast, however, Williams and Cavanagh (1983), Richards et al. (1985), and Koenig et al. (1994) reported no differences in the amount of variability in ground reaction force and COP patterns over repeated trials for golfers of different playing abilities. A possible explanation for these discrepancies is that, since ground reaction forces represent the algebraic sum of the forces exerted by all body segments and that different combinations of body segment motions can produce very similar ground reaction force patterns, these measurements may not be sufficiently sensitive enough to capture subtle differences in body segment motions over iterative performance trials.

Of perhaps greater significance than whether the amount of intra-individual variability exhibited differs with expertise is how intra-individual variability changes throughout the duration of the golf swing. Indeed, the patterning of variability during different phases of the swing is of interest because it can provide an insight into how the swing is regulated and controlled. Koenig et al. (1994) reported that a common trend among the low-, mid-, and high-handicap golfers they studied was the increasing variability in ground reaction forces from address to the midpoint of the downswing, followed by a decrease during the impact phase, and then a further increase during the follow-through. More recently, Morrison et al. (2014) reported that intra-individual variability of clubhead trajectories of low-handicap male golfers hitting drives increased from address to the top of the backswing but decreased from the start of the downswing to impact. Horan et al. (2011) also reported a sequential and progressive decrease in intra-individual variability of hand and clubhead trajectories during the downswing for skilled male and female golfers. However, both groups exhibited greater amounts of variability in pelvis and thorax motions during the same period, with female golfers exhibiting the most. Taken together, these findings suggest that there is a general organisation of all body segments during the backswing, transition, and early downswing, followed by a perceptually guided zeroing in of the more distal segments during the late downswing to maximise spatial precision at impact. These findings support the theoretical assertions of Latash (1996) that the central nervous system is principally concerned with the outcome of an action rather than how the degrees of freedom (e.g., muscles, segments, and joints) comprising an action are assembled and how they interact.

The studies reviewed so far in this section have all been concerned with the *amount* of intra-individual variability in the golf swing, either at key moments (e.g., top of backswing, mid-downswing, and impact) or how it changes during different phases. However, there is a growing realisation that the *structure* of intra-individual variability is of potentially greater significance in understanding system control (refer to Newell & Slifkin, 1998; Latash et al., 2002; Newell & James, 2008). To date, however, only one study, to our knowledge, has considered the structure of intra-individual variability in the golf swing. Following on from their earlier work, Morrison et al. (2016) examined the interaction of the lead arm and club over repeated drives performed by low- and mid-handicap golfers. Using uncontrolled manifold analysis to decompose movement variability into variance components that do (so-called 'bad' or 'dysfunctional' variability) and do not (so-called 'good' or 'functional' variability) affect performance outcome (refer to Scholz & Schöner, 1999, for a detailed description), it was found that low-handicap golfers exhibited greater proportions of good variability than intermediate golfers, thus suggesting that better golfers are able to exploit abundant degrees of freedom and produce more flexible movement solutions. It was argued that, rather than developing an invariant technique, increased proficiency in golf may be characterised by greater control over abundant degrees of freedom and increased synergy strength, which is harmonious with the assertions of Wu and Latash (2014).

Summary

In this section, we have summarised the extant literature on inter- and intra-individual movement variability in the golf swing. Although there are clearly some commonalities between golfers regardless of skill level, a moderate-to-large amount of inter-individual variability exists even among the swings of expert golfers. As would be expected, more-skilled golfers generally exhibit less intra-individual variability than their less-skilled counterparts, although there is some evidence to suggest that high-handicap golfers are just as consistent as low-handicap golfers for some variables (e.g., ground reaction forces). A distinct patterning of intra-individual variability appears to be apparent across different skill levels, with golfers of all abilities exhibiting relatively large amounts of intra-individual variability during the late backswing and early downswing phases before progressively decreasing to lower amounts as impact nears. Although the number of studies that have considered the structure of intra-individual variability is extremely limited, there is some preliminary evidence to suggest that compensatory variability is an integral feature of achieving successful performance outcomes, but more research is needed on this complex topic.

Practical relevance of movement variability and implications for the game

So far, in this chapter, we have summarised the scientific literature that has considered inter- and intra-individual movement variability in the golf swing and discussed the theoretical relevance of movement variability. In this penultimate section, we discuss the practical relevance of movement variability, specifically its implications for golf biomechanics research, golf club design, development, and fitting, as well as golf coaching practice.

Implications for golf biomechanics research

The preceding sections of this chapter provide strong rationale and justification for examining intra- and inter-individual movement variability in the golf swing. However, conventional empirical approaches that have been adopted in many biomechanical investigations of the golf swing are generally not well suited to analysing these important aspects of golf performance. A major issue with many extant studies is the habitual reduction or collapsing of biomechanical time series measurements to single data points, such as the peak angular velocity of a joint or the angular displacement of a body segment at a key moment (e.g., Chu et al. 2010), to facilitate statistical analysis. Although this practice is commonplace in applied sports biomechanics research and considered appropriate if these time-discrete metrics or 'performance parameters' (Bartlett, 1999) are derived from a hierarchical or deterministic model of performance,[3] the removal of the remaining data points precludes insight into how a particular body segment moves throughout the swing, and, more importantly, how multiple body segments move in relation to each other throughout the swing, over iterative shots. In other words, this approach provides very little information about how body segments are coordinated and controlled during the swing (refer to Sparrow, 1992, for elaboration).

A further issue is that most studies of the golf swing have adopted cross-sectional, group-based, research designs, whereby a very limited number of trials are collected, either from a single group of golfers who are homogeneous in terms of skill level (e.g., Burden et al., 1998) or from two or more groups of golfers who are heterogeneous in terms of skill level (e.g., Zheng et al., 2008) and/or some other characteristic, such as gender (e.g., Egret et al., 2006). In a single-group design, performance parameters are typically correlated with some performance criterion or outcome measure, such as clubhead speed or ball speed, whereas in a multiple-group design, mean differences in performance parameter data are calculated across groups. However, the pooling of individual data to analyse central tendencies and dispersions can mask or obscure inter-individual variability. In effect, group-based research designs focus on establishing an 'average' response for the 'average' golfer in the group, resulting in the de-emphasis of the individual golfer. Furthermore, the reliance on a single 'best' or a putatively more 'representative' average trial in these group-based research designs precludes the analysis of intra-individual variability (e.g., James & Bates, 1997).

To overcome the aforementioned issues and provide further insight into the role and functionality of movement variability in the golf swing, alternative empirical approaches need to be explored. One approach that has featured in several recent dynamical systems investigations of human movement, which could be useful for examining inter- and intra-individual movement variability in the golf swing, is coordination profiling (Button et al., 2006). This approach combines analytical methods, such as continuous relative phase (e.g., Lamb & Stöckl, 2014), vector coding (e.g., Tepavac & Field-Fote, 2001), and self-organising maps (e.g., Lamb & Bartlett, 2013), which are capable of examining multiple time series datasets simultaneously, with a repeated-measures research design. By adopting these more innovative approaches, golf researchers will be better equipped to analyse how patterns of coordination and control vary throughout the golf swing within and between golfers of different skill levels.

Implications for golf club design, development, and fitting

The presence and impact of movement variability has largely been overlooked in the design, development, and fitting of golf clubs. Most golf equipment manufacturers evaluate their latest prototypes using electromechanical robots to ascertain whether their new designs can provide tangible performance benefits. The perceived advantage of using robots over human golfers is that they are able to swing the golf club in exactly the same way over repeated trials, so any variance in shot outcome can be attributed to the equipment rather than variance introduced by the golfer. However, this approach ignores that the club–golfer system represents a biomechanical system, not a purely mechanical system, and that different golfers with comparable clubhead speeds can, and typically do, apply forces and torques to their clubs in different ways when performing the same golf shot, which will affect the behaviour of the club and the precision of shot outcomes (Stefanyshyn & Wannop, 2015).

Although variability in the forces and torques applied to the golf club, as well as the variability in the patterns of coordination and control causing the variability in those forces and torques, has seldom received coverage in the scientific literature, several studies have reported variability in shaft deflection patterns within and among golfers. Cochran and Stobbs (1968) presented preliminary findings that suggested that shaft deflection patterns may be uniquely matched to each golfer and that better players are likely to exhibit greater consistency over repeated shots in these shaft deflection patterns. Similarly, Lee et al. (2002) reported the existence of 'strain signatures' or 'kinetic fingerprints' for individual golfers while also noting that shaft deflection patterns tended to be more variable in less-skilled golfers over repeated shots, particularly during the backswing-to-downswing transition. In a larger study, Butler and Winfield (1994) identified three broad categories of shaft deflection patterns that most of the golfers studied fitted into and presented exemplar data for three golfers with shaft deflection profiles that are representative of these categories (Figure 5.3). It was suggested that these shaft deflection plots might be useful in a club fitting capacity. For example, the golfer who generated the 'single peak' shaft deflection profile may benefit from stiffer shafts and/or different lie angles than the golfer who generated the 'double peak' shaft deflection profile.

Based on the aforementioned empirical findings, it would appear that the prototype evaluation procedures traditionally adopted by golf equipment manufacturers, which involve the use of electromechanical robots to swing test clubs in a uniform way, may lack external validity as they do not adequately replicate the shaft deflection patterns exhibited by the majority of golfers. The introduction of more customisable electromechanical robots, such as those described by Harper et al. (2008) and Roberts et al. (2010), may help to overcome this limitation and enable golf equipment manufacturers to test golf clubs under loading patterns more representative of those produced by actual golfers. The pursuit of other, more efficacious methods for evaluating golf clubs takes on even greater significance when one considers research that has shown that static shaft bending tests, which are often used by club fitters, have very little, if any, correspondence to actual shaft deflection patterns generated by golfers (e.g., Chou & Roberts, 1994; Mather et al., 2000).

Implications for golf coaching practice

Considering the amount of inter- and intra-individual movement variability observable in the swings of even the most elite golfers, major tasks for the coaching practitioner are, firstly, to differentiate technical faults from idiosyncrasies and, secondly, to prescribe an achievable modification to technique that, following a period of extended practice, will lead to the production of consistently better performance outcomes, particularly under the often-intense psychological pressures of competition. As alluded to earlier in this chapter, a common strategy adopted by many coaching practitioners is to compare their students' swings to the perceived 'perfect' or 'ideal' swing depicted in many golf coaching manuals or exhibited by a champion golfer to identify faults and prescribe fixes (e.g., Sherman et al., 2001; Smith et al., 2015). However, this approach, in effect, perpetuates the idea that all variability is error or noise that requires reducing or eliminating. Even putatively more scientific approaches, such as the one described by Mann and Griffin (1998), which uses a composite model ('ModelPro') derived from the average of 100 US PGA, LPGA, and Senior PGA tour players as 'the' template or criterion golf swing that all golfers should strive to achieve, have the same goal of coaching out inter- and intra-individual movement variability and, thus, are similarly limited.

Since there is currently no way of objectively establishing what the best or optimal swing is for a specific golfer[4], it is necessary for coaching practitioners to explore other, more heuristic approaches in an attempt to modify technique to improve performance. One approach might be to use club delivery parameters as augmented information to channel the golfer's search towards his or her own optimal swing (e.g., Newell et al., 1989; Newell & McDonald, 1992). As the shot outcome is directly related to the initial launch conditions, which are, in turn, directly related to club delivery parameters (refer to Tuxen, 2009, for a description of the 'ball flight laws'), data obtained from launch monitor technology can provide guidance about the types of technical adjustments that may be required to obtain more-desirable club delivery parameters at impact. Since different patterns of coordination and control can produce the same club delivery parameters, and because

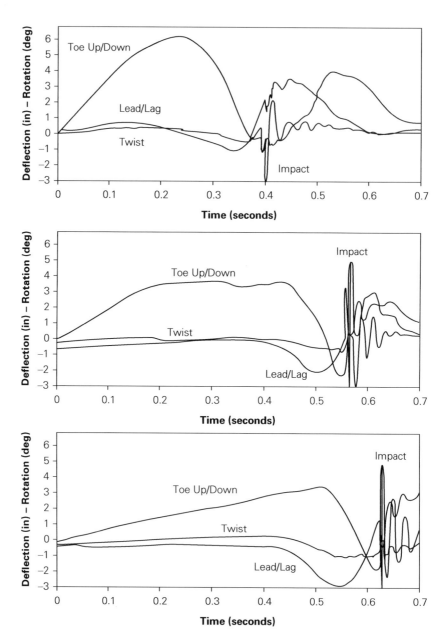

Figure 5.3 Shaft deflection patterns exhibited by three golfers, all of whom used the same golf club and produced the same clubhead speed (46 m·s⁻¹). Positive 'toe-up/-down' deflection represents toe up deflection; positive 'lead/lag' deflection represents forward shaft bend; and positive 'twist' deflection represents a closed clubface. These 'single peak' (top), 'double peak' (middle), and 'ramp–like' (bottom) profiles are also representative of three broader categories of shaft deflection patterns exhibited by most golfers.

Source: Reproduced from Butler and Winfield, 1994, with permission.

it is difficult to predict whether a prescribed technical change will lead to consistently better club delivery for a particular golfer owing, in part, to their unique 'intrinsic dynamics' (e.g., Kostrubiec et al., 2012), a viable pedagogic strategy might be to manipulate physical and instructional constraints (refer to Chow et al., 2016 for elaboration) and observe how club delivery parameters change. Once more desirable club delivery parameters have been achieved, the golfer can attempt to iteratively recreate the pattern of coordination and control that produced those more desirable club delivery parameters. This form of (guided) discovery learning has been shown to be effective when learning other sports actions (e.g., Vereijken & Whiting, 1990), but further research is required to verify its efficacy when making technical adjustments to the golf swing.

Summary and future directions

In this chapter, we have reviewed the literature on, and discussed the role of, inter- and intra-individual movement variability in the golf swing and its implications for golf biomechanics research, golf club design, development, and fitting, as well as golf coaching practice. Rather than being unwanted error or noise, as would typically be the interpretation from an information processing theoretical perspective, dynamical systems theory suggests that movement variability may both afford, and be a reflection of, great flexibility and adaptability in the movement system, which enables the golfer to perform effectively in a variety of performance contexts. While we are not suggesting that all movement variability is good, we are, however, suggesting that not all movement variability is bad. Accordingly, we recommend that future research should focus on establishing the functionality of movement variability by examining the relationship between joint/segment coupling variability and outcome variability, both within and between individual golfers of different skill levels, using some of the innovative analytical approaches and emerging measurement technologies highlighted in this chapter.

Acknowledgements

We would like to thank Jonathan Wall for permitting use of the images that feature in Figure 5.1.

Notes

1 The term 'movement variability' is used in this chapter to denote variations in motor output exhibited by a golfer (intra-individual) or golfers (inter-individual) over iterative shots under approximately the *same* environmental and task conditions. Other studies (e.g., Phillips et al., 2012) have used 'movement variability' to denote variations in motor output exhibited by performers over iterative performance trials under *different* environmental or task conditions, but, in our view, this interpretation is incorrect.

2 Some researchers (e.g., Carson & Collins, 2014) have injudiciously attempted to integrate the largely disparate and incompatible principles and concepts of information processing and dynamical systems theories to explain the role of movement variability in the technical refinement of the golf swing. However, this approach is fundamentally incorrect and does not show good understanding of the basic tenets of either theoretical framework.

3 MacKenzie (2014) suggested that hierarchical or deterministic models could offer a sound basis for golf instruction and provide further insight into the mechanics of the golf swing. However, since these models are *performance* models – not *technique* models (Lees, 2002) – they cannot readily account for technical features such as segmental sequencing, whereby the interaction among body segments is often profoundly indeterminate (i.e., body segments can, and typically do, interact in different ways to produce the same outcome).

4 There have been numerous attempts in the scientific literature to establish the optimal golf swing using mathematical modelling or computer simulation (refer to Betzler et al., 2008, for a review). However, these predominantly theoretical approaches have only been able to provide general, rather than individual-specific, coordination solutions, in part, because they have not taken into account a full range of interacting

constraints that act to shape the patterns of coordination and control that define the golf swing (Glazier & Davids, 2009). Consequently, the practical utility of these simulations in a coaching context has been limited.

References

Abernethy, B.; Neal, R.; Moran, M. & Parker, A. (1990) Expert-Novice Differences in Muscle Activity During the Golf Swing, In: A. Cochran (Ed.) *Science and Golf: Proceedings of the First World Scientific Congress of Golf*, London: E & FN Spon, pp. 54–60.

Ball, K. & Best, R. (2007) Different Centre of Pressure Patterns Within the Golf Stroke I: Cluster Analysis, *Journal of Sports Sciences*, 25 (7), 757–770.

Barclay, J. & McIlroy, W. (1990) Effect of Skill Level on Muscle Activity in Neck and Forearm Muscles During the Golf Swing, In: A. Cochran (Ed.) *Science and Golf: Proceedings of the First World Scientific Congress of Golf*, London: E & FN Spon, pp. 49–53.

Bartlett, R. (1999) *Sports Biomechanics: Reducing Injury and Improving Performance*, London: E & FN Spon.

Bartlett, R.; Wheat, J. & Robins, M. (2007) Is Movement Variability Important for Sports Biomechanists? *Sports Biomechanics*, 6 (2), 224–243.

Betzler, N.; Monk, S.; Wallace, E.; Otto, S. & Shan, G. (2008) From the Double Pendulum Model to Full-Body Simulation: Evolution of Golf Swing Modeling, *Sports Technology*, 1 (4–5), 175–188.

Brisson, T. & Alain, C. (1996) Should Common Optimal Movement Patterns Be Identified as the Criterion to Be Achieved? *Journal of Motor Behavior*, 28 (3), 211–223.

Burden, A.; Grimshaw, P. & Wallace, E. (1998) Hip and Shoulder Rotations During the Golf Swing of Sub-10 Handicap Players, *Journal of Sports Sciences*, 16 (2), 165–176.

Butler, J. & Winfield, D. (1994) The Dynamic Performance of the Golf Shaft During the Downswing, In: A. Cochran & M. Farrally (Eds.) *Science and Golf II: Proceedings of the World Scientific Congress of Golf*, London: E & F Spon, pp. 259–264.

Button, C.; Davids, K. & Schöllhorn, W. (2006) Coordination Profiling of Movement Systems, In: K. Davids; S. Bennett & K. Newell (Eds.) *Movement System Variability*, Champaign, IL: Human Kinetics, pp. 133–152.

Carlsöö, S. (1967) A Kinetic Analysis of the Golf Swing, *Journal of Sports Medicine and Physical Fitness*, 7 (2), 76–82.

Carson, H.; Collins, D. & Richards, J. (2014) Intra-Individual Movement Variability During Skill Transitions: A Useful Marker? *European Journal of Sport Science*, 14 (4), 327–336.

Chou, A. & Roberts, O. (1994) Golf Shaft Flex Point – An Analysis of Measurement Techniques, In: A. Cochran & M. Farrally (Eds.) *Science and Golf II: Proceedings of the World Scientific Congress of Golf*, London: E & FN Spon, pp. 278–283.

Chow, J.; Davids, K.; Button, C. & Renshaw, I. (2016) *Nonlinear Pedagogy in Skill Acquisition: An Introduction*, London: Routledge.

Chu, Y.; Sell, T. & Lephart, S. (2010) The Relationship Between Biomechanical Variables and Driving Performance During the Golf Swing, *Journal of Sports Sciences*, 28 (11), 1251–1259.

Cochran, A. & Stobbs, J. (1968) *The Search for the Perfect Swing*, London: Heinemann.

Davids, K.; Bennett, S. & Newell, K. (Eds.) (2006) *Movement System Variability*. Champaign, IL: Human Kinetics.

Egret, C.; Nicolle, B.; Dujardin, F.; Weber, J. & Chollet, D. (2006) Kinematic Analysis of the Golf Swing in Men and Women Experienced Golfers, *International Journal of Sports Medicine*, 27 (6), 463–467.

Evans, K. & Tuttle, N. (2015) Improving Performance in Golf: Current Research and Implications From a Clinical Perspective, *Brazilian Journal of Physical Therapy*, 19 (5), 381–389.

Faisal, A.; Selen, L. & Wolpert, D. (2008) Noise in the Nervous System, *Nature Reviews Neuroscience*, 9 (4), 292–303.

Farrally, M.; Cochran, A.; Crews, D.; Hurdzan, M.; Price, R.; Snow, J. & Thomas, P. (2003) Golf Science Research at the Beginning of the Twenty-First Century, *Journal of Sports Sciences*, 21 (9), 753–765.

Gatt, C.; Pavol, M.; Parker, R. & Grabiner, M. (1998) Three-Dimensional Knee Joint Kinetics During a Golf Swing: Influences of Skill Level and Footwear, *American Journal of Sports Medicine*, 26 (2), 285–294.

Gearon, J. (1970) *A Comparison of the Golf Drive of Sanders and Weiskopf*, Unpublished Msc Thesis, Massachusetts: University of Massachusetts.

Glazier, P. (2011) Movement Variability in the Golf Swing: Theoretical, Methodological, and Practical Issues, *Research Quarterly for Exercise and Sport*, 82 (2), 157–161.

Glazier, P. & Davids, K. (2009) Constraints on the Complete Optimization of Human Motion, *Sports Medicine*, 39 (1), 15–28.

Harper, T.; Roberts, J.; Jones, R. & Carrott, A. (2008) Development and Evaluation of New Control Algorithms for a Mechanical Golf Swing Device, *Proceedings of the Institution of Mechanical Engineers, Part I: Journal of Systems and Control Engineering*, 222 (6), 595–604.

Hatze, H. (1986) Motion Variability—Its Definition, Quantification, and Origin, *Journal of Motor Behavior*, 18 (1), 5–16.

Hatze, H. (2002) The Fundamental Problem of Myoskeletal Inverse Dynamics and Its Implications, *Journal of Biomechanics*, 35 (1), 109–115.

Horan, S.; Evans, K. & Kavanagh, J. (2011) Movement Variability in the Golf Swing of Male and Female Skilled Golfers, *Medicine and Science in Sports and Exercise*, 43 (8), 1474–1483.

Hosea, T.; Gatt, C.; Galli, K.; Langrana, N. & Zawadsky, J. (1990) Biochemical [sic] Analysis of the Golfer's Back, In: A. Cochran (Ed.) *Science and Golf: Proceedings of the First World Scientific Congress of Golf*, London: E & FN Spon, pp. 43–48.

James, C. & Bates, B. (1997) Experimental and Statistical Design Issues in Human Movement Research, *Measurement in Physical Education and Exercise Science*, 1 (1), 55–69.

Kelso, J. (1995) *Dynamic Patterns: The Self-Organization of Brain and Behavior*. Cambridge, MA: MIT Press.

Koenig, G.; Tamres, M. & Mann, R. (1994) The Biomechanics of the Shoe-Ground Interaction in Golf, In: A. Cochran & M. Farrally (Eds.) *Science and Golf II: Proceedings of the World Scientific Congress of Golf*, London: E & FN Spon, pp. 40–45.

Komi, E.; Roberts, J. & Rothberg, S. (2008) Measurement and Analysis of Grip Force During a Golf Shot, *Proceedings of the Institution of Mechanical Engineers, Part P: Journal of Sports Engineering and Technology*, 222 (1), 23–35.

Kostrubiec, V.; Zanone, P.-G.; Fuchs, A. & Kelso, J. (2012) Beyond the Blank Slate: Routes to Learning New Coordination Patterns Depend on the Intrinsic Dynamics of the Learner—Experimental Evidence and Theoretical Model, *Frontiers in Human Neuroscience*, 6, Article 222.

Lamb, P. & Bartlett, R. (2013) Neural Networks for Analysing Sports Techniques, In: T. McGarry; P. O'Donoghue, & J. Sampaio (Eds.) *Routledge Handbook of Sports Performance Analysis*, London: Routledge, pp. 225–236.

Lamb, P. & Stöckl, M. (2014) On the Use of Continuous Relative Phase: Review of Current Approaches and Outline for a New Standard, *Clinical Biomechanics*, 29 (5), 484–493.

Langdown, B.; Bridge, M. & Li, F.-X. (2012) Movement Variability in the Golf Swing, *Sports Biomechanics*, 11 (2), 273–287.

Langlais, S. & Broker, J. (2014) Grip Pressure Distributions and Associated Variability in Golf: A Two-Club Comparison, *Sports Biomechanics*, 13 (2), 109–122.

Latash, M. (1996) The Bernstein Problem: How Does the Central Nervous System Make Its Choices? In: M. Latash & M. Turvey (Eds.) *Dexterity and Its Development*, Mahwah, NJ: Lawrence Erlbaum Associates, pp. 277–303.

Latash, M.; Scholz, J. & Schöner, G. (2002) Motor Control Strategies Revealed in the Structure of Motor Variability, *Exercise and Sport Sciences Reviews*, 30 (1), 26–31.

Leadbetter, D. & Huggan, J. (1990) *The Golf Swing*, London: Harpercollinswillow.

Lee, N.; Erickson, M. & Cherveny, P. (2002). Measurement of the Behavior of a Golf Club During the Golf Swing, In: E. Thain (Ed.) *Science and Golf IV: Proceedings of the World Scientific Congress of Golf*, London: Routledge, pp. 374–386.

Lees, A. (2002) Technique Analysis in Sports: A Critical Review, *Journal of Sports Sciences*, 20 (10), 813–828.

Li, F.-X. & Turrell, Y. (2002) Control of Grip Force in Interceptive Sport Actions, In: K. Davids; G. Savelsbergh; S. Bennett, & J. Van der Kamp (Eds.) *Interceptive Actions in Sport: Information and Movement*, London: Routledge, pp. 301–310.

MacKenzie, S. (2014) Professionalism, Golf Coaching and a Master of Science Degree: A Commentary, *International Journal of Sports Science and Coaching*, 9 (4), 841–844.

Mann, R. & Griffin, F. (1998) *Swing Like a Pro: The Breakthrough Scientific Method of Perfecting Your Golf Swing*, New York, NY: Broadway Books.

Mather, J.; Smith, M.; Jowett, S.; Gibson, K. & Moynihan, D. (2000) Application of a Photogrammetric Technique to Golf Club Evaluation, *Sports Engineering*, 3 (1), 37–47.

McTeigue, M.; Lamb, S.; Mottram, R. & Pirozzolo, F. (1994) Spine and Hip Motion Analysis During the Golf Swing, In: A. Cochran & M. Farrally (Eds.) *Science and Golf II: Proceedings of the World Scientific Congress of Golf*, London: E & FN Spon, pp. 50–58.

Morrison, A.; McGrath, D. & Wallace, E. (2014) Changes in Club Head Trajectory and Planarity Throughout the Golf Swing, *Procedia Engineering*, 72, 144–149.

Morrison, A.; McGrath, D. & Wallace, E. (2016) Motor Abundance and Control Structure in the Golf Swing, *Human Movement Science*, 46, 129–147.

Neal, R.; Abernethy, B.; Moran, M. & Parker, A. (1990) The Influence of Club Length and Shot Distance on the Temporal Characteristics of the Swings of Expert and Novice Golfers, In: A. Cochran (Ed.) *Science and Golf: Proceedings of the First World Scientific Congress of Golf*, London: E & FN Spon, pp 36–42.

Nesbit, S. (2005) A Three Dimensional Kinematic and Kinetic Study of the Golf Swing, *Journal of Sports Science and Medicine*, 4 (4), 499–519.

Newell, K. (1986) Constraints on the Development of Coordination, In: M. Wade & H. Whiting (Eds.) *Motor Development in Children: Aspects of Coordination and Control*, Dordrecht, The Netherlands: Martinus Nijhoff, pp. 341–360.

Newell, K. & McDonald, P. (1992) Searching for Solutions to the Coordination Function: Learning as Exploratory Behavior, In: G. Stelmach & J. Requin (Eds.) *Tutorial in Motor Behavior II*, Amsterdam, The Netherlands: North-Holland, pp. 517–532.

Newell, K. & Corcos, D. (Eds.) (1993) *Variability and Motor Control*, Champaign, IL: Human Kinetics.

Newell, K. & Slifkin, A. (1998) The Nature of Movement Variability, In: J. Piek (Ed.) *Motor Behavior and Human Skill: A Multidisciplinary Approach*, Champaign, IL: Human Kinetics, pp. 143–160.

Newell, K. & James, E. (2008) The Amount and Structure of Human Movement Variability, In: Y. Hong & R. Bartlett (Eds.) *Handbook of Biomechanics and Human Movement Science*, London: Routledge, pp. 93–104.

Newell, K.; Kugler, P.; van Emmerik, R. & McDonald, P. (1989) Search Strategies and the Acquisition of Coordination, In: S. Wallace (Ed.) *Perspectives on the Coordination of Movement*, Amsterdam, The Netherlands: North-Holland, pp. 85–122.

Phillips, E.; Portus, M.; Davids, K. & Renshaw, I. (2012) Performance Accuracy and Functional Variability in Elite and Developing Fast Bowlers, *Journal of Science and Medicine in Sport*, 15 (2), 182–188.

Plagenhoef, S. (1971) *Patterns of Human Motion: A Cinematographic Analysis*, Englewood Cliffs, NJ: Prentice-Hall.

Plagenhoef, S. (1983) Golf Research Projects, In: J. Terauds (Ed.), *Biomechanics in Sports: Proceedings of the International Symposium of Biomechanics in Sports*, Del Mar, CA: Academic Publishers, pp. 167–189.

Richards, J.; Farrell, M.; Kent, J. & Kraft, R. (1985) Weight Transfer Patterns During the Golf Swing, *Research Quarterly for Exercise and Sport*, 56 (4), 361–365.

Roberts, J.; Harper, T. & Jones, R. (2010) Development of a Golf Robot for Simulating Individual Golfer's Swings, *Procedia Engineering*, 2 (2), 2643–2648.

Sanders, R. & Owens, P. (1992) Hub Movement During the Swing of Elite and Novice Golfers, *International Journal of Sports Biomechanics*, 8 (4), 320–330.

Schmidt, R. (1985) The Search for Invariance in Skilled Movement Behavior, *Research Quarterly for Exercise and Sport*, 56 (2), 188–200.

Sherman, C. & Finch, C. (1999) The Ideal Golf Swing: An Evaluation of Its Mechanics and Relationship to Injury Risk, *Safety Science Monitor*, 3 (2), 1–7.

Sherman, C.; Sparrow, W.; Jolley, D. & Eldering, J. (2001) Coaches' Perceptions of Golf Swing Kinematics, *International Journal of Sport Psychology*, 31 (3), 257–270.

Scholz, J. & Schöner, G. (1999) The Uncontrolled Manifold Concept: Identifying Control Variables for a Functional Task, *Experimental Brain Research*, 126 (3), 289–306.

Slater-Hammel, A. (1948) Action Current Study of Contraction-Movement Relationships in Golf Stroke, *Research Quarterly*, 19 (3), 164–177.

Slifkin, A. & Newell, K. (1998) Is Variability in Human Performance a Reflection of System Noise? *Current Directions in Psychological Science*, 7 (6), 170–177.

Smith, A.; Roberts, J.; Wallace, E.; Kong, P. & Forrester, S. (2015) Golf Coaches' Perceptions of Key Technical Swing Parameters Compared to Biomechanical Literature, *International Journal of Sports Science and Coaching*, 10 (4), 739–755.

Smith, T.; Henning, R.; Wade, M. & Fisher, T. (2015) *Variability in Human Performance*. Boca Raton, FL: CRC Press.

Sparrow, W. (1992) Measuring Changes in Coordination and Control, In: J. Summers (Ed.) *Approaches to the Study of Motor Control and Learning*, Amsterdam, The Netherlands: North-Holland, pp. 147–162.

Stefanyshyn, D. & Wannop, J. (2015) Biomechanics Research and Sport Equipment Development, *Sports Engineering*, 18 (4), 191–202.

Stergiou, N. (Ed.) (2016) *Nonlinear Analysis for Human Movement Variability*, Boca Raton, FL: CRC Press.

Tepavac, D. & Field-Fote, E. (2001) Vector Coding: A Technique for Quantification of Intersegmental Coupling in Multicyclic Behaviors, *Journal of Applied Biomechanics*, 17 (3), 259–270.

Tuxen, F. (2009) The Impact of John Jacobs on Golf Coaching: A Commentary, *International Journal of Sports Science and Coaching*, 4 (Supplement 1), 39–49.

Vereijken, B. & Whiting, H. (1990) In Defence of Discovery Learning, *Canadian Journal of Sport Sciences*, 15 (2), 99–106.

Wallace, E.; Grimshaw, P. & Ashford, R. (1994) Discrete Pressure Profiles of the Feet and Weight Transfer Patterns During the Golf Swing, In: A. Cochran & M. Farrally (Eds.) *Science and Golf II: Proceedings of the World Scientific Congress of Golf*, London: E & FN Spon, pp. 26–32.

Wallace, E.; Kingston, K.; Strangwood, M. & Kenny, I. (2008) Golf Science, In: T. Reilly (Ed.) *Science and Sports: Bridging the Gap*, Maastricht, The Netherlands: Shaker Publishing, pp. 94–107.

Wicks, A.; Knight, C. & Neighbors, J. (1998) Identification of the "Sweet Spot" for Golf Clubs, *Proceedings of the 16th International Modal Analysis Conference*, 2, 1803–1806.

Williams, K. (2004) Relationships Between Ground Reaction Forces During the Golf Swing and Ability Level, In: M. Hubbard; R. Mehta, & J. Pallis (Eds.) *The Engineering of Sport – Volume 1*, Sheffield, UK: International Sports Engineering Association, pp. 189–195.

Williams, K. & Cavanagh, P. (1983) The Mechanics of Foot Action During the Golf Swing and Implications for Shoe Design, *Medicine and Science in Sports and Exercise*, 15 (3), 247–255.

Williams, K. & Sih, B. (2002) Changes in Golf Clubface Orientation Following Impact with the Ball, *Sports Engineering*, 5 (2), 65–80.

Wu, Y.-H. & Latash, M. (2014) The Effects of Practice on Coordination, *Exercise and Sport Sciences Reviews*, 42 (1), 37–42.

Zheng, N.; Barrentine, S.; Fleisig, G. & Andrews, J. (2008) Kinematic Analysis of Swing in Pro and Amateur Golfers, *International Journal of Sports Medicine*, 29 (6), 487–493.

6

HOW THE SHAFT OF A GOLF CLUB INFLUENCES PERFORMANCE

Sasho MacKenzie

Introduction

The golf shaft is a mediator between the golfer and clubhead during the swing. A primary role of the shaft in a golf club is to allow the golfer to deliver the clubhead to the ball with a specific amount of kinetic energy. For most full swings, greater kinetic energy is desired. A second purpose is to facilitate the delivery of the clubhead to the ball such that, at impact, the clubhead is travelling in a specific direction with a specific orientation and the intended spot on the face makes contact with the ball. Said another way, the shaft can influence the position, velocity, and orientation of the clubhead relative to the ball at impact (MacKenzie & Boucher, 2015). These clubhead kinematics have a near-causative relationship with the impact kinetics, which determines the initial velocity and spin of the ball. The initial velocity and spin of the ball are the primary determinants of its trajectory. This is important because the fundamental objective of any particular golf shot can be represented by its trajectory. A ball's trajectory is simply the path the ball traces out during the shot and includes all features such as the curve, carry distance, bounces, and final resting location. Not only must a proficient golfer be able to generate specific trajectories, but the variability in reproducing a particular trajectory, on command, should also be as low as possible. While most advances of the golf ball towards the hole do not *require* a specific trajectory, it can be reasoned that certain trajectories offer a higher probability of success depending on the conditions. For example, curving around a tree instead of going through it, or sending a bunker shot on a high trajectory to avoid the lip of the trap. There is also a clear benefit to maximizing the trajectory length off the tee with a driver. In 2016, on the PGA Tour, the top eight in strokes gained off the tee all averaged >300 yards in driving distance, which was 10 yards more than the average driving distance in 2016 (PGA Tour, 2017).

The purpose of this chapter is to understand how a shaft can influence the golf ball's trajectory and the golfer's ability to repeat that trajectory with a low amount of variability when that shot is required. The chapter is organized by shaft properties; how these properties are quantified and typical ranges for these properties are mentioned. More importantly, the influence of these properties on clubhead delivery, and thus the ball's trajectory, is discussed. It should be noted that this chapter is focussed almost entirely on driver shafts, which is a reflection of the previous literature in the area.

Shaft mass, centre of mass, and mass distribution

The options for shaft materials and design processes in 2017 allows for a wide range of potential shaft masses (~30–130 g). For a shaft of given length, manufactures are also able to move the centre of mass (CoM) up or down the shaft by a few inches. The distribution of mass is represented by a property called the moment of inertia (MOI). The MOI of a striking implement seems to have more relevance to swing motion than the implement's mass (Daish, 1965; Reyes & Mittendorf, 1998; Smith et al., 2003; Cross & Bower, 2006; White, 2006; Cross & Nathan, 2009); therefore, further explanation of the property is warranted. MOI is the rotational equivalent of mass; mass resists changes in linear motion, while MOI resists changes to an object's angular motion. An object's resistance to change in linear motion remains invariant regardless of how it is being moved. This is not the case for angular motion. An object's resistance to change in rotational motion will depend on the chosen axis of rotation. The farther that the mass is spread out around a particular axis, the greater is the resistance to change in motion about that axis. Twisting a club about the long axis of the shaft is relatively easy as most of the mass is located relatively close to that axis. Rotating the club about an axis perpendicular to the shaft is more challenging because, on average, the mass is distributed further from that axis. The MOI of an object undergoing motion that is not perfectly planar, such as a golf club, is represented by a nine-element MOI matrix. This is necessary to account for the fact that the instantaneous axis of rotation of the club is continually changing throughout the swing.

Within constraints, it is possible to vary the mass, CoM location, and MOI independently of other properties such as length and stiffness. With respect to club delivery, altering these inertial properties of the shaft will primarily exert its influence simply by altering these same properties for the overall club. For example, the whole club's CoM could be moved closer to the butt by using a *shaft* with a CoM closer to the butt, or by using a *grip* with a CoM closer to the butt.

Increasing the mass of the shaft will increase the overall inertia of the club (i.e., both the mass and MOI). All else being equal, from a mechanics standpoint, increasing the inertia of the club will theoretically result in a reduction in the clubhead speed that a given golfer can deliver to the ball at impact (MacKenzie et al., 2016). Most previous research has demonstrated that increasing the inertia of a striking implement will reduce the speed obtained at impact (Daish, 1965; Reyes & Mittendorf, 1998; Smith et al., 2003; Cross & Bower, 2006; White, 2006; Cross & Nathan, 2009; MacKenzie et al., 2016). However, Haeufle (2012) recruited 12 golfers to investigate the influence of increasing shaft mass by adding 22 g of mass at a distance of 355 mm from the butt. Although they found no difference in clubhead speed, it is possible that the change in mass/MOI was not large enough to create a meaningful effect. For a given clubhead speed at impact, an increase in clubhead mass will result in an increase in ball speed (Daish, 1972; Jorgensen, 1994; MacKenzie et al., 2016); however, the same cannot be said for shaft mass. During impact, the ball is in contact with the clubhead for a very short period of time (~.00045 s), which seems to prevent much of the shaft mass from playing a role in the impact dynamics.

There also seems to be some evidence to support the notion that increasing the overall inertia of the club (either through shaft mass or otherwise) will influence the clubhead direction of travel and orientation at impact. MacKenzie et al. (2016) investigated the influence of clubhead mass on ball trajectory. They found that increasing the inertia of the club tended to open the face and, to a lesser extent, shift the clubhead path right at impact (for right-handed golfers). Specifically, increasing clubhead mass from 174 g to 200 g resulted in average ball resting locations that were approximately 20 yards farther to the right. This difference was attributed to overall changes in club inertia. All 18 participants were right handed and were proficient players (handicap: 1.7 ± 2.2). It should be noted that the study was designed in such a way as to prevent participants from adapting to the particular club inertia, thus demonstrating *tendencies*. It is quite likely that golfers of this calibre could adjust their swing to negate the influence of the manipulated clubhead mass.

Further, there is anecdotal commentary on the PGA Tour, which implies that heavier golf clubs can be swung more consistently (Johnson, 2014), resulting in less-variable ball finishing positions. This notion is supported by recent research demonstrating that rods with higher moments of inertia were swung in a more consistent manner (Schorah et al., 2014). MacKenzie et al. (2016) also demonstrated this finding. Collectively, across all participants, there appeared to be a trend of improved consistency as clubhead mass increased; however, these results were not statistically significant. Interestingly, when ordered by clubhead speed, a trend did seem evident, in that participants with higher clubhead speeds were relatively more consistent with the heavier condition. Further, if a different participant population was used (e.g., junior golfers), it is quite likely that improved consistency would be associated with lighter golf clubs.

Shaft stiffness

Previous research suggests that clubhead speed and orientation at impact can be influenced by shaft stiffness, likely via shaft deflection (MacKenzie & Sprigings, 2009; Worobets & Stefanyshyn, 2012; Betzler et al., 2012; MacKenzie & Boucher, 2015). Overall shaft stiffness is typically quantified using two common techniques. One method uses a shaft frequency analyzer, which measures the number of cycles per minute (cpm) when a shaft is clamped at the butt and put into oscillation with a weight secured to the tip. A stiffer shaft will have a higher cpm. The frequency of golf shafts range between approximately 200–400 cpm. The second method involves securing the butt end of the shaft and applying a known force to the tip to create a bend in the shaft. Shafts with the highest measurements of deflection are considered the most flexible, while those shafts with the lowest deflection are considered the stiffest. There are also more thorough methods, known as shaft profiling, which quantify the stiffness of a shaft at regularly spaced intervals along the length. This is relevant in understanding kick point, which is discussed later.

The amount of speed that a shaft adds to the clubhead for a particular swing, relative to a theoretically rigid shaft, is referred to as kick velocity (MacKenzie & Sprigings, 2009). Specifically, kick velocity is the rate at which the clubhead is moving from a lagging into a leading position at impact (Figure 6.1). Shaft deflection during the swing has typically been partitioned into lead/lag and toe-up/-down directions based on a reference frame fixed in the grip of the club (Butler & Winfield, 1994; MacKenzie & Sprigings, 2010). Kick velocities reported in the literature for the driver have typically been in the range of 4–5% of the total clubhead speed (Butler & Winfield, 1994; Horwood, 1994; MacKenzie & Sprigings, 2009). However, the role of shaft stiffness in generating clubhead speed cannot be understood solely through kick velocity. Previous research suggests that shaft deflection influences the kinematics at the grip end of the club as well as the clubhead (MacKenzie & Sprigings, 2009; Osis & Stefanyshyn, 2012).

The lack of quantifying the shaft's influence on *both* clubhead and grip kinematics was likely the primary reason why earlier research into the changes in clubhead speed associated with changes in shaft stiffness was unclear. Worobets and Stefanyshyn (2012) compared five shafts of varying stiffness while using the same clubhead and determined that shaft flex did not have an overall systematic effect on clubhead speed. However, at the individual level, for the majority of the golfers they tested (27/40), shaft stiffness was reported to have a statistically significant influence on clubhead speed. On average, for these 27 golfers, there was a 2.6% increase in clubhead speed between the flexes with the highest and the lowest clubhead speed for each golfer individually. Importantly, without information on grip kinematics, it cannot be

Lead deflection   Toe-down deflection

Figure 6.1   Planes of shaft deflection based on a grip reference frame.

definitively determined whether the changes in clubhead speed were a result of altered shaft dynamics, modified grip kinematics, or both. Betzler et al. (2012) compared two drivers with meaningful differences in shaft stiffness ('ladies' vs 'x-stiff') and determined that the majority of their participants (17/20) generated higher clubhead speed with the more flexible shaft. The result was statistically significant, but the average increase in clubhead speed with the flexible shaft (0.4%) was not meaningful.

According to MacKenzie and Sprigings (2009), who used computer simulation techniques, a greater kick velocity with a flexible shaft, relative to a stiff shaft, may not result in a greater clubhead speed if the flexible shaft is associated with a slower grip speed. This concept was supported by MacKenzie and Boucher (2017) in comparing two driver shafts with disparate levels of stiffness. All 33 of their participants generated greater kick velocities with the more-flexible shaft; however, the more-flexible shaft was also associated with significantly slower grip angular velocity at impact, which resulted in no significant differences in clubhead speeds between the shafts (Figure 6.2). Similar to Worobets et al. (2012) and Betzler et al. (2012), despite no overall differences, MacKenzie and Boucher (2017) found that at the individual level, approximately half of their participants demonstrated a statistically significant difference between shafts in terms of clubhead speed.

As demonstrated by three recent studies, shaft flex also influences clubhead orientation at impact, specifically, loft, face angle, and lie (Betzler et al., 2012; Worobets & Stefanyshyn, 2012; MacKenzie & Boucher, 2017). Worobets and Stefanyshyn (2012) reported no systematic difference in loft across their five test shafts; however, there was a significant influence in 11 out of their 40 subjects. The average difference between the flexes with the highest and lowest loft within each of these 11 subjects was 2.5°; importantly, the higher loft was not necessarily associated with the

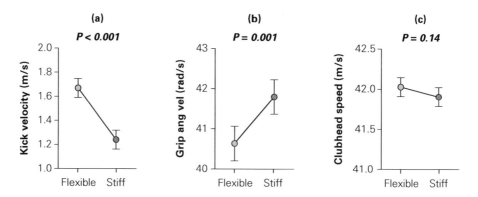

Figure 6.2   Kick velocity, grip angular velocity, and clubhead speed.

Note: $P < 0.05$ indicates a statistically significant difference.

more-flexible shaft. Lie angle increased systematically with increasing shaft stiffness, with the stiffest shaft being associated with a lie angle that was 1.4° more upright, on average, in comparison to the most flexible shaft. Worobets and Stefanyshyn (2012) reported no systematic difference in face angle across their five test shafts. Betzler et al. (2012) did find small, but statistically significant, differences between two disparate levels of shaft stiffness in terms of loft (0.44° more loft for the 'x-stiff' shaft) and face angle (0.65° more open for the 'ladies' shaft). The majority of their participants (13/20) achieved higher loft with the stiffer shaft. This finding is at odds with the remaining literature and may be related to the fact that different clubheads were used for each shaft condition. These authors did not report lie angle. For either of these studies, it is not known how much of the differences in clubface angles at impact was due to changes in shaft deflection, compared to changes in grip orientation. MacKenzie and Boucher (2017) employed a novel methodology, which allowed them to determine how much of the differences in clubface angles at impact were due to changes in shaft deflection, compared to changes in grip orientation. For example, the amount of delivered loft solely due to shaft deflection was referred to as bend loft. Each of their 33 participants – representing a wide range of abilities and clubhead speeds – executed 14 drives with a stiff shaft and 14 with a more-flexible shaft. In comparing the two shafts of disparate levels of stiffness, they found that the more-flexible shaft was deflected to a greater extent at impact, which tended to increase the loft and the lie angle (in the toe-down direction); however, the more-flexible shaft was also associated with a grip orientation that tended to neutralize the influence of

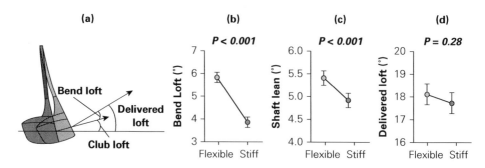

Figure 6.3   Bend loft, shaft lean, and delivered loft.

Note: $P < 0.05$ indicates a statistically significant difference.

shaft deflection (Figure 6.3). They provided two probable explanations regarding how shaft stiffness influenced grip kinematics. It was possible that participants used the same motor pattern with each shaft, but due to the varied bending profiles, each shaft applied a unique reaction force pattern to the golfer, which in turn resulted in altered grip kinematics. It was also possible that some participants felt a difference between the shafts, which resulted in a shaft stiffness-specific motor pattern being implemented during the swing.

Kick point

Shafts do not bend uniformly and the location of maximum bending along the length of a shaft when an external load is applied is known as the shaft's kick point. The kick point is typically determined by statically loading a shaft and noting the location, on the bent shaft, which is furthest from a line joining the two ends of the shaft. The static kick point has been reported to be located between 40 and 60% of the length of the shaft when measured from the tip (Mather et al., 2000). It is generally believed that, for a given level of overall shaft flex, a lower kick point (closer to the clubhead) increases delivered loft at impact, while a higher kick point reduces delivered loft. A shaft with a higher kick point might also be referred to as having a stiff tip.

Attempts have been made to assess the influence of kick point on ball flight (Chou & Roberts, 1994). Chou and Roberts (1994) conducted a well-designed study that included live golfer and robotic testing on six driver shafts (three steel, three composite), which were intended to represent a wide range of kick points while keeping other shaft characteristics as similar as possible. They also measured the kick point using three unique methods (1 – axial loading of the shaft, 2 – cantilever beam while clamping the butt, and 3 – cantilever beam while clamping the tip). They concluded that none of the three flex point-measuring methods were very accurate or consistent in predicting relative changes in ball launch characteristics. However, it should be pointed out that measured kick points differed by a maximum of 5% of shaft length between the highest and lowest kick point shafts. Depending on the measurement method, the kick points ranged from 40–44% (Method 3) to 43–48% (Method 2). These kick points all appear to be on the low end of the continuum. Interestingly, the authors reported a potentially meaningful relationship between shaft CoM and ball trajectory, with the shaft CoMs closer to the tip being associated with higher trajectories. Mather et al. (2000) used photogrammetry to track 12 points along the length of the shaft during the downswing and compute a dynamic kick point – using a radius of curvature measurement – just prior to ball contact. All five of their tests shafts, which covered a range of flexes, demonstrated a dynamic kick point that was very close to the tip (~10% of length) at impact. This may partially explain the findings of Chou and Roberts (1994). Unfortunately, only two swings per shaft were measured, and no static kick point measurements were reported. Joyce et al. (2013) also determined dynamic kick points of shafts just prior to impact. Somewhat similar to Mather et al. (2000), they found that dynamic kick points at impact were closer to the tip (~4% closer) compared to static kick points. However, unlike Mather et al., dynamic kick points at impact were still very close to the middle of the shaft. The fact that Mather et al. used the minimum radius of curvature point is the likely reason for dynamic kick points being located relatively close to the tip. Joyce et al. (2014) attempted to determine the influence of static kick point on clubhead delivery and ball launch variables. They reported that the high kick point shaft was associated with a significantly different attack angle (2° steeper), spin rate (550 rpm greater), and launch angle (2° lower). Unfortunately, the two test shafts differed marginally in kick point location relative to the tip (55.3 vs 58.4%: recall that kick point can vary between 40 and 60%) but differed meaningfully in other parameters, such as shaft mass (22 g difference) and CoM location (2.4 cm difference). Haeufle et al. (2012) actually used a 22 g discrepancy to test for the effect of shaft mass on performance. In my opinion, an experimental study that maximizes differences in kick point (say 45 vs 55%) while minimizing other shaft properties is still necessary to address this area of inquiry. The predictive value of various static kick point measurement methods (e.g., radius of curvature) on clubhead delivery parameters, which builds on the research of Chou et al., should also be assessed.

Shaft torque

In the golf industry, shaft torque refers to a shaft's resistance to torsional twisting. It is typically measured by determining how much the shaft twists, in degrees, when the butt is clamped and 1 ft-pound (1.36 Nm) of torque is applied to the tip. A 'low torque' driver shaft might twist less than 2°, while a high torque driver shaft could twist more than 6°. Although it is somewhat possible to manipulate shaft torque independently of shaft stiffness, it is typical to see more-flexible shafts with a higher torque rating and stiffer shafts with a lower torque rating.

There are currently no published findings regarding the influence of shaft torque on clubhead or ball kinematics. While the shaft certainly does twist during the swing, the best available evidence suggests that it may twist much less than what is measured during a typical shaft torque test. Butler and Winfield (1994) used shear strain gauges to measure the amount of shaft twist during driver swings. They concluded that during the entire downswing, the shaft did not twist more than 0.6° and that at impact, the twist was approximately 0.5° in a direction that would tend to close the clubface. These findings would suggest that the torque a golfer applies about the long axis of the grip is typically less than what is applied in a standard shaft torque test (1.36 Nm). This is in agreement with unpublished inverse dynamics measurements conducted in the Sports Biomechanics Laboratory of St. Francis Xavier University, Canada, in 2016. A group of 33 male golfers – with average clubhead speeds ranging from 80 to 120 mph – were measured hitting 28 drives. The maximum about-the-shaft torque value, applied at any point in the downswing, was 0.49 ± 0.16 Nm. The twist values reported by Butler and Winfield make sense considering these torque values. Perhaps the MOI about the long axis of the club is so small that larger about-the-shaft torques are difficult to apply unless the shaft is clamped at one end.

So, although shafts do twist about their long axis during the swing, the magnitude might be so small that a meaningful influence might be difficult to detect when comparing shafts with different torque ratings. That being said, despite no published research, it is generally accepted that shaft torque has an important influence on the feel of a golf club, perhaps even more so than overall stiffness. Higher torque shafts will feel 'softer' than lower torque shafts with the same overall flex properties. The feel of a club can have important implications for performance (Haeufle et al., 2012; MacKenzie & Boucher, 2015; MacKenzie & Boucher, 2017).

Shaft length

Varying the shaft length is the primary method for eliciting changes in clubhead speed while allowing a golfer to make a nominally similar swing. This, along with changes in clubhead loft, facilitates a golfer to hit shots of varying distances. A set of golf irons typically follows a 1.3 cm increase in length between consecutively lower-numbered clubs. For example, the shaft of a three-iron is approximately 9 cm longer than the shaft of a pitching wedge. Given the same linear and angular velocities of the grip, a longer shaft will be associated with more clubhead speed. For this reason, of the 14 clubs allowed in a bag, drivers are built with the longest shaft (with the exception of some putters). The Rules of Golf, as approved by the R&A Rules Limited and the United States Golf

Association [Appendix II 1c (length), effective 1 January 2016], state that the overall maximum club length (excluding putters) must not exceed 48" (×1.219 m).

Not only does shaft length have a direct and meaningful influence on performance, but it also tends to affect many other shaft/club properties, which subsequently have an influence on performance. Suppose two identical 48" shafts are manufactured and ready to go as part of a driver assembly. One of the shafts is installed without trimming, while the second shaft is installed at a trimmed length of 45". This second shaft will have less inertia, have a different centre of gravity location, and will also be stiffer. In addition, if fitted with the same grip and clubhead, the 45" shaft will also meaningfully reduce the overall club MOI. So, length can influence other variables. Yet, it is quite possible for a manufacturer to make adjustments to those parameters independent of length. However, it is important to note that if two shafts have the same mass and MOI, but are of different lengths, the longer shaft will still result in the whole club having a higher MOI.

When assessing the shaft length research, it is important to note the control variables. At one extreme, completely different drivers could be tested, making it challenging to determine the specific influence of length (Lacy et al., 2012). For example, Lacy et al. (2012), used four test drivers that varied meaningfully in length, as well as in clubhead mass, loft, flex, and MOI, in order to assess the influence of shaft length on ball launch characteristics. Studies such as this suffer from internal validity issues; it is very challenging to determine which club property influenced performance. At the other extreme would be a computer simulation study in which only shaft length is manipulated. In a study like this, external validity becomes a concern, since it is not practical to manipulate actual clubs in this constrained manner. While studies at both ends have the potential to provide useful information, in my opinion, perhaps it would be reasonable to at least use the same (or nominally indistinguishable) clubhead (Wallace et al., 2007). Arguments could then be made for further controlling properties such as shaft stiffness and shaft mass. In general, these comments apply to studying practically any golf club property.

A few principles can be drawn from a collective reflection of the shaft length research (Cochran & Stobbs, 1968; Reyes & Mittendorf, 1998; Werner & Greig, 2000; Wallace et al., 2007; Kenny et al., 2008; Lacy et al., 2012). If club inertia and CoM location were held constant, then clubhead speed would increase with increasing shaft length (Cochran & Stobbs, 1968). In reality, if a club is lengthened via shaft length, the CoM will move further from the grip and club inertia will increase, which means the same energy input from the golfer may not generate higher clubhead speed. It is also evident that other impact variables will be influenced by shaft length. For example, the location on the clubface with which the ball makes contact will become more variable with increases in shaft length and may also show a systematic bias relative to the face. There also might be systematic changes in other impact variables, such as delivered loft, and clubhead path. Both the variable and the systematic changes at impact mean that increases in clubhead speed may not be associated with increases in golf ball displacement as the ball speed may decrease and the launch angle and ball spin could become less favourable due to the changing conditions of impact. Like many club properties, shaft length will not just influence the outcome of a given swing but will also influence how the golfer swings the club. For example, a longer shaft will typically result in a 'flatter' swing plane (Coleman & Anderson, 2007). It seems certain that the optimal driver length for maximizing clubhead speed will depend on the other club properties as well as the particular golfer. Further, two golfers may generate their peak clubhead speeds with drivers of the same length, but when further considering ball displacement and accuracy, their 'optimal' driver lengths may be very different. Determining the 'optimal' shaft length will be specific to the individual. For example, Brooke Henderson (64" tall) of the LPGA Tour was playing a 48" driver (the maximum length allowed) with a D8 swing weight during the 2016 season, in which she won the 2016

Women's PGA Championship (Ping, 2016a). In contrast, Bubba Watson (75" tall) was playing a 44.5" driver with a D4 swing weight in 2016 (Ping, 2016b). One presumes that, for these players, their drivers are reasonably well suited to maximizing performance.

Shaft alignment relative to the club face

The Rules of Golf state that, at any point along its length, the shaft must bend in such a way that the deflection is the same regardless of how the shaft is rotated about its longitudinal axis (USGA & R&A Rules Limited, 2016). However, such a shaft is difficult to manufacture in practice and it is generally accepted within the industry that a typical golf shaft does not meet this requirement.

When the orientation of a shafts puts the 'spine' of the shaft directly within the plane of deflection during a standard shaft deflection board measurement, then deflection is minimized. The side of the cross-section of a golf shaft with the thickest wall is often referred to as the spine (Rancourt et al., 2010). For those advocating the benefits of spine aligning, the general idea is to assemble each club in a set such that the spine of every shaft is in the same orientation relative to the clubface. Some advocate aligning the spine within the toe–up/toe–down bending plane, while others advocate aligning the spine within the lead/lag bending plane (Figure 6.1). Changing the stiffness of the shaft relative to these planes would theoretically have implications for clubhead kinematics at impact since deflection in the lead/lag and toe–up/toe–down direction leading up to impact would be different (MacKenzie, 2011). For example, aligning the spine within the lead/lag bending plane would increase shaft stiffness in this plane and tend to reduce clubface loft at impact. On the contrary, aligning the spine within the toe–up/toe–down bending plane would tend to increase loft, which would be associated with a higher vertical launch angle. Findings by Rancourt et al. (2010) support this hypothesis. They compared both alignment possibilities as well as a third 'random' alignment condition in live player testing with three identical five-irons. They determined that aligning the spine within the toe–up/toe–down plane resulted in a vertical launch angle that was 0.75° and 0.91° greater than that with the lead/lag aligned and randomly aligned shafts, respectively. While the vertical launch angle was significantly different, there were no significant differences for carry distance between methods, which was likely due to minor offsetting differences in ball speed and ball spin. Therefore, there does appear to be some evidence suggesting that spine aligning can have a systematic influence on clubhead delivery. However, the only practical benefit would be to achieve better distance gapping between clubs, and there is not much evidence to suggest a meaningful effect in this regard.

Another claim from spine-aligning advocates is that non-aligned shafts cause off-line bending and twisting during the golf swing, which causes an increase in shot dispersion (SST PURE, 2016). It is not clear what is meant by off-line bending and twisting since the shaft deflects meaningful amounts in all directions. As such, there will always be 'off-line' bending. Regardless of the logic behind the hypothesis, it is still possible that aligning results in less variability in performance. However, to the contrary, Rancourt et al. (2010) found that the lead/lag-aligned spine generated the most variability in vertical launch (compared to the other conditions), while the toe–up/toe–down align method generated the most variability in carry distance. This is in agreement with Werner and Greig (2000), who found that maximizing changes in spine alignment with drivers moved the average ball finish location a negligible amount and did not appreciably increase dispersion. What seems to be missing from previous spine alignment research studies is a quantification of how much the spine influences the bending stiffness for the particular shafts used in the study. For example, future studies could report the shaft frequency (cpm) with the spine aligned in the deflection plane and rotated 90° to the deflection plane.

Summary and future directions

The shaft is a highly influential club component with numerous properties that can play key roles in fitting a club to a particular golfer in an effort to make a systematic change in golf ball trajectory. There is, however, a paucity of evidence to suggest that shaft parameters can be adjusted to improve the consistency aspect of performance. A recognized source of inconsistency associated with the full swing is the use of multiple clubs – designed with varying mechanical properties – in order to produce systematic changes to ball trajectory (gapping) when a nominally similar swing is employed. In general, the process of achieving appropriate gapping between clubs within a set while simultaneously making different clubs feel the same during the swing is referred to as *matching*. Several shaft parameters are routinely used to match clubs within a set or within a segment of a set (e.g., long irons). As recently mentioned, all shaft spines can be oriented in the same fashion, relative to the face, throughout a set. Shaft mass and CoM location can be manipulated to achieve swing weight (or MOI) parity within a set. Shaft stiffness can also be adjusted to have the same value or follow a consistent trend within a set (frequency matching). Another practice is to use clubs that are matched for length in an attempt to achieve improved consistency. There is no available research suggesting that any of these practices reduces the variability that results from switching between full swing clubs during a round of golf.

Robotic testing reveals relatively clear relationships between each shaft property and club-head delivery. When the neurobiological nuances of a human golfer are called upon to supply the kinetics to the grip of the club, those clear relationships become considerably stirred. Yet, the probability is still high that the correct mix of shaft properties can result in meaningful and persistent improvements to performance. Future research should focus on isolated testing of individual shaft parameters with both robots and humans. Once clear relationships are established, focus should be shifted to the more challenging task of understanding how these variables interact when optimizing performance for individual golfers.

References

Betzler, N.; Monk, S.; Wallace, E. & Otto, S. (2012) Effects of Golf Shaft Stiffness on Strain, Clubhead Presentation and Wrist Kinematics, *Sports Biomechanics*, 11 (2), 223–238.

Butler, J. & Winfield, D. (1994) The Dynamic Performance of the Golf Shaft During the Downswing, In: A. Cochran & M. Farrally (Eds.) *Science and Golf II: Proceedings of the World Scientific Congress of Golf*, London: E & F Spon, pp. 259–264.

Chou, A. & Roberts, O. (1994) Golf Shaft Flex Point – An Analysis of Measurement Techniques, In: A. Cochran & M. Farrally (Eds.) *Science and Golf II: Proceedings of the World Scientific Congress of Golf*, London: E & F Spon, pp. 278–284.

Cochran, A. & Stobbs, J. (1968) *The Search for the Perfect Swing*, London: Morrison & Gibb Ltd.

Coleman, S. & Anderson, D. (2007) An Examination of the Planar Nature of Golf Club Motion in the Swings of Experienced Players, *Journal of Sports Sciences*, 25 (7), 739–748.

Cross, R. & Bower, R. (2006) Effects of Swing-Weight on Swing Speed and Racket Power, *Journal of Sports Sciences*, 24 (1), 23–30.

Cross, R. & Nathan, A. (2009) Performance Versus Moment of Inertia of Sporting Implements, *Sports Technology*, 2 (1–2), 7–15.

Daish, C. (1965) The Influence of Clubhead Mass on the Effectiveness of a Golf Club, *Bulletin of the Institute of Physics and the Physical Society*, 16 (9), 347–349.

Daish, C. (1972) *The Physics of Ball Games: The Sportmens' Guide to Impact, Swing, Stroke, Rolling and Bounce*, Lincoln, UK: English University Press.

Haeufle, D.; Worobets, J.; Wright, I.; Haeufle, J. & Stefanyshyn, D. (2012) Golfers Do Not Respond to Changes in Shaft Mass Properties in a Mechanically Predictable Way, *Sports Engineering*, 15 (4), 215–220.

Horwood, G. (1994) Golf Shafts – A Technical Perspective, In: A. Cochran & M. Farrally (Eds.) *Science and Golf II: Proceedings of the World Scientific Congress of Golf*, London: E & FN Spon, pp. 247–258.

Johnson, E. (2014) *Accuracy, Feel Explain Why Some PGA Tour Players Have Gone to Heavier Driver Shafts*, Available at www.Golfdigest.Com/Blogs/The-Loop/2014/01/Pga-Tour-Heavier-Driver-Shafts.Html (Accessed February 02, 2016).

Jorgensen, T. (1994) *The Physics of Golf*, New York, NY: American Institute of Physics Press.

Joyce, C.; Burnett, A. & Matthews, M. (2013) A New Method to Identify the Location of the Kick Point During the Golf Swing, *Journal of Applied Biomechanics*, 29, 779–784.

Joyce, C.; Burnett, A.; Reyes, A. & Herbert, S. (2014) A Dynamic Evaluation of How Kick Point Location Influences Swing Parameters and Related Launch Conditions, *Proceedings of the Institution of Mechanical Engineers, Part P: Journal of Sports Engineering and Technology*, 228 (2), 111–119.

Kenny, I.; Wallace, E. & Otto, S. (2008) Influence of Shaft Length on Golf Driving Performance, *Sports Biomechanics*, 7 (3), 322–332.

Lacy, T.; Yu, J.; Axe, J. & Luczak, T. (2012) The Effect of Driver Mass and Shaft Length on Initial Golf Ball Launch Conditions: A Designed Experimental Study, *Procedia Engineering*, 34, 379–384.

Mackenzie, S. (2011) How Does Shaft Flexibility Affect the Delivery of the Clubhead to the Ball? *The Journal of Applied Golf Research*, 3 (2), 46–77.

Mackenzie, S. & Boucher, D. (2015) Golfer Specific Responses to Shaft Stiffness: Implications for Optimizing Loft During Driver Fitting, *Journal of Applied Golf Research*, 1 (4), 1–17.

Mackenzie, S. & Boucher, D. (2017) The Influence of Golf Shaft Stiffness on Grip and Clubhead Kinematics, *Journal of Sports Sciences*, 35 (2), 105–111.

Mackenzie, S.; Ryan, B. & Rice, A. (2016) The Influence of Clubhead Mass on Clubhead and Golf Ball Kinematics', *International Journal of Golf Science*, 4 (2), 136–146.

Mackenzie, S. & Sprigings, E. (2009) Understanding the Role of Shaft Stiffness in the Golf Swing, *Sports Engineering*, 12 (1), 13–19.

Mackenzie, S. & Sprigings, E. (2010) Understanding the Mechanisms of Shaft Deflection in the Golf Swing, *Sports Engineering*, 12 (2), 69–75.

Mather, J.; Smith, M.; Jowett, S.; Gibson, K. & Moynihan, D. (2000) Application of a Photogrammetric Technique to Golf Club Evaluation, *Sports Engineering*, 3 (1), 37–47.

Osis, S. & Stefanyshyn, D. (2012) Golf Players Exhibit Changes to Grip Speed Parameters During Club Release in Response to Changes in Club Stiffness, *Human Movement Science*, 31 (1), 91–100.

PGA Tour (2017) *PGA Tour Statistics: Strokes Gained – Off the Tee*, Available at www.Pgatour.Com/Stats/Stat.02567.2016.Html (Accessed February 03, 2017).

Ping (2016a) *Ping Tour Staff: Brooke Henderson – What's in Brooke's Bag* [Homepage of Ping.Com], [Online]. Available at www.Ping.Com/Tour/Prodetails.Aspx?Id=19068 (Accessed August 01, 2016).

Ping (2016b) *Ping Tour Staff: Bubba Watson – What's in Bubba's Bag* [Homepage of Ping.Com], [Online]. Available at www.Ping.Com/Tour/Prodetails.Aspx?Id=2750 (Accessed August 01, 2016).

Rancourt, J.; Millard, M. & Mcphee, J. (2010) Player Testing and Statistical Analysis of Two Different Methods for Spine-Aligning Golf Club Shafts, *Procedia Engineering*, 2 (2), 3355–3360.

Reyes, M. & Mittendorf, A. (1998) A Mathematical Swing Model for a Long-Driving Champion, In: M. Farrally & A. Cochran (Eds.) *Science and Golf III: Proceedings of the World Scientific Congress of Golf*, Champaign, IL: Human Kinetics, pp. 13–19.

Schorah, D.; Choppin, S. & James, D. (2014) Effect of Moment of Inertia and Physical Profile on Restricted Motion Swing Speed, *Procedia Engineering*, 72 (5), 93–98.

Smith, L.; Broker, J. & Nathan, A. (2003) A Study of Softball Player Swing Speed, In: A. Subic; P. Trivailo, & F. Alam, *Sports Dynamics Discovery and Application*, Melbourne, Australia: RMIT University, pp. 12–17.

SST PURE (2016) *Golf Shaft Analysis and Alignment*. Available at http://Sstpure.Com/#About (Accessed August 01, 2016).

USGA & R&A Rules Limited (2016) *The Rules of Golf*, Far Hills, NJ: USGA and R&A Rules Limited. Available at www.usga.org/articles/2015/10/usga--r-a-release-2016-edition-of-the-rules-of-golf.html

Wallace, E.; Otto, S. & Nevill, A. (2007) Ball Launch Conditions for Skilled Golfers Using Drivers of Different Lengths in an Indoor Testing Facility, *Journal of Sports Sciences*, 25 (7), 731–737.

Werner, F. & Greig, R. (2000) *How Golf Clubs Really Work and How to Optimize Their Designs*, Jackson, WY: Origin, Inc.

White, R. (2006) On the Efficiency of the Golf Swing, *American Journal of Physics*, 74 (12), 1088–1094.

Worobets, J. & Stefanyshyn, D. (2012) The Influence of Golf Club Shaft Stiffness on Clubhead Kinematics at Ball Impact, *Sports Biomechanics*, 11 (2), 239–248.

PART II

Skill learning and technology

Introduction

The importance of skill and learning, which are so central to many sports, is arguably no more pronounced than it is in golf. With coaches spending such a high proportion of their time focussing on the area when working with players, the wide variety of resources available in this area is hardly surprising. These resources range from books to professional courses, to teaching aides that incorporate the latest technology. Notable examples include swing trainers and launch monitors, which have had a profound effect on teaching practice in the sport. Although the influence of the coach on the rate of student learning is unquestionable regardless of whether they choose to utilise these resources, with such a variety of content available, they face a difficult task in determining how best to apportion their time with players.

This part of the handbook provides a resource for skill and learning in golf by summarising and reviewing the scientific literature available in the sport. Much research has been carried out since Fitts and Posner first developed their theory of motor skill acquisition in 1967, which proposed cognitive, associative and autonomous stages of learning. However, despite the volume of work undertaken, it is clear that much more is needed in order to verify the relevance of some of the purported approaches for use in golf. Readers will note that a substantial portion of the research included in the chapters have origins in motor learning displayed in other non–golf contexts.

Despite the variety of topics covered in this part of the handbook, multiple recurring themes are evident. One such common theme is the call from multiple authors to externally validate results discovered in laboratory environments by determining the extent to which they transfer to player behaviour in competition. Further, it is apparent that only limited research has been undertaken investigating elite players, in particular, within *in situ* environments. Further still, it is evident that very few longitudinal studies have been undertaken with players of varying abilities to date. While such research is difficult to undertake for a variety of reasons (i.e., participant access and dropout, costs and so on), it is clear that much work is needed in order for our understanding of learning rates and athlete progression to be improved. One way in which these developments will be progressed will undoubtedly be through furthered collaboration between academic institutions and golfing organisations. Partnership models whereby university researchers are actively embedded within sporting organisations are gaining popularity in other sports and may allow for the divide between research and practice to be reduced. Thus, although the authors contributing to this part originate from a range of backgrounds, the message is consistent and clear across the chapters: more work is needed in order to ensure that the research they and others working in the area are producing is made available to those in the field. I am confident that this part of the handbook will go some way to addressing this problem.

Leading off this part, Pauls, Bertram and Guadagnoli discuss the influence that technology has had on coaching practice and research in 'Is Technology the Saviour or the Downfall of Modern Golf Instruction?' Specifically, the lack of information currently available with respect to how utilisation of technology is approached by the athletes themselves is discussed. As an outcome of the review, the authors call for a framework to be used to guide the use of technology across various stages of the learning pathway.

Next, Wulf, Orr and Chauvel present their chapter on 'Optimizing Golf Skill Learning'. Here, the considerable body of research investigating the motivational and attentional factors previously revealed as relevant to motor learning is reviewed. In summation, the authors reiterate the importance of three variables in particular (performance expectancy, autonomy support and attentional focus) and highlight the implications that these have for practitioners.

In the third chapter of the part, Poolton and Masters discuss 'Putting Implicit Motor Learning into Practice'. The chapter specifically focusses on two areas of investigation, the theory of reinvestment and implicit motor learning. The authors discuss how the research published to date has shown that conscious control of movement coordination heightens the possibility for skill failure. Support for an implicit approach is provided based on its ability to develop resilience in the performer to situational challenges such as pressure that occur in high levels during competition. Design principles are also provided with respect to planning activities to enhance implicit motor learning.

Next, Christina and Alpenfels' chapter 'Factors Influencing the Effectiveness of Modelling Golf Technique' discusses the body of work that has been accumulated with respect to observational modelling of the golf swing, whereby processes relating to attention and retention are applied in order to form an effective cognitive representation of the modelled swing. The approach shows benefits in learning motor tasks across a variety of sports.

In the chapter by Bertram, Guadagnoli and Marteniuk, 'The Stages of Learning and Implications for Optimized Learning Environments', the authors summarise the research relating to the importance of relative automaticity in golf performance. The 'optimal challenge' framework is discussed with reference to guiding the design of efficient learning environments, with specific evidence-based strategies also presented for maintaining automaticity in skilled players.

Next, Robertson provides a chapter relating to how we measure and assess skill in practice settings, 'Skill Assessment in Golf'. This commences with a summary and critical review of the existing work published to date on skill assessment of golfers. The second half delivers literature-based guidance as to how the quality of skill assessments can be measured, thus providing a resource for coaches and researchers in making informed decisions on test design and selection in their respective settings.

To finish the part, Robertson and Farrow consider the literature with respect to 'Designing Optimal Golf Practice Environments'. A range of theories and concepts proposed in the literature are summarised in a manner suitable for use by practitioners. Specificity of practice / representative learning design, monitoring player progression and ensuring optimal athlete overload are three such topic areas covered. The chapter rounds out by summarising the work undertaken to date on preventing skill reversibility and achieving variety in skill-specific training sessions.

In summary, the 'Skill Learning' part of this handbook represents an important resource for researchers, practitioners and students alike. We are confident that the content contained within will challenge readers to improve the way they train and develop players. However, we are also hopeful that it will serve as a stimulus for further research and development in the area of skill acquisition, refinement and practice design.

Sam Robertson
Victoria University, Australia

7

IS TECHNOLOGY THE SAVIOUR OR THE DOWNFALL OF MODERN GOLF INSTRUCTION?

Aaron L. Pauls, Christopher P. Bertram and Mark A. Guadagnoli

Introduction

The use of technology in golf instruction is a hotly debated topic. The underlying debate largely centres around the notion that modern coaches and players are overly reliant on technology. This can result in the creation of the 'mechanical' player who spends too much time and effort thinking about the golf *swing* and not enough time focusing on the golf *shot*. By contrast, Jordan Spieth has been highlighted as a 'non-mechanical player'. This conclusion is echoed in his quote after his 2015 Masters victory in which he stated: "We try to keep the technicality to a minimum. I grew up playing (on the course) a lot more than I did hitting balls on the range, the same thing over and over again" he said. Through this chapter, we explore the use of technology in teaching as an entry point into the broader conversation of motor learning research, specifically, the concept of feedback as a learning tool. The basic premise of the chapter is that launch monitors, video cameras, force plates, or the coaches themselves are neither the villain of golf improvement, nor are they necessarily its saviour. The key, as we discuss, is not the source of the information per se, but rather *how* it is used (i.e., the frequency or content of use), and *who* it is used by (i.e., the skill level of the player). Relevant literature from the field of motor learning is reviewed and recommendations presented for appropriate use of technology in the teaching, learning, and maintenance of the golf swing.

Review of literature

It has long been known that feedback is a critical component to efficient learning. Typically, this feedback is received from two sources: intrinsic feedback, which is derived from proprioceptors and/or other sensory pathways; and augmented feedback, which comes from a source external to the body. Augmented feedback is supplemental information obtained in addition to what one could get on their own (Schmidt & Lee, 1999). For example, in addition to what a player felt, saw, and heard (intrinsic feedback), an instructor may augment this information with sources of feedback, such as verbal instruction, video feedback, launch monitor data, and so on.

As discussed later, augmented feedback is often beneficial because learners can struggle with interpreting intrinsic feedback and using it as the sole means for improving skill. For example, asking a novice player where his/her hands were positioned at the top of their backswing will often yield inaccurate information because novices are typically unable to interpret their body's intrinsic feedback. The complexity of a multi-limb, multi-joint movement such as the golf swing produces a myriad of proprioceptive stimuli, and the accurate interpretation of these stimuli is a significant challenge in the learning process. As such, learner-appropriate augmented feedback can be a valuable tool in expediting skill acquisition.

Content of feedback

Information regarding the outcome of a motor performance (i.e., a golf swing) is considered essential to the acquisition and development of a skill (Adams, 1971). When performance feedback is not immediately available from sensory feedback, the performer must rely on external feedback sources. The content of augmented feedback is given or received in two forms, quantitatively or qualitatively. In 1971, Adams defined quantitative feedback as containing numerical values, while qualitative information simply lacks the use of numerical values. A coach can, for instance, provide general feedback using qualitative information (i.e., direction of error) or be more precise by providing quantitative information (i.e., magnitude of error) regarding a trial. The two feedback forms can best be understood using an example pertaining to a golfer hitting an approach shot landing on the green near the flag. Without any augmented feedback, or strictly relying on intrinsic feedback sources, one may only be able to decipher very general information such as the direction in which the ball missed the flag (i.e., right, left, long, or short). The availability of augmented feedback, more specifically quantitative feedback, provides a more detailed description of the error magnitude. When both of these information sources are provided, the golfer has a comprehensive understanding of the direction and magnitude associated with the error of the golf shot. The question arising from the availability of augmented feedback is which form is more effective for acquiring and developing motor skills associated with golf: qualitative or quantitative?

A seminal study in motor learning by Magill and Wood (1986) examined the effects of feedback precision when learning a simple hand–positioning task. Participants moved their hand through a series of wooden blocks over 120 trials. Over the first 100 trials, participants were assigned to one of two feedback groups: Group A received qualitative and Group B received quantitative feedback. Analysis of the results demonstrated that initially, both feedback types provide the necessary information to elicit an increase in performance. However, as practice was prolonged, quantitative feedback proved increasingly beneficial for further performance improvements by way of smaller errors in performance requiring more precise information for correction. This examination of feedback precision displayed findings suggesting that the two feedback forms are effective at different stages of the learning process. During the initial stages of learning, both feedback forms provide the basic error information required for the learner to make motor movement corrections. However, as movement errors begin to decrease, qualitative feedback no longer provides the precision of information necessary to make corrections (i.e., information is too vague). At this point, it seems as though the more precise information that quantitative feedback provides to the learner is more valuable with respect to further minimizing of performance errors.

Although feedback can be provided using strictly qualitative or quantitative information, any combination of the two can be used to provide a level of precision that is optimal for a given performer's skill level. The idea existing that a specific range of precision is important to improvement is not a new one. What was first introduced by Bilodeau in 1966 has now been supported by a series of experiments. The first came from a study in 1974, wherein Rogers provided subjects one, two, three, or four numerical digits to describe trials on a motor performance task (four digits being very precise). The results from the experiment support the theory that augmented feedback is most valuable when delivered with an optimal level of precision that is completely dependent upon the performing individual. Furthermore, additional studies provide supporting evidence for the notion that an optimal feedback precision level exists (Gill, 1975; Newell & Kennedy, 1978).

More recently, Guadagnoli and Lee (2004) proposed the Challenge Point Framework, which suggests that motor learning depends on the level of challenge arising from the interaction of the performer's processing capabilities, task difficulty, and practice conditions (i.e., contextual interference). This framework serves as a predictor of the challenge present during practice and whether that matches the information-processing capabilities of the learner. According to the Challenge Point Framework, a certain degree of challenge is necessary in order to engage the cognitive processes needed for motor learning. Whereas learning can be maximized when the correct degree of difficulty is matched with the learner's processing capabilities, the learning process can also be hindered when the difficulty is too low or high. One way in which the challenge present during practice can be altered is by the content of the augmented feedback provided. For example, a challenge that is too high for a given learner (i.e., the information-processing capabilities are not sufficient to decipher the available information) can be manipulated from very precise information to less precise in order to decrease the level of challenge present, creating a more appropriate match of challenge to processing capabilities. As one improves and the challenge becomes too easy, the incorporation of more precise feedback can increase the challenge and once again create a more appropriate match.

Frequency of feedback

Frequency of feedback for this paper will be referred to in terms of augmented feedback and is described simply as how often this feedback source is used. For example, one can use augmented feedback at a high frequency, such as after each trial, or at a much lower rate of every 10th trial. For decades now, the scheduling of feedback has been examined using a collection of tasks attempting to discover what is most effective for performance improvements. Some feedback schedules that have been used previously include after every trial (100%), after every fifth trial (20%), or in a fading fashion wherein more feedback is provided early on in practice and gradually decreases throughout. This begs the question; how can feedback best be scheduled in order to elicit the greatest improvement possible?

Across a period of decades, numerous studies have been completed observing the effects that feedback frequency produces in the process of motor skill learning/development. In a review paper published by Salmoni et al. (1984), the authors outlined the different effects on learning and performance that are dependent upon the rate of feedback administration. For example, when feedback is provided on 100% of acquisition trials (practice trials), performance is superior during the practice phase (Bilodeau & Bilodeau, 1958; Ho & Shea, 1978). However, when participants are asked to perform the same task a day later in the absence of feedback, a decrease in performance is observed. Furthermore, when comparing the 100% feedback group to a progressively decreasing feedback group (i.e., more feedback was provided early in the practice phase and systematically reduced throughout), the opposite is true. That is, the fading schedule of feedback results in poorer performance during practice followed by a performance superior to that of the 100% feedback group during a delayed-retention test (Taylor & Noble, 1962; Baird & Hughes, 1972).

One major laboratory-based experiment contributing to the conclusion that a reduced feedback frequency is more optimal (i.e., feedback on <100% of trials) was conducted by Winstein and Schmidt (1990). These researchers inspected the outcomes that various feedback frequencies have on learning a relatively simple arm rotation task. Participants were divided into one of two groups receiving feedback after either 50% or 100% of the trials, with the 50% group's feedback gradually decreasing throughout the acquisition phase. The task required participants to sit at a table grasping a lever while resting their forearm on a pad. The pad was mounted to the table underneath the elbow, allowing for the lever to rotate around an axis. Participants were then instructed to produce a desired movement pattern consisting of four elbow flexion and extension segments to be completed in <800 milliseconds. Feedback on this motor task was provided via a computer screen displaying the accuracy of each trial relative to the ideal movement pattern. Similar to the conclusions drawn earlier, a 24-hour delayed retention test resulted in a greater performance from the group receiving the fading feedback schedule. In fact, the fading feedback group performed the task with one-third less error during the delayed-retention test.

Additionally, Sparrow and Summers (1992) examined the effectiveness of various feedback frequencies, including 100% (feedback on every trial), 33%, 20%, 10%, and a group receiving a mixture of predetermined frequencies (i.e., 50% for the first third of trials, 25% for the second third, and 10% for the final third). Feedback was provided on a task using an apparatus requiring participants to slide a ball bearing horizontally across a groove composed of two steel rods. The goal of the task was to stop the ball bearing as accurately as possible at a predetermined length selected by the experimental group. To ensure that feedback was withheld for participants on certain trials, a blindfold was placed around the head, and any feedback regarding trial distance was given verbally. Analysis of the data showed a strong benefit for a high feedback frequency (100%) at the initial 2-minute delayed retention test. However, on the second retention the following, the roles reversed, demonstrating greater performance from those groups receiving limited feedback (i.e., 33, 20, and 10%). These findings further suggest that limiting feedback during the acquisition or practice phase results in poor performance initially but facilitates greater improvements during subsequent delayed-testing phases.

More recently, feedback scheduling data has been taken from simple motor tasks in a laboratory and examined using more complex motor tasks. One such experiment by Ishikura (2008) used a putting task to study the effects that feedback frequency produces in the learning process. In the study, participants were required to putt a golf ball on a man-made approximately 10 feet putting green. The goal of the task was to stop the golf ball on a line that had been drawn on the putting surface exactly 10 feet from the starting position. Participants were given 60 trials during practice, for which half were permitted feedback regarding the result of every putt (100% frequency) while the second group received information regarding only 33% of trials. Resulting data showed that both feedback conditions showed improvements in performance from the pretest to the post-test phase on both a 10-minute and a 24-hour delayed post-test, indicating that either of the feedback forms works for initial improvement. However, and more importantly, the error produced in both of the retention tests was much smaller in the 33% feedback group than in the 100% feedback group. The implication of this data is that receiving limited amounts of feedback provides greater benefits to one's putting performance in the long run.

Various theories have been brought forward attempting to explain why putting limits on feedback can result in increased motor performance. The Guidance Hypothesis offers a logical explanation for why more feedback is not always the better option, outlining how a learner can become dependent on augmented feedback that improves performance during initial practice but ultimately deteriorates during gameplay (Magill, 2007). In other words, the guidance provided by an excessive rate of feedback offers an immediate reward (i.e., superior performance during practice) but leads to a reliance on such feedback, resulting in poor gameplay performance when augmented feedback is withdrawn (Salmoni et al., 1984; Lee et al., 1990).

A study by Butki and Hoffman (2003) investigated how the quantity/timing of feedback could affect how participants learned a golf-putting task. The task required participants to putt a golf ball along a man-made putting green, attempting to stop the golf ball at a target hole drawn on the carpet 3 m from the starting position. Three feedback conditions were used: a continuous feedback group, and groups being deprived of some feedback on 50% (50/50) and 100% (0/50) of feedback trials. As expected, performance during practice favoured the participants in the continuous feedback condition, while the groups with the 50/50 and 0/50 limited feedback conditions displayed improved performance during retention testing. While both the latter groups deprived of certain feedback aspects outperformed the continuous feedback condition during final testing, the greatest performance was seen in the 0/50 condition. The authors provide an explanation for these results using the Guidance Hypothesis, stating that the 0/50 condition was given very limited feedback, which required them to rely on their own intrinsic sources. As a result, they were better able to perform the task when no feedback was provided during the final testing. Similarly, Salmoni et al. (1984) describe that the detriment occurring with guidance is due to neglect of the intrinsic sources of feedback that are available on each practice or gameplay trial. During practice, the learner's attention is focussed solely on the augmented feedback due to its frequent availability. However, once the environment transitions from practice to gameplay, the intrinsic sources are still available but the augmented feedback has been withdrawn. The learner is now left with only feedback sources that are intrinsic, and due to the mistreatment of these sources, the learner is rendered unable to interpret this data.

In a learning versus performance review, Soderstrom and Bjork (2015) discuss the implications of the Guidance Hypothesis on motor learning. In their review, the authors outline studies that support the results of Butki and Hoffman (2003), stating that practising a skill without excessive guidance often leads to greater learning and subsequent performance than does being guided. Soderstrom and Bjork (2015) suggest that one method to maximize the use of practice and augmented feedback is to introduce small tests or quizzes periodically, in which augmented feedback is withheld from the learner. These test trials where no feedback is provided serve as problem-solving opportunities similar to those that occur during gameplay. In order to successfully solve such problems, the learner must develop the skills and learn how to make use of the intrinsic information sources present to make the corrections necessary for future successful trials.

Technology

Thus far, the discussion of augmented feedback has been limited to the kinds of verbal feedback one might receive from a coach or instructor. Increasingly, however, modern golf instruction makes use of technology to supplement the learning environment. Many of the technological advancements used in the game today include launch monitoring systems, force plates, and high-definition video cameras. While these devices provide an abundance of information, the same guidelines governing verbal feedback (content/frequency) should be applied to the use of digital devices, ensuring they are used correctly. The ability of digital devices to provide such large quantities of information regarding each trial leads people to believe they are beneficial. For example, the use of a video camera provides information on many different aspects of a swing, including posture, set-up, swing plane, and body rotations. However, what remains unclear is just how and when such technology ought to be best utilized.

One study that investigated this issue comes from Bertram et al. (2007). Both novice and skilled golfers were randomly placed into one of three conditions: self-guided (control) group, verbal plus video feedback group, or a verbal-feedback-only group. Over a series of practice sessions, each group received their assigned feedback type and were then tested to determine the effect of feedback type on swing characteristics. The results of the study showed that the positive impact of using video feedback was only seen in the skilled players. While the authors suggested that adding video feedback can be useful for some players, they cautioned about the risk of overwhelming more novice players with too much information.

Further on the effects of video feedback use, Guadagnoli et al. (2002) looked at the effects of video feedback on learning the golf swing. The authors recruited novice golfers and placed them into one of three groups: video feedback group, verbal feedback group, or self-guided (control) group. Novice golfers were asked to participate in four 90-minute practice sessions, receiving feedback according to their assigned condition. After the four practice sessions were finished, subjects completed two post-tests: one immediately upon completion of their fourth practice session and a second 2 weeks later. On the initial post-test, the two instruction groups performed worse than the self-guided group. However, 2 weeks later, on the second post-test, both feedback groups' performance was superior to that of the self-guided group, with the video feedback condition performing the best. These results are interpreted to indicate that video feedback is an effective means for practice, but the positive effects may take some time to present themselves. A possible explanation for this is the period of consolidation between the two post-tests, allowing the newly learned information to fortify in the brain.

Recommendations

In order to maximize the information presented in this chapter, an example of how best to use sources of feedback can be valuable for the reader. In this section, a scenario of a golfer looking to make a change to their golf swing (see Figure 7.1) will be provided and then an outline of how three different golfers (i.e., high, middle, and low handicap) should use feedback and technology to make these swing changes is suggested. Let us imagine that a right-handed golfer is on the driving range accompanied by different sources of technology (i.e., Trackman, video camera, and so on) and a coach ready to help make swing changes. This golfer particularly struggles with a slight pull of the golf ball, one starting out left of the target and flying on a relatively straight path that ends up missing the target to the left. The problem can be fixed by swinging the club on a path that is more inside to outside, starting the ball on a path slightly more to the right. Now that the golfer understands what the correction to be made is, how should this player use technology and feedback to maximize the benefits of his/her practice session?

High handicap (12+)

Feedback content: The use of qualitative (general information) feedback most likely fits into the player's ideal range of precision, not too challenging while still providing adequate information for correction (Newell & Kennedy, 1978; Guadagnoli & Lee, 2004).

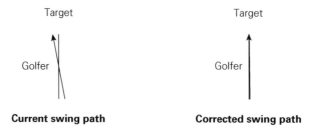

Figure 7.1 Depiction of a hypothetically flawed swing path (left) and a corrected swing path (right).

Feedback frequency: Feedback should be provided initially at a rate of roughly 60–75% of trials, gradually reducing the frequency throughout the practice session. Allows the golfer some trials where they must search for answers using intrinsic feedback (Taylor & Noble, 1962; Baird & Hughes, 1972; Winstein & Schmidt, 1990).

Technology: The use of technology should be limited; however, a video camera can be useful if used according to the content/frequency recommendations outlined earlier. The focus should remain solely on changing the swing path only (Guadagnoli et al., 2002).

Mid handicap (5–11)

Feedback content: A mixture of qualitative and quantitative information should be used to provide a challenge level appropriate for this skill level (Magill & Wood, 1986; Guadagnoli & Lee, 2004).

Feedback frequency: At this intermediate stage of development, feedback is recommended to be provided in the range of 30–50% of practice trials. Throughout the practice session, augmented feedback should be reduced to encourage the use of intrinsic feedback sources to correct flaws with each trial (Salmoni et al., 1984; Butki & Hoffman, 2003; Soderstrom & Bjork, 2015).

Technology: Technology should be used at this stage to provide general information regarding the swing change. A video of their swing, in addition to some general swing direction information from a Trackman regarding the correction, can be helpful (Guadagnoli et al., 2002; Bertram et al., 2007).

Low handicap (0–4)

Feedback content: For the minor adjustments these players will be making, it is important to be very precise when giving feedback. Numerical values will be beneficial towards correcting motor movements to the appropriate extent (Bilodeau, 1966; Rogers, 1974; Gill, 1975; Newell & Kennedy, 1978; Magill & Wood, 1986).

Feedback frequency: Feedback at this level should be kept to a minimum, roughly at a rate of <30% to begin. Similar to both other handicap groups, systematically decreasing feedback throughout practice is recommended. Practice should be completed by withdrawing the aid of augmented feedback and allowing for the golfer to develop intrinsic feedback sources (Salmoni et al., 1984; Sparrow & Summers, 1992; Ishikura, 2008).

Technology: If available, technology should be used in some form. The use of Trackman and various other computer programs to provide very detailed information regarding direction, speed, angles, and degrees of the swing are advantageous when making such minor swing adjustments (Bertram et al., 2007).

Implications for the game

In this chapter, the debate on technology use in teaching has been explored. The literature shows that in some cases, technology can be beneficial to learning, while in other cases, it can be detrimental. The key determinant of the effectiveness of technology is not the source of the information, but how it is used and by whom. The premise of this chapter is that the existing literature on feedback in motor learning can help dictate how technology can be used for one's benefit. If technology is used appropriately and in accordance with the principles of feedback use outlined herein, it can be a great benefit to the teaching and learning of the game of golf. Not only does the application of technology have the potential to greatly decrease the acquisition and performance learning curves, but it also has the added benefit of making learning more fun and can keep learners engaged. We contend that the proper use of technology, according to evidence-based principles, is good for the game of golf and can help optimize the learning environment.

Summary and future directions

This chapter began by questioning whether technology as a source of augmented feedback provides benefits or becomes a hindrance towards learning the game of golf. Upon reviewing relevant literature in the field of motor learning and feedback, the conclusion is that technology is neither the villain nor the saviour for golf instruction. Rather, its effectiveness lies in how one chooses to use technology as a source of feedback. The incorrect use of technology during practice (i.e., rely on it too frequently) can be harmful towards improving one's game. However, the proper use of technology offers many benefits that optimize the learning environment and stimulate a great deal of game improvement. The take-home message from the literature reviewed in this chapter is that the instruction and learning of golf can be greatly enhanced by the use of technology. The responsibility is on the user to learn and apply the correct uses of technology in order to produce the potential performance benefits it can provide.

Future research into the field of motor learning and the effects of augmented feedback is required to gain a better understanding. Much of the research in this area was conducted prior to the year 2000, before much of the technology we have today was available. The use of technology by individuals is so prevalent in golf (and indeed most sports) that it can be potentially misused if the user does not have the proper understanding of how to use it or, at the very least, some appropriate parameters within which to operate. Future studies need to look more specifically at the use of technology in golf, using a variety of skill levels alongside various age groups. The benefit of this line of research would allow those who teach the game of golf to greatly improve the way in which they use technology and ultimately to become better instructors.

References

Adams, J. (1971) A Closed-loop Theory of Motor Learning, *Journal of Motor Behavior*, 3 (2), 111–150.

Baird, I. & Hughes, G. (1972) Effects of Frequency and Specificity of Information Feedback on Acquisition and Extinction of a Positioning Task, *Perceptual and Motor Skills*, 34 (2), 567–572.

Bertram, C.; Marteniuk, R. & Guadagnoli, M. (2007) On the Use and Misuse of Video Analysis, *International Journal of Sports Science and Coaching*, 2 (1), 37–46.

Bilodeau, E. (1966) *Acquisition of Skill.* New York, NY: Academic Press.

Bilodeau, E. & Bilodeau, I. (1958) Variable Frequency of Knowledge of Results and the Learning of a Simple Skill, *Journal of Experimental Psychology*, 55 (4), 379–383.

Butki, B. & Hoffman, S. (2003) Effects of Reducing Frequency of Intrinsic Knowledge of Results on the Learning of a Motor Skill, *Perceptual and Motor Skills*, 97 (2), 569–580.

Gill, D. (1975) Knowledge of Results Precision and Motor Skill Acquisition, *Journal of Motor Behavior*, 7 (3), 191–198.

Guadagnoli, M.; Holcomb, W. & Davis, M. (2002) The Efficacy of Video Feedback for Learning the Golf Swing, *Journal of Sports Sciences*, 20 (8), 615–622.

Guadagnoli, M. & Lee, T. (2004) Challenge Point: A Framework for Conceptualizing the Effects of Various Practice Conditions in Motor Learning, *Journal of Motor Behavior*, 36 (2), 212–224.

Ho, L. & Shea, J. (1978) Effects of Relative Frequency of Knowledge of Results on Retention of a Motor Skill, *Perceptual and Motor Skills*, 46 (3 Pt 1), 859–866.

Ishikura, T. (2008) Reduced Relative Frequency of Knowledge of Results Without Visual Feedback in Learning a Golf Putting Task 1, 2, *Perceptual and Motor Skills*, 106 (1), 225–233.

Lee, T.; White, M. & Carnahan, H. (1990) On the Role of Knowledge of Results in Motor Learning: Exploring the Guidance Hypothesis, *Journal of Motor Behavior*, 22 (2), 191–208.

Magill, R. (2007) *Motor Learning and Control: Concepts and Applications* (8th Ed.), Columbus, OH: McGraw-Hill.

Magill, R. & Wood, C. (1986) Knowledge of Results Precision as a Learning Variable in Motor Skill Acquisition, *Research Quarterly for Exercise and Sport*, 57 (2), 170–173.

Newell, K. & Kennedy, J. (1978) Knowledge of Results and Children's Motor Learning, *Developmental Psychology*, 14 (5), 531–536.

Rogers, C. (1974) Feedback Precision and Postfeedback Interval Duration, *Journal of Experimental Psychology*, 102 (4), 604–608.

Salmoni, A.; Schmidt, R. & Walter, C. (1984) Knowledge of Results and Motor Learning: A Review and Critical Reappraisal, *Psychological Bulletin*, 95 (3), 355–386.

Schmidt, R. & Lee, T. (1999) *Motor Control and Learning: A Behavioural Emphasis* (3rd Ed.), Champaign, IL: Human Kinetics.

Soderstrom, N. & Bjork, R. (2015) Learning Versus Performance: An Integrative Review, *Perspectives on Psychological Science*, 10 (2), 176–199.

Sparrow, W. & Summers, J. (1992) Performance on Trials Without Knowledge of Results (KR) in Reduced Relative Frequency Presentations of KR, *Journal of Motor Behavior*, 24 (2), 197–209.

Taylor, A. & Noble, C. (1962) Acquisition and Extinction Phenomena in Human Trial-and-error Learning Under Different Schedules of Reinforcing Feedback, *Perceptual and Motor Skills*, 15 (1), 31–44.

Winstein, C. & Schmidt, R. (1990) Reduced Frequency of Knowledge of Results Enhances Motor Skill Learning, *Journal of Experimental Psychology: Learning, Memory, and Cognition*, 16 (4), 677–691.

8

OPTIMIZING GOLF SKILL LEARNING

Gabriele Wulf, Steven Orr and Guillaume Chauvel

Introduction

Golf skills are arguably among the most complex sports skills. Although 'complexity' is notoriously difficult to define, the high precision requirements involved in hitting a golf ball, coupled with a relatively high clubhead speed, and the countless degrees of freedom involved in a coordinated action of the whole body are criteria that most would probably agree constitute complex skills. Both novice and professional golfers alike know the challenges this sport entails. To assist them in overcoming those challenges, different approaches to teaching have been developed by golf professionals, often based on their own experience and the perceived success of their methods (e.g., Jimmy Ballard, Butch Harmon, and David Leadbetter). For instance, David Leadbetter has built 28 golf academies across 11 countries that promote his methods and drills.

Motor learning researchers are concerned with understanding the factors that influence the learning of motor skills, i.e., that is, relatively permanent changes in motor skill as a result of practice (Schmidt & Lee, 2011). Learning is typically measured by delayed (i.e., 24 hours or more) retention or transfer tests. The knowledge generated through studies that examine the effects of certain variables on skill learning can help practitioners to design effective practice conditions. The understanding of how learning is affected by different types of variables or instructional methods has seen some significant developments over the past few years. Specifically, three factors that are critical for optimal motor learning have been identified, and these are central to a new theory of motor learning, the OPTIMAL (Optimizing Performance Through Intrinsic Motivation and Attention for Learning) theory (Wulf & Lewthwaite, 2016). Two of the key factors are motivational in nature, *enhanced expectancies* for performance and *autonomy support*, and one is related to the performers' attention, an *external focus of attention*. In this chapter, we review findings related to each factor, with particular consideration for golf-specific studies. We also provide examples of how golf instructors and coaches may incorporate those variables in their work with their clients and athletes.

Enhancing expectancies

Being confident in one's ability to perform well is critical for optimal motor performance, and this is immediately obvious in golf. Circumstances that enhance learners' expectations of future success in golf can potentiate even more success (Rosenqvist & Scans, 2015). Thus, providing learners with a heightened sense of confidence, or self-efficacy, is key to effective long-term changes in performance (i.e., learning) and sustained performance at a higher level. Expectancies for performance can be enhanced in various ways. In the motor learning literature, different manipulations have been used to increase learners' performance expectancies. For example, in several studies, feedback was provided on trials with relatively small errors versus larger errors (e.g., Chiviacowsky & Wulf, 2007; Clark & Ste-Marie, 2007; Chiviacowsky et al., 2009; Saemi et al., 2012). Even though, intuitively, one might expect feedback to be more effective when it is provided after less successful trials, in studies, learning was consistently facilitated when feedback was given on more accurate trials. Thus, highlighting good performances and essentially ignoring poor trials resulted in higher self-efficacy (e.g., Saemi et al., 2012) and more effective learning than the opposite. Even simple statements suggesting that peers typically do well on a given task (Wulf et al., 2012, Experiment 2), encouraging statements about the learner's performance or aspects of the skill that are performed well, or about general improvement (Wulf et al., 2010) will likely suffice to promote learning.

Increasing learners' perceptions of success during practice can be achieved through other means as well. For example, setting criteria that purportedly indicate good performance, but that can be reached relatively easily, can raise learners' expectancies and facilitate learning. In a study by Trempe et al. (2012), the learning of a visuo-motor task was enhanced when participants were given a relatively easy goal compared with a more difficult goal. Participants with the easy goal achieved that goal more frequently, and thus experienced more success during the practice phase, than did those with the difficult goal. When the groups were retested the next day (retention test), the easy-goal group performed more accurately than the difficult-goal group. Thus, after memory consolidation had a chance to take place (i.e., 24 hours later), the success experienced during practice in the former group manifested itself in enhanced learning.

Mechanisms underlying the enhanced expectancy effect

High performance expectancies prepare the mover for successful movement at cognitive, motivational, neurophysiological, and neuromuscular levels. This ensures that goals are effectively coupled with desired actions – termed *goal–action coupling* in the OPTIMAL theory (Wulf & Lewthwaite, 2016). Enhanced expectancies may also serve as a buffer against responses that would detract from optimal performance, such as distracting thoughts or self-referential thinking (refer section on External focus of attention).

Golf-specific studies

A few studies have demonstrated how enhancing performance expectancies can lead to more effective learning of golf skills. In one study, novice golfers performed a putting task where the target was surrounded by two concentric circles (Palmer et al., 2016). One group was instructed that putting within the larger circle would constitute 'good' golf putts, whereas another group was informed that balls ending up in the smaller circles would be considered 'good' putts. The group for whom the larger circle was identified had smaller deviations from the target in practice than did the group with the higher standard definition of success (smaller circle). More importantly, in delayed retention and transfer tests, with the circles removed, these group differences were maintained. Thus, making learners feel successful during practice resulted in more effective learning. Enhanced performance expectancies likely also play a role in other interventions designed to allow learners to experience success. Putting practice with increasing distances from the hole, sometimes called "errorless" practice (Maxwell et al., 2001), has been shown to result in fewer putting errors relative to putting with increasing distances ('errorful' practice), as well as improved retention test performance (for similar results with older adults, refer Chauvel et al., 2012).

Visual illusions affecting the perceived size of the hole can also influence accuracy in golf putting. In a few studies (Witt et al., 2012; Wood et al., 2013; Chauvel et al., 2015), the golf hole was surrounded either by larger circles, making the hole appear smaller, or by small circles, making the hole appear larger (Ebbinghaus illusion). As first demonstrated by Witt et al. (2012), when the golf hole appeared larger, participants produced more accurate putts than when the hole was surrounded by larger circles (refer also Wood et al., 2013). In a follow-up study, Chauvel et al. used a delayed retention test to determine whether the performance-enhancing effects would be relatively permanent and independent of the presence of the visual illusions. Learning was indeed enhanced in the group that practiced with a perceived larger hole compared with a group that experienced a smaller-looking hole. Moreover, in the group with the perceived larger hole, self-efficacy was higher. Thus, enhancing learners' performance expectancies by making the hole appear larger resulted in more effective learning of the putting task. Overall, it is striking how easily performance and learning can be affected by performers' expectancies.

Implications for golf

These findings have important implications for coaching. They suggest that it may be helpful for coaches to reconsider a number of factors that are considered standard practice in coaching. These include the predominance for offering feedback on unsuccessful trials instead of successful ones, or how they set up challenges for pupils with regards to task difficulty. For example, with beginners, there is often an emphasis on wanting to hit the ball a reasonable distance early in the learning process. For a coach, creating a distance goal that is relatively easy, coupled with enhanced expectancy of what is deemed to be acceptable at that stage of learning, can have a significant impact on early success experience. When setting challenges that involve accuracy, e.g., in short game or putting, coaches will often use tees or markers to demarcate the target zone for a pupil. In order to evoke greater learning and performance, coaches could consider making these tasks easier and lower the challenge level that they normally set in the future. Furthermore, the findings have implications for bringing beginners into the game. With the number of new participants in golf dropping (Sports Marketing Surveys, 2015) and one of the reasons cited for this being the perceived difficulty of the game (Syngenta, 2014), the ability for coaches to lower this barrier to entry through early success cannot be understated. Enhanced performance expectancies are also critical for golfers practicing for, or warming up before, a competition. Setting simple and attainable goals during the warm-up, e.g., can serve to boost confidence. Moreover, after a successful putt, not putting again from the same location, or ending the warm-up with a successful shot, can help players enhance their expectancies for performance in the tournament.

Autonomy support

Autonomy support is another motivational variable that appears to be indispensible for optimal learning (Wulf & Lewthwaite, 2016). The need to be autonomous, i.e., being able to make one's own choices, is considered a fundamental psychological need (e.g., Deci & Ryan, 2008). Conditions that support individuals' need for autonomy have been shown to increase motivation, performance, or learning in a variety of situations (e.g., Reeve & Tseng, 2011). In the motor learning literature, practice conditions in which learners are allowed to make certain decisions themselves – termed self-controlled practice – have consistently been shown to have beneficial effects on learning relative to control conditions (for reviews, refer Wulf, 2007). For instance, giving learners the opportunity to request feedback when practising a motor task (e.g., Janelle et al., 1997), letting them decide when to use an assistive device (e.g., Hartman, 2007; Wulf, 2007), or choose the number of practice trials (Post et al., 2014) has been shown to enhance learning. In addition, the type of instructional language (i.e., autonomy support-ive versus controlling) has been found to have an impact on motor learning. Hooyman et al. (2014) varied the way in which instructions for performing a novel motor task were presented. Instructions that gave the learners a sense of choice (i.e., autonomy-supportive language) led to superior learning than instructions that offered little option for how to execute the skill (i.e., controlling language).

The motivational nature of these effects – i.e., choices contributing to the satisfaction of learn-ers' need for autonomy – was first highlighted by Lewthwaite and Wulf (2012). Interestingly, and in accordance with this view, even minor and seemingly insignificant choices have been found to facilitate learning (e.g., Wulf et al., 2014a; Lewthwaite et al., 2015). For example, in a study by Wulf and Adams (2014), participants were asked to perform three different balance tasks. In a choice group, participants were allowed to choose the order in which they wanted to perform those tasks. In the control group, each participant's order was determined, unbeknown to them, by what their assigned counterpart in the choice group had selected. The choice group showed superior balance performance on all tasks, compared with the control group, through-out the practice phase and, more importantly, on a delayed retention test with a fixed order of tasks. Thus, the ability to choose the task order during practice enhanced balance learning. In another study (Wulf et al., 2014b), participants who were able to choose the order of tasks subsequently chose to complete more sets and repetitions than did control group participants. Thus, an additional benefit of giving learners choices is that it can increase their motivation to practise – which might have additional indirect benefits for learning.

It is even more striking that giving individuals choices that are *incidental* to the motor task to be learned have been shown to have a positive effect on learning (e.g., Wulf et al., 2014a). In one experiment (Lewthwaite et al., 2015, Experiment 2), balance learning was enhanced in a group in which participants were given a choice related to another task they would practice afterwards, and in which they were asked their opinion as to which of two pictures should be hung in the laboratory. Relative to a control group that was simply informed of the second task or the picture to be hung, the choice group demonstrated more effective learning of the balance task. These findings demonstrate that giving learners choices – even small ones or ones that are not directly related to the task – has the capacity to facilitate motor skill learning.

Mechanisms underlying the autonomy support effect

Potential consequences of autonomy support include facilitation of performance through enhanced processing of task errors and greater self-regulatory responsiveness (Legault & Inzlicht, 2013). Moreover, some evidence for a beneficial reduced self-focus comes from findings that participants who were able to choose when to use a balance pole on a balance task (Chiviacowsky et al., 2012) reported being less nervous than participants who were also able to use the pole but could not choose when to use it. Indirect effects of autonomy support include the opportunity to enhance expectations for performance. For example, learners able to control the delivery of feedback typically report asking for feedback when they assumed their performance was relatively successful (e.g., Chiviacowsky & Wulf, 2002). Thus, autonomy support seems to contribute to goal–action coupling by enhancing performance expectancies (Wulf & Lewthwaite, 2016).

Golf-specific studies

Choices as trivial as the colour of objects to be used (e.g., ball colour) have been shown to lead to more effective motor learning (e.g., Wulf et al., 2014a). This includes one study (Lewthwaite et al., 2015, Experiment 1) in which allowing novice golfers to choose the colour of golf balls led to more effective learning of a putting task than not giving them that choice. More specifically, in the choice group, learners were able to choose the golf ball colour (white, orange, or yellow) before each 10-trial block during the practice phase, which consisted of 60 trials. In a control group, learners were provided balls of the same colour that an assigned counterpart in the choice group had used. Choice of ball colour resulted in superior learning, as measured by a retention test 1 day later, in which both groups had to use white balls. Thus, simply being able to choose the colour positively affected learning.

Implications for golf

The effects of autonomy support have considerable implications for golfers and coaches. Throughout the pupil–coach relationship, the coach has many opportunities to support pupils' need for autonomy, thereby affecting their learning. For example, a coach can allow the pupil to choose which target to aim at, in which order to work on the agreed tasks for the coaching session, or which section of the practice field to hit from. When offering augmented feedback, a common tool used by coaches is video replay and, more recently, launch monitors. Coaches can offer choice as to whether a pupil looks at good or bad trials, as well as how frequently they look at them. Furthermore, when asking the pupils to hit clubs in a random order, the pupil could be given a choice as to the order of clubs. When golfers are practicing or performing certain shots (e.g., chip shot), leaving the choice of the club to be used from a specific location up to the player may lead to better outcomes than prescribing the club. Similarly, letting a player decide on the strategy with which he or she wants to play a certain hole may be more effective than trying to dictate the strategy. For coaches working with teams of players, offering choice to players on things such as team order, selection of playing partners, the amount of time needed to warm up, and even incidental choice such as team colours also appear to provide an opportunity for enhanced learning and performance.

External focus of attention

As most golfers will be able to attest, their attentional focus plays a key role in performance. Indeed, an individual's focus of attention, or concentration, is a critical variable in any complex motor activity. However, the need for high precision in golf (e.g., hitting the sweet spot of the clubhead) typically makes the consequences of a less-than-optimal attentional focus immediately obvious. Over the past 2 decades, many studies have shown that adopting an external focus, i.e., concentrating on the intended movement effect (e.g., on the environment), enhances motor performance and learning compared with an internal focus on body movements (e.g., Wulf et al., 1998; for a review, refer Wulf, 2013). An external focus might be one that is directed at the motion of an implement (e.g., racquet, ball, skis, discus, or kayak), even a sticker attached to the body (e.g., chest), a target, the force exerted against the ground, or an image such as thependulum-like motion of a golf club. Compared with an internal focus (e.g., arms, shoulders, hips), an external focus enhances movement effectiveness (e.g., movement accuracy, consistency) and efficiency (as measured by force production, muscular activity, heart rate, and oxygen consumption). This benefit to performance and learning has been demonstrated for a wide variety of skills, including sport skills (e.g., soccer, volleyball, basketball, swimming, running, kayaking, and gymnastics). The effect is independent of the task, performer's skill level, age, or (dis)ability. In essence, by adopting an external focus, a higher skill level is reached in less time (refer Wulf, 2013, for a full review of these).

Mechanisms underlying the external focus effect

An external, relative to an internal, focus appears to have a dual advantage by (a) directing attention to the task goal and (b) reducing a self-focus (for more details, refer Wulf & Lewthwaite, 2016). Therefore, an external focus is another important contributor to goal–action coupling (Wulf & Lewthwaite, 2016). The result of adopting an external focus is greater automaticity (Wulf et al., 2001) as indicated, e.g., by an increased use of fast, reflexive movement adjustments (Wulf et al., 2001), more effective dual-task performance, and greater movement fluidity (e.g., Kal et al., 2013). A focus on movement effects that occur at a greater distance from the body – and are presumably more easily distinguishable from body movements – result in even greater automaticity (Wulf, 2013). In contrast, an internal focus facilitates access to the self (McKay et al., 2015) and presumably results in 'micro-choking' episodes (Wulf & Lewthwaite, 2010), i.e., widespread, inefficient activation of the muscular system, disruption of automaticity, and the use of more conscious control of movements. The consequence is a constrained movement pattern that can be seen when a basketball player 'short-arms' a free throw, or when a golfer leaves a putt short. Finally, it should be noted that, by reliably producing more successful performance outcomes and ease of movement, an external attentional focus contributes to enhanced expectancies (e.g., Shafizadeh et al., 2013) – thus providing another indirect advantage for learning.

Golf-specific studies

Several studies have examined the effects of different attentional foci in golf. In the first study, Wulf et al. (1999) used a pitch shot to compare learning in different groups of novices who were asked to focus on either the swing of their arms (internal focus) or the swing of the club (external focus). On a retention test, the external focus group demonstrated greater accuracy in hitting a target than the internal focus group. Those findings were later extended by Wulf and Su (2007, Experiment 1), who found that the same external focus instructions were more effective not only relative to the internal focus instructions, but also relative to no focus instructions (control group). In a second experiment by Wulf and Su, highly skilled golfers with an average handicap of zero were asked to adopt the same foci (internal, external, and control). The golfers completed 20 shots under each of the three focus conditions. Interestingly, these experts also showed the greatest accuracy when they were asked to focus on the club motion (external). Focussing on their arms (internal) and even adopting their typical focus (control condition) resulted in similar and reduced accuracy.

To examine the distance effect, Bell and Hardy (2009) compared the performance of skilled golfers under three focus conditions, namely, the wrist (internal), clubface (proximal external), and the intended ball trajectory and landing point (distal external). As predicted, participants demonstrated the greatest accuracy in hitting a target in the distal external, followed by the proximal external, followed by the internal focus condition. In addition, the performance advantage seen with a distal focus was maintained under pressure (e.g., evaluation by a PGA professional, publication of scores, possibility of winning a prize).

Two recent studies examined the effects of attentional focus instructions on the learning of movement form in golf (An et al., 2013; Christina & Alpenfels, 2014). In the An et al. (2013) study with novice golfers, the instructions were aimed at increasing the angle between the shoulders and pelvis during the downswing – a characteristic of skilled performance – which can be achieved by encouraging a forward weight shift. External focus instructions to 'push against the left side of the ground' resulted in a greater increase in that angle on a delayed retention test than did internal focus instructions to shift their weight to the left foot, or no focus instruction (control group) (Figure 8.1a). Importantly, the carry distance of the ball was increased by the external focus instruction as well (Figure 8.1b). Thus, a single external focus instruction enhanced both movement form and outcome. Christina and Alpenfels (2014) recently showed that experienced golfers learned to change their swing path more effectively with external rather than internal focus instructions. In two studies, using a six-iron in Study 1 and a driver in Study 2, the authors showed that an inside–out swing path was retained best with an external focus of attention cue.

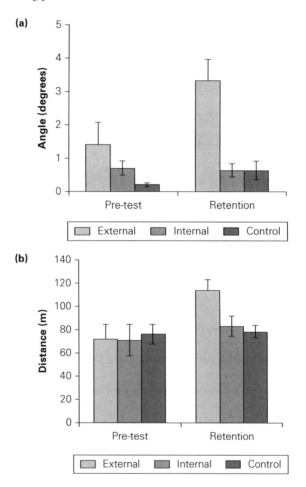

Figure 8.1   Results of the study by An et al. (2013). Different groups of novice golfers hit golf balls under external focus, internal focus, or control conditions (refer text for more details). The practice phase (not shown here) included 100 trials. The pre-test and retention test (after 3 days) consisted of 10 trials each.

Source: Adapted from An et al. 2013, p. 6.

Implications for golf

For coaches, making use of external cues consistently will improve both the ability to make changes in movement form and facilitate improvements in performance more rapidly. Challenges coaches may face in implementing these small changes in how their coaching ques are delivered will be familiarity but also the creativity to devise relevant tasks and metaphors that draw their pupils to the movement effect rather than the movement itself. For example, when using video feedback, a coach might feel that a faulty hip or shoulder action may be the primary contributor to poor movement form, and it is often easiest to simply ask the pupil to focus on that. However, focussing on the movement of the club or on hitting a certain part of the golf ball may be an alternative cue that will facilitate the change in hip movement required. For coaches working with elite-level players, using external cues effectively can yield considerable gain, particularly, when taking advantage of the distance effect by emphasizing distal attentional cues such as the target or flight of the ball. In preparing elite players for competition, training them to understand their most relevant and meaningful cues, and then ensuring that this becomes part of their pre-tournament preparation, can offer competitive golfers a performance advantage. On the course, it is often recommended that player not think about the swing (e.g., technical modifications to work on during practice). However, elite players are able to use 'technical keys' (e.g., images) on the course to ensure the implementation of technical changes without using internal cues. Using external swing thoughts that are more distal in nature and that are focussed tightly on the movement effect, such as 'hit a high draw', 'land it pin high', or 'start it on the tree on the left', allows the player to maintain the technical aspects during the swing (e.g., try to keep the clubhead moving down the target line after impact) without disrupting automaticity. Many coaches also use various training aids to enhance performance. Rather than using them to merely to try and force the learner into a desired position, the attentional focus findings give coaches a new perspective for their use (i.e., how to use a certain training aid to help the learner understand the desired movement effect even more clearly).

Summary and future directions

We have discussed three factors for motor skill learning that are central to a new theory of motor learning, the OPTIMAL theory (Wulf & Lewthwaite, 2016): enhanced expectancies, autonomy support, and an external focus of attention. The importance of each factor for enhancing performance and learning has been demonstrated in numerous studies, including golf-related studies. While each of these variables plays an important role in and of itself, recent findings show that they have additive effects (Wulf et al., 2014a; Pascua et al., 2015; Wulf et al., 2015), with the presence of all three variables leading to the most effective learning outcomes (Wulf et al., 2017). Golf coaches can easily take advantage of these effects. They require little more than small changes in the way they give instructions or feedback – and, of course, some creativity. Giving their clients (small) choices, delivering feedback at their request, providing success experience, avoiding references to body movements, and instead directing their attention externally can go a long way in terms of facilitating learning. The resulting movement success may even create a *virtuous cycle*, with overall positive consequences for learning, motivation, and participation in the game of golf.

References

An, J.; Wulf, G. & Kim, S. (2013) Increased Carry Distance and X-Factor Stretch in Golf Through an External Focus of Attention, *Journal of Motor Learning and Development*, 1 (1), 2–11.

Bell, J. & Hardy, J. (2009) Effects of Attentional Focus on Skilled Performance in Golf, *Journal of Applied Sport Psychology*, 21 (2), 163–177.

Chauvel, G.; Maquestiaux, F.; Hartley, A.; Joubert, S.; Didierjean, A. & Masters, R. (2012) Age Effects Shrink When Motor Learning is Predominantly Supported by Nondeclarative, Automatic Memory Processes: Evidence From Golf Putting, *The Quarterly Journal of Experimental Psychology*, 65 (1), 25–38.

Chauvel, G.; Wulf, G. & Maquestiaux, F. (2015) Visual Illusions can Facilitate Sport Skill Learning, *Psychonomic Bulletin & Review*, 22 (3), 717–721.

Chiviacowsky, S. & Wulf, G. (2002) Self-Controlled Feedback: Does It Enhance Learning Because Performers Get Feedback When They Need It? *Research Quarterly for Exercise and Sport*, 73 (4), 408–415.

Chiviacowsky, S. & Wulf, G. (2007) Feedback After Good Trials Enhances Learning, *Research Quarterly for Exercise and Sport*, 78 (2), 40–47.

Chiviacowsky, S.; Wulf, G.; Lewthwaite, R. & Campos, T. (2012) Motor Learning Benefits of Self-Controlled Practice in Persons with Parkinson's Disease, *Gait & Posture*, 35 (4), 601–605.

Chiviacowsky, S.; Wulf, G.; Wally, R. & Borges, T. (2009) KR After Good Trials Enhances Learning in Older Adults, *Research Quarterly for Exercise and Sport*, 80 (3), 663–668.

Christina, R. & Alpenfels, E. (2014) Influence of Attentional Focus on Learning a Swing Path Change, *International Journal of Golf Science*, 3 (1), 35–49.

Clark, S. & Ste-Marie, D. (2007) The Impact of Self-as-a-Model Interventions on Children's Self-Regulation of Learning and Swimming Performance, *Journal of Sports Sciences*, 25 (5), 577–586.

Deci, E. & Ryan, R. (2008) Self-Determination Theory: A Macrotheory of Human Motivation, Development, and Health, *Canadian Psychology*, 49 (3), 182–185.

Hartman, J.M. (2007) Self-controlled Use of a Perceived Physical Assistance Device During a Balancing Task, *Perceptual and Motor Skills*, 104, 1005–1016.

Hooyman, A.; Wulf, G. & Lewthwaite, R. (2014) Impacts of Autonomy-Supportive Versus Controlling Instructional Language on Motor Learning, *Human Movement Science*, 36, 190–198.

Janelle, C.; Barba, D.; Frehlich, S.; Tennant, L. & Cauraugh, J. (1997) Maximizing Performance Effectiveness Through Videotape Replay and a Self-Controlled Learning Environment, *Research Quarterly for Exercise and Sport*, 68 (4), 269–279.

Kal, E.; van der Kamp, J. & Houdijk, H. (2013) External Attentional Focus Enhances Movement Automatization: A Comprehensive Test of the Constrained Action Hypothesis, *Human Movement Science*, 32 (4), 527–539.

Legault, L. & Inzlicht, M. (2013) Self-Determination, Self-Regulation, and the Brain: Autonomy Improves Performance by Enhancing Neuroaffective Responsiveness to Self-Regulation Failure, *Journal of Personality and Social Psychology*, 105 (1), 123–138.

Lewthwaite, R.; Chiviacowsky, S.; Drews, R. & Wulf, G. (2015) Choose to Move: The Motivational Impact of Autonomy Support on Motor Learning, *Psychonomic Bulletin & Review*, 22 (5), 1383–1388.

Lewthwaite, R. & Wulf, G. (2012) Motor Learning Through a Motivational Lens, In: N. Hodges & A. Williams (Eds.) *Skill Acquisition in Sport: Research, Theory & Practice* (2nd Ed.), London: Routledge, pp. 173–191.

Maxwell, J.; Masters, R.; Kerr, E. & Weedon, E. (2001) The Implicit Benefit of Learning Without Errors, *Quarterly Journal of Experimental Psychology*, 54 (4), 1049–1068.

McKay, B.; Wulf, G.; Lewthwaite, R. & Nordin, A. (2015) The Self: Your Own Worst Enemy? A Test of the Self-Invoking Trigger Hypothesis, *Quarterly Journal of Experimental Psychology*, 68 (9), 1910–1919.

Palmer, K.; Chiviacowsky, S. & Wulf, G. (2016) Enhanced Expectancies Facilitate Golf Putting, *Psychology of Sport and Exercise*, 22, 229–232.

Pascua, L.; Wulf, G. & Lewthwaite, R. (2015) Additive Benefits of External Focus and Enhanced Performance Expectancy for Motor Learning, *Journal of Sports Sciences*, 33 (1), 58–66.

Post, P.; Fairbrother, J.; Barros, J. & Kulpa, J. (2014) Self-Controlled Practice Within a Fixed Time Period Facilitates the Learning of a Basketball Set Shot, *Journal of Motor Learning and Development*, 2 (1), 9–15.

Reeve, J. & Tseng, C.M. (2011) Cortisol Reactivity to a Teacher's Motivating Style: The Biology of Being Controlled Versus Supporting Autonomy, *Motivation and Emotion*, 35, 63–74.

Rosenqvist, O. & Skans, O. (2015) Confidence Enhanced Performance? – The Causal Effects of Success on Future Performance in Professional Golf Tournaments, *Journal of Economic Behavior & Organization*, 117, 281–295.

Saemi, E.; Porter, J.; Ghotbi-Varzaneh, A.; Zarghami, M. & Maleki, F. (2012) Knowledge of Results After Relatively Good Trials Enhances Self-Efficacy and Motor Learning, *Psychology of Sport and Exercise*, 13 (4), 378–382.

Schmidt, R. & Lee, T. (2011) *Motor Control and Learning* (5th Ed.), Champaign, IL: Human Kinetics.

Shafizadeh, M.; Platt, G. & Bahram, A. (2013) Effects of Focus of Attention and Type of Practice on Learning and Self-Efficacy in Dart Throwing, *Perceptual and Motor Skills*, 117 (1), 182–192.

Sport Marketing Surveys (2015) *2014 Golf Participation Figures*, Available at www.Sportsmarketingsurveysinc. Com/Sports-Marketing-Surveys-Inc-Announces-2014-Golf-Participation-Figures/ (Accessed February 22, 2016).

Syngenta (2014) *Growing Golf in the UK*, Available at www.Greencast.Co.Uk/Uk/News/General/News-2014/Growing-Golf-In-The-Uk-Download-Your-Free-Report.Aspx (Accessed February 22, 2016).

Trempe, M.; Sabourin, M. & Proteau, L. (2012) Success Modulates Consolidation of a Visuomotor Adaptation Task, *Journal of Experimental Psychology: Learning, Memory, and Cognition*, 38 (1), 52–60.

Witt, J.; Linkenauger, S. & Proffitt, D. (2012) Get Me Out of This Slump! Visual Illusions Improve Sports Performance, *Psychological Science*, 23 (4), 397–399.

Wood, G.; Vine, S. & Wilson, M. (2013) The Impact of Visual Illusions on Perception, Action Planning, and Motor Performance, *Attention, Perception, & Psychophysics,* 75 (5), 830–834.

Wulf, G. (2007) Self-Controlled Practice Enhances Motor Learning: Implications for Physiotherapy, *Physiotherapy*, 93 (2), 96–101.

Wulf, G. (2013) Attentional Focus and Motor Learning: A Review of 15 Years, *International Review of Sport and Exercise Psychology*, 6 (1), 77–104.

Wulf, G. & Adams, N. (2014) Small Choices Can Enhance Balance Learning, *Human Movement Science*, 38, 235–240.

Wulf, G.; Chiviacowsky, S. & Cardozo, P. (2014a) Additive Benefits of Autonomy Support and Enhanced Expectancies for Motor Learning, *Human Movement Science*, 37, 12–20.

Wulf, G.; Chiviacowsky, S. & Drews, R. (2015) External Focus and Autonomy Support: Two Important Factors in Motor Learning Have Additive Benefits, *Human Movement Science*, 40, 176–184.

Wulf, G.; Chiviacowsky, S. & Lewthwaite, R. (2010) Normative Feedback Effects on Learning a Timing Task, *Research Quarterly for Exercise and Sport*, 81 (4), 425–431.

Wulf, G.; Chiviacowsky, S. & Lewthwaite, R. (2012) Altering Mindset Can Enhance Motor Learning in Older Adults, *Psychology and Aging*, 27 (1), 14–21.

Wulf, G.; Freitas, H. & Tandy, R. (2014b) Choosing to Exercise More: Small Choices Can Increase Exercise Engagement, *Psychology of Sport and Exercise*, 15 (3), 268–271.

Wulf, G.; Höß, M. & Prinz, W. (1998) Instructions for Motor Learning: Differential Effects of Internal Versus External Focus of Attention, *Journal of Motor Behavior*, 30 (2), 169–179.

Wulf, G.; Lauterbach, B. & Toole, T. (1999) Learning Advantages of an External Focus of Attention in Golf, *Research Quarterly for Exercise and Sport*, 70 (2), 120–126.

Wulf, G. & Lewthwaite, R. (2010) Effortless Motor Learning? An External Focus of Attention Enhances Movement Effectiveness and Efficiency, In: B. Bruya (Ed.) *Effortless Attention: A New Perspective in Attention and Action*, Cambridge, MA: MIT Press, pp. 75–101.

Wulf, G. & Lewthwaite, R. (2016) Optimizing Performance Through Intrinsic Motivation and Attention for Learning: The OPTIMAL Theory of Motor Learning, *Psychonomic Bulletin & Review*, 23 (5), 1382–1414.

Wulf, G.; Lewthwaite, R.; Cardozo, P. & Chiviacowsky, S. (2017) Triple Play: Additive Contributions of Enhanced Expectancies, Autonomy Support, and External Attentional Focus to Motor Learning, *Quarterly Journal of Experimental Psychology*, Doi: 10.1080/17470218.2016.1276204.

Wulf, G.; McNevin, N. & Shea, C. (2001) The Automaticity of Complex Motor Skill Learning as a Function of Attentional Focus, *Quarterly Journal of Experimental Psychology*, 54 (4), 1143–1154.

Wulf, G. & Su, J. (2007) External Focus of Attention Enhances Golf Shot Accuracy in Beginners and Experts, *Research Quarterly for Exercise and Sport*, 78 (4), 384–389.

9

PUTTING IMPLICIT MOTOR LEARNING INTO GOLF PRACTICE

Jamie Poolton and Rich Masters

Introduction

Conveniently, in the context of this handbook, the putting green has been a preferred testing ground for two allied avenues of investigation, which together aim to understand the mechanisms that underlie how best to develop resilient motor skills. *The theory of reinvestment* recognises that traditional learning environments incite cognitive activity that leads to the deliberate storage and recall of technical knowledge. In response to pressure, performers use the knowledge to consciously control coordination of their movements in an attempt to perform successfully. Ironically, reinvesting knowledge in this way can heighten the potential for skill failure (Masters & Maxwell, 2008). *Implicit motor learning* has been proposed as a means to inoculate performers against the negative impact of reinvestment (Masters, 1992). Implicit motor learning interventions prevent accumulation of technical knowledge and so deny performers an opportunity to reinvest. As a consequence, motor performance is resilient to challenges such as pressure (Masters & Poolton, 2012). This chapter offers a golf-centric overview of empirical, mostly laboratory-based work in the area. Emerging from the overview are design principles for implicit motor learning interventions, which inform player–coach interactions and the planning of practice activities, as well as the best use of commercially touted brain-training aids. We urge practitioners to use the principles to put implicit motor learning into practice.

Cognitive engagement in skill learning

Like no other sport, golf fosters problem-solving behaviour. The game is inherently difficult. Multiple interdependent body parts require organisation in order to apply the appropriate force onto the ball, and a miniscule 1-degree error at ball contact can be an 80-yard error down the fairway. Golf is also self-paced, affording more time between trials than most individual sports to search for an effective solution. Players' inclination to engage in systematic problem solving is overtly evident on the practice ground and the putting green, and this has been demonstrated empirically.

During practice, novice players tend to take longer over putt preparation (and execution) if the previous putt was missed than if it was holed (Lam et al., 2010a). Experimental paradigms (probe reaction times; Lam et al., 2010a) and neuroscientific measures (frontal-central alpha power by electroencephalogram [EEG]; Cooke et al., 2014) imply that this extra time is a function of cognitive intervention, presumably to formulate a solution to correct the error, and is accompanied by visible "tinkering" with putting technique between shots (Lam et al., 2010b). Error correction behaviour of this kind ostensibly results in the storage and manipulation of technical information (Maxwell et al., 2001), because when (extreme) measures are taken to deny learners the opportunity to use feedback (both visual and kinaesthetic) to adjust their technique, they find it harder to describe the putting action (e.g., Maxwell et al., 2003).

On face value, cognitive engagement in skill learning seems inevitable and represents a fruitful mental investment. The technical know-how cultivated and supplemented by well-intended coaches affords players advanced problem-solving capability. However, Masters (1992) argued that the availability of technical knowledge can ultimately be counterproductive.

Cognitive intervention under pressure

Masters (1992) asked novice players to practice short-range putts (1.50 m) on an indoor green with a shallow incline. Four hundred practice putts were made across 4 days. One group of players was provided a list of technical instructions, while another group was left to their own devices. Players in both groups progressed to the extent that they made about every other putt. Furthermore, players were able to recall considerable amounts of technical information that they viewed as important for hitting a perfect putt. However, an anxiety-raising pressure manipulation tended to have a negative effect on performance. This was in stark contrast to the performance of the group of players who did not appear to have access to very much technical information. Masters (1992) proposed that the availability of technical knowledge afforded conscious control over interdependent parts of the putting stroke that ordinarily functioned in "an automatic, effortless, implicit nature" (p. 344).

Pressure likely evokes conscious control as an attempt by players to perform at their best (Moran, 2012) but manifests in disturbed coordination of movement, causing putts to be missed. The preferred term for this phenomenon became reinvestment (Masters, 1992; Masters et al., 1993), i.e., the performer reinvests technical knowledge that had been acquired during practice. These original ideas have generally held up against empirical scrutiny (e.g., Hardy et al., 1996; Gucciardi & Dimmock, 2008; Toner & Moran, 2011). For instance, Beilock et al. (2004) found that deliberately instructing skilled players (handicap <8) to "monitor their swing and attempt to keep their club head straight as it travelled toward the target" (p. 375) was harmful to putting accuracy. In a subtler test of the phenomenon, the same researchers manipulated preparation time under the premise that "time affords [skilled players] the counterproductive opportunity to explicitly attend to and monitor automated execution processes" (p. 378) or, in our terminology, the opportunity to *reinvest*. Beilock et al. (2004) contrasted the putting accuracy of skilled players when they were allowed as much time as they wanted to prepare and execute the putt to the situation when they were forced to putt within 3 seconds. The time constraints resulted in better putting performance, probably due to the diminished opportunity players had to cognitively intervene in their own movements.

A more direct attempt to index reinvestment was conducted by Zhu et al. (2011) using EEG measurement of co-activation (or coherence) between brain regions associated with verbal–analytical processing (T3) and motor planning (Fz) (Deeny et al., 2003). A sample of players who had missed putts frequently during practice (approximately one out of three putts) displayed heightened T3–Fz co-activation levels when preparing to putt under pressure than at baseline (no pressure manipulation), suggesting that pressure stimulated cognitive intervention in putt preparation.

The propensity to reinvest technical knowledge is considered an individual personality trait that can be quantified psychometrically using different scales (Masters et al., 1993). One iteration, the Movement-Specific Reinvestment Scale (MSRS), comprises dimensions of personality that characterise concern about the "style" of movement – *movement self-consciousness* – and the act of reinvesting as it was originally conceived – *conscious motor processing* (Masters & Maxwell, 2008). Reinvestment scales offer practitioners a tool with which to identify players vulnerable to the effects of pressure (e.g., Maxwell et al., 2006) or who are likely to cognitively (over)engage in skill learning (Zhu et al., 2011). The conscious motor processing dimension of the MSRS has also been adapted to function as a state measure of reinvestment that captures a person's propensity for cognitive (over)engagement during specific golf putting performances (Cooke et al., 2011; Vine et al., 2013).

If reinvestment mediates the relationship between pressure and performance, the challenge for practitioners is to design learning environments that help guard players against the potentially negative consequences of reinvestment.

Implicit motor learning

If, in passing from novice to expert, or unpractised to practised, explicit learning can be minimized, the performer will have less conscious knowledge of the rules for execution of the skill, and will be less able to reinvest his or her knowledge in time of stress.

(Masters, 1992, p. 345)

Given the appetite of learners to problem solve and of practitioners to instruct, Masters's not insignificant challenge was to devise a learning environment that stifled cognitive (over)engagement in skill learning. Masters's initial solution was to occupy cognitive resources with an irrelevant distractor. He had novice players hit 400 practice putts from 1.50 m while attempting to continuously call out letters of the alphabet in a random order. After practice, learners recalled very little technical knowledge of the golf putt. The dual-task intervention seemed fit for the purpose. Crucially, putting proficiency did improve as a function of practice. Moreover, an anxiety-raising pressure manipulation had no disruptive impact on putting performance (refer Hardy et al., 1996, for verification of the findings). The feasibility of *implicit motor learning* had been established.

These findings challenged the commonly held view that cognitive engagement is a prerequisite for learning complex motor skills. Instead, evidence began to mount for an alternative dual-pathway model that proposed that implicit and explicit motor learning could occur simultaneously and from the onset of practice, with the contribution of each dependent on the design of the learning environment (Masters & Maxwell, 2004).

Using a dual-task intervention to cause implicit motor learning did come with drawbacks, however. The learning curve of players engaged in dual-task practice was shallower than that in players who received technical instructions or learnt through trial and error. To ascertain whether dual-task learners would eventually "catch up", Maxwell et al. (2000) embarked on a longitudinal study. Novice players hit *three thousand*[1] 3 m putts over 5 days while at all times carrying out a continuous backward-counting task. Learning was compared to a sample of self-guided discovery learners. Although dual-task learners trailed discovery learners throughout practice, a test of skill retention 3 days later found no differences. Dual-task learners did catch up. Remarkably, even after 3000 putts, dual-task learners recalled limited technical knowledge of the mechanics of the putting stroke.

While theoretically interesting, dual-task interventions are practically limited. Secondary task demands need to be sufficiently high to successfully inhibit cognitive engagement in learning

(MacMahon & Masters, 2002); however, field-based tests suggest that if the secondary task is too challenging, learners will disengage from it and attend primarily to the motor skill (Gabbett et al., 2014). Practitioners could consider making the task more relevant to the learner (e.g., preferred object list, Gabbett et al., 2014; recite songs or rhymes, Capio et al., 2013) or relevant to the context in which the learner is operating (Poolton et al., 2016). For example, cognitive resources could be occupied with tactical elements of the game or psychological skills training exercises. Context-relevant tasks have the added benefit of making best use of practice time by offering a two-for-one skill training session.

Implicit motor learning principles for coach instruction

An alternative approach is to occupy cognitive resources with task-relevant, movement outcome-centred aspects of the task (Wulf, 2013). Wulf et al. (1999) have shown that careful rewording of technical instructions to focus attention on the direct outcome of a movement generally benefits skill learning. For example, after receiving a demonstration and conventional technical instruction on the fundamentals of a 15 m pitch shot, novice players instructed to "focus on the pendulum-like motion of the *club*" outperformed players instructed to "focus on the swinging motion of the *arms*" in a delayed retention test (Wulf et al., 1999). The same external focus instruction was also found to elicit performance gains for skilled players relative to performance with internal focus instruction or when no instruction was provided (Wulf & Su, 2007). Armed with considerable empirical evidence, Wulf has resolutely argued that coaching points that direct attention to movement components constrain action by disturbing automatic (implicit) processes (Wulf, 2013). The *constrained-action hypothesis* also states that a deliberate focus on the outcome of movement "allows the motor system to more naturally self-organize" (Wulf et al., 2001, p. 1143).

With this argument in mind, we asked whether instructions to focus on movement outcomes lowered cognitive involvement in learning (Poolton et al., 2006b). Novice players were simply instructed to focus either on the "swing of their hands" or on the "swing of the putter head" for 300 practice putts. Players instructed to focus on the putter head recalled less technical knowledge than those instructed to focus on their hands. Furthermore, the purposeful loading of cognitive resources with an irrelevant secondary task did not affect the number of putts made by players instructed to focus on the putter-head, but it did cause more putts to be missed by those instructed to focus on their hands. The negative effect of the secondary task load indicates that the latter group was dependent on cognitive resources to support performance. Taken together, the findings imply that provision of a *single* carefully worded instruction to just focus on the putter head successfully stifled cognitive engagement and thus promoted implicit learning of the putt (refer also Poolton et al., 2007).

For the literal-minded readers, it is important to be clear that an instruction to *focus on* the outcome of a movement does not necessarily mean *look at*. That is, attention is not necessarily aligned with gaze fixation (Ryu et al., 2012). However, in some cases, an exact interpretation may carry implicit learning benefits. Vine et al. have investigated the feasibility of training novice and experienced golfers to lengthen the duration of their final gaze fixation prior to movement initiation (refer Vine et al., 2011, for a review) – a period known as quiet eye. In one such study, quiet eye duration of novice players was successfully trained via explicit instructions. Following putting practice, quiet eye-trained players reported limited access to technical knowledge about the putting stroke, as well as lower scores on the conscious motor processing dimension of the MSRS than the group that had been guided by technical instructions throughout practice. Conscious motor processing scores provided an index of each player's perceived cognitive engagement in putting performance. Furthermore, quiet eye-trained players' putting accuracy, quiet eye duration, and self-reported conscious motor processing score were not influenced by the imposition of a multifaceted pressure manipulation. Vine et al. (2013) proposed quiet eye training as "a means to implicit motor learning" (p. 367).

Included within the design of Vine et al.'s (2013) study was a group of learners who were provided a single analogical instruction to "keep your body still like a grandfather clock and use your arms the same way that the pendulum of the clock operates" (p. 386). Analogical instructions do not challenge the learner to piece together, and make sense of, a rich list of technical information. Instead, effective analogical instructions present technical knowledge in a pre-packaged form (refer Liao & Masters, 2001), which is less biomechanically prescriptive than verbal instructions. Despite some evidence that use of analogical instruction does not necessarily reduce the deployment of cognitive resources during practice (Lam et al., 2009a), after practice, learners have limited recall of technical knowledge (e.g., Lam et al., 2009b) and tend not to be affected by the introduction of additional cognitively demanding tasks (e.g., Poolton et al., 2006a), which is congruent with implicit learning. Vine et al. (2013) reported that the *grandfather clock* analogy resulted in the report, on average, of a single piece of technical information; the self-report of relatively low conscious processing scores that were not raised by pressure; sustained quiet eye durations under pressure; and crucially, robust putting performance. In short, the evidence implied that the grandfather clock analogy promotes implicit learning of the putting stroke.

The grandfather clock analogy is reminiscent of Wulf et al.'s (1999) instruction to "focus on the pendulum-like motion of the club" cited earlier. The significant difference is that the grandfather clock instruction makes reference to the *body* and the use of the *arms* (focus on the movement), rather than the motion of the putter (focus on the movement outcome). Empirical investigation of analogical instruction has generally guarded against reference to body segments (Liao & Masters, 2001; Lam et al., 2009a); however, interpretation of Vine et al.'s (2013) data suggests that this does not compromise implicit learning.

An implicit motor learning principle for the design of practice activities

If error correction is the primary stimulus for cognitive (over)engagement in skill learning, then the simplest way to curtail cognitive activity is to create practice activities that promote successful performance outcomes. Maxwell et al. (2001) empirically tested this idea. Putts were made extremely easy at the start of practice by placing balls just 0.25 m from the hole. After each subsequent block of 50 putts, the balls were placed 0.25 m further from the hole, with practice ending with 2 m putts. This practice structure successfully reduced the occurrence of errors in practice compared to putting schedules that had learners putt the same number of balls from the same distances but in a different distance order (random or a systematic decrease in putt difficulty). Relatively more putts continued to be made by error-reduced learners in both a post-test (2 m) and a distance transfer test (3 m) by the group of players who experienced more successful performance outcomes in practice. Moreover, consuming cognitive resources with an irrelevant secondary task had no effect on performance, implying that the putt was learnt implicitly. Surprisingly, the learners' ability to recall detailed technical information implied otherwise. Maxwell et al. attributed the accrual of technical knowledge to error correction behaviour in response to the noticeable rise in putting errors from distances longer than 0.75 m.

A second study showed that novice learners putting from 0.25 m to 0.75 m missed, on average, 1 in 10 putts, demonstrated relatively few visible adjustments to technique, made relatively few indicative statements of error correction behaviour, and showed greater resilience to an additional cognitive load than novice learners who missed, on average, 6 of 10 putts from 1.75 m to 1.25 m. Practice designs that reduce putting outcome errors early in practice seem to promote implicit motor learning. Moreover, Poolton et al. (2005) later verified that cognitive engagement in skill learning following an opening bout of error-reduced practice did not appear to confound the initial implicit learning of the putt.

More recent tests of the resilience of error-reduced learners to reinvestment have attempted to induce cognitive engagement by using unfamiliar and unusual putters (Lam et al., 2010b) or the application of pressure (Zhu et al., 2011), but without success. For example, Zhu et al. showed that EEG T3–Fz coherence levels, used as an index of reinvestment, were not heightened by pressure. Error-reduced practice designs appear to inoculate players against reinvestment.

By design, error-reduced practice provides learners with a "history of successful experiences" (Bunker & Williams, 1986, p. 235), which builds confidence. Recent unpublished data found that despite similarities in putting proficiency, players who used error-reduced practice reported higher confidence in their capability to make 2.50 m putts than players who missed frequently during practice (constant practice from 2.50 m) (Masters et al., 2012), suggesting that error-reduced practice approaches are also good for player self-confidence.

For teaching professionals, a recent application of the error-reduced practice principle is noteworthy. Deficits in the cognitive function of older adults (>59 years) means a reduced capacity to correct putting errors and likely explains compromised learning gains from practice designs that do not manage the frequency of errors (Chauvel et al., 2012). This appears to be remedied by error-reduced practice. Chauvel et al. (2012) showed that older adults' putting success both during and after error-reduced practice (0.25 m–1 m putts) was equivalent to their younger counterparts (<32 years). The study illustrates the potential utility of implicit learning interventions for practitioners working with groups with cognitive limitations, such as the elderly, children, or learners with intellectual disability.

A final finding of note is yet to be replicated in golf. Recently acquired data from the practice session of a far-aiming throwing task implies that error-reduced practice designs promote higher trial-to-trial movement variability of the upper arm than more error-strewn designs (van Ginneken et al., in press). Participants' tendency to consciously control their movements, as measured by the MSRS, was also associated with movement variability. Those with a weaker disposition tended to show greater variability between throws, although following an error-reduced practice design did weaken the relationship. Together, the findings imply that suppression of cognitive engagement in skill learning leads to the production of less-consistent movement patterns. However, this need not be viewed negatively. Indeed, movement variability is considered by some (e.g., non-linear pedagogists) as a valuable constituent of practice, which better prepares the motor system to adapt to perturbations of movement (e.g., caused by a gust of wind) or the challenges of competition (Davids et al., 2007). Future research needs to evaluate the value of practice designs that (implicitly) promote movement variability during practice of the putting stroke.

A new (brain) wave of training aids

Advances in technology present the possibility that brain activity can be reliably, cheaply, and unobtrusively monitored via wireless electroencephalography (EEG). Researchers have used EEG systems to identify cortical correlates of optimal putting performance by differentiating the brain activity of experts compared to that of novices (Baumeister et al., 2008; Cooke et al., 2014), as well as when putts are made compared to when putts are missed (Arns et al., 2008; Babiloni et al., 2008; Cooke et al., 2014). The implication then is that desirable patterns of brain activity can be trained using EEG systems that provide immediate on-line feedback of activity in key areas of the brain. Typically, training asks learners to attempt to extinguish an auditory tone that represents sub-optimal brain activity before stroke initiation. Ring et al. (2015) showed that recreational golfers can be trained to regulate their brain activity prior to the initiation of a putt after as little as 3 hours of neurofeedback training; although performance gains were not evident. Arns et al. (2008), however, showed that feedback of customised *optimal* brain activity profiles increased the chance of a putt being holed. It, therefore, seems plausible for practitioners to begin using wireless EEG technology to objectively gauge their players' level of cognitive involvement in putt preparation on the practice green, or even out on the course. Furthermore, consideration of the research will help practitioners to set desirable brain activity parameters for neurofeedback training (e.g., low T3-Fz coherence to promote implicit motor learning).

More controversially, brain activity can be modulated directly by transcranial direct current stimulation (tDCS), which is a non-invasive technique that selectively excites or suppresses areas of the cerebral cortex. Recently, Zhu et al. (2015) used tDCS to suppress neural activity associated with cognitive functioning during practice. This study primarily provided theoretical insight, although Zhu et al. (2015) were guilty of premature speculation on the practical utility of the technique. Rigorous, systematic empirical investigation is needed to fully understand the effectiveness of tDCS intervention, as well as the longer-term consequences of repetitive brain stimulation. Our study administered an electrical current in a controlled laboratory environment by a trained technician. Safety guidelines constrained practice to a single 20-minute bout of putting, which was enough time to comfortably make 70 practice putts. Practical application of tDCS is, therefore, limited by technical expertise, time constraints, and uncertainty around the long-term effects. Practitioners need to exercise caution when offered tDCS as a training tool.

Implications for the game and future research

Despite its successes, advocates of implicit motor learning have conceded that "the chances of maintaining implicit motor learning over the many years that it takes to become an expert seem remote" (Masters et al., 2002, p. 138). Encouragingly, a short initial bout of implicit motor learning at the beginning of the learning journey could be sufficient to bestow benefits of learning implicitly even if cognitive engagement follows (Poolton et al., 2005).

While the implication of such findings is exciting for the coaching of novices, players are often delivered to practitioners with some degree of golfing experience and technical knowledge. Only after sampling the game will most players seek professional guidance. Practitioners may want to quickly establish their added value or want to engage the learner by giving them something to *work on*. Technical instruction is hard to resist. After the lesson, technical knowledge affords problem solving in response to error, injury, or impairments to the players' natural swing or putting stroke. In short, cognitive (over)engagement seems inevitable. The possibility of offsetting this known threat to optimal performance via the insertion of bouts of implicit motor learning is, therefore, of practical significance. A test of the real-world impact of implicit learning interventions is overdue.

If practitioners are already convinced by the potential of implicit motor learning, their challenge as facilitators of learning is to engage learners in activities and player–coach interactions that progress them towards their goals while suppressing cognitive engagement in skill learning. This can be achieved by the careful manipulation of space, such as the distance from or the size of the target (Maxwell et al., 2001), by adaptations of equipment (e.g., length, weight, and head size of the club; Buszard et al., 2014), or by shot time constraints that take away the opportunity for time-consuming cognitive processes (Beilock et al., 2004).

The design of "implicit" practice activities needs to be accompanied by constructively aligned player–coach interactions (Muir et al., 2011). For instance, Poolton et al. (2005) found that the implicit benefits of an error-reduced practice design were overshadowed by the provision of a set of technical instructions. The research suggests that the provision of technical instruction/ feedback needs to be diluted as much as possible and carefully phrased to deflect attention away from performance mechanics. Analogical instruction or instructions that engage the learner in a salient external component of the task, such as the outcome of the movement (e.g., putter or path of the ball) or *quiet-eyeing* the ball, appear fit for this purpose. Care should also be taken with practitioners' use of questioning as a device to assess and/or deepen player understanding (Muir et al., 2011), as it ultimately might lead to cognitive engagement and technical knowledge accrual. Besides, from an implicit learning perspective, observation of movement is a better indicator of a player's understanding of technique than the recall of technical coaching points.

Implicit motor learning design should also consider the personality traits of the individual player. For instance, reinvestment disposition may help identify individuals most susceptible to skill failure (Masters et al., 1993) and/or most likely to engage cognitive resources in skill learning (Zhu et al., 2011; Malhotra et al., 2015). Psychometric profiling, therefore, helps the practitioners better understand the player in order to tailor their intervention accordingly.

A final thought is whether the principles of implicit learning outlined in this chapter generalise to other facets of the game. It is likely that teaching professionals will have, perhaps implicitly, applied many of the principles described in their practice. Peter Lightbrown (2010), for example, advocates a teaching philosophy of the swing that directs attention to the abstract sensations of "balance, relaxation and rhythm" (p. 77) rather than highlighting key swing flaws and fixes (refer Poolton & Masters, 2010, for a short commentary on Lightbrown's approach). The golf swing has such a high level of organisational complexity because of the need to coordinate so many interdependent parts that it seems likely that learning would benefit from practice environments that allow the body to self-organise (Davids et al., 2007; Wulf, 2013). Whether the penchant for problem solving can be quashed when the skill is so complex is a question for future research.

Summary

The body of work presented in this chapter supports the view commonly attributed to William James that "the greatest weapon against stress is our ability to choose one thought over another." A player's ability to "*choose*" not to reinvest in technical knowledge helps safeguard him/her against pressure-induced skill failure. This inclination can be influenced by implicit motor learning. The overarching rule of thumb emerging from research in this area is that learning environments should be designed with the objective of limiting cognitive (over)engagement in learning. This can be achieved via carefully worded instructions and intelligently designed practice activities. The big question for teaching professionals is does implicit learning work in practice? Can it really be a great weapon against the stress induced by club or professional competition?

Note

1 Maxwell et al.'s longitudinal study was part of a program of PhD work by the late Jon Maxwell (supervised by Masters), which made exclusive use of golf putting to answer theoretical questions. Upon completion of his thesis, Jon acknowledged that his work "took a lot of balls … 49,542 to be precise!" (Maxwell, 2001). Jon contributed greatly to the empirical work and theoretical thinking presented in this chapter.

References

Arns, M.; Kleinnijenhuis, M.; Fallahpour, K. & Breteler, R. (2008) Golf Performance Enhancement and Real-life Neurofeedback Training Using Personalized Event-Locked EEG Profiles, *Journal of Neurotherapy*, 11 (4), 11–18.

Babiloni, C.; Del Percio, C.; Lacoboni, M.; Infarinato, F.; Lizio, R.; Marzano, N.; Crespi, G.; Dassù, F.; Pirritano, M.; Gallamini, M. & Eusebi, F. (2008) Golf Putt Outcomes Are Predicted by Sensorimotor Cerebral EEG Rhythms, *The Journal of Physiology*, 586 (1), 131–139.

Baumeister, J.; Reinecke, K.; Liesen, H. & Weiss, M. (2008) Cortical Activity of Skilled Performance in a Complex Sports Related Motor Task, *European Journal of Applied Physiology*, 104 (4), 625–631.

Beilock, S.; Bertenthal, B.; McCoy, A. & Carr, T. (2004) Haste Does Not Always Make Waste: Expertise, Direction of Attention, and Speed Versus Accuracy in Performing Sensorimotor Skills, *Psychonomic Bulletin & Review*, 11 (2), 373–379.

Bunker, L. & Williams, J. (1986) Cognitive Techniques for Improving Performance and Building Confidence, In: J. Williams (Ed.) *Applied Sport Psychology, Personal Growth to Peak Performance*, Palo Alto, CA: Mayfield.

Buszard, T.; Farrow, D.; Reid, M. & Masters, R. (2014) Scaling Sporting Equipment for Children Promotes Implicit Processes During Performance, *Consciousness and Cognition*, 30, 247–255.

Capio, C.; Poolton, J.; Sit, C.; Eguia, K. & Masters, R. (2013) Reduction of Errors During Practice Facilitates Fundamental Movement Skill Learning in Children with Intellectual Disabilities, *Journal of Intellectual Disability Research*, 57 (4), 295–305.

Chauvel, G.; Maquestiaux, F.; Hartley, A.; Joubert, S.; Didierjean, A. & Masters, R. (2012) Age Effects Shrink When Motor Learning Is Predominantly Supported by Nondeclarative, Automatic Memory Processes: Evidence From Golf Putting, *The Quarterly Journal of Experimental Psychology*, 65 (1), 25–38.

Cooke, A.; Kavussanu, M.; Gallicchio, G; Willoughby, A.; Mcintyre, D. & Ring, C. (2014) Preparation for Action: Psychophysiological Activity Preceding a Motor Skill as a Function of Expertise, Performance Outcome, and Psychological Pressure, *Psychophysiology*, 51 (4), 374–384.

Cooke, A.; Kavussanu, M.; McIntyre, D.; Boardley, I. & Ring, C. (2011) Effects of Competitive Pressure on Expert Performance: Underlying Psychological, Physiological, and Kinematic Mechanisms, *Psychophysiology*, 48 (8), 1146–1156.

Davids, K.; Button, C. & Bennett, S. (2007) *Dynamics of Skill Acquisition: A Constraints-Led Approach*, Champaign, IL: Human Kinetics Publishers.

Deeny, S.; Hillman, C.; Janelle, C. & Hatfield, B. (2003) Cortico-Cortical Communication and Superior Performance in Skilled Marksmen: An EEG Coherence Analysis, *Journal of Sport and Exercise Psychology*, 25 (2), 188–204.

Gabbett, T.; Poolton, J. & Masters, R. (2014) Training to 'Draw-and-Pass' in Elite Rugby League: A Case Study, In: A. Lane; R. Godfrey; M. Loosemore, & G. Whyte (Eds.) *Case Studies in Sport Science and Medicine*, London: Createspace, pp. 143–147.

Gucciardi, D. & Dimmock, J. (2008) Choking Under Pressure in Sensorimotor Skills: Conscious Processing or Depleted Attentional Resources? *Psychology of Sport and Exercise*, 9 (1), 45–59.

Hardy, L.; Mullen, R. & Jones, G. (1996) Knowledge of Conscious Control of Motor Actions Under Stress, *British Journal of Psychology*, 87 (4), 621–636.

Lam, W.; Maxwell, J. & Masters, R. (2009a) Analogy Learning and the Performance of Motor Skills Under Pressure, *Journal of Sport and Exercise Psychology*, 31 (3), 337–357.

Lam, W.; Maxwell, J. & Masters, R. (2009b) Analogy Versus Explicit Learning of a Modified Basketball Shooting Task: Performance and Kinematic Outcomes, *Journal of Sports Sciences*, 27 (2), 179–191.

Lam, W.; Masters, R. & Maxwell, J. (2010a) Cognitive Demands of Error Processing Associated with Preparation and Execution of a Motor Skill, *Consciousness and Cognition*, 19 (4), 1058–1061.

Lam, W.; Maxwell, J. & Masters, R. (2010b) Probing the Allocation of Attention in Implicit (Motor) Learning, *Journal of Sports Sciences*, 28 (14), 1543–1554.

Liao, C.-M. & Masters, R. (2001) Analogy Learning: A Means to Implicit Motor Learning, *Journal of Sports Sciences*, 19 (5), 307–319.

Lightbrown, P. (2010) Discovering Golf's Innermost Truths: A New Approach to Teaching the Game, *Annual Review of Golf Coaching,* 5 (2), 77–87.

MacMahon, K. & Masters, R. (2002) The Effects of a Secondary Task on Implicit Motor Skill Performance, *International Journal of Sport Psychology,* 33 (3), 307–324.

Malhotra, N.; Poolton, J.; Wilson, M.; Omuro, S. & Masters, R. (2015) Dimensions of Movement-Specific Reinvestment in Practice of a Golf Putting Task, *Psychology of Sport & Exercise*, 18, 1–8.

Masters, R. (1992) Knowledge, Knerves and Know-How: The Role of Explicit Versus Implicit Knowledge in the Breakdown of a Complex Motor Skill Under Pressure, *British Journal of Psychology*, 83 (3), 343–358.

Masters, R.; Law, J. & Maxwell, J. (2002) Implicit and Explicit Learning in Interceptive Actions, In: K. Davids; G. Savelsbergh; S. Bennett, & J. Van der Kamp (Eds.) *Interceptive Actions in Sport: Information and Movement*, London: Routledge, pp. 126–143.

Masters, R. & Maxwell, J. (2004) Implicit Motor Learning, Reinvestment and Movement Disruption: What You Don't Know Won't Hurt You? In: N. Hodges & A. Williams (Eds.) *Skill Acquisition in Sport: Research, Theory and Practice*, London: Routledge, pp. 207–228.

Masters, R. & Maxwell, J. (2008) The Theory of Reinvestment, *International Review of Sport and Exercise Psychology*, 1 (2), 160–183.

Masters, R.; Polman, R. & Hammond, N. (1993) Reinvestment: A Dimension of Personality Implicated in Skill Breakdown Under Pressure, *Personality and Individual Differences*, 14 (5), 655–666.

Masters, R. & Poolton, J. (2012) Advances in Implicit Motor Learning, In: N. Hodges & A. Williams (Eds.) *Skill Acquisition in Sport: Research, Theory and Practice* (2nd Ed.), London: Routledge, pp. 59–76.

Masters, R.; Poolton, J.; Omuro, S. & Ryu, D. (2012) Errorless Learning: A History of Success or a Future of Doubt? *6th Australasian Skill Acquisition and Research Group Meeting (ASARG)*, June 30–July 1, 2012, Melbourne, Australia.

Maxwell, J. (2001) *The Roles of Implicit and Explicit Processes During the Performance and Acquisition of Motor Skills*, Unpublished PhD Thesis, Birmingham: University of Birmingham.

Maxwell, J.; Masters, R. & Eves, F. (2000) From Novice to Know-How: A Longitudinal Study of Implicit Motor Learning, *Journal of Sports Sciences*, 18 (2), 111–120.

Maxwell, J.; Masters, R. & Eves, F. (2003) The Role of Working Memory in Motor Learning and Performance, *Consciousness & Cognition*, 12 (3), 376–402.

Maxwell, J.; Masters, R.; Kerr, E. & Weedon E. (2001) The Implicit Benefit of Learning Without Errors, *The Quarterly Journal of Experimental Psychology A*, 54 (4), 1049–1058.

Maxwell, J.; Masters, R. & Poolton, J. (2006) Performance Breakdown in Sport: The Roles of Reinvestment and Verbal Knowledge, *Research Quarterly for Exercise and Sport*, 77 (2), 271–276.

Moran, A. (2012) *Sport and Exercise Psychology: A Critical Introduction* (2nd Ed.), London: Routledge.

Muir, B.; Morgan, G.; Abraham, A. & Morley, D. (2011) Developmentally Appropriate Approaches to Coaching Children, In: R. Bailey & I. Stafford (Eds.) *An Introduction to Coaching Children in Sport*, New York, NY: Routledge, pp. 17–37.

Poolton, J. & Masters, R. (2010) Discovering Golf's Innermost Truths: A New Approach to Teaching the Game – A Commentary, *Annual Review of Golf Coaching*, 5 (2), 119–123.

Poolton, J.; Masters, R. & Maxwell, J. (2005) The Relationship Between Initial Errorless Learning Conditions and Subsequent Performance. *Human Movement Science*, 24 (3), 362–378.

Poolton, J.; Masters, R. & Maxwell, J. (2006a) The Influence of Analogy Learning on Decision-Making in Table Tennis: Evidence From Behavioural Data, *Psychology of Sport & Exercise*, 7 (6), 677–688.

Poolton, J.; Maxwell, J.; Masters, R. & Raab, M. (2006b) Benefits of an External Focus of Attention: Common Coding or Conscious Processing? *Journal of Sports Sciences*, 24 (1), 89–99.

Poolton, J.; Maxwell, J.; Masters, R. & van der Kamp, G. (2007) Moving with an External Focus: Automatic or Simply Less Demanding? *Bewegung Und Training*, 1, 43–44.

Poolton, J.; Zhu, F.; Malhotra, N.; Leung, G.; Fan, J. & Masters, R. (2016) Multitask Training Promotes Automaticity of a Fundamental Laparoscopic Skill Without Compromising the Rate of Skill Learning, *Surgical Endoscopy*, 30 (9), 4011–4018.

Ring, C.; Cooke, A.; Kavussanu, M.; McIntyre, D. & Masters, R. (2015) Investigating the Efficacy of Neurofeedback Training for Expediting Expertise and Excellence in Sport, *Psychology of Sport and Exercise*, 16, 118–127.

Ryu, D.; Abernethy, B.; Mann, D. & Poolton, J. (2012) The Role of Central and Peripheral Vision in Expert Decision Making, *Perception*, 42 (6), 591–607.

Toner, J. & Moran, A. (2011) The Effects of Conscious Processing on Golf Putting Proficiency and Kinematics, *Journal of Sports Sciences*, 29 (7), 673–683.

Van Ginneken, W.; Poolton, J.; Capio, C.; van der Kamp, J.; Choi, S.-Y. & Masters, R. (In Press) Conscious Control is Associated with Freezing of Mechanical Degrees of Freedom During Motor Learning, *Journal of Motor Behavior*.

Vine, S.; Moore, L.; Cooke, A.; Ring, C. & Wilson, M. (2013) Quiet Eye Training: A Means to Implicit Motor Learning, *International Journal of Sport Psychology*, 44 (4), 367–386.

Vine, S.; Moore, L. & Wilson, M. (2011) Quiet Eye Training: The Acquisition, Refinement and Resilient Performance of Targeting Skills, *European Journal of Sport Science*, 14 (1), 235–242.

Wulf, G. (2013) Attentional Focus and Motor Learning: A Review of 15 Years, *International Review of Sport and Exercise Psychology*, 6 (1), 77–104.

Wulf, G.; Lauterbach, B. & Toole, T. (1999) The Learning Advantages of an External Focus of Attention in Golf, *Research Quarterly for Exercise and Sport*, 70 (2), 120–126.

Wulf, G.; McNevin, N. & Shea, C. (2001) The Automaticity of Complex Motor Skill Learning as a Function of Attentional Focus, *The Quarterly Journal of Experimental Psychology A*, 54 (4), 1143–1154.

Wulf, G. & Su, J. (2007) An External Focus of Attention Enhances Golf Shot Accuracy in Beginners and Experts, *Research Quarterly for Exercise and Sport*, 78 (4), 384–389.

Zhu, F.; Poolton, J.; Wilson, M.; Maxwell, J. & Masters, R. (2011) Neural Co-Activation as a Yardstick of Implicit Motor Learning and the Propensity for Conscious Control of Movement, *Biological Psychology*, 87 (1), 66–73.

Zhu, F.; Yeung, A.; Poolton, J.; Lee, T.; Leung, G. & Masters, R. (2015) Cathodal Transcranial Direct Current Stimulation Over Left Dorsolateral Prefrontal Cortex Area Promotes Implicit Motor Learning in a Golf Putting Task, *Brain Stimulation*, 8 (4), 784–786.

10

FACTORS INFLUENCING THE EFFECTIVENESS OF MODELLING GOLF TECHNIQUE

Bob Christina and Eric Alpenfels

Introduction

Learning a new behaviour by watching the performance modelled by others (e.g., expert models) or oneself (self or learning model) is referred to as *observational learning* or *modelling*. There is ample research evidence revealing the beneficial effects of modelling on learning motor tasks and various sport skills when *key factors* are operating to help students engage in *attention* and *retention* processes to form an effective *cognitive representation* of the modelled technique (Bandura, 1986, 1997; for reviews, refer McCullagh et al., 2012; Ste-Marie et al., 2012; McCullagh et al., 2013). Whether these beneficial effects also hold for learning golf technique when the key factors are functioning is still a matter of some uncertainty because of the lack of research evidence available. This chapter focusses on what the evidence says about how these key factors influence the effectiveness of modelling technique and discusses how that information can be applied to facilitate the learning of golf technique.

What is the purpose of modelling technique?

It has been common practice in golf to use criterion (expert) models of an 'ideal' swing that students were expected to learn to imitate. Most of these models came directly from great players (e.g., Hogan, 1957) and a few were scientifically based (e.g., Cochran & Stobbs, 1968). Several models were computer generated based on the best characteristics of the swings of >100 US PGA, LPGA and Senior PGA tour players (Mann & Griffin, 1998). Students were expected to learn the criterion model of the 'ideal' swing that was selected by viewing it on video as often as needed and also by comparing the characteristics of their own swing with those of the criterion model as a basis for detecting and correcting errors. Moreover, this practice has been facilitated in recent years by the increased reliance on launch monitor data and improved split-screen video analysis (Kostis, 2016).

One concern with this practice is that learning to imitate a criterion model's swing, especially those characteristics that are incompatible with the student's own swing identity (i.e., special intrinsic dynamics) and learning capabilities, ignores the differences in structural (e.g., height, mass, strength, and flexibility) and functional (physiological and psychological) constraints within and between individual students, which produce differences in the swing variability

(Glazier, 2010, 2012). While certain movement variability should be reduced because it may be detrimental to swing performance, other movement variability should be embraced because it reflects how the golfer uniquely satisfies the confluence of constraints acting on performance in the best possible way. The key is knowing which structural and physical constraints are the most influential in determining the effectiveness of a student's swing before deciding on whether to 'coach out' or 'make use' of the variability observed (Glazier, 2012).

This alternative approach views the ideal swing as one that works best for the student (i.e., considers the student's structural and functional constraints) rather than some criterion model that should be imitated in its entirety. One top golf teacher who is an advocate of this approach holds that 'There's no one swing for everybody, but everybody needs one swing' (Kostis, 2013, p. 45). Glazier (2012) and Kostis (2016) prefer to see a swing that is fundamentally sound (i.e., has the essential characteristics of a criterion model), but that retains some of the student's own swing identity by making use of the structural and functional constraints that contribute to the effectiveness of his or her swing because it is likely to be trusted under pressure. With this approach, the purpose of modelling a skilled swing is *not* to have students learn to imitate all its characteristics, but to help them get a 'picture' of what an effective swing looks like and become aware of its general make-up and essential characteristics (Glazier, 2010). Armed with this information and instructional guidance, students can learn to discover how to develop their own 'ideal' swing, i.e., a swing that works best for them based on their own unique structural and functional constraints (Glazier, 2011, 2012; Langdown et al., 2012).

Who should model technique?

Although combining expert and novice modelling (mixed observation) has been found to facilitate the learning of a novel motor task more than modelling with either a novice or an expert model alone (Andrieux & Proteau, 2013, 2014), more research is needed to determine the extent to which this effect holds for golf technique. There is sufficient evidence, however, indicating that either novice or expert modelling facilitates motor and sport skill learning more than teaching without modelling (McCullagh et al., 2011; Ste-Marie et al., 2012; McCullagh et al., 2013). This beneficial effect is likely to occur when the student perceives (a) the *status* and *competence* of the expert model to be creditable (Baron, 1970; McCullagh, 1986; George et al., 1992), and (b) *similarities* between the expert model and himself/herself (Landers & Landers, 1973; Gould & Weiss, 1981; McCullagh, 1987; Lirgg & Feltz, 1991). For instance, a student is more likely to focus attention on the model's performance and be motivated to learn if the person modelling the swing (a) is admired and has swing characteristics the student wants to acquire; (b) has swing characteristics that are largely compatible with the student's swing identity; (c) swings from the same side; (d) is the same gender; (e) is about the same age; and (f) has similar physical characteristics.

Of course, the actual functional and perceived similarities are at a maximum when one serves as one's own expert or novice learning model (Holmes & Calmels, 2008), and this is more effective for facilitating learning than by observing others, except when technique essentials must be modelled by others (Dowrick & Raieburn, 1995; Starek & McCullagh, 1999; Totsika & Wulf, 2003; Onate et al., 2005; Clark & Ste-Marie, 2007). Thus, if one cannot perform the skilled technique essentials well enough to serve as one's own expert model, learning can still be facilitated by watching others (expert models). Novices are dependent on someone else (expert) to model skilled technique, unless a feed-forward, expert self-model is used, in which the video of a student's swing is edited to remove the flaws so that the student sees a video of himself/herself performing a skilled swing without the flaws (Dowrick, 1999).

A feed-forward, expert self-model can be created using special video software to edit the flawed swing movements and replace them with correct movements. The resulting effect is that one could serve as one's own expert model to observe one's own swing with corrections that are not yet learned but are possible to learn based on one's repertoire of movement capabilities. Some evidence has revealed the beneficial effects of this feed-forward, expert self-model for learning sports skills (Boyer, 1987; Melody, 1990; Bradley, 1993; Winfrey & Weeks, 1993), but these studies did not determine its effects on the learning of golf skills. Nonetheless, to be able to see what one's own swing would look like when it is skilled would seem to be the ideal model to facilitate learning. However, further research is needed to determine whether feed-forward, expert self-models facilitate the learning of golf technique substantially more than either traditional expert or novice models or combining them.

On what should students focus their attention?

There is a dearth of research on this topic and much more research is needed, but typically, the modelled technique essentials on which students focus depend on what their teachers and coaches want them to learn. For instance, novices could be given several video demonstrations of a tour player's driver swing to help them to get a mental picture and become aware of the general character and essential characteristics of a skilled swing. With each repeated showing, one or two key essential characteristics of the swing are pointed out for the students to *attend to, process,* and *remember* so that the essential characteristic(s) can be *applied* when attempting to learn their own swing. Often, with experienced players who have a swing flaw, a video of a tour player's swing (expert model) is shown while explaining how to correct the flaw. And, sometimes video swings of several tour players are shown while pointing out how all of them are in about the same position at a certain point during the swing, which is different from the student's flawed swing position.

What students attend to while viewing a video of a skilled swing also depends on whether teachers or coaches are going to have their students focus on internal or external cues when physically practising to learn their swing. If students are going to use internal cues, they should focus their attention on viewing the swing movements themselves (e.g., getting your left shoulder under your chin at the end of the backswing so that your back faces the target); whereas if they are going to use external cues they should focus on viewing the effects of the swing movements (e.g., clubhead movement on the backswing relative to the target line). Of course, students could focus on both internal and external cues when practising their swing.

There is substantial evidence revealing that having students focus their attention on external cues often facilitates learning to improve outcome performance (Wulf, 2007a, 2007b) and movement form (Lawrence et al., 2011; Christina & Alpenfels, 2014) more than instructing them to focus on internal cues. This holds for both novice and skilled performers (Wulf & Su, 2007; Bell & Hardy, 2009). Apparently, movements are planned and controlled in relation to their effects or outcomes (Prinz, 1997), and focussing attention on the effects rather than movements that produce the effects provides more congruence between movement planning and control on the one hand, and the desired effects on the other (Wulf et al., 2001).

What instructional guidance should accompany technique presentations?

Various kinds of instructional guidance can be used *before, during,* and *after* a technique presentation to facilitate the student's observational experience (Ste-Marie et al., 2012). Although there is some scientific evidence supporting the effectiveness of a few of them in helping students attend to, process, and remember the key aspects of a technique modelled, more research is needed before definitive recommendations can be made about the most effective ways to use them.

Typically, verbal instruction and/or cues as well as visual cues are given *before* a technique presentation to prepare students by *setting the stage* for what they are about to see and to what they should attend (e.g., key swing essentials) during the presentation (Rose & Christina, 2006). Andrieux and Proteau (2016) found that informing students of the demonstration quality beforehand facilitated learning more than when it was given after each demonstration. This finding is consistent with the evidence revealing that the nature of instructions given to students before observing a presentation modifies the neural structures they use during actual observation (Grezes et al., 1998). Moreover, verbal and visual cues given before the presentation have been found to facilitate learning in adults and children (Al-Abood et al., 2002; Ste-Marie et al., 2002) and are recommended, especially when there is too much information for students to process if these cues are given during the presentation.

Traditionally, verbal cues (one or two words or succinct statements), verbal instruction (statements or full sentences of instruction) (Landin, 1994), and visual cues are given *during* demonstrations to direct the student's attention to the key swing characteristics. Visual cues are things such as (a) pointing at a key swing characteristic or (b) using video graphics (e.g., lines, arrows, and circles) to highlight key swing characteristics. Verbal cues and verbal instruction given in conjunction with a demonstration have been shown to facilitate learning in adults as have visual cues given in support of verbal cues (Meaney, 1994; Janelle et al., 2003; Kampiotis & Theodorakou, 2006). Moreover, observational learning was facilitated more when a demonstration with knowledge of results (KR) was followed by a demonstration without KR (Andrieux & Proteau, 2014). Students who benefit from verbal and/or visual guidance quite often are those who are inexperienced at processing visual information from a video presentation and, hence, are simply not knowledgeable enough to identify, prioritize, and explain the key swing characteristics that have to be learned. Of course, the content of this guidance must be appropriate relative to the student's age, developmental level, and background experience (Ste-Marie et al., 2002).

Point-light displays (PLDs – only show moving dots that reflect the motion of key joints of a model's moving body) have been used *during* a presentation to place emphasis on showing relative motion. Although one study found it to be more effective than a video model (Scully & Carnegie, 1998), most have produced equivocal findings (Ste-Marie et al., 2012). Thus, the effectiveness of video or live models relative to PLD models for facilitating learning will have to be determined by future research. However, video, live, animated, or virtual models have been found to have the same effects on motor learning (Feltz et al., 1979; Ste-Marie et al., 2012), which is convenient because the video models provide some special advantages (e.g., slow motion, stop action, and split screen) over live models (Franks & Maile, 1991).

How much information should be provided and how precise should it be?

How much of the modelled technique on which to focus depends on how much each student can effectively process (e.g., understand) and remember at the moment. This varies among students because of individual differences in factors, such as their cognitive capabilities, motivation to learn, previous experiences and learning, and developmental level. Students are likely to effectively process more new information when (a) one or two key cues are introduced *before* and again *during* the presentation rather than overloading students with too many cues (Al-Abood et al., 2002; Ste-Marie et al., 2002); (b) previous cues have been effectively processed and remembered before adding another cue (Hicks, 1975; Landin, 1994); (c) the explanations that supplement visual presentations are simple, brief, accurate, and direct (Siedentop, 1991; Landin, 1994); (d) the new information can be effectively related to their background knowledge, skills, and experiences (Rose & Christina, 2006); and (e) the new movement information is easy to understand.

Moreover, how much information can be effectively processed and remembered depends on the extent to which the instructional information accompanying the visual presentation literally describes the details of the swing characteristics, for instance, providing precise information about a model's right-handed swing by *literally* describing the cues in quantitative terms (e.g., notice that the left elbow is at 180° at set-up and 174° at the top of the backswing) or less-precise information by simply describing the cues in *qualitative* terms (e.g., notice that the left elbow is straight at set-up and nearly straight at the top of the backswing). Students are likely to remember information described in simpler, qualitative, or figurative terms than literal precise quantitative terms (Rose & Christina, 2006).

Typically, the more *precise* the information accompanying a visual technique presentation, the more effective is the learning, up to the point at which students are unable to effectively process and apply it to improve their performance (Rose & Christina, 2006). In addition, students can usually process a greater amount of and more precise information as they advance through the stages of motor learning. Furthermore, more precise information has been found to be more beneficial for older children than for younger children (Thomas et al., 1979). More research is needed before specific statements can be made about how much information should accompany golf technique presentations and how precise it should be. In the meantime, however, it is reassuring to know that students have a way of letting their teachers and coaches know when the information being provided is too much or too little and/or too precise or too vague (Rose & Christina, 2006).

How often and when should modelled technique be viewed?

Too much essential information is contained in a modelled swing presentation to be effectively processed and remembered in one or two viewings. So, how *often* should a presentation be viewed? The evidence suggests that more modelled presentations are needed to facilitate learning when teachers or coaches are controlling when students view them (Sidaway & Hand, 1993; Ste-Marie et al., 2012), whereas fewer are needed when students are in control (Wrisberg & Pein, 2002; Wulf et al., 2005). This evidence suggests that students should have considerable input into when they see technique presentations for at least two reasons. First, they would be viewing the technique presentations when they need them, and second, fewer presentations would be required to facilitate learning than if they had no input at all. After viewing the presentations, students should be asked to recall and recognize the essential technique information that was pointed out to ensure that it has been appropriately processed and remembered.

Essentially, a modelled technique should be shown the number of times it takes for a student to effectively process, remember, and apply the key points of information being taught. This number will vary with (a) the differences in students' processing and remembering capabilities, (b) the stage of learning, (c) how well the new information relates to the students' background, and (d) complexity of the information demonstrated. For instance, typically a modelled swing needs to be seen more often (a) early in learning and less often as learning progresses, and (b) when the swing information is more rather than less complex to process (understand) and apply. But, how much and why the number varies as a function of these factors will have to be determined by future research.

The limited amount of research investigating *when* skilled technique presentations should be viewed has studied the learning effects of providing demonstrations before, during, and after the physical practice of the technique to be learned. The evidence available suggests that viewing a modelled technique demonstration before students begin physical practice and then again, as needed, during a lesson or practice session is likely to facilitate motor and golf skill learning (Landers, 1975; Ste-Marie et al., 2002; Andrieux & Proteau, 2013, 2014). However, further research is needed to determine the most appropriate time(s) to provide skilled technique presentations to optimize learning.

At what speed should a video of modelled technique be observed?

The evidence suggests that the complexity of the technique characteristics being observed and processed is an important factor to consider (Ste-Marie et al., 2012). For example, for more complex skill information (e.g., golf swing), slow motion is likely to facilitate learning aspects of the swing related to coordination (movement form) and relative timing (i.e., temporal ratios or the time of each segment of the swing relative to the total time of the whole swing). However, it may be less helpful for learning the features of the swing related to the manipulation of control factors such as absolute timing (i.e., overall swing speed) and absolute force production (e.g., overall force applied) that are needed to produce effective swing variations.

The limited available evidence (Ste-Marie et al., 2012) suggests that a skilled swing should be first presented several times in real-time speed so that students can see and get an idea of what the swing's spatial and temporal characteristics look like. Seeing a skilled swing demonstrated in real time is likely to help beginning students with learning the absolute timing and force production of their own swing. After viewing the swing in real time, observing it several times in slow motion enables students to see and become aware of how the movements are coordinated in space and time (e.g., body, limb, and club positions at different times during the swing), which can be used when learning to develop the coordination of their own swing movements. Of course, a video of a modelled swing presentation in real time, slow motion, and stop action can be provided for students at any time during learning. Teachers and coaches will have to use their judgment and rely on input from their students to determine the appropriate presentation speeds and when to provide them.

At what angle(s) should a modelled technique presentation be viewed?

Typically, the two viewing angles that are used to show a modelled golf swing technique to students are the objective view (front view) and target-line view. The objective view enables a student to see the swing with the model's face and chest facing the student's face and chest. The target-line view enables a student to observe the swing from behind the target line. Other available angles that are probably used less with golfers are the mirror view, overhead view, and the subjective view. The mirror view involves the golfer facing the model as in the objective view, but the model's swing would be performed as though the golfer was seeing his or her own swing in a mirror. The overhead view is one where the swing is seen from above the model. And, the subjective view is opposite of the objective view and enables a student to see the swing from behind the model. The limited amount of research available has focussed on objective, subjective, and mirror views (Ste-Marie et al., 2012).

A study by Ishikura and Inomata (1995) found that a modelled seven-step movement sequence was acquired faster from a subjective view than from the objective and mirror views. This finding is consistent with what Roshal (1961) found using a modelled knot-tying task. However, a similar study by Sambrook (1998) was unable to replicate Roshal's finding, and Smith (2004) found no differences between learning a driver swing from the objective view of an expert model and learning the same from a multi-view perspective (front, back, left, and right). Moreover, retention performance was similar for the three views in the study by Ishikura and Inomata (1995). Thus, although there is some evidence revealing faster acquisition for the subjective view than for the objective and mirror views, that advantage is not evident in retention performance. Perhaps the subjective view made the tasks easier to acquire because they were seen from the same directional perspective in which they had to be performed and hence, required less cognitive processing (e.g., translation) than seeing the modelled movements from the objective and mirror views (Ishikura & Inomata, 1998). Further, less cognitive processing may have led to a weaker memory representation of the learned tasks than the objective and mirror views, which required additional cognitive processing in which the tasks are processed at a 'deeper' cognitive level. However, further research is needed before the validity of this explanation can be ascertained.

The limited evidence available suggests that a modelled golf swing should be viewed from a subjective view. Unfortunately, doing so would prevent students from seeing and learning about spatial and temporal movement information, which is essential for learning. For instance, viewing a swing presentation facing the back of the model (subjective view) would prevent students from seeing much-needed movement information that is only available when facing the model (e.g., hands, wrists, arms, and all or most of the club) or from behind the target line (e.g., swing path). Viewing a modelled swing facing the model would prevent students from seeing information that can only be seen from the other viewing angles. Thus, while some movement information about the swing can be seen from all of the viewing angles, other swing information can only be seen from one of them. More research is needed before scientifically based recommendations can be made about the most effective viewing angle(s) for students to observe a modelled swing.

Implications for the game

There is ample evidence to suggest that acquiring golf techniques benefits from observational learning. However, until substantially more observational learning research on golf techniques becomes available, the findings emanating from observational learning research using motor task and sport skill techniques must be used to generalize effective applications to the modelling of golf techniques. Specifically, knowing what the *key factors* are and how they operate to facilitate the observational learning of motor task and sport skill techniques provides an evidence-based foundation for their efficacious manipulation when modelling golf techniques. Appropriate manipulation of these key factors helps students *attend to, process, remember,* and develop a *cognitive representation* of the golf technique or correction that can be effectively used when physically practising to learn their own 'ideal' technique or learn to correct a previously acquired one.

Effective manipulation of the key factors to model golf techniques should contribute to the development of a stronger cognitive representation, resulting in a deeper level of observational learning than ineffective manipulation or no modelling at all. One would expect the stronger cognitive representation to enhance the effectiveness of physical practice of the modelled golf technique leading to a deeper level of golf technique learning. If this is true, one would predict that effective manipulation of the key factors would result in the need for less practice to acquire the technique than if modelling was used with ineffective manipulation or no modelling at all. Moreover, if the effective manipulation leads to deeper level of learning, one would also expect that retention and transfer of that learning would be better.

Observational practice of modelled golf techniques should be beneficial to use when a player is between practice sessions or unable to physically practise due to factors such as injury or poor weather conditions. This observational practice could even help maintain or even strengthen retention during periods of no physical practice, which, in turn, could facilitate the further learning or refinement of golf technique when the player returns to physical practice. Teaching or coaching with effective modelling of golf technique is likely to ensure at the outset that students understand, practise, and learn the technique essentials that are being modelled rather than some nonessentials that would result in flawed technique. In other words, they would learn the 'right things' rather than the 'wrong things' from the outset. Lastly, playing performance could benefit from observing self-modelled golf techniques before rounds. Of course, further research is needed before the validity of the preceding statements made in this section can be ascertained.

Summary and future research directions

There is ample evidence revealing the beneficial learning effects of modelling technique when key factors such as the most appropriate purpose, focus of attention, instructional guidance, amount and precision of information presented, and the frequency, angle, and speed of model presentations are effectively operating. However, most of the evidence emanates from research on motor tasks and sports skills other than golf. Future research is needed to determine the extent to which these beneficial effects hold for learning golf technique when the key factors are present. More specifically, research is needed to answer many questions such as those that follow. What are the most effective kinds of instructional guidance to use when modelling golf technique? What is the appropriate amount and precision of information to use in relation to the complexity of the technique being modelled on the one hand and the students' processing and remembering capabilities, the stage of learning, and background on the other? What are the learning effects of giving students more control over when and how often the modelled technique is seen? What is the best time to show modelled technique presentations in real time, slow motion, and stop action? What are the most effective angle(s) to view modelled technique presentations? Furthermore, what is the extent to which feed-forward, expert self-models facilitate learning relative to traditional expert models. Central to all of this research is understanding how and the extent to which these key factors influence the golfers' ability to attend to, process, and remember the general make-up and essential characteristics of the modelled technique so that an effective cognitive representation can be developed.

Acknowledgements

Funding for this chapter was provided by the Education Department of the PGA of America.

Appreciation is extended to Penny McCullagh for her comments on a previous version of this chapter.

References

Al-Abood, S.; Bennett, S.; Hernandez, F.; Ashford, D. & Davids, K. (2002) Effects of Verbal Instructions and Image Size on Visual Search Strategies in Basketball Free Throw Shooting, *Journal of Sports Sciences*, 20 (3), 271–278.
Andrieux, M. & Proteau, L. (2013) Observation Learning of a Motor Task: Who and When, *Experimental Brain Research*, 229 (1), 125–137.
Andrieux, M. & Proteau, L. (2014) Mixed Observation Favors Motor Learning Through Better Estimation of the Model's Performance, *Experimental Brain Research*, 232 (10), 3121–3132.
Andrieux, M. & Proteau, L. (2016) Observational Learning: Tell Beginners What They Are About to Watch and They Will Learn Better, *Frontiers in Psychology*, 29, 7–51.
Bandura, A. (1997) *Self-efficacy: The Exercise of Control*, New York, NY: W. H. Freeman.
Bandura, A. (1986) *Social Foundations of Thought and Action: A Social Cognitive Theory*, Englewood Cliffs, NJ: Prentice-Hall.

Baron, R. (1970) Attraction Toward the Model and Model's Competence as Determiners of Adult Initiative Behavior, *Journal of Personality & Social Psychology*, 14 (4), 345–351.

Bell, J. & Hardy, J. (2009) Effects of Attentional Focus on Skilled Performance in Golf. *Journal of Applied Sport Psychology*, 21, 163–177.

Boyer, B. (1987) *Using the Self-as-a-Model with Video Editing in Athletic Performance*, Unpublished MA Thesis, Stockton, CA: University of the Pacific.

Bradley, R. (1993) *The Use of Goal-setting and Positive Self-modeling to Enhance Self-efficacy and Performance for the Basketball Free Throw*, Unpublished Phd Thesis, College Park, MD: University of Maryland.

Christina, R. & Alpenfels, E. (2014) Influence of Attentional Focus on Learning a Swing Path Change, *International Journal of Golf Science*, 3 (1), 35–49.

Clark, S. & Ste-Marie, D. (2007) The Impact of Self-as-a-Model Interventions on Children's Self-regulation of Learning and Swimming Performance, *Journal of Sports Sciences*, 25 (5), 577–586.

Cochran, A. & Stobbs, J. (1968) *The Search for the Perfect Swing*, New York, NY: Lippincott.

Dowrick, P. (1999) A Review of Self-modeling and Related Interventions, *Applied and Preventative Psychology*, 8 (1), 23–39.

Dowrick, P. & Raieburn, J. (1995) Self-modeling: Rapid Skill Training for Children with Physical Disabilities, *Journal of Developmental and Physical Disabilities*, 7 (1), 25–37.

Feltz, D.; Landers, D. & Raeder, U. (1979) Enhancing Self-efficacy in High Avoidance Motor Tasks: A Comparison of Modeling Techniques. *Journal of Sport Psychology*, 1, 112–122.

Franks, I. & Maile, L. (1991) The Use of Video in Sport Skill Acquisition, In: P. Dowrick (Ed.) *Practical Guide to Using Video in the Behavioral Sciences*, New York, NY: Wiley, pp. 231–243.

George, T.; Feltz, D. & Chase, M. (1992) Effects of Model Similarity on Self-efficacy and Muscular Endurance, *Journal of Sport & Exercise Psychology*, 14 (3), 237–248.

Glazier, P. (2010) Augmenting Golf Practice Through the Manipulation of Physical and Informational Constraints, In I. Renshaw; K. Davids, & G. Sabelsbergh (Eds.) *Motor Learning in Practice: A Constraints Approach*, London: Routledge, pp. 187–198.

Glazier, P. (2011) Movement Variability in the Golf Swing: Theoretical, Methodological, and Practical Issues, *Research Quarterly for Exercise and Sport*, 82 (2), 157–161.

Glazier, P. (2012) *The Perfect Golf Swing: Dispelling the Myth*, Available at www.Mytpi.Com/Articles/Swing/The_Perfect_Golf_Swing_Dispekling_The_Myth (Accessed June 15, 2016).

Gould, D. & Weiss, M. (1981) Effects of Model Similarity and Model Talk on Self-efficacy and Muscular Endurance, *Journal of Sport Psychology*, 3 (1), 17–21.

Grezes, J.; Costes, N. & Decety, J. (1998) Top-Down Effect of Strategy on the Perception of Human Biological Motion: A PET Investigation, *Cognitive Neuropsychology*, 15 (6), 553–582.

Hicks, R. (1975) Intrahemispheric Response Competition Between Vocal and Unimanual Performance in Normal Adult Human Males, *Journal of Comparative and Physiological Psychology*, 89 (1), 50–60.

Hogan, B. (1957) *The Modern Fundamentals of Golf*, New York, NY: AS Barnes.

Holmes, P. & Calmels, C. (2008) A Neuroscientific Review of Imagery and Observation Use in Sport, *Journal of Motor Behavior*, 40 (5), 433–445.

Ishikura, T. & Inomata, K. (1995) Effects of Angle of Model-Demonstration on Learning of a Motor Skill, *Perceptual & Motor Skills*, 80 (2), 651–658.

Ishikura, T. & Inomata, K. (1998) An Attempt to Distinguish Between Two Reversal Processing Strategies for Learning Modeled Motor Skill, *Perceptual & Motor Skills*, 86 (3), 1007–1015.

Janelle, C.; Champenoy, J.; Coombes, S. & Mousseau, M. (2003) Mechanisms of Attentional Cueing During Observational Learning to Facilitate Motor Skill Acquisition, *Journal of Sports Sciences*, 21 (10), 825–838.

Kampiotis, S. & Theodorakou, K. (2006) The Influence of Five Different Types of Observation Based Teaching on the Cognitive Level of Learning, *Kinesiology*, 38 (2), 116–125.

Kostis, P. (2013) The Rules of Improvement, *Golf Magazine*, 55 (11), 45.

Kostis, P. (2016) More Is Less, *Golf Magazine*, 58 (3), 38.

Landers, D. (1975) Observational Learning of a Motor Skill: Temporal Spacing of Demonstrations and Audience Presence, *Journal of Motor Behavior*, 7 (3), 281–287.

Landers, D. & Landers, D. (1973) Teacher Versus Peer Models: Effects of Model's Presence and Performance Level on Motor Behavior, *Journal of Motor Behavior*, 5 (3), 129–139.

Landin, D. (1994) The Role of Verbal Cues in Skill Learning, *Quest*, 46 (3), 299–313.

Langdown, B.; Bridge, M. & Li, F.-X. (2012) Movement Variability in the Golf Swing, *Sports Biomechanics*, 11 (2), 273–287.

Lawrence, G.; Gottwald, V.; Hardy, J. & Khan, M. (2011) Internal and External Focus of Attention in a Novice Form Sport, *Research Quarterly for Exercise and Sport*, 82 (2), 431–441.

Lirgg, C. & Feltz, D. (1991) Teacher Versus Peer Models Revisited: Effects on Motor Performance and Self-efficacy, *Research Quarterly for Exercise and Sport*, 62 (2), 217–224.

Mann, R. & Griffin, F. (1998) *Swing Like a Pro: The Breakthrough Scientific Method of Perfecting Your Swing*, New York, NY: Broadway Books.

McCullagh, P. (1986) Model Status as a Determinant of Observational Learning and Performance, *Journal of Sport Psychology*, 8 (4), 319–331.

McCullagh, P. (1987) Model Similarity Effects on Motor Performance, *Journal of Sport Psychology*, 9 (3), 249–260.

McCullagh, P.; Law, B. & Ste-Marie, D. (2012) Modeling and Performance, In: S. Murphy (Ed.) *The Oxford Handbook of Sport and Performance Psychology*, New York, NY: Oxford University, pp. 250–272.

McCullagh, P.; Ste-Marie, D. & Law, B. (2013) Modeling: Is What You See What You Get? In: J. Vanraalte & B. Brewer (Eds.) *Exploring Sport and Exercise Psychology* (3rd Ed.), Washington, DC: American Psychological Association, pp. 139–162.

Meaney, K. (1994) Developmental Modeling Effects on the Acquisition, Retention, and Transfer of a Novel Motor Task, *Research Quarterly for Exercise and Sport*, 65 (2), 31–39.

Melody, D. (1990) The Influence of Self-modeling Upon Free-Throw Shooting, *Dissertation Abstracts International*, 52 (2), 478.

Onate, J.; Guskiewic, K.; Marshall, S.; Guiliani, C.; Yu, B. & Garrett, W. (2005) Instruction of Jump-Landing Technique Using Videotape Feedback Altering Lower Extremity Motion Patterns, *American Journal of Sports Medicine*, 33 (6), 831–842.

Prinz, W. (1997) Perception and Action Planning, *The European Journal of Cognitive Psychology*, 9, 129–154.

Rose, D. & Christina, R. (2006) *A Multilevel Approach to the Study of Motor Control and Learning* (2nd Ed.), New York, NY: Pearson.

Roshal, S. (1961) Film-Mediated Learning with Varying Representation of the Task: Viewing Angle, Portrayal of Demonstration, Motion, and Student Participation, In: A. Lumsdaine (Ed.) *Student Responses in Programmed Instruction*, Washington, DC: National Academy of Sciences – National Research Council, pp 155–175.

Sambrook, T. (1998) Does Visual Perspective Matter in Imitation? *Perception*, 27 (12), 1461–1473.

Scully, D. & Carnegie, E. (1998) Observational Learning in Motor Skill Acquisition: A Look at Demonstrations, *The Irish Journal of Psychology*, 19 (4): 472–485.

Sidaway, B. & Hand, J. (1993) Frequency of Modeling Effects on the Acquisition and Retention of a Motor Skill, *Research Quarterly for Exercise and Sport*, 64 (1), 122–126.

Siedentop, D. (1991) *Developing Teaching Skills in Physical Education*, Mountain View, CA: Mayfield.

Smith, J. (2004) *Effects of Video Modeling on Skill Acquisition in Learning the Golf Swing*, Unpublished MSc Thesis, Utah: Brigham Young University.

Starek, J. & McCullagh, P. (1999) The Effect of Self-modeling on the Performance of Beginner Swimmers, *The Sport Psychologist*, 13 (3), 269–287.

Ste-Marie, D.; Clark, S. & Latimer, A. (2002) Contributions of Attention and Retention Processes in the Observational Learning of a Motor Skill by Children, *Journal of Human Movement Studies*, 42, 317–333.

Ste-Marie, D.; Law, B.; Rymal, A.; Jenny, O.; Hall, C. & McCullagh, P. (2012) Observation Interventions for Motor Skill Learning and Performance: An Applied Model for the Use of Observation, *International Review of Sport and Exercise Psychology*, 5 (2), 1–32.

Thomas, J.; Mitchell, B. & Solomon, M. (1979) Precision Knowledge of Results and Motor Performance: Relationship to Age, *Research Quarterly*, 50 (4), 687–698.

Totsika, V. & Wulf, G. (2003) The Influence of External and Internal Foci of Attention on Transfer to Novel Situations and Skills, *Research Quarterly for Exercise and Sport*, 74 (2), 220–225.

Winfrey, M. & Weeks, D. (1993) Effects of Self-modeling on Self-efficacy and Balance Beam Performance, *Perceptual & Motor Skills*, 77 (3), 907–913.

Wrisberg, C. & Pein, R. (2002) Note on Learners' Control of Frequency of Model Presentation During Skill Acquisition, *Perceptual & Motor Skills*, 94 (3), 792–794.

Wulf, G. (2007a) Attentional Focus and Motor Learning: A Review of 10 Years of Research, *E-Journal Bewegung Und Training*, 1, 4–14.

Wulf, G. (2007b) *Attention and Motor Skill Learning*, Champaign, IL: Human Kinetics.

Wulf, G.; McNevin, N.H. & Shea, C. (2001) The Automaticity of Complex Motor Skill Learning as a Function of Attention, *Quarterly Journal of Experimental Psychology*, 54 (4), 1143–1154.

Wulf, G.; Raupach, M. & Pfeiffer, F. (2005) Self-controlled Observational Practice Enhances Learning, *Research Quarterly for Exercise and Sport*, 76 (1), 107–111.

Wulf, G. & Su, J. (2007) An External Focus of Attention Enhances Golf Shot Accuracy in Beginners and Experts, *Research Quarterly for Exercise and Sport*, 78 (4), 384–389.

11

THE STAGES OF LEARNING AND IMPLICATIONS FOR OPTIMIZED LEARNING ENVIRONMENTS

Christopher P. Bertram, Mark A. Guadagnoli
and Ronald G. Marteniuk

Introduction

The purpose of this chapter is to provide an overview of the stages that learners of all motor tasks – including golf – go through on their way to becoming skilled players, or in some cases, elite players at the collegiate, national, or professional level. We present a learner-centred model based on the notion that the progression through the learning stages in golf involves an ever-decreasing reliance on conscious attention, ideally leading to a state of relative automaticity. During the early stages of learning, golfers rely heavily on information-processing mechanisms and conscious problem-solving processes. However, as skill increases, less attention is needed for the execution of the swing itself, thus freeing up cognitive resources, which can be focussed more effectively on task-relevant, external stimuli. We, furthermore, discuss the concept of *optimal challenge* (Guadagnoli & Lee, 2004) as a framework for helping to guide decision-making around the key factors in the design of more efficient learning environments. The implications for instructional philosophy and best practice within each of the stages of learning are discussed, as well as specific, evidence-based strategies for maintaining the often-fleeting state of automaticity in highly skilled golfers.

Review of literature

Learning in three stages: the Fitts and Posner model (1967)

Whether it is riding a bike, playing an instrument, or swinging a golf club, learning a new skill is a complex process fraught with physical, mental, and emotional challenges at every step along the pathway to proficiency. A sport such as golf presents unique challenges to the learner in that it requires a precise blend of power and precision, with a margin of acceptable error that borders, at times, on the seemingly impossible.

While the inherent difficulty of the game has undoubtedly contributed to the decline in participation rates in recent years, it has simultaneously spawned unprecedented growth in 'game improvement' industries such as training aids, measurement technologies, coaching, and a host of other performance improvement specialists. It is, however, perplexing to learn that despite advances in training techniques, equipment design, and the astounding ability to measure and record the minutiae of the golf swing, the average handicap has not changed appreciably in recent decades. In fact, a case could be made that the level of analysis currently available to players at all levels could in fact be making the game *more* difficult to learn (Bertram et al., 2007).

On a more optimistic note, since the 1980s, there have been tremendous gains in the basic understanding of human learning and the resulting changes in the central and peripheral nervous systems. As it pertains to golf, the field of *motor learning* has likewise been building a detailed and well-documented theoretical framework to describe the process of motor skill acquisition, as well as providing evidence-based accounts for how to create environments that are more conducive to learning.

Among the first researchers to formulate models for human motor learning were Fitts and Posner (1967). These authors proposed that the process of motor skill acquisition happens in a continuum of three stages: cognitive, associative, and autonomous. The first stage of learning is referred to as the *cognitive* stage, during which learners spend much of their time and attention on cognitive problem solving, verbal self-talk (Adams, 1971), and attempts to interpret errors in performance. In golf, a player in the cognitive stage is working hard to understand details such as how to hold the club properly, the differences in length and loft of the various clubs, and/or how to properly sequence the multitude of body segments necessary to make a proper golf swing. In many cases, a player at this stage is also taking in basic information from a coach or instructor and having to assimilate this feedback into his/her rapidly expanding cognitive framework for how to adequately perform the skill. Much of the player's attention at this stage is understandably focussed internally on processing information and problem solving, and as a result, actual performance is characteristically poor in terms of accuracy and consistency (Wallace & Haggler, 1979). It is also important to remember that a beginner's emotional state can be quite fragile during the cognitive stage of learning (Mouton, 2016) and, therefore, instructors should be mindful of setting achievable goals early on and maintaining an especially positive tone in their interactions with the player.

As the learning process progresses, Fitts and Posner (1967) suggest that learners then transition from the cognitive stage into stage two: the *associative* stage. Around this time, a person has formed the basis of a foundation for how to perform a given skill and starts trying to *associate* his/ her internal concept of the movement with the feedback they get from the environment as well as from their own proprioceptive feedback as the actual movement unfolds. This intermediate stage of learning is where a majority of the refinement of a skill takes place and where, unfortunately, the vast majority of golfers plateau in their pursuit of a lower handicap. It is the stage where the bulk of all practice happens. It is the place where most coaching happens, and where most lessons are paid for. It is the time when players are trying to take what they know (or think they know) and translate that knowledge into straighter, more consistent golf shots and more fluid putting strokes. Referring back to the idea that transitions through the stages of learning involve a gradual shift in the focus of one's attention (Beilock et al., 2002), those in the associative stage are caught in a difficult place as they attempt to share their attention between *thought* and *action*. Given that most research in psychology suggests that attention is a resource with a limited capacity (Magill, 2014), it is understandable that the experience of being in the associative stage of learning is often one of information overload and great frustration, which ultimately leads to very little in the way of true learning in a sport such as golf. However, if properly managed, performance during the associative stage of learning will begin to show signs of improvement whether that be in terms of increased overall accuracy, decreased variability, or increased error detection.

The third and final stage of the Fitts and Posner (1967) learning model is the *autonomous* stage. At this point in the learning process, the execution of motor skills becomes seemingly automatic, and the ability to allow free-flowing movements to unfold can occur with very little in the way of conscious effort or attention. Being autonomous in movement is the feeling most people experience when performing everyday tasks such as walking, signing their names, or reaching out to pick up a cup of water. In golf, however, being autonomous in movement is, unfortunately, something that escapes the vast majority of players. If one was to define being autonomous in golf as a player who is a scratch handicap or better, 2016 statistics suggest this would include <2% of all players in that category (United States Golf Association [USGA], 2016). If more lenient in the definition and including those with handicaps of 10 or better in the autonomous category, that would still exclude approximately 75% of all players. In other words, golf is hard. However, for some, that small minority of players who can challenge or even break par with regularity, the movements associated with swinging a golf club are, indeed, seemingly automatic. At this stage, the golf swing becomes more efficient, more repeatable, and therefore the quality and consistency of golf shots become more desirable. In terms of attention, autonomous movements can largely be executed free of conscious thought, and those same attention resources can instead be used to focus externally on a target or an intended target line.

It is important to note that we are not intending for the definition of automaticity presented herein to be used synonymously or interchangeably with the concept of 'flow state' or 'the zone', which are often described in the sport psychology literature (Swann et al., 2012). These terms are generally reserved for the rare moments in sport (or other performance arenas) when athletes feel fully 'connected' to their activity and success seems effortless. While the notions of flow states are undoubtedly linked to Fitts and Posner's autonomous stage of learning, they are unique, success-centred phenomena that go beyond the scope of the current chapter.

Why an understanding of learning matters

Having now provided an overview of the Fitts and Posner model, it is perhaps worthwhile to pause and reflect on why an understanding of how learning happens is so important in the discussion of golf instruction (or teaching, more generally). First, having a basic, conceptual understanding of what a player is experiencing at a cognitive level throughout the learning process is crucial for the instructor. The 'learning curve' in golf is anything but smooth, and the result can be a process filled with setbacks and frustration. For the instructor, understanding the stages of learning brings an expanded awareness to the coach/player relationship and provides new tools and vocabulary to the more human side of learning. For example, a coach who observes a highly skilled player becoming overly analytical on the course might recognize that the player is operating more on an associative level as opposed to the more optimal autonomous level. This new layer of understanding and awareness on the part of the instructor could then lead to more productive discussions with the player through a process similar to cognitive behavioural coaching (Palmer & Szymanska, 2007). This approach views the relationship between coach and pupil as a collaboration built on empathy and open dialogue.

A second – and perhaps more important – reason why it is vital for instructors to understand the stages of learning is that this knowledge should absolutely inform how the coaches teach and design learning environments. Current research clearly indicates that the way lessons and/or practice sessions are designed for beginners should be much different than the learning environment that is set up for the advanced player (Shea et al., 1990). In other words, the learning environment ought to be learner-centred and guided by the stage of learning that an individual is currently occupying. This might seem obvious or instinctual to some coaches, but the simple truth is skilled players too often employ practice methods better suited to beginners, and instructors too often use instructional language with a novice player that would be much more appropriate for an advanced player. In the next section, we provide an overview of some of the key research in motor learning in the area of practice and feedback, as well as discuss how they relate specifically to the stages of learning.

The learning environment

In the field of motor learning, the 'learning environment' is typically defined as the place where practice occurs and/or the place where time is spent with a coach or instructor. In golf, key practice considerations include concepts such as contextual interference (Shea & Morgan, 1979) or what has more commonly become known through terminology comprising *blocked* versus *random* practice (among other related manipulations). In addition to practice design, the learning environment often involves an exchange of information – or feedback – with a coach or instructor. Learning environments in golf can (and often do) include additional, supplemental sources of feedback, such as launch monitors, video cameras, force plates, or other training aids. Research in motor learning – specifically in the areas of *practice* and *feedback* – has provided a wealth of data around the issue of optimal learning environments and can serve as a guide for instructors attempting to incorporate evidence-based practices into their own learning environments.

Practice and contextual interference

Even before the twentieth century, scientists were exploring the nature of the learning process and the acquisition of skill (e.g., Bryan & Harter, 1897). However, >80 years would pass between these initial studies and systemic investigations into the impact of different practice schedules on learning. A significant early contribution came from Shea and Morgan (1979), who were the first among many to describe what has now become known as the *contextual interference effect*. Contextual interference is a term used to describe the interference that results from practising a variety of tasks or versions of a task within the context of a single practice situation. In other words, low levels of contextual interference can be established by having a player practise the same task repeatedly within a block of trials (i.e., blocked practice). Higher levels of contextual interference can be established by practising several tasks in a random order (i.e., random practice). Importantly, Shea and Morgan established a key finding in motor learning research: blocked practice tends to lead to better performance during practice, but a greater degree of *learning* results from random practice, and the latter was therefore determined to be a more optimal method of practice. This key finding eloquently illustrated that observations made during training are not necessarily indicative of learning – a phenomenon known more widely today as the performance-learning paradox (refer Soderstrom & Bjork, 2013, for a review). Within the context of golf, Shea and Morgan's results suggest that repetitive, blocked practice will yield good performance on the range but will not necessarily transfer to lower scores on the golf course or significant learning in general. It would appear as though the benefits of simple repetition in the practice setting are short-lived and provide little more than a false sense of security when abilities are later put to the test.

An important supplement to the traditional understanding of contextual interference was provided by Guadagnoli et al. (1999) with their finding that optimal practice, in terms of variability and contextual interference, is dependent upon the skill level of the learner. Their study involved a golf putting task and demonstrated that novice participants (i.e., beginners) who practised under a repetitive, blocked practice protocol learned more than novice subjects who practised under a more variable random practice protocol. The experienced players, however, showed the opposite effect. These more skilled players who practised under a random protocol learned more than experienced subjects who practised under a blocked protocol. In other words, the typical finding that random practice leads to greater learning was only true for *skilled players*. Beginners, on the other hand, appeared to be better suited for a learning environment that allowed them to practise with a greater amount of repetition that blocked practice affords. Presumably, blocked practice provided the most appropriate challenge for novice performers and random practice provided the most appropriate challenge for experienced performers. Therefore, it was concluded that performers in the early stages of learning benefit from a reduction in extraneous challenge; however, as the performer becomes more proficient, added challenge is beneficial (Guadagnoli & Lee, 2004). This study clearly demonstrated that an optimal learning environment is dependent upon the skill level of the performer and, thus, implies that different practice strategies need to be utilized for players with different levels of ability. Similar results showing the beneficial effects of random practice for skilled performers have also been demonstrated in other applied settings such as baseball (Hall et al., 1994), learning to play a musical instrument (Stambaugh, 2011) and numerous laboratory-based movement tasks (e.g., Wulf & Lee, 1993; Green & Sherwood, 2000; Simon, 2007).

Feedback

It has long been known that feedback coming from an external source (e.g., a coach; technology) is critical in skill development (Adams, 1987; Schmidt & Lee, 2011). Such feedback is needed because many performers cannot adequately evaluate errors on their own. This is particularly true with performers in the cognitive stage of development, who are yet to establish an adequate reference of correctness in their movement abilities. In short, until one has developed an adequate cognitive representation of a skill, a model must be provided for them and this model most often comes in the form of external feedback. In the scientific literature, this feedback is known as knowledge of results (KR). A variety of studies have examined the most appropriate KR frequency and schedule, and these studies have been progressively pointing to an overarching principle of optimal feedback. For example, Schmidt et al. (1990) found that an optimal KR was task specific. That is, the more complex the task, the more immediate that the KR should be given. Guadagnoli et al. (1996) extended this line of thinking by investigating the relationships among KR, task complexity, and performer experience. They found that optimal KR depends on the level of the performer and the complexity of the task. For a complex task, or a novice performer, KR should be given more immediately than for a simple task or an experienced performer. That is, Guadagnoli et al. (1996) suggested that optimal KR is dependent on the relative task difficulty, with relative task difficulty being defined as the difficulty of the task relative to the person performing it. For example, a novice golfer trying to make a 4-foot putt on the practice green may find that task very difficult. A PGA professional attempting the same putt may find it relatively easy. In this example, the relative task difficulty for the professional is much lower than for the novice. On the other hand, a 4-foot putt for a novice and a 12-foot putt for the professional may have the same relative difficulty. In short, KR should be matched to the relative task difficulty.

Another important consideration relating to feedback in learning is the content of the feedback itself in terms of the amount of technical detail provided. Seminal work in this area was conducted by Magill and Wood (1986). These authors investigated this issue by varying the content of the feedback in tasks involving trying to complete a complex movement pattern within a specified amount of time. One group of participants in the study received qualitative feedback about their performance (e.g., 'that trial was too slow'), while a second experimental group received more detailed quantitative feedback (e.g. 'that trial was 250 ms too slow'). While ultimately the group that was given the more detailed information performed better (and learned more), the key finding once again was that the content of information used in a learning environment should be tailored to the skill level of the learner. More specifically, the results of the study showed that having access to more detailed, numerical feedback only became beneficial once the movement was well practised. In other words, during the early stages of learning, detailed technical information was of little value. The results of Magill and Wood (1986), as well as other more recent publications (Swinnen, 1996; Williams & Hodges, 2005), are particularly relevant to modern golf instruction, where, owing to advances in technology and swing analysis, access to detailed information is so readily available. While it may be tempting to allow beginners access to detailed biomechanical, impact, or ball flight information, current research clearly advises against it. Instructors would be better served by steering less-skilled players away from the minutiae of their golf swings and instead focussing on more general fundamentals or broader swing concepts. On the other hand, more highly skilled players who have reached the autonomous level of learning are theoretically better equipped – from a cognitive standpoint – to process more complex information. Still however, care should be taken to prevent the learner from becoming overly reliant on feedback. Winstein and Schmidt (1990) and other researchers have demonstrated that as the skill level increases, feedback is most beneficial when it is presented less frequently.

Optimal challenge and the stages of learning

In 2004, the *Challenge Point Framework for motor learning* (Guadagnoli & Lee, 2004) was published, providing an overarching principle for practice and learning. This model can also be applied to optimal feedback across the stages of learning. The essence of the framework is that for efficient learning to take place, the individual must be *optimally challenged*. This notion of optimal challenge (also known as Optimal Challenge Point or OCP) is critical and relates directly to the stages of learning. For any given task, task OCP varies depending upon the complexity of the task and the skill of the learner. If a task is simple (or of low complexity), then practice difficulty should be increased to result in an appropriate challenge for the learner. However, if a task is more complex, the challenge may need to be decreased, at least with an inexperienced performer. This particular finding has been demonstrated in a variety of motor settings with a variety of populations, such as Parkinson's patients (Onla-or & Winstein, 2008) and children with certain speech sound disorders (Hitchcock & Mcallister, 2015)

Over-challenging or under-challenging will produce inefficient learning. Over-challenging often creates a high degree of failure, which is not ideal as it tends to overwhelm a learner's ability to process information (Bertram et al., 2007) and can demotivate the learner. Conversely, under-challenging the player may *feel* good because it produces a great deal of success, but that feeling (and the success) is short-lived. An example of the latter would be a situation where a skilled golfer practises by hitting twenty 9-irons in a row, from the same perfect lie, to the same target. Of course, the majority of those shots will be hit well, but once that same player steps onto the golf course, that good feeling can quickly turn to frustration when a single nine-iron shot, hit under pressure, to a tucked pin is not perfectly executed.

Considering that OCP is a task- and learner-specific tool, it can be viewed as dynamic and will ultimately shift as a learner increases in proficiency. To account for this shift, practice difficulty should be increased to form an appropriate challenge. Once a learner is proficient in a task, and performance becomes efficient with little failure, learning is no longer optimized at that level of difficulty and should be increased. This concept of optimal challenge can be directly manipulated by feedback or KR. All things being equal, more feedback provides more guidance, thus making a task relatively easier. For individuals in the early stage of learning, feedback should be provided frequently as this provides the appropriate challenge for the individual without over-challenging them. As the learner progresses, the frequency of feedback should decrease, thus requiring the performer to rely more on his/her intrinsic feedback. This will challenge the performer more, and it is this challenge that will result in continued learning. For individuals in the autonomous stage of learning, it is suggested that feedback is not required. Rather, at this stage, the learner has a substantial internal model for skilled movement. The learners should be able to evaluate their response with accuracy. As such, at this stage, it is suggested that the learners tell their coach how they performed and have the coach confirm or deny the assessment. This challenge will provide a great learning opportunity for the skilled golfer. Indeed, it has been long known that, when a performer is in a later stage of learning, the cognitive system's ability to group information improves and thus the learner can more efficiently handle a more demanding practice protocol (Shannon & Weaver, 1949). As such, this increased challenge of withholding feedback for skilled golfers should appropriately challenge the learner.

Implications for the game

A greater understanding of the stages of learning is vital for instructors seeking to fully develop their teaching philosophy and, ultimately, how effective they are in facilitating meaningful changes in the abilities of their students. As discussed, using the stages of learning and the Challenge Point Framework as guideposts for instruction would have tremendous implications for how the game of golf is taught and, therefore, how quickly improvements in performance might be realized. A commitment to a learner-centred instruction approach allows for the creation of learning environments that are purposefully and specifically tailored to the skill level of the player.

In terms of the novice player (i.e., one who is in the cognitive stage of learning), the aforementioned research suggests that practice time should involve a good deal of repetition and blocked practice. This practice should also involve frequent yet easy-to-understand intervention from the instructor with the aim of helping the player establish the conceptual understanding of the game, which will eventually form the basis of the swing fundamentals. Then, as the player starts to become more proficient and moves into the associative stage, the learning environment should be adjusted to employ gradually increasing amounts of random practice in an attempt to adequately challenge the player and maintain the desirable difficulties that true learning demands. Furthermore, feedback from the instructor during the associative stage should start to become slightly more detailed and perhaps more technical but should be given *less frequently*. Recalling that a learner in the associative stage is exploring his/her movements and processing the sensations and results internally, time and space should be allowed at this point to allow the players to reflect on their own ideas without interruption. During this critical time, instructors need to resist the temptation to constantly intervene and must instead allow the players to seek their own solutions to problems – even if that means occasional failure. Being mindful that the associative stage is usually accompanied by a good deal of frustration, instructors must guard against becoming a crutch for the player and instead adopt more of a guided-discovery approach to instruction (e.g., Raab et al., 2009).

Finally, for players reaching an autonomous, or even expert, stage of learning, the environment must again be adjusted to suit their level of ability. Generally speaking, practice for skilled players should incorporate variability and randomness wherever possible (Guadagnoli & Bertram, 2015). On the range, this could mean having a player frequently changing clubs, aiming to different targets, and/or adjusting ball flight trajectories. With putting, similar random practice principles could be introduced by ensuring that new lines or targets are constantly being selected, essentially challenging the player to not hit the same putt twice. In terms of instructor feedback, players in the autonomous stage are, by and large, better able to process detailed, technical information from their coaches, but as we have alluded to earlier in the chapter, research clearly suggests that such feedback should be used sparingly. Players at this stage should be encouraged to find their own solutions, thus promoting the kind of robust and durable understanding that can stand alone and allow for optimal performance to occur in the absence of the instructor. In essence, the level of challenge that is brought about through the combination of variability/randomness in practice, coupled with independent self-reflection, is more optimal for skilled players and promotes the kinds of conditions that are most likely to increase learning and ultimately transfer to the competitive environment.

A final note relating to the Fitts and Posner (1967) model would be to remember that the learning process exists on a continuum and that the stages are not fixed. An important example of this would be those times when a highly skilled player encounters repeated struggles with a part (or parts) of their game. Perhaps they are fighting a persistent hook with their full swing, or maybe they are having ongoing difficulty with their short game. During these challenging times, it is essential for the instructor to recognize that their highly skilled student is no longer performing in the autonomous state that they have become accustomed to, and conscious thought has – perhaps necessarily – crept back into what is ideally a more automatic process. At such times, it would be advisable to readjust the learning environment to one better suited to an associative stage player (i.e., more blocked practice drills, more frequent feedback). These adjustments should be temporary however, and efforts should be made to quickly realign the learning environment to one more ideally suited to the skilled player. In other words, once a player has begun to feel comfortable with the new movement or technique and is performing consistently under blocked conditions with frequent feedback, it is essential that practice sessions return to an appropriate level of challenge in terms of increased variability and the tapering of feedback.

Summary and future directions

The goal of this chapter was to provide instructors with a conceptual overview of the stages that players go through as they progress through the learning process. Furthermore, we presented a learner-centred model for instruction based on the idea that learning environments – in terms of practice design and instructional content – ought to be designed according to principles derived from current motor learning literature. More specifically, we reviewed how the optimal Challenge Point Framework can help guide decision-making within the learning environment. We discussed that during the early stages of learning, golfers rely heavily on information-processing mechanisms and conscious problem–solving processes. As such, instruction at this stage should be simpler in terms of content and be utilized frequently; moreover, practice should focus on repetitive drills that reinforce fundamentals. However, as the player's skill increases, less attention is needed for the execution of the swing itself, thus freeing up cognitive resources that can ideally be focussed on more task-relevant external stimuli such as an intended target or ball flight. At this stage of learning, instruction (in terms of feedback) can be more technical in nature but should be less frequent to allow for a greater degree of learner-centred reflection and problem solving. Practice for the skilled player should avoid repetition, incorporate variability wherever possible, and should seek to challenge the player in ways that resemble actual playing or competitive conditions. In conclusion, the research reviewed clearly indicates that kinds of information or the types of practice drills that are helpful for a novice can be useless or even detrimental for the more skilled player (and vice versa). The evidence-based instructional framework presented indicates that the stages of learning should be the foremost consideration when designing optimal learning environments. Future research in the area should further investigate issues such as i) variability during warm-up and practice, as well as ii) feedback scheduling as they pertain to enhanced learning environments and performance outcomes in golfers of all skill levels.

References

Adams, J. (1971) A Closed-Loop Theory of Motor Learning, *Journal of Motor Behavior*, 3 (2), 111–150.

Adams, J. (1987) A Historical Review and Appraisal of Research on the Learning, Retention, and Transfer of Human Motor Skills, *Psychological Bulletin*, 101 (1), 41–74.

Beilock, S.; Wierenga, S. & Carr, T. (2002) Expertise, Attention, and Memory in Sensorimotor Skill Execution: Impact of Novel Constraints on Dual-Task Performance and Episodic Memory, *Quarterly Journal of Experimental Psychology*, 55A (4), 1211–1240.

Bertram, C.; Marteniuk, R. & Guadagnoli, M. (2007) On the Use and Misuse of Video Analysis, *International Journal of Sports Science and Coaching*, 2 (1), 37–46.

Bryan, W. & Harter, N. (1897) Studies in the Physiology and Psychology of the Telegraphic Language, *Psychology Review*, 4 (1), 27–53.

Fitts, P. & Posner, M. (1967) *Human Performance*, Belmont, CA: Brooks/Cole.

Green, S. & Sherwood, D. (2000) The Benefits of Random Variable Practice for Accuracy and Temporal Error Detection in a Rapid Aiming Task, *Research Quarterly for Exercise and Sport*, 71 (4), 398–402.

Guadagnoli, M. & Bertram, C. (2015) Optimizing Practice for Performance Under Pressure, *International Journal of Golf Science*, 3 (2), 119–127.

Guadagnoli, M.; Dornier, L. & Tandy, R. (1996) Optimal Summary Knowledge of Results: The Influence of Task Related Experience and Complexity, *Research Quarterly for Exercise and Sport*, 67 (2), 239–248.

Guadagnoli, M.; Holcomb, W. & Weber, T. (1999) The Relationship Between Contextual Interference Effects and Performer Expertise on the Learning of a Putting Task, *Journal of Human Movement Studies*, 37 (1), 19–36.

Guadagnoli, M. & Lee, T. (2004) Challenge Point: A Framework for Conceptualizing the Effects of Various Practice Conditions in Motor Learning, *Journal of Motor Behavior*, 36 (2), 212–224.

Hall, K.; Domingues, D. & Cavazos, R. (1994) Contextual Interference Effects with Skilled Baseball Players, *Perceptual and Motor Skills*, 78 (3), 835–841.

Hitchcock, E. & Mcallister Byun, T. (2015) Enhancing Generalisation in Biofeedback Intervention Using the Challenge Point Framework: A Case Study, *Clinical Linguistics & Phonetics*, 29 (1), 59–75.

Magill, R. (2014) *Motor Learning and Control: Concepts and Applications* (10th Ed.), New York, NY: McGraw-Hill.

Magill, R. & Wood, C. (1986) Knowledge of Results Precision as a Learning Variable in Motor Skill Acquisition, *Research Quarterly for Exercise and Sport*, 57 (2), 170–173.

Mouton, A. (2016) Performance Coaching in Sport, Music, and Business: From Gallwey to Grant, and the Promise of Positive Psychology, *International Coaching Psychology Review*, 11 (2), 129–142.

Onla-or, S. & Winstein, C. (2008) Determining the Optimal Challenge Point for Motor Skill Learning in Adults with Moderately Severe Parkinson's Disease, *Neurorehabilitation and Neural Repair*, 22 (4), 385–395.

Palmer, S. & Szymanska, K. (2007) Cognitive Behavioural Coaching: An Integrative Approach, In: S. Palmer & A. Whybrow (Eds.) *Handbook of Coaching Psychology: A Guide for Practitioners*, London: Routledge, pp. 86–117.

Raab, M.; Masters, R.; Maxwell, J.; Arnold, A.; Schlapkohl, N. & Poolton, J. (2009) Discovery Learning in Sports: Implicit or Explicit Processes? *International Journal of Sport and Exercise Psychology*, 7 (4), 413–430.

Schmidt, R.; Lange, C. & Young, D. (1990) Optimizing Summary Knowledge of Results for Skill Learning, *Human Movement Science*, 9 (3), 325–348.

Schmidt, R. & Lee, T. (2011) *Motor Control and Learning: A Behavioural Emphasis*, (5th Ed.), Champaign, IL: Human Kinetics.

Shannon, C. & Weaver, W. (1949) *The Mathematical Theory of Communication*, Urbana, IL: University of Illinois Press.

Shea, C.H.; Kohl, R. & Indermill, C. (1990) Contextual Interference: Contributions of Practice, *Acta Pyschologica*, 73 (2), 145–157.

Shea, J. & Morgan, R. (1979) Contextual Interference Effects on the Acquisition, Retention, and Transfer of a Motor Skill, *Journal of Experimental Psychology: Human Learning and Memory*, 5 (2), 179–187.

Simon, D. (2007) Contextual Interference Effects with Two Tasks, *Perceptual and Motor Skills*, 105 (1), 177–183.

Soderstrom, N. & Bjork, R. (2013) Learning Versus Performance, In: D. Dunn (Ed.) *Oxford Bibliographies Online: Psychology*, Available at www.oxfordbibliographies.com/view/document/obo-9780199828340/obo-9780199828340-0081.xml

Stambaugh, L. (2011) When Repetition Isn't the Best Practice Strategy: Effects of Blocked and Random Practice Schedules, *Journal of Research in Music Education*, 58 (4), 368–383.

Swann, C.; Keegan, R.; Piggott, D. & Crust, L. (2012) A Systematic Review of the Experience, Occurrence, and Controllability of Flow States in Elite Sport, *Psychology of Sport and Exercise*, 13 (6), 807–819.

Swinnen, S. (1996) Information Feedback for Motor Skill Learning: A Review, In: H. Zelaznik (Ed.) *Advances in Motor Learning and Control*, Champaign, IL: Human Kinetics, pp. 37–66.

USGA (2016) Men's Handicap Index Statistics, Available at www.Usga.Org/Handicapping/Handicap-Index-Statistics/Mens-Handicap-Index-Statistics-D24e6096.Html (Accessed March 12, 2016).

Wallace, S. & Hagler, R. (1979) Knowledge of Performance and Learning of a Closed Motor Skill, *Research Quarterly*, 50 (2), 265–271.

Williams, A. & Hodges, N. (2005) Practice, Instruction and Skill Acquisition in Soccer: Challenging Tradition, *Journal of Sport Sciences*, 23 (6), 637–650.

Winstein, C. & Schmidt, R. (1990) Reduced Frequency of Knowledge of Results Enhances Motor Skill Learning, *Journal of Experimental Psychology: Learning, Memory, and Cognition*, 16 (4), 677–691.

Wulf, G. & Lee, T. (1993) Contextual Interference in Movements of the Same Class: Differential Effects on Program and Parameter Learning, *Journal of Motor Behavior*, 25 (4), 254–263.

12

SKILL ASSESSMENT IN GOLF

Sam Robertson

Introduction

The use of performance assessment is commonplace in most sports with participants of all ages and ability levels. Such assessments typically consist of a measurement or a series of measurements that are used to determine the sport-specific ability of a particular individual (Currell & Jeukendrup, 2008). Performance assessment can be used to determine the strengths and weaknesses of an individual (Pyne et al., 2005; Robertson et al., 2013), identify a talented potential athlete (Ali, 2011, Lidor et al., 2009) or help to determine the effectiveness of an implemented coach intervention (Currell et al., 2009; Robertson et al., 2012). Despite relatively common use, skill assessment has, nonetheless, experienced some debate in the literature (Lidor et al., 2005; Anshel & Lidor, 2012). One major criticism relates to the use of testing that does not accurately reflect the demands of competition, which in turn can lead to incorrect conclusions being made relating to the ability of a performer (Lidor et al., 2005). When used to inform decision-making in talent identification settings, early assessment of players may also lead to their premature de-selection from the sport. Therefore, establishing the measurement qualities of an assessment prior to use or development can help to avoid these potential pitfalls. This chapter provides a review of research that has utilised skill assessments in golf, as well as develops an awareness and understanding of the advantages and disadvantages relating to their use. This chapter also delivers literature-based guidance as to how the quality of a skill assessment can be measured. Readers can use this information to make informed decisions on test selection in coaching and research settings.

Skill measurement in golf

As in many sports, consensus on the importance and merits of skill assessment in golf is yet to be reached. Although used for a variety of purposes in coaching and research environments, because no assessment is perfect, debate is likely to continue with respect to their benefits in these contexts. As a sport, golf has a history of using skill data obtained from multiple sources to help analyse performance, inform practice plans and enhance media coverage. Recent improvements to technologies used in the sport have, in particular, seen the ability for feedback on skilled performance to be obtained more rapidly than was previously available. At the elite level, one of the most pertinent examples is the ShotLink™ system, which was first implemented on the United States Professional Golfers Association (US PGA) Tour in 2008. Incorporating radar and laser technologies, this system has enabled a range of descriptive information relating to every shot played on the tour to be obtained, including the distance, wind and lie. Performance and outcome benchmarks relating to different players, holes and tournaments can also be tracked longitudinally.

The increased use of technologies off the course, in particular as teaching aids, has also allowed for growth in the collection of skill data. Initially only accessible to elite players, launch monitors present one such example of these aids and are now used commonly by many coaches to supplement their work with players on the range. The influence of these devices on the evolution of coaching practice is undeniable. For instance, for assessing the ability of a player to hit the ball to a target 150 m away prior to launch monitor availability, a coach or assistant would have been required to stand where the shot landed, mark the location and measure the shot using manual methods. By using a radar-based launch monitor, combined with sophisticated computer software, this information is now readily available to coach and/or player in near-real time all while remaining standing on the practice tee.

Skill assessment in golf

While the collection of skill data using these means is now relatively commonplace, skill assessment also has a long history of use by coaches in the field. A multitude of texts exists in circulation, each outlining multiple tests and drills designed to assess most of the components of the game, such as driving, iron play, short game and putting. Further, many coaches and golf organisations have developed their own versions of skills tests, with the intention of assessing the abilities of players across a variety of levels. More recently, many commercially available launch monitors discussed in the previous section also have skill tests built into their software. While some of these experience considerable popularity in the field, the measurement properties of these tests (including their reliability and validity) have largely not been established, meaning that their ability to accurately assess golf skill remains unknown.

Putting

Putting assessments are by far the most prevalent in the literature comparative to the other main golf skills. Many of these have been undertaken in a 'test/re-test' format, often in order to determine the influence of a psychological intervention on subsequent performance. For example, Daou et al. (2016) undertook an accuracy and distance-based putting task on an indoor artificial surface in order to determine how the expectation of having to teach the skill to another individual altered their own performance, along with their level of information processing. In this example, the target represented two small pieces of white masking tape. Using a similar task, Iso-Ahola et al. (2016) aimed to determine whether differences existed in putting performance in individuals when switching between different types of putters. In determining the impact that enhanced expectancies have on subsequent putting performance, Palmer et al. (2016) incorporated circular targets of different diameters (0.14 m and 0.07 m) for putts undertaken over 1.50 m also on an indoor surface.

Contextual interference, which refers to how the repeated alteration of different tasks during practice affects motor learning, has also extensively used putting assessments. For instance, Porter et al. (2007) compared the differences between low, medium and high levels of contextual interference on both practice and test performance. Their assessment consisted of participants undertaking 3.2 m long putts on an indoor carpet surface to concentric circle targets, with points awarded for each shot based on the circle in which it finished. In a similar investigation, Land et al. (2014) developed an assessment that consisted of multiple putts undertaken from five different distances between 2 m and 5 m, with the order for each individual randomised. A differing example comes from Doan et al. (2006), who developed an assessment to determine the influence of strength training on putting performance in elite collegiate players. The task consisted of 15 putts undertaken from 4.6 m, with performance defined as the ability of the player to control the distance of each shot.

To date, only one example for reporting the measurement properties of the test itself exists in the literature. Robertson et al. (2015) developed a putting assessment to assess the ability of players to perform over six different distances ranging from 3 feet to 25 feet. The order in which shots were performed was randomised, meaning that participants did not have the opportunity to obtain a practice read of the putt. The authors concluded that a minimum of six putts from each distance was required to sufficiently gain a representation of a player's ability from that location. Despite undertaking the test on an outdoor putting green, the surface was flat, meaning that the ability of players to perform over varying terrain was not assessed.

The above examples provide insight into the manner in which putting has been assessed in the literature to date. The protocols implemented vary in their design; however, the quality of each may be interpreted differently depending on the intended use of the test. For instance, undertaking an assessment on a carpeted surface indoors removes the variability caused by external factors outdoors; however, the transfer of findings to 'real-world' scenarios may be questionable. Although fulfilling these criteria, competition-like designs may suffer from an inability to distinguish 'signal from the noise' and thus may require multiple trials in order for accurate inferences to be made. Irrespective of the design, when using outdoor environments, contextual information exerting a potential influence on the putting skill should also be collected, such as the green speed between repeated days of testing, or the additional assessment of players on different slopes.

Iron play

Limited work has been undertaken with respect to the assessment of golf iron play in non-competitive settings. The TrackMan™ Combine represents perhaps the most high-profile commercial offering, with players required to perform six shots to nine different distances from 55 m to 165 m, as well as driver (60 shots total). Participants are scored on their ability to land the ball close to the target. Although experiencing considerable popularity and many professional tour players recording high scores, the measurement properties of the test are yet to be reported.

Using the TrackMan ™ Combine as a template, Robertson et al. (2013) developed the Approach-Iron Skill Test. Using the same shot distances (55, 65, 75, 85, 95, 105, 125, 145, 165 m and driver) as the TrackMan Combine (excluding the driver), participants were scored on the percent error index (PEI) of each shot. The PEI metric is calculated as the resultant distance a ball has remaining to its intended target divided by the distance from which the ball was originally hit (Pelz, 1999). A second example from Robertson et al. (2012) is the 'Nine-Ball Skills Test', which was based on a variation of the Nine-Ball Drill commonly used by coaches. Unlike the abovementioned example, this test aims to assess a player's ability to control ball shape and trajectory while maintaining accuracy. Players are required to hit an accurate shot (again defined by PEI) while hitting one of nine different shot types using a six-iron club. These include various combinations of straight, draw and fade shots each hit at low, 'normal' or high trajectories.

A limitation of iron-play assessments proposed in the literature to date is that, typically, repeated shots are played from an identical location, even if the length is varied between each shot. These shots are also typically performed from the same (normally flat) ball lie. Utilising 360° practice tees can enable the shot direction to be also varied, thereby exposing the player to varying wind directions and targets. However, in order to undertake this in a time-efficient manner, multiple launch monitors would need to be used concurrently (one for each direction), which in most cases is impractical. This provides an example whereby the design of an assessment consisting of more competition-like conditions can often come at the expense of feasibility.

Driving

Considerable debate exists with respect to defining driving performance; this not only relates to practice settings but also in competition. In his review paper, Hellström (2009) reports average driving distance, driving accuracy (percentage of fairways hit in a round) and total driving (magnitude of differences between players on the previous two metrics) as the most commonly used metrics to define this construct. With relation to skill assessment in the research, driving distance has been the most prominent outcome measure of skill in a range of golf-specific interventions. One such example comes from Green et al. (2015), who assessed whether light aerobic warm-up improved driving performance when undertaken prior to driving. In this example, drive accuracy was defined as the perpendicular distance of the resting ball from a target placed 260 m from the tee on a driving range for 10 trials. The distances of each drive were also determined.

Elsewhere, biomechanical parameters have also been reported in place of driving distance as a measure of driving performance. For instance, Myers et al. (2008) assessed players over five trials in an indoor facility, using ball velocity as the sole outcome measure. Similarly, Chu et al. (2010) also defined driving performance using ball velocity in their study assessing upper body swing biomechanics. Elsewhere, Fletcher and Hartwell (2004) used a combination of both club velocity and driving distance in their assessment of whether strength training was advantageous for improving golf performance.

Similar to iron play assessments, published protocols to date have not varied the direction of drives in testing, choosing to implement blocked conditions from a single location. Further, randomisation of landing targets has not been utilised, which results in the lack of task variation and thus calls into question the strength of validity of the assessments. While useful for purposes of data collection, the use of indoor driving facilities also remove external stimuli from being considered by the performer, thus the transfer of findings into competition scenarios may be questionable.

Pitching and chipping

A number of formal assessments of short game have been reported in the literature; largely, these have been used to determine the effect of different experimental interventions on performance. One example comes from Pates and Maynard (2000), who implemented a hypnotic-based intervention with participants in order to determine whether it could improve chipping performance. Participants undertook 12 chip shots from 20 m with performance measured as the radial distance from the hole where each shot stopped. A monetary reward was provided to the best performing participant, with the intention of this design component to increase participant task motivation. Bell and Hardy (2009) prescribed participants five blocks of 10 pitch shots to determine the effect that different anxiety conditions exerted on performance. Similar to the previous example, a 20 m shot distance was utilised, with performance determined by the radial distance the ball had remaining to the hole. A financial incentive was also provided.

Both studies utilised outdoor flat fairway and green areas in order to produce a competition-like environment for the testing. Perkins-Ceccato et al. (2003) examined the influence of internal and external attention instructions on the performance of a pitch shot undertaken by groups of high- and low-skilled players. The pitch shot was undertaken using a nine-iron club, with targets signified by a pylon located at distances of 10 m, 15 m, 20 m and 25 m. Stevenson et al. (2007) aimed to determine the influence that trust training could exert on a variety of golf performance measures. Among others, a pitch shot assessment was undertaken on a practice green using a similar protocol as in the previous example (six attempts to a 25 m target). Performance measurement was determined by calculating the perpendicular distance the ball finished to the target. In another psychologically oriented investigation, Brouziyne and Molinaro (2005) investigated the influence that mental imagery could exert on skill learning in a task consisting of 13 wedge shots played to 50 m. Scoring of each shot was based on the final location of the ball in relation to the pin target, with four × 2 m 'zones' set up around the target. A final example comes from Porter et al. (2007), who examined how contextual interference affected learning of the golf pitch shot in novice adults. Three concentric circles spaced 0.4 m apart were used as targets for 160 pitch shots hit from a carpeted surface at a distance of 10.6 m. The effectiveness of the intervention was based on the ability of participants to improve their scoring in the task between test and re-test sessions.

Summary

It is evident from the work reviewed in this chapter that skill assessments reported in the research to date have largely been used to determine the benefit of a given intervention, particularly in a test and re-test format. For instance, a researcher may design an assessment of an accuracy-based motor skill, test a given sample of a population and then undertake a reassessment at a later date in order to determine the efficacy of the intervention. Prior to the widespread use of technologies to measure player skill, many of these assessments focussed on relatively closed golf skills (such as putting) performed in relatively controlled environments (such as indoors on completely flat carpeted surfaces). Such implementations facilitate easier analysis of the performance (i.e., whether a player holed a putt, or the distance the putt finished from an intended target). Further, allowing for relative control of the environment can allow for the influence of random effects on the intervention outcomes to be minimised. However, these very design considerations can also draw criticisms of such testing. Specifically, by controlling the testing environment in the abovementioned manner, it may be argued that the skill being assessed is different to that which is undertaken in competition. Therefore, obtaining a balance between designing assessments that capture the unique conditions associated with competition and ensuring reproducibility of testing results remains a challenge for researchers moving into the future.

Evaluating the skill assessment

Given its benefits (whether actual or perceived), it is likely that skill assessment will continue to be utilised at most levels of sports participation and research. In ensuring that appropriate inferences are made from such results, it is of importance that the assessment chosen or designed is of a suitable quality. To this end, the ability to transfer the findings from the research above to 'real-world' settings depends largely on the measurement properties of the test itself.

Fortunately, determination of the measures that should be considered when undertaking this exercise has received considerable attention. Much of this work is grounded in traditional measurement theory, whereby a ranking or recommendation for a test is provided

TEST QUALITY

RELIABILITY	VALIDITY
Stability	Content
Re-test reliability	Discriminant
Intra-rater reliability	Convergent
Inter-rater reliability	Concurrent
Internal consistency	Predictive

RESPONSIVENESS	FEASIBILITY
Responsiveness/sensitivity	Interpretability
Minimum important difference/smallest	Familiarity required
worthwhile change	Scoring complexity
Floor and ceiling effects	Completion complexity
	Cost
	Duration

Figure 12.1　A framework for informing skill assessment selection and development.

based on its ability to fulfil certain pre-defined criteria. Of particular prominence in this area, Currell and Jeukendrup (2008) considered the components of test validity, reliability and sensitivity that should be considered when assessing a sports performance measurement. Hopkins (2000) and Atkinson and Nevill (1998) have explored a similar topic from a statistical technique perspective. With specific reference to assessments of sporting skill, Robertson et al. (2014) reviewed skills tests (including three from golf) based on various quality characteristics similar to these examples. More recently, a framework has been developed for use by practitioners and researchers to guide their decision-making in test selection or development (Robertson et al., 2017). Consisting of 4 categories and 19 items, Figure 12.1 illustrates this framework, with each item described in greater detail in the following text. When selecting or designing a new test, practitioners can evaluate its quality based on the extent to which an assessment fulfils these features. Although not all features included in the framework are necessary to be fulfilled in order for a test to be useful, nonetheless, it provides a useful guide for this type of exercise.

Validity

The validity of a performance test can be considered in many forms, the most well known of which is perhaps *face validity*. This refers to how effective a test appears to be but does not include any systematic evaluation. While scientifically considered a relatively weak method of evaluating a test, nonetheless, this form is crucial in ensuring that a test receives uptake in the field. Irrespective of whether a test is well designed, if coaches, practitioners and players do not see its initial value, it is likely to be destined for a very limited uptake. A second form of validity is *construct validity*. Put simply, this refers to the extent to which scores obtained on one test relate to those measuring a different construct (Streiner et al., 2014). For instance, if a test of putting skill were designed to discriminate between players of different ability levels, we would expect that a professional player would perform better on the test than an amateur. The extent to which this holds true can then be used to determine the level of construct validity the test has. *Content validity* refers to how well a specific assessment measures that which it intends to measure (Terwee et al., 2010). For example, if designing an assessment of a player's short game, a test showing good content validity may include a variety of shot types (i.e., flop, chip and pitch) from a range of different lies and slopes, rather than a single task. It is often assessed based on expert consensus, or using ratings obtained from coaches. *Convergent validity* is based on the notion that results from two assessments that theoretically should be related to each other are, in fact, related to each other (Streiner et al., 2014). For example, it would be expected that an assessment examining a player's putting ability from 2 m would show a strong relationship with the same player's ability from this distance in competition. While similar to the above, *concurrent validity* refers to how well results from the assessment relate to an alternate, previously validated measure of the same construct (Streiner et al., 2014). The difference to convergent validity is that both assessments are administered at the same time. For instance, certain biomechanical parameters collected during putting may show a strong relationship with corresponding performance. The final item to be considered under the validity category is *predictive validity*. This refers to how well scores on the test relate to another measure of a similar construct, which is administered at a future point in time. As such, it is one of the more powerful forms of validity to determine. However, it is also one of the most difficult. For instance, if a player's performance on a given test shows a strong relationship with his/her tournament performance at a later date in the future, then this has considerable implications (particularly at the higher level) for selection onto a team or in informing talent identification.

Reliability

The *re-test reliability* of a skill assessment is perhaps the most common measurement property considered under this category. It can be determined by evaluating the consistency of a performer's results over repeated rounds of testing. This is often established over a period of days or weeks and may include both systematic and random error in the test as well as 'true' changes in performance (Terwee et al., 2010). Practically, this could include undertaking the same assessment 1 week apart with a player, during a regular lesson time. The systematic error in the assessment could be limited by ensuring that any technology used is appropriately set up, while the amount of variation in player performance can be reduced by ensuring that testing is undertaken in the same environmental conditions and at the same time of day. *Stability,* although similar to the above construct, refers solely to the participants themselves, with assessment error removed. It is also typically measured on a longer time scale, often months or even years. For instance, if a player completed a putting assessment on one occasion each yearly quarter, his/her stability would be defined as the extent to which their performance stayed the same across this time period. Two further forms to consider are *intra-rater* and *inter-rater reliability*. The former typically relates to scenarios whereby a subjective human assessment is being made and can be defined as the agreement (consistency) among two or more trials administered or scored by the same individual (Baumgartner & Jackson, 1998). In a talent identification example, this might refer to the ability of a coach to evaluate the same player consistently upon repeated viewings of his/her training or competition performance. Inter-rater reliability is similar, but is differentiated by considering the agreement between different individuals rather than of the same individual. In the abovementioned example, this might consist of the extent to which two or more coaches evaluate the same player at a single time point, based on pre-defined criteria. The final form of reliability to consider is *internal consistency*. In classic terms, this is defined as the degree of inter-relatedness among test components that intend to measure the same characteristic (Mokkink et al., 2010). We might consider a scenario whereby a setting testing battery is designed to evaluate a range of golfing skills (i.e., a range of putting or chip shots from different distances).

By assessing the extent to which scores on each component of the test are related, an evaluation of its internal consistency can be made. For example, if evaluation of players putting from 1 m is similar to that from 1.5 m, then one of these distances may be removed from the assessment based on the assessment's internal consistency.

Responsiveness

Although some disagreement exists in the literature, both *responsiveness* and *sensitivity* are often used interchangeably. They refer to the ability of an assessment to detect actual and worthwhile improvements over time (i.e., between initial and subsequent rounds of testing) (Guyatt et al., 1987). On a related note, the *minimum important difference (MID)* and *smallest worthwhile change (SWC)* are two measures used to indicate the smallest change or difference in a test result that is considered practically meaningful or important (Copay et al., 2007). The final item included under this category is *floor and ceiling effects*. This refers to the ability of an assessment to distinguish between individuals at the lower (floor) and upper (ceiling) extremities of performance (Mokkink et al., 2010). For instance, if a test is designed that is too easy for a given group of participants (i.e., they are able to achieve a maximum score or performance), then this would represent a ceiling effect. An example of a floor effect would be that in which the test is so difficult that an unacceptable proportion of participants are unable to record even a low score.

Feasibility

The fourth and final category to consider when evaluating a skill assessment is its feasibility. One important feasibility item is *interpretability*. This refers to the extent to which practical meaning can be assigned to the assessment result (Mokkink et al., 2010). The level of *familiarity required* also represents an important consideration, particularly when working in the field. For instance, if it is expected that players will improve on the test over repeated assessments, then it is important to hold at least one (or potentially multiple) training session(s) earlier to ensure that any subsequent results do not reflect these improvements. The *complexity* of an assessment relates to how hard a test is to set up and complete (i.e., technology may be required as part of the administration of the assessment). This component also extends to the scoring of the assessment; for instance, also whether it is simple to obtain or whether it requires some sophisticated measurement and/or calculations. While not always a consideration at the elite level, the *cost* associated with undertaking the test is often also an important component. For example, irrespective of the quality of the test, if it is overly expensive to run, it will be infeasible for amateur- or community-level organisations to run. The final item relates to the *duration* or length of the assessment itself. It is self-evident that when looking to assess multiple players within a single session, the shorter the test, the better it is. However, an overly long assessment may also induce excessive fatigue in the performer, which may or may not be a desirable aspect of the design.

Summary and future directions

The level of detail obtained from skill assessment will continue to increase concomitantly as golf technology and resources grow. However, researchers and coaches holding themselves to higher standards with respect to how drills and assessments are designed and implemented will ensure that the evidence behind what makes players improve is increased. While researchers will always strive for a level of environmental control over their testing environments, greater adherence to the key characteristics stated in this chapter will allow for greater transfer of research findings into the applied domain.

Achieving this increased quality will also ensure that greater credence is placed on the results obtained from skill assessments in future. In particular, assessments that are indistinguishable from a practice drill should be sought after, as they provide the coach with the ability to obtain regular insight into the progression or regression of a player, with minimum disruption to valuable training time. With such well-developed tools available, the ability of coaches to assess the effectiveness of implemented interventions becomes enhanced. If administrators are able to place trust in the findings of these tests, obtaining discrete, objective measures of multiple players' ability levels in a single testing session becomes a reality. This has considerable positive ramifications for talent identification practices.

Assessing longitudinal progression of players in valid and reliable settings is a useful tool for any coach working in development. As technology continues to improve, the ability for crucial process and outcome information to be collected with ease and precision will increase. Skills testing will need to continue to not only display the characteristics shown in this chapter but also interact with technologies to remain relevant. For instance, signals obtained from lightweight, tattoo-like sensors will be common to provide real-time biofeedback into the movements and performance of players. While such technologies are unavailable for players during competition, practice and testing environments will represent the most appropriate platforms in which to take advantage of these developments.

References

Ali, A. (2011) Measuring Soccer Skill Performance: A Review, *Scandinavian Journal of Medicine & Science in Sports*, 21 (2), 170–183.

Anshel, M. & Lidor, R. (2012) Talent Detection Programs in Sport: The Questionable Use of Psychological Measures, *Journal of Sport Behavior*, 35 (3), 239–266.

Atkinson, G. & Nevill, A. (1998) Statistical Methods for Assessing Measurement Error (Reliability) in Variables Relevant to Sports Medicine, *Sports Medicine*, 26 (4), 217–238.

Baumgartner, T. & Jackson, A. (1998) *Measurement for Evaluation in Physical Education and Exercise Science*, Boston, MA: WCB/McGraw-Hill.

Bell, J. & Hardy, J. (2009) Effects of Attentional Focus on Skilled Performance in Golf, *Journal of Applied Sport Psychology*, 21 (2), 163–177.

Brouziyne, M. & Molinaro, C. (2005) Mental Imagery Combined with Physical Practice of Approach Shots for Golf Beginners, *Perceptual and Motor Skills*, 101 (1), 203–211.

Chu, Y.; Sell, T. & Lephart, S. (2010) The Relationship Between Biomechanical Variables and Driving Performance During the Golf Swing, *Journal of Sports Sciences*, 28 (11), 1251–1259.

Copay, A.; Subach, B.; Glassman, S.; Polly, D. & Schuler, T. (2007) Understanding the Minimum Clinically Important Difference: A Review of Concepts and Methods, *The Spine Journal*, 7 (5), 541–546.

Currell, K.; Conway, S. & Jeukendrup, A. (2009) Carbohydrate Ingestion Improves Performance of a New Reliable Test of Soccer Performance, *International Journal of Sport Nutrition*, 19 (1), 34–46.

Currell, K. & Jeukendrup, A. (2008) Validity, Reliability and Sensitivity of Measures of Sporting Performance, *Sports Medicine*, 38 (4), 297–316.

Daou, M.; Lohse, K. & Miller, M. (2016) Expecting to Teach Enhances Motor Learning and Information Processing During Practice, *Human Movement Science*, 49, 336–345.

Doan, B.; Newton, R.; Kwon, Y. & Kraemer, W. (2006) Effects of Physical Conditioning on Intercollegiate Golfer Performance, *The Journal of Strength & Conditioning Research*, 20 (1), 62–72.

Fletcher, I. & Hartwell, M. (2004) Effect of an 8-Week Combined Weights and Plyometrics Training Program on Golf Drive Performance, *The Journal of Strength & Conditioning Research*, 18 (1), 59–62.

Green, A.; Dafkin, C.; Kerr, S. & Mckinon, W. (2015) The Effects of Walking on Golf Drive Performance in Two Groups of Golfers with Different Skill Levels, *Biology of Exercise*, 11 (1), 13–25.

Guyatt, G.; Walter, S. & Norman, G. (1987) Measuring Change Over Time: Assessing the Usefulness of Evaluative Instruments, *Journal of Chronic Diseases*, 40 (2), 171–178.

Hellström, J. (2009) Competitive Elite Golf, *Sports Medicine*, 39 (9), 723–741.

Hopkins, W. (2000) Measures of Reliability in Sports Medicine and Science, *Sports Medicine*, 30 (1), 1–15.

Iso-Ahola, S.; Dotson, C.; Jagodinsky, A.; Clark, L.; Smallwood, L.; Wilburn, C.; Weimar, W. & Miller, M. (2016) Improving Performance by Anchoring Movement and "Nerves", *Human Movement Science*, 49, 239–247.

Land, W.; Frank, C. & Schack, T. (2014) The Influence of Attentional Focus on the Development of Skill Representation in a Complex Action, *Psychology of Sport and Exercise*, 15 (1), 30–38.

Lidor, R.; Côté, J. & Hackfort, D. (2009) ISSP Position Stand: To Test or Not to Test? The Use of Physical Skill Tests in Talent Detection and in Early Phases of Sport Development, *International Journal of Sport and Exercise Psychology*, 7 (2), 131–146.

Lidor, R.; Falk, B.; Arnon, M.; Cohen, Y.; Segal, G. & Lander, Y. (2005) Measurement of Talent in Team Handball: The Questionable Use of Motor and Physical Tests, *The Journal of Strength & Conditioning Research*, 19 (2), 318–325.

Mokkink, L.; Terwee, C.; Patrick, D.; Alonso, J.; Stratford, P.; Knol, D.; Bouter, L. & De Vet, H. (2010) The COSMIN Checklist for Assessing the Methodological Quality of Studies on Measurement Properties of Health Status Measurement Instruments: An International Delphi Study, *Quality of Life Research*, 19 (4), 539–549.

Myers, J.; Lephart, S.; Tsai, Y.; Sell, T.; Smoliga, J. & Jolly, J. (2008) The Role of Upper Torso and Pelvis Rotation in Driving Performance During the Golf Swing, *Journal of Sports Sciences*, 26 (2), 181–188.

Palmer, K.; Chiviacowsky, S. & Wulf, G. (2016) Enhanced Expectancies Facilitate Golf Putting, *Psychology of Sport and Exercise*, 22, 229–232.

Pates, J. & Maynard, I. (2000) Effects of Hypnosis on Flow States and Golf Performance, *Perceptual and Motor Skills*, 91 (3 Supplement), 1057–1075.

Pelz, D. & Frank, J. A. (1999) *Dave Pelz's short game bible: Master the finesse swing and lower your score* (Vol. 1), New York, NY: Doubleday.

Perkins-Ceccato, N.; Passmore, S. & Lee, T. (2003) Effects of Focus of Attention Depend on Golfers' Skill, *Journal of Sports Sciences*, 21 (8), 593–600.

Porter, J.; Landin, D.; Hebert, E. & Baum, B. (2007) The Effects of Three Levels of Contextual Interference on Performance Outcomes and Movement Patterns in Golf Skills, *International Journal of Sports Science & Coaching*, 2 (3), 243–255.

Pyne, D.; Gardner, A.; Sheehan, K. & Hopkins, W. (2005) Fitness Testing and Career Progression in AFL Football, *Journal of Science and Medicine in Sport*, 8 (3), 321–332.

Robertson, S.; Burnett, A. & Cochrane, J. (2014) Tests Examining Skill Outcomes in Sport: A Systematic Review of Measurement Properties and Feasibility, *Sports Medicine*, 44 (4), 501–518.

Robertson, S.; Burnett, A. & Newton, R. (2013) Development and Validation of the Approach-Iron Skill Test for Use in Golf, *European Journal of Sport Science*, 13 (6), 615–621.

Robertson, S.; Burnett, A.; Newton, R. & Knight, P. (2012) Development of the Nine-Ball Skills Test to Discriminate Elite and High-level Amateur Golfers, *Journal of Sports Sciences*, 30 (5), 431–437.

Robertson, S.; Gupta, S.; Kremer, P. & Burnett, A. (2015) Development and Measurement Properties of a Putting Skill Test for High-Level Golf, *European Journal of Sport Science*, 15 (2), 125–133.

Robertson, S.; Kremer, P.; Aisbett, B.; Tran, J. & Cerin, E. (2017) Consensus on Measurement Properties and Feasibility of Performance Tests for the Exercise and Sport Sciences: A Delphi Study, *Sports Medicine-Open*, 3 (1), 2.

Stevenson, J.; Moore, B.; Pinter, M.; Stephenson, P.; Liley, M.; Elliot, D. & Brossman, M. (2007) Effects of Trust Training on Tee and Pitch Shots in Golf, *International Journal of Sports Science & Coaching*, 2 (1 Supplement), 47–66.

Streiner, D.; Norman, G. & Cairney, J. (2014) *Health Measurement Scales: A Practical Guide to Their Development and Use*, Oxford, UK: Oxford University Press.

Terwee, C.; Mokkink, L.; Van Poppel, M.; Chinapaw, M.; Van Mechelen, W. & De Vet, H. (2010) Qualitative Attributes and Measurement Properties of Physical Activity Questionnaires, *Sports Medicine*, 40 (7), 525–537.

13

DESIGNING OPTIMAL GOLF PRACTICE ENVIRONMENTS

Sam Robertson and Damian Farrow

Introduction

Practice is arguably regarded as the most integral component in the development of expertise in sport. In golf, a large proportion of the time spent on practice focusses on the acquisition and refinement of technical skills. In order to identify the types of practice settings that best facilitate learning, the task and environmental characteristics of these contexts should be measured and monitored longitudinally. This in turn allows coaches to optimise the design of their practice drills, based on player responses to these prescribed stimuli. A variety of approaches that can be used for this purpose have been reported in the literature, which will be discussed in detail throughout this review. The review also provides a summary of the skill acquisition literature to directly inform the creation of efficient and effective learning environments for players. Specifically, it is proposed that practice design should be considered using five separate components, namely, i) specificity (also referred to as representative learning), ii) progression, iii) overload, iv) reversibility and v) movement variability/practice variety. Existing empirical evidence is provided to support how these practice environments can be systematically manipulated over time, based on information relating to the player responses, thereby potentially improving the quality of skill acquisition and refinement.

Review of current research

The aim of training (or practice) in most sports is to develop a range of capabilities that are required in order to participate in the sport at a given level. In golf, these capabilities have been categorised under five separate domains: technical, physical, tactical, mental and life skills (Smith, 2010). All these factors interact and influence the performance of a player in both practice and competition states. In the context of this review, skill is considered as a player's technical execution and adaptability, perceptual–cognitive proficiency, and his/her capacity to process numerous types of information concurrently and consequently undertake efficient movement (Baker & Farrow, 2015; Farrow & Robertson, 2016). Although skill is undoubtedly technical in nature, its expression can be considered as a combination of factors from the abovementioned five domains interacting to produce the given movement (Smith, 2010).

A recent review of skill acquisition in high-performance sports outlined the need for a more systematic approach to designing and measuring the characteristics of practice environments, along with an evaluation of their long-term efficacy (Farrow & Robertson, 2016). Although the golf science literature represents a rapidly growing field (refer Farrally et al., 2003, and Hellström, 2009, for useful reviews of this content), limited work exists with respect to optimal practice design. Providing a detailed summary of the content that is available, in the context of what has been undertaken in sport, more broadly, is therefore important. Information from both the golf-specific and general sport literature is summarised herein under the five components mentioned in the Introduction. Recommendations are also provided as to how these components can be utilised by coaches to design, measure and assess the effectiveness of their prescribed practice interventions.

Practice specificity and representative learning

One of the most commonly researched characteristics relating to skill practice environments is training *specificity*. Simply, this term has been used to refer to the extent to which the practice prescribed relates to that normally experienced by the participant in competition (Henry, 1968; Proteau, 1992). In coaching parlance, specificity has often been referred to as 'train how you play'. Despite a large amount of research being undertaken in the area, the predominant volume of this work has been limited to laboratory environments. It is therefore perhaps unsurprising that the degree of specificity required for a practice environment to confer enhanced learning for the participants remains somewhat unresolved (Tremblay, 2010).

Recently, *representative learning design* has been offered as an alternative theoretical approach to specificity (Brunswik, 1956; Pinder et al., 2011). This term refers to the extent to which the practice environment reflects the behavioural requirements of a given task (Davids et al., 2013). Pinder et al. (2011, p. 151) describe representative learning as 'the constraints of training and practice need to adequately replicate the performance environment so that they allow learners to detect affordances for action and couple actions to key information sources within those specific settings'. The constraints referred to in the definition are generally categorised as relating to the task, individual or environment (Newell, 1986). Under this model in golf, a task constraint could relate to the type of skill being performed in practice, the equipment used or any adjusted rules as part of the practice drill or performance. An individual constraint could refer to the physical characteristics of the players themselves. For instance, if a player displays reduced rotation of the thoracic spine, then he/she may need to adapt his/her movement in a compensatory manner in order to undertake certain shots effectively. An environmental constraint, on the other hand, relates to the situations that the player is practising in and may include the type of grass, the wind speed and direction, or even the sand conditions in the practice bunkers.

In golf, research has examined how manipulation of these types of constraints can lead to changes in movement execution and skilled performance, with putting being the predominant focus to date. For instance, Dias et al. (2014a) looked at the influence of different slopes and distances on the variability expressed by a variety of parameters in the putting stroke, such as the duration of the backswing and the speed of the clubhead. A second example using a similar protocol showed that through manipulation of these task constraints, players are forced to develop multiple unique movement solutions, referred to as 'functional variability' (Dias et al., 2014b). Despite this, more work is clearly needed in golf relating to how manipulation of the abovementioned (and other) constraints in practice could lead to enhanced learning outcomes for the participant. The paucity of research in this area to date is surprising given that, in golf, the ball is not moving at the point of impact and does not involve direct interaction with an opponent prior to or during skill execution. Therefore, the effect of the simple manipulation of certain constraints in practice on performance would theoretically be easier to determine than in more dynamic team sports (i.e., how the lie of the ball alters a player's skilled performance with a six-iron). What is also unclear is how the manipulation of different constraints during learning translates into a player ultimately producing an altered competition performance. For instance, in the abovementioned example, a coach may determine that manipulation of a given constraint translates to improved practice performance over time for a player. However, information confirming whether this improved performance at practice transfers to actual competition is also not yet available in golf.

What is evident, however, is that the systematic and reliable measurement of constraints during practice can open up a range of possibilities for the coach (Farrow & Robertson, 2016). Specifically, obtaining an understanding of how a player performs under different combinations of these factors can determine his/her relative strengths and weaknesses. For example, repeated practice sessions reveals that a player is performing poorly with iron shots when the wind is directed over the right shoulder; then, this can be intentionally factored into future practice sessions. As a second step, the coach can develop refined practice drills that target those areas most prioritised based on competition data. For instance, if it was discovered that the same wind conditions were experienced regularly by the player in competition, then the decision to target practice under this environmental constraint could be further validated.

Progression

When considering progression in the context of practice environments, a range of metrics (i.e., improved performance or ability to tolerate larger amounts of practice) can be used to define the concept. Of course, in the ultimate sense, progression can refer to the actual performance improvements displayed by an athlete in competition. These types of associations are commonly made in sport. For instance, if a player is spending more time practising putting and experiences a concurrent improvement in putting performance in competition, it is easy (logical?) to assume a relationship between the two. However, without ongoing, reliable measurement, such assumptions are prone to human bias and/or a lack of recall (Franks & Miller, 1986; Laird & Waters, 2008). Specifically, the coach or player may only remember those relationships that they want to remember! More feasibly, for the purposes of practice evaluation, progression of the player in the context of practice can be taken to refer to his/her performance under the same conditions. For instance, if a drill prescribed by a coach is repeated regularly by a player in consecutive practice sessions, progression could be taken to mean an improvement of performance in this drill. Of course, it should be noted that not all practice exercises undertaken by golfers are classified as 'performance drills' – some may be focussed more on learning, others on technique alterations. Apart from a performance focus (and arguably of even more practical use for coaches), progression in practice can also be considered as the capacity of the player to undertake and ultimately tolerate increased skill loads. These loads have been measured using a variety of formats in the literature, including the ability of a player to undertake higher repetition volume, an increase in task representativeness (as noted earlier) or an ability to tolerate higher levels of mental exertion. This work is summarised below.

Perhaps the most well-known theory relating to progression is that of deliberate practice (Ericsson et al., 1993). The deliberate practice theory contends that the ability of a player to develop mechanisms that improve his/her processing capabilities, and consequently, the player's skill development is directly linked to the extensive amount of training that he/she undertakes. Perhaps the most publicised example comes from Ericsson et al. (1993), wherein it was contended that performers aiming to achieve expert status in a given skill actively seek out practice environments that include goals that are set above their existing performance levels. However, despite this (and importantly from a practical perspective), the authors also state that the coach should play an integral part of the organisation and sequencing of the activities that an individual undertakes in order to achieve progression. This includes determining when increases in the difficulty of practice should be implemented. Through appropriate measurement and analysis of the contextual factors relating to practice using the abovementioned specificity/representative learning design approach, the accuracy with which these increases are implemented can be optimised.

Considerable debate exists with respect to the comprehensiveness with which the deliberate practice theory explains the development of expertise (Hambrick et al., 2014). Most notably, the theory has been criticised for its inability to explain individual differences in progression rates (Hambrick et al., 2014); most notably in chess (Gobet & Campitelli, 2007; Howard, 2012) and music (Meinz, 2000). Further, determining differences in practice type and quality between individuals longitudinally has not been undertaken in a sufficiently detailed manner, thereby making direct comparisons between these progression rates difficult. Consequently, related approaches with respect to progression have also been proposed in the literature. One such example is the Challenge Point Framework (Guadagnoli & Lee, 2004). Although advocated for use in golf (Guadagnoli & Lindquist, 2007), empirical evidence is needed with respect to its efficacy in the sport (refer Pollock et al., 2014, for an example in athlete rehabilitation). Nonetheless, the framework may provide coaches with a means of describing the effects of practice conditions on skill learning when combined with the concurrent athlete response. The framework centres on gaining an understanding of the interaction between information made available to the performer during skill execution and the actual difficulty of the skill (in both relative and actual terms). Once this is determined (often through trial and error), a 'challenge point' can be prescribed that ensures that the athlete progresses. An example might include the prescription of a short game drill, whereby the participant is required to finish the ball within a set distance/radius to an intended target (i.e., a flagstick). If the drill is too difficult (and the player repeatedly 'fails' at the task), the level of interest, performance and motivation exhibited by the player will likely be reduced (Guadagnoli & Lee, 2004). The obvious flow-on effect of this may also be a reduction in the learning rate of the player. Thus creating an environment that ensures that the athlete is adequately challenged, but not to excessive levels, represents a potentially useful example of the framework for golf.

Overload

A range of intensity- and temporal-based measures have been used to define overload in practice (discussed specifically later). These can include a number of the external measures described in the previous sections, such as the volume of practice undertaken or the relative and absolute intensity of this practice. Internal measures, such as the rated difficulty of the session by the participant themselves can also be considered. Whichever measure(s) is selected however, the predominant question relating to overload remains similar; that the association between this concept and skill acquisition/refinement is something worth understanding and ultimately manipulating.

From a longitudinal perspective, in many team-based sports, where predefined pre-season and in-season training periods are well established, practice overload can be systematically progressed or manipulated. This is typically implemented in order to coincide with critical junctures in the competition period (i.e., to peak for play-offs or final matches). This occurs in much the same manner as *periodisation* (Fleck, 1999); a training planning and prescription methodology that has origins in the physical preparation literature. Although periodisation has experienced some use in golf (Smith, 2010), the differences in tournament scheduling compared to professional team sports may mean that tactical periodisation (Crespo, 2011) may be of value in future work. This form is popular in soccer and tennis, consisting of different components of the game being practised more heavily than others at certain stages of the competitive season and thus might also be suitable for the types of scheduling prevalent in golf.

With respect to practice environments, skill practice load and overload have been mainly considered in two different ways. The first of these is *cognitive effort* (Marcora et al., 2009), which could be considered an example of an internal load measure as discussed earlier. Cognitive effort can be defined as the mental work an individual does when making decisions and which are underpinned by movement (Lee et al., 1994). Thus, this concept centres on the contention that cognition is an integral factor in how humans learn motor skills. Therefore, how cognitive effort relates to the type and magnitude of practice undertaken by an individual is important to note when undertaking the training prescription process.

Examples of cognitive effort in the literature have predominantly focussed on two main areas. The first typically involves individuals aiming to solve a given technical problem relating to execution of a skill. In golf, e.g., this may be a player working on making an adjustment to swing technique in order to perform a particular shot type. The second relates to the ability of an individual to process information to drive his/her decision-making in a complex environment. In golf, this might relate to the type of shot an individual decides to play, or the club he/she selects based on the conditions they perceive in a given competition situation. This could include the wind velocity and direction, the ball lie or the context of a player's round with respect to the leader board. Theoretically, the more complex the scenario is, the more the cognitive effort required is.

There is some evidence to suggest that high periods of demanding cognitive load are directly associated with performance decline (Nederhof et al., 2006). Additionally, simple measures such as a reduction in reaction time can provide an indication of an individual having reached a point of critical overload (or overreaching) (Nederhof et al., 2006). However, limited work has been undertaken on measuring the response of the participation with respect to the acute or chronic loads associated with skill practice. Despite this, some measures exist in other areas that may be readily importable into this domain for this purpose. For example, the session rate of perceived exertion (sRPE) measure used in physical training (American College of Sports Medicine, 2016) requires individuals to rate the difficulty of a practice or training session on a scale, often ranging between one and ten. Although simplistic, the implementation of a similar approach in skill practice could provide an early solution to obtaining this measurement.

Another area of the skill acquisition literature that has considered the influence of cognitive load in skill practice has been work examining the *contextual interference* effect (refer Brady, 2008, and Barreiros et al., 2007, for reviews). This body of work is centred on the notion that practice that requires high cognitive effort may negatively affect practice performance but will ultimately lead to enhanced skill retention and transfer to competition. In contrast, for practice undertaken in settings where lower mental effort is required, the performance will be higher yet transfer comparatively worse to competition (Magill & Hall, 1990). The predominant examples used in this work to distinguish between low and high cognitive load have been through implementations of blocked and random practice, respectively. For example, a blocked practice approach might consist of 20 × five-iron shots hit consecutively, which would generate a relatively low amount of cognitive load. In contrast, a random practice approach might include alternating from driver to five-iron, then to wedge and nine-iron and so on, in turn producing a higher cognitive load for the learner.

Research has shown that high contextual interference practice can lead to improvements in coordinated movements in tasks such as pitching and putting (Porter et al., 2007). In putting, a systematic and gradual increase in contextual interference has been shown to lead to greater skill learning in novices compared to learning through either blocked or random practice alone (Porter & Magill, 2010). It is worth noting that this gradual increase approach (and in some cases, a blocked approach alone) has actually been shown to be sufficient and, in some ways, preferable when working with novices (Wulf & Shea, 2002). This is due to the demands on the performer already being substantial, especially if the new skill is complex.

Of course, one of the challenges when implementing contextual interference in practice is that if the conditions are not appropriately monitored, progression (or a lack thereof) may be overstated depending on the nature in which the practice is scheduled. For example, an extended block of low contextual interference practice may result in an appearance of improved performance, whereas in reality, once the skill is transferred to a different context, such as a competition setting, the performance of the practised skill declines. Further work remains to be completed in this area particularly as it relates to golf practice. The relative high complexity of a golf swing may result in a sufficient amount of cognitive load being evoked such that the amount of random practice required is less than what is typically purported from the research literature where generally simple skills have been used. Clearly, careful consideration of the players' skill level and performance response to such practice is critical in setting such practice (Guadagnoli & Lee, 2004)

From a longitudinal perspective, the accumulated effects of prolonged periods of practice and its relation to the rate of learning have been investigated in the literature since the nineteenth century (e.g., Bryan & Harter, 1897). A power function was proposed (also referred to as the law of diminishing returns), where performers experience substantial skill improvements during initial practice; however, over time, this rate is diminished. Thus, more time and effort are required by the performer in order to continue to achieve incremental minor improvements. Earlier work in this area considered this phenomenon simply with respect to the time spent on a given task, with limited benefits revealed once an individual exceeded more than 4 hours of practice on a day (Welford, 1968). Contemporary perspectives on this issue have shifted to a focus on the interaction between practice quality and quantity. In simple terms, the conditions set in practice should be at a minimum level, whereby the performer is meaningfully loaded or overloaded in such a way that maintaining skill performance is challenging. When a period of stability in skill performance is observed, the coach should consider this as a sign to alter aspects of practice under his/her control to further challenge the player. This might include the organisation of the session, the level of feedback and information provided to the performer or even the structure of the practice itself.

Reversibility

The principle of reversibility centres on the idea that performers will experience some reduction in their performance levels once certain practice activities are ceased or reduced (Grout & Long, 2009). It can also be taken to refer to these reductions being reversed once regular practice is recommended. What is challenging with respect to the measurement of reversibility is that, often, it is difficult to determine the degree of learning that has been achieved in a given session, unless identical sessions are repeated consecutively. This is often not ideal practically. Further, when practice sessions are spaced, it is often too difficult to determine whether any improvements made will be maintained between sessions, or whether some reversibility will occur. As has been stated throughout this review, the systematic and reliable measurement of factors relating to the practice session or drill (such as the nature of the environment or specific detail relating to the task) can help to determine these effects more accurately.

In sports performance research, the predominant method used to determine a level of skill learning or reversibility has been through skill retention or transfer assessment (Magill & Anderson, 2007). Retention testing assesses the ability of an individual to perform a given skill following a predetermined period of no practice. This aims to separate the 'normal' variability exhibited by individuals when undertaking skilled actions from any actual alterations to their 'true' performance. However, in the field, this can be problematic, as it is often difficult and potentially unethical to request players to cease practice activities for an extended period of time, particularly if a reversible effect is anticipated. However, some of the problems experienced in the application of retention testing in a practical setting are overcome if a transfer test is used. A transfer test relies on the measurement of the skill in a different context to inform the coach of a skill's stability. In sport, competition performance is the most logical 'transfer test' condition and in turn, metric of interest. One challenge with the reliance solely on competition performance outcomes as one's learning metric is that it can be difficult to directly connect a specific period of practice or use of a specific drill/intervention with the corresponding change in competition performance. Consequently, it is also suggested that transfer tests are developed that can be used more routinely in the practice setting. For example, if a player has been working on a technical element of the swing such as keeping the face angle of the club more closed at the point of impact, this can be recorded using a variety of clubs/shots to ascertain whether the change in technique is club/shot specific or more generalisable. In summary, transfer testing of this kind is the 'gold standard' metric for assessing skill development. In most instances in golf, skill is evidenced by a player's capacity to adapt his/her swing to different circumstances based on different weather conditions, ball location or course layout. This adaptability is best examined by a combination of transfer testing approaches that couple game performance measurement with routine well-controlled transfer testing in the daily training environment.

Movement variability and practice variety

An early example advocating the benefits of movement variability comes from Bernstein (1967), who discusses the concept of 'repetition without repetition'. This is based on the contention that all human movement contains inherent variance and thus no two actions performed will be exactly the same. Specifically, as the performer adapts to his/her ever-changing surroundings, so too will his/her body and inter-limb coordination be different (Reed & Bril, 1996). Based on this position, it would be considered impractical to repeat a specific, invariant movement with high repetition and monotony during practice as it is unlikely to be exactly repeated in competition. Consequently, Bernstein contended that it was more appropriate to focus on solving a problem rather than aiming to repeat a solution. The notion of variability in the golf swing technique has received considerable support in the literature (Dias et al., 2014a) and has been well summarised by Glazier (2011).

Practice variety in golf has been well investigated in a range of settings. Early work by Moxley (1979) showed that children who completed variable practice were advantaged compared to non-variable practice condition. Interestingly, even for skills considered to be low in variability, practice with variety is regarded as beneficial. The abovementioned contextual interference effect provides an example of a case wherein work on the variety of practice has progressed. Differential practice (Schollhorn et al., 2006) represents a further example of how practice can be varied. Using this approach, the same skill is practised throughout a given session; however, the method of execution is altered. For example, an iron shot might be performed repeatedly towards a target at the same distance; however, multiple swing planes, grips, ball flights and trajectories are used in order to achieve the same outcome. This approach is based on the notion that this exploration provides greater skill stability, which may have a flow-on effect on performance (Savelsbergh et al., 2010). However, given the relative infancy of the differential practice approach in sport, further research is required before it can be strongly advocated for coaches to implement into practice.

Implications for the game

The ability of coaches to systematically account for the concepts discussed in this review is undoubtedly a challenge in many senses. The time taken to design, prescribe, assess and evaluate the practice environment as well as the player's response to such stimuli is an onerous task. Further, staying up to date with the latest research in this dynamic and rapidly expanding area is often problematic for many working in the field, due to not only time availability but also access to literature (refer Farrow et al., 2013, for a review). It is recommended that coaches and golf programmes develop strong working relationships with academic institutions and/or researchers to assist with these areas. For example, a critical element is contextualising skill development across a longitudinal player development model. Clearly, golf is a complex sport that requires significant investment from players over many years to develop the requisite skills to be successful. While there is commentary on the long-term physical preparation of athletes, there is much less information on the micro-structure of long-term skill development. It is suggested that coaches and players could collaborate with applied sports researchers to document their training approaches and thus begin to shed some light on the dynamic nature of physical development and how this may influence a player's capacity to learn or execute a particular skill. Further, in the instance that many of the principles outlined are adhered to on a grand scale, a range of improvements for the sport could be observed. For novices, the use of variable practice and problem-based learning (as opposed to repetitive practice) may encourage greater enjoyment and thus participation in the game, most likely along with improved performance. The use of more systematic approaches to practice design by coaches could also improve their work efficiency; planning (and evaluating) sessions could then become a more productive and worthwhile process. At the elite level, improving the practice habits and approaches of current players could take current performance standards seen on the professional tours to a whole new level.

Summary and future directions

This review has summarised a variety of skill practice-related research undertaken in golf, as well as other sports. It is clear that much more research is required in golf, and in sport in general, to gain a stronger understanding of how practice influences competition, particularly longitudinally. In future, this will be facilitated through many of the constraints relating to skill practice being directly measurable in real time through improvements to wearable technologies. Automated collection of data generated by these technologies, which can then in turn be reported to the coach/player directly, would allow practice to be designed with an unprecedented level of specificity. However, the quality of practice prescription and completion in the field will be dependent on the willingness of coaches to obtain access to and uptake information such as that delivered in this chapter. Additionally, given the considerable gaps identified here, it is clear that longitudinal research into the influence of practice design on the rate of skill learning in situ is required and should be a priority in future.

References

American College of Sports Medicine (2016) *ACSM's Guidelines for Exercise Testing and Prescription*, Philadelphia, PA: Wolters Kluwer.

Baker, J. & Farrow, D. (2015) A [Very Brief] Review of the Historical Foundations of Sport Expertise: An Introduction to the Handbook, In: J. Baker & D. Farrow (Eds.) *The Routledge Handbook of Sports Expertise*, London: Routledge, pp. 1–8.

Barreiros, J.; Figueiredo, T. & Godinho, M. (2007) The Contextual Interference Effect in Applied Settings, *European Physical Education Review*, 13 (2), 195–208.

Bernstein, N. (1967) *The Co-ordination and Regulation of Movements*, Oxford, UK: Permagon Press.

Brady, F. (2008) The Contextual Interference Effect and Sport Skills, *Perceptual and Motor Skills*, 106 (2), 461–472.

Brunswik, E. (1956) *Perception and the Representative Design of Psychological Experiments*, Berkeley, CA: University of California Press.

Bryan, W. & Harter, N. (1897) Studies in the Physiology and Psychology of the Telegraphic Language, *Psychological Review*, 4 (1), 27–53.

Crespo, M. (2011) Tactical Periodisation in Tennis: An Introduction, *International Tennis Federation Coaching & Sport Science Review*, 53 (19), 16–18.

Davids, K.; Araújo, D.; Vilar, L.; Renshaw, I. & Pinder, R. (2013) An Ecological Dynamics Approach to Skill Acquisition: Implications for Development of Talent in Sport, *Talent Development & Excellence*, 5 (1), 21–34.

Dias, G.; Couceiro, M.; Barreiros, J.; Clemente, F.; Mendes, R. & Martins, F. (2014a) Distance and Slope Constraints: Adaptation and Variability in Golf Putting, *Motor Control*, 18 (3), 221–243.

Dias, G.; Mendes, R.; Couceiro, M.; Gomes, R.; Clemente, F. & Martins, F. (2014b) Video Analysis of Left and Right Breaking Putts, *International Journal of Golf Science*, 3 (1), 78–89.

Ericsson, K.; Krampe, R. & Tesch-Römer, C. (1993) The Role of Deliberate Practice in the Acquisition of Expert Performance, *Psychological Review*, 100 (3), 363–406.

Farrally, M.; Cochran, A.; Crews, D.; Hurdzan, M.; Price, R.; Snow, J. & Thomas, P. (2003) Golf Science Research at the Beginning of the Twenty-First Century, *Journal of Sports Sciences*, 21 (9), 753–765.

Farrow, D.; Baker, J. & Macmahon, C. (2013) *Developing Sport Expertise: Researchers and Coaches Put Theory into Practice* (2nd Ed.), Abingdon, UK: Routledge.

Farrow, D. & Robertson, S. (2016) Development of a Skill Acquisition Periodisation Framework for High-Performance Sport, *Sports Medicine*, 1–12.

Fleck, S. (1999) Periodized Strength Training: A Critical Review, *The Journal of Strength & Conditioning Research*, 13 (1), 82–89.

Franks, I. & Miller, G. (1986) Eyewitness Testimony in Sport, *Journal of Sport Behavior*, 9 (1), 38–46.

Glazier, P. (2011) Movement Variability in the Golf Swing: Theoretical, Methodological, and Practical Issues, *Research Quarterly for Exercise and Sport*, 82 (2), 157–161.

Gobet, F. & Campitelli, G. (2007) The Role of Domain-Specific Practice, Handedness, and Starting Age in Chess, *Developmental Psychology*, 43 (1), 159–172.

Grout, H. & Long, G. (2009) *Improving Teaching and Learning in Physical Education*, London: Mcgraw-Hill Education.

Guadagnoli, M. & Lee, T. (2004) Challenge Point: A Framework for Conceptualizing the Effects of Various Practice Conditions in Motor Learning, *Journal of Motor Behavior*, 36 (2), 212–224.

Guadagnoli, M. & Lindquist, K. (2007) Challenge Point Framework and Efficient Learning of Golf, *International Journal of Sports Science & Coaching*, 2 (1 Supplement), 185–197.

Hambrick, D.; Oswald, F.; Altmann, E.; Meinz, E.; Gobet, F. & Campitelli, G. (2014) Deliberate Practice: Is That All It Takes to Become an Expert? *Intelligence*, 45, 34–45.

Hellström, J. (2009) Competitive Elite Golf, *Sports Medicine*, 39 (9), 723–741.

Henry, F. (1968) Specificity vs. Generality in Learning Motor Skill, In: R. Brown, Jr. & G. Kenyon (Eds.) *Classical Studies in Physical Activity*, Englewood Cliffs, NJ: Prentice-Hall, pp. 328–331.

Howard, R. (2012) Longitudinal Effects of Different Types of Practice on the Development of Chess Expertise, *Applied Cognitive Psychology*, 26 (3), 359–369.

Laird, P. & Waters, L. (2008) Eyewitness Recollection of Sport Coaches, *International Journal of Performance Analysis in Sport*, 8 (1), 76–84.

Lee, T.; Swinnen, S. & Serrien, D. (1994) Cognitive Effort and Motor Learning, *Quest*, 46(3), 328–344.

Magill, R. & Anderson, D. (2007) *Motor Learning and Control: Concepts and Applications* (Vol. 11), New York: Mcgraw-Hill.

Magill, R. & Hall, K. (1990) A Review of the Contextual Interference Effect in Motor Skill Acquisition, *Human Movement Science*, 9 (3), 241–289.

Marcora, S.; Staiano, W. & Manning, V. (2009) Mental Fatigue Impairs Physical Performance in Humans, *Journal of Applied Physiology*, 106 (3), 857–864.

Meinz, E. (2000) Experience-Based Attenuation of Age-Related Differences in Music Cognition Tasks, *Psychology and Aging*, 15 (2), 297–312.

Moxley, S. (1979) Schema: The Variability of Practice Hypothesis, *Journal of Motor Behavior*, 11 (1), 65–70.

Nederhof, E.; Lemmink, K.; Visscher, C.; Meeusen, R. & Mulder, T. (2006) Psychomotor Speed, *Sports Medicine*, 36 (10), 817–828.

Newell, K. (1986) Constraints on the Development of Coordination, *Motor Development in Children: Aspects of Coordination and Control*, 34 (30), 341–360.

Pinder, R.; Davids, K.; Renshaw, I. & Araújo, D. (2011) Representative Learning Design and Functionality of Research and Practice in Sport, *Journal of Sport and Exercise Psychology*, 33 (1), 146–155.

Pollock, C.; Boyd, L.; Hunt, M. & Garland, S. (2014) Use of the Challenge Point Framework to Guide Motor Learning of Stepping Reactions for Improved Balance Control in People With Stroke: A Case Series, *Physical Therapy*, 94 (4), 562–570.

Porter, J. & Magill, R. (2010) Systematically Increasing Contextual Interference Is Beneficial for Learning Sport Skills, *Journal of Sports Sciences*, 28 (12), 1277–1285.

Porter, J.; Landin, D.; Hebert, E. & Baum, B. (2007) The Effects of Three Levels of Contextual Interference on Performance Outcomes and Movement Patterns in Golf Skills, *International Journal of Sports Science & Coaching*, 2 (3), 243–255.

Proteau, L. (1992) On the Specificity of Learning and the Role of Visual Information for Movement Control, *Advances in Psychology*, 85, 67–103.

Reed, E. & Bril, B. (1996) The Primacy of Action, In: M. Latash & M. Turvey (Eds.) *Development, Dexterity and Its Development*, Mahwah, NJ: Lawrence Erlbaum, pp. 431–451.

Savelsbergh, G.; Kamper, W.; Rabius, J.; De Koning, J. & Schöllhorn, W. (2010) A New Method to Learn to Start in Speed Skating: A Differencial Learning Approach, *International Journal of Sport Psychology*, 41 (4), 415–427.

Schollhorn, W.; Beckmann, H.; Michelbrink, M.; Sechelmann, M.; Trockel, M. & Davids, K. (2006) Does Noise Provide a Basis for the Unification of Motor Learning Theories? *International Journal of Sport Psychology*, 37 (2/3), 186–206.

Smith, M.F. (2010) The Role of Physiology in the Development of Golf Performance, *Sports Medicine*, 40 (8), 635–655.

Tremblay, L. (2010) Visual Information in the Acquisition of Goal-Directed Action, In: D. Elliott & M. Khan (Eds.) *Vision and Goal-Directed Movement Neurobehavioral Perspectives*, Leeds, UK: Human Kinetics, pp. 281–291.

Welford, A. (1968) *Fundamentals of Skill*, London: Methuen.

Wulf, G. & Shea, C. (2002) Principles Derived From the Study of Simple Skills Do Not Generalize to Complex Skill Learning, *Psychonomic Bulletin & Review*, 9 (2), 185–211.

PART III

Performance development

Introduction

The intended audience of this book knows that for a game with such a simple scoring system based on a basic goal, namely, to get the ball in the hole for each of the 18 holes, golf certainly is hard. Certainly and hopefully, the goal of most golfers is to have an enjoyable outdoor sporting outing with friends. Golf is a wonderful game to play. But, frustrations abound once 'going low' becomes the golfer's focus. Perhaps the previous sentence was my experience with the game of golf!

Professional performance development ideas, systems, and – of course – 'secrets', whether focussed on the beginner or the professional, seemingly are unlimited. Without question, there are tremendous resources and golf coaches across the globe, such as those reading this text right now. Considering, as mentioned above, that the intended audience for this book is golf professionals, sports scientists, and the like, it is most likely that you are looking for more than just an infomercial or 'quick fix' for your golf game or golf coaching. In this part of this wonderful academic resource book, Performance Development, it is our hope that you find comfort in scientific performance development as opposed to one more 'unlocked secret' from 'masters' found via infomercials.

The authors are a great mixture of academics, practitioners, and golf enthusiasts. Three of the chapters focus on putting. As calculated by Bridge and Middleton, 99% of all professional golf holes (stroke play) end with the putter putting the ball into the hole. Hence, understanding putting is of great importance. Bridge and Middleton themselves review the physical science of putting. Their focus is on solving the direction and distance problem that confounds novice and professionals alike when trying to finish each golf hole. In doing so, Bride and Middleton focus on the physics of putting, aim point and green reading, direction/alignment, and putt distance control. The authors provide several practical implications that will help improve the putting instruction.

Lochbaum et al., in the second chapter of this part, discuss the psychology of putting. More specifically, they examine the literature on interventions and psychology constructs with novice golfers. Their chapter provides brief historical information as well as details of many studies that are clustered into the following topics: attention, imagery, pressure, and achievement motivation. The authors use meta-analytical techniques and results in their interpretations to help frame the strategies that are most beneficial for a coach or performance academy director to rely on with beginner golfers.

Carey et al. review the perceptual-cognitive or 'reading the green' putting literature. The authors state upfront in their chapter that 'reading the green' is difficult. Thus experts with their superior putting abilities have much to teach the rest of us. Their chapter reviews studies, most of which have been recently published, on their chosen topic. The literature base includes tour professionals as participants. Though the research base is only in the beginning stages, Carey et al. provide concrete strategies that should appeal to the readers of this book.

Of course, one's approach to performance development is vital to improvement as well as enjoyment and motivation for continued golf participation. Hence, the last two contributed chapters concern approaches to golf coaching. Gordon and Nair review the strength-based approach prominent within the positive psychology movement, whereas Carson and Collins review performance development from a biopsychosocial perspective.

More specifically, Gordon and Nair provide a historical overview of the Positive Psychology movement and how to apply the strength-based approach to golf coaching. Their chapter certainly makes one think to rethink golf coaching. Gordon and Nair provide a step-by-step example of the strength-based approach that is informative and understandable. Last, in this part, Carson and Collins provide a review of approaches centred on the contexts of making golf game modifications. Certainly, as the authors state early on in their chapter, the implementation of refinements is a great challenge, especially when the focus is on tweaking a well-automatized movement pattern. In their chapter, Carson and Collins strongly argue for an interdisciplinary approach to golf coaching. They end by presenting their intriguing Five-A Model that should stimulate thoughts among golf coaches and managers.

In summary, as you will read, a great deal of valuable scientific information with sprinkles of practical advice is found within the five chapters in this performance development part. One common take-home point found in the chapters covering putting is that future research needs to focus on putting under real conditions. Far too often, most likely because of convenience and the elimination of variability, researchers study golf putting on artificial turfs without undulations (unless examining reading 'breaks').

Concerning golf coaching and our two chapters on approaches to golf, tradition comes across as a common barrier. Golf is a game wherein improvements are frustrating and celebrations of great moments are clouded with shanks, duck hooks, lost balls, and chunks. How coaching approaches affect performance development is unknown in golf. Researchers have rarely tested coaching approaches and certainly have not tested multiple approaches within the same research paradigm. More research in this area is also strongly encouraged.

Even with the limitations and future needs, the hope is that you are either encouraged as a golfer to put into practice scientifically derived performance improvement strategies or encouraged as a researcher to further the science of golf. If you are unable to remember the advice found within this part, find space in your golf bag and carry this book with you on the course!

Marc Lochbaum
Texas Tech University, TX, USA

14

PUTTING

A direction–distance problem

Matthew W. Bridge and Nicholas Middleton

Introduction

The putter is the most used club in a golfer's bag. Typically, 40–45% of shots in elite golf are taken using the putter (Karlsen, 2010), but it is only in contact with the ball for approximately half a millisecond on an 18-foot putt (Hurrion, 2009). If we were to take this event time across 45% of a par 72 round (32 putts), this would mean that a golfer influences the ball when putting for only 0.016 seconds in a round of golf that may last upwards of 4 hours. While Broadie (2012) has argued that long game contributes more to scoring difference on the PGA Tour than putting, based upon PGA Tour statistics, 99% of the time the ball is putted into the hole[1]. This clearly illustrates the fine degree of control at impact required to determine the output of the most decisive shot in golf. Numerous areas are important in putting, and Karlsen (2010) has suggested a deterministic hierarchical model of these factors, as illustrated in Figure 14.1.

The first comprehensive work on the science of putting was carried out by the retired US Airforce Colonel Horace A. Templeton, who published *Vector Putting – The Art & Science of Reading Greens and Computing Break* – in 1984. In his work, Templeton (1984) covers all the areas that are proposed in the deterministic model of Karlsen (2010) about 24 years later.

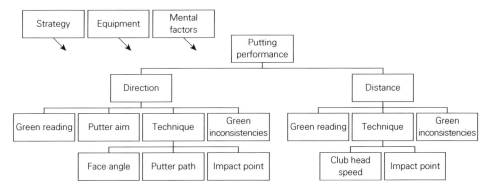

Figure 14.1 Deterministic model of the factors affecting putting performance. Mental factors, equipment and strategy can affect performance throughout the model (Karlsen, 2010, p. 7).

Source: Reproduced with permission from Karlsen, 2010.

Although Templeton is little known in the golf industry, he served as the project manager for the top-secret Lockheed Martin SR-71 supersonic Blackbird spy plane. He applied the same scientific tenets during his investigations into putting. In the 1980s, he produced the first-ever fully functioning putting simulator designed for a television broadcast, which he programmed using relatively primitive computers. As with Karlsen's (2010) model and Penner's (2002) calculated putt solutions, Templeton (1984) found putting outcome to be determined by the launch vector quotients of the start line and speed. This combination of start line and speed has a limited number of solutions governed by the capture speed of the hole. This is the problem that a golfer must solve to hole the ball. This interrelatedness of distance control (speed) and putt direction is illustrated by the work of Karlsen and Nilsson (2008a), who showed that green reading accounts for 60% of distance variability in golf putting. After considering this putting problem itself, the current chapter examines research on areas that govern its solution, focussing on those that a golfer or coach might influence.

Review of current research

The physics of putting

From a task point of view, holing the ball is fairly simple in that the ball must cross the rim of the hole measuring 4.24 inches in diameter at such a speed that it falls into the hole. It is, in fact, the only shot in golf in which for a successful outcome, the ball has to change its path immediately by 90° in the vertical plane. Some models have been proposed for analysing ball motion across the green in the literature, with the primary difference between them related to how the frictional force acting on the ball is accommodated. This ranges from the use of separate coefficients of friction for each of the sliding and rolling phases of a putt (Lorensen & Yamrom, 1992), to friction being seen as a constant over the length of a putt (Alessandrini, 1995) and the ball being considered as rolling throughout the entire trajectory of the putt, with a retarding force during the rolling phase (Penner, 2002). Grober (2011) added to Penner's (2002) motion of putting by including a generalised parameter for the putting surface affecting the putt trajectory; the product of the Stimp distance and the gradient of the green. One difficulty with this approach is that there is no published data on the initial launch speed of the ball from a Stimpmeter, although it has been reasoned that it has an initial speed of 1.83 m·s⁻¹ (Holmes, 1986). While it is clear from observations that the ball undergoes an initial period of sliding before rolling, this has not yet been fully captured in a model due to the inherent difficulties in terms of impact conditions and putter head design affecting the sliding distance (Pope et al., 2014).

The capture of the ball by the hole has been thoroughly considered by Holmes (1991), who found that in the case of a putt entering the hole at the centre of the rim, the maximum speed that it can have at this point and still be captured is 1.63 m·s⁻¹ (Holmes, 1991). For balls that cross the rim off-centre, the capture speed is less than this value. The difficulty with the approach taken by Holmes (1991) was that it did not consider whether the capture speed changes with a sloping green, instead focussing on a planar surface with no gradient. Penner (2002) found that for uphill and downhill putts, the critical capture speed increases and decreases, respectively – on a 5% slope, the uphill speed becomes 1.71 m·s⁻¹ and the downhill speed is 1.56 m·s⁻¹.

Both Mahoney (1982) and Penner (2002), by modelling the launch direction and speed of a putt and the subsequent trajectory, have suggested that the probability of holing a downhill putt is higher than that for an uphill putt of the same length. Penner (2003) suggests that this is caused by offline trajectories tending to converge back towards the target line in downhill putts and the opposite occurring in uphill putts. It is, of course, important to note that this is somewhat at odds with most golfers' preference for an uphill putt, which Penner (2003) suggests is possibly the result of a downhill miss leaving a longer second putt than an uphill one. However, observations from ShotLink data show that for a given distance, uphill putts are indeed more likely to be holed (Broadie, 2014). An interesting finding from the same analysis is that the probability of a putt being holed is more a function of distance than break (unless slope is severe and green speed is fast). Shorter putts across a slope are more likely to be holed than longer putts up a slope, again somewhat at odds with golfers' preferences (Broadie, 2014).

Putt aiming point and green reading

The work of Templeton (1984) emphasised the importance of green reading and proposed the introduction of Greens Maps that featured notation that enabled the golfer to determine the key factors of the launch vector. His pioneering work proposed that symmetries existed on the Green, for instance, all putts equidistant from the hole on a planar surface effectively share the same aiming point, which lies on a line referred to as the 'Zero Break Line'. This is the direction of the slope as it intersects the hole and represents the maximum slope through the hole. He also made an allowance he termed the 'Gravity Factor' to account for the change in aiming point for uphill versus downhill putts, something that can be linked to the differing capture speeds of Penner (2002). Grober (2011) found that Templeton's (1984) aiming point gradually enlarged as putt distance increased, with putts equidistant from the hole and within an arc spanning $\pm30°$ from the ball forming a subset that share a common aiming point. When these aiming points are mapped around a hole, a diamond shape is formed, which is centred directly on Templeton's (1984) 'Zero Break Line' above the hole (Grober, 2011).

Beyond this published work on the point at which a putt should be aimed, there is also the AimPoint® method, which is claimed to be the world's number one green reading system (www.aimpointgolf.com), and while it is clearly in use on all the major professional tours, there has been no independent evaluation of its effect on green reading. Pelz (1994) examined the green reading of all levels of players, finding that only about 25% of the break on a given putt is read and compensation occurs through aim and technique. Karlsen and Nilsson (2008a) suggest that these stroke compensations, such as aiming left at address and opening the club face at impact, should be avoided; although such compensations have been shown in skilled golfers (van Lier, 2011).

To the authors' knowledge, only one peer-reviewed article attempts to evaluate a method of green reading. MacKenzie and Sprigings (2005) looked at the efficacy of the plumb-bob green-reading method. This method sees the golfer stand behind the ball perpendicular to the slope, straddling a line that bisects his/her stance, the ball, and the hole. The player then holds the putter at arm's length and allows gravity to pull the shaft of the club to a true vertical alignment. The shaft is then aligned with the ball using the golfer's dominant eye, resulting in the upper end of the shaft being on the high side of the hole and thus indicating the slope of the green (MacKenzie & Sprigings, 2005). The authors found that unless the putt was across a planar surface upon which the player also stood, this method would provide an incorrect indication of the break. Alongside this, they found that participants failed to stand perpendicular to the slope, which resulted in a median error of ±0.08 cm in under/over-reading for a 1.4 m putt. It should be noted the participants in the study were not active golfers and while there should not be a difference in the ability to stand perpendicular to a slope (MacKenzie & Sprigings, 2005), it may be that active golfers develop an 'adapted method' as a result of trial and error on the course and practice green. However, it is evident that the utilisation of this method will not allow a golfer to accurately read a putt across a green with two or more slopes across the path of the ball or where the golfer's feet are not on the same slope as the putt.

From the perspective of vision, green reading is one of the most complicated skills in golf (Dalton, 2013). To accurately solve the distance–direction putting problem, a player must be able to judge putt distance and contours of the green and have a knowledge of the speed of the green through observation of the outcomes of previous putts on the course or practice green. While slope and contours of the green can also be judged kinaesthetically through a player's feet; vision is an important element in these predictions (Dalton, 2013). Through the use of this visual and other information, a player must predict how the ball will roll across the green and choose an appropriate starting line for the putt and starting speed for the ball. Dalton (2013) discusses how stereopsis is important for judging the distance between the ball and the hole, and colour perception and contrast sensitivity (Templeton, 1984) are important to judge slopes and contours of a putting green. It has also been suggested that visual perception of the same slanted surface can lead to a systematic underestimation of the slope over time; this process of normalisation (Bergman & Gibson, 1959) could lead to errors in green reading if a player spends too long looking at a contour.

The green reading gaze behaviour of 45 golfers, including touring professionals, elite amateurs (+1 handicap) and club golfers (10 handicap), for a simulated putt was reported by Campbell and Moran (2014). Participants were asked to precisely identify the aim line of their putt after viewing it from six different positions during a virtual tour of the green. Based upon Pelz (1994), the optimal read was calculated (15 cm) and the golfers' reads were assessed as being accurate in the range of 5–25 cm. This range was used, as it was argued that through adjustment of putt speed, all of these reads could be holed (Campbell & Moran, 2014). Moreover, 76.5% of professionals were accurate compared to 57.1% of amateurs, but no significant difference in the proportion of accurate reads was found between groups. This finding may be the result of the accuracy tolerance being 20 cm, as the authors showed no calculation for the efficacy of this reading. While the study is limited in that it was a simulated putt on a computer screen, it does suggest that expertise in green reading has a visual perceptive element and opens the potential for training in this area within golf.

Considering the paucity of academic work looking at different green reading methods, there is considerable scope for academics and golf professionals to come together in this area. With gaze behaviour having been found to differ between professional and club-level golfers in both the number and duration of fixations (Campbell & Moran, 2014), inclusion of these measurements in an on-course evaluation of green reading would be of use.

Putt direction and alignment

Two different visual alignment errors can occur in putting: the alignment of the ball to the start line and the face of the putter relative to this line at address (Dalton, 2013). The first of these assumes that a player has some sort of alignment marking on the ball that he/she uses to align the putter at address, but this is by no means the case for all golfers. The second places emphasis on stroke mechanics that require the golfer to return the putter to the same face alignment at impact as when addressing the ball.

One of the earliest studies looking at aligning the putter to the target was carried out by Sidowski et al. (1973). It was found that for a flat surface, the error of novice golfers from the centre of the hole was <1 inch on a 2-foot putt, but, on average, 4 inches on a 6-foot putt, which would lead to a missed putt (Sidowski et al., 1973). The difficulty here is that the authors provided no data as to whether this error was to the left or right of the centre of the hole. Two further conditions found that the inclusion of a ball at address on the 6-foot putt reduced error in alignment to 2 inches (Sidowski et al., 1973). Given that this data looked at novice golfers, the role of putter alignment with the ball and target in early learning should not be ignored in golf coaching and should be encouraged in instructional programmes.

Aiming inaccuracies have been reported, with McGlynn et al. (1990) finding that 64% of players (2 handicap to novice) aimed consistently left of the target. This tendency was also found by Karlsen and Nilsson (2008b), who reported a mean aim direction of $0.8\pm1.8°$ left in 32 amateur players (handicaps +3 to 35). In contrast to this, Marquardt (2007) found a tendency to aim to the right of the target ($0.35\pm1.56°$) in 99 professional players, in agreement with Karlsen's (2003) findings in elite amateur players. These inaccuracies may be a result of eye alignment; with aim being found to be significantly correlated with this (MacKay, 2008). Meanwhile, van Lier (2011) looked at head inclination, and therefore corresponding eye alignment; reporting that players aim the putter with greater accuracy when the head position is constrained such that it is directly above the ball and where the head rotates in a plane perpendicular to the ground running though the true aim line between the ball and the hole.

It has been suggested that golfers should seek consistency of aim rather than the accuracy of the aim itself since coaching aim direction is relatively easier compared to improving the consistency of aim (Karlsen & Nilsson, 2008b). This suggestion is supported by the observation that highly skilled players may compensate for the rightward errors in aim seen in novices by adjusting their aim through feedback from previous putting experiences (van Lier, 2011). In addition, players who have more variability in their aim (less precise) combine this with a higher deviation in their aim (less accuracy), with aim variability in elite players (handicap +0.4) being <1° ($0.92 \pm 0.25°$, Karlsen & Nilsson, 2008c). Variation in the initial ball start direction has been found to be 0.6°, which is lower than the variation in aim on short putts; therefore, players should concentrate on aiming of the putter face for short putts rather than aiming the ball (Karlsen & Nilsson, 2008a).

The use of differing putter alignment strategies and their effect on the accuracy of aim have been examined by Potts and Roach (2001), who compared a player's aim of the putter when standing over the putt to that taken when standing behind the line of a putt in the position a caddy might take if providing a line for a player. Low- (2–11) and mid-handicap (12–24) golfers were unable to match their conventional aiming accuracy using the caddy-related technique, with significantly more error made. Interestingly, the novice golfers in the study showed a reverse trend, with the horizontal aiming being slightly more accurate, perhaps illustrating a learned effect in the regular golfers. It does also suggest that any caddy providing a line for a player from behind needs to practise this skill since if the caddies are regular golfers, they are likely to be less accurate here compared to being over the ball. It is important that learning to aim the putter takes place with the putter and with a subsequent stroke as it has been shown that the training of perception of aim line does not transfer to the action of aiming the putter and subsequent performance (van Lier et al., 2011).

Many manufacturers place 'aiming lines' on their putter heads and players may typically draw a line on their ball. Shim et al. (2012) looked at the effects of using a line drawn on the ball to align the ball to target and on putting success. The authors found that there was no effect on the alignment of using a line on the ball. Interestingly, habitual users of this technique were no more accurate than non-users. Considering putter design, it has been found that, while golfers prefer mallet putter heads for aiming, they tend to aim better with blade designs (Karlsen & Nilsson, 2008b), although the sample used here was small compared to the range of handicaps covered. In contrast, McGlynn et al. (1990) found the addition of three parallel aiming lines to a mallet putter head to be of benefit to alignment, but Sidowski et al. (1973) found no effect of marking on a blade-headed putter.

Player distance control

Green reading accounts for about 60% of distance variability in putting, with green inconsistencies (6%) and technique (34%) providing the remainder of the variation (Karlsen & Nilsson, 2008a), suggesting that any practice of distance control should incorporate green reading.

The velocity of the putter at impact is important in governing the distance that a golf ball travels as it determines the initial launch speed of the ball. Sim and Kim (2010) and Delay et al. (1997) both found that experts had a lower club velocity at impact than novices and that this resulted in greater accuracy (Sim & Kim, 2010). This may be the consequence of experts' ability to control acceleration through impact, while novices do not, resulting in a stronger, more-consistent impulse being imparted to the ball at impact (Sim & Kim, 2010). In contrast, Delay et al. (1997) have suggested that this lower velocity is the result of experts achieving a better launch of the golf ball at impact, with consequential improvement to ball trajectory. Sim and Kim (2010) suggest that this is due to the expert player increasing the rise angle through impact, resulting in the ball entering the rolling phase earlier, although they present no data to support this factor. In considering the aspect of launch angle, it is also interesting to note the findings of Pope et al. (2014) that a negatively lofted putter promoted earlier roll of the ball and the most consistent distance. This is somewhat at odds with industry targets of loft of 1–4° with a rising stroke (Pope et al., 2014).

Players must ensure that they do not adopt the strategy of 'dead weight' putting, where the terminal velocity of the ball coincides with the edge of the hole, because surface artefact and grain can lead to the ball deviating from the intended line (Templeton, 1984). To combat this, it is commonly recommended to play the ball at a velocity to finish 12 inches past the centre of the hole (Templeton, 1984) to 17 inches past the hole (Pelz, 2000). These distances equate to the optimal hole capture speeds that the same authors suggest and as discussed earlier. This leaves open the question as to how a player should approach a putt ensuring that the ball reaches the hole at a velocity to go somewhere 12–17 inches past.

While avoiding the error of leaving the ball short is an obvious answer, de la Peña et al. (2008) found avoidant instructions in novices, e.g. 'don't leave the ball short of the hole', resulted in an over-compensatory behaviour by players when planning to putt the ball past the hole. Following this, Toner et al. (2013) looked at the effect of avoidant instructions in golf putting on the performance of low- and high-skilled golfers. On a breaking putt, golfers were instructed to hole the ball but not to miss on a particular side. There was no effect of avoidant instructions on the highly skilled golfers, but the performance of lower-skilled golfers was reduced as a result, with significant adjustments to stroke path and impact point, which accompanied an over-compensatory behaviour (Toner et al., 2013).

When preparing to putt, golfers often pick an aiming point around the hole to focus on during preparation and alignment. With novice golfers, it is more likely that their ball will stop in this area relative to the hole, e.g., an aiming focus in front of the hole results in the ball finishing short (Binsch et al., 2009). While not repeated in experienced golfers, this suggests that instructions on where to look before putting can influence the likelihood of the ball ending up in an area, an important finding since if the ball does not reach the hole, it has no chance of success. Another visual consideration is the direction of a golfer's gaze during the stroke. Binsch et al. (2009) looked at gaze prior to the stroke, and MacKenzie et al. (2011) looked at the effects of focussing on the hole or the ball throughout the stroke execution. Comparing the differing gaze techniques, the authors found practice with either strategy to significantly improve putting success. While focussing on the hole resulted in a significant reduction in putter speed variability, compared to focussing on the ball, there were no changes in the quality of impact parameters.

Technique

The ultimate goal of the putting stroke is to have a technique that can repeatedly start the ball along the desired target line with an appropriate speed to solve the distance–direction problem. The ability to repeatedly start the ball on a similar target line has been shown to be correlated with handicap, a lower handicap being associated with lower variability (Karlsen et al., 2008).

Initial start direction of the ball is governed by the face angle of the putter, the putter path and the impact point on the face, the biggest influence being the face angle (Pelz, 2000), with Nilsson and Karlsen (2006) finding horizontal miss-hits had little effect. Face alignment at impact has been shown to determine 80–83% of the initial start direction of the ball (Pelz, 2000; Karlsen et al., 2008), club path 17% and impact point 3% (Karlsen et al., 2008). Karlsen (2010) details how unpublished data from Nilsson and Karlsen (2006) showed that for every 1 cm off the midline of the putter, only a 0.34° error in initial ball direction occurred, suggesting that this should be of lesser focus for coaches. Some coaches suggest that start line error caused by the face of the putter affecting different parts of the dimpled surface of the golf ball (dimple error) can be important, but Richardson et al. (2017) found this not to be so in golfers or a mechanical putting device. Given the importance of face alignment at impact, a face change of <±1.5° from address to impact is part of an optimal putting strategy in elite players, with no change being optimal for start direction consistency (Karlsen et al., 2008), something that is close to the −0.05° result found in PGA Tour players (Marquardt, 2007).

In modelling the technique required to repeatedly and accurately deliver the club to the ball, Brooks (2002) examined three different putting strokes, with the start line as a reference and the putter head path moving as follows: straight back–straight through, inside-to-straight-through and inside-to-inside. While no conclusion was made as to the best approach, a backswing that moves the putter head inside the start line, resulting in the face being open to the start line at the end of the backswing, was recommended (Brooks, 2002). An inside path on the backswing is the commonest in PGA Tour players (Marquardt, 2007), but this gives rise to the problem of returning the face to the same orientation as at address. Pelz (2000) suggested a straight back–straight through stroke, where the putter face remains square to the intended start line, as being the best approach. While this would potentially take away the problem of controlling the rotation of the face to and through the impact, it would require a biomechanically complex action to achieve (Karlsen et al., 2008).

Two separate putting techniques were identified by McLaughlin and Best (2013) through cluster analysis of golfers' centre of pressure (CoP) movements, namely, arm putting and body putting. Also looking at CoP, Hurrion (2009) found amateurs had a greater proportion of their weight on the right foot (59.6%) compared to European Tour professionals, whose weight distribution was more even (right foot: 51.7%). Although there was no significant difference in stance width, there was a trend for a wider stance to result in less deviation of the CoP during the stroke. CoP deviation was significantly greater for amateurs, something indicative of lower stability during the stroke (Hurrion, 2009). McLaughlin et al. (2008) also found differences in CoP movement between golfers of differing skill levels. Low-handicap (0–9) players exhibited significantly lower lateral CoP movement than the mid- (10–18) and high- (18–27) handicap players in the backswing phase, while high-handicap players showed significantly more CoP movement in the downswing. However, these differences were not related to putting performance.

The putting stroke has been described as a double pendulum system, with the hands holding the club, which moves symmetrically back and forth past the impact point, while the shoulders roll in an up–down pattern (Neal & Wilson, 1985; Grober, 2009). In contrast to this, Delay et al. (1997) and Sim and Kim (2010) have found that expert players exhibit an asymmetrical putting stroke, with a shorter backswing than follow-through, although whether the experts in these groups could truly be classified as being so is debatable. However, this pattern has been found to be normal in PGA Tour players, with the backswing only being 36% of the forward swing length (Marquardt, 2007). Kinematic parameters around the putter head and CoP have been extensively studied, but there is little analysis of how the golfer moved to produce these movements. Richardson (2015) found that low variability in body segmental rotations was related to low variability in initial stroke direction. However, the difficulty here was that the author only looked at a level straight 3.2-metre putt, somewhat at odds with what a golfer will experience on a green.

Implications for the game

It is hoped that this chapter has highlighted some areas that coaches and players might consider relevant in their practice and skill acquisition, but our aim is not to be prescriptive about any element, since putting is an aspect of the game where every player has the opportunity to develop an individualised approach. Players and coaches should consider the following two actions as having potential to improve performance: aiming the face of the putter rather than aligning the ball on short putts (Karlsen & Nilsson's, 2008a) and, from the work of the same authors, the incorporation of green reading as a key of practice of distance control. While the literature has not and should not identify an optimal technique, and it is unlikely that a sole technique will exist, as highlighted by the modelling work of Brooks (2002) and the Tour player observations of Marquardt (2007) it is suggested that coaches look to develop an inside-to-inside stroke with a club face that returns to the address position at impact (Karlsen et al., 2008) and a low CoP deviation during a player's stroke (Hurrion, 2009).

Coaches and players should consider the role of gaze, and specifically where it is directed during putting (Binsch et al., 2009); moreover, coaches should be careful in using explicit avoidant instructions (Toner et al., 2013). While the 'drive for show, putt for dough' adage is less important to performance than previously thought (Broadie, 2012), golfers still have to hole the ball in the majority of the main Tour playing formats. In devoting time to learning and putting practice, they should consider the work of Evans et al. (2008), who found that 40 minutes of putting practice resulted in significant changes in full swing kinematics, altering swing duration, as well as pelvic and torso rotation. This most likely stems from the very different postural positions of the two skills (Evans et al., 2008).

Summary and future directions

Putting is a simple problem to determine the correct start line and speed of the ball. When solved, this produces the appropriate launch vector that delivers the ball into the hole. While putting is a skill often examined in research, being easy to control experimentally and with less movement variation than in full swing (Richardson, 2015), it is most commonly used as a vehicle to examine theoretical positions rather than to contribute to knowledge on performing and coaching golf. As such, those with interest in the area must discern the true reasons for the use of putting in any study when interpreting its findings. This is particularly poignant since there are very few studies in which a breaking putt or real grass is utilised rather than a flat putt on an artificial surface.

This observation highlights another key area in which progress can be made in putting research through the incorporation of more ecologically valid conditions and representative tasks (Pinder et al., 2011). There is considerable scope for work in the area of green reading, with very little currently known, something highlighted by one of the World's top putting coaches and a coach to many Major winners (Kenyon, 2008). A challenge for researchers is for their work to have an impact upon golf and its coaching; to do so, it must be seen by both coaches and players to be relevant and within their setting; something that is often missing from the majority of current work.

Note

1 Based upon the PGA Tour 'Total Hole Outs' statistic (http://www.pgatour.com/stats/stat.350.2016. html), which encompasses shots holed from off the green or fringe. Using the data from 184 players, the total hole-outs as a percentage of holes played was calculated and deducted from 100%, to provide an indication of the number of shots holed when not using a putter.

References

Alessandrini, S. (1995) A Motivational Example for the Numerical Solution of Two-Point Boundary-Value Problems, *SIAM Review*, 39 (3), 423–427.
Bergman, R. & Gibson, J. (1959) The Negative After-Effect of the Perception of a Surface Slanted in the Third Dimension, *The American Journal of Psychology*, 72 (3), 364–374.
Binsch, O.; Oudejans, R.; Bakker, F. & Savelsbergh, G. (2009) Unwanted Effects in Aiming Actions: The Relationship Between Gaze Behavior and Performance in a Golf Putting Task, *Psychology of Sport and Exercise*, 10 (6), 628–635.
Broadie, M. (2012) Assessing Golfer Performance on the PGA TOUR, *Interfaces*, 42 (2), 146–165.
Broadie, M. (2014) *Every Shot Counts*, New York, NY: Gotham Books.
Brooks, R. (2002) Is It a Pendulum, Is It a Plane? Mathematical Models of Putting, In: E. Thain (Ed.) *Science and Golf IV: Proceedings of the World Scientific Congress of Golf*, New York, NY: Routledge, pp. 127–141.
Campbell, M. & Moran, A. (2014) There Is More to Green Reading than Meets the Eye! Exploring the Gaze Behaviours of Expert Golfers on a Virtual Golf Putting Task, *Cognitive Processing*, 15 (3), 363–372.
Dalton, K. (2013) *The Vision Strategy of Golf Putting*, Unpublished PhD Thesis, Birmingham, UK: Aston University.
de La Peña, D.; Murray, N. & Janelle, C. (2008) Implicit Overcompensation: The Influence of Negative Self-Instructions on Performance of a Self-paced Motor Task, *Journal of Sports Sciences*, 26 (12), 1323–1331.
Delay, D.; Nougier, V.; Orliaguet, J. & Coello, Y. (1997) Movement Control in Golf Putting, *Human Movement Science*, 16 (5), 597–619.
Evans, K.; Refshauge, K.; Adams, R. & Barrett, R. (2008) Swing Kinematics in Skilled Male Golfers Following Putting Practice, *Journal of Orthopaedic & Sports Physical Therapy*, 38 (7), 425–433.
Grober, R. (2009) Resonance in Putting. *Eprint Arxiv:0903.1762* [Online], Available at https://Arxiv.Org/Abs/0903.1762v1 (Accessed August 30, 2016).
Grober, R. (2011) The Geometry of Putting on a Planar Surface. *Eprint Arxiv:1106.1698* [Online], Available at https://Arxiv.Org/Abs/1106.1698v1 (Accessed August 24, 2016).
Holmes, B. (1986) Dialogue Concerning the Stimp Meter, *The Physics Teacher*, 24 (7) 401–404.
Holmes, B. (1991) Putting: How a Golf Ball and Hole Interact, *American Journal of Physics*, 59 (2), 129–136.
Hurrion, P. (2009) A Biomechanical Investigation into Weight Distribution and Kinematic Parameters During the Putting Stroke, *International Journal of Sports Science & Coaching*, 4 (1 Supplement), 89–105.
Karlsen, J. (2003) *Golf Putting: An Analysis of Elite-Players Technique and Performance*, Unpublished MSc Thesis, Norway, Europe: Norwegian School of Sport Sciences.
Karlsen, J. (2010) *Performance in Golf Putting*, Unpublished PhD Thesis, Norway, Europe: Norwegian School of Sport Sciences.
Karlsen, J. & Nilsson, J. (2008a) Distance Variability in Golf Putting Among Highly Skilled Players: The Role of Green Reading. *International Journal of Sports Science & Coaching*, 3 (1 Supplement), 71–80.
Karlsen, J. & Nilsson, J. (2008b) Golf Players Prefer Mallet Putters for Aiming, but Aim More Consistent with Blade Putters, In: D. Crews & R. Lutz (Eds.) *Science and Golf V: Proceedings of the World Scientific Congress of Golf*, Meza, AZ: Energy in Motion, pp. 402–407.
Karlsen, J. & Nilsson, J. (2008c) A New Method to Record Aiming in Golf Putting – Applied to Elite Players, In: D. Crews & R. Lutz (Eds.) *Science and Golf V: Proceedings of the World Scientific Congress of Golf*, Meza, AZ: Energy in Motion, pp. 395–401.
Karlsen, J.; Smith, G. & Nilsson, J. (2008) The Stroke Has Only a Minor Influence on Direction Consistency in Golf Putting Among Elite Players, *Journal of Sports Sciences*, 26 (3), 243–250.

Kenyon, P. (2008) Distance Variability in Golf Putting Among Highly Skilled Players: The Role of Green Reading: A Commentary, *International Journal of Sports Science & Coaching*, 3 (1 Supplement), 81–83.

Lorensen, W. & Yamrom, B. (1992) Golf Green Visualisation, *IEEE Computer Graphics & Applications*, 12 (1), 35–44.

MacKay, J. (2008) An Analysis of Eye and Club Face Alignment at Address in Putting, In: D. Crews & R. Lutz (Eds.) *Science and Golf V: Proceedings of the World Scientific Congress of Golf*, Meza, AZ: Energy in Motion, pp. 202–207.

MacKenzie, S. & Sprigings, E. (2005) Evaluation of the Plumb-Bob Method for Reading Greens in Putting, *Journal of Sports Sciences*, 23 (1), 81–87.

MacKenzie, S.; Foley, S. & Adamczyk, A. (2011) Visually Focusing on the Far Versus the Near Target During the Putting Stroke, *Journal of Sports Sciences*, 29 (12), 1243–1251.

Mahoney, J.F. (1982) Theoretical Analysis of Aggressive Golf Putts, *Research Quarterly for Exercise and Sport*, 53 (2), 165–171.

Marquardt, C. (2007) The SAM Puttlab: Concept and PGA Tour Data, *International Journal of Sports Science & Coaching*, 2 (1 Supplement), 101–120.

McGlynn, F.; Jones, R.; Kerwin, D. & Cochran, A. (1990) A Laser Based Putting Alignment Test, In: A. Cochran (Ed.) *Science and Golf I: Proceedings of the First World Scientific Congress of Golf*, Champaign, IL: Human Kinetics, pp. 70–75.

McLaughlin, P. & Best, R. (2013) Taxonomy of Golf Putting: Do Different Golf Putting Techniques Exist? *Journal of Sports Sciences*, 31 (10), 1038–1044.

McLaughlin, P.; Best, R. & Carlson, J. (2008) Movement of the Centre of Pressure (COP) in the Putting Stroke, In: D. Crews & R. Lutz (Eds.) *Science and Golf V: Proceedings of the World Scientific Congress of Golf*. Meza, Arizona: Energy in Motion, pp. 239–244.

Neal, R. & Wilson, B. (1985) 3D Kinematics and Kinetics of the Golf Putting, *International Journal of Biomechanics*, 1 (3), 221–232.

Nilsson, J. & Karlsen, J. (2006) A New Device for Evaluating Distance and Directional Perforamnce of Golf Putters, *Journal of Sports Sciences*, 24 (2), 143–147.

Pelz, D. (1994) A Study of Golfers Abilities to Read Greens, In: A. Cochran & M. Farrelly (Eds.) *Science and Golf II. Proceedings of the World Scientific Congress of Golf*, London: E & F.N. Spon, pp. 180–185.

Pelz, D. (2000) *Dave Pelz's Putting Bible*, New York, NY: Doubleday.

Penner, A. (2002) The Physics of Putting, *Canadian Journal of Physics*, 80 (2), 83–96.

Penner, A. (2003) The Physics of Golf, *Reports on Progress in Physics*, 66 (2), 131–171.

Pinder, R.; Davids, K.; Renshaw, I. & Araújo, D. (2011) Representative Learning Design and Functionality of Research and Practice in Sport, *Journal of Sport and Exercise Psychology*, 33 (1), 146–155.

Pope, J.; James, D.; Wood, P. & Henrikson, E. (2014) The Effect of Skid Distance on Distance Control in Golf Putting, *Procedia Engineering*, 72, 642–647.

Potts, A. & Roach, N. (2001) A Laser-Based Evaluation of Two Different Alignment Strategies Used in Golf Putting, In: P. Thomas (Ed.) *Optimising Performance in Golf*, Brisbane: Australian Academic Press, pp. 104–111.

Richardson, A. (2015) *Biomechanics of the Golf Swing and Putting Stroke*, Unpublished PhD Thesis, Luton, UK: University of Hertfordshire.

Richardson, A.; Mitchell, A. & Hughes, G. (2017) The Effect of Dimple Error on the Horizontal Launch Angle and Side Spin of the Golf Ball During Putting, *Journal of Sports Sciences*, 35 (3), 224–230.

Shim, J.; Miller, G. & Lutz, R. (2012) Use of Ball Line as an Alignment Aid in Putting, *International Journal of Golf Science*, 1 (2), 71–80.

Sidowski, J.; Carter, K. & O'Brien, T. (1973) Variables Influencing "Lining Up the Shot" in Golf Putting. *Perceptual and Motor Skills*, 37 (1), 39–44.

Sim, M. & Kim, J.-U. (2010) Differences Between Experts and Novices in Kinematics and Accuracy of Golf Putting, *Human Movement Science*, 29 (6), 932–946.

Templeton, H. (1984) *Vector Putting*, Fort Worth, TX: Vector Putting Inc.

Toner, J.; Moran, A. & Jackson, R. (2013) The Effects of Avoidant Instructions on Golf Putting Proficiency and Kinematics, *Psychology of Sport and Exercise*, 14 (4), 501–507.

Van Lier, W. (2011) *Visual Perception and Action in Golf Putting*, Unpublished PhD thesis, Hogeschool Van Amsterdam: University of Applied Sciences.

Van Lier, W.; Van Der Kamp, J.; Van Der Zanden, A. & Savelsbergh, G. (2011) No Transfer of Calibration Between Action and Perception in Learning a Golf Putting Task, *Attention, Perception, & Psychophysics*, 73 (7), 2298–2308.

15

THE BEGINNING GOLFER

Psychological techniques and constructs affecting putting performance

Marc Lochbaum, Zişan Kazak Çetinkalp and Landry Actkinson

Introduction

Golf is a global game. Effective ways to improve golf performance, especially putting, the club that is mostly likely used the most, are of value. Commercial putting programmes abound, as does, of course, advice – wanted or unwanted – from fellow golfers. Besides solid putting mechanics, what else should a beginning golfer know about putting? A body of scientific research, most of which is experimental, exists on the psychological techniques or constructs affecting putting performance. Hence, the purpose of this chapter is to quantify this body of literature. By using effect-size values and through grouping the literature into common topics, it will be possible to suggest concrete psychological techniques that will positively benefit the beginning golfer's putting performance. To achieve this, 30 scientific papers, spanning eight different countries, were identified, with beginning golfers as participants putting with a variety of applied psychological topics. Nearly all of the participants in these studies were university students. Studies fit into the following topic areas: attention, imagery, pressure, and achievement motivation. There was also one study examining social support and one with a very comprehensive intervention. The effect-size values clearly indicated the importance of an external focus of attention, being more confident than one's fellow golfers, approaching putting in a positive manner, using any golf-related imagery, avoiding ironic or avoidance thoughts, and feeling supported. It appeared that pressure, for the most part, did not affect the novice golfer's performance simply due to a floor effect during the control condition. Considering the large meaningfulness found in many of the studies, novice golfers should find one technique to be beneficial among the many options for laboratory short, flat putts. Hopefully, the effectiveness of the techniques extends to the golf course.

Review of current research

As stated, the intention of this chapter is to appropriately group the research and use effect-size metrics to provide beginning golfers with effective suggestions to improve their putting performance. To achieve this, a brief methodology precedes the review.

Literature search and inclusion criteria

Each author conducted independent literature searches and worked together to finalize the included articles. Articles retained for this review met the following inclusion criteria: (a) at least one group of participants had to be novice golfers; (b) a sport psychology intervention or construct was used in conjunction with golf putting; and (c) an objective measure (e.g., putts holed, distance of error from hole) of golf putting performance was reported.

Effect-size guidelines

Standard effect-size guidelines for the social sciences were followed. It was possible, for nearly all of the studies, to find and/or calculate r, Cohen's d, Hedge's g, or ηp^2 (partial eta squared). The following interpretation were used: $r \leq 0.10$ as small, 0.30 as medium, and ≥ 0.50 as large (Cohen, 1990); Cohen's d and Hedge's g 0.2 was considered small, 0.5 as medium, and >0.8 as large (Cohen, 1990); and ηp^2 was interpreted as follows: 0.01 as small, 0.06 as moderate, and >0.14 as large (Green & Salkind, 2008). Within the tables, the magnitude of the effect size is provided to help guide the conclusions of the effectiveness of the interventions on golf putting performance. All extracted data are available from the first author.

Description of retained studies

Of the 40 studies that initially appeared to meet all inclusion criteria, 30 were retained. The sample range was 5–175, with the mean sample size being nearly 51, with a large variation (mean sample size = 50.93±42.62). Nearly all participants were university-aged undergraduate and graduate students. In the studies with both male and female participants ($n = 23$), the overall percentage was fairly even on average at 53.83%, though there was a large range (13%–83%). The studies and mostly likely the participants came from the USA ($n = 11$), the UK ($n = 8$), Japan ($n = 3$), Germany ($n = 2$), The Netherlands ($n = 2$), France ($n = 1$), Australia ($n = 1$), and Hong Kong ($n = 1$). We were unable to discern one investigation as the authors were from different countries (Beattie et al., 2014). The distance of the putts was mainly short 4–5 footers and were nearly all flat putts on artificial turf. Only Lochbaum and Smith (2015) conducted their work on a golf course grass putting green with natural breaks and undulations. The investigations were categorized into the following topics: attention, imagery, pressure, and achievement motivation. Two investigations did not fall into one of the four topics. Rees and Freeman (2010) studied social support. Their work strongly suggested that receiving social support improved putting performance. Beauchamp et al. (1996) investigated a comprehensive cognitive–behavioural programme. In addition to being unable to categorize this final investigation, we were unable to determine the meaningfulness of the cognitive–behavioural programme for novice golfers' putting.

Attention and the novice golfer

Attention has been a topic in the psychological literature since the late 1800s. William James (1890, pp. 403–404) defined attention as 'the taking possession by the mind, in clear and vivid form, one out of what seem several simultaneously possible objects or train of thought'. Many different models have been proposed to explain how we choose to focus our selective attention. When examining performance or skill learning, the topic is not *how* but *where* we choose to focus our selective attention. Nideffer's (1976) Test of Attentional and Interpersonal Style (TAIS) received a great amount of research focus. Though certainly intuitively appealing, evidence supporting the TAIS never seemed to emerge. However, certainly one of the two main dimensions, the direction from external to internal, has had a long-lasting impact in attention research as a mechanism by which attention affects performance. There seems little question that an external focus of attention positively benefits performance when compared to an internal focus of attention. Likewise, the ironic effect is another mechanism by which selective attention affects performance. Simply stated, ironic mental processes theory (Wegner, 1994) is based on the premise that successful thought management relies on the following two cognitive processes: automatic and controlled. For instance, while performing, unwanted thoughts, such as 'don't miss', are automatically scanned and replaced by the controlled processes. The controlled processes that are available to correct an unwanted thought may be impaired by a taxed attentional system. Thus, the unwanted thought becomes the dominant thought. For instance, the 'don't miss it short' thought is not replaced because the novice golfer is overwhelmed with attempting to read the green, listen to others in his or her foursome provide advice, and, on top of that, the wind is strong and blowing into the performer. In short, the putt is then left way short!

As Table 15.1 identifies, six studies that researched external and internal focus of attention were found: three studies that researched ironic mental process theory, and one study with avoidant thoughts that logically fit into ironic mental process theory. Clearly, an external focus of attention is superior to an internal focus of attention. Certainly, the mechanisms underlying the reasons for this consistently large meaningful result are beyond the concern of the novice golfer and the space provided in this chapter. Suffice to say, novice golfers should externally focus when putting. Concerning the ironic mental processing studies, the effect appears medium in magnitude. When putting, the novice golfer should focus externally and leave out thoughts of not doing this or that. Nike is probably still correct after all of these years with their 'Just do it' slogan as opposed to 'Do not just do it'.

Table 15.1 Summary of attention studies

Reference	Result	Performance impact	Advice
Wegner et al. (1998)	Ironic mental processing influenced golf performance as it caused the undesired effect (putting past the hole).	Medium	Tell yourself to putt the ball in the hole, not past or short of the hole.
Beilock et al. (2001)	Replacing negative images (ironic in nature) with positive images every so often improves performance, more so than trying on every putting attempt.	Medium	Be sure to replace negative images with positive ones every so often. Do not try too hard!
Binsch et al. (2009)	Ironic mental processing influenced golf performance by causing the undesired effect (putting past the hole), and visual gaze was important to this effect.	Small	Fixate your gaze on where you would like the ball to stop.

(Continued)

Table 15.1 (Continued)

Reference	Result	Performance impact	Advice
Vine and Wilson (2010)	Quiet eye training is effective in minimizing pressure.	Large	Learning the quiet eye technique is of value as it involves simply focussing on the hole and then the ball before putting (so hold an external focus of attention).
Neumann and Thomas (2011)	Putting without any attentional focus instructions, with a performance or outcome focus, is better for performance when compared to process, or trust your body attentional foci when putting.	Medium to large	Just putt it or have performance/outcome focus.
Toner et al. (2013)	Engaging in avoidant thoughts is detrimental to putting performance.	Medium	Engage in neutral-to-positive thoughts.
Munzert et al. (2014)	An external focus of attention (compared to an internal focus) leads to improved performance (reduced absolute error from putting target) by way of improved putting stroke movement (more pendulum like).	Large	Focus on the ball, not on yourself.
Land et al. (2014)	An external focus of attention leads to improved performance because it develops, largely, a complete mental representation of the task.	Large	Focus on the ball, not on yourself.

Imagery and the novice golfer

As Jack Nicklaus once said, 'I never hit a shot even in practice without having a sharp in-focus picture of it in my head' (Kremer & Moran, 2013, p. 92). The impact of mental practice or imagery on sport performance has been a widely researched topic since before even the great Jack Nicklaus began playing golf. Vealey and Greenleaf (2009, p. 267) define imagery as 'a mental process that uses all of the senses to create or recreate experiences in the mind'. Though not every sense has to be used for effective imagery, the general idea certainly is to create a mental representation that mimics reality. Further reading into Nicklaus's thoughts on imagery points to how he constructed his golf shots close to reality before swinging. Concerning the effectiveness of imagery on performance, Feltz and Landers (1983) were able to include 60 studies dating back to the 1950s in their mental practice meta-analysis, with the conclusion that mental practice or imagery is moderately better than no practice at all. A scan of the imagery or mental practice literature certainly suggests that interest has maintained and/or even grown since Feltz and Landers' meta-analysis.

As Table 15.2 identifies, six studies that researched imagery and the novice golfer's putting performance were located. The studies examined imagery from some perspectives and/or the qualities of imagery. Most likely due to the variety of research questions, the meaningfulness

Table 15.2 Summary of imagery studies

Reference	Result	Performance impact	Advice
Kornspan et al. (2004)	Pre-performance imagery and positive self-talk improve performance but no more than simply practising compared to the no-practice group.	Large	Be sure to use pre-performance imagery or positive self-talk if unable to practise.
Peluso et al. (2005)	Compared to a control group, all forms of imagery and self-talk improve performance.	Small to large	Be sure to imagine success and engage in positive self-talk prior to and even while putting.
Ramsey et al. (2008)	Facilitative imagery improves putting performance (putts holed) compared to the debilitative imagery group and the control group. Using no imagery is better than using debilitative imagery.	Small to medium	Be sure to use facilitative imagery.
Beilock and Gonso (2008)	More time available for imaging was beneficial to putting performance.	Large	Take your time when putting is the bottom line.
Forlenza et al. (2013)	Improved performance (short-distance putts made) favoured using any imagery (slow, real time, and fast) compared to the control group at post-test evaluation.	Medium	See yourself at any mental speed making short-range putts.
	Imagery use was not as effective compared to controls of longer putts.	Negligible	
Williams et al. (2013)	LSRT is effective in improving putting performance (both holed and distance error).	Large	Read up on LSRT and learn the techniques.

of imagery for putting performance ranged from negligible to large. As with the results of Feltz and Landers, imagery is not better than physical practice as found by Kornspan et al. (2004). However, certainly, if one has the time to image, it is worth using before putting, and using the layered stimulus and response training (LSRT) appears to be worth the novice golfer's time.

Pressure and the novice golfer

Investigating the effects of pressure and/or interventions to elevate its debilitating effects is very logical because – whether real or simply perceived – pressure putts are found on the golf course! Though different theories abound as to why pressure is debilitating and though pressure/anxiety/stress may be facilitative in nature (Jones, 1995), choking models and/or single constructs from choking models (self-consciousness) were the focus of the included studies. Choking under pressure in academic circles is attributed to Baumeister's (1984) work. Choking under pressure models incorporate, for the most part, attentional and drive theories (Baumeister & Showers, 1986). Attentional theories of choking under pressure describe how automatic processes such as a routine putt suddenly require the performer's attention and/or divert the performer's attention away from a small nuance such as a small break in the putt. In golf, there are many examples of golfers missing a routine short putt to win an event. For instance, an apparent high-stake golfing major breakdown was Dustin Johnson's three-putt on the 18th green at the 2015 U.S. Open.

Drive theory explanations for choking under pressure have been around for >100 years. The inverted-U theory (Yerkes & Dodson, 1908) and Easterbrook's cue utilization theory (1959) are two such drive-based theories used to explain choking under pressure. Especially for more complex or fine motor-skilled movements such as putting, both predict that arousal and/or pressure is facilitative up to a point, after which they become very debilitative. Certainly, many other drive or arousal-based theories and models exist, such as the cusp catastrophe model, and the reader is encouraged to seek out more of these models and theories. The basic point for the current review is that the included experiments attempted to manipulate pressure to induce the choking and, in some cases, to provide an intervention to reduce the chance of choking under pressure.

Eight studies, as detailed in Table 15.3, were included in this review. For the most part, the effect sizes were small in magnitude. The main issues seemed to be that by definition, the novice golfers were simply not very good at the initial putting task. Thus, there was little room for decrements to occur during pressure conditions. Even the prospects of losing or earning money did not influence performance! A few of the investigations did have an experienced group of golfers. The experienced golfers' putting performances were far superior to the novice golfers' putting performances in both the control and pressure conditions. Simply stated, novice golfers have little room for the immediate decrement in performance as a result of a pressure condition or manipulation. Of note, it seemed that distracting thoughts were effective (Balk et al., 2013) and could be a reasonable strategy for the novice golfer when facing self-perceived high-pressure situations on the golf course.

Table 15.3 Summary of pressure studies

Reference	Result	Performance impact	Advice
Kinrade et al. (2010)	Pressure slightly impairs performance. Moreover, engaging in reinvesting or being high in public self-consciousness negatively affects performance when going from low- to high-pressure putting conditions.	Small Reinvesting: small Public self-consciousness: medium	Your low- and high-pressure putting will not differ much, so do not worry about pressure putting. Think neutral-to-positive external thoughts and know your limitations in public.
Tanaka and Sekiya (2010a)	The putting task was very complex. Based on the score possible, the novice putters were not very good.	>Small	Pressure will not affect your difficult putts.
Tanaka and Sekiya (2010b)	Pressure certainly did not help putting performance.	No effect size	Perceived pressure will impair your performance in that you will not get better.
Cooke et al. (2010)	Perceiving pressure (associated with increased anxiety, mental effort, and energy expended) negatively affects putts holed, though this does not negatively affect radial error.	Medium	Keep holing putts in perspective.

Tanaka and Sekiya (2011)	Cash reward does not help improve performance very much. The threat of shock based on putting performance is not very likely on the golf course.	<Small	Keep your money in your pocket.
Land and Tenenbaum (2012)	Distractions did not affect putting performance a great deal (which, compared to skilled performers, was very low. Hence, getting worse might not have been possible with pressure).	Small	The good news is your low- and high-pressure putting may not differ, so do not sweat the pressure putts.
Balk et al. (2013)	Engaging in distracting thoughts is an effective strategy to improve performance under pressure.	Large	Focus on something other than the magnitude of the putt.
	Reappraising the situation in a positive manner slightly neutralizes the negative effect of pressure on putting performance.	Small	
Malhotra et al. (2015)	Losing *earned* money as a source of anxiety does not worsen golf putting performance.	Small	Keep your money in your pocket. It does not help or hurt, so do not waste it.

Motivation theories and the novice golfer

Certainly, motivation is a key factor in any achievement context. Feelings of hope, competence, and situational confidence are all certainly needed to play golf! The literature in this area contains three dominant motivational theories in sport psychology: attribution theory (Weiner, 1985), self-efficacy theory (Bandura, 1997), and approach-avoidance achievement goal theory (Elliot & MacGregor, 2001).

Attribution theory examines the impact of causal attribution patterns on achievement and performance through emotions. In sport, attributions are the specific reasons performers ascribe to outcomes such as making an important putt as well as missing an important putt. Three attribution dimensions affect future behaviours by influencing the expectancy of future success. The locus of causality dimension relates to whether the attributed cause is internal or external to the performer. The stability dimension (permanent or temporary) relates to the performer's perception of the temporal duration of the attributed cause. Last, the personal controllability dimension refers to the performer's belief as to control (yes or no) of the attributed cause. The combinations of attribution dimensions determine feelings of hope or hopelessness for future success. Performers who use internal, controllable, and unstable (ICU) causes to explain a failure are more likely to hold on to future success expectancies. For instance, a poor putting round is attributed to lack of concentration, an ICU cause. Hence, the performer may improve his or her concentration and be hopeful. However, if a performer attributes a failure to an internal, uncontrollable, and stable (IUS) cause such as low putting ability, then future expectancy for a good putting round are slim. Likewise, for attributes with an external, uncontrollable, and stable cause, such as tough putting greens, the performer will have low expectancy for success on the same or similar greens in the future.

The approach-avoidance achievement goal framework posits two goals, mastery and performance, which are crossed with the approach-avoidance dimension, producing four distinct ways in which competence is defined and viewed. Competence based on the mastery-approach goal is defined by a focus on task-based attainment such as improving upon one's record of putts per round, whereas competence based on the mastery-avoidance goal is defined by avoiding more putts per upcoming round. From the performance goal perspective, the performance-approach goal defines competence based on normative achievements, such as fewer putts within a foursome, whereas the performance-avoidance goal defines competence based on avoiding displays of normative incompetence, such as not being the worst putter in one's foursome. Specific to sport, Lochbaum and Gottardy's (2015) meta-analysis provided evidence that both the mastery- and performance-approach goals are moderately related to performance, with the performance contrast score (performance-approach minus performance-avoidance scores) being moderately large in relation to performance.

For the majority of modern-day applied sport psychology, situation-specific self-confidence has been extensively studied from Bandura's (1977) self-efficacy theory. Self-efficacy is typically and simply defined as the strength of one's beliefs in one's ability to meet the situational demands to obtain a desired outcome or goal. Self-efficacious thoughts are influenced by previous experiences, vicarious experiences, social persuasion, and interpretation of physiological factors (e.g., butterflies in one's stomach). Moritz et al. (2000) conducted a meta-analysis on self-efficacy (Bandura, 1997) and sport performance. They reported a mean correlation of 0.38 across 45 studies and 102 correlations. Though significant moderators were found, such as objectivity of performance, concordance between measures, time of assessment, and familiarity of the task to the participants, none changed the effect-size interpretation from moderate to large. Since the time of these meta-analyses, a body of research has emerged, which questions exactly how important efficacy assessments are to performance *within* participants as opposed to the traditional cross-sectional or *between*-participants reporting of data.

This section (Table 15.4) discusses some articles that obtained moderate-to-moderately large effect sizes. Competence is defined by wanting to win (performance-approach achievement goal) and ascribing success to IUC factors is advised for the beginning golfer. From the self-efficacy studies, we learned that novice golfers greatly overestimate their putting skills. Hence, for a novice, the impact of confidence is negligible, but among novices, self-efficacy has a large effect. However, changes in putting confidence via practice manipulations should be researched further, in conjunction with other proven applied psychological techniques. It seems that the conditions under which one learns to putt affects confidence/positive expectancies and, ultimately, performance.

Table 15.4 Summary of motivation theory studies

Reference	Result	Performance impact	Advice
Le Foll et al. (2008)	A functional attribution style is better for performance than a dysfunctional style.	At trait level: medium	Ascribing success to internal, controllable, and unstable factors (a functional style) is better for putting performance.

Beattie et al. (2011)	Among participants, higher-efficacious participants (magnitude and strength of efficacy) made more putts, though all participants overestimated putting performance.	Medium to large	Be more confident than anyone in your foursome. Do not worry about your confidence, just putt.
	Within a participant, self-efficacy did not predict subsequent performance.	Negligible	
Beattie et al. (2014)	Self-efficacy magnitude is a mental factor when performing under dynamic learning conditions (change in the break, distance of putt) for continued improvement. For static putting (no change in the break, distance of putt), self-efficacy is not important.	Small	Move your ball around while practising putting to create a realistic picture of the game and tell yourself you believe you can make the putts.
Lochbaum and Smith (2015)	Thoughts of being excited to beat others more than wanting to avoid getting beat and wanting to personally improve more than avoiding getting worse lead to improved performance.	Performance-approach goal: medium Mastery-approach goal: small	Write down the thought of being excited on a notecard and read it while on the putting green.
Palmer et al. (2016)	Providing more opportunities for putting success during learning (larger putting hole radius) leads to improved performance.	Retention: large Transfer: large	When practising, create a larger radius around the hole.

Implications for the game

Golf is a difficult game to learn and play if one's standards are to play par golf. Professional golfers make the game seem so easy to play at par compared to the reality of the beginning golfer. The novice golfer is probably unaware that most golfers are unable to break 90 within their lifetime. Unless one holes out from off the green or simply quits before holing out, the last putt is the last chance for a positive experience. Thus, putting is important for more than just a lower score, but for a feel-good feeling walking to the car park, clubhouse, or home. Based on the reviewed studies by grouped topics, some implications for the novice golfer are presented.

The attentional focus has a large impact on putting performance in novice golfers. Novice golfers should focus externally as opposed to internally. Focussing on ball speed or the line of the putt is a simple and effective performance-enhancing strategy. Though certainly something discussed within all sports as a huge benefit, confidence – unfortunately – within a novice golfer from putt to putt does not improve performance. The novice golfer seems to greatly overestimate his or her putting ability. However, it is of great value to be the most confident golfer within a group of novice golfers on the green when putting. The most confident putter in a group will perform best. Thus, if you are a beginning golfer, be the most confident putter in your group. Furthermore, concerning confidence and putting, one should practise putting on a greater area (i.e., putting hole size).

The impact of facilitative imagery on putting performance appears large. There are exceptions, but novice golfers should engage in imagery (e.g., visualizing making a putt) before putting. Certainly, novice golfers should not engage in debilitative imagery. If one has a debilitative image, it is better to just putt the ball without an image. It is also better to just putt the ball regardless of perceived importance because pressure does not affect the novice's putting performance. Though this result seems illogical, the most likely reason that putting performance does not suffer much more with pressure is that the novice golfer is simply a poor putter. Thus, based on the research with cash prizes, the novice golfer should not gamble! The one area of concern with pressure is related to a disposition for high public self-consciousness.

Concerning thought patterns, certainly, a clear facilitative thought is better than 'don't putt it short/long' or 'don't miss' thoughts. Though only documented in one study, intentionally providing social support positively affects putting performance. Golfers should always support each other, especially following the advice to not gamble! Providing social support may have a large and positive meaningful impact on putting performance. Last, though there are few comprehensive interventions for the novice golfer, it appears that programmes that integrate applied psychological techniques during practice will positively benefit the novice golfer.

Summary and future directions

There are some statements about each covered topic in this review that merit a summary sentence or two. For instance, external focus of attention should always be an intervention condition as it seems to very meaningfully benefit a novice's putting performance. Understanding the impact of this very meaningful attentional focus strategy, relative to other strategies within the same research paradigm, would further research concerned with improving novice golfers' putting performance and, thus, the overall golfing experience. Currently, we only know that an external focus of attention is much better than an internal focus of attention. From the research on confidence, we learn that novice golfers greatly overestimate their putting skills. Hence, for a novice, the impact of confidence is negligible. However, changes in putting confidence via practice manipulations should be researched further in conjunction with other proven applied psychological techniques. It seems that the conditions under which one learns to putt affects confidence/positive expectancies and, ultimately, performance. Imagery research has been extensive and very detailed.

Future directions point to using facilitative imagery in real golfing conditions. Focussing on pressure manipulations is not a fruitful area of research as novice golfers simply do not have the putting skills to be affected positively or negatively by pressure if the putt is of any difficulty. Last, thoughts do affect putting performance. In all of the areas reviewed, future research directions point strongly to moving from the laboratory setting to the golf course.

References

Balk, Y.; Adriaanse, M.; De Ridder, D. & Evers, C. (2013) Coping Under Pressure: Employing Emotion Regulation Strategies to Enhance Performance Under Pressure, *Journal of Sport and Exercise Psychology*, 35 (4), 408–418.

Bandura, A. (1997) *Self-Efficacy: The Exercise of Control*, New York, NY: Freeman.

Baumeister, R. (1984) Choking Under Pressure: Self-consciousness and Paradoxical Effects of İncentives on Skillful Performance, *Journal of Personality and Social Psychology*, 46 (3), 610–620.

Baumeister, R. & Showers, C. (1986) A Review of Paradoxical Performance Effects: Choking Under Pressure in Sports and Mental Tests, *European Journal of Social Psychology*, 16 (4), 361–383.

Beattie, S.; Fakehy, M. & Woodman, T. (2014) Examining the Moderating Effects of Time on Task and Task Complexity on the Within Person Self-efficacy and Performance Relationship, *Psychology of Sport and Exercise*, 15 (6), 605 610.

Beattie, S.; Lief, D.; Adamoulas, M. & Oliver, E. (2011) Investigating the Possible Negative Effects of Self-efficacy Upon Golf Putting Performance, *Psychology of Sport and Exercise*, 12 (4), 434–441.

Beauchamp, P.; Halliwell, W.; Fournier, J. & Koestner, R. (1996) Effects of Cognitive-behavioral Psychological Skills Training on the Motivation, Preparation, and Putting Performance of Novice Golfers, *The Sport Psychologist*, 10 (2), 157–170.

Beilock, S.; Afremow, J.; Rabe, A. & Carr, T. (2001) "Don't Miss!" The Debilitating Effects of Suppressive Imagery on Golf Putting Performance, *Journal of Sport and Exercise Psychology*, 23 (3), 200–221.

Beilock, S. & Gonso, S. (2008) Putting in the Mind Versus Putting on the Green: Expertise, Performance Time, and the Linking of Imagery and Action, *The Quarterly Journal of Experimental Psychology*, 61 (6), 920–932.

Binsch, O.; Oudejans, R.; Bakker, F. & Savelsbergh, G. (2009) Unwanted Effects in Aiming Actions: The Relationship Between Gaze Behavior and Performance in a Golf Putting Task, *Psychology of Sport and Exercise*, 10 (6), 628–635.

Cohen, J. (1990) Things I Have Learned (So Far), *American Psychologist*, 45 (12), 1304–1312.

Cooke, A.; Kavussanu, M.; Mcintyre, D. & Ring, C. (2010) Psychological, Muscular and Kinematic Factors Mediate Performance Under Pressure, *Psychophysiology*, 47 (6), 1109–1118.

Easterbrook, J. (1959) The Effect of Emotion on Cue Utilization and the Organization of Behavior, *Psychological Review*, 66 (3), 183–201.

Elliot, A. & McGregor, H. (2001) A 2 × 2 Achievement Goal Framework, *Journal of Personality and Social Psychology*, 80 (3), 501–519.

Feltz, D. & Landers, D. (1983) The Effects of Mental Practice on Motor Skills, Learning and Performance: A Meta-Analysis, *Journal of Sport Psychology*, 5 (1), 25–57.

Forlenza, S.; Weinberg, R. & Horn, T. (2013) Imagery Speed and Self-efficacy: How Fast (Or Slow) to Go? *International Journal of Golf Science*, 2 (2), 126–141.

Green, S. & Salkind, N. (2008) *Using SPSS for Windows and Macintosh: Analyzing and Understanding Data*, Upper Saddle River, NJ: Pearson/Prentice Hall.

James, W. (1890) *The Principles of Psychology* (Vol. 1), New York, NY: Henry Holt and Company.

Jones, G. (1995) More than Just a Game: Research Developments and Issues in Competitive Anxiety in Sport, *British Journal of Psychology*, 86 (4), 449–478.

Kinrade, N.; Jackson, R. & Ashford, K. (2010) Dispositional Reinvestment and Skill Failure in Cognitive and Motor Tasks, *Psychology of Sport and Exercise*, 11 (4), 312–319.

Kornspan, A.; Overby, L. & Lerner, B. (2004) Analysis and Performance of Pre-performance Imagery and Other Strategies on a Golf Putting Task, *Journal of Mental Imagery*, 28 (3–4), 59–74.

Kremer, J. & Moran, A.P. (2013) *Pure Sport: Practical Sport Psychology* (2nd Ed.), New York, NY: Routledge.

Land, W. & Tenenbaum, G. (2012) An Outcome-and Process-oriented Examination of a Golf-specific Secondary Task Strategy to Prevent Choking Under Pressure, *Journal of Applied Sport Psychology*, 24 (3), 303–322.

Land, W.; Frank, C. & Schack, T. (2014) The Influence of Attentional Focus on the Development of Skill Representation in a Complex Action, *Psychology of Sport and Exercise*, 15 (1), 30–38.

Le Foll, D.; Rascle, O. & Higgins, N. (2008) Attributional Feedback-induced Changes in Functional and Dysfunctional Attributions, Expectations of Success, Hopefulness, and Short-term Persistence in a Novel Sport, *Psychology of Sport and Exercise*, 9 (2), 77–101.

Lochbaum, M. & Gottardy, J. (2015) A Meta-analytic Review of the Approach–avoidance Achievement Goals and Performance Relationships in the Sport Psychology Literature, *Journal of Sport and Health Science*, 4 (2), 164–173.

Lochbaum, M. & Smith, C. (2015) Making the Cut and Winning a Golf Putting Championship: The Role of Approach-avoidance Achievement Goals, *International Journal of Golf Science*, 4 (1), 50–66.

Malhotra, N.; Poolton, J.; Wilson, M.; Uiga, L. & Masters, R. (2015) Examining Movement-specific Reinvestment and Performance in Demanding Contexts, *Journal of Sport and Exercise Psychology*, 37 (3), 327–338.

Moritz, S.; Feltz D.; Fahrbach, K. & Mack, D. (2000) The Relation of Self-efficacy Measures to Sport Performance: A Meta-Analytic Review, *Research Quarterly for Exercise and Sport*, 71 (3), 280–294.

Munzert, J.; Maurer, H. & Reiser, M. (2014) Verbal-motor Attention-focusing Instructions Influence Kinematics and Performance on a Golf-putting Task, *Journal of Motor Behavior*, 46 (5), 309–318.

Neumann, D. & Thomas, P. (2011) Cardiac and Respiratory Activity and Golf Putting Performance Under Attentional Focus Instructions, *Psychology of Sport and Exercise*, 12 (4), 451–459.

Nideffer, R. (1976) Test of Attentional and Interpersonal Style, *Journal of Personality and Social Psychology*, 34 (3), 394–404.

Palmer, K.; Chiviacowsky, S. & Wulf, G. (2016) Enhanced Expectancies Facilitate Golf Putting, *Psychology of Sport and Exercise*, 22, 229–232.

Peluso, E.; Ross, M.; Gfeller, J. & Lavoie, D. (2005) A Comparison of Mental Strategies During Athletic Skills Performance, *Journal of Sports Science and Medicine*, 4 (4), 543–549.

Ramsey, R.; Cumming, J. & Edwards, M. (2008) Exploring a Modified Conceptualization of Imagery Direction and Golf Putting Performance, *International Journal of Sport and Exercise Psychology*, 6 (2), 207–223.

Rees, T. & Freeman, P. (2010) Social Support and Performance in a Golf-putting Experiment, *The Sport Psychologist*, 24 (3), 333–348.

Tanaka, Y. & Sekiya, H. (2010a) The Influence of Audience and Monetary Reward on the Putting Kinematics of Expert and Novice Golfers, *Research Quarterly for Exercise and Sport*, 81 (4), 416–424.

Tanaka, Y. & Sekiya, H. (2010b) The Relationships Between Psychological/Physiological Changes and Behavioral/Performance Changes of a Golf Putting Task Under Pressure, *International Journal of Sport and Health Science*, 8, 83–94.

Tanaka, Y. & Sekiya, H. (2011) The Influence of Monetary Reward and Punishment on Psychological, Physiological, Behavioral and Performance Aspects of a Golf Putting Task, *Human Movement Science*, 30 (6), 1115–1128.

Toner, J.; Moran, A. & Jackson, R. (2013) The Effects of Avoidant Instructions on Golf Putting Proficiency and Kinematics, *Psychology of Sport and Exercise*, 14 (4), 501–507.

Vealey, R. & Greenleaf, C. (2009) Seeing Is Believing: Understanding and Using Imagery in Sport, In: J. Williams (Ed.), *Applied Sport Psychology: Personal Growth to Peak Performance* (6th Ed.), New York, NY: Mcgraw-Hill, pp. 267–304.

Vine, S. & Wilson, M. (2010) Quiet Eye Training: Effects on Learning and Performance Under Pressure, *Journal of Applied Sport Psychology*, 22 (4), 361–376.

Wegner, D. (1994) Ironic Processes of Mental Control, *Psychological Review*, 101 (1), 34–52.

Wegner, D.; Ansfield, M. & Pilloff, D. (1998) The Putt and the Pendulum: Ironic Effects of the Mental Control of Action, *Psychological Science*, 9 (3), 196–199.

Weiner, B. (1985) An Attributional Theory of Achievement Motivation and Emotion, *Psychological Review*, 92 (4), 548–573.

Williams, S.; Cooley, S. & Cumming, J. (2013) Layered Stimulus Response Training Improves Motor Imagery Ability and Movement Execution, *Journal of Sport and Exercise Psychology*, 35 (1), 60–71.

Yerkes, R. & Dodson, J. (1908) The Relation of Strength of Stimulus to Rapidity of Habit-Formation, *Journal of Comparative Neurology and Psychology*, 18 (5), 459–482.

16

PERCEPTUAL-COGNITIVE EXPERTISE IN GOLF PUTTING

Laura M. Carey, Robin C. Jackson, Malcolm M. Fairweather, Joe Causer and A. Mark Williams

Introduction

In golf putting, 'reading the green' is a difficult task. A study of university golfers completing 3-m putts found that they were significantly worse on severely breaking (11% success) and moderately breaking putts (41% success) than on flat putts (51% success) (Wilson & Pearcy, 2009). This chapter focusses on the perceptual-cognitive phase of putting preparation, the period in which golfers make decisions about the optimal path from the ball position to the hole, taking into consideration the slope, break, and green contours (Campbell & Moran, 2014). In this phase, golfers attempt to determine the correct aim line and required force before taking up their putting stance in preparation for the putting stroke (van Lier et al., 2011).

The aim of the chapter is to synthesise existing work to highlight how superior performance in putting has been captured and to consider findings in relation to expertise. To place this in context, there are few studies on this aspect of golf putting, and researchers have highlighted the need to recognise that "successful putting entails more than proficient movement control, but requires . . . skillful perception" (van Lier et al., 2011, p. 349). Golf putting is a complex perceptual-cognitive skill owing to unpredictable environmental factors, such as the strength and direction of the wind, the influence of other weather conditions on ambient light and putting surface characteristics, and the variable topology and grain of the green. It is, therefore, likely that the ability to 'read' a putt and select the most appropriate strategy is a significant determinant of expertise in putting (Pelz, 1994; Karlsen & Nilsson, 2008).

Review of current research

Observation of world-class golf putters operating within the rules that govern their behaviour reveals an evaluation process that is time constrained, ordered, and predictable. Accordingly, the expert performance approach, originally proposed by Ericsson and Smith (1991; refer also Williams & Ericsson, 2005) can be applied to compare the demands of expert golf putting with scientific studies in this area. A systematic review framework was applied based on the operational definition of the perceptual-cognitive phase of golf putting. Consistent with this definition, eye movements and other behaviours that occur after the golfer has taken up his/her putting stance are not considered in this chapter. Ten studies focussing on the perceptual-cognitive phase of golf putting were identified, of which four focussed on visual aspects of reading the slope of the green and six focussed more broadly on thought processes during this preparation phase (for a summary, refer Table 16.1). This section will first focus on findings regarding perceptual judgment accuracy and errors in green reading and will then consider evidence for the processes underlying performance.

Accuracy of perceptual judgments

Of the studies that have focussed on judging the slope or 'break' of a putt, two examined expertise effects (Pelz, 1994; Campbell & Moran, 2014), one focussed on alignment errors using the 'plumb-bob' technique (MacKenzie & Sprigings, 2005), and one examined the contribution of green reading to putt distance variability in skilled golfers (Karlsen & Nilsson, 2008). These studies primarily focussed on performance measures, with the exception of Campbell and Moran, who also analysed concurrent visual gaze behaviour. Karlsen and Nilsson used a mathematical formula to estimate the proportion of variability in putt distance judgments explained by errors in green reading, putting technique, and green inconsistency. They tested 43 skilled golfers' ability to judge distance on 40 putts, encompassing a variety of lengths and slopes, and used data from 30 repeated putts to the same target to calculate variability attributable to technique. Using simple subtraction, they calculated that green reading variability was the largest contributor to putt distance error in the 40-putt test, accounting for 60% of the variance, considerably more than variability in putting technique (34%) and inconsistencies of the putting surface (6%). These results clearly establish the importance of the perceptual-cognitive phase of putt preparation in skilled golfers but not the extent to which it differs across the expertise spectrum.

Table 16.1 Summary of the 10 identified studies exploring perceptual-cognitive expertise in golf putting. Handicap data refer to mean values

Authors	Participants	Measures	Task	Results
Pelz (1994)	Amateurs ($n = 179$), PGA club professionals ($n = 128$), and PGA Tour professionals ($n = 6$)	Estimation of putt break	4–40 holes; straight-to-severely sloped putts of 3–4.5 m.	Accuracy: Tour professionals > club professionals > amateurs.
MacKenzie and Sprigings (2005)	Golf experience not specified ($n = 31$)	Plum-bob separation; perpendicular stance alignment error	Reading 6 × 1.4 m putts (0° or 10° slope) from platform (−10° to 12°).	Significant error when judging from sloped platform; error in judging perpendicular stance.
Karlsen and Nilsson (2008)	High-skilled ($N = 43$, handicap = 2.8)	Putt distance variability	40 putts, 2.2–19.3 m (uphill, downhill with right and left breaks) on two-tiered grass practice green.	Predictors: green reading (60%) > technique (34%) > green inconsistency (6%).

Cotterill et al. (2010)	International amateurs (*n* = 6, handicap = +1.5)	Retrospective think-aloud protocols	Driving, chipping, and putting video clips.	Shot selection: task demands and task variability influenced planning.
Calmeiro and Tenenbaum (2011)	Beginners (*n* = 3, no handicap) and experienced (*n* = 3, 0–18 handicap)	Concurrent verbal reports	20 × 12 ft putts (uphill, downhill with right and left breaks); 4 positions; grass practice green.	Experienced > beginners for gathering information, planning, knowledge of results, and diagnostic statements.
Campbell and Moran (2014)	Tour professionals (*n* = 17), elite amateurs (*n* = 14, handicap = +1.1), and club amateurs (*n* = 14, handicap = 10.3)	Visual search behaviour; slope judgment accuracy	Reading a single putt from six positions in a virtual environment.	Tour professionals and elite amateurs made fewer fixations of longer duration.
Whitehead et al. (2015) Study 1	Skilled (*n* = 30, handicap = 5.3), and novices (*n* = 30, no handicap)	Concurrent verbal reports	30 × 3 m putts; indoor artificial surface.	Skilled > novices for information gathering and planning statements.
Whitehead et al. (2015) Study 2	Skilled (*N* = 6, handicap = 5.5).	Concurrent and retrospective (10 min, 24 hr, 48 hr) verbal reports.	Six holes on a golf course.	Low similarity between themes identified using think-aloud and interview protocols.
Whitehead et al. (2016) Study 1	High skilled (*n* = 6, handicap = 4.2), and low skilled (*n* = 6, handicap = 20.2)	Concurrent verbal reports	Six holes on a golf course.	Planning thoughts: high-skilled > low- skilled.
Whitehead et al. (2016) Study 2	High skilled (*n* = 8, handicap = 2.3) and moderately skilled (*n* = 8, handicap = 9.6)	Concurrent verbal reports	Six holes in practice and competition.	High-skilled > moderately skilled for thoughts per putt, planning, and evaluation statements.

Regarding expertise effects, Pelz (1994) asked >179 amateurs, 128 club professionals, and 6 professional tour players to estimate the influence of lateral slope by indicating where they perceived their aim line should be in relation to the hole. Golfers judged a variable number of straight-to-severely sloping putts ranging from 3 m to 4.5 m in length taken to several of 40 hole locations. Pelz reported that all participants systematically underestimated the break of putts, on average reporting just 25% of the true break regardless of skill level. Although the error decreased, participants continued to underestimate the break in regard to how they aligned the putter and the initial direction of the ball after contact. For putts with a break of >15 cm, participants were far more likely to miss 'below' the hole (>84%) than above the hole (<9%). Furthermore, professional tour players were found to be 2% more accurate than club professionals and 5% more accurate than amateurs.

In a more controlled test of green reading using a single putting green displayed in virtual reality, professional golfers were found to be more accurate at reading the greens than elite amateurs and club golfers (Campbell & Moran, 2014). In this study, participants were asked to 'tour' the green using six set positions, then report precisely where they would aim to hole the putt. They were allowed 6 seconds at each position, following a circular route from crouching behind the ball to looking from the left side (standing), crouching behind the hole, standing behind the hole, looking from the right side, then lastly standing behind the ball. Campbell and Moran found that the professional golfers were accurate in reading 76.5% of putts, which was significantly higher than the accuracy attained by elite amateur and club golfers (57%).

Golfers use a variety of ways to read the green. Popular methods include 'plumb-bob'(MacKenzie & Sprigings, 2005) and the certified-instructor-taught method of 'AimPoint' (AimPoint, 2016). In the 'plumb-bob' method, the golfer straddles an imaginary line between the hole, the ball, and him/herself, then hangs the putter at arm's length to align the bottom on the golf shaft with the centre of the ball (Foston, 1992). There is little formal evaluation of these methods; however, MacKenzie and Sprigings (2005) found that the plumb-bob method was inaccurate when the slope where the reading was taken from differed from the slope between the ball and the hole. In addition, they found that half the participants deviated by at least 1.5° when attempting to take up a perpendicular stance to a platform angled 10° from the horizontal. The slopes in this study were extremely severe (8°–12°) and approximately five to seven times above the recommended limit of 1.7° for real putting greens (Lemons, 2008), so the practical significance of these findings is questionable. Nonetheless, the error in stance for a 10° slope was calculated to be equivalent to 8 cm of break for a 1.4 m putt. As standing perpendicular to the green is critical when using this method, even small errors may be potentially significant at the elite level.

Processes underlying perceptual-cognitive expertise

Six studies have employed verbal protocols to explore perceptual-cognitive processes underlying decision-making (Cotterill et al., 2010; Calmeiro & Tenenbaum, 2011; Whitehead et al., 2015; Whitehead et al., 2016). By analysing verbal protocols, researchers gain insight into performers' thought processes, and this requires participants to report their thoughts and explain their actions before, during, or after the performance of the task. From this research, differences between higher- and lesser-skilled golfers have been identified. Calmeiro and Tenenbaum (2011) analysed concurrent verbal protocols from three novice and three experienced golfers as they completed 12-foot putts from four positions. The researchers grouped verbalisations into 'gathering information' (the search for relevant characteristics of the environment) and 'planning' (defining actions or strategies) and found that experienced golfers made significantly more of both types of statements than the beginner golfers. This finding was replicated in a larger-scale study of skilled golfers who were found to make more frequent comments in regard to gathering information and planning shots (Whitehead et al., 2015; Whitehead et al., 2016). Furthermore, high-skilled golfers made more frequent use of planning statements than low-skilled golfers when putting on the course (Whitehead et al., 2016, Study 1).

An important consideration when conducting research using verbal protocols is whether different methodologies yield the same information. Cotterill et al. (2010) used interpretive phenomenological analysis to gather in-depth data from six elite amateur golfers on the psychological strategies used in their pre-performance routines for driving, putting, and chipping. Regarding reading the green, the interviews revealed how the nature of the green can influence shot strategy and how one player attempted to visualise the path the ball would take rather than reading the line of the putt. Research on the decision-making processes in golf putting has revealed important differences between concurrent and retrospective verbal reports. Whitehead et al. (2015, Study 2) recorded concurrent 'think-aloud' Level 3 verbalisations from six skilled golfers and conducted three interviews 10 minutes, 24 hours, and 48 hours after the participants completed a truncated round of six holes on a golf course. Overall, the concurrent verbal reports yielded more in-depth data in comparison to retrospective reports from the interviews. The themes identified using the concurrent and retrospective methods were very different, with similarity scores ranging from 38% to 41%. Verbalisations for the themes 'Score' and 'Pre-performance activity' (including thoughts about putt sequence, planning the putt, and identifying a target to aim for) were mentioned less in the retrospective interviews than in the think-aloud condition. These findings highlight the possible limitations associated with retrospective reports, such as reliability and recall accuracy (Cumming et al., 2005), as well as the potential for response bias (Shiffman et al., 1997). Concurrent verbal protocols therefore currently offer the best method for capturing golfers' verbalisable thought processes in their natural environment and, with it, the opportunity to use highly representative putting task (Magill, 2000).

In extending their research to consider the impact of competitive pressure, Whitehead et al. (2016, Study 2) examined differences in concurrent verbal reports as participants played six holes on a golf course in practice and competition formats. In the competition round, prizes of £100, £70, and £30 were offered to those finishing in the top three and participants were told that individual scores would be reported back to all participants the following week. For putting during practice, the proportion of holes on which the high-skilled group made planning statements (76%) and evaluation statements (88%) was significantly higher than the same for the moderately skilled group (40% and 56%, respectively). Under competitive pressure, the high-skilled group also made planning statements on more holes (79%) than the moderately skilled golfers (46%). These results suggest that higher-skilled players gather additional verbalisable planning and evaluation information. However, further research is required to establish a causal link with performance.

To evaluate information sources golfers draw from as they read the green, Campbell and Moran (2014) used eye tracking technology in a virtual reality study. Consistent with results from other sports, these data revealed that more-skilled players (professionals and elite amateurs) made fewer fixations of longer duration than less-skilled (club) players. However, there was no difference between groups regarding where they looked. The sample as a whole spent approximately half their time fixating on the immediate region of the target and approximately 35% of their time fixating on the 2-foot area leading to the target, with <15% of their time spent looking at the ball. Considered alongside group differences in green reading accuracy and thought processes inferred from verbal reports, this finding implies that green reading expertise is more to do with how long information is processed than simply knowing the information sources on which to focus.

Limitations in current perceptual-cognitive research

To consider the applicability of these studies to world-class competitive golfers, it is important to consider the representativeness of the putting tasks used alongside potential methodological limitations. Factors such as the playing surface and response requirements affect task representativeness, while the number of participants, how their putting expertise is determined, and testing protocol are also important methodological concerns. Attention to these factors helps ensure that researchers do not unintentionally limit the understanding of perceptual-cognitive expertise and associated skill-based differences (Dicks et al., 2009).

Task representativeness. Depending on the specific research question, the full demands of green reading are likely best captured when the putting surface (and variability) is the same as that experienced on golf courses. Of the studies focussed on perceptual aspects of green reading, two were conducted on grass putting greens (Pelz, 1994; Karlsen & Nilsson, 2008), one used a putting green displayed in virtual reality (Campbell & Moran, 2014), and one used wooden platforms (MacKenzie & Sprigings, 2005). Of the studies focussed on thought processes, five were conducted on grass putting greens either on a golf course (Cotterill et al., 2010; Whitehead et al., 2015, Study 2; Whitehead et al., 2016) or in a practice area (Calmeiro & Tenenbaum, 2011), and one study used an artificial putting surface (Whitehead et al. 2015, Study 1). Regarding the putting surface, response requirements were therefore highly representative for most studies. Adding further quantitative information about green speed and slope would help facilitate comparison with conditions experienced in elite-level competition.

The design and response requirements across the 10 identified studies included assessment over a range of slopes and distances, assessment of putts of the same distance but different slopes, assessment of multiple putts of the same distance, and assessment of a single putt in a virtual environment. In the on-course studies, some task designs were more highly representative as participants competed against each other in a natural environment, adhering to the rule requirement for 40 seconds per putt and employing a full pre-putt routine. While this might not always be possible or desirable, it is important to note the requirement for information gathering is largely eliminated when repeated putts are taken from the same position. For example, Karlsen and Nilsson (2008) found that distance variation on a 6-m putt reduced substantially from the first to the second attempt but very little in 29 subsequent attempts, with no significant change in the last 15 attempts. Conversely, the study conducted on an indoor artificial putting surface used more participants but was less representative and used multiple putts from the same distance.

Methodological limitations. Regarding the expertise of participants, the studies recruited participants ranging from novices to highly skilled golfers and included tour professionals, club professionals, elite amateurs, low-handicap golfers, and individuals with no previous golf experience. This range of expertise may help build a cross-sectional picture of how perceptual-cognitive variables differ as golfers become more proficient; however, different criteria have been applied when ascribing group labels. For example, golfers classified as 'novices' range from those with no previous playing experience to those with a mean handicap of approximately 20. Similarly, the label 'skilled' has been applied to golfers ranging in handicap from 18 to 5.3 and 'highly skilled' to groups with mean handicaps from 4.2 to plus 1.5. An additional limitation of classifying players by golf handicap is that handicap reflects all aspects of golf play and so may lack sensitivity as an indicator of putting expertise. The participants' current playing and practice activity (e.g., hours per week), current competitive level, and accumulated years of competitive playing experience were not reported in all studies. Having more detailed knowledge about golfers' practice and playing experience would provide additional information that might help researchers better delineate participants. For example, golfers with a richer variety of competitive playing experience would have been exposed to a greater variety of green surfaces and contours that may enhance their perceptual-cognitive expertise (Kenyon, 2008).

In regard to group size, one should be cautious about making inferences about the relevant populations when group size is small, and this has been the case in many of the studies reviewed. Exceptions include the study by Pelz (1994), which examined slope reading in hundreds of amateur golfers and club professionals but also included a group of six tour professionals. Whitehead et al. (2015, Study 1) also used large groups ($n = 30$) in their comparison of concurrent verbal protocols in skilled and novice golfers. In contrast, group sizes of three were used in the Calmeiro and Tenenbaum (2011) study and groups of three to eight were used in other studies that analysed verbal protocols (Cotterill et al., 2010; Whitehead et al., 2015, Study 2; Whitehead et al., 2016). In addition, some studies lacked comparison or control groups that would have facilitated skill-based comparisons.

Research on how players gather information from a range of sources as they plan to putt will only be accurate insofar as the task includes relevant sources of information. If a key source of information is degraded or missing, this may affect an individual's ability to explore and process the perceptual-cognitive information they would use on the golf course. Considering task representativeness on a macro level, virtual reality technology gives researchers the opportunity to present, manipulate, and control topographical features of the green in a precise and systematic manner. The virtual environment also lends itself to gathering verbal report and/or eye tracking data, which help further understanding of the perceptual-cognitive processes underlying green reading judgments. Campbell and Moran's (2014) study provides a taste of the potential of this area. On a micro level, the 'fidelity' of virtual environments (i.e., their ability to accurately represent the [visual] environment they depict) is critical. An examination of how behavioural markers of perceptual-cognitive expertise differ in real and virtual environments is needed to advance understanding in this area.

Concurrent verbal protocols require participants to report their thoughts in a continuous 'think-aloud' manner (Ericsson & Simon, 1993). Importantly, the evidence thus far indicates that capturing concurrent verbal reports before putting does not impair subsequent performance. Specifically, Whitehead et al. (2015, Study 1) compared the performance of novices and skilled golfers who were assigned to one of three groups: Level 2 verbalisation (say what you are thinking at all times before and after the execution of the putt); Level 3 verbalisation (same as Level 2 with additional explanations provided for actions); or a control group. Participants completed 3-m putts on an artificial surface, and Whitehead et al. found that performance was the same across the three conditions. While this is encouraging, the detrimental effect of 'reinvesting' conscious control during proceduralised actions is well established (Masters, 1992; Flegal & Anderson, 2008), therefore, as this area of research develops, it is important to ensure that there is no 'contagion' from obtaining verbal protocols while players prepare to putt. For example, Kinrade et al. (2010) developed a scale designed to measure individual differences in the propensity for reinvesting when making decisions. In their study examining verbal protocols in golf putting, Whitehead et al. (2016, Study 2) found that scores on the decision reinvestment subscale were strongly correlated with the increase in comments on technical instruction when under competitive pressure in a group of high-skilled players.

Implications for the game

The conclusions that can be drawn at this stage are necessarily tentative, as research in this area is in its infancy. Nonetheless, the studies reviewed in this chapter have revealed differences between high- and less-skilled golfers in the green reading process. Specifically, as they read the green during practice and competition, higher-skilled golfers engage in significantly more planning than do lesser-skilled golfers. Professionals are also more accurate than amateurs in their ability to judge the break of a putt (Pelz, 1994; Campbell & Moran, 2014), while the difficulty of the putt sometimes affects skilled players' putt strategy, such as whether or not to lag the putt (Cotterill et al., 2010). Expertise differences are reflected in some aspects of visual attention – more-skilled players make fewer fixations of longer duration – but not in regard to the distribution of time they spend focussing on different areas. Collectively, these findings highlight the need to extend understanding of the nature of differences in perceptual-cognitive processes and how they are acquired.

In this chapter, we have argued that capturing the perceptual-cognitive demands of 'real-world' putting is crucial for developing a full understanding of the processes underlying expert putting preparation. Using a range of qualitative and quantitative research methods and multiple dependent variables (e.g., combining verbal protocols with eye-tracking and behavioural measures, and potentially electroencephalogram [EEG]) will help develop a more comprehensive understanding of observed behavioural effects. It would also help establish clearer links between thought content (and associated inferences), different perceptual-cognitive strategies, subsequent judgment accuracy, alignment accuracy, and, ultimately, putting performance. Understanding these links will allow researchers to make and test specific predictions about interventions that help establish causality, a crucial step towards making evidence-based recommendations to coaches and golfers.

In developing a more comprehensive understanding, there are three further considerations. First, the influence of age on the acquisition, retention, and deterioration of perceptual-cognitive expertise is yet to be examined in golf. Longitudinal research recording changes in perceptual-cognitive expertise over time, as well as research comparing the perceptual-cognitive expertise of players in junior, adult, and senior age groups (including Senior Tour Players), will further enhance understanding in this area. Second, researchers have calculated that caddies help to improve scoring by approximately one stroke per round after controlling for player quality, weather, tournament round, and course changes (Coate & Toomey, 2014). The way in which golfers use their caddie – either as a source of perceptual-cognitive expertise or as a source of feedback for their judgments – together with how perceptual-cognitive expertise develops in caddies themselves, remains under-explored. Third, it is likely that tour players develop highly refined perceptual-cognitive knowledge about greens while competing and can use this knowledge to improve their performance and to better adapt to the conditions. At this stage, knowledge on how the golfer acquires perceptual-cognitive expertise within a round or across a competition or from competition to competition, wherein the green characteristics can significantly vary, is currently unknown. It would be of interest to examine the perceptual-cognitive strategies employed by tour players and the influence of these strategies on performance (current and future). For example, televised and live observations of golfers playing on the US Professional Golfers' Association (PGA) and European Tours highlight that successful putters employ the perceptual-cognitive strategy of tracking the ball post-putt. Advantages in visually tracking the ball throughout its journey to the hole may include useful online feedback relative to the putting action, and secondly, through the tracking response, a golfer can gain information about the green's surface and potentially recognise environmental variation, including topography and pace variations. To track the ball, the golfer's head and eye movements need to be scaled and timed to the external motion of the ball. Research into dynamic visual acuity (or an individual's ability to track a moving object) has found that dynamic acuity increases with practice (Long & Riggs, 1991). To develop evidence-based recommendations that can help inform golfers and coaches, a greater understanding on how much practice a golfer needs to develop an effective tracking response and perceptual-cognitive expertise is required. It is also unknown whether tracking your opponent's/playing partner's putt can help you to gain knowledge to inform your future putt on the same surface. Examining both performance and associated perceptual-cognitive processes and strategies associated with the transfer to novel conditions would further enhance knowledge in this area and help to define the perceptual-cognitive phases in golf putting, such as preparation and post-putt phases.

Summary and future directions

When designing perceptual-cognitive studies, it is important that the task is representative, so that findings can be applied to the real world. A representative task might involve high variability in terms of putt difficulty (e.g., slope and distance), performed on a grass putting surface, using a regulation size hole, with each participant using his/her putter and preferred golf ball. Participants might also be required to adhere to PGA Tour regulations and be free to move around the green, as they would do in a 'real-world' circumstance. Alternatively, and depending on the research question, it may be appropriate to design a task that allows researchers to manipulate certain variables systematically in a controlled environment. Finally, qualitative research such as detailed interviews with targeted individuals, e.g., the best 'green readers' in the world or current tour players, would be highly informative, especially considering that it is not currently possible to recreate the reality of tour level putting in a research laboratory setting. The circumstance of a tour player preparing to putt on the 18th green, knowing that the consequences of holing the putt means a life-changing difference (both financially and in future opportunities) is very different from the associated competitive pressure generated in the current research. At this time, research on the perceptual-cognitive aspects of golf putting is limited. As more systematic and ecologically valid research is reported, with more representative task designs and different (or combined) methodologies, a more comprehensive evidence base will be established. This enhanced knowledge will enable researchers to make stronger evidence-based recommendations to golfers, coaches, and practitioners.

References

AimPoint (2016) *AimPoint. Get the Facts*, Available at www.aimpointgolf.com/ (Accessed February 20, 2016).

Calmeiro, L. & Tenenbaum, G. (2011) Concurrent Verbal Protocol Analysis in Sport: Illustration of Thought Processes During a Golf-Putting Task, *Journal of Clinical Sport Psychology*, 5 (3), 23–236.

Campbell, M. & Moran, A. (2014) There Is More to Green Reading than Meets the Eye! Exploring the Gaze Behaviours of Expert Golfers on a Virtual Golf Putting Task, *Cognitive Processing*, 15 (3), 363–372.

Coate, D. & Toomey, M. (2014) Do Professional Golf Tour Caddies Improve Player Scoring? *Journal of Sports Economics*, 15 (3), 303–312.

Cotterill, S.; Sanders, R. & Collins, D. (2010) Developing Effective Pre-performance Routines in Golf: Why Don't We Ask the Golfer? *Journal of Applied Sport Psychology*, 22 (1), 51–64.

Cumming, J.; Hall, C. & Starkes, J. (2005) Deliberate Imagery Practice: The Reliability of Using a Retrospective Recall Methodology, *Research Quarterly for Exercise and Sport*, 76 (3), 306–314.

Dicks, M.; Davids, K. & Button, C. (2009) Representative Task Designs for the Study of Perception and Action in Sport, *International Journal of Sport Psychology*, 40 (4), 506–524.

Ericsson, K. & Simon, H. (1993) *Protocol Analysis: Verbal Reports as Data*, Cambridge, MA: MIT Press.

Ericsson, K.A. & Smith, J. (1991) Prospects and Limits of the Empirical Study of Expertise: An Introduction, In: K.A. Ericsson & J. Smith (Eds.) *Toward a General Theory of Expertise: Prospects and limits*, New York, NY: Cambridge University Press, pp. 1–38.

Flegal, K. & Anderson, M. (2008) Overthinking Skilled Motor Performance: Or Why Those Who Teach Can't Do, *Psychonomic Bulletin & Review*, 15 (5), 927–932.

Foston, P. (1992) *The Encyclopedia of Golf Techniques: The Complete Step-by-step Guide to Mastering the Game of Golf*, Philadelphia, PA: Courage Books.

Karlsen, J. & Nilsson, J. (2008) Distance Variability in Golf Putting among Highly Skilled Players: The Role of Green Reading, *Annual Review of Golf Coaching*, 3 (1), 71–80.

Kenyon, P. (2008) Distance Variability in Golf Putting among Highly Skilled Players: The Role of Green Reading, *Annual Review of Golf Coaching*, 3 (1), 81–84.

Kinrade, N.; Jackson, R.; Ashford, K. & Bishop, D. (2010) Development and Validation of the Decision-specific Reinvestment Scale, *Journal of Sports Sciences*, 28 (10), 1127–1135.

Lemons, J. (2008) Putting Green Speeds, Slopes, and "Non-conforming" Hole Locations, *USGA Green Section Record*, (July–August), 21–25.

Long, G. & Riggs, C. (1991) Training Effects on Dynamic Visual Acuity with Free-head Viewing, *Perception*, 20, 363–371.

MacKenzie, S. & Sprigings, E. (2005) Evaluation of the Plumb-bob Method for Reading Greens in Putting, *Journal of Sports Sciences*, 23 (1), 81–87.

Magill, R. (2000) Augmented Feedback in Motor Skill Acquisition, In: R. Singer; H. Hausenblas, & C. Janelle (Eds.) *The Handbook of Research on Sport Psychology*, New York, NY: John Wiley & Sons, pp. 86–114.

Masters, R. (1992) Knowledge, Knerves and Know-How: The Role of Explicit Versus Implicit Knowledge in the Breakdown of a Complex Motor Skill Under Pressure, *British Journal of Psychology*, 83, 343–358.

Pelz, D. (1994) A Study of Golfers' Abilities to Read Greens, In: A. Cochran & M. Farrally (Eds.) *Science and Golf II: Proceedings of the 1994 World Scientific Congress of Golf*, London: E & FN Spon, pp. 180–185.

Shiffman, S.; Hufford, M.; Hickox, M.; Paty, J.; Gnys, M. & Kassel, J. (1997) Remember that? A Comparison of Real-time Versus Retrospective Recall of Smoking Lapses, *Journal of Consulting and Clinical Psychology*, 65 (2), 292–300.

van Lier, W.; van der Kamp, J. & Savelsbergh G. (2011) Perception and Action in Golf Putting: Skill Differences Reflect Calibration, *Journal of Sport & Exercise Psychology*, 33 (3), 349–369.

Whitehead, A.; Taylor, J. & Polman, R. (2015) Examination of the Suitability of Collecting in Event Cognitive Processes Using Think Aloud Protocol in Golf, *Frontiers in Psychology*, 6 (1083), 12.

Whitehead, A.; Taylor, J. & Polman, R. (2016) Evidence for Skill Level Differences in the Thought Processes of Golfers During High and Low Pressure Situations, *Frontiers in Psychology*, 6 (1974), 12.

Williams, A. & Ericsson, K. (2005) Perceptual-cognitive Expertise in Sport: Some Considerations When Applying the Expert Performance Approach, *Human Movement Science*, 24 (3), 283–307.

Wilson, M. & Pearcy, R. (2009) Visuomotor Control of Straight and Breaking Golf Putts, *Perceptual & Motor Skills*, 109 (2), 555–562.

17

POSITIVE PSYCHOLOGY AND GOLF

Sandy Gordon and Jay-Lee Nair

Introduction

As alluded to by Maslow's (1954) early philosophical works as well as the contemporary views offered by Seligman (1999, 2011), human endeavours are characterised as fixing weaknesses. Arguably, deficit-based approaches to human development in all sports, including the delivery of traditional psychological skills by sport psychologists, predominate and typically focus on identifying athletes' weaknesses and fixing them. In contrast, practitioners in the disciplines of positive psychology (PP) and applied sport psychology (ASP) are beginning to examine the optimal functioning of human beings using strengths-based interventions. In this chapter, the authors present a case for this new strengths-based approach to enhancing human performance in golf and illustrate how such an approach can be introduced to leaders and policymakers, as well as to both coaches and golfers. Specifically, four applications of strengths-based interventions in golf are provided: 1) a strengths-based debrief process, 2) a strengths-focussed golf game analysis, 3) strengths-based questions for exploring a player's weaknesses and strengths, and 4) strengths identification profiling.

A strengths-based approach

Contemporary and popular writers on golf psychology (Cohn, 2001; Hemmings et al., 2007; Rotella, 2008; Valiante, 2013) primarily document means of dealing with problem thinking and analysing mental weaknesses. Subsequently, the readership, including golf coaches and golfers themselves, rarely consider studying success, i.e., what golfers do well and what can be learned from achievement. Recent writing on PP applications in sport (e.g., Park-Perin, 2010; Gordon & Gucciardi, 2011) has highlighted that, in contrast to weakness- or deficit-based leadership, strengths-based approaches are about identifying (spotting) and exploiting an individual's strengths, which – according to Linley et al. (2010a, p. 67) – have two elements: "delivering a high level of performance . . . and experiencing a sense of energy when you are doing it". In other words, a strength is something an individual is both good at and passionate about. During a strengths-based approach, the focus is on what is already working and because strengths are part of basic human nature – every individual has strengths and deserves respect for having them – the areas of greatest potential are considered to lie in the areas of an individual's greatest strengths. When applying a strengths-based approach in the context of golf, it can be assumed that while golfers *can*, of course, develop from working on their weaknesses, change and sustained improvement are only possible when golfers are *also* working on their strengths.

Strengths-based leadership, such as coaching, can be regarded as being both an approach (i.e., strengths are used more effectively in the attainment of goals) and as a value-adding outcome (i.e., strengths-based coaching is used to enable the realisation and development of an individual's strengths) (Linley & Harrington, 2006; Gordon, 2008a, 2008b; Linley et al., 2009; Driver, 2011). Non-sport research has shown that, in addition to being more confident, having higher levels of energy and vitality (Govindji & Linley, 2007), and being more likely to achieve their goals (Linley et al. 2010a), individuals who use their strengths are more effective at developing and growing themselves than people who do not (Sheldon et al. 2002). Research by Linley et al. (2010a) also demonstrates that those individuals who use their strengths more often are happier, have higher self-esteem, experience less stress, are more resilient, perform better at work, and are more engaged in what they are doing.

The case *for* using a strengths-based approach to enhancing performance is quite compelling, particularly so when leaders and coaches are specifically engaged to 'develop talent'. Talent development requires an understanding that talented people are very good at reflection (good thinkers) (Mainwaring, 2009; Sharp & Hodge, 2011; Toogood, 2012) and they also exploit their strengths through strong self-awareness, which is turned into their advantage. While talented individuals often fail, they learn quickly to convert setbacks into opportunities. They also have an urge for personal growth, meaning and purpose in all that they do, and a general feeling of being on the move (Robertson & Abbey, 2003). Following Linley and Joseph (2004), Lopez and Snyder (2009), Biswas-Diener (2010), Driver (2011), Cameron and Spreitzer (2012), and Hawkins (2012), a summary of the contrasting assumptions of strengths-based approaches to human development and traditional psychological skills training approaches is illustrated in Table 17.1.

Table 17.1 Contrasts between strengths-based and traditional leadership assumptions

Assumptions (technical, tactical, physical, and mental performance areas)	Strengths-based approach	Traditional approach
Assessment norms	Self-referenced standards or comparison to elite models that highlight similarities and promote positive modelling.	Contrast to elite models and professional standards that highlight discrepancies
Type of coaching required	Proactive	Remedial
	Exploit existing strengths	Fix existing weaknesses
Coach philosophy	Strengths spotting	Problem identification
Learning process	Coaching	Training
	Athlete-directed	Coach/expert led and directed
Individual players (all skill levels)	Players are resourceful, have inherent strengths, and have experienced success	Require expert assistance in addressing inherent weaknesses and dealing with failures
Training focus & resource/ attention allocation	Strengths	Weaknesses
	Use strengths to compensate for weaknesses and energise action.	Weaknesses are inherent and need constant attention and management

In accordance with PP traditions, the strengths-based philosophy is about looking for 'what is strong' (strengths spotting) as opposed to 'what is wrong' (identifying problems). However, in their study of the Titleist Performance Institute (TPI), Gulgin et al. (2014) reported that coaches schooled in modern physical assessments, such as the level 1 movement screening analysis, typically look for and assess weaknesses and highlight a player's deficiencies in terms of strength, flexibility, and balance associated with the 14 different golf swing faults based on comparisons to elite prototypes. Subsequently, coaches become experts at analysing genetic dysfunction and its impact on swing mechanic deviations from the elite models/standards. This approach to assessment and training of physical performance perpetuates the assumption that an individual's weaknesses are inherent and require constant attention and management. Also, it emphasises the gap and deviation from normative standards set by top performers, which can negatively affect confidence over time.

The guiding standard philosophy and practice in a traditional golf lesson are to identify problems in an individual's golf swing. The contemporary learning process is often facilitated by incorporating slow motion capture of an individual's golf swing and providing the visual comparison of an elite prototype, demonstrating the ideal mechanics to highlight discrepancies. Subsequently, the focus of the training process is on fixing weaknesses, which reinforces block practice and attentional resources directed primarily towards technical analysis. Linley (2008) and Linley et al. (2010a) have demonstrated in non-sport environments that a development plan focussed on fixing weaknesses is de-energising and, rather than creating a 'want to' approach, creates a 'must do' approach to training, aligned with a controlling form of motivation associated with higher levels of stress and dissatisfaction.

The problem-centred focus of traditional golf teaching and coaching on the practice range can also influence on-course processes. For example, the conclusion often reached by golfers who are not experiencing the outcomes they would like is '*I'm not playing well and feeling disappointed, so I must be playing badly*'. Such emotional reasoning might appear natural, but it represents crooked thinking as golfers are mistaking feelings for facts, which can subsequently derail performance. Figure 17.1 illustrates a player's typical on-course actions and reactions associated with a traditional coaching approach following poorly executed golf shots. Technical coaching, focussed on problem identification, can influence post-shot analysis on the golf course, during which the player is more likely to look for and assess weakness in the swing following a poor shot. When problem identification in technical performance dominates the learning process and training activities, it primes an internal dialogue and analysis fixated on swing faults and what is going wrong, rather than what the player is doing well in the present moment. As a consequence, players are more likely to experiment with corrections from one shot to the next, which may explain why players of all levels experience the phenomenon 'paralysis by analysis' on the golf course. The player is preoccupied with technical thoughts following a poor shot, consequently switching from a task-oriented and target focus to task-irrelevant cues, leading to cognitive interference, deterioration in movement, faulty skill execution, and ultimately a poor performance. Confidence and perceived control over one's game is low in players with this type of focus and reinforces the assumption that only an expert-directed didactic learning process is suited to improve overall performance.

On the other hand, when a golfer is exposed to a strengths-based approach in training, following a poor shot on the golf course, the player is focussed on using strengths to compensate for weaknesses, promoting solution-focussed thinking, as illustrated in Figure 17.2. Instead of being consumed by crooked thinking and technical thoughts around identifying and fixing mistakes, the player is primed to draw on task-relevant cues that produce optimal movement. For example, if a player is aware that a strength in his/her swing is the tempo when errors occur on the golf

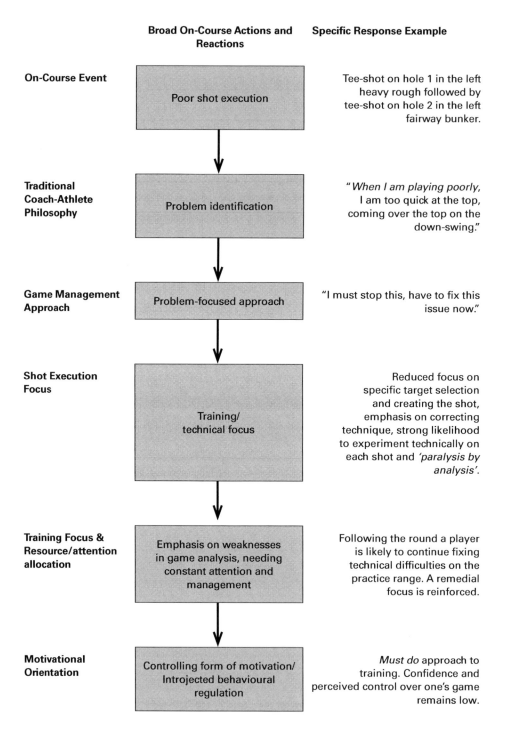

	Broad On-Course Actions and Reactions	**Specific Response Example**
On-Course Event	Poor shot execution	Tee-shot on hole 1 in the left heavy rough followed by tee-shot on hole 2 in the left fairway bunker.
Traditional Coach-Athlete Philosophy	Problem identification	"*When I am playing poorly*, I am too quick at the top, coming over the top on the down-swing."
Game Management Approach	Problem-focused approach	"I must stop this, have to fix this issue now."
Shot Execution Focus	Training/ technical focus	Reduced focus on specific target selection and creating the shot, emphasis on correcting technique, strong likelihood to experiment technically on each shot and *'paralysis by analysis'*.
Training Focus & Resource/attention allocation	Emphasis on weaknesses in game analysis, needing constant attention and management	Following the round a player is likely to continue fixing technical difficulties on the practice range. A remedial focus is reinforced.
Motivational Orientation	Controlling form of motivation/ Introjected behavioural regulation	*Must do* approach to training. Confidence and perceived control over one's game remains low.

Figure 17.1 Chain reaction of on-course actions and reactions associated with a traditional approach following a typical on-course event.

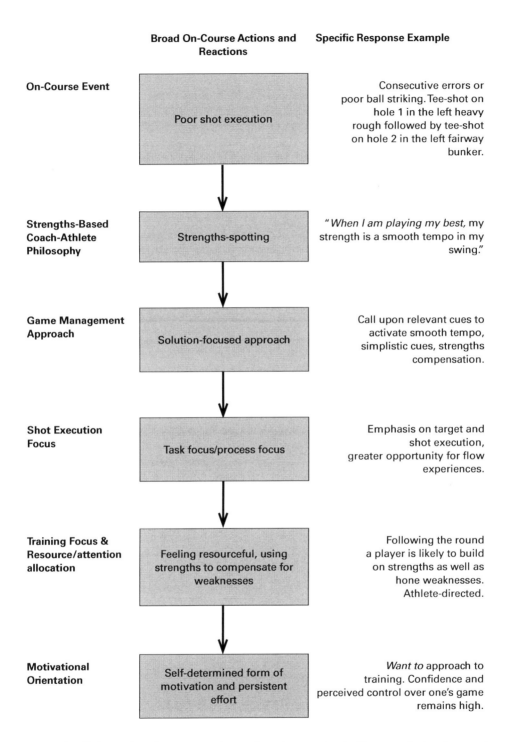

Broad On-Course Actions and Reactions

Specific Response Example

On-Course Event

Poor shot execution

Consecutive errors or poor ball striking. Tee-shot on hole 1 in the left heavy rough followed by tee-shot on hole 2 in the left fairway bunker.

Strengths-Based Coach-Athlete Philosophy

Strengths-spotting

"*When I am playing my best,* my strength is a smooth tempo in my swing."

Game Management Approach

Solution-focused approach

Call upon relevant cues to activate smooth tempo, simplistic cues, strengths compensation.

Shot Execution Focus

Task focus/process focus

Emphasis on target and shot execution, greater opportunity for flow experiences.

Training Focus & Resource/attention allocation

Feeling resourceful, using strengths to compensate for weaknesses

Following the round a player is likely to build on strengths as well as hone weaknesses. Athlete-directed.

Motivational Orientation

Self-determined form of motivation and persistent effort

Want to approach to training. Confidence and perceived control over one's game remains high.

Figure 17.2 Chain reaction of on-course actions and reactions associated with a strengths-based approach following a typical on-course event.

course, he/she will more likely be primed to call up relevant cues that focus on producing good tempo. Rather than focussing on and over-analysing the problem, he/she will utilise his/her strengths to compensate and whisper simplistic cues such as 'smooth at the top' or 'easy transition'. Such an approach to error correction can be taught on the range and, subsequently, on the course, it facilitates choking-resistant players whose autonomy and confidence remain intact.

We are *not* suggesting that the traditional approach to golf coaching should be entirely replaced. Rather we are recommending that a multi-system approach be considered as optimal, whereby strengths-based approaches can serve to buffer and balance some of the potential negative consequences of a uni-dimensional coaching methodology focussed exclusively on problem identification and fixing existing weaknesses.

Implications for the game

In this section, we present four applications of the strengths-based approach that illustrate the principles of PP in action.

Application 1

The first application introduces 'GOOD, BETTER, HOW', which is a powerful strengths-based debrief process, where golfers are first asked to recall 'three good things' that happened during a particular round, then one thing they would like to do 'better', followed by ideas on 'how' they would subsequently practise. Readers will recognise how dramatically different (and refreshing) this process compares to traditional post-game reflections comprising endless lists and evidence of gross incompetence, hapless effort, and of course 'bad luck'. The 'GOOD, BETTER, HOW' approach to debriefing is derived from Marriott and Nilsson's (2011) VISION54 programme, named after the idea that golfers who make 18 birdies on a par-72 course would shoot a 54. The VISION54 concept is also a metaphor for building belief in golfers of all abilities and encourages them to consider and understand ways in which they are consistent when they play well, to reflect on their great golfing qualities, to imagine what it is like to play their best, and to write down things they do, think, see, and feel when they play well. In the following example, the GOOD, BETTER, HOW approach to debriefing is used to capture the learning and reflection process of a young golfer following her golf round.

> *Good:* Can you recall three things you did well today?
> Player: First, I remained calm after poor shots and mistakes, and I did not get frustrated or upset. I carried on with a good attitude in today's round. Second, I had a focussed warm-up; I gave myself enough time and did not rush. Third, I putted well and saved par a number of times from about 4 feet.
> *Better:* What one thing would you like to do better?
> Player: My focus during slow play. I didn't handle long waits well. I got caught up talking with my playing partners, and my mind drifted, and I lost focus on the next shot.
> *How:* How will you go about handling this better in the future?
> Player: I will take my time to go through all my steps for preparing the next shot, re-calculating the distance and accounting for the wind, take extra practice swings to feel loose again and get focussed on the present.

It seems acceptable and normal for golfers to focus their attention and even ruminate on errors made in the most recent performance, as well as to disregard or downplay successful events.

The GOOD, BETER, HOW debriefing approach (Marriott & Nilsson, 2011) offers a simplistic framework for reflection that brings awareness to successful moments associated with a player's strengths. The language used to explore elements for remedial focus aligns with a growth mindset that encourages learning opportunities from identifying mistakes and emphasising self-improvement rather than simply pointing out what went *wrong* or needs correcting. The final reflection point, *HOW,* is crucial for establishing autonomy in the approach to player development, which facilitates feelings of empowerment and reinforces the strengths-based assumption, highlighted in Table 17.1, that all players are resourceful.

Application 2

To introduce a strengths-based focus to a professional male golfer, the authors asked him to reflect on his strengths 'off the tee', 'around the green', and 'approach to the green', as well as what he could do differently at practice to work on and exploit these strengths. His responses are illustrated in Table 17.2.

Table 17.2 Strengths-based conversation with male professional golfer

	My strengths are . . . I feel strong when I am . . . (doing this)	*Things I can do to build on my off-the-tee strengths, put myself into situations where I am in my element are . . .*
Off the tee	When I am playing a fade. In between distances – when I dial down my yardage and focus on feeling a smooth swing.	To train my tee shots mostly by simulating tournament play under greater pressure, setting up challenging scenarios, and setting up tight fairways in the space on the range.
Approach to green	My six-irons into the green from the fairway with a little draw. I feel strong when I can see clearly the line from the ball to the target on the green. In between wedge shots – when I have a number in my head (yardage) and I see and feel the distance matching perfectly the feel of my backswing and the yardage to the pin.	Focussing on the visualisation of my shot more at the beginning of my pre-shot routine. Taking more time to see the line of the shot and committing to that.
Around the green	Flop shots behind bunkers and slopes – stopping the ball in a short space. When the lie is tough. When I am using my imagination and feel free to be creative with the shot. When I am in the bunker – any bunker shot. Challenging lies. When I am reading the lie – feeling natural/ instinctive in adjusting my club face and ball position to create the shot.	Incorporate new drills and practice situations in my short game practice habits (tough lies, challenging spaces) that call for creativity in my shot making and reduce a technical focus.

Application 3

In the following example, a low-handicap female golfer was asked a series of strengths-based questions related to both her perceived weaknesses and strengths. These are listed in Table 17.3.

Table 17.3 Strengths-based questions and player responses for both weaknesses and strengths

---

Strengths-based coaching of a perceived *weakness.*

Consider if the *weakness* is 'performance critical'; does it matter?

Player: I can hit it long and play a power game, but my weakness is in course management and taking calculated risks. It is performance critical. I have a tendency to want to play high-risk shots when they are difficult to pull off and a miss will have big consequences.

How does it affect you, impact your game, your feelings?

Player: I can get frustrated quickly, which then leads to more errors. I am often in a good position and then I create trouble for myself.

Where are you now in terms of improving the weakness on a scale: 1 (terrible) – 10 (no problems); __/10

Player: 3/10. It's an issue. I haven't formulated a clear plan or strategy to minimise it.

What would improvement look like e.g., if you moved up one notch?

Player: My game would be less volatile, I would have less blow-up holes (high scores on a few holes), and emotionally I know I would be calmer with less frustration.

How have you successfully addressed this weakness in the past?

Player: When I take more time to assess the shot and look at all my options, instead of rushing into it mindlessly going for the Tiger line. I do this well when I have a caddy because we talk through the shot together.

Can you 'compensate it away' by using your strengths in other areas? If so, how?

Player: Yes. My strength is my ability to hit it longer than most girls, which means that I have many viable options off the tee and I don't need to take the driver all the time to be in a good position. I need to marshal this strength to allow me to manage any course well.

To achieve the change you want, what will you need to commit to doing differently?

Player: I need to adjust what I am doing during my shot-selection phase of my pre-shot routine. I need to look for multiple options and take responsibility for talking myself through my options when I'm on my own.

How will you go about doing this?

Player: I can practise taking more time, generate options, and assess the outcome.

How will you measure change? What indicators of improvement will you use?

Player: I could use a stopwatch to assess the timing of my routine with the goal of making this sequence slightly longer to allow for adequate assessment.

Who can help you?

Player: My caddy, coach, or playing partners can help with observation work.

How will I/others know you have achieved it?

Player: Changes in timing of my routine and observing my assessment phase on every shot should indicate whether I am achieving my goal. In terms of statistics, I should see fewer double-bogeys and experience fewer moments of frustrations.

What will hold you back? What excuses will you use to not achieve this goal?

Player: The only thing that will hold me back is the excitement I feel when I see a high-risk shot as an opportunity to bomb the driver over the trees on a tight fairway. I will have to stick to my plan of assessment first.

Strengths-based coaching of a perceived *strength.*

Let's brainstorm how to find a way to exploit this strength.

Player: I play my best golf and I feel energised when I am under pressure. I love playing under pressure.

How have you successfully used this strength more in the past?
Player: In the past, I have successfully used this strength when I am intensely focussed on the shot or the moment and feel a sense of urgency and determination to achieve my goal.

Who do you know has this strength and uses it well? What do they do?
Player: Phil Mickelson, Tiger Woods, and Morgan Pressel. They show fearsome focus on every shot from the preparation phase to their committed execution when under the pump. They play aggressive and without hesitation.

If you were using it more, what would this look like?
Player: I would be drawing this strength into game situations when I don't feel as much external pressure. Finding a way to replicate that same intensity and sense of urgency that facilitate great shot making in my game.

Where would you say you are now on a 1 – 10 scale (1 = not using it; 10 = using all the time)?
Player: _5_/10

What would it look like if you moved up one notch?
Player: I would play aggressive and look more focussed over every shot during times when I don't perceive any real external pressure.

What opportunities are there for increasing the frequency of use? How can you stretch yourself?
Player: There are opportunities in every game and every shot to engage my competitive drive. Simulating game scenarios and mini tests in training drills can also stretch myself.

To achieve the change you want, what will you need to commit to doing differently?
Player: I will not wait for circumstances to present themselves but instead start setting goals that challenge and test me in rounds.

How will you go about doing this?
Player: I will not judge certain shots or holes as easy or hard, but instead see the challenge in every shot and as an opportunity to create the best shot I have ever played.

How will you measure change? What indicators of improvement will you use?
Player: Intensity of focus and determination and an assessment of how challenged I felt on the day. Quality of shot making and number of sub-par holes.

Who can help you?
Player: I could ask for feedback from my caddy or playing partners and ask my practice partners to set up mini challenges with me.

How will I/others know you have achieved it?
Player: Changes in intensity of focus and feeling more energised. An increase in number of birdies per round.

What will hold you back? What excuses will you use to not achieve this goal?
Player: General laziness to challenge and test myself when circumstances do not create the pressure for me.

Application 4

This application illustrates how strengths identification profiling, utilising the Realise2 model (R2; Linley et al., 2010b), can be utilised with individuals to facilitate and guide discussion around a player's goals and to generate action plans for further growth and development. Briefly, the R2 model considers strengths as things you do well, *and* that energise us, such as *Realised Strengths* that we get to do regularly, or *Unrealised Strengths* that we don't get as much opportunity to use and yet are our greatest areas for development. *Learned Behaviours,* on the other hand, are activities we are good at but drain us of energy, which is particularly relevant for elite/professional athletes because if activities are not energising, doing them repeatedly can lead to an increasing sense of feeling disengaged. Finally, *Weaknesses* are things we are not good at and also drain us. Subsequently, from the model, the best advice is to *marshal realised strengths* by using them differently to best effect; *maximise unrealised strengths* by finding opportunities to use them more; *moderate learned behaviours* by not using them too much, and *minimise weaknesses* by finding ways to stop having to focus on them at all.

To *maximise unrealised strengths*, Linley et al. (2010b) suggest asking R2 profile respondents to reflect on the following questions: *Identify your unrealised strengths*, e.g., 'Which of your unrealised strengths are you most passionate about using? Which will make the most difference to you in achieving your goals?' *Find the opportunity*, e.g., 'Which strengths will help you get things done or fill the gap in golf?' *Practise* e.g., 'If you haven't used this strength much before, you might need to practise it. Notice when you learn things quickly and easily, a true sign of a strength and potential for growth'. *Develop*, e.g., 'Improve your use of the strength even more with formal learning and development as required. Who has this strength and uses it successfully? What can you learn from them?' *Expand your reach*, e.g., 'As you improve, take on bigger or more challenging shots'. *Evaluate*, e.g., 'As you maximise an unrealised strength, evaluate how you get on. Ask for feedback. Did you get the results you expected? What have you learned? What can you improve?'

To apply the R2 model and adapt the above reflection questions to golf, one of the authors utilised the results from the R2 Strengths Profiler, represented in Figure 17.3, with an experienced tour player. Both the questions used and the player's responses are illustrated in Table 17.4.

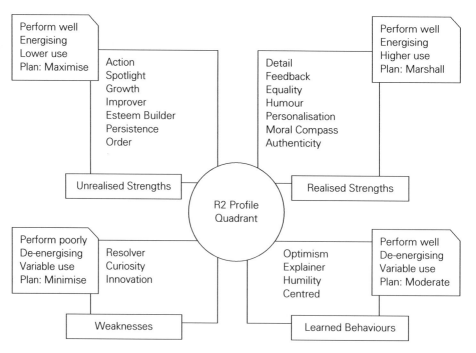

Figure 17.3   Example of the Realise2 strengths profile quadrant results, illustrating an experienced tour player's *Unrealised Strengths*, *Realised Strengths*, *Learned Behaviours*, and *Weaknesses*.

Source: Adapted from Linley (2010).

Table 17.4 Strengths-based questions exploring how to maximise *Unrealised Strengths* based on a Realise2 strengths profile. Refer Figure 17.3 to review the full Realise2 strengths profile, illustrating *Unrealised Strengths, Realised Strengths, Learned Behaviours,* and *Weaknesses*

Based on your results from the R2 Strengths Profiler, which of your unrealised strengths are you most passionate about using?

Player: Order – Being well organised and having everything in place at work and home. *Improver* – Not accepting how things are done and looking for ways to develop myself further. *Action* – Getting started immediately and being comfortable with forward momentum.

Which will make the most difference to you in achieving your goals this year on tour?

Player: I've been on the tour for 12 years. I know how to make cuts, but this year, I want to be in the winner's circle again. To do that, I will need to maximise my unrealised strength in *Improver,* as well as identify and develop ways to do things differently and more effectively. My strengths in *Action* can allow me to get started and *Persistence* to keep going when changes are challenging, knowing it takes effort and determination.

What are you doing when you have engaged these qualities more frequently in the past?

Player: I feel great when I am on tour and I think this is because I can more easily engage my strength of *Order*. It comes naturally because everything is set up around my tee times and I keep my plans strict and simple. I know where I have to be and what to do every minute of the day and I love that feeling. I don't use this strength as often away from the tour and I get off-track with my training and competing social arrangements.

When can you engage these strengths more often and how can you use them on and off the course this year?

Player: In my training habits and time away from tour events. Strict timing for starting and finishing training, planning ahead with my social arrangements. . . a focussed orderly schedule is important this year. I am good at getting my training done (action) every day, but my focus could be much better, I sometimes drag it out longer than it needs to be, going through the motions and doing what I feel like doing rather than sticking to a solid drill plan. If I bring *Order* to it, my focus would be more intense and my action more effective.

How can you improve the use of the strength even more, who do you need to involve, what resources do you need in place?

Player: Keeping a diary, calendar, and writing down my drills the night before training is key to bringing more *Order, Persistence,* and focus into my practice habits this year. Sharing these plans with my coach and sport psychologist and conducting reflection sessions will help me develop this further and keep me accountable for following through with it.

Can you use these strengths in bigger and more complex activities this year?

Player: Creating an annual performance plan is something I have wanted to do but haven't, and this is a project that I could use my strength of *Order* and *Persistence* to develop and continue to implement.

As you maximise your unrealised strengths, how will you evaluate your progress?

Player: If I am spending time organising my practice drills and keeping a log in advance, then I know I'm on track. Doing this will elevate my quality of training, which should translate to more top 10 finishes and possibly holding the trophy in a tournament this year.

Summary and future directions

The purpose of this chapter was to adapt a strengths-based approach specifically to golf. Currently, leaders, policymakers, and golf practitioners, including accredited coaches and psychologists, seem to ignore or forget the fact that regardless of outcomes, all golfers are successful in some way and are resourceful human beings. Traditionally, remedial approaches that focus on 'fixing weaknesses' have characterised the type of leadership thought to be appropriate, which typically involves 'training and telling' by an 'expert practitioner', who dominates the engagement. In contrast, a strengths-based proactive approach and learning process is more of a collaborative partnership, and the leader's expertise lies in assisting 'golfers as experts' by exploiting as well as identifying their strengths.

We encourage readers to consider the principles and strategies that have been presented and reflect on how they could be adapted for their use. We also encourage golf science practitioners to explore further and conduct research on the efficacy of these strengths-based approaches, as there is currently no evidence base for using applied PP principles in golf. Finally, we believe strengths-based approaches will soon be used in combination with the traditions of 'old school' methodologies to inform better and balance assumptions in the golf industry about how to motivate and inspire all participants.

For the future, upon reading this chapter, golf leaders, policymakers, coaches, and players are invited to consider the following questions:

1 When engaged in human development, which theoretical leadership assumptions do you currently employ? How and when might you consider adopting a strengths-based approach?
2 "You will find what you look for". Do you spot the strengths of those you work with or focus only on detecting weaknesses and faults? Which focus characterises your approach – strengths or weaknesses?
3 Reflect on how you might develop the strengths of individuals by shifting priorities from 'fixing weaknesses' to 'exploiting strengths'.
4 Could you embed strengths-based dialogue during your conversations? When might this be most useful and with whom, e.g., older or younger, novice or elite, male or female participants?

References

Biswas-Diener, R. (2010) *Practicing Positive Psychology Coaching*, Hoboken, NJ: John Wiley & Sons.
Cameron, K. & Spreitzer, G. (Eds.) (2012) *The Oxford Handbook of Positive Organizational Scholarship*, New York, NY: Oxford University Press.
Cohn, P. (2001) *Going Low: How to Break Your Individual Golf Scoring Barrier by Thinking Like a Pro*, New York, NY: Contemporary Books.
Driver, M. (2011) *Coaching Positively: Lessons for Coaches From Positive Psychology*, Maidenhead, UK: Open University Press.
Gordon, S. (2008a) An Appreciative Inquiry Coaching Approach to Developing Mental Toughness, In: D. Drake; D. Brennan, & K. Gørtz (Eds.) *The Philosophy and Practice of Coaching: Insights and Issues for a New Era*, Chichester, UK: Wiley, pp. 128–144.
Gordon, S. (2008b) Appreciative Inquiry Coaching, *International Coaching Psychology Review*, 3 (1), 17–29.
Gordon, S. & Gucciardi, D. (2011) Strengths-based Approach to Coaching Mental Toughness, *Journal of Sport Psychology in Action*, 2 (3), 143–155.
Govindji, R. & Linley, P. (2007) Strengths Use, Self-concordance and Well-being: Implications for Strengths Coaching and Coaching Psychologists, *International Coaching Psychology Review*, 2 (2), 143–153.
Gulgin, H.; Schulte, B. & Crawley, A. (2014) Correlation of Titleist Performance Institute (TPI) Level 1 Movement Screens and Golf Swing Faults, *Journal of Strength and Conditioning Research*, 28 (2), 534–539.
Hawkins, P. (2012) *Creating a Coaching Culture*, Maidenhead, UK: Open University Press.
Hemmings, B.; Mantle, H. & Ellwood, J. (2007) *Mental Toughness for Golf: The Minds of Winners*, Swindon, UK: Green Umbrella.
Linley, A. (2008) *Average to A+: Realizing Strengths in Yourself and Others*, Coventry, UK: CAPP.
Linley, P. (2010). *Realise2: Technical Report*, Coventry, UK: CAPP.

Linley, P. & Harrington, S. (2006) Strengths Coaching: A Potential-guided Approach to Coaching Psychology, *International Coaching Psychology Review*, 1 (1), 37–46.

Linley, P. & Joseph, S. (Eds.) (2004) *Positive Psychology in Practice*, Hoboken, NJ: John Wiley & Sons.

Linley, P.; Nielsen, K.; Wood, A.; Gillett, R. & Biswas-Diener, R. (2010a) Using Signature Strengths in Pursuit of Goals: Effects on Goal Progress, Need Satisfaction, and Well Being, and Implications for Coaching Psychologists, *International Coaching Psychology Review*, 5 (1), 8–17.

Linley, A.; Willars, J. & Biswas-Diener, R. (2010b) *The Strengths Book: Be Confident, Be Successful, and Enjoy Better Relationships by Realising the Best of You*, Coventry, UK: CAPP.

Linley, P.; Woolston, L. & Biswas-Diener, R. (2009) Strengths Coaching with Leaders, *International Coaching Psychology Review*, 4 (1), 37–48.

Lopez, S. & Snyder, C. (Eds.) (2009) *Oxford Handbook of Positive Psychology* (2nd Ed.), New York, NY: Oxford University Press.

Mainwaring, L. (2009) Working with Perfection, In: K. Hays (Ed.) *Performance Psychology in Action*, Washington, DC: American Psychological Association, pp 139–160.

Marriott, L. & Nilsson, P. (2011) *Play Your Best Golf Now*, New York, NY: Gotham.

Maslow, A. (1954) *Motivation and Personality*, New York, NY: Harper.

Park-Perin, G. (2010) Positive Psychology, In: S. Hanrahan & M. Andersen (Eds.) *Routledge Handbook of Applied Sport Psychology: A Comprehensive Guide for Students and Practitioners*, London: Routledge, pp 141–149.

Robertson, A. & Abbey, G. (2003) *Managing Talented People*, Harlow, UK: Pearson Education.

Rotella, R. (2008) *Your 15th Club: The Inner Secret to Great Golf*, Sydney, Australia: Simon & Schuster.

Seligman, M. (2011) *Flourish*, Sydney, Australia: Heinemann.

Seligman, M. (1999) The President's Address, *American Psychologist*, 54, 559–562.

Sharp, L.-A. & Hodge, K. (2011) Sport Psychology Consulting Effectiveness: The Sport Psychology Consultant's Perspective, *Journal of Applied Sport Psychology*, 23 (3), 360–376.

Sheldon, K.; Kasser, T.; Smith, K. & Share, T. (2002) Personal Goals and Psychological Growth: Testing an Intervention to Enhance Goal-Attainment and Personality Integration, *Journal of Personality*, 70 (1), 5–31.

Toogood, K. (2012) Strengthening Coaching: An Exploration of the Mindset of Executive Coaches Using Strengths-Based Coaching, *International Journal of Evidence Based Coaching and Mentoring*, (Special Issue No. 6), 72–87.

Valiante, G. (2013) *Golf Flow*, Urbana Champaign, IL: Human Kinetics.

18

REFINING MOTOR SKILLS IN GOLF

A biopsychosocial perspective

Howie J. Carson and Dave Collins

Introduction

For all golfers, especially those committed to a performance pathway, progression is not constant across involvement (MacNamara et al., 2010b). Undoubtedly, novices become more skilled with practice, largely through improvements in technical proficiency and consistency (Gentile, 1972). Indeed, skill acquisition theory explains this relative permanence of skill as resulting from increased automaticity (Fitts & Posner, 1967), a hallmark of learnt skills as execution processes become committed to subconscious control (Beilock et al., 2004). Notably, however, long-term performance gains are sometimes more difficult to achieve as practice volume increases, irrespective of skill level – often termed a 'performance plateau'.

In fact, once skills are automatized, implementing refinements, or tweaks, presents not only the more significant but also more common challenge for golfers. Thus, players may wish to make changes across a broad front, for instance, to improve proficiency, in response to new equipment regulations (e.g., shallower grooves), course demands (e.g., lengthened holes), improved competitors, ageing, or prevent/return from injury. Indeed, fixing ineffective but well-automatized movements constitutes a significant part of some coaches' everyday role (as opposed to teaching the acquisition of new skills). Furthermore, if golfers are willing to commit to making these modifications, it would seem desirable that they be long-lasting and robust under highly pressurized conditions.

Considering the importance of successful refinement to skills that are already learnt, long-practised, and well established, these challenges have, however, received surprisingly scant research attention (e.g., Schack & Bar-Eli, 2007). Accordingly, this chapter is targeted at assisting coaches working with experienced players, whether seasoned 15-handicappers or Tour professionals. Specifically, it aims to review and critique three key dimensions to achieving successful skill refinement. Firstly, the need for an interdisciplinary perspective towards player development; secondly, the role of planning and the nature of the coach's decision-making processes; and thirdly, the training programme required. In the following sections, implications and future research directions are offered for applied coaching practice in skill refinement.

Review of current research
The importance of an interdisciplinary perspective

As science support has become a common feature across sports, recognition has emerged for the ways in which disciplines may collaborate and integrate with the job of the coach. However, despite important and well-argued papers making this point some time ago (e.g., Burwitz et al., 1994), uni- and multidisciplinary models still predominate. In short, truly interdisciplinary approaches, where specialists work in an integrated fashion, with strong, effective communication and towards commonly agreed objectives, are still the exception. If golfers, coaches, support practitioners, and managers would rather consult nutritionists about food, fitness consultants about training, and psychologists about mental challenges, they fail to notice that elements of all three and their interactions will typically underpin performance issues. Using this silo approach neglects the increasingly accepted fact that almost all human issues are both complex and biopsychosocial in nature. Indeed, interactions between these different elements often play an even greater part in determining behavior and outcomes than the distinct factors themselves.

An example may add clarity. A golfer may report problems with maintaining attentional focus, which, after careful evaluation, can be largely attributed to an overuse of simple carbohydrates at breakfast and poor hydration on course. Dietary changes are made, with the player announcing to her/his friends and family that she/he has decided to really work holistically on her/his game. In such a case (and not exclusive to golf; cf. Collins et al., 1993), performance may well improve resulting from changes in biochemistry (the Bio), expectancy effects, better body image in the golfer (the Psycho), and increased support, plus expectancy impacts from her/his peers (the Social). A well-informed support group will work with the golfer and coach to optimize the impact of a change, exploiting all three elements and the interactions to maximize performance effects. Importantly, the particular blend of bio, psycho, and social will vary depending on many factors, for example, across golfers, the state of the change (e.g., early or later in the intervention), and the influence of those practitioners suggesting/driving the change.

The origin of knowledge is another important consideration. Regarding the science underpinning the change (which may itself be multifaceted), consumers need to be aware of the originators' intentions. As shown by Collins and Kamin (2012), scientists can be motivated by work through, of, or for sport. Therefore, research will look to examine rather fundamental effects through the use of golf situations. For example, consider much of the work on implicit learning (e.g., Maxwell et al., 2000), where novices learn a very simple putting task (e.g., flat 10 ft. putt). In such cases, the authors' motivation is to increase their knowledge of implicit learning through use of a golf-like task. It would, therefore, be questionable to uncritically transfer and apply these results to work with Tour professionals. By contrast, the Five-A Model (Carson & Collins, 2011), which is addressed later, was developed for application using what is known as a pragmatic approach (cf. Giacobbi Jr. et al., 2005). Add to these sources the bewildering array of gurus and experts available through social media (MacNamara & Collins, 2015) and the challenge becomes even greater. Sound advice is to always be aware of the source and intention of the advice, applying a dose of healthy critique, or even scepticism, to ideas before they are tried and tested with performers.

These concerns notwithstanding, it is an important realization that coaching for technical refinement should be fundamentally biopsychosocial in nature and exist within an ongoing player–coach relationship. Accordingly, the skilled coach should be aware of the contribution of each of the three elements, as well as their interactions, towards player performance and progress. Coaching is certainly not one-dimensional or unidisciplinary, even if so many of the coaching and performance aids currently on the market are!

So, what might a truly biopsychosocial approach look like? Imagine that coach and player have decided to implement technical change. The predominant focus of the coach is, traditionally at least, on the bio – the technical change itself. Building on previous points, a comprehensive treatment will also address the other two elements. The coach will address the psycho by ensuring the golfer's confidence in the change, by maintaining confidence in progress, and by generating a positive view of the outcome to ensure motivation. From a social perspective, the coach will work to gain support for change from the golfer's immediate group. Avoiding dissenting voices as the change is made is essential. These ideas are now extended into the early stages of technical refinement, a time when the psychosocial dimensions are particularly important.

Planning and decision-making

The need for a comprehensive biopsychosocial approach is particularly apparent in the early stages of refinement. Without careful and considered analysis, plus a strong selling job, there is a significant risk that the wrong decisions will be taken or, just as damaging, good decisions not followed through. Accordingly, coach and player will first need to ensure due diligence when considering making a change, weighing up the pros and cons of refinement against other options (cf. Toner et al., 2012). Crucially, one must ask if the change is worth it. Subsequent sections will testify that technical tweaks take time, especially when the skill must be reautomatized to ensure pressure-proofing. Accordingly, many considerations come into play, such as the player's age and when s/he needs to peak next; that is, how long until peak performance is next required. This is hard enough working with Olympic sports, for example, tweaking a judo player's throw can take 6 months. For golfers, where a 6-month absence from, or underperformance on, the Tour may necessitate requalification, the decision is even more complex.

Once these difficulties are addressed, it is then possible to get into even more devilish detail. How will the refinement take place? Can some waymarks be set so that progress can be monitored and demonstrated to all concerned? Will any specialists be brought in to help and, if so, does the need to get individuals completely trusted by the player add additional time to the planned schedule? Hopefully, this brief tour through the challenges of change is sufficient to evidence how carefully such decisions need to be made. Ultimately, coaches' and players' accounts show that changes are all too often initiated without sufficient thought (Carson et al., 2013). Indeed, coaches may often keep fiddling with skills inappropriately through a desire to contribute when the situation is a perfect environment for 'less is more'! Elements of role clarity, presentational bias, and authority often play a part in this tendency (Mallett & Pyke, 2008), which the wise coach will resist. Thus, in the present context, coaches must generate positive psychosocial support for change, a commitment and desire in the player, in parallel to the more usual bio (in this case, technical and mechanical) focus.

It is hoped that the need for a clear underpinning process is emerging. With elements of macro (overarching) and meta (thinking about) cognition, coaches in every sport, and certainly one as technically focussed as golf, can benefit from the development and application of more structured higher-order thinking. Thus, in the example above, the coach will use macrocognitive approaches to drive a process of decision-making, design, and implementation of technical change. Additionally, s/he will use metacognitive techniques to reflect on the process, making adjustments appropriately but not so regularly that the player is disrupted in making the change.

Interested readers should refer to an examination of these processes in adventure sports (e.g., Collins & Collins, 2015), which clearly demonstrates transfer at both macro and meta levels.

As these and other papers demonstrate, macro and metacognitive approaches are best considered under the umbrella approach of professional judgment and decision-making (PJDM). At its simplest, PJDM stresses the importance for a coach to consider the 'why' as much as, or even more than, the 'what' and 'how' of coaching. Inevitably, therefore, alternatives are always framed and critically considered, generating a more expertise-based approach to coaching. Indeed, this approach is viewed as taking coaching beyond the overly structured and reproductive system of competencies, which currently predominates in many coach accreditation programmes (Collins et al., 2015a).

In this regard, it is worth stating that such levels of macro and metacognition are characteristics of professions (cf. Winter & Collins, 2016). As Carr (1999) explains, when distinguishing teaching as a profession, the existence of a distinct knowledge base and clear autonomy of practice are key characteristics. Similarly, optimum golf coaching should be built on a specific and highly individual blend of techniques, drawn from a large library of knowledge on the basis of careful and ongoing reflection and weighing up of options.

Therefore, reflecting these twin ideas of biopsychosocial and PJDM, the next section presents a systemic structure within which the fine-tuning can take place. As another comparison, this structure provides the basic recipe against which the creative chef/coach can develop a refined and bespoke solution to meet the specific needs of each particular player. To push the principles of meta and macrocognition, a five-part process is suggested, which can be used at major decision-making stages. Accordingly, the truly reflective coach will follow this checklist:

- 'I have decided to . . .'
- 'Because . . .'
- 'But I considered these options . . .'
- 'And would have taken this alternative if the circumstances were changed to . . .'
- 'I will check my decision in X months and, if I was right, would expect to see . . .'

Consequently, alternatives are always considered and evaluated, countering the tendency to go with recipe approaches that have reportedly worked for others. There is a real tendency to equate the quality of performer outcome with the quality of coach input ('she's a great performer, so he must be a great coach'! cf. Nash et al., 2012) and golf is equally susceptible to this bias. The best counter is to always critically consider alternatives, to check with peers on the whys and wherefores of how they are coaching, and to regularly review progress against predicted benchmarks. Bear these factors in mind during the review of the structure and design of refinement-focussed interventions in the next section.

Training programme

A third review addresses the mechanistic underpinnings necessary to generate long-term permanent and pressure-resistant refinement, thereby providing the important declarative knowledge of 'what needs to be done' and 'why', as well as the procedural knowledge of 'how to do it'. Unfortunately, many golfers struggle to bring about such change for a variety of reasons. Despite this inherent difficulty, however, coaching interventions must be able to cater to such possibilities and exploit these mechanisms on an individual basis as part of the approach, if they are to provide a first-class service to their clients. Of course, not all elements of training will be different for each golfer. On the contrary, common practices (or at least similar practices with common aims) will be apparent, acting as primary facilitators of the change process as a function of human nature (refer also Prochaska & Prochaska, 1999). Understanding these basic principles should, therefore, be the starting point for further coach development in this area.

Addressing one crucial facilitator, and forming the focus of critique offered here, is the type of motor control required for long-term permanent and pressure-resistant outcomes. As identified earlier, the development of automaticity is a fundamental part of the skill acquisition process, resulting in the largely effortless, automatic, and efficient (although in our present example perhaps erroneous, or at least suboptimal) execution of movement (Fitts & Posner, 1967). There are many advantages of automaticity when performing motor skills. For example, it enables attention to be directed towards changeable shot, weather, and game conditions without having to also overly focus on controlling the movement components (not that attention paid internally towards the movement always results in a negative outcome; refer Bortoli et al., 2012). Briefly, because attentional capacity is finite, automatization releases resources to focus on task-relevant information. In the short term, automaticity even prevents golfers from stabilizing what would normally be considered ineffective technique for the majority of shots experienced: when, for instance, executing from a severely steep incline or hitting out from underneath a bush. Therefore, the important message here is that the most practised technique, rather than the most recent technique, is the version most likely to persist within a golfer's repertoire.

Accordingly, skill refinement should be considered a high-risk intervention and distinct from skill acquisition (i.e., developing automaticity) and performance (i.e., exploiting already existing levels of automaticity), due largely to the competition associated with a golfer's already well-established technique (Kostrubiec et al., 2006). In fact, the more experienced the golfer is at executing a technique and/or the greater the number of changes made previously (a distinct possibility if frequently switching coaches), the stronger/greater number of sources of competition there will be. It is on this basis that critique is warranted towards several proposals within the literature that suggest that strategies for skill acquisition and performance can be and/or are applicable to the experienced athlete when making a refinement. Specifically, consider the use of an external focus of attention (i.e., directing attention away from body movement; Wulf, 2016) and implicit motor learning (i.e., practising a skill without accruing explicit knowledge of the movement; Masters, 1992; Rendell et al., 2011). Notably, both approaches have also recently been challenged regarding their usefulness and application outside of the experimental setting and for sports requiring a variety of complex skills (refer Gabbett & Masters, 2011, Toner & Moran, 2015); but, in the present context, this critique will be limited purely to occasions of refinement.

By definition, both strategies involve not consciously attending to any body movements in an effort to prevent interference with automatic, subconscious execution processes (McNevin et al., 2003). Furthermore, implicit learning aims to inhibit explicit knowledge generation about the skill and, therefore, prevent the possibility of conscious reinvestment and skill breakdown under high-anxiety conditions (Masters & Maxwell, 2008). However, should the golfer's automatized control remain unchanged, it would be difficult to see how small refinements could be made long-term permanent and pressure-resistant since the already well-established version would continue to exert strong competition. Moreover, even if a skill were to be already acquired via implicit training, how would a technique change even work using additional implicit methods? Coaches should be cautious when observing apparent success during coaching sessions with the said approaches, since often these can be lost after a short break or when attempting to transfer the new move onto the golf course. Moreover, the consistency of a movement's automaticity explains this occurrence (Carson & Collins, 2016a), with some suggesting that the skill acquisition process be beneficially prevented from achieving full automatization across the entire movement; in other words, too much automatization is a bad thing (cf. Toner & Moran, 2015). Indeed, this would certainly concur with characteristics of elite-level athletes' performances (e.g., Nyberg, 2015; Christensen et al., 2016), which provide the possibility to access skill components should they be necessary to maintain performance of a task at hand (e.g., intentionally execute a draw rather than a fade), and, therefore, counter any long-term advantages of always executing with an external focus of attention or under an implicit design. In summary, the proposal that one type of motor control strategy is absolutely beneficial for acquiring, performing, and refining motor skills is absolutely unrealistic and undesirable in absolutely every case. In short, it depends!

Alternatively, successful skill refinement requires a non-linear, transitory process. Notably, the Five-A Model proposed by Carson and Collins (2011) – a five-stage process designed to promote long-term permanence and pressure resistance – expressly encourages conscious deautomatization of the technical aspect (not every aspect of movement) requiring modification within the early 'awareness' stage (Christina & Corcos, 1988; Beilock et al., 2002; Oudejans et al., 2007). That is, of course, having already conducted a case formulation to decide whether refinement is necessary, what to refine, how, why, and when during the previous stage of 'analysis' (cf. the previous section). Accordingly, the golfer actively retrieves, through a narrow internal focus of attention, the flawed aspect of the memory representation and inevitably experiences a temporary regression in motor control. Such practice is, therefore, entirely counter to implementing a completely external focus of attention or implicit strategy (e.g., dual-task condition), but essential if it is to undergo permanent modification.

Of course, deautomatization can be very frustrating for the golfer as performance dips (Carson & Collins, 2016b). Therefore, it is crucial to ensure buy-in and trust between golfer and coach, as described in the previous section. Indeed, a thorough analysis would have confirmed that a golfer was 'change-ready', equipped with the mental skills to employ the required techniques (e.g., internal imagery), and sufficiently well supported by their caddie, psychologist, family, manager, teammates, and/or friends to maintain focus on and motivation for the job at hand. Given the potential for mixed messages within a close multi-stakeholder environment, however, the coach would be wise to set ground rules regarding role clarity and interaction among the support team (Collins & Collins, 2011). Indeed, a disruptive effect is easily misunderstood as poor coaching to the uninformed golfer, so consistent messages can help to enhance a subjective norm (Ajzen, 1991) and intention to stay committed.

Empirically, available data demonstrate the reality of this awareness process as not necessarily being immediate within the training session (Carson & Collins, 2015). Instead, golfers may need several sessions of focussed effort to fully deautomatize the targeted swing aspect. The primary aim at this stage, however, is not the modification of movement, but simply to deautomatize the movement's control as a 'kick start' to the process.

To assist in this goal, studies (e.g., Collins et al., 1999; Hanin et al., 2002; Carson et al., 2014) have supported the use of contrast training (i.e., purposefully alternating between the flawed and desired version techniques) concurrently with intentional cueing and direct questioning. Not only does this approach call the established version into consciousness, it also generates a targeted new version – although initially weak (relative to the existing version) – within the motor memory trace. Additionally, Carson et al. (2016) showed that several found it more effective to consciously initiate refinements when hitting in front of a net versus onto an outdoor driving range, thereby reducing environmental distractions to permit a more internally directed and less outcome-oriented focus. While such practice might not be the case for all golfers, empirical study is yet to confirm this. Data certainly support the former contention, in that lower inter-trial movement variability of individually targeted refinements was found in the former condition, thus indicating a higher level of conscious control.

So, if using the Five-A Model, having deautomatized the erroneous technique and created the realization of what needs to change, progress is required through a gradual stage of 'adjustment' in which the new version of the technique becomes more accurate, comfortable, and accepted while concurrently representing a distinct 'departure' from the original, unwanted movement. Such an effect relies on increasing the practice volume of the new version by tapering out contrasts with the original and reintroducing more representative golf environments (e.g., driving range/golf course). Presenting a best-attempt self-model (e.g., on an electronic tablet; Carson & Collins, 2015) at this stage can prime the golfer and drive the modification of the memory representation, as well as provide a source of motivation (Carson et al., 2014). Once consistently achieved, gradual reautomatization must take place through a reduction of conscious control towards the targeted technical aspect, within the '(re)automation' stage. This process allows for the less-associated aspects of the refinement to 'settle in' with the new version of the skill, whereby the entire movement is primed holistically through patterns of rhythmic thought (e.g., mood words), therefore acting as a 'source of information' (MacPherson et al., 2008, p. 289). MacPherson et al. (2009) also explain such cognitions as providing a 'screen' from potentially maladaptive thoughts, that is, a positive distraction. Finally, as a proactive step, the skill must be pressure-proofed against all weathers, including negative symptoms of anxiety. Combination training (Collins et al., 1999; Carson & Collins, 2015), that is, combining physical exertion with a high degree of technical challenge, has been employed to offer the double benefit of increased performance outcome and perceived proficiency.

Notably, there are many factors to consider during use of the Five-A Model, too many to cover in detail here. As such, we recommend interested readers to other informative texts (refer Hanin et al., 2002; Carson & Collins, 2011; Toner et al., 2012; Carson & Collins, 2014, 2016b). What we hope to have achieved, however, is a position against a 'one size fits all' approach.

Implications for the game

Given the need for such a comprehensive approach to refining skills, there are clearly many significant implications, including the training of the coach, the use and integration of any support specialists, and the prerequisite characteristics of the golfer. Addressing the former, a PJDM approach will focus on generating a case formulation, as well as implementing and auditing working practice, therefore requiring a sufficiently broad declarative and procedural understanding of sport sciences as a whole. The effective coach will not solely specialize; rather, training must facilitate knowledge across the '-ologies' and be in context for optimum impact. Coaches will be encouraged and provided with a range of opportunities to think critically when evaluating research/evidence-based practice, discover the important factors that coaching decisions depend on, and conduct meaningful, light-on-description self-reflections referencing their intention for impact, with ongoing auditing processes involved. Indeed, these components will form an important aspect of coach accreditation, with frequent, less-formal, and articulated justification characterizing the style of interaction between assessor and coach. The authors suggest that the development of both macro and metacognitive skills in this way provides a stronger basis for lifelong development and an overall more capable workforce.

The use and integration of support team dynamics will also have strong implications. Indeed, it is not uncommon for the too many ologists involved – each with their own working agenda, desire to prove their discipline's worth, and understanding of the issue – to create unwanted conflict (Collins et al., 2015b). While critical debate is of course a positive characteristic of high-performance environments (Burke, 2011), it must be carefully mediated by the coach at the right times to ensure that it offers only a beneficial impact to both the intervention design and auditing process. In fact, such appreciation also applies to other stakeholders, such as management staff, especially at the elite level, who often have the final say when it comes to finances and support provision. Ideally, the support team will function with a shared understanding and common goals, putting the golfer at the forefront of any decision made. As such, collaboration with, for instance, performance institutes, must be oriented for golf. Presentation of ideas and feedback to the golfer must be consistent, even if there exist hard-core debate and discussion behind the scenes. Therefore, establishing role clarity before the refinement is initiated is increasingly important to knowing exactly who does what, with whom, and when.

From the golfer's perspective, technical refinement can be characterized as a transition. Since transitions often present a significant degree of difficulty and challenge (Collins & MacNamara, 2012), it is important that golfers can overcome any trauma imposed. Indeed, recent talent development research has identified several psychobehavioural skills (Psychological Characteristics for Developing Execellence; MacNamara et al., 2010a) that, when developed for and deployed at, these critical periods assist athletes to successfully negotiate the inevitable rocky road ahead. Indeed, exemplar characteristics include resilience, imagery, commitment, coping under pressure and with setbacks, goal setting, and social skills (Kamin et al., 2007; MacNamara et al., 2008; Sarkar & Fletcher, 2014). Accordingly, as a precursor to implementing refinement, coaches should ensure that golfers are sufficiently prepared during the skill acquisition process, through the development of these skills, to overcome known future transitions such as injury, expectations of playing in higher-status teams/Tours, and technical refinement. Notably, while these specific characteristics are yet to be empirically tested as holding relevance during skill refinement with experienced athletes, current work in golf suggests elements of self-presentation bias and confidence in using mental imagery, at least, have a significant impact on the level of intervention outcome (Carson & Collins, 2015).

Summary and future directions

This chapter has challenged coaches and researchers to consider new perspectives when helping golfers refine already long-practised and well-established skills. Fundamentally, this has meant acknowledging the limitations of skill acquisition and performance knowledge for use during this starkly different task. Additionally, there is a need to broaden the application of coaches' (and other stakeholders', including management at the elite level) understanding to cater for inherent and complex biopsychosocial interactions (this latter point also being pertinent to skill acquisition and performance outcomes). Therefore, the use of an expertise (PJDM) approach was suggested as an alternative to acting on a competency-driven basis. It is not anticipated that such a transition could be easy within the golf-coaching profession, especially considering its long-standing and historic roots: it will require a significant change in culture, development, and assessment structure, as well as service provision for some coaches working with some players. Accordingly, future work should seek to assess the meta and macrocognitive skills of coaches as exemplar standards of practice at different stages of professional development and when working towards different player outcomes. Equally, there is a need for greater testing of the Five-A Model with a range of golfers and a range of intended technical changes. While research to date has explored many of its elements, including longitudinal tracking, greater attention towards its validation would be much welcomed. Finally, any innovations that golf development bodies can implement towards growth in this area of research and practice are awaited with much interest.

References

Ajzen, I. (1991) The Theory of Planned Behavior, *Organizational Behavior and Human Decision Processes*, 50 (2), 179–211.

Beilock, S.; Bertenthal, B.; Mccoy, A. & Carr, T. (2004) Haste Does Not Always Make Waste: Expertise, Direction of Attention, and Speed Versus Accuracy in Performing Sensorimotor Skills, *Psychonomic Bulletin & Review*, 11 (2), 373–379.

Beilock, S.; Carr, T.; Macmahon, C. & Starkes, J. (2002) When Paying Attention Becomes Counterproductive: Impact of Divided Versus Skill-Focused Attention on Novice and Experienced Performance of Sensorimotor Skills, *Journal of Experimental Psychology: Applied*, 8 (1), 6–16.

Bortoli, L.; Bertollo, M.; Hanin, Y. & Robazza, C. (2012) Striving For Excellence: A Multi-Action Plan Intervention Model for Shooters, *Psychology of Sport and Exercise*, 13 (5), 693–701.

Burke, V. (2011) Organizing for Excellence, In: D. Collins; A. Button & H Richards, (Eds.) *Performance Psychology: A Practitioner's Guide*, Oxford, UK: Elsevier.

Burwitz, L.; Moore, P. & Wilkinson, D. (1994) Future Directions for Performance-Related Sports Science Research: An Interdisciplinary Approach, *Journal of Sports Sciences*, 12 (1), 93–109.

Carr, D. (1999) Professional Education and Professional Ethics Right to Die or Duty to Live? *Journal of Applied Philosophy*, 16 (1), 33–46.

Carson, H. & Collins, D. (2011) Refining and Regaining Skills in Fixation/Diversification Stage Performers: The Five-A Model, *International Review of Sport and Exercise Psychology*, 4 (2), 146–167.

Carson, H. & Collins, D. (2014) Effective Skill Refinement: Focusing on Process to Ensure Outcome, *Central European Journal of Sport Sciences and Medicine*, 7 (3), 5–21.

Carson, H. & Collins, D. (2015) Tracking Technical Refinement in Elite Performers: The Good, the Better, and the Ugly, *International Journal of Golf Science*, 4 (1), 67–87.

Carson, H. & Collins, D. (2016a) The Fourth Dimension: A Motoric Perspective on the Anxiety–Performance Relationship, *International Review of Sport and Exercise Psychology*, 9 (1), 1–21.

Carson, H. & Collins, D. (2016b) Implementing the Five-A Model of Technical Change: Key Roles for the Sport Psychologist, *Journal of Applied Sport Psychology*, 28 (4), 392–409.

Carson, H.; Collins, D. & Jones, B. (2014) A Case Study of Technical Change and Rehabilitation: Intervention Design and Interdisciplinary Team Interaction, *International Journal of Sport Psychology*, 45 (1), 57–78.

Carson, H.; Collins, D. & Macnamara, Á. (2013) Systems for Technical Refinement in Experienced Performers: The Case From Expert-level Golf, *International Journal of Golf Science*, 2 (1), 65–85.

Carson, H.; Collins, D. & Richards, J. (2016) Initiating Technical Refinements in High-level Golfers: Evidence for Contradictory Procedures, *European Journal of Sport Science*, 16 (4), 473–482.

Christensen, W.; Sutton, J. & Mcilwain, D. (2016) Cognition in Skilled Action: Meshed Control and the Varieties of Skill Experience, *Mind and Language*, 31 (1), 37–66.

Christina, R. & Corcos, D. (1988) *Coaches Guide to Teaching Sport Skills*, Champaign, IL: Human Kinetics.

Collins, D. & Collins, J. (2011) Putting Them Together: Skill Packages to Optimize Team/Group Performance, In: D. Collins; A. Button, & H. Richards (Eds.) *Performance Psychology: A Practitioner's Guide*, Oxford, UK: Elsevier.

Collins, D. & Kamin, S. (2012) The Performance Coach, In: S. Murphy (Ed.) *The Oxford Handbook of Sport and Performance Psychology*, New York, NY: Oxford University Press.

Collins, D. & MacNamara, Á. (2012) The Rocky Road to the Top: Why Talent Needs Trauma, *Sports Medicine*, 42 (11), 907–914.

Collins, D.; Burke, V.; Martindale, A. & Cruickshank, A. (2015a) The Illusion of Competency Versus the Desirability of Expertise: Seeking a Common Standard for Support Professions in Sport. *Sports Medicine*, 45 (1), 1–7.

Collins, D.; Carson, H. & Cruickshank, A. (2015b) Blaming Bill Gates AGAIN! Misuse, Overuse and Misunderstanding of Performance Data in Sport, *Sport, Education and Society*, 20 (8), 1088–1099.

Collins, D.; Doherty, M. & Talbot, S. (1993) Performance Enhancement in Motocross: A Case Study of the Sport Science Team in Action, *The Sport Psychologist*, 7 (3), 290–297.

Collins, D.; Morriss, C. & Trower, J. (1999) Getting It Back: A Case Study of Skill Recovery in an Elite Athlete, *The Sport Psychologist*, 13 (3), 288–298.

Collins, L. & Collins, D. (2015) Integration of Professional Judgement and Decision-making in High-Level Adventure Sports Coaching Practice, *Journal of Sports Sciences*, 33 (6), 622–633.

Fitts, P. & Posner, M. (1967) *Human Performance*, Belmont, CA: Brooks/Cole Publishing Company.

Gabbett, T. & Masters, R. (2011) Challenges and Solutions When Applying Implicit Motor Learning Theory in a High Performance Sport Environment: Examples From Rugby League, *International Journal of Sports Science and Coaching*, 6 (4), 567–575.

Gentile, A. (1972) A Working Model of Skill Acquisition with Application to Teaching, *Quest*, 17 (1), 3–23.

Giacobbi, P., Jr.; Poczwardowski, A. & Hager, P. (2005) A Pragmatic Research Philosophy for Applied Sport Psychology, *The Sport Psychologist*, 19 (1), 18–31.

Hanin, Y.; Korjus, T.; Jouste, P. & Baxter, P. (2002) Rapid Technique Correction Using Old Way/New Way: Two Case Studies with Olympic Athletes, *The Sport Psychologist*, 16 (1), 79–99.

Kamin, S.; Richards, H. & Collins, D. (2007) Influences on the Talent Development Process of Non-classical Musicians: Psychological, Social and Environmental Influences, *Music Education Research*, 9 (3), 449–468.

Kostrubiec, V.; Tallet, J. & Zanone, P.-G. (2006) How a New Behavioral Pattern Is Stabilized with Learning Determines Its Persistence and Flexibility in Memory, *Experimental Brain Research*, 170 (2), 238–244.

MacNamara, Á. & Collins, D. (2015) Twitterati and Paperati: Evidence Versus Popular Opinion in Science Communication, *British Journal of Sports Medicine*, 49 (19), 1227–1228.

MacNamara, Á.; Button, A. & Collins, D. (2010a) The Role of Psychological Characteristics in Facilitating the Pathway to Elite Performance Part 1: Identifying Mental Skills and Behaviors, *The Sport Psychologist*, 24 (1), 52–73.

MacNamara, Á.; Collins, D. & Button, A. (2010b) The Role of Psychological Characteristics in Facilitating the Pathway to Elite Performance Part 2: Examining Environmental and Stage-Related Differences in Skills and Behaviors, *The Sport Psychologist*, 24 (1), 74–96.

MacNamara, Á.; Holmes, P. & Collins, D. (2008) Negotiating Transitions in Musical Development: The Role of Psychological Characteristics of Developing Excellence, *Psychology of Music*, 36 (3), 335–352.

MacPherson, A.; Collins, D. & Morriss, C. (2008) Is What You Think What You Get? Optimizing Mental Focus for Technical Performance, *The Sport Psychologist*, 22 (3), 288–303.

MacPherson, A.; Collins, D. & Obhi, S. (2009) The Importance of Temporal Structure and Rhythm for the Optimum Performance of Motor Skills: A New Focus for Practitioners of Sport Psychology, *Journal of Applied Sport Psychology*, 21 (S1), 48–61.

Mallett, C. & Pyke, F. (2008) Coaching the Best, *Sports Coach*, 30 (1), 6–8.

Masters, R. (1992) Knowledge, Knerves and Know-how: The Role of Explicit Versus Implicit Knowledge in the Breakdown of a Complex Motor Skill Under Pressure, *British Journal of Psychology*, 83 (3), 343–358.

Masters, R. & Maxwell, J. (2008) The Theory of Reinvestment, *International Review of Sport and Exercise Psychology*, 1 (2), 160–183.

Maxwell, J.; Masters, R. & Eves, F. (2000) From Novice to No Know-how: A Longitudinal Study of Implicit Motor Learning, *Journal of Sports Sciences*, 18 (2), 111–120.

McNevin, N.; Shea, C. & Wulf, G. (2003) Increasing the Distance of an External Focus of Attention Enhances Learning, *Psychological Research*, 67 (1), 22–29.

Nash, C.; Martindale, R.; Collins, D. & Martindale, A. (2012) Parameterising Expertise in Coaching: Past, Present and Future, *Journal of Sports Sciences*, 30 (10), 985–994.

Nyberg, G. (2015) Developing a "Somatic Velocimeter" – The Practical Knowledge of Freeskiers, *Qualitative Research in Sport, Exercise and Health*, 7 (1), 109–124.

Oudejans, R.; Koedijker, J. & Beek, P. (2007) An Outside View on Wulf's External Focus: Three Recommendations, *E-Journal Bewegung Und Training* [Online], 1, Available at www.Ejournal-But.De.

Prochaska, J. & Prochaska, J. (1999) Why Don't Continents Move? Why Don't People Change? *Journal of Psychotherapy Integration*, 9 (1), 83–102.

Rendell, M.; Farrow, D.; Masters, R. & Plummer, N. (2011) Implicit Practice for Technique Adaptation in Expert Performers, *International Journal of Sports Science and Coaching*, 6 (4), 553–566.

Sarkar, M. & Fletcher, D. (2014) Psychological Resilience in Sport Performers: A Review of Stressors and Protective Factors, *Journal of Sports Sciences*, 32 (15), 1419–1434.

Schack, T. & Bar-Eli, M. (2007) Psychological Factors of Technical Preparation, In: B. Blumenstein; R. Lidor, & G. Tenenbaum (Eds.) *Psychology of Sport Training*, Münster, Germany: Meyer & Meyer Sport, pp. 62–103.

Toner, J. & Moran, A. (2015) Enhancing Performance Proficiency at the Expert Level: Considering the Role of "Somaesthetic Awareness", *Psychology of Sport and Exercise*, 16 (Pt 1), 110–117.

Toner, J.; Nelson, L.; Potrac, P.; Gilbourne, D. & Marshall, P. (2012) From "Blame" To "Shame" in a Coach–Athlete Relationship in Golf: A Tale of Shared Critical Reflection and the Re-Storying of Narrative Experience, *Sports Coaching Review*, 1 (1), 67–78.

Winter, S. & Collins, D. (2016) Applied Sport Psychology: A Profession? *The Sport Psychologist*, 30 (1), 89–96.

Wulf, G. (2016) An External Focus of Attention is a Conditio Sine Qua Non for Athletes: A Response to Carson, Collins, and Toner (2015), *Journal of Sports Sciences*, 34 (14), 1293–1295.

19

GOLF ANALYTICS

Richard J. Rendleman, Jr.

Introduction

This chapter reviews recent studies that have used golf performance data to gain insight into the game of golf. Although not reviewed in this chapter, performance data have also been used to study broader issues related to labour and behavioural economics, risk-taking, and the economics of tournament design. These include studies by the following authors: Brown (2011), who shows that during his prime, Tiger Woods's presence in a Professional Golfers' Association (PGA) TOUR event may have caused other tournament participants to give less effort and perform at a substandard level; Pope and Schweitzer (2011), who show that when putting, PGA Tour players are influenced by the par assigned to the hole; Hickman and Metz (2015), who find that the putting performance of players on the last hole of a PGA Tour event deteriorates as a function of the amount of money that is on the line; Ehrenberg and Bognanno (1990), who find strong support for the proposition that the level and structure of prizes in PGA Tour events influence player performance; and Guryan et al. (2009), who find no evidence that the ability or skill level of a professional golfer's playing partner(s) affects his performance.

Almost all recent golf analytics research has drawn on ShotLink data, described below, and in some cases, data collected by hand or from the Internet. Starting in 2004, the PGA Tour has made data from its ShotLink archives available for academic research. Presently, ShotLink data related to PGA Tour competition include the following:

1   Event-level, 1983–2016. For each PGA Tour-sanctioned event, it includes a list of participants, their total scores, finishing positions, money winnings, FedExCup Points, and a number of event-level performance-related summary statistics, such as sand saves, putts made from various distances, etc.

2   Round-level, 1983–2016. For each PGA Tour-sanctioned event, it includes a list of participants by round. For each participant, data include the player's 18-hole score, a course identification number, course par, course yardage (per course scorecard), tee time, and numerous round-specific scoring statistics.

3   Hole-level, 1983–2016. For each PGA Tour-sanctioned event, it includes a list of participants by round and hole. For each hole, data include a course identification number, the player's score, the par for the hole, card yardage, actual yardage, the hole sequence number

(if starting on hole 10, the sequence number for hole 10 is 1), and numerous player–hole-specific performance measures such as driving distance, putts taken, etc.

4   Shot-level, 2003–2016. Since 2003, the PGA Tour has been using a laser-based system to record ball positions of every shot at most events sponsored by the Tour. Each shot record includes a Global Positioning System (GPS)-type coordinate position and description of the ball's position (e.g., fairway, rough, bunker, water, etc.). In principle, one could start with shot-level data to create many of the performance measures summarized in the hole-, round-, and event-level files.

The ShotLink archives also include event-, round-, and hole-level data for the Champions (senior) Tour for most years in the period 1983–2016 and for the Web.com Tour for most years for the period 1990–2016. In addition, round-level scoring data are available for several international professional tours. Finally, the archives include miscellaneous data such as weekly Official World Golf Rankings (OWGR), as well as points and scoring data related to the final stage of the PGA Tour Qualifying Tournament (Q-school).

Review of recent research

Skill versus luck

This section begins by reviewing studies that have focussed, either directly or indirectly, on the issue of skill versus luck in golf. When an average golfer is asked to identify specific sources of luck in golf, the usual answer is 'good and bad bounces, balls lying within divots, unexpected wind gusts, etc.' It could be argued that the luck factor goes well beyond good and bad breaks and has more to do with body mechanics, or the natural variation in one's swing. The human body, not even Tiger Woods in his prime, can produce the same swing all the time. This view is consistent with the view of Connolly and Rendleman (2008, p. 81), who state as follows: 'We believe that professional golfers think of luck as sources of variation in scoring outside a player's direct and conscious control.'

Consider a typical PGA Tour player, who – in 2016 – hits his drive an average of 290 yards (refer PGA Tour, 2016a). Broadie (2014) has estimated that for a typical PGA Tour player, the angular error relative to the intended target in connection with drives is approximately 3.4°, and in unpublished work, he arrived at a similar number (3.475°) but also shows that the angular error is approximately normally distributed. Using Broadie's 3.4° value, this would suggest that 290-yard drives for typical PGA Tour players would fall $290 \times \tan(3.4) \times 2 \approx 34$ yards to the left or right of the intended target 95% of the time.

Now, try to visualize a circle, centred on the intended driving target, with a radius of 34 yards, the drive shot pattern of a typical PGA Tour player. (Actual shot patterns tend to be more elliptical than circular, but that distinction is not critical in this illustration.) Skill is the ability to hit a drive 290 yards on average maintaining a shot pattern that varies within 34 yards of the intended target 95% of the time. Luck, on the other hand, determines where the ball finishes within the intended shot pattern. A player's score in a given round reflects the cumulative effect of a player's skill and all random outcomes, both favourable and unfavourable, within his various shot patterns – those associated with his drives, his long and short approach shots to the green, his play from green-side bunkers, his putting, etc. In essence, if natural random variation in a player's shot outcomes works in his favour, the player has been lucky. A player may think that he played well in a given round when all that was really going on was favourable random variation within the various patterns of the shots that define his skills.

This is why it is so rare for a PGA Tour player to shoot an exceptionally low score such as 61 or 62 followed by a similar or even better score in the next round.

To gain further insight into the luck factor, consider the following 'experiment', summarized by Rendleman (2016). After the first round of a typical PGA Tour event played on a single course, put the players into two groups. Group 1 includes players whose scores were in the top half (lowest) after the first round, and Group 2 includes those whose first-round scores were in the bottom half, with ties broken randomly. Compute the average first-round score for each group. Next, compute the average second-round score for the same two player groups.

Now consider how a player might be included in one of the two groups. First, those in Group 1 might be more skilled than those in Group 2. Second, those in Group 1 might have experienced more favourable random variation in scoring ('good luck') in round 1 relative to those in Group 2. If skill alone is what determines a player's group placement after round 1, then (all other factors being the same) one would expect the difference in the two mean group scores to be approximately the same in rounds 1 and 2. On the other hand, if luck alone is what determines group placement, one would expect the average second-round score to be approximately the same for both groups, implying that the difference in mean group scores would be approximately zero. More realistically, if a combination of skill and luck is what determines first-round group placement, one would expect the difference in average second-round scores to be less than the difference in average first-round scores.

This characterization represents an example of the classic 'regression to the mean' phenomenon. Whenever a performance outcome, in this case, an 18-hole golf score, is measured with error or is subject to random variation, extreme values of the outcome observed in one set of observations will tend to regress towards their true mean values in a second set. (In his best-selling book, *Thinking Fast and Slow*, Kahneman (2011) uses the same example of first- and second-round scoring in golf tournaments to illustrate regression to the mean but does not present any specific results.) If deviations between players' actual scores and expected scores (i.e., residual scores) are not correlated between rounds 1 and 2, the difference in mean scores for the two groups in round 2 should represent an unbiased estimate of the difference in true group means. (Connolly and Rendleman (2008) actually find very weak evidence of positive first-order autocorrelation in 18-hole residual scores.)

In 519 PGA Tour events played on a single course over the 2002–2014 seasons, the difference in mean first-round scores for players in Groups 1 and 2 was 4.67 strokes, but the difference in mean second-round scores for the same two player groups was only 0.74 strokes. Assuming residual scoring is uncorrelated between rounds 1 and 2, this 'experiment' suggests that Group-1 players were 0.74 'better' than Group-2 players, on average. So why did players in Group 1 perform 4.67 strokes better on average than Group-2 players in round 1 when they were only 0.74 strokes better? – because Group-1 players had better luck, or more favourable random variation in scoring, in round 1.

In the same study, it is shown that under certain assumptions, the ratio of the mean difference in scoring in round 2 to that in round 1 – in this case, 0.74/4.67 = 0.159 – can be interpreted as the cross-sectional variance of mean 18-hole scores across players as a proportion of the total variance in 18-hole scoring. This, in turn, suggests that at the PGA Tour level, luck plays a larger role than player skill differences in determining the best and worst 18-hole scores in a given tournament round. In the study, the same Group-1/Group-2 experiment is conducted for other golfer populations, and it is shown that as the general skill level within a given competition decreases, differences in player skills becomes more important in determining 18-hole scoring outcomes. For example, for the New Hampshire Senior Championship (for men 55 years of age or older), the ratio of the mean difference in Group-1 vs Group-2 scoring in round 2 to that in round 1 is 0.547.

It is important to note that the Group-1/Group-2 experiment does not identify which specific players are the best, nor does it identify specific sources of random variation in scoring such as good and bad bounces, balls lying within divots, or balls finishing favourably or unfavourably within individual players' shot patterns. Instead, it simply shows that luck, or random variation in scoring, plays a role in golf, even when played at the highest level. No player, not even Tiger Woods in his prime, can escape the impact of luck.

Even though the Group-1/Group-2 experiment does not allow one to identify specific player skill levels and sources of random variation in scoring, individual player skill for PGA Tour players can be estimated directly using the following or similar model. Following Broadie and Rendleman (2013), who estimate mean neutral individual player scores in 2-year windows to examine potential bias in the OWGR, let us assume that each player, i, is endowed with a fixed skill level that generates an expected neutral score of μ_i per 18-hole round. Each round (j)–course (k) combination, $\{j, k\}$, has a fixed level of difficulty that causes the expected score of each player to be $\delta_{j,k}$ strokes higher than in a round that is otherwise neutral. (This model structure reflects that courses vary by PGA Tour event and in some cases by round within a given PGA Tour event.) Therefore, the actual score of player i in round j on course k, $s_{i,j,k}$, is modelled as follows:

$$s_{i,j,k} = \mu_i + \delta_{j,k} + \varepsilon_{i,j,k},$$

where $\varepsilon_{i,j,k}$ is the usual error term. One can then use ordinary least squares (OLS) regression, as specified in the following equation, to estimate each individual player's mean neutral score while simultaneously controlling for the relative difficulty of the rounds in which the scores are recorded.

$$s_{i,j,k} = \mu_i P_i + \delta_{j,k} R_{j,k} + \varepsilon_{i,j,k}$$

In this equation, P_i is a matrix of dummy variables that identifies players, and $R_{j,k}$ is a matrix of dummies that identifies the interaction of round and course. The terms μ_i and $\delta_{j,k}$ are estimated simultaneously as fixed effects using one-zero indicator variables for players and round–course combinations. As specified, dummy indicators for one player or one round–course combination must be omitted. For ease of interpretation, assume that dummy indicators associated with the first round–course combination are omitted; therefore, μ_i can be interpreted as the estimated score of player i when playing round–course combination $\{j = 1, k = 1\}$.

Although the second equation does not take specific information about course setup, weather conditions, and so on into account, their mean effects on scoring should be reflected in the $\delta_{j,k}$ estimates. Slight variations of the equation include those by Berry (2001) and Broadie (2012), who estimate $\delta_{j,k}$ as random effects, and by Connolly and Rendleman (2008, 2009, 2012a, & 2012b), who estimate time-varying player skill, while simultaneously estimating random round–course and player–course effects and first-order autocorrelation in individual player residual scores.

In two separate studies, Connolly and Rendleman (2008), covering the 1998–2001 PGA Tour seasons, and Connolly and Rendleman (2009), covering the period 2003–2009, asked the following question. For active players whose skill levels were estimated via the regression equation, how would a player have performed in a given tournament if one substituted his regression-based predicted scores for his actual scores? (More specifically, Connolly & Rendleman [2008] estimate individual player skills as time-dependent cubic spline functions.) Stated differently, how would a player have performed in a given tournament if he just played his normal game? As it turns out, in both studies, Tiger Woods was the only player on the

PGA Tour who could have won a tournament by just playing normally. For example, over the 2002–2009 period, Connolly and Rendleman estimate that Woods could have won 13 events by just playing his normal game (11 of the 13 are events he actually won, but two are events he did not win but could have won if he had played to his norm.) All other players would have had to have experienced some degree of favourable random variation in scoring (i.e., good luck) to have won. In fact, in both studies, Connolly and Rendleman estimate that the typical winner on the PGA Tour experienced approximately 10 strokes of favourable random variation in scoring per four-round event.

Why was Woods the only player who was capable of winning a PGA Tour event without experiencing any luck? Because his skill level was so much greater than that of the other players on Tour. For example, over the 2003–2009 period, Connolly and Rendleman estimate that, on average, Woods's statistically based expected score was 1.19 strokes per round lower than that of the next-best player, Vijay Singh, and 1.93 strokes per round lower than that of the 10th-best player, Stewart Cink. Due to skill alone, Woods had at least a $1.19 \times 4 \approx 5$-stroke 72-hole advantage over the next-best player in any tournament field before anyone even teed it up!

In another study, Connolly and Rendleman (2011) are concerned about the impact of luck in connection with the series of tournaments known as Q-School, used to determine PGA Tour eligibility at the end of each PGA Tour season. As presently structured, Q-School consists of four stages, Pre-Qualifying, which started in 2006, and Stages 1–3. Except for the final stage, each stage of Q-School is broken into a number of competitions conducted at different tournament sites, with a portion of the field at each site continuing on to the next stage. Those who do not advance from early-stage competition are eliminated and have no opportunity to reenter the competition until the following year. Although many professionally untested golfers must begin Q-School in Pre-Qualifying, a number of golfers enter Q-School in its later stages based on their success in prior Q-School competitions and/or positions on the PGA Tour and affiliated Web.com Tour money lists.

Using simulation, in combination with their 2008 regression-based skill estimation model, Connolly and Rendleman estimate that among the most highly skilled players in a given year's Q-School competition, many will not succeed in qualifying for the Tour due to unfavourable random variation in scoring (Type I errors), and many players of substantially lower skill will actually qualify (Type II errors) due to favourable random variation. More specifically, Connolly and Rendleman estimate that among the players entering Q-School in Pre-Qualifying with skill comparable to that of a top-25 PGA Tour player, the median qualifying rate is approximately 70%. This implies that approximately 30% of players who would otherwise have become household names on Tour, get knocked out in Q-School due to bad luck. At the same time, many players of much lower skill are likely to experience favourable random variation in scoring and actually qualify for the Tour. In 2013, the PGA Tour changed Q-School to become a qualifying series for the Web.com Tour rather than a qualifier for direct entry onto the PGA Tour. The Connolly–Rendleman study was among the analytical and competitive factors that Tour officials considered in arriving at their final decision. Simply put, it is much more difficult to 'luck out' and finish among the top 25 money winners after a year on the Web.com Tour, and thereby become eligible to participate on the PGA Tour, than to gain PGA Tour entry, mainly by luck, after a few stages of Q-School.

Bias in the OWGR

The question of whether the OWGR is biased against players on the PGA Tour has been raised by Broadie and Rendleman (2013). Although there appears to be no official stated purpose for the ranking system, John Paul Newport (2012) states:

the first thing to know about the OWGR is that its primary purpose is not to identify the world's No. 1, or even the top 10. It is to set the fields for golf's major championships and other big tournaments in a fair, transparent manner.

Following Newport's stated purpose, the authors attempt to determine whether the OWGR system provides fair and unbiased rankings for players across all the major international tours. They consider a ranking system to be unbiased 'if two otherwise identical golfers who happen to play on different tours have the same (or very similar) world rankings. That is, a ranking system is unbiased if a golfer is neither rewarded nor penalized because of the tour affiliation of the tournaments he plays' (Broadie & Rendleman, 2013, p. 128).

Using regression specification (the second equation), Broadie and Rendleman estimated μ_i, which they refer to as the 'score-based skill estimate' (SBSE), for each individual player in separate 2-year sub-periods (2003–04, 2005–06, 2007–08, & 2009–10) for all active players internationally, using 18-hole scoring data for almost all events on the PGA Tour, European Tour, Asian Tour, Australasia Tour, Sunshine Tour, Japan Tour, Nationwide Tour, and Challenge Tour. At the end of each sub-period, they ranked each player based on his SBSE. They also obtained Sagarin rankings applicable to the end of each 2-year sub-period. (They employed 2-year sub-periods, since OWGR points and rankings are based on performance over rolling 2-year windows.)

For each sub-period, Broadie and Rendleman assigned each player a primary tour affiliation based on the number of regular (non-major and World Golf Championships [WGC]) events in which he participated on the various tours covered in their data. They then formed two groups of players in connection with each sub-period, those whose primary tour affiliation was the PGA Tour and those whose primary tour affiliation was one of the other tours. Finally, they compared the SBSE ranks and OWGRs as well as Sagarin rankings and OWGRs for PGA Tour players and non-PGA Tour players. Based on a comparison of SBSE ranks and OWGRs, Broadie and Rendleman found that:

> a golfer whose primary tour affiliation is the PGA Tour is penalized an average of 37 OWGR rankings positions relative to non-PGA Tour affiliated golfers. … [T]he magnitude of the … bias in the OWGR is large and statistically significant.
>
> (2013, p. 134)

Although not quite as dramatic, similar results are obtained when comparing Sagarin rankings and OWGRs.

Strokes gained

Consider a player whose ball is in position 'A' on the course, a position from which PGA Tour players average 3.2 strokes to finish the hole. Position 'A' could be the tee box on a long par–3, or according to Broadie (2014, p. 85), a position in the fairway 201 yards from the pin or a position in the rough 150 yards from the pin. The player then hits his shot from position 'A' to position 'B,' a position on the green 30 feet from the pin, where, according to Broadie (2014, p. 37), Tour players average 1.98 strokes to complete the hole. In this case, the player, hitting from position 'A' to position 'B,' would have gained $3.2 - 1.98 - 1 = 0.22$ strokes relative to an average Tour player. The player started at a position where the average score to finish was 3.2 and ended at a position where the average score to finish is 1.98, but it took the player one stroke to get from 'A' to 'B'; therefore, the player gained 0.22 strokes. In a sense, it is like he started at a position where par was 3.2 and ended at a position where par was 1.98, thereby gaining 0.22 strokes relative to par.

Continuing with the same example, assume that the same player makes his putt from 30 feet. In this case, he would have gained $1.98 - 0 - 1 = 0.98$ strokes from putting. Overall, he would have gained $0.22 + 0.98 = 1.2$ strokes, 0.22 strokes from his shot from position 'A' and 0.98 from his putt. The resultant 1.2 strokes gained overall is consistent with the player having taken two strokes to finish the hole from a position where players average 3.2.

In previous studies (Broadie, 2008, 2012) and in the book, *Every Shot Counts* (Broadie, 2014), Broadie lays out the framework for his strokes gained metric, which is now being used as a standard performance measure on the PGA Tour. More specifically, since being introduced by the Tour in 2011, Strokes Gained-Putting (SGP), which measures strokes gained from putts only (in the example above, the player's SGP would have been +0.98 strokes) 'has been hailed by players and pundits alike as the most accurate, meaningful way to present player putting efficiency' (PGA Tour, 2016b). (SGP was also developed independently by Fearing et al. in 2011.) In addition to SGP, in 2014, the PGA Tour introduced Strokes Gained Tee to Green (SGT2G), which, as the name suggests, measures strokes gained from the tee to the green, excluding strokes gained from putting after reaching the green. In the example above, if position 'A' were the tee box, SGT2G would be +0.22 strokes. More recently, the PGA Tour expanded the strokes gained measures it reports to include off-the-tee, approach-the-green, and around-the-green statistics.

SGP is clearly superior to the more traditional statistic, average putts per green in regulation, as a measure of putting performance, since the latter does not differentiate between putts made from different distances – a putt made from 6 inches would be treated the same as a putt made from 50 feet. Moreover, it mixes putting performance with performance from off the green. For example, a player who one-putts from 6 inches does not do so because he putted well but, instead, because he hit an excellent shot into the green.

Using the strokes gained metric, Broadie refutes several heretofore commonly held beliefs about the game. For example, commentators often say that a player would rather his ball finish in a greenside bunker than in the rough at an equivalent distance. However, Broadie (2012, p. 151) shows that 'when the distance to the hole is less than 15 yards or greater than 34 yards, sand shots have larger average strokes to complete the hole than shots from the rough from the same distance. In the range from 15 yards to 34 yards, sand shots are easier than shots from the rough, on average.'

Similarly, many who follow professional golf believe that the best players gain most of their advantage from putting. Broadie, however, provides convincing evidence that it is not putting but, instead, the long game, that distinguishes the best PGA Tour players from the rest of the field. For example, over the 2003–2010 seasons, Tiger Woods gained an average of 3.20 strokes per round relative to an average PGA Tour player. For Woods, the 3.20 strokes gained included 2.08 strokes gained per round from his long game (rank = 1), 0.42 from his short game (rank = 16), and 0.70 from putting (rank = 3). Similar patterns were observed for the best 10 players. On average, they gained 1.84 strokes per round relative to the average Tour player, 1.20 strokes from the long game, 0.42 strokes from the short game, and 0.22 strokes from putting (Broadie, 2012).

Implications for the game

Skill versus luck

From a psychological standpoint, it is important for all golfers, both professional and amateur, to recognize that although golf is primarily a game of skill, it also includes an element of luck. Unlike poker, which also combines skill and, to a much larger extent, luck, the luck element in golf is not directly observable. A poker player knows when he/she has been dealt a lucky hand. A golfer, on the other hand, who sinks two 30-foot putts in the same round does not necessarily see this as a good luck outcome, nor does a player who misses an 8-foot putt necessarily view this as a reasonable adverse random variation in scoring. (According to Broadie [2014, p. 55], PGA Tour players sink only 7% of their putts from 30 feet, scratch golfers sink 6% of their putts from the same distance, and golfers who score 90 per 18 holes, on average, sink 2% of their putts from 30 feet. He also shows that PGA Tour players miss half their putts from 8 feet, scratch golfers miss 59% of their 8-foot putts, and 90-golfers miss 73% of their putts from 8 feet). Since luck outcomes in golf, especially those arising from imprecise body mechanics, are not easy to recognize, a golfer is likely to internalize the luck factor, becoming over-confident after experiencing favourable random variation in scoring and disappointed after experiencing unfavourable random outcomes. However, similar to a professional poker player who has learned not to personalize the luck factor, to the extent that a golfer understands that certain outcomes in golf are beyond a player's control, he/she should become a better player.

In designing tournament competition, it is important to recognize that if the objective is to identify the best golfer or to align tournament finishing positions in the approximate order of player skill, it may take a number of rounds to eliminate or sufficiently reduce the luck element in competition to ensure that the best player, or at least one of the best players, wins. Inasmuch as player skill differences appear to be large in low-level amateur competition, such as the New Hampshire Senior Championship, a four-round event may be sufficient to identify the best players(s). On the other hand, in PGA Tour competition, where player skills are more homogeneous and luck plays a large role in determining outcomes in any given round, it could take many four-round events to identify the best players. Consistent with this notion, Connolly and Rendleman (2012a) find that the FedExCup Points and Playoffs system, which essentially ranks and rewards players over a full season of play, does an excellent job in identifying and rewarding the best players on Tour, although the points reset, which is applied going into the last event in the Playoffs, regardless of the number of FedExCup Points a player might have accumulated, impairs selection efficiency to some degree.

Bias in the OWGR

If the OWGR is biased against players on any tour, it should be fixed. Otherwise, some players who *should* be eligible to play in golf's most prestigious events, including majors and WGC events, will be left out. With today's technology and extensive worldwide scoring data, there is no reason to retain a system that is based on an arbitrary set of rules put into place years ago to rank players and determine eligibility for golf's most important events. (Refer Broadie & Rendleman [2013, pp. 127–128], for a description of the underlying mathematics of the OWGR system.)

Strokes gained

Clearly, Broadie's strokes gained metric has the potential to help professional golfers better understand their strengths and weaknesses. In fact, in his book, Broadie cites several examples in which PGA Tour players, using the strokes gained system, were surprised to learn about specific deficiencies and strong points in their games.

Now, knowing some of the numbers behind Broadie's SGP, when you miss an 8-foot putt, you might not get upset like you could have done in the past, since you know that even the best players on the planet miss putts of this length half the time!. If you were a higher-level amateur player capable of driving the ball 300 yards, you might find it interesting to compare your play to that of the pros, as outlined in Broadie's book. If your 300-yard drive gained you 0.15 strokes relative to a drive from the same position for a regular PGA Tour player, you might find this to be very informative, especially if you were a young player with aspirations to play on Tour.

Summary and future directions

The recent availability of golf-related performance data, especially ShotLink data made available by the PGA Tour, has made it possible to study golf in ways that heretofore were impossible. We now know much more about player skill differences at the professional level and the extent to which luck comes into play in determining winners and losers from week to week. We now know much more about how to structure qualifying for the PGA Tour to mitigate the influence of both good and bad luck. We now know the extent to which the OWGR system is biased and that it is in dire need of repair, and with Broadie's strokes gained system, we now know how to assess player performance at the most micro level.

As mentioned at the beginning of this chapter, economists have been using golf data to study broader issues related to labour and behavioural economics, risk-taking, and the economics of tournament design. With ShotLink, we now have access to an incredibly rich dataset for examining human behaviour and performance under extreme pressure when the stakes are high and, in some instances, entire livelihoods are on the line. Although ShotLink will surely provide more insight into the game of golf in years to come, its most significant contributions may come in behavioural economics, where we may have just scratched the surface.

References

Berry, S. (2001) How Ferocious Is Tiger? *Chance*, 14 (3), 51–56.

Broadie, M. (2008) Assessing Golfer Performance Using Golfmetrics, In: D. Crews & R. Lutz (Eds.) *Science and Golf V: Proceedings of the 2008 World Scientific Congress of Golf*, Mesa, AZ: Energy in Motion, pp. 253–262.

Broadie, M. (2012) Assessing Golfer Performance on the PGA TOUR, *Interfaces*, 42 (2), 146–165.

Broadie, M. (2014) *Every Shot Counts*, New York, NY: Gotham Books.

Broadie, M. & Rendleman, R., Jr. (2013) Are the Official World Golf Rankings Biased? *Journal of Quantitative Analysis in Sports*, 9 (2), 127–140.

Brown, J. (2011) Quitters Never Win: The (Adverse) Incentives Effects of Competing with Superstars, *Journal of Political Economy*, 119 (5), 982–1013.

Connolly, R. & Rendleman, R., Jr. (2008) Skill, Luck and Streaky Play on the PGA TOUR, *Journal of the American Statistical Association*, 103 (1), 74–88.

Connolly, R. & Rendleman, R., Jr. (2009) Dominance, Intimidation, and "Choking" on the PGA Tour, *Journal of Quantitative Analysis in Sports*, 5 (3), Article 6.

Connolly, R. & Rendleman, R., Jr. (2011) Going for the Green: A Simulation Study of Qualifying Success Probabilities in Professional Golf, *Journal of Quantitative Analysis in Sports*, 7 (4), Article 7.

Connolly, R. & Rendleman, R., Jr. (2012a) Tournament Selection Efficiency: An Analysis of the PGA TOUR's Fedexcup, *Journal of Quantitative Analysis in Sports*, 8 (4), 1–31.

Connolly, R. & Rendleman, R., Jr. (2012b) What It Takes to Win on the PGA Tour (If Your Name Is "Tiger" Or If It Isn't), *Interfaces*, 42 (6), 554–576.

Ehrenberg, R. & Bognanno, M. (1990) Do Tournaments Have Incentive Effects? *Journal of Political Economy*, 98 (6), 1307–1324.

Fearing, D.; Acimovic, J. & Graves S. (2011) How to Catch a Tiger: Understanding Putting Performance on the PGA TOUR, *Journal of Quantitative Analysis in Sports*, 7 (1), 1–45.

Guryan, J.; Kroft, K. & Notowidigdo, M. (2009) Peer Effects in the Workplace: Evidence From Random Groupings in Professional Golf Tournaments, *American Economic Journal: Applied Economics*, 1 (4), 34–68.

Hickman, D. & Metz, N. (2015) *The Impact of Pressure on Performance: Evidence From the PGA Tour.* Working paper, February.

Kahneman, D. (2011) *Thinking Fast and Slow*, New York, NY: Farrar, Straus and Giroux.

Newport, J. (2012) Why Scientists Love to Study Golf, *New York Times*, Available at Http://Online.Wsj.Com/Article/SB10001424052702304636404577299702668540234.Html (Accessed May 3, 2012).

PGA Tour (2016a) Available at www.Pgatour.Com/Stats/Stat.101.Html (Accessed February 29, 2016).

PGA Tour (2016b) Available at www.Pgatour.Com/Stats/Academicdata/Shotlink.Html (Accessed February 29, 2016).

Pope, D. & Schweitzer, M. (2011) Is Tiger Woods Loss Averse? Persistent Bias in the Face of Experience, Competition, and High Stakes, *American Economic Review*, 101 (1), 129–157.

Rendleman, R., Jr. (2016) *The Paradox of Skill: Lessons From Golf*, Working Paper, February 2016.

PART IV

Psychological techniques for success

Introduction

Golf is a game that, for many, has been illuminated through greater access to technical and strategic information, biomechanical knowledge, and performance statistics. The consequence of this proliferation of accessible knowledge is that, perhaps less obviously accessible knowledge (such as what is going on in the heads of golfers), has been given less attention than perhaps warranted considering its potential impact on performance.

This part on the psychology of golf considers a broad range of topics that will help inform those interested in supporting both participation and performance in this simple bat-and-ball sport that brings pleasure to so many. The subject matter will be directly relevant to a wide range of individuals and groups, e.g., students of golf science, coaches, consultants supporting players, or players themselves. Equally, policymakers, governing bodies, academy managers, or performance directors can benefit from the information presented. To illustrate the wide-ranging relevance, the individual chapter topics focus on the following: specific techniques to help improve performance regardless of ability level; the importance of understanding the drivers behind engagement in golf, and the specific personal motives and consequences; the individual differences in psychological skill use, preferences in terms of learning styles, and how these moderate effects of skill teaching. The final two chapters consider aspects of golf psychology that have been minimally considered within the mainstream sport psychology literatures, namely, mental health and well-being of golfers, and the psychophysiology of golfers.

It has been reported that putting accounts for approximately 40% of all strokes taken on the golf course. It is not surprising, therefore, that research concerned with gaze control in the production and control of the putting stroke has received considerable attention. Vine and Wilson describe a simple technique of focusing on the back of the ball for about 1 second prior to initiating the stroke. Evidence is presented that contrasts the eye movements between novice and experienced golfers, and in turn how gaze control can be influenced by competition pressure and anxiety. Finally, directions are given on how to optimise gaze control to improve/refine performance, and to ensure that it remains resilient under pressure.

Jack Nicklaus, the most successful professional golfer in the modern era, was an early advocate of imagery, and he often described 'going to the movies' to represent his use of imagery as he prepared for practice and competition. In the second chapter, there is again an emphasis on utilising a specific skill to enhance performance. Cumming et al. present a convincing case for the benefits of imagery in sport and golf and, in doing so, they provide evidence that validates a revised model to describe imagery use. Having reviewed the research, they give concrete recommendations on how to improve golfers' imagery practice.

The next two chapters are concerned with the process of motivation in golf. The former sets motivation at the front and centre of understanding the 'why' of involvement and continued engagement in golf. In considering two of the most popular contemporary motivational theories, namely, the self-determination theory (Deci & Ryan, 1985) and Elliot's (1999) hierarchical goal model, the author provides a context and direction for supporting healthy engagement and long-term participation in golf. In explicitly identifying intrinsic motivation (where engagement is underpinned by rewards inherent within the activity, e.g., learning, enjoyment, personal improvement, and meeting personal challenges) and greater internalisation of motives as the objective of any interventions, this chapter concludes with some guidance on how adaptive motivation can be supported. The second motivation chapter adopts an approach that has dominated motivational research for the past 30 years and yielded >300 research papers (Roberts, 2012). Sachau et al. report on descriptive research that examines the dispositional criteria that individuals use for evaluating competence, i.e., the goal orientations of active, recreational golfers. Specifically, they are concerned with how these individuals engage with the game and how goal orientations are related to the ways in which golfers think about themselves (self-esteem, contingencies of self-worth), become attached to the game (obsessive and harmonious passion), and behave ethically in competition (self-handicapping and sandbagging). Similar to the previous chapter, they conclude with some directions for a psychologically healthy approach to the game.

While the chapters to date highlight either specific guidelines for using psychological skills (quiet eye and imagery) or guidance on appropriate motives and goals, Thomas et al. highlight the need to consider individual differences when tailoring interventions to support effective performance. They actively question whether the same psychological skills training (PST) programme is equally effective for all clients and specifically concern themselves with specific cognitive processes that are used to optimise golf performance, as well as the role of individual differences in these. They explicitly review research on the basic psychological skills of self-talk and imagery and thereafter provide a case of individually targeted interventions. Next, they consider individual learning styles, and based on mainstream educational and cognitive psychology research, extrapolate that, in the sports context, athletes may benefit from instructions tailored to their learning style (e.g., visual, verbal, kinaesthetic). The research group then presents research exploring information-processing preferences in golfers and note the ability of experts to switch attention through different modalities according to the demands of the task, before finally considering how the cognitive processes reviewed can be combined to optimise performance in golf.

There is little doubt that there are numerous physical and mental benefits of participation in sport. However, sports performers at the top level, like their less-able counterparts, suffer from conditions such as stress and burnout, and these are often exacerbated by a narrow and exclusive athlete identity. In their chapter exploring mental health, Douglas and Carless draw upon much of their own research to highlight that sport performers at the top level are not immune to mental illness. They observe that while more and more high-profile sports people talk publically about mental illness, they largely remain shrouded by stigma, denial, or silence. Furthermore, athletes living with a mental illness face additional issues such as clinicians and governing organisations who do not understand these conditions in the context of sport. The authors review the literature on mental health and illness and discuss how mental health can be placed at risk in pursuit of sporting excellence. They conclude by charging organisations to take a collective responsibility for the mental health and illnesses of their athletes.

There is an interesting point made by Thomas et al. – in their chapter on individual differences – that brain mapping using functional magnetic resonance imaging (fMRI) during skill execution suggests that different types of imagery processes activate different neural processes. This highlights how sport psychologists are beginning to consider psychophysiology as a method through which to illuminate our understanding of the mechanisms through which psychological skills may influence performance. The focus of the final chapter in the psychology part focusses explicitly on the psychophysiology of golf performance; Crews and Cheetham's objective is to promote understanding of the measures used in the discipline (i.e., electroencephalogram [EEG], heart rate, and electrodermal responses [EDRs] of the skin) and the implications thereof. As a starter, they outline the measures recorded during golf performance and compare these between elite and non-elite players, as well as effective/less-effective performances, while also examining these under conditions of stress. Within their reviews of these measures, Crews and Cheetham highlight their relevance to sport broadly, and specifically to golf, and how interventions (e.g., neurofeedback, electrical stimulation, and biofeedback) can be used to reduce stress and improve performance. They conclude by arguing that greater efficiency in cognitive processing is associated with best performance in experts, while acknowledging that research is in its infancy. However, wearable sensing devices are beginning to be readily available to researchers, and these may be useful in further enlightening the link between brain patterns and performance.

While there is an explicit intention to target this text at a wide range of golf-related audiences, each of the chapters has emphasised the need to continually develop the knowledge base through continued research; this final paragraph will summarise the future research directions that have been highlighted across the psychology chapters.

Much of the research that has been conducted in sport psychology, by necessity, has utilised the available resources of novice golfers or undergraduate sport students. There is a consistent call for research to be conducted with elite, and especially truly elite, golfers to validate research with top performers. At the other end of the spectrum, commonly, researchers argue for a consistent focus on the psychosocial development of younger golfers; these individuals are the lifeblood of our game, and research needs to recognise the value of promoting both enjoyment as well as talent development. While research can develop knowledge, effectively transmitting that information cannot always be assumed. Our contributors consistently make the point that delivering the message to the various stakeholders, whether through coaches, psychologists, or organisations requires an acknowledgment of the dynamics of these relationships, but also sensitivity to the individual differences of those receiving the messages. Finally, as psychological intervention research evolves, there is a need to understand how the mental skills we promote influence performers at a cortical and neurological level; this is perhaps the next stage to ensuring that the mechanisms through which improvements occur can be understood.

Kieran Kingston
Cardiff Metropolitan University, Wales

References

Deci, E. & Ryan, R. (1985) *Intrinsic Motivation and Self-Determination in Human Behavior*, New York, NY: Plenum.

Elliot, A. (1999) Approach and Avoidance Motivation and Achievement Goals, *Educational Psychologist*, 34 (3), 169–189.

Roberts, G. (2012) Motivation in Sport and Exercise From an Achievement Goal Theory Perspective: After 30 Years, Where Are We? In: G. Roberts & D. Treasure (Eds.) *Advances in Motivation in Sport and Exercise*, Champaign, IL: Human Kinetics, pp. 5–58.

20

THE QUIET EYE IN GOLF PUTTING

Sam Vine and Mark Wilson

Introduction

Putting can be one of the most difficult and frustrating parts of the game of golf, yet when mastered, it can have a hugely positive impact on scoring and handicap. It is arguably the most important shot in a golfer's repertoire, accounting for an estimated 40% of all strokes made during a round (Professional Golfers' Association Tour Website, 2016). Despite the fact that it is the shortest and simplest swing that a golfer has to make, the requirements for precision and the binary nature of success and failure make putting the most interesting aspect of the game of golf from a psychomotor perspective. It is not surprising, therefore, that one of the most enduring adages in golf is that you 'drive for show; but putt for dough'.

A range of motor control and sport psychology literature highlights that four psychomotor abilities are needed for accurate putting. First, the golfer must be able to predict the proposed path or line of the putt in relation to the position of the ball and the hole, as well as the slope of the green (Campbell & Moran, 2014). Second, the golfer must be able to hold this information in working memory and call upon a suitable motor programme to match stroke tempo and length with the requisite stroke force to achieve the desired distance (Mann et al., 2011). Third, the putting stroke must be performed with sufficient precision to propel the ball along the correct line towards the hole (MacKenzie & Sprigings, 2005). Fourth, these processes must occur unhindered under the demands of competitive pressure (Wilson, 2012). Given these considerable demands on the human psychomotor system, it is perhaps not surprising that even elite golfers only successfully hole about 29% of putts from a distance of 10–15 feet (Professional Golfers' Association Tour Website, 2016). In understanding how golfers can putt more accurately and more consistently, research has focussed on the role of vision in the production and control of the putting stroke.

With advances in eye tracking technology, it is now possible to gain an insight into how experts use vision to plan and control skilled movements, as well as how contingencies like competitive pressure can disrupt efficient processing (e.g., Panchuk et al., 2015). One of the most important components of vision that has been related to proficient putting is gaze control, i.e., the movements of the eyes around the visuomotor workspace (refer Vickers, 2007). The aim of this chapter is to synthesise the scientific literature that has examined the link between gaze control and putting performance, with focus on a specific form of gaze and motor control coupling known as the Quiet Eye (QE; Vickers, 1996). First, we discuss the literature showing that the way in which experienced and novice golfers control their eye movements during the putt is very different. Second, we discuss the effect that competitive pressure and anxiety can have on the gaze control of putters and outline how this affects performance. Third, we discuss how it is possible to learn how to optimise gaze control to improve or refine performance and, via QE training (QET), to remain resilient under pressure.

The QE: a key variable in supporting putting performance

The first study to examine the QE in golf putting was carried out by Vickers (1992). In this study, expert and novice golfers performed putts while wearing a head-mounted eye tracker. During the alignment phase of the putt, experts (with an average handicap of 6.2) tended to make quick fixation shifts between the hole and the ball to determine the putt trajectory. These fixations were focussed at the centre of the hole and on the back of the ball. In contrast, novices (with an average handicap of 14.1) had less-structured fixations and looked in a variety of locations around the hole, on the green, behind the ball, or on the clubhead. Experts also had differing visual control while making the putt, keeping their eyes steady on the back of the ball for about 2 seconds prior to initiating the back swing and maintaining this fixation throughout the swing until just after contact with the ball. Novices, in contrast, sometimes followed the putter as it moved or had scattered fixations around the ball; moreover, they tended to allow their gaze to move towards the hole before they had struck the ball. This steady final fixation that the experts used was later termed the QE.

The QE has been defined as the final fixation towards a relevant target prior to the execution of the critical phase of movement (Vickers, 1996). It has since been adopted as a measure of optimal visual attentional control in visuomotor tasks as varied as golf putting (Vine et al., 2011), football penalty kicks (Wilson et al., 2010), ice hockey goal tending (Panchuk & Vickers, 2006), shooting (Moore et al., 2014), and throwing and catching (Wilson et al., 2013). The QE is proposed to represent a critical period of cognitive processing during which the parameters of the movement such as force, direction, and velocity are fine-tuned and programmed (Vickers, 1996). It is during this period that sensory information is synthesised with the mechanisms necessary to both plan (pre-programme) and control (online) the appropriate motor response. For example, when putting, golfers need to programme the necessary direction and force needed to propel the ball along the right line and length towards the hole. Some of this information is processed prior to swinging (i.e., during the pre-performance routine) and some of this processing occurs during the swing (i.e., controlling the swing of the putter as the putt unfolds). Generally, experts have longer QE durations than non-experts and successful attempts have longer QE durations than unsuccessful attempts (refer Wilson et al., 2015, for a more recent review). For example, Wilson and Pearcey (2009) examined the QE durations of golfers during straight and breaking putts and found that performers had significantly longer QE durations on successful (1700 ms) compared to unsuccessful (1200 ms) putts.

Researchers have proposed a number of reasons for why the QE might be important in supporting successful putting performance:

1   *Pre-programming*

The QE provides the brain with a quiet moment to process distance and line cues, while minimising distraction from other environmental cues. Vickers (2011) postulates that experts are better able to maintain the longer-duration QE that helps to sustain the organisation and control of this information. Indeed, Mann et al. (2011) found that expert golfers' longer QE durations were associated with a neural measure indexing good control of attention in the seconds prior to the swing. This measure, known as the Bereitschaftspotential, is derived from electroencephalogram (EEG) recordings and has been associated with movement preparation. The same study by Mann et al. also found that expert golfers, compared to novice golfers, had greater electrical activation in the right–central regions of the brain, which are related to visuospatial processing. Both of these measures (the Bereitschaftpotential and activation on the right side of the brain) appear to link the QE to more focussed and efficient processing of information obtained from the visual system.

2   Online control

The fact that the QE remains on the target up to (and beyond) contact suggests that it is also providing an online control function – helping to guide putter-to-ball contact. Recent research suggests that this is an important function for ensuring accurate performance. Vine et al. (2015) asked experienced golfers to putt while looking through a liquid crystal screen that could change between clear and opaque during the putt depending on the starting conditions (Figure 20.1). This meant that it was possible to change whether the golfer could or could not see through the screen either early in the planning phase (before the putter moved) or in the movement phase. Putting performance was disrupted more when golfers had no visual information to guide putter–ball contact (vision during the swing), compared to the situation when early information (vision when the putter was placed behind the ball) was occluded.

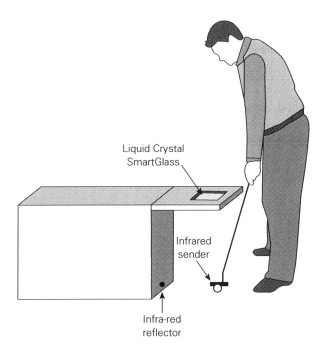

Figure 20.1   A diagram of the experimental set-up showing key elements of the occlusion method used in the study by Vine et al. (2015, p. 87): (a) infrared reflector; (b) LC SmartGlass™; and (c) infrared sender.

In addition to helping a golfer optimise his/her attentional control from a visuomotor perspective – in terms of synthesising information to plan and control the putt – the QE may also help in a more general sense. By focussing on a single external cue (a dimple on the back of the ball), it is more difficult for attention to wander towards disruptive internal cues (Kremer & Moran, 2008). In this way, a golfer can 'stay in the present' rather than focus on concerns about the outcome or the mechanics of the putt. Both of these alternative thought processes have been implicated in the dreaded experience of choking under pressure (refer Wilson, 2012, for a review). While the QE may, therefore, sound incredibly obvious, we have found that even very experienced golfers do not always manage to maintain this optimal attentional control, especially when under pressure.

The QE and performance under pressure

Self-paced sports, like golf, are interesting from a psychological perspective as they provide sufficient thinking time for worry and anxiety to disrupt performance when pressure (e.g., a big competition or a final putt to win) is raised. These performance disruptions have been colloquially termed 'choking' in both the sporting press and the sport psychology literature. Choking can be defined as 'an acute and considerable decrease in skill execution and performance when self-expected standards are normally achievable, which is the result of increased anxiety under perceived pressure' (Mesagno & Hill, 2013, p. 273).

A growing body of evidence is emerging, which highlights the critical role that QE plays in choking under pressure. Across the target sports, such as shotgun shooting (Causer et al., 2011), dart throwing (Nibbeling et al., 2012), basketball free throw shooting (Wilson et al., 2009), and biathlon shooting (Vickers & Williams, 2007), the QE has been shown to be shortened or disrupted by anxiety and performance pressure. These findings have been explained in terms of the predictions of a theory first developed for mainstream psychology, namely, the attentional control theory (ACT; Eysenck et al., 2007), and since developed more specifically for sport (ACTS; Eysenck & Wilson, 2016). A central assumption of the ACT is that we should distinguish between two attentional systems (Corbetta & Shulman, 2002).

First, there exists a top–down, goal-directed attentional system (dorsal attention network), which is important for response or action selection and is involved in linking relevant stimuli to appropriate motor responses. Second, a stimulus-driven attentional system (ventral attention network) is recruited during the detection of salient and unattended stimuli. In essence, the ACTS suggests that anxiety increases the influence of the stimulus-driven system (ventral attention), making individuals more distractible, at the expense of goal-directed control (dorsal attention). While these distractions may be both external (environmental) or internal (body mechanics, distracting thoughts), in terms of QE, this increased sensitivity of ventral attention is likely to disrupt efficient QE processing and subsequent visuomotor performance (Eysenck & Wilson, 2016).

A recent test of this effect in golf putting used a novel shootout manipulation, where 50 single-handicap golfers were asked to make the same 5 foot putt on a level putting green until they missed (Vine et al., 2013). They were put under pressure by instructions designed to increase the ego-threatening nature of the putt (i.e., financial incentives and penalties for poor performance) and they performed the putts in their own time. While there was a wide range of successful performance – the number of consecutive successful putts ranged from 3 to 237 (mean = 23.06) – what was interesting was the pattern across the group between the QE of their

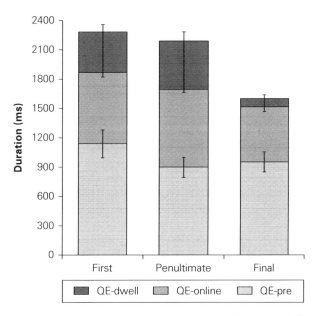

Figure 20.2 Mean (± s.e.m.) duration of the pre-programming (steady gaze on ball before swing starts), online control (from swing initiation to ball contact), and dwell (after ball contact) components of the overall quiet eye duration (QED; sum of the three sub-phases) for the first, penultimate, and final putts of the shootout.

Source: Reproduced with permission from Vine et al., 2013, p. 1991.

last putt (the one that missed) and that of the first and the penultimate putts (the last successful one) (Figure 20.2).

What is noticeable from Figure 20.2 is that the QE duration of the final putt was significantly less than that on the other two putts (dropping from 2.2 seconds to 1.6 seconds). The other interesting point was that this difference was driven primarily by a reduction in the late phases of the QE (online control and dwell) and not the early phase (initial pre-programming). In effect, the golfers broke off their QE durations too early on the putt they missed (and started to look towards the target) compared to when they did not miss. A long QE duration (online control & dwelling in particular) prior to and during task performance may therefore be needed to suppress competing stimuli/thoughts and allow the dorsal network to carry out the action as planned (Wilson, 2012). Indeed, Vickers and Williams (2007) found that elite biathletes who increased their QE duration during simulated competition, compared with that during practice, were less susceptible to the adverse effects of anxiety. As such, the authors suggested that the act of allocating attention externally to critical task information (via the QE) may insulate athletes from the debilitating effects of anxiety. The big question is, can a long QE be developed/trained?

The QE: training for optimal attentional control

Not only has the QE been shown to be indicative of superior performance and as sensitive to the influence of anxiety, but it also has been demonstrated to be trainable (Vine et al., 2014). Indeed, compared to traditional training instructions, QET has been shown to (1) speed up the learning process of novices, (2) improve putting performance under pressure, and (3) help skilled golfers to improve their putting statistics in competitions. The following paragraphs will describe and discuss this research evidence further.

QET for novices

Vine and Wilson (2010) were the first to examine the effectiveness of QET for novice performers. In this study, novice golfers were divided into two groups; QE trained (gaze-focussed instructions) and control (technique-focussed instructions; Table 20.1), and they performed 10-foot putts, numbering totally 360, over a period of 4 days. Learning was assessed using retention tests 2 days later, where no guidance or instructions were provided. Although both groups improved over the training period, the QE-trained group demonstrated a larger training effect and had lower radial error on their retention test putts (their putts were closer to the hole). Importantly, when both groups were then put under pressure test conditions, the QE-trained group still performed better. The duration of QE seemed to be an important factor in explaining these differences in performance, predicting 36% of the variance in performance during the test phase. However, this study was not able to examine what processes might change during learning and under pressure; therefore, a follow-up study was designed.

The follow-up study (Moore et al., 2012) sought to understand *how* QET might affect putting performance so effectively. It therefore replicated the training interventions used in the Vine and Wilson (2010) study, while assessing additional measures of cardiovascular and forearm muscular activity from participants in the seconds leading up to each putt, as well as kinematic data from the putter head itself during the putt. Findings showed that QE-trained participants learned faster than their technically trained counterparts and were able to maintain their performance under pressure, whereas the technical-trained group performed significantly worse. The authors were also able to shed light on some of the reasons why the QE might be so important in aiming skills, like putting. The radial error data can be seen in Figure 20.3; acceleration of the putter along the x-axis (perpendicular to the direction of ball travel) is one of the key measures of putting kinematics. The similar shapes of both graphs reveal how

Table 20.1 Technical instructions from a leading golf putting coach (Dave Pelz), whereas the QET instructions only focus on desired gaze behaviour at timings that are similar to the technical instructions

QET instructions	Technical instructions
Assume stance and ensure that gaze is on the back of the ball	Stand with legs hip width apart and keep your head still
After setting up, fixate the hole (fixation should be made no more than three times)	Maintain relaxation of shoulders and arms
Your final fixation should be on the back of the ball and for no longer than 2–3 seconds	Keep the putter head square to the ball
No gaze should be directed to the clubhead or shaft during the putting action	Perform a pendulum-like swing and accelerate through the ball
Your fixation should remain steady for 200–300 ms after contact with the ball	Maintain a still head after contact

Source: Adapted from Vine and Wilson, 2010; and Moore et al., 2012.

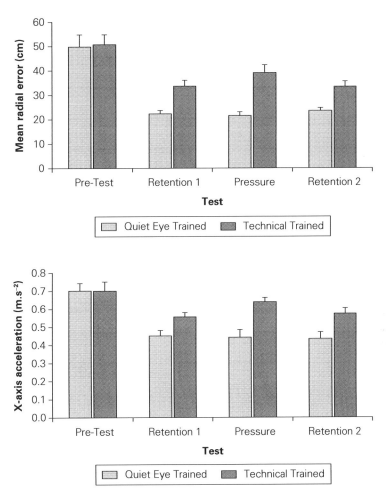

Figure 20.3 Mean (SE) radial error (cm) and x-axis clubhead acceleration (ms⁻²) for the quiet eye-trained and technical-trained groups in the study by Moore et al. (2012, p. 1010), during pretest, retention tests, and pressure test.

the QE-trained participants learned how to move their putter in a more efficient (less jerky) way after training (bottom graph), and this helped them to be more accurate (top graph). This finding suggests that QET can craft changes in movement kinematics to more expert-like patterns – despite not including any instructions about putter movement – and that this learning is resilient under pressure. Importantly, these changes are greater and more resilient than what can be achieved using typical, technical-focussed instructions.

Another exciting finding from the Moore et al. (2012) study was that the QE instructions also created changes in the psychophysiological state of the novice golfers, in effect making them more relaxed. Figure 20.4 reveals the cardiac (top) and muscle (bottom) activity data from the participants, expressed as change scores from a nominal 'origin', 6 seconds prior to putter–ball contact. What is fascinating is that both groups had similar profiles at baseline (panel A), but that the QE-trained group changed their levels of tension after training, whereas the technical-trained participants did not (panel B). Furthermore, this is despite not receiving any explicit

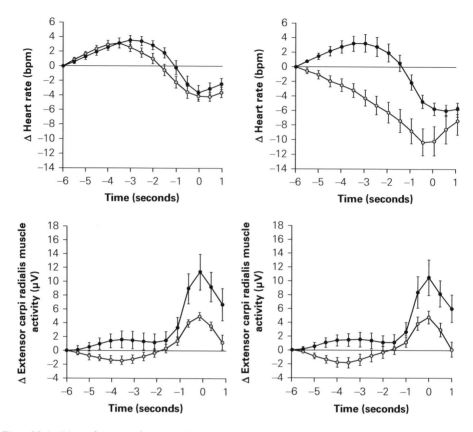

Figure 20.4 Mean changes in heart rate (top row) and forearm muscular activity (bottom row) in the 6
seconds leading up to putter–ball contact and 1 second after, in the baseline condition (A –
before training) and retention condition (B – after training), for QE-trained (grey circles) and
technically trained (black circles) groups (± s.e.m.)

Source: From Moore et al. (2012, p. 2011). Reproduced with permission from Moore et al., 2012, p. 2011.

instructions about relaxation. Additionally, data collected on the psychological responses to
stress from these groups of golfers (Moore et al., 2013) also revealed that the QE-trained group
had a more positive response to the pressure situation than their technically trained counterparts.
Specifically, they evaluated the pressure as a challenge (believing they had the resources to cope
with the demands) compared to the technical-trained group who evaluated it as a threat (believing that the demands of the situation outweighed their coping resources). The overall message
from the study is that QET appears to have significant benefits for individuals seeking to learn
the skill of golf putting and that these benefits seem to arise from a combination of attentional
alterations (longer QE durations), mechanical alterations (smoother putting action), physiological alterations (reduced heart rate and muscular tension), and psychological alterations (more
productive stress responses).

While these results are exciting from a research perspective, these novice participants may
never touch a putter again after the study finished. It would be more interesting if current
golfers could apply a similar learning experience onto the course. Additionally, we know
that total novices have the most room for improvement (gains are easier to make early in
learning), so the effects found in the studies by Vine et al. may not be so meaningful in more

experienced performers. What would happen if you applied QET to single-handicap golfers for example?

QET for experts

In 2011, Vine et al. (2011) performed a brief QET intervention (1 hour long) with 22 low-handicap golfers (with an average handicap of 2.7). Thus, 11 golfers were assigned to a QET group, while 11 equally skilled golfers were assigned to a control group. All subjects were first asked to capture their putting performance data from 10 competitive rounds of golf, before coming into the laboratory for training. Both training groups started by viewing their own gaze data from putts taken on the putting green in the laboratory and were asked to verbalise what they noticed with regard to their own gaze control. Next, after taking some more putts, both groups viewed a video of their gaze control alongside that of an elite prototype who exhibited the critical QE as found in past gaze research (e.g., Vickers, 1992; Wilson & Pearcey, 2009). At this stage only, the QET group received additional verbal instructions that directed their attention towards the critical aspects of the video. We highlighted the differences in their gaze and the elite prototype and further emphasised the importance of the steadiness and timing of the final fixation (as in our instructions to novices – Table 20.1).

Both groups of golfers were then required to perform a series of putts from 10 feet under high- and low-pressure conditions, during which their performance and eye movements were recorded. This enabled us to calculate a performance score for each subject, consisting of his/her percentage number of putts holed and their radial error on missed shots (centimetres from the hole). We also calculated the QE for each participant on each shot. Following this laboratory-putting test, participants were again asked to record their putting statistics for 10 competitive rounds of golf in the following 3 months.

The results of the laboratory part of the study supported the benefits of QET for skilled golfers. Unsurprisingly, there were no differences in performance or QE at pre-test, with both groups holing about 50% of their 10-foot putts and using optimal QE durations of about 2 seconds. Even after only 1 hour of training, however, the QE-trained group significantly increased their QE durations (>2.8 seconds) and performance (>60% putts holed) and, in addition, maintained these scores under pressure. In contrast, the control group did not see the improvements in the retention test and experienced a shortening of the QE under pressure, which likely explains their performance change. When comparing putting performance under pressure, it is interesting to note that the QE-trained group holed 60% of their putts, whereas the control group now only holed 35% of their putts.

The most critical finding of this study was that the performance advantages of QET also transferred to the golf course (as measured by putting statistics collected over 10 competitions before and after the laboratory visit). After training, the QE-trained group made 1.9 fewer putts per round, compared to the pre-training phase, whereas the control group showed no change in their putting statistics. Considering their handicaps, such an improvement is certainly meaningful (two shots per round!) and points the way for more research into the real-life benefits of QET for golfers of various levels. We still need to better understand *how* the QE supports more accurate putting performance (especially under pressure) and disentangle some of the psychological and technical benefits we have found in our studies.

The body of work presented is persuasive in making a case that accurate golf putting is underpinned by the QE gaze strategy, and this seems to reflect efficient control of attentional, physical, and psychological systems. Successful putts, especially those under pressure conditions, seem to be associated with longer and better-maintained QE durations. While the QE might be a characteristic of expertise, it can be trained, and this can result in more resilient performance under pressure. At an individual level, however, how can golfers, coaches, and sport psychologists apply these exciting findings about QET, especially because few will have access to expensive eye trackers? We tackle some of these issues in the next section.

Implications for the game – applying QE

As researchers, it is important to measure the QE accurately using eye trackers, and undoubt-edly, 'gaze' videos make for useful training resources for immediate directed feedback (as in Vine et al., 2011). However, this does not mean that you cannot benefit from a QE approach. The first step is to simply give it a go the very next time you are on your practice putting green. Once you have finished aligning yourself with the hole, focus with all your mental energy on a dimple at the back of the ball for about 1 second before initiating the stroke. Maintain this 'laser-like' focus as you make your backswing and foreswing and right through impact, pausing with your gaze on the ball's 'previous' location for a brief period after it has been sent on its way. After you have practiced a few times, reflect on what your mind is doing while you are putting – where is your attention? What thoughts are going through your mind? What body sensations are you aware of? How good was the contact? If you really like to provide yourself with some 'evidence' that you are doing this well (but don't have access to an eye tracker), then a simple video camera, positioned close to the face, will give a proxy indication of the stability of the eye and the head during putting.

Hopefully, you will recognise that your attention is much more focussed in the moment and not on irrelevant or threatening cues or thoughts. As with any new technique, it will take time to practise and become comfortable, so incorporate the QE into your putting pre-shot routine (you could modify the one we use in our research – Table 20.1). A useful drill while embedding the QE is to score the contact you made on the ball (1–10) *before* you look up to see where it went. This will help you maintain the 'QE dwell period' that we found to be a key predictor of missed putts in one of our studies (Figure 20.2) and help develop your awareness of any putting technique flaws.

Summary and future directions

In this article, we have provided you an overview of the research relating to QE and golf. We have highlighted a range of evidence that suggests that the QE is an important factor in accurate and consistent putting. We have also provided some practical information regarding ways in which the QE technique can be applied to your own game. The great irony is that we often are good at applying techniques when we do not necessarily 'need' them (on the practice green) but 'forget' to use them just when it could be most useful (a match-winning 6-footer). It takes men-tal 'energy' to consistently use a QE strategy – especially when anxious (when we are potentially more distractible) and more likely to make mental errors. For example, it is very easy when putting under pressure to think back in time to previous mistakes, or forward in time to what the consequences might be if the putt goes in (or misses!). While such thought processes are a natural part of performing in a competitive environment, they are unlikely to help you with the task at hand: we cannot undo the past and we cannot control the future! Instead, the QE fixa-tion may help you to maintain your focus, whereby it can help you provide the foundation for a successful putt (maintaining a more relaxed body and a more focussed mind). Start today and incorporate the QE fixation into your pre-putt routine to see if you can 'focus with a quiet eye, putt with a quiet mind' (Wilson & Richards, 2010).

Research examining the QE, in putting and other sporting tasks, is growing in popularity. This is important, as many unanswered and important research questions remain. For example, research is needed to examine truly elite golfers, to ensure that our current understanding of the role of gaze behaviour in putting is correct. Second, further research is needed to better understand precisely what the QE is doing on a cortical and neurological level. Finally, more work is needed to establish precisely how QET can best affect the teaching and coaching of golfing skills. In particular, if this research is to influence golf coaching and performance, then methods of delivery that do not require the use of expensive eye tracking technology need to be developed.

References

Campbell, M. & Moran, A. (2014) There Is More to Green Reading than Meets the Eye! Exploring Gaze Behaviours of Expert Golfers on a Virtual Golf Putting Task, *Cognitive Processing*, 15 (3), 363–372.

Causer, J.; Holmes, P.; Smith, N. & Williams, A. (2011) Anxiety, Movement Kinematics, and Visual Attention in Elite-Level Performers, *Emotion*, 11 (3), 595–602.

Corbetta, M. & Shulman, G. (2002) Control of Goal-Directed and Stimulus-Driven Attention in the Brain, *Nature Reviews Neuroscience*, 3 (3), 201–215.

Eysenck, M.; Derakshan, N.; Santos, R. & Calvo, M. (2007) Anxiety and Cognitive Performance: Attentional Control Theory, *Emotion*, 7 (2), 336–353.

Eysenck, M. & Wilson, M. (2016) Sporting Performance, Pressure and Cognition: Introducing Attentional Control Theory: Sport, In: D. Groome & M. Eysenck (Eds.) *An Introduction to Applied Cognitive Psychology*, London: Routledge, pp. 329–350.

Kremer, J. & Moran, A. (2008) *Pure Sport: Practical Sport Psychology*, London: Routledge.

MacKenzie, S. & Sprigings, E. (2005) Evaluation of the Plumb-bob Method for Reading Greens in Putting, *Journal of Sports Sciences*, 23 (1), 81–87.

Mann, D.; Coombes, S.; Mousseau, M. & Janelle, C. (2011) Quiet Eye and the Bereitschaftspotential: Visuomotor Mechanisms of Expert Motor Performance, *Cognitive Processing*, 12 (3), 223–234.

Mesagno, C. & Hill, D. (2013) Definition of Choking in Sport: Re-Conceptualization and Debate, *International Journal of Sport Psychology – Performance Under Pressure, 44 (4),* 267–277.

Moore, L.; Vine, S.; Cooke, A.; Ring, C. & Wilson, M. (2012) Quiet Eye Training Expedites Motor Learning and Aids Performance Under Heightened Anxiety: The Roles of Response Programming and External Attention, *Psychophysiology*, 49 (7), 1005–1015.

Moore, L.; Vine, S.; Freeman, P.; Cooke, A.; Macintyre, D.; Ring, C. & Wilson, M. (2013) Quiet Eye Training Promotes Challenge Appraisals and Aids Performance Under Elevated Anxiety, *International Journal of Sport and Exercise Psychology*, 11 (2), 169–183.

Moore, L.; Vine, S.; Smith, S.; Smith, A. & Wilson, M. (2014) Quiet Eye Training Improves Small Arms Maritime Marksmanship, *Military Psychology*, 26 (5–6), 355–365.

Nibbeling, N.; Oudejans, R. & Daanen, H. (2012) Effects of Anxiety, a Cognitive Secondary Task, and Expertise on Gaze Behavior and Performance in a Far Aiming Task, *Psychology of Sport and Exercise*, 13 (4), 427–435.

Panchuk, D. & Vickers, J. (2006) Gaze Behaviors of Goaltenders Under Spatial – Temporal Constraints, *Human Movement Science*, 25 (6), 733–752.

Panchuk, D.; Vine, S. & Vickers, J. (2015) *Eye Tracking Methods in Sport Expertise*, In: J. Baker & D. Farrow (Eds.) *Routledge Handbook of Sport Expertise*, London: Routledge, pp. 176–186.

Professional Golfers' Association Tour Website (2016) Available at www.pgatour.com/

Vickers, J. (1992) Gaze Control in Putting, *Perception*, 21 (1), 117–132.

Vickers, J. (1996) Visual Control When Aiming At a Far Target, *Journal of Experimental Psychology: Human Perception and Performance*, 22 (2), 342–354.

Vickers, J. (2007) *Perception, Cognition and Decision Making: The Quiet Eye in Action*, Champaign, IL: Human Kinetics.

Vickers, J. (2011) Mind Over Muscle: The Role of Gaze Control, Spatial Cognition, and the Quiet Eye in Motor Expertise, *Cognitive Processing*, 12 (3), 219–222.

Vickers, J. & Williams, A. (2007) Performing Under Pressure: The Effects of Physiological Arousal, Cognitive Anxiety, and Gaze Control in Biathlon, *Journal of Motor Behaviour*, 39 (5), 381–394.

Vine, S.; Lee, D.; Moore, L. & Wilson, M. (2013) Quiet Eye and Choking: Online Control Breaks Down At the Point of Performance Failure, *Medicine and Sciences in Sport and Exercise*, 45 (10), 1988–1994.

Vine, S.; Lee, D.; Walters-Symons, R. & Wilson, M. (2015) An Occlusion Paradigm to Assess the Importance of the Timing of the Quiet Eye Fixation, *European Journal of Sport Sciences*, 17(1), 85–92.

Vine, S.; Moore, L. & Wilson, M. (2011) Quiet Eye Training Facilitates Competitive Putting Performance in Elite Golfers, *Frontiers in Psychology*, 2 (8), 1–9.

Vine, S.; Moore, L. & Wilson, M. (2014) Quiet Eye Training: The Acquisition, Refinement and Resilient Performance of Targeting Skills, *European Journal of Sport Science*, 14 (S1), S235–S242.

Vine, S. & Wilson, M. (2010) Quiet Eye Training: Effects on Learning and Performance Under Pressure, *Journal of Applied Sport Psychology*, 22 (4): 361–76.

Wilson, M. (2012) Anxiety: Attention, the Brain, the Body and Performance, In: S. Murphy (Ed.) *The Oxford Handbook of Sport and Performance Psychology*, New York, NY: Oxford University Press, pp. 173–190.

Wilson, M.; Causer, J. & Vickers, J. (2015) Aiming for Excellence: The Quiet Eye as a Characteristic of Expert Visuomotor Performance, In: J. Baker & D. Farrow (Eds.) *The Routledge Handbook of Sport Expertise*, London: Routledge, pp. 22–37.

Wilson, M.; Miles, C.; Vine, S. & Vickers, J. (2013) Quiet Eye Distinguishes Children of High and Low Motor Coordination Abilities, *Medicine & Science in Sports & Exercise*, 45 (6), 1144–1151.

Wilson, M. & Pearcey, R. (2009) On the Right Line: The Visuomotor Control of Straight and Breaking Golf Putts, *Perceptual and Motor Skills*, 109 (2), 555–562.

Wilson, M. & Richards, H. (2010) Putting It Together: Skill Packages for Pressure Performance, In D. Collins; A. Abbott, & H. Richards (Eds.), *Performance Psychology*, Edinburgh, UK: Elsevier, pp 333–356.

Wilson, M.; Vine, S. & Wood, G. (2009) The Influence of Anxiety on Visual Attentional Control in Basketball Free Throw Shooting, *Journal of Sport and Exercise Psychology*, 31 (2), 152–168.

Wilson, M.; Wood, G. & Vine, S. (2010) Anxiety, Attentional Control and Performance Impairment in Penalty Kicks, *Journal of Sport and Exercise Psychology*, 31 (6), 761–775.

21

GOLFERS' IMAGERY USE

Jennifer Cumming, Elliott Newell and Fredrik Weibull

Introduction

I never hit a shot even in practice without having a sharp in-focus picture of it in my head.

(Jack Nicklaus, 1974, p. 79)

Imagery is an important mental technique used by golfers to enhance learning and performance, and its systematic use is both a marker of talent development and expertise (e.g., Cumming & Hall, 2002; Brouziyne & Molinaro, 2005). Imagery can improve the learning and execution of golf shots (e.g., Brouziyne & Molinaro, 2005) as well as influence key psychological variables such as confidence (e.g., Hammond et al., 2012), focus (e.g., Ploszay et al., 2006) and flow experiences (e.g., Nicholls et al., 2005). This range of positive outcomes coupled with the flexibility with which it can be used has led to imagery becoming a popular strategy in golf (e.g., Bernier & Fournier, 2010; Cotterill et al., 2010). Moreover, imagery represents a key marker of success in sport, leading to learning and performance enhancement over the short term as well as supporting long-term talent development.

Guided by the revised applied model of imagery use (RAMDIU; Cumming & Williams, 2012, 2013), this chapter reviews research to explain who, where, when, what, why, and how golfers' image. Recommendations are provided on how to improve the effectiveness of golfers' imagery, including the role golf professionals can have in encouraging players' imagery use, and strategies for overcoming common imagery problems.

Review of current research

RAMDIU was developed by Cumming and Williams (2012, 2013) following a review of over 20 years of research and by incorporating relevant aspects of earlier applied models (e.g., Martin et al., 1999; Guillot & Collet, 2008). It focuses on deliberate as opposed to spontaneous images and consists of seven components to consider when developing effective imagery interventions: (a) Who; (b) Where and When; (c) Why; (d) What and How; (e) Personal Meaning; (f) Imagery Ability; and (g) Outcomes. The main proposition of this model is that its components interact to determine whether effective imagery will occur; that is, whether the intended function(s) (Why) of the imagery match the actual outcome(s) achieved. For example, self-efficacy enhancements occur when a golfer uses imagery to increase confidence in their bunker shots. As explained in the following subsections, both individual (Who) and situational (Where and When) factors will inform the function(s) of a golfer's imagery use. In turn, the content (What) and characteristics (How) of this imagery should fulfil the intended function(s) in a personally meaningful way. The golfer's imagery ability will also determine the extent to which outcomes are achieved as well as influence choices individuals make regarding what and how to image. As a relatively recent addition to the literature, the evidence base to support these propositions made by RAMDIU is still limited. Drawing from the extant research, the following sections will provide a review of this evidence in relation to the sport of golf.

Who

The 'Who' component of the RAMDIU describes the individual characteristics of the imager. Imagery is as a highly personal experience, and Why, What and How imagery is used is largely dependent on Who is imagining (Ahsen, 1984). Relevant individual characteristics include the golfer's experience in using imagery and their skill level (e.g., novice vs. expert). For example, golfers with a lower handicap used imagery more frequently than golfers with a higher handicap (Gregg & Hall, 2006). Dispositional characteristics such as achievement goal orientation, trait confidence, trait competition anxiety, and narcissism will also have an impact on golfers' imagery use (Cumming & Williams, 2012, 2013). Interventions should, therefore, consider the psychological profile of the golfer alongside their demographic information. To illustrate, an experienced golfer with a high task achievement and low ego orientation profile may not benefit from outcome-based images (e.g., winning, outperforming others) that are incongruent with their motivational tendencies. Instead, they may prefer more process-focused images (e.g., improving skills and strategies) to fulfil a motivational function.

Where and When

As a flexible strategy that can be used anywhere and anytime, it is unsurprising that athletes report using imagery in a wide variety of situations. Davies et al. (2014) highlighted a number of time periods within the competitive golf experience when imagery can be used, including pre-tournament tactical planning, pre-tournament technical change/refinement, pre-shot routines, post-shot analysis, and in-game strategising and decision making. Imagery may positively contribute to performance, psychological state and attentional control at these times points in competition and also in training. In addition to these sport-specific contexts, golfers may also use imagery during periods of rehabilitation, in breaks or their off-season, or when travelling to tournaments (e.g., Cumming & Hall, 2002; Driediger et al., 2006).

Why

The functions served by imagery are broadly categorised as cognitive and motivational, with each operating at specific and general levels (Paivio, 1985; Hall et al., 1998). The two cognitive functions involve learning and executing skills (cognitive-specific) or strategies (cognitive-general). By contrast, the three motivational functions involve using organising goal-related behaviour (motivational specific), promoting positive beliefs and cognitions (motivational general mastery), and regulating stress, anxiety and arousal (motivational general arousal). Research has largely remained focussed on these reasons for using imagery although other functions, such as promoting recovery from injury, have also been identified (Ievleva & Orlick, 1991).

The extant literature indicates that, in general, golfers employ imagery most frequently for a motivational general mastery function, followed by cognitive-specific and cognitive-general functions. The least used functions are motivational general arousal and motivational specific (Gregg & Hall, 2006). Similarly, Bernier and Fournier (2010) found that elite golfers reported using imagery to learn or perfect their swing (e.g., to check amplitude of backswing), to evaluate a shot, to prepare strategies and tactics (e.g., club and/or shot selection), to focus (e.g., selectively attend to relevant information and avoid overthinking the technical aspects of the shot), and to manage their psychological states (e.g., enhancing their confidence, managing arousal). To gain more fully from using imagery, educational components of interventions could help make golfers more aware of the motivational benefits of using imagery to assist with setting goals and making plans for achieving them.

What

The content of golfers' images describes what they see in their mind's eye, hear in their mind's ear, feel with their mind's touch, and so on. It is highly personal to the golfer and usually constructed based on their experiences. There is no limit to what a golfer might image, but the tendency is to focus on the swing and the results of this action (Bernier & Fournier, 2010). Imagery content can also reflect the other functions described above using the rule of thumb 'what you see is what you get' (Martin et al., 1999). A golfer may image themselves winning an event, being interviewed by the media, and receiving congratulations from their fellow players to serve a motivational specific function. However, it is important to be aware that imagery content does not necessarily need to match the function this explicitly. Due to the highly personal nature of imagery, a golfer might find that the same image can serve a different function or even multiple functions. For example, imaging the perfect swing could potentially serve cognitive specific, motivational specific and motivational general mastery functions. For example, a golfer may use visual imagery when planning a strategy at the start of a hole to arrive at the green. Their visualisation of the desired flight of the ball for each shot in sequence may serve a cognitive general purpose for the golfer for whom the image represents clarity of tactical approach to a sequence of shots that are considered within their capability. The same image, however, may be used by another golfer for motivational and confidence purposes because their desired strategy pushes them to the limits of their perceived capability.

Golfers are also not limited to imagery content that fits neatly into Paivio's (1985) framework and can draw on an extensive range of images, including anatomical, appearance, health and healing, and pain management (Cumming & Williams, 2012, 2013). From an applied perspective, imagery content will be effective if it serves the intended function(s), but what is imaged may differ between individuals and situations. To serve a motivational general mastery function, one individual may prefer to image themselves managing the symptoms they associate with pre-tournament nerves, whereas another may focus on previewing a successful round. For this reason, recent advice on imagery script development highlights the importance of tailoring the content of imagery to meet the unique needs of the imager (Williams et al., 2013b).

How

The How element of RAMDIU describes the different delivery methods available to golfers for receiving imagery interventions and the characteristics of their imagery experience. Because there is often a close relationship between what is imaged and how this imagery is done, both are represented in the same element within RAMDIU (Cumming & Williams, 2012, 2013).

However, the exact nature of the relationship between What and How still needs to be established by future research.

How: Characteristics

Imagery characteristics are the different ways to describe the imagery experience (Cumming & Williams, 2012, 2013). These mainly refer to the speed, duration, modality, perspective, angle, and agency of the images. With respect to speed, images can be generated in slow motion, real time, or fast time. Imaging in real time more closely approximates the actual experience, and helps to make this imagery more realistic and effective (Holmes & Collins, 2001). However, O and Hall (2013) found that athletes slow their images down to review and fine-tune skills, assist with strategy planning, enhance confidence and focus, as well as to calm down. Similarly, speeding up images helped with strategy planning under pressure, and confidence. Furthermore, fast-motion images can serve an energising function as well as help fast-forward through parts of the performance.

Another temporal characteristic is the duration of the imaged performance. Researchers compare the duration of the image to the executed movement (i.e., mental chronometry). Smaller discrepancies are inferred to represent more accurate imagery, whereas larger discrepancies may indicate problems in the imagery process (Cumming et al., 2016). Koyama et al. (2009) found that, although the duration of mental imagery was less than actual duration for both the skilled and unskilled golfers, skilled golfers had longer imagery of the flight phase. Timing golfers' imagery may, therefore, be a useful monitoring and evaluation tool to complement the self-report scaling more commonly used to assess ease, vividness, and controllability.

In the absence of external stimulus input, golfers are able to experience different perceptions in the mind's ear (i.e., auditory imagery), the mind's noise (i.e., olfactory imagery), the mind's skin (i.e., tactile imagery), the mind's eye (i.e., visual imagery), and so on (Kosslyn et al., 2006). These different senses can be combined to produce more vivid and realistic images. Within sport research, visual and kinaesthetic are the two modalities that have featured most predominately (Cumming & Williams, 2012). Recognising the importance of both, Tiger Woods once said, "You have to see the shots and feel them through your hands" (Pitt, 1998, p. 5).

Visual imagery contains information about what the individual sees through their mind's eye, which can be viewed from either a first-person perspective (1PP; i.e., through their own eyes) or a third-person perspective (3PP; i.e., external observer of the action). Within sport research, 1PP has been found to benefit well-learned tasks and those depending on the perceptual information available. In contrast, 3PP is considered more useful for tasks emphasising technical form or body shape (Hardy, 1997). For 3PP, single or multiple angles can also provide different sources of visual information (e.g., behind, in front, side on). Cumming and Williams (2012) further suggested that specific or multiple angles may enhance the effects of 3PP by providing visual information not otherwise available during 1PP.

Although golfers may display preferences for using one viewing perspective over the other, there is an advantage to being able to alternate between perspectives and/or viewing angles to match the nature of the task or desired outcomes of the imagery. For example, a golfer might evaluate weather and course conditions using 3PP and then mentally rehearse the shot and resulting ball flight path with 1PP. In support, players interviewed by Bernier and Fournier (2010) reported mostly using 1PP because it provided specific information to assist with the performance, whereas 3PP was used mainly to gain additional information about the environment.

A final characteristic of note is the behavioural agency or authorship of the visual image (Ruby & Decety, 2001; Holmes & Calmels, 2008). Regardless of viewing perspective, a golfer can image their performance (i.e., agent of one's behaviour) or that of another golfer (i.e., another person is the agent of the action). However, in 1PP this would involve mentally stepping into the shoes of another golfer to predict and understand their actions (Jeannerod, 2006). In 3PP, by contrast, the golfer might take the position of an audience member to review mentally the shot taken by another competitor.

How: Delivery

Different theories explain how images are formed in the mind (e.g., bioinformational theory, functional equivalence theory, symbolic learning theory). But, it is agreed that images can originate from internal and/or external sources and then reside in our conscious awareness (Murphy et al., 2008). Internally generated images are typically based on one's knowledge and experiences and drawn from long-term memory. Images can also be constructed from working memory such as in the case of a golfer who uses the motor or sensory traces of a just executed swing to image subsequently that same movement (Koyama et al., 2009). In contrast, externally generated images can be 'cued' by different perceptual stimuli (e.g., sights, sounds, smells and tastes) or verbal instruction (e.g., imagery script). Regardless of the source, images are then processed in working memory through inspection, transformation, and maintenance (Kosslyn, 1995).

Understanding that imagery is constructed in different ways helps to inform what methods are used to deliver imagery interventions such as guided imagery scripts (see Williams et al., 2013b, for detailed guidance on how to plan, deliver and evaluate personalised scripts). RAMDIU suggests that characteristics of both the individual (e.g., experience level) and the situation (e.g., demands of a particular course) should be considered when determining how an intervention is delivered. Effective imagery will then occur if the generated content meets the intervention goals. Take, for example, the situation of an experienced golfer playing a round on a challenging course for the first time. His pre-tournament imagery will likely be more effective when memories of past successful tournaments are combined with studying video footage of a previous year's tournament. Collectively this information can then be used to construct a realistic preview of his performance despite not having played the course previously. Upon arrival at the tournament, walking the course or doing practice rounds will lead the golfer to update these images based on new information as it is gained (e.g., pin placement, weather conditions). In this case, the golfer can combine long-term memories with external sources of information and new experiences to maximise the potential for a vivid and realistic image of their upcoming performance. By doing so, he will likely benefit from the sense of accomplishment resulting from rehearsing a successful performance before it has even occurred – an important source of self-efficacy (Bandura, 1997).

The above example also illustrates how golfers may draw from available resources to enhance the quality of their imagery. Two factors to consider are whether these will provide information about the physical nature of the task and the environment within which it is performed. As explained by the PETTLEP model (Holmes & Collins, 2001; also see Table 21.1 as well as Wakefield & Smith, 2012, for a full description of its elements), the imagery experience should be made as physical as possible to match the real-life situation. A golfer might involve recalling the kinaesthetic sensations felt when performing a drive off the tee. This image can also be primed by adopting the pre-shot position, holding the appropriate club, making small gestures or movements, and wearing the same shoes and clothes. Imagery carried out where the real-life performance will take place is also easier to generate. When this is not possible, golfers can take advantage of modern technology by accessing photos, video footage, audio recordings, and even topographical maps of the course (Anuar et al., 2016).

Table 21.1 Elements of the PETTLEP model (Holmes & Collins, 2001)

Element	Definition	Example
Physical	Physical nature of imagery, including body position, clothing and sport equipment specific to task/situation.	Adopt position to drive off tee, holding onto the club, and feel yourself move through the swing.
Environment	Physical environment where imagery is performed.	Perform imagery at the golf course.
Task	Characteristics of the task and expertise level.	Preview shot appropriate for your level, course and weather conditions.
Timing	Temporal nature of imagery (slow motion vs. real time vs. fast motion).	Image shot in real time.
Learning	Imagery content evolves with learning and refinement of behaviour.	Adapt imaged shot technique in response to feedback.
Emotion	Affective and emotional response to situation.	Feel calm and in control of shot being taken.
Perspective	Visual perspective adopted (1PP vs. 3PP) according to personal preferences and/or function of the imagery.	View the action using 1PP.

Related to PETTLEP imagery, observing the movement to be executed is another effective imagery aid for delivering imagery interventions. Providing movement observation either live or recorded will facilitate the imagery experience by providing golfers with clear and vivid instructions of what they are imaging. This aid may be particularly useful for relatively inexperienced golfers who find it difficult to create images of themselves performing. A smartphone or tablet can be used to record and review a golfer's own performance or that of another golfer. After viewing this footage, the golfer can be guided to accurately recreate the desired aspects of their performance in their imagery. Interestingly, research has shown that movement observation can make it easier to generate both visual images and kinaesthetic images. However, the observation perspective used to film the movement (i.e., first vs. third person) should correspond with the visual imagery perspective (Williams et al., 2011; also see Wright et al., 2015).

Imagery ability

Within sport, imagery ability is defined as "an individual's capability of forming vivid, controllable images and retaining them for sufficient time to effect the desired imagery rehearsal" (Morris et al., 2005, p. 60). The ability to create accurate mental representations of intended shots is associated with high performance in golf (Finn, 2008; Hellström, 2009). Moreover, the effectiveness of golfers' imagery use is influenced by this ability (Hall et al., 1992; Robin et al., 2007). Indeed, research has demonstrated that imagery ability moderates the relationship between imagery use and its intended outcomes, with greater benefits occurring for those with a better ability to generate and control images (Goss et al., 1986; Cumming, 2008). Bernier and Fournier (2010) found that elite golfers were able to manipulate their image content to meet the perceived demands of the situation. For a particularly challenging shot, for example, golfers in this study reduced the speed of their image and adapted the angle from which they 'see' it.

Due its importance, golfers will benefit from methods for improving their imagery ability. Layered Stimulus Response Training (LSRT; Williams et al., 2013a) is one such technique. LSRT was developed based on bioinformational theory (Lang, 1977) and involves the golfer building an image in increasing layers of detail. The layers consist of different types of infor-mation: (a) stimulus propositions (characteristics of the imagery scenario; e.g., ball lands in a bunker); (b) response propositions (the physiological responses to the stimulus; e.g., increased heart rate and muscle tension); and (c) meaning propositions (the relationship between stimulus and response propositions; e.g., scared of hitting the shot). The practitioner/researcher helps the participant to decide on what details to include in each layer, with the gradual improvements helping to make the scene more vivid and more meaningful for the participant (for a more detailed description of how to use this technique, see Cumming et al., 2016).

Outcomes

The final element of RAMDIU depicts the four main types of imagery outcomes experi-enced by athletes: (1) motor learning and performance; (2) strategies and problem-solving; (3) psychological outcomes; and (4) injury rehabilitation (Guillot & Collett, 2008). However, it is also possible for imagery to result in outcomes beyond those proposed by RAMDIU.

Within golf, most research demonstrating the effectiveness of imagery for improving motor learning and performance has focused on the short game, namely putting (Woolfolk et al., 1985; Smith & Holmes, 2004) and chipping (Brouziyne & Molinaro, 2005; Smith et al., 2008). These studies have consistently found imagery to have a positive effect on performance for both nov-ice and experienced golfers. Supporting the idea that imagery is a useful supplement to physical practice (Hall, 2001), combining both types of practice, is also more effective than physical practice or imagery practice alone.

On strategies and problem-solving, few studies have directly addressed this issue within golf. However, it is likely that golfers will use imagery to help plan their course strategy (e.g., whether to aim for accuracy or distance), assist them with decision-making (e.g., shot selection, where to strategically position the ball), and effectively adapt to different course conditions (e.g., fast vs. slow greens). A golfer might use imagery to consider their approach to a difficult hole by previewing the possible outcomes of either playing to the middle of the green or the pin by taking into account details of the hole's design (e.g., distance, hazards, out-of-bounds borders).

Research supports golfers' use of imagery for obtaining psychological outcomes, including emotional control (Kirschenbaum et al., 1998), intrinsic motivation (Martin & Hall, 1995), flow states (Nicholls et al., 2005), and self-efficacy (Short et al., 2002). Imagery also appears to help improve symptoms of the yips (Bell et al., 2009), which are involuntary twitches, jerks or freezing that can affect the initiation or execution of fine motor movements (Milne & Morrison, 2015). It does so by targeting related psychological factors (e.g., negative thoughts, somatic anxiety symptoms, lack of confidence and concentration disruption) (Smith et al., 2000).

Imagery can also play a role in helping golfers to prevent an injury or recover from one. Among professionals, injuries are commonly located in the lower back or wrist and result from overuse (i.e., high frequency of golf swings) or poor technique (McHardy et al., 2006). Imagery may help players manage their pain and promote healing, but also to serve as a substitute for any missed physical practice when injured (Driediger et al., 2006). It may also help prevent further injury by enabling players to improve their technique and fix bad habits (Hall, 2001) as well as manage the emotional distress that can accompany injury and support psychological readiness to return to play (Podlog et al., 2014).

Although outcomes from imagery interventions are found to be mostly positive in nature, it should be noted that imagery can also sometimes have negative or unintended effects. Imaging oneself missing the hole, for example, can hamper performance as well as self-efficacy beliefs (Short et al., 2002). Trying to suppress such images (e.g., "don't image the ball going in the water") can also inadvertently and negatively affect players' performance (Beilock et al., 2001; Ramsey et al., 2008). However, unintended outcomes can also be desirable in nature. A participant in Nicholls et al.'s (2005) study did not perceive the imagery intervention to help improve chipping performance. However, the imagery did help to improve his concentration. As suggested by RAMDIU, practitioners are advised to check whether the content of players' images is serving the intended function(s) and facilitating desired outcomes.

Implications for the game

General tips and recommendations

In addition to those suggestions outlined above, more general advice can also be given for developing imagery interventions for golfers.

1   **Eyes open vs. eyes closed**: Most individuals find it easier to image as clearly and vividly as possible with their eyes closed and when they try to incorporate relevant senses (e.g., sights, sounds).
2   **Personally meaningful**: Actively involve golfers in the development of their imagery interventions. According to RAMDIU, personal meaning serves as a bridge between the content and function of golfers' imagery. What golfers image will also be influenced by individual preferences and situational demands (Cumming & Williams, 2012, 2013).
3   **Shared experiences**: As well as providing anecdotal reports from well-known golfers about their imagery use, discussions between players can be used to encourage sharing of ideas as to what and how to image. This group work can help golfers to learn from each other as well as debunk any existing myths about imagery.
4   **Duration of imagery sessions**: For a golfer new to imagery, they should be encouraged to aim for short but high-quality periods of imaging before gradually extending the rehearsal period. Similar to physical skills, regular and systematic imagery practice will likely lead to greater benefits (Cumming & Hall, 2002).
5   **Evaluate imagery**: We recommend evaluating the golfer's imagery experience, whether this is during an LSRT exercise or following script rehearsal. Rating scales can be used as immediate feedback as well as other more objective measures (e.g., mental chronometry, biofeedback).

Overcoming common imagery problems

A common imagery problem occurs when golfers are unable to generate and/or maintain the desired image (Cumming et al., 2016). Some may find it difficult to incorporate certain sensations or details into their image (e.g., "I see just blackness" or "It is fuzzy and unclear") or hold it in their mind for a certain period. Golfers who experience problems might be less likely to use imagery or use it ineffectively and, therefore, miss out on the many benefits outlined above. LSRT and other techniques such as observing video clips of desired movements can help to resolve these issues. Alternatively, a golfer may wish to use positive self-talk to help cue the desired image or reverse the effects of an undesirable image (Cumming et al., 2006).

Summary and future research recommendations

In conclusion, imagery is a complex, personal and multifaceted process characterised by who, where, when, why, and what is imaged. Better golfers will more likely be aware of their preferred imagery process (i.e., their meta-imagery skills) and be able to adapt the content and characteristics of their imagery to the function required by the situation (Bernier and Fournier, 2010). However, novice golfers or those less familiar with using imagery may benefit from more structured support, including LSRT and imagery scripts, to help them develop these skills. Research has focussed mostly on the short game; for a more robust evidence base, further research is also warranted on the long game as well as to test out the predictions of RAMDIU across a range of skill levels and situations. Few studies have systematically explored golfers' imagery use within the injury rehabilitation setting despite the many potential benefits. Another suggestion is to focus on younger golfers and investigate the role imagery may play over time in their talent and psychosocial development. That is, many exciting avenues are open for exploration to help further understanding of effective imagery use in golf.

References

Ahsen, A. (1984) ISM: The Triple Code Model for Imagery and Psychophysiology, *Journal of Mental Imagery*, 8 (4), 15–42.

Anuar, N.; Cumming, J. & Williams, S. (2016) Effects of Applying the PETTLEP Model on Vividness and Ease of Imaging Movement, *Journal of Applied Sport Psychology*, 28 (2), 185–198.

Bandura, A. (1997) *Self-efficacy: The Exercise of Control*, New York, NY: Freeman.

Beilock, S.; Afremow, J.; Rabe, A. & Carr, T. (2001) "Don't Miss!" The Debilitating Effects of Suppressive Imagery on Golf Putting Performance, *Journal of Sport and Exercise Psychology*, 23 (3), 200–221.

Bell, R.; Skinner, C. & Fisher, L. (2009) Decreasing Putting Yips in Accomplished Golfers via Solution-focused Guided Imagery: A Single-subject Research Design, *Journal of Applied Sport Psychology*, 21(1), 1–14.

Bernier, M. & Fournier, J. (2010) Functions of Mental Imagery in Expert Golfers, *Psychology of Sport and Exercise*, 11 (6), 444–452.

Brouziyne, M. & Molinaro, C. (2005) Mental Imagery Combined with Physical Practice of Approach Shots for Golf Beginners, *Perceptual and Motor Skills*, 101 (1), 203–211.

Cotterill, S.; Sanders, R. & Collins, D. (2010) Developing Effective Pre-performance Routines in Golf: Why Don't We Ask the Golfer? *Journal of Applied Sport Psychology*, 22 (1), 51–64.

Cumming, J. (2008) Investigating the Relationship Between Exercise Imagery, Leisure-time Exercise Behavior, and Self-efficacy, *Journal of Applied Sport Psychology*, 20 (2), 184–198.

Cumming, J.; Cooley, S.; Anuar, N.; Kosteli, M.; Quinton, M.; Weibull, F. & Williams, S. (2016) Developing Imagery Ability Effectively: A Guide to Layered Stimulus Response Training, *Journal of Sport Psychology in Action*, 8 (1), 23–33.

Cumming, J. & Hall, C. (2002) Deliberate Imagery Practice: Examining the Development of Imagery Skills in Competitive Athletes, *Journal of Sport Sciences*, 20 (2), 137–145.

Cumming, J.; Nordin, S.; Horton, R. & Reynolds, S. (2006) Examining the Directional Component of Imagery and Self-talk Strategies on Performance and Self-efficacy, *The Sport Psychologist*, 20 (3), 257–274.

Cumming, J. & Williams, S. (2012) The Role of Imagery in Performance, In: S. Murphy (Ed.) *Handbook of Sport and Performance Psychology*, New York, NY: Oxford University Press, pp. 213–232.

Cumming, J. & Williams, S. (2013) Introducing the Revised Applied Model of Deliberate Imagery Use for Sport, Dance, Exercise, and Rehabilitation, *Movement and Sport Sciences*, 82 (4), 69–81.

Davies, T.; Collins, D. & Cruickshank, A. (2014) So What Do We Do with the Rest of the Day? Going Beyond the Pre-shot Routine in Professional Golf, *International Journal of Golf Science*, 3 (2), 163–175.

Driediger, M.; Hall, C. & Callow, N. (2006) Imagery Use by Injured Athletes: A Qualitative Analysis, *Journal of Sports Sciences*, 24 (3), 261–271.

Finn, J. (2008) An Introduction to Using Mental Skills to Enhance Performance in Golf: Beyond the Bounds of Positive and Negative Thinking, *International Journal of Sports Science, and Coaching*, 3 (1), 255–269.

Goss, S.; Hall, C.; Buckolz, E. & Fishbourne, G. (1986) Imagery Ability and the Acquisition and Retention of Movements, *Memory and Cognition*, 14 (6), 469–477.

Gregg, M. & Hall, C. (2006) The Relationship of Skill Level and Age to the Use of Imagery by Golfers, *Journal of Applied Sport Psychology*, 18 (4), 363–375.

Guillot, A. & Collet, C. (2008) Construction of the Motor Imagery Integrative Model in Sport: A Review and Theoretical Investigation of Motor Imagery Use, *International Review of Sport and Exercise Psychology*, 1 (1), 31–44.

Hall, C. (2001) Imagery in Sport and Exercise, In: R. Singer; H. Hausenblas, & C. Janelle (Eds.) *Handbook of Sport Psychology*, New York, NY: Wiley, pp. 529–549.

Hall, C.; Buckolz, E. & Fishburne, G. (1992) Imagery and the Acquisition of Motor Skills, *Canadian Journal of Sport Sciences*, 17 (1), 19–27.

Hall, C.; Mack, D.; Paivio, A. & Hausenblas, H. (1998) Imagery Use by Athletes: Development of the Sport Imagery Questionnaire, *International Journal of Sport Psychology*, 29 (1), 73–89.

Hammond, T.; Gregg, M.; Hrycaiko, D.; Mactavish, J. & Leslie-Toogood, A. (2012) The Effects of a Motivational General-mastery Imagery Intervention on the Imagery Ability and Sport Confidence of Inter-collegiate Golfers, *Journal of Imagery Research in Sport and Physical Activity*, 7, 1–20.

Hardy, L. (1997) The Coleman Roberts Griffith Address: Three Myths about Applied Consultancy Work, *Journal of Applied Sport Psychology*, 9 (2), 277–294.

Hellström, J. (2009) Psychological Hallmarks of Skilled Golfers, *Sports Medicine*, 39 (10), 845–856.

Holmes, P. & Calmels, C. (2008) A Neuroscientific Review of Imagery and Observation Use in Sport, *Journal of Motor Behavior*, 40 (5), 433–445.

Holmes, P. & Collins, D. (2001) The PETTLEP Approach to Motor Imagery: A Functional Equivalence Model for Sport Psychologists, *Journal of Applied Sport Psychology*, 13 (1), 60–83.

Ievleva, L. & Orlick, T. (1991) Mental Links to Enhanced Healing: An Exploratory Study, *The Sport Psychologist*, 5 (1), 25–40.

Jeannerod, M. (2006) *Motor Cognition*, Oxford, UK: Oxford University Press.

Kirschenbaum, D.; Owens, D. & O'Connor, E. (1998) Smart Golf: Preliminary Evaluation of a Simple, Yet Comprehensive, Approach to Improving and Scoring the Mental Game, *The Sport Psychologist*, 12 (3), 271–282.

Kosslyn, S. (1995) Mental Imagery, *Visual Cognition: An Invitation to Cognitive Science*, 2, 267–296.

Kosslyn, S. (2005) Mental Images and the Brain, *Cognitive Neuropsychology*, 22 (3/4), 333–347.

Kosslyn, S.; Thompson, W. & Ganis, G. (2006) *The Case for Mental Imagery*, New York, NY: Oxford University Press.

Koyama, S.; Tsuruhara, K. & Yamamoto, Y. (2009) Duration of Mentally Simulated Movement Before and After a Golf Shot, *Perceptual and Motor Skills*, 108 (1), 327–338.

Lang, P. (1977) Imagery in Therapy: An Information-Processing Analysis of Fear, *Behavior Therapy*, 8 (5), 862–886.

Martin, K. & Hall, C. (1995) Using Mental Imagery to Enhance Intrinsic Motivation, *Journal of Sport and Exercise Psychology*, 17 (1), 54–69.

Martin, K.; Moritz, S. & Hall, C. (1999) Imagery Use in Sport: A Literature Review and Applied Model, *The Sport Psychologist*, 13 (3), 245–268.

McHardy, A.; Pollard, H. & Luo, K. (2006) Golf Injuries', *Sports Medicine*, 36 (2), 171–187.

Milne, D. & Morrison, G. (2015) Cognitive Behavioural Intervention for the Golf Yips: A Single-case Design, *Sport and Exercise Psychology Review*, 11 (1), 20–33.

Morris, T.; Spittle, M. & Watt, A. (2005) *Imagery in Sport*, Champaign, IL: Human Kinetics.

Murphy, S.; Nordin, S. & Cumming, J. (2008) Imagery in Sport, Exercise and Dance In: T. Horn (Ed.) *Advances in Sport and Exercise Psychology*, Champaign, IL: Human Kinetics, pp. 297–324.

Nicholls, A.; Polman, R. & Holt, N. (2005) The Effects of Individualized Imagery Interventions on Golf Performance and Flow States, *Athletic Insight*, 7 (1), 43–64.

Nicklaus, J. (1974) *Golf My Way*, New York, NY: Simon & Schuster.

O, J. & Hall, C. (2013) A Qualitative Analysis of Athletes' Voluntary Image Speed Use', *Journal of Imagery Research in Sport and Physical Activity*, 8 (1), 1–12.

Paivio, A. (1985) Cognitive and Motivational Functions of Imagery in Human Performance, *Canadian Journal of Applied Sport Sciences*, 10 (4), 22–28.

Pitt, N. (1998) Out of the Woods, *Sunday Times (Sport)*, 19 July.

Ploszay, A.; Gentner, N.; Skinner, C. & Wrisberg, C. (2006) The Effects of Multisensory Imagery in Conjunction with Physical Movement Rehearsal on Golf Putting Performance, *Journal of Behavioral Education*, 15 (4), 247–255.

Podlog, L.; Heil, J. & Schulte, S. (2014) Psychosocial Factors in Sports Injury Rehabilitation and Return to Play, *Physical Medicine and Rehabilitation Clinics of North America*, 25 (4), 915–930.

Ramsey, R.; Cumming, J. & Edwards, M. (2008) Exploring a Modified Conceptualization of Imagery Direction and Golf Putting Performance, *International Journal of Sport and Exercise Psychology*, 6 (2), 207–223.

Robin, N.; Dominique, L.; Toussaint, L.; Blandin, Y.; Guillot, A. & Her, M. (2007) Effects of Motor Imagery Training on Service Return Accuracy in Tennis: The Role of Imagery Ability, *International Journal of Sport and Exercise Psychology*, 5 (2), 175–186.

Ruby, P. & Decety, J. (2001) Effect of Subjective Perspective Taking During Simulation of Action: A PET Investigation of Agency, *Nature Neuroscience*, 4 (5), 546–550.

Short, S.; Bruggeman, J.; Engel, S.; Marback, T.; Wang, L.; Willadsen, A. & Short, M. (2002) The Effect of Imagery Function and Imagery Direction on Self-efficacy and Performance on a Golf-putting Task, *The Sport Psychologist*, 16 (1), 48–67.

Smith, A.; Malo, S.; Laskowski, E.; Sabick, M.; Cooney III, W.; Finnie, S. B.; Crews, D.; Eischen, J.; Hay, I.; Detling, N. & Kaufman, K. (2000) A Multidisciplinary Study of the "Yips" Phenomenon in Golf, *Sports Medicine*, 30 (6), 423–437.

Smith, D. & Holmes, P. (2004) The Effect of Imagery Modality on Golf Putting Performance, *Journal of Sport and Exercise Psychology*, 26 (3), 385–395.

Smith, D.; Wright, C. & Cantwell, C. (2008) Beating the Bunker: The Effect of PETTLEP Imagery on Golf Bunker Shot Performance, *Research Quarterly for Exercise and Sport*, 79 (3), 385–391.

Wakefield, C. & Smith, D. (2012) Perfecting Practice: Applying the PETTLEP Model of Motor Imagery, *Journal of Sport Psychology in Action*, 3 (1), 1–11.

Williams, S.; Cooley, S. & Cumming, J. (2013a) Layered Stimulus Response Training Improves Motor Imagery Ability and Movement Execution, *Journal of Sport and Exercise Psychology*, 35 (1), 60–71.

Williams, S.; Cooley, S.; Newell, E.; Weibull, F. & Cumming, J. (2013b) Seeing the Difference: Developing Effective Imagery Scripts for Athletes, *Journal of Sport Psychology in Action*, 4 (2), 109–121.

Williams, S.; Cumming, J. & Edwards, M. (2011) The Functional Equivalence Between Movement Imagery, Observation, and Execution Influences Imagery Ability, *Research Quarterly for Exercise and Sport*, 82 (3), 555–564.

Woolfolk, R.; Parrish, M. & Murphy, S. (1985) The Effects of Positive and Negative Imagery on Motor Skill Performance, *Cognitive Therapy and Research*, 9 (3), 335–341.

Wright, D.; Mccormick, S.; Birks, S.; Loporto, M. & Holmes, P. (2015) Action Observation and Imagery Training Improve the Ease with Which Athletes Can Generate Imagery, *Journal of Applied Sport Psychology*, 27 (2), 156–170.

22

DEVELOPING AND MAINTAINING MOTIVATION IN GOLF

Kieran Kingston

Introduction

A perusal of the mainstream sport psychology journals suggests that, while golf is a fruitful vehicle for research in sport psychology, much of this research utilises golf-related tasks (e.g., putting or chipping) to explore the effects of discrete psychological skills (e.g., imagery or goal-setting) or to demonstrate skill learning under different conditions (e.g., focus of attention, competitive anxiety, social facilitation, etc.). There have been a number of other psychology-related studies in the sport, exploring such concepts as attributions, social support and participation; however, many of these types of studies have tended to use golf as a vehicle for theory testing, rather than necessarily aiming to inform those engaged within the game.

The purpose of this chapter is to consider the topic of motivation; concepts under this umbrella term have been front and centre in general psychology for decades as well as, more recently, in the sport and exercise psychology domain. Though theoretical perspectives on motivation in sport are numerous, the objective here is to review research into motivation that, in our view, can help inform our understanding of constructive motivation in the sport of golf. Insight into the processes that facilitate adaptive engagement in activities can help students, scientists, coaches and organisations concerned with golf at all levels to provide a more supportive environment for initial engagement, continued participation and sporting excellence (Kingston et al., 2006).

As we have alluded to above, there is a general lack of breadth into the psychological research in golf; this is no different when we consider the concept of motivation. Much of the research has adopted a social-cognitive view and focused on achievement goals (Nicholls, 1989). Consequently, though we will consider that research published in golf, for the theoretical aspects we are focusing on here, and given the relative scarcity of research in the areas of interest much of the information supporting our arguments comes from golf-specific studies, direct research in the sport, or in the absence of that, research in achievement settings (e.g., education or physical activity) which can be applied directly to sport.

In terms of the structure and organisation of this particular chapter, in the process of sourcing knowledge relevant to our chosen theoretical areas, we will briefly describe the existing research that has been conducted in sport and, where applicable, review that research which has used golf as the sport of interest. Having reflected on the current state of knowledge and clarified the specific threats to motivation for golfers across ages and ability levels, the emphasis will be on how this knowledge can support the aim of promoting long-term motivation and adaptive views of engagement in the sport of golf. Finally, there will be a summary in which we will consider the directions of potential research in the future.

Review of literature

It is often argued that the term motivation is both overused and vague. Roberts (2012) suggests that definitions of motivation are either too broad, such that they incorporate the whole field of psychology, or so narrow that they explain almost nothing. For example, if you take its use in everyday life, motivation is synonymous with arousal and can be illustrated through the motivational tirades of football managers. Similarly, motivation is often portrayed as reflective of confidence – the winning attitude that inspires great performance, or perhaps simply a matter of positive thinking. Unfortunately, most of these simplistic portrayals do not begin to capture the complexity and richness of motivational matters (Roberts, 2012). Despite these variations in conceptualisation, and the directions they lead researchers, an assumption shared by most motivational theorists is that motivation is actually a process – one that influences the initiation, direction, magnitude, perseverance and continuation and quality of goal-directed behaviour (Maehr & Zusho, 2009). In such cases, behaviours are 'driven' through the goals individuals possess and the personal meaning they attach to the process of pursuing these.

The degree to which athletes engage in goal-directed effort and persist over a period of time is critical to learning and performance, and the motivation displayed by athletes is underpinned by numerous factors. Roberts (2001) alludes to these in describing motivation as those personality factors, social variables and cognitions which act in situations where one is evaluated, competes against others, or attempts to attain a standard of excellence. Further, in order to start to predict and understand human behaviour in sport, it is critical in turn to understand the complex dynamic psychological processes that underlie motivated behaviour. From an applied perspective, according to Ryan and Deci (2000), this motivational process is the key determinant behind every action taken and every effort exerted in sport; it is, therefore, a pre-eminent concern to those who have an interest in promoting engagement, striving and performance in sports such as golf.

Theoretical perspectives

The most popular contemporary theories of motivation in sport and exercise are based on social-cognitive or organismic perspectives. Though most motivational research in the physical activity context over the past 35 years has adopted a social-cognitive approach, specifically utilising achievement goal theory (Nicholls, 1989), organismic approaches are, according to Roberts, experiencing a resurgence largely through the popularising of Deci and Ryan's (1985) self-determination theory (SDT) and Elliott's (1999) model of approach and avoidance goals. The emphases of this chapter are these organismic approaches.

Achievement goal theorists adopting Nicholls' (1989) approach commonly identify two distinct orientations towards evaluating competence – a performance goal focus where they seek to demonstrate competence relative to others, and a mastery goal focus where development of self-referenced competence and task mastery are the objective. Though there is some variation in terms used (e.g., task and ego), the essence of the goals of action remain the same.

While it is beyond the scope of this chapter to review the approximate 300 studies that have examined achievement goals in the context of sport and exercise, based on the recent comprehensive review by Roberts (2012), some important conclusions can be drawn. When individuals evaluate their competence relative to others (i.e., they are ego-involved), they are likely to engage in motivationally maladaptive behaviours; this is especially the case when perceptions of competence are lower, or they are concerned with evaluation. Effort and persistence are diminished, satisfaction and enjoyment suffers, peer relationships are placed at risk, and withdrawal is likely. In contrast, when competence is evaluated through setting self-referenced goals, learning or task engagement (i.e., the individual is mastery/task involved), effort and persistence are maintained, satisfaction and enjoyment are higher, peer relationships and social interactions are more constructive, and participants feel more positive about themselves or the task (Roberts, 2012). These conclusions should not be interpreted to mean that utilising social comparison-based criteria for evaluating competence cannot be beneficial; the point is that, while high perceptions of competence may lead to such goals having a positive influence, they are more fragile and can lead to maladaptive striving when achievement is threatened (Dweck & Leggett, 1988). The next chapter by Dan Sachau considers the effects of dispositional task and ego involvement (goal orientations) in detail. Nevertheless, this chapter will briefly review a small number of studies that have considered achievement goals in the context of golf.

In terms of goal orientations in golfers; for beginners, mastery goals facilitate interest and persistence and, when manipulated can promote better performance than ego/performance goals. (Steinberg et al., 2000). Similarly, in recreational golfers, task involvement is positively related to happiness and excitement, while ego involvement was correlated with dejection (Dewar & Kavussanu, 2011). For collegiate golfers, Kuczka and Treasure (2005) identified that perceptions that a team environment was supportive of self-referenced goals and learning was negatively related to seeking to make excuses for upcoming performance (self-handicapping). Finally, in recreational golfers, higher levels of task orientation have been associated with peak performance states and absorption in an activity (Oh, 2001; cf. Sachau et al., 2013). In the context of learning, Spray et al. (2006) found that students who were told their goals were to 'learn and master the techniques of golf putting' (a task goal) performed better than students who were told that their goal was to 'outperform other students in the school in golf putting' (an ego-oriented goal). These findings mirror the achievement goal research reviewed by others (e.g., Roberts et al., 2007; 2012), i.e., mastery/task goals largely promote positive effects, and ego/performance goals put performers at risk motivationally.

Prior to the turn of the millennium, in the domain of sport and exercise, achievement goals were almost exclusively discussed in terms of a dichotomous mastery (task) versus performance (ego) goal distinction (Nicholls, 1984; Dweck, 1986). However, emerging research from both academic and more recently sport domains indicates that the utility of the achievement goal construct can be enhanced by distinguishing appetitive (approach) and aversive (avoidance) achievement goals (e.g., Elliot and McGregor, 2001; Conroy et al., 2006); it is to that work that we now focus our attention.

Approach/avoidance goals

Competence lies at the heart of the achievement goal construct. Achievement goals may be differentiated on two basic dimensions of competence: according to how it is *defined* and according to how it is *valenced* (Elliot, 1999). The conventional distinction between performance and mastery goals is grounded in how individuals define competence and research adopts an appetitive view of goals, where behaviour is instigated by a positive, desirable possibility to demonstrate competence. Performance goals define competence in terms of the performance of others (normative comparisons), whereas mastery goals define competence in terms of self-referenced criteria (i.e., acquiring knowledge and understanding or improving personal performance). In this traditional view, goals vary only as a function of whether competence is defined relative to others or the self. In a later iteration of their original framework, Elliot and McGregor (2001) proposed a 2 × 2 Achievement Goal model, where activity within an achievement setting could be focused not only to the positive possibility that one would like to approach competence, but also to a negative possibility that one would like to avoid incompetence. They used the term competence 'valence' to describe these positive or negative possibilities. As Elliot and Harackiewicz (1994) suggest, people can be motivated by a desire to appear more competent to themselves or others, but also by a fear of appearing less competent.

The 2 × 2 achievement goal framework (Elliot & McGregor, 2001) comprises four distinct achievement goals: Mastery approach goals represent striving to approach absolute or intrapersonal competence, e.g., striving to master a specific skill or learn more about a task. Mastery avoidance goals, while similarly self-referenced, represent striving to avoid absolute or intrapersonal incompetence, e.g., striving to not do worse than one has done previously, or to illustrate that personal abilities are diminishing. Performance approach goals represent striving to demonstrate normative competence, e.g., outperforming or demonstrating greater skills than others. Performance avoidance goals represent striving to avoid normative incompetence, e.g., striving to avoid doing worse than others. This framework is presumed to comprehensively cover the content universe of competence-based goals in achievement settings (Elliot, 1999; Conroy et al., 2003). Furthermore, it is argued that competence is a direct antecedent of these intentions. High competence perceptions are posited to lead to approach goals, and low competence perceptions lead to avoidance goals.

Although they highlight a number of concerns regarding the scope of the literature particularly within a physical activity context, Papaioannou et al's. (2012) review highlights a number of important research findings. Mastery approach goals had positive effects on self-determined forms of motivation (Conroy et al., 2006) and are associated with intrinsic interest in tasks, satisfaction and interest, whereas performance approach goals have less consistent positive and some negative effects. The recent meta-analysis of Lochbaum and Gottardy (2015) suggested that approach avoidance goals are meaningful and important in understanding and improving performance, while avoidance goals, though less impactful, should not be discounted due to their potential negative motivational effects. The magnitude of effects of these on performance equates to popular performance enhancement techniques such as imagery and goal-setting (Lochbaum & Smith, 2015).

A number of researchers into motivation in golf (e.g., Bois et al., 2009; Schantz & Conroy, 2009; Lochbaum & Smith, 2015) have adopted this approach avoidance perspective (Elliot & Church, 1997; Elliot, 1999). The results of this work suggests that mastery approach goals have inconsistent relationships with performance, while avoidance goals negatively predict performance in professional (Bois et al., 2009) and collegiate (Schantz & Conroy, 2009) golfers. Lochbaum and Smith's more recent (2015) study, albeit with students taking golf classes, reinforced and expanded these findings by suggesting better performances were associated with greater endorsement of approach goals (mastery or performance), and worse performance with greater endorsement of avoidance goals. Despite the inconsistencies of this work when applied to the context of golf, when considered in light of other sport research (e.g., Lochbaum & Gottardy, 2015), the implications of this work are clear. Goals where the focus of the individual is on avoiding demonstrating a lack of competence (avoidance goals) undermine performance, whereas those that target attaining competence – for example, my goal is to putt better than I have previously, or to putt better than everyone else in my group, are likely to be effective in enhancing performance (Lochbaum & Smith, 2015).

While it is important to identify strategies to reduce the negative impact of such goals (e.g., imagery, cognitive restructuring, etc.) more effective would be addressing their antecedents. In addition to concerns about evaluation and self-esteem, one important antecedent which is receiving greater attention in the sport domain is fear of failure. Fear of failure is the dispositional desire to avoid experiencing failure. According to Wilkman et al. (2014), it is associated with poorer sporting performance in both adolescents and adults. Further, Conroy et al. (2007) suggest it can result in maladaptive learning and performance behaviours and long-term reductions in intrinsic motivation through anxiety, self-protective withdrawal, disrupted concentration and a loss of task focus. Research in the academic domain has shown that fear of failure positively predicts avoidance goals and striving-based social comparison goals (performance approach), yet is unrelated to mastery approach goals in the academic domain (Elliot & Church, 1997; Elliot & McGregor, 2001).

One method for changing fear of failure is to introduce appropriate goal-setting practices, for example, a focus on mastery approach goals. These goals produce better behaviour and experience with no recourse to the consequences of failure (Wilkman et al., 2014). Following their 12-week intervention with adolescent athletes trained in the use of mastery approach goals, results indicated a significant reduction in fear of failure; however, it should be noted that this was only a short-term effect if the systematic use of mastery approach goals ceased.

In summary, from what we have come to understand about this refined approach to exploring achievement goals in sport, goals should clearly focus on self-referenced intentions with regard to skill development and learning. The objective of using such goals is to facilitate the development of competence within the individual, and to reduce the potential for the negative consequences of comparing personal performance with that of others. Mastery approach goals have the potential to promote intrinsic and self-determined motivation (which will be considered shortly), satisfaction and enjoyment, and effort and persistence. Furthermore, athletes can be trained to use these goals in a structured manner to develop esteem and to reduce fear of failure.

Self-determination approach

Currently, one of the most popular theoretical areas from both a research and an applied perspective is SDT (Deci & Ryan 1985); it has proved effective in illuminating our understanding of motivational processes in physical activity and sport (Sarrazin et al., 2007), and the associated cognitive, affective (i.e., emotional) and behavioural outcomes. For these reasons, it is especially relevant for those concerned with promoting motivation in the sports domain.

Whereas much of the motivational research in sport has contrasted types of goals or outcomes and suggested that these have different behavioural and affective consequences, SDT takes a different approach. SDT differentiates content of goals with the regulatory processes through which they are pursued, making predictions for variations in content and for processes. Specifically, it uses the concept of innate psychological needs, and argues that the critical issue in the effects of goal pursuit concerns the degree to which they are able to satisfy their basic psychological needs as they pursue and attain their valued objectives (Ryan & Deci, 2000).

At the heart of SDT is the concept of intrinsic motivation. Individuals may engage in an activity for a variety of both internally and externally driven reasons; however, there is compelling evidence that those who do so for more self-determined motives, and in particular for intrinsic reasons, may accrue particular benefits (Kingston et al., 2006). Intrinsic motivation describes an inclination to master, to explore through spontaneous interest, and involves engaging in activities voluntarily (personal volition) in the absence of material rewards or external pressures and constraints (Ryan & Deci 2000). Intrinsic motivation is the most self-determined type of motivation and leads to greater persistence, more effort exerted during practices and games, higher enjoyment, less boredom and less drop-out from sport (Pelletier et al., 1995). Furthermore, research by Vink et al. (2015) highlighted the benefits of skill development that can be accrued through the development of intrinsic motivation. In a sample of 162 adolescent team sport athletes, intrinsic motivation has been found to have a mutually predictive relationship with practice designed with a clear goal of improving a particular skill (deliberate practice).

Intrinsic motivation can be regarded as the most constructive type of motivation, and it exists when we internalise our reasons for engaging in a goal-directed activity. The concepts of intrinsic motivation and internalisation are closely linked. While intrinsic motivation can be defined as engaging in an activity for the inherent rewards of that activity (as opposed to being driven at least partly by some external sources), internalisation is a developmental process whereby individuals come to identify themselves, assimilate and reconstitute formerly external reasons for engaging in activities. To illustrate, one might be driven to engage in an exercise program because there is a known value to being fit and healthy. Though engagement can be attributed (to a degree) to external reasons, prolonged engagement with such an activity may in time lead to the individual identifying themselves with being a fit and healthy person. For this individual, for whom engagement with exercise programs now reflects part of who they are, the reasons (or to use the term the regulations of behaviour, from SDT) have become internalised. Internalisation is not an automatic process, when behaviours are referred to as becoming more internalised; they reflect the personal view that one is more self-determined when engaging in the activity. Goal-directed activities can differ in the extent to which they are self-determined – that is, the extent to which they are pursued with a full sense of personal volition and choice.

Intrinsic motivation and largely internalised extrinsic motives are the bases for self-determined behaviour. However, athletes high in intrinsic motivation may also legitimately be high in more externally regulated forms of motivation (extrinsic reasons). It is unclear whether more self-determined motives buffer against the negative effects of more externally influenced motives; nevertheless, it does suggest that considering 'recipes' of motives in the context of such factors as perceived competence may be fruitful. Despite this caveat, the evidence is compelling; promotion of intrinsic motivation and more self-determined extrinsic motives are most likely to encourage adaptive task behaviours, cognitions and affective responses.

Within SDT, Deci and Ryan (1985) present a number of sub-theories. One such component aspect, basic needs theory, proposes that three universal psychological needs – the needs for competence, autonomy and relatedness – are fundamental to promoting motivation and psychological well-being. According to SDT, individuals experience intrinsic motivation when their innate and fundamental needs for autonomy (perceptions of agency and control), competence (perceptions of ability) and relatedness (perceptions of connectedness to others) are satisfied (Deci & Ryan, 2000). The satisfaction of the need for autonomy involves the experience of choice and the feeling that one is self-initiating in determining one's actions (De Charms, 1968; Vallerand & Losier, 1999). The satisfaction of the need for competence is fulfilled by interacting effectively with one's environment (White, 1959) to bring about desired effects and outcomes – to experience mastery (Kingston et al., 2006). The fulfilment of the need for relatedness comes from feeling connected to, and having a sense of mutual respect and reliance in relation to others (Baumeister & Leary, 1995).

In the context of sport, a number of studies (e.g., Pelletier et al., 2001; Sarrazin et al., 2002; Guzmán & Kingston, 2012) have shown that need satisfaction predicted self-determined motivation. Moreover, it also has been reported that need satisfaction has a direct effect on intention to continue participation in their chosen sport (Guzmán & Kingston, 2012) and on sport commitment (Lukwu & Guzmán, 2011). A considerable amount of research has examined the link between motives varying in degree of self-determination and a variety of outcomes in sport, such as dropout (Pelletier et al., 2001; Sarrazin et al., 2002), burnout (Cresswell & Eklund, 2005), intention to continue participation (Guzmán & Kingston, 2013), and sportspersonship orientations (e.g., Lukwu & Guzmán, 2011). Consistently, the results from this research suggests that greater use of more self-determined motives is associated with positive consequences, while negative outcomes are associated with less or non-self-determined motives.

More recently, Schaefer et al. (2016) explored the link between autonomous (self-determined) and controlled motivation with anxiety and mental toughness in one-hundred and seventy-three competitive golfers. Results suggested that participant golfers with higher levels of autonomous motivation had lower levels of competitive anxiety, and higher levels of mental toughness. Furthermore, they suggested that it is possible that self-determined motivation protects athletes from competitive anxiety through the development of mental toughness. Unsurprisingly, therefore, the promotion of high levels of intrinsic motivation and more self-determined motives should be a primary objective for anyone interested in the development and maintenance of sport participation and the development of skills (i.e., coaches). The mechanism for this promotion lies, according to SDT, in the facilitation of the three basic psychological needs – autonomy, competence and relatedness.

Autonomy-supportive coaching

The coach–athlete relationship is an important predictor of athletes' motivation and consequential performance (Mageau & Vallerand, 2003). Specifically, and according to SDT, the extent to which coaches fulfil their athletes' psychological needs has strong implications for their motivation, cognition and well-being in the sporting context (Mageau & Vallerand, 2003; Reinboth et al., 2004).

Autonomy support refers to the degree to which coaches encourage athletes to take initiative in sport and be active problem-solvers, provide meaningful rationales for necessary limits, and take an athlete rather than coach perspective (Mageau & Vallerand, 2003). Such coaching behaviours have been shown to encourage younger athletes to endorse external events as personally meaningful (internalise them) and, thus, cultivate their engagement through more self-determined motives. In addition, autonomy support from coaches has been found to positively influence athletes' perceptions of autonomy, persistence and well-being (e.g., Pelletier et al., 1995; Reinboth, et al., 2004; Conroy & Coastworth, 2007) and to predict attentive, effortful, persistent and active participation in sport (e.g., Sarrazin et al., 2002). Autonomy-supportive coaches acknowledge athletes' feelings and perspectives, allow them to be involved in the decision-making process within specific rules and limits, provide non-controlling informational feedback, avoid controlling behaviours while minimising the use of pressure, and prevent ego-involvement in athletes (Deci & Ryan, 1987; Grolnick & Ryan, 1989; Mageau & Vallerand, 2003). This openness to the views of athletes may include listening to, and acting upon, athletes' ideas, offering them opportunity to take initiative and make choices while providing them with meaningful rationales for necessary limits (Reeve, 2006). Similarly, providing adequate structure that fosters the need competence is also known to be important (Grolnick & Ryan, 1989). This may include providing rules and constraints prior to an activity, giving support and informational feedback during and after an activity (Reeve, 2006). According to Curran et al. (2013), this structure provides fertile conditions for athletes' self-regulation via the concurrent facilitation of autonomy and competence.

In a study involving interviews with 11 high school coaches, Iachini et al. (2010) explored coach views on strategies to support basic needs. To support competence perceptions, content analysis suggested that positive verbal communication (encouragement/reinforcement), use of self-set goals, emphasis on individual opportunities to be successful while ignoring mistakes, and a personal style which was relaxed positive and constructive were critical elements for facilitating perceptions of competence. For relatedness support, the coaches described strategies associated with effective management of social interactions, creating unity through team building activities (both in and away from the sport), an emphasis on the concept of 'team', and peer mentoring. Mageau and Vallerand (2003) produced a framework through which, it was argued, the coach could positively impact athlete's basic psychological needs. Accordingly, they identified seven key qualities of autonomy-supportive coaching: (a) providing athletes with choice, (b) giving opportunities for initiative-taking, (c) using a democratic leadership style, (d) giving a rationale for their actions, (e) showing concern for the athlete both on and off the field, (f) giving constructive feedback, and (g) fostering a task-oriented sport environment. Although there should be educational support for coaches and encouragement to adopt a reflective approach to their practice, it is incumbent upon the coaches across all levels to work hard and be creative in searching for ways to provide an environment that continues to support the innate needs of competence, autonomy and relatedness for their charges. By doing so, they provide opportunities for the development of intrinsic interest in activities, promote effort and persistence, and reduce the likelihood of disengagement with activities.

To summarise this section, SDT is an increasingly popular and useful theoretical framework through which to consider basic needs and their consequential effects on intrinsic motivation. For example, threats, deadlines, directives, pressured evaluation and imposed goals have been shown to undermine intrinsic motivation, whereas choice, acknowledgment of feelings, and opportunities for self-direction have been associated with increases in intrinsic motivation (for a fuller review, see Ryan & Deci, 2000). The relationships outlined in SDT suggest that social conditions, such as supportive coaching behaviors, may promote an athlete's basic psychological needs (Mageau & Vallerand, 2003; Hollembeak & Amorose, 2005). In particular, autonomy-supportive coaching has been shown to positively influence these key predictors of well-being and effective motivational functioning (Amorose & Horn, 2000).

Implications for golfers

Promoting competence

The importance of competence perceptions cannot be underplayed. Both theoretical perspectives and the research that has been conducted to explore these emphasise the critical role that a belief in one's ability to be successful has on behaviours, associated thoughts and feelings, and overall psychological well-being.

To promote athletes' sense of competence, coaches should promote self-evaluation through self-referenced improvement and the degree to which effort and resilience are demonstrated in training and competition. They could also encourage athletes to reflect on personal performance indicators; for example, there are numerous ways in golf to monitor performance statistics, but simple strategies like monitoring the number of putts made in succession from 5 feet, or the number of times a good chip shot saves you a stroke while playing in competition or practice provides real and meaningful competence-based information on skill development. Furthermore, ensuring instructions are clearly focused and realistically challenging will help promote problem-solving and engagement with the task through play (which also facilitates the need to be volitional or autonomous). The key here is that young golfers in particular (but golfers at any age would also benefit) should internalise their engagement. If early in their involvement with a sport, they come to view challenging themselves through play as part and parcel of what it takes to improve, this will ensure that skill practice is always seen as valued, and that they associate themselves with this behaviour. The positive implications for long-term involvement and performance are obvious given the research described previously.

Mastery goals

Mastery approach goals reflect an emphasis on self-referent improvement, mastery and effort; these goals also predict athletes' satisfaction of the basic needs of competence and relatedness (Reinboth et al., 2004). According to Duda (2001), the reason a mastery focus fosters perceptions of competence is because the self-referenced criteria (e.g., effort) which underlie competence judgments and consequent feelings of success, are more controllable and achievable compared to social-normative-based criteria, such as winning.

A systematic goal-setting training program promoting mastery approach goals, similar to that utilised by Wilkman et al. (2014), would likely serve a useful educational purpose and promote effective goal-setting practices in the short term. The key for effective goal-setting is that the goals should be predominantly self-referenced (e.g., process goals which focus on technique or behaviours; see Kingston and Hardy, 1997 for a goal-setting-based intervention study in golf), and athletes should engage with them in a reflective manner systematically to ensure they remain challenging and appropriate for the individual's ability and the context. Those engaging with goals need to ensure that they are able to utilise short-term skill-based stepping stones in pursuit of their wider performance objectives, and that the behaviours required to facilitate goal achievement become internalised and habitual. Coaches supporting golfers can utilise performance statistics and personal skill development as the basis for promoting self-referenced goals; the role of coaches and those managing training programs is to create environments where players focus on self-referenced targets, and what they need to do to improve skills rather than how they compare to others. Furthermore, goals should be sufficiently flexible to ensure barriers can be addressed and that well-intentioned goal plans are not derailed because they cannot be adjusted to accommodate personal and situational changes.

Organising and managing practice

As we have alluded to on a number of occasions throughout this chapter, the coach and those managing the practice and training environment play a central role in promoting motivation in their athletes. Among other things, autonomy-supportive coaches allow them to be involved in the decision-making process within specific rules and limits. Giving choice does not mean that the coach or leader relinquishes management of the coaching environment. Far from it, the guidance of coach remains central to the learning experience; choice in this context refers to choosing the boundaries or targets in skill games. From a motivational point of view, the less prescriptive the coach, the more intrinsically motivating the task. Golf is a perfect game for shifting the goal-posts while practicing. The key to maintaining and promoting intrinsic motivation is to allow the golfer to have opportunities to feel they are becoming more competent, while allowing them to make choices during practice.

In terms of practice at an individual level, the reciprocal relationship between goal-directed practice and intrinsic motivation should not be ignored. High-quality practice, focused explicitly on developing skills, is motivationally far more constructive than less-focused practice of greater quantity. The key for golfers, whether at the range, on the putting green, or practicing on the course, is that practice should have a clear objective in terms of skill development and structure. Having a few holes practice on a summer evening, for example, will be of most benefit when there is a clear focus for the practice. For example, if 30–50-yard pitch shots are the focus, then one should not be overly concerned with the consequences of hitting errant shots in that situation, rather create situations that enable one to test this skill under a variety of conditions.

Summary and future directions

The purpose of this chapter was to consider two theoretical perspectives that, in our view, could help inform understanding of constructive motivation in the sport of golf. While motivation in golf beyond the traditional dichotomy of achievement goals has largely escaped the attentions of researchers, we sought to draw upon the wider sport literature to inform our discussion. Our reviews highlighted some common issues, but also some robust messages that transcended theoretical perspectives. Most notably the promotion of competence, use of self-referenced goals, and need for those responsible for guiding future generations of golfers to have autonomy support as the bedrock of coaching practice.

Coaches can foster the three basic needs in a number of ways; for autonomy, athletes should be given choices and options. For example, they may provide information to solve a problem or learn a new skill, but should allow them to do it in their own way. To promote competence, coaches should help athletes self-monitor performance standards and focus on self-referenced improvement and the degree to which effort is exerted in training and competition. Finally, to satisfy the need for relatedness, coaches should accept, care for and value players as individuals, rather than solely as performing athletes (Reinboth & Duda, 2004).

Any review – even one such as this which, by necessity, is less comprehensive than it might be – raises further questions, and it is to these potential future research directions that we will turn in concluding this chapter.

It might appear obvious to suggest that more research into the motivation of golfers is required – but it is! At a general level, testing psychological theory and concepts on this particular population can help practitioners, but also sport scientists who have a captive audience for their work. More specifically, based on this review, we suggest that the following selected areas warrant exploration to inform both theory and applied practice.

- Antecedents of avoidance goals – understanding the factors that lead individuals to use avoidance goals (e.g., lower self-esteem, perfectionism, social evaluation), and in particular the role of fear of failure in this process, could help support the motivation of golfers at all levels, but also retain those individuals who either choose not to engage or engage initially but then withdraw.
- Helping coaches support athlete needs – as Curran et al. (2014) put it, there should be a greater focus among sport psychologists, in particular, on the evaluation of interventions aimed at enhancing coaches' ability to recognise and support the psychological needs of their young athletes. It is perfectly reasonable to highlight the role of coaches and make recommendations about how they should use certain strategies to help their athletes. Unfortunately, less attention is paid to helping coaches to implement, adapt and evaluate the effectiveness of these strategies. Research is needed to help coaches support their athletes in this area.
- Exploring the effects needs thwarting – although research into basic needs in sport continues apace, more recently, researchers have proposed that dissatisfaction with needs should also be

considered. Dissatisfaction with basic needs exerts substantially different effects on well-being than satisfaction (Sheldon & Hilpert, 2012). For those athletes motivationally at risk, need dissatisfaction could undermine both positive experiences and satisfaction of basic needs.

References

Amorose, A. & Horn, T. (2000) Intrinsic Motivation: Relationships with Collegiate Athletes' Gender, Scholarship Status, and Perceptions of Their Coaches' Behaviour, *Journal of Sport and Exercise Psychology*, 22 (1), 63–84.

Baumeister, R. & Leary, M. (1995) The Need to Belong: Desire for Interpersonal Attachments as a Fundamental Human Motivation, *Psychological Bulletin*, 117 (3), 497–529.

Bois, J.; Sarrazin, P.; Southon, J. & Boiche, J. (2009) Psychological Characteristics and Their Relations to Performance in Professional Golfers, *The Sport Psychologist*, 23 (2), 252–270.

Conroy, D. & Coastworth, J. (2007) Assessing Autonomy-Supportive Coaching Strategies in Youth Sport, *Psychology of Sport and Exercise*, 8 (5), 671–684.

Conroy, D.; Elliot, A. & Hofer, S. (2003) A 2 x 2 Achievement Goals Questionnaire for Sport: Evidence for the Factorial Invariance, Temporal Stability, and External Validity, *Journal of Sport and Exercise Psychology*, 25 (4), 456–476.

Conroy, D.; Kaye, M. & Coastworth, J. (2006) Coaching Climates and the Destructive Effects of Mastery Avoidance Goals on Situational Motivation, *Journal of Sport and Exercise Psychology*, 28 (1), 69–92.

Conroy, D.; Kaye, M.P. and Fifer, A.M. (2007) Cognitive Links Between Fear of Failure and Perfectionism, *Journal of Rational-Emotive and Cognitive Behavioural Therapy*, 4, 237–253.

Cresswell, S. & Eklund, R. (2005) Motivation and Burnout among Top Amateur Rugby Players, *Medicine and Science in Sports and Exercise*, 37 (3), 469–477.

Curran, T.; Appleton, P.; Hill, A. & Hall, H. (2013) The Mediating Role of Psychological Need Satisfaction in Relationships Between Types of Passion for Sport and Athlete Burnout, *Journal of Sports Sciences*, 31 (6), 597–606.

Curran, T.; Hill, A.; Hall, H. & Jowett, G. (2014) Perceived Coach Behaviours and Athletes' Engagement and Disaffection in Youth Sport: The Mediating Role of the Psychological Needs, *International Journal of Sport Psychology*, 45 (6), 559–580.

De Charms, R. (1968) *Personal Causation: The Internal Affective Determinants of Behavior*, New York, NY: Academic Press.

Deci, E. & Ryan, R. (1985) *Intrinsic Motivation and Self-determination in Human Behaviour*, New York, NY: Plenum.

Deci, E. & Ryan, R. (1987) The Support of Autonomy and the Control of Behavior, *Journal of Personality and Social Psychology*, 53 (6), 1024–1037.

Deci, E. & Ryan, R. (2000) The "What" and "Why" of Goal Pursuits: Human Needs and the Self-determination Theory, *Psychological Inquiry*, 11 (4), 227–268.

Dewar, A. & Kavussanu, M. (2011) Achievement Goals and Emotions in Golf: The Mediating and Moderating Role of Perceived Performance, *Psychology of Sport and Exercise*, 12 (5), 525–532.

Duda, J. (2001) Achievement Goal Research in Sport: Pushing the Boundaries and Clarifying Some Misunderstandings, In: G. Roberts (Ed) *Advances in Motivation in Sport and Exercise*, Champaign, IL: Human Kinetics, pp. 129–182.

Dweck, C. (1986) Motivational Processes Affecting Learning, *American Psychologist*, 41 (10), 1040–1048.

Dweck, C. & Leggett, E. (1988) A Social-cognitive Approach to Motivation and Personality, *Psychological Review*, 95 (2), 256–273.

Elliot, A. (1999) Approach and Avoidance Motivation and Achievement Goals, *Educational Psychologist*, 34 (3), 169–189.

Elliot, A. & Church, M. (1997) A Hierarchical Model of Approach and Avoidance Achievement Motivation, *Journal of Personality and Social Psychology*, 72 (1), 218–232.

Elliot, A. & Harackiewicz, J. (1994) Goal Setting, Achievement Orientation, and Intrinsic Motivation: A Mediational Analysis, *Journal of Personality and Social Psychology*, 66 (5), 968–980.

Elliot, A. & McGregor, H. (2001) A 2 x 2 Achievement Goal Framework, *Journal of Personality and Social Psychology*, 80 (3), 501–519.

Grolnick, W. & Ryan, R. (1989) Parent Styles Associated with Children's Self-regulation and Competence in School, *Journal of Educational Psychology*, 81 (2), 143–154.

Guzmán, J. & Kingston, K. (2012) Prospective Study of Sport Dropout: A Motivational Analysis as a Function of Age and Gender, *European Journal of Sport Sciences*, 12 (5), 431–442.

Guzmán, J. & Kingston, K. (2013) Coaches' Need Satisfaction and Self-determination Predict Perceived Promotion of Athletes' Well-being, *Wulfenia*, 20 (4), 107–120.

Hollembeak, J. & Amorose, A. (2005) Perceived Coaching Behaviors and College Athletes' Intrinsic Motivation: A Test of Self-determination Theory, *Journal of Applied Sport Psychology*, 17 (1), 20–36.

Iachini, A.; Amorose, A. & Anderson-Butcher, D. (2010) Exploring High School Coaches' Implicit Theories of Motivation From Self-determination Theory Perspective, *International Journal of Sports Science & Coaching*, 5 (2), 291–308.

Kingston, K. & Hardy, L. (1997) Effects of Different Types of Goals on Processes That Support Performance, *The Sport Psychologist*, 11 (3), 277–293.

Kingston, K.; Harwood, C. & Spray, C. (2006) Contemporary Approaches to Motivation in Sport, In: S. Hanton & S. Mellalieu (Eds.) *Literature Reviews in Sport Psychology*, New York, NY: Nova Science Publishers, pp. 159–197.

Kuczka, K. & Treasure, D. (2005) Self-handicapping in Competitive Sport: Influence of the Motivational Climate, Self-efficacy, and Perceived Importance, *Psychology of Sport and Exercise*, 6 (5), 539–550.

Lochbaum, M. & Gottardy, J. (2015) A Meta-analytic Review of the Approach-avoidance Achievement Goals and Performance Relationship in the Sport Psychology Literature, *Journal of Sport and Health Science*, 4 (2), 164–173.

Lochbaum, M. & Smith, C. (2015) Making the Cut and Winning a Golf Putting Championship: The Role of Approach-avoidance Achievement Goals, *International Journal of Golf Science*, 4 (1), 50–56.

Lukwu, R. & Guzman, J. (2011) Sport Commitment and Adherence: A Social-cognitive Analysis, *International Journal of Sport Science*, 25 (7), 277–286.

Maehr, M. & Zusho, A. (2009) Achievement Goal Theory: The Past, Present and Future, In: K. Wentzel & A. Wingfield (Eds.) *Handbook of Motivation in School*, New York, NY: Taylor Francis, pp. 77–104.

Mageau, G. & Vallerand, R. (2003) The Coach–Athlete Relationship: A Motivational Model, *Journal of Sports Sciences*, 21 (11), 881–954.

Nicholls, J. (1984) Achievement Motivation: Conceptions of Ability, Subjective Experience, Task Choice, and Performance, *Psychological Review*, 91 (3), 328–346.

Nicholls, J. (1989) *The Competitive Ethos and Democratic Education*, Cambridge, MA: Harvard University Press.

Oh, S. (2001) *Flow in Golf: Motivation, Orientation and Challenge Determinants*, Unpublished Dissertation, College of Forestry and Consumer Science, Virginia, USA: West Virginia University.

Papaioannou, A.; Zourbanos, N.; Krommidas, C. & Ampatzoglou, G. (2012) The Place of Achievement Goals in the Social Context of Sport: A Comparison of Nicholls' and Elliot's Models, In: G. Roberts & D. Treasure (Eds.) *Advances in Motivation in Sport and Exercise*, Champaign, IL: Human Kinetics, pp. 59–90.

Pelletier, L.; Fortier, M.; Vallerand, R. & Brière, N. (2001) Associations among Perceived Autonomy Support, Forms of Self-regulation, and Persistence: A Prospective Study, *Motivation and Emotion*, 25 (4), 279–306.

Pelletier, L.; Fortier, M.; Vallerand, R.; Tuson, K.; Brière, N. & Blais, M. (1995) Toward a New Measure of Intrinsic Motivation, Extrinsic Motivation and Amotivation in Sports: The Sport Motivation Scale (SMS), *Journal of Sport and Exercise Psychology*, 17 (1), 35–53.

Reeve, J. (2006) Teachers as Facilitators: What Autonomy-supportive Teachers Do and Why Their Students Benefit, *The Elementary School Journal*, 106 (3), 225–236.

Reinboth, M. & Duda, J. (2004) The Motivational Climate, Perceived Ability, and Athletes' Psychological and Physical Well-being: A Longitudinal Perspective, *The Sport Psychologist*, 18 (3), 237–251.

Reinboth, M.; Duda, J. & Ntoumanis, N. (2004) Dimensions of Coaching Behaviour, Need Satisfaction, and the Psychological and Physical Welfare of Young Athletes, *Motivation and Emotion*, 28 (3), 297–313.

Roberts, G. (2001) *Advances in Motivation in Sport and Exercise*, Champaign, IL: Human Kinetics.

Roberts, G. (2012) Motivation in Sport and Exercise From an Achievement Goal Theory Perspective: After 30 Years, Where Are We? In: G. Roberts & D. Treasure (Eds.) *Advances in Motivation in Sport and Exercise*, Champaign, IL: Human Kinetics, pp. 5–58.

Roberts, G.; Treasure, D. & Conroy, D. (2007) Understanding the Dynamics of Motivation in Sport and Physical Activity: An Achievement Goal Interpretation, In: G. Tenenbaum & R. Eklund (Eds.) *Handbook of Sport Psychology* (3rd Ed.), Hoboken, NJ: Wiley, pp. 3–30.

Ryan, R. & Deci, E. (2000) Self-Determination Theory and the Facilitation of Intrinsic Motivation, Social Development, and Well-being, *American Psychologist*, 55 (1), 68–78.

Sachau, D.; Simmering, L.; Ryan, W. & Adler, M. (2013) Goal Orientation of Recreational Golfers, *International Journal of Golf Science*, 2 (2), 95–115.

Sarrazin, P.; Boiché, J. & Pelletier, L. (2007) A Self-determination Theory Approach to Dropout in Athletes, In: M. Hagger & N. Chatzisarantis (Eds.) *Intrinsic Motivation and Self-determination in Exercise and Sport*, Champaign, IL: Human Kinetics, pp. 229–242.

Sarrazin, P.; Vallerand, R.; Guillet, E.; Pelletier, L. & Cury, F. (2002) Motivation and Dropout in Female Handballers: A 21-Month Prospective Study, *European Journal of Social Psychology*, 32 (3), 395–418.

Schaefer, J.; Vella, S.; Allen, M. & Magee, C. (2016) Competition Anxiety, Motivation, and Mental Toughness in Golf, *Journal of Applied Sport Psychology*, 28 (3), 309–320.

Schantz, L. & Conroy, D. (2009) Achievement Motivation and Intra Individual Affective Variability During Competence Pursuits: A Round of Golf as a Multi-level Data Structure, *Journal of Research in Personality*, 43 (3), 472–481.

Sheldon, K. & Hilpert, J. (2012) The Balanced Measure of Psychological Needs (BMPN) Scale: An Alternative Domain General Measure of Need Satisfaction, *Motivation and Emotion*, 36 (4), 439–451.

Spray, C.; Wang, C.; Biddle, S. & Chatzisarantis, N. (2006) Understanding Motivation in Sport: An Experimental Test of Achievement Goal and Self-determination Theories, *European Journal of Sport Science*, 6 (1), 43–51.

Steinberg, C.; Singer, R. & Murphey, M. (2000) The Benefits to Sport Achievement When a Multiple Goal Orientation is Emphasized, *Journal of Sport Behavior*, 23 (4), 407–423.

Vallerand, R. & Losier, G. (1999) An Integrative Analysis of Intrinsic and Extrinsic Motivation in Sport, *Journal of Applied Sport Psychology*, 11 (1), 142–169.

Vink, K.; Lennart, R. & Kis, K. (2015) Intrinsic Motivation and Individual Deliberate Practice Are Reciprocally Related: Evidence From a Longitudinal Study of Adolescent Team Sport Athletes, *Psychology of Sport and Exercise*, 16, 1–6.

White, R. (1959) Motivation Reconsidered: The Concept of Competence, *Psychological Review*, 66 (5), 297–333.

Wilkman, J.; Stelter, R.; Melzer, M.; Hauge, M.–L. & Elbe, A. (2014) Effects of Goal Setting on Fear of Failure in Young Elite Athletes, *International Journal of Sport and Exercise Psychology*, 12 (3), 185–205.

23

MASTERS OF THE GAME

Goal orientations of recreational golfers

*Daniel Sachau, Luke Simmering, Amy Harris, Max Adler
and Warren Ryan*

Introduction

A golfer's *goal orientation* refers to the way the player normally defines competence. One way to assess competence is via social comparison. Some golfers think of themselves as competent when they perform better than others; this focus on normative comparisons is referred to as an *ego* orientation. Another way to define competence is via intrapersonal comparison. Some golfers think of themselves as competent when they learn something new or improve their skills; this mastery focus is referred to as *task orientation* (Nicholls, 1984, 1989). In this chapter, we examine how goal orientations are related to the ways golfers think about themselves (self-esteem, contingencies of self-worth), are attached to the game (obsessive and harmonious passion) and behave ethically in competition (self-handicapping and sandbagging).

Review of current research

The goal orientation framework most commonly used by sport psychologists is Joan Duda's model (Duda, 1989, 1992; Duda & Nicholls, 1992). Duda treats *task* and *ego* orientation as orthogonal traits, which means that individuals can be high on both, low on both, or have a dominant orientation. In their research, Duda and colleagues found that athletes who scored high on measures of task orientation tended to have higher levels of intrinsic interest in their sport (Duda et al., 1995), were more likely to cooperate with teammates (Duda et al., 1992), and saw a closer connection between effort and success (Duda & Nicholls, 1992; Treasure & Roberts, 1994) compared to athletes who scored low on task orientation. Athletes who scored high on ego orientation were more likely to believe that success is tied to ability rather than effort, were less open to instructional feedback (Cury et al., 1997), were prone to higher levels of competitive trait anxiety (Biddle et al., 2003), and were more likely to believe that people should participate in sport to enhance their social status (Duda, 1989).

Achievement goals have been studied as traits and as states. That is, researchers make a distinction between goal *orientation* which reflects an athlete's preference for goals across a wide variety of settings, and goal *involvement* which represents the athlete's task or ego goals for a particular sport, task or setting (Nicholls, 1989; Duda, 2001). In addition, researchers have examined achievement goals at the group level. Goal *climate* refers to the extent to which a team is focused on task or ego goals (Ames, 1992).

A number of researchers have studied golfer achievement goals. Steinberg et al. (2000) found that when instructors gave golf students task goals, thus heightening task involvement, the students showed greater interest in a putting activity and persisted longer than students who were not given task goals. Dewar and Kavussanu (2011) surveyed 200 recreational golfers finding that task involvement was positively related to golfer happiness and excitement, and negatively related to dejection. Ego involvement was negatively correlated with happiness and was positively related to dejection and anxiety when golfers performed poorly, but was unrelated to these variables when golfers performed well. Oh (2001) found that task orientation was positively correlated to the frequency with which players experienced flow while playing; flow is the state of deep levels of concentration and enjoyment in an activity (Csikszentmihalyi, 1990).

Achievement goals have also been studied with regard to their effects on player performance. Spray et al. (2006, p. 45) found that students who were told their goals were to "learn and master the techniques of golf putting" (a task goal) performed better than students who were told that their goal was to "outperform other students in the school in golf putting" (an ego goal). Creating individual player goal 'profiles', Kingston and Hardy (1997) found that golfers who scored high on ego orientation and low on task orientation performed worse than players who scored high task/high ego, low ego/low task or high ego/low task orientation. Further, in a study of golf goal climate, Kuczka and Treasure (2005) surveyed 30 collegiate golf teams. The authors found that the more players thought their team was task-oriented, the less likely the individual players were to self-handicap.

Studying the malleability of task and ego scores, Kingston and Swain (1998) found that both professional and amateur golfers' ego orientation scores increased as the players moved from pre-season to practice sessions, to pre-tournament. For the non-professionals, the transition from pre-season to pre-competition also involved a drop in task orientation scores. This indicates that goal orientations, while often described as possessing stability over time and being relatively enduring (Roberts, 2012), can vary by setting and time.

Over the last few years, our team has been studying golfer goal orientations and their relationships with a variety of other trait-like measures relevant to sport. In our first study of golfer goal orientation (Sachau et al., 2013), we created a six-item ego orientation scale and six-item task orientation scale and distributed the measures to over 2,400 members of the Minnesota Golf Association (MGA). Participants read the stem, "In order to enjoy a round of golf among friends I need to _____:" and then they indicated their agreement with the following items on a five-point scale. Ego-oriented items read: Play better than the golfers in my group, outplay my companions, win (have the lowest score; or win the most skins, holes or money in my group), have the lowest net score in my group, impress others with my play, have others see me make good shots (ego scale $\alpha = .80$). Task-oriented items read: Work hard at my game, make a change to my game that really seems to help, learn from my opponents, learn something new, see improvement in my game, try my best (task scale $\alpha = .87$). On reviewing the results, we found there were minor gender and age differences such that females and older golfers scored higher on task orientation and lower on ego orientation than their counterparts. Scores on the task and ego orientation scales were positively correlated to each other but were differentially related to measures of golf engagement.

More specific examination of the data indicated that players who scored high on the task scale were more likely to train and learn about golf by taking golf fitness courses, practicing at a range, practicing at a simulator, practicing at home, and reading about golf. Thus, players who scored high on task orientation appear more concerned about improving their game than players who scored low on the scale. Golfers who scored high on the ego scale played more golf than golfers who scored low. Scores on both ego and task orientation were negatively correlated with handicap (positively correlated with ability).

To supplement this literature review, we aggregated data from the study mentioned above with data from five other studies we had conducted involving members of the MGA. Just over 88% of the participants in the aggregated data set were male. The typical participant was 55 years of age, he/she had been playing golf for 35 years, and had a 12.25 handicap index. These golfers played 10 rounds per month (median). It should be noted that the participants in the data set were thus more active and skilled than the typical recreational golfer, but the participants in the aggregated data set were representative of a very large group of avid players.

Self-esteem

The first question we consider is this: is goal orientation related to a player's self-esteem? If a high level of task orientation is indeed a healthier approach to the game, as some claim (Nicholls, 1984), then task orientation might be more positively related to self-esteem than is ego orientation. There has been research to support this possibility. People with low self-esteem tend to have more negative reactions to failure than do people with high self-esteem (Baumeister & Tice, 1985; Mackinnon et al., 2015). Brown and Dutton (1995) note that individuals with high self-esteem are more likely to reject or dismiss the negative implications of failure. Thus, individuals with high self-esteem take failure less personally than do people with low self-esteem. However, across a variety of goal orientation studies, ego orientation has been positively correlated with self-esteem (Gencer, 2010). Perhaps athletes with high self-esteem are more comfortable using social comparison as the basis for self-evaluation than those with low self-esteem, especially because they presumably perceive a greater opportunity to succeed against their opponents.

In the aggregated data set, we found that self-esteem was not strongly correlated with either goal orientation scale. This may be because self-esteem scores were negatively skewed which would limit the potential correlation between self-esteem and any variable. It could also be the case that goal orientations are more highly related to the source of self-esteem rather than the level of self-esteem. We examine this issue in the next section.

Contingent self-worth

The Contingencies of Self-Worth Scale was developed by Jennifer Crocker and her colleagues (Crocker & Wolfe, 2001; Crocker, 2002; Crocker et al., 2003) to assess the extent to which people find self-worth from seven sources: social approval, physical appearance, outdoing others in competition, academic competence, family love and support, being a virtuous or moral person, and God's love. These domains of self-worth divide into internal sources: academic competence, family love/support, being a virtuous or moral person, God's love; and external sources: social approval, physical appearance, and outdoing others in competition. We ask, do people who score high on task orientation rely on internal sources, and people who score high on ego orientation rely on external sources for self-worth?

Our team (Harris, 2014; Harris et al., 2014) borrowed and modified items from Crocker's scale to tailor a questionnaire to adult golfers. We included measures of social approval, physical appearance, outdoing others in competition, golf competence (rather than academic competence), family love/support, and being virtuous/moral. Studying MGA members, we found that the task orientation was not significantly correlated with any of the CSW variables.

Table 23.1 Correlations with goal orientations

		Task orientation	Ego orientation
CSW appearance	r	.08	.16*
	n	191	189
CSW competition	r	.08	.46***
	n	195	193
CSW virtue	r	−.04	−.15*
	n	194	192
CSW approval	r	.07	.03
	n	194	191
CSW family	r	.12	.07
	n	190	188
CSW golf	r	.14	.31***
	n	191	188
Self-esteem	r	.10	−.14
	n	194	192
Harmonious passion	r	.16*	.24***
	n	196	194
Obsessive passion	r	.09	.30***
	n	194	192
Sandbagging scale	r	.08	.28***
	n	570	570
Golf sandbagging interpersonal	r	−.03	.28***
	n	585	587
Golf sandbagging normative beliefs	r	.02	.09*
	n	589	590
Self-handicapping	r	−.11**	.21***
	n	578	578

*$p < .05$, **$p < .01$, ***$p < .001$

The ego orientation scale was, as we predicted, positively correlated with CSW competition, CSW appearance, and CSW golf. Ego orientation was negatively but only modestly correlated with CSW virtue. See Table 23.1.

The results of this study fit with the notion that individuals who score high on ego orientation are more externally oriented than their counterparts. The problem with self-worth being contingent on external sources is that self-esteem is vulnerable when external conditions change (Niiya & Crocker, 2008). Players hit slumps. Age takes a toll on driver distances. Even the best professional players occasionally fail to make the tournament cut. If a player's self-esteem is tied to success in competition, they may respond very poorly when they play badly.

Passion

According to Vallerand and his colleagues (2003, 2007), one has *passion* for an activity if it is highly valued, occupies a large amount of the person's energy, and is central to the person's identity (Vallerand & Houlfort, 2003; Mageau et al., 2011). Vallerand argues that passion can take two forms: harmonious passion and obsessive passion. People with harmonious passion participate out of intrinsic interest and the desire to fulfill needs for autonomy, competence, and relatedness (Deci & Ryan, 1985). Harmonious passion is positively related to life satisfaction and positive affect (Gustafsson et al., 2011), and is negatively related to symptoms of burnout (Curran et al., 2013). In contrast to harmonious passion, athletes with an obsessive passion participate because of a felt obligation to participate (Vallerand et al., 2003; Mageau et al., 2011). The obsessively passionate seek competence in order to maintain feelings of self-worth (Crocker & Wolfe, 2001; Vallerand et al., 2003, 2007; Stenseng & Dalskau, 2010).

Researchers have examined obsessive passion among participants of a wide variety of sports. These authors find that for the obsessively passionate, self-esteem, feelings of self-worth, and emotional reactions fluctuate with successful and unsuccessful performances (Crocker & Wolfe, 2001; Mageau et al., 2011; Curran et al., 2013). Harris et al. (2014) found that golfers with an obsessive passion for golf scored higher on CSW competence and CSW golf. Players who scored high on harmonious passion scored higher on CSW competition and golf competence, but also scored higher on CSW family support and CSW virtue. Thus, harmonious and obsessive passion were related to deriving one's self-esteem from golf and competition, but only harmonious passion was related to deriving ones self-esteem from family and virtue.

Because they seem to derive self-worth from external sources, we predicted that players who score high on obsessive passion would also score high on ego orientation. Players who derive their self-worth from internal sources would score high on task orientation. The results of our studies were partially consistent with this prediction; as expected, ego orientation was positively correlated with obsessive passion, and task orientation was correlated with harmonious passion. The inconsistency is that ego orientation was also positively correlated to harmonious passion. This correlation is intriguing, and while potentially attributable to sample demographics, (high perceptions of competence, high life satisfaction, etc.) this warrants further research.

Researchers have found that although obsessive passion is positively correlated with liking and participating in an activity (Vallerand et al., 2003; Vallerand & Houlfort, 2003), obsessive passion can lead to emotional exhaustion, negative affect, rigid persistence on tasks, and stress (Gustafsson et al., 2011; Curran et al., 2013). Coaches and teachers may thus want to watch players who score high on ego orientation, as they may be inclined to develop an obsessive passion for the game.

The next question we examine is: do task and ego orientations relate to ethical behavior on the course? Some research suggests that an emphasis on ego goals might motivate unethical behavior (Schweitzer et al., 2004). Two types of unethical behavior, sandbagging and self-handicapping, are examined.

Sandbagging

Sandbaggers pretend to be less competent than they really are. More specifically, "sandbagging is a self-presentation strategy involving the false claim or feigned demonstration of inability used to create artificially low expectation for the sandbagger's performance" (Gibson & Sachau, 2000, p. 56). Golfers sandbag when they intentionally inflate their handicaps and then enter into a competition or wager.

There are two primary reasons to sandbag. One obvious reason, is to increase the chance of winning (Shepperd & Socherman, 1997). If a player enters a tournament with a handicap that is higher than it should be, the player will have more strokes removed from his/her score than is fair. The second reason that players sandbagging is to reduce performance pressure (Gibson & Sachau, 2000; Gibson et al., 2002; Gibson, 2007). A player who broadcasts an artificially high handicap has an easier time 'living up to' performance expectations observers might hold for the player, and might therefore avoid appearing less competent than they would appear without sandbagging.

In a study of over 2,400 golfers, our team (Sachau et al., 2014) found that golfers who scored higher on a 12-item sandbagging (Gibson & Sachau, 2000) scale (high sandbaggers) thought that sandbagging (claiming an artificially high handicap) was more common than did players who scored low on the scale; sandbaggers think most people sandbag. We also found that high sandbaggers were more likely than low sandbaggers to admit to using interpersonal sandbagging on the course (e.g., complaining about a non-existent pain, intentionally hitting bad shots to fool an opponent, etc.).

Sandbagging can be used to gain an unfair advantage in a competition and to reduce performance pressure. Both of these motives would be more salient to the golfer who scores high on ego orientation. We would thus predict that sandbagging would be more common for those who score high on ego orientation. This prediction is supported by research that shows that athletes who score high on ego orientation are more likely to cheat (Nicholls, 1989; Sage & Kavussanu, 2007), less likely to engage in prosocial behavior (Kavussanu & Duda, 2007), and more likely to believe that deceptive tactics are the causes of success in sport (Duda & Nichols, 1992; Roberts et al., 1996).

In the aggregated data set, players who scored high on the ego orientation scale did indeed score higher on the trait sandbagging scale. Players who scored high on the ego orientation scale were also more likely to use interpersonal sandbagging on the course than players who scored low on ego orientation. We found only a modest a relationship between ego orientation and beliefs about the frequency of sandbagging. Task orientation was not significantly related to sandbagging behaviors or beliefs.

The message from these results is clear. Players who score high on ego orientation may be more likely to sandbag than their counterparts. At a general level, sandbagging is a problem because it equates to cheating. Sandbagging undermines the handicap system and leads to unfair matches. In addition, sandbagging may keep players from addressing weaknesses in their game and thus prevents them from reaching their full potential.

Self-handicapping

Self-handicapping is a term Berglas and Jones (1978) used to describe a self-presentation strategy involving intentionally erecting impediments to one's own success. For instance, a self-handicapping student might drink heavily the night before an exam. The self-handicapping runner might avoid practice. The motive for self-handicapping lies in the attributions that observers make about the self-handicapper (Berglas & Jones, 1978). If before a tournament, a player broadcasts that she has not practiced and then performs poorly, observers are likely to attribute the poor performance to the lack of practice instead of a lack of ability. The self-handicapper's image and self-esteem are thus preserved. On the other hand, if the self-handicapper performs well, observers might marvel at the performance, and wonder just how much skill the player must have if she can perform so well despite the handicap? In sum, self-handicapping causes observers to discount ability attributions for failure but augment ability attributions for success (Berglas & Jones, 1978).

Researchers have examined self-handicapping in a wide variety of competitive settings. They find, for instance, that some swimmers will self-handicap by intentionally reducing the number of practices they attended before an important swimming event (Rhodewalt et al., 1984). Basketball players (Coudevylle et al., 2008) will self-handicap by withdrawing effort during practice.

Within golf, Rhodewalt et al. (1984), found that some would self-handicap by reducing practice effort before an important golf event. Prapavessis and Grove (1998) demonstrated that golfers with low self-esteem were more likely to claim handicaps than golfers with high self-esteem. Others (e.g., Thill & Curry, 2000; Kuczka & Treasure, 2005) found that self-handicapping was more likely to occur in contexts where social comparison based goals were being emphasized (ego oriented climate).

In the combined data set, and consistent with prediction and earlier studies on self-handicapping among golfers, ego orientation was positively correlated with scores on the self-handicapping scale which is a trait like measure of the propensity to self-handicap (Rhodewalt, 1990). Task orientation was negatively correlated with scores on the self-handicapping scale.

Self-handicapping frustrates coaches and instructors because it prevents them from diagnosing a player's full potential. It may also prevent players from facing their own skill deficits, which may again undermine their opportunities to realize their full potential. Promoting personal skill development and challenge, rather than emphasizing competence relative to others, is likely to reduce the tendency of golfers to self-handicap.

Implications for the game

Across our studies, golfers who scored higher on ego orientation were more likely to have an obsessive passion for the game. Their self-worth was more likely to be dependent on golf and competition, and they were more likely to sandbag and self-handicap than players who scored low on ego orientation. This would seem to be a less healthy approach to the game. If ego orientation is indeed associated with a less healthy approach to the game, it is worthwhile to discuss ways that coaches, parents, and instructors might shape the goal orientation of young players. In other words, instructors, parents, and golf team coaches should consider creating a task-oriented motivational climate (see Duda & Balaguer, 2007). They can do this by:

- Emphasizing that success depends more on effort and practice than it does on raw athletic ability.
- Rewarding hard work and practice.
- Emphasizing player *personal bests* rather than success in competition.
- Be instructive rather than punitive when players make mistakes.
- Resist cultivating rivalries between players.
- Focus attention on all players rather than just the most successful players.
- Encourage players to teach and offer each other advice.
- Focus player efforts on correcting their weaknesses rather than rehearsing their strengths.
- Focus player attention on process (ball trajectory, swing, spin control, beautiful shots) rather than just score.
- Encourage players to experiment with various shots and clubs.
- Encourage players to embrace mistakes as learning opportunities.

Although ego orientation was associated with a variety of negative personality traits in our studies, ego orientation was also positively related to ability, golf frequency, and a harmonious passion for the game. If ego orientation is related to player success, then the question for coaches, parents, and teachers should be, how does one harness the positive aspects of ego orientation while minimizing the negative? Most of the problems associated with ego orientation occur when players feel less competent (Duda, 1992). Coaches, parents, and instructors working with players who score high on ego orientation should:

- Provide social support when golfers encounter slumps. Players who score high on ego orientation may question their own potential in these circumstances.
- Keep an eye on players who may become discouraged as he or she moves from a life stage where he or she has a great deal of time for golf to a stage where family and work responsibilities cut into practice. Not performing at one's best may be discouraging for the players

who score high on ego orientation. This is particularly true for players whose self-worth is contingent on playing golf well.

- Watch players who score high on ego orientation as they may be inclined to obsessive passion, sandbagging, and self-handicapping.

Summary and future directions

We used the most common conceptualization of two, orthogonal goal perspectives as a framework for our research. A number of theorists, however, suggest more nuanced approaches that incorporate approach and avoidance goal. One such approach (VandeWalle & Cummings, 1997) distinguishes goals of those individual who seek to demonstrate their competence (classified as ego approach goals) from those whose objective is to avoid demonstrating incompetence (ego avoidance goals). Elliot and Harackiewicz (1994) suggest that approach and avoidance goals can also apply to task orientation. Their model thus includes combinations of task and ego, approach and avoidance. The seemingly inconsistent results related to ego orientation in this chapter might have been teased apart if we had identified golfers who were ego-approach (desire to appear more competent than others) and ego-avoidant (desire to not appear less competent than others).

What we did not find were many strong relationships between task orientation and the variables we studied. This may be because players in our studies generally had high scores on task orientation and there may have been a problem with restriction of range. We do not know if the high scores reflect social desirability in our scale, or if players in our studies, who typically had 30 years of golf experience, had stayed with the game because they were interested in mastery and learning. We would like to think so, but task orientation scales are often negatively skewed, and we should include a greater number of novice and casual golfers in future samples.

Although, their approach does not necessarily address issues with subscale integrity, a number of researchers have argued that a more conceptually coherent approach to studying orthogonal task and ego orientations, may be to examine how various *combinations* of scores on task and ego orientation scales relate to performance (e.g., Fox et al., 1994; Hodge & Petlichkoff, 2000). These researchers, who focus on player goal profiles, consistently show that a high level of task orientation is desirable, irrespective of levels of ego orientation (cf. Roberts, 2012). The benefits of a high level of task orientation had been espoused consistently, and the correlation data presented here supports those views.

There are, however, a variety of questions yet to be answered regarding golfer goal orientation. Some of these questions relate to coaching and instruction. For instance, to what extent can coaches, instructors, and parents shape the goal orientation of players? Should these authority figures try to discourage ego orientation in players? How does goal orientation affect the interaction between player and coach? Does a coach who scores high on ego-orientation work well with players who score high on ego orientation? Some of the research questions yet to be answered relate to player development. Do older players define competence differently than young players? Do goal orientations change as player's age and/or become more skilled? Other unanswered questions are related to resilience. Does scoring high on goal orientation increase the chance that young players will experience negative affect and/or burnout, especially when they hit progress plateaus? Are tournament players who score high on ego orientation more likely to withdraw from a tournament when they have a bad round and are no longer in contention? Then there are questions about goal orientation and social interaction. For many recreational players, golf is a social rather than competitive event; it provides a chance to spend time with friends. Are goal orientations even relevant for these players? Does the golfer who scores high on ego orientation 'play well with others'? How do the players who score high on ego orientation partner with players who score high on task orientation?

Ultimately, instructors and coaches may benefit from assessing the goal orientations of their golfers. The measures provide insights into the ways that players perform, find satisfaction in the game, define competence, derive self-worth, and behave ethically on the course.

References

Ames, C. (1992) Achievement Goals, Motivational Climate, and Motivational Processes, In: G. Roberts (Ed.) *Motivation in Sport and Exercise*, Champaign, IL: Human Kinetics Publishers, pp. 161–176.

Baumeister, R. & Tice, D. (1985) Self-esteem and Responses to Success and Failure: Subsequent Performance and Intrinsic Motivation, *Journal of Personality*, 53 (3), 450–467.

Berglas, S. & Jones, E. (1978) Drug Choice as a Self-handicapping Strategy in Response to Non-contingent Success, *Journal of Personality and Social Psychology*, 36 (4), 405–417.

Biddle, S.; Wang, J.; Kavussanu, M. & Spray, C. (2003) Correlates of Achievement Goal Orientations in Physical Activity: A Systematic Review of Research, *European Journal of Sports Science*, 3 (5), 1–19.

Brown, J. & Dutton, K. (1995) The Thrill of Victory, the Complexity of Defeat: Self-esteem and People's Emotional Reactions to Success and Failure, *Journal of Personality and Social Psychology*, 68 (4), 712–722.

Coudevylle, G.; Martin Ginis, K. & Famose, J.-P. (2008) Determinants of Self-handicapping Strategies in Sport and Their Effects on Athletic Performance, *Social Behavior and Personality*, 36 (3), 391–398.

Crocker, J. (2002) The Costs of Seeking Self-esteem, *Journal of Social Issues*, 58 (3), 597–615.

Crocker, J.; Luhtanen, R.; Cooper, M. & Bouvrette, A. (2003) Contingencies of Self-worth in College Students: Theory and Measurement, *Journal of Personality and Social Psychology*, 85, (5), 894–908.

Crocker, J. & Wolfe, C. (2001) Contingencies of Self-worth, *Psychological Review*, 108 (3), 593–623.

Csikszentmihalyi, M. (1990) *Flow: The Psychology of Optimal Experience*, New York, NY: Harper and Row Publishers.

Curran, T.; Appleton, P.; Hill, A. & Hall, H. (2013) The Mediating Role of Psychological Need Satisfaction in Relationships Between Types of Passion for Sport and Athlete Burnout, *Journal of Sports Sciences*, 31 (6), 597–606.

Cury, F.; Famose, J. & Sarrazin, P. (1997) Achievement Goal Theory and Active Search for Information in a Sport Task, In: R. Lidor & M. Bar-Eli (Eds.) Innovations in Sport Psychology: Linking Theory and Practice. *Proceedings of the IX World Congress in Sport Psychology: Part I*. Netanya, Israel: Ministry of Education Culture and Sport, pp. 218–220.

Deci, E. & Ryan, R. (1985) *Intrinsic Motivation and Self-determination in Human Behavior*, New York, NY: Plenum.

Dewar, A. & Kavussanu, M. (2011) Achievement Goals and Emotions in Golf: The Mediating and Moderating Role of Perceived Performance, *Psychology of Sport and Exercise*, 12 (5), 525–532.

Duda, J. (1989) The Relationship Between Task and Ego Orientation and the Perceived Purpose of Sport among Male and Female High School Athletes, *Journal of Sport and Exercise Psychology*, 11 (3), 318–335.

Duda, J. (1992) Motivation in Sport Settings: A Goal Perspective Approach, In: G. Roberts (Ed.) *Motivation in Sport and Exercise*, Champaign, IL: Human Kinetics, pp. 57–92.

Duda, J. (2001) Achievement Goal Research in Sport: Pushing the Boundaries and Clarifying Some Misunderstandings, In: G. Roberts (Ed.) *Advances in Motivation in Sport and Exercise*, Champaign, IL: Human Kinetics, pp. 129–182.

Duda, J. & Balaguer, I. (2007) The Coach Created Motivational Climate, In: S. Jowett & D. Lavalee (Eds.) *Social Psychology of Sport*, Champaign, IL: Human Kinetics, pp. 117–130.

Duda, J.; Chi, L.; Newton, M.; Walling, M. & Catley, D. (1995) Task and Ego Orientation and Intrinsic Motivation in Sport, *International Journal of Sport Psychology*, 26 (1), 40–63.

Duda, J.; Fox, K.; Biddle, S. & Armstrong. N. (1992) Children's Achievement Goals and Beliefs about Success in Sport, *British Journal of Educational Psychology*, 62 (3), 313–323.

Duda, J. & Nicholls, J. (1992) Dimensions of Achievement Motivation in Schoolwork and Sport, *Journal of Educational Psychology*, 84 (3), 1–10.

Elliot, A. & Harackiewicz, J. (1994) Goal Setting, Achievement Orientation, and Intrinsic Motivation: A Mediational Analysis, *Journal of Personality and Social Psychology*, 66 (5), 968–980.

Fox, K.; Goudas, M.; Biddle, S.; Duda, J. & Armstrong, N. (1994) Children's Task and Ego Goal Profiles in Sport, *British Journal of Educational Psychology*, 64 (2), 253–261.

Gencer, E. (2010) The Relationship Between Locus of Control, Self-esteem and Goal Orientation, Motivational Climate in Badminton Players, *Ovidius University Annals, Series Physical Education And Sport/Science, Movement and Health*, 10 (2), 157–162.

Gibson, B. (2007) The Role of Individual Differences in Sandbagging on Selective Avoidance of Self-evaluative Information, *Journal of Research in Personality*, 41 (2), 481–487.

Gibson, B. & Sachau, D. (2000) Sandbagging as a Self-presentational Strategy: Claiming to Be Less than You Are, *Personality and Social Psychology Bulletin*, 26 (1), 56–70.

Gibson, B.; Sachau, D.; Doll, B. & Shumate, R. (2002) Sandbagging in Competition: Responding to the Pressure of Being the Favorite, *Personality and Social Psychology Bulletin*, 28, (8), 1119–1130.

Gustafsson, H.; Hassmen, P. & Hassmen, N. (2011) Are Athletes Burning Out with Passion? *European Journal of Sport Science*, 11 (6), 387–395.

Harris, A. (2014) *Ramifications of Taking the Game Too Seriously*, Unpublished MA Thesis, Mankato, MN: Minnesota State University.

Harris, A.; Sachau, D. & Kamphoff, C. (2014) *Taking It Personally: Examining Negative Reactivity on the Golf Course*, 29th Annual Conference of the American Association of Applied Psychologists, Las Vegas, NV.

Hodge, K. & Petlichkoff, L. (2000) Goal Profiles in Sport Motivation: A Cluster Analysis, *Journal of Sport and Exercise Psychology*, 22 (3), 256–272.

Kavussanu, M. & Duda, J. (2007) Goal Orientations and Moral Identity as Predictors of Prosocial and Antisocial Functioning in Male Association Football Players, *Journal of Sport Sciences*, 24 (5), 455–466.

Kingston, K. & Hardy, L. (1997) *Do Goal Orientation Profiles Impact Upon Competition Performance?* Unpublished Manuscript, University of Wales, Bangor, UK.

Kingston, K. & Swain, A. (1998) Goal Orientations and State Goals: Research in Golf and Implications for Performance, In: M. Farrally & A. Cochran (Eds.) *Science and Golf III*. Champaign, IL: Human Kinetics, pp 150–157.

Kuczka, K. & Treasure, D. (2005) Self-handicapping in Competitive Sport: Influence of the Motivational Climate, Self-efficacy, and Perceived Importance, *Psychology of Sport and Exercise*, 6 (5), 539–550.

Mackinnon, S.; Smith, S. & Carter-Rogers, K. (2015) Multidimensional Self-esteem and Test Derogation After Negative Feedback, *Canadian Journal of Behavioural Science*, 47 (1), 123–126.

Mageau, G.; Carpenter, J. & Vallerand, R. (2011) The Role of Self-esteem Contingencies in the Distinction Between Obsessive and Harmonious Passion, *European Journal of Social Psychology*, 41 (6), 720–729.

Nicholls, J. (1984) Achievement Motivation: Conceptions of Ability, Subjective Experience, Task Choice, and Performance, *Psychological Review*, 91 (3), 328–346.

Nicholls, J. (1989) *The Competitive Ethos and Democratic Education*, Cambridge, MA: Harvard University Press.

Niiya, Y. & Crocker, J. (2008) Mastery Goals and Contingent Self-worth: A Field Study, *International Review of Social Psychology*, 21 (1), 135–155.

Oh, S.-Y, (2001) *Flow in Golf: Motivation, Orientation and Challenge Determinants*, Unpublished PhD Thesis, West Virginia, USA: West Virginia University.

Prapavessis, H. & Grove, J. (1998) Self-Handicapping and Self-esteem, *Journal of Sport Applied Psychology*, 10 (2), 175–184.

Rhodewalt, F. (1990) *The Self-Handicapping Scale. Available From the Department of Psychology*, Salt Lake City, UT: University of Utah.

Rhodewalt, F.; Saltzman A. & Wittmer J. (1984) Self-handicapping among Competitive Athletes: The Role of Practice in Self-esteem Protection, *Basic and Applied Social Psychology*, 5 (3), 197–209.

Roberts, G. (2012) Motivation in Sport and Exercise From an Achievement Goal Theory Perspective: After 30 Years, Where Are We? In: G. Roberts & D. Treasure (Eds.) *Advances in Motivation in Sport and Exercise*, Champaign, IL: Human Kinetics, pp. 5–58.

Roberts, G.; Treasure, D. & Kavussanu, M. (1996) Orthogonality of Achievement Goals and its Relationship to Beliefs about Success and Satisfaction in Sport, *The Sport Psychologist*, 10 (4), 398–408.

Sachau, D.; Simmering, L.; Ryan, W. & Adler, M. (2013) Goal Orientation of Recreational Golfers, *International Journal of Golf Science*, 2 (2), 95–115.

Sachau, D.; Simmering, L.; Ryan, W. & Adler, M. (2014) Sandbagging: Faking Incompetence on the Golf Course, *International Journal of Golf Science*, 3 (1), 78–89.

Sage, L. & Kavussanu, M. (2007) Multiple Goal Orientations as Predictors of Moral Behavior in Youth Soccer, *Sport Psychologist*, 21 (4), 417–437.

Schweitzer, M.; Ordonez, L. & Douma, B. (2004) Goal Setting as a Motivator of Unethical Behavior, *Academy of Management Journal*, 47 (3), 422–432.

Shepperd, J., & Socherman, R. (1997) On the Manipulative Behavior of Low Machiavellians: Feigning Incompetence to "Sandbag" an Opponent, *Journal of Personality and Social Psychology*, 72 (6), 1448–1459.

Spray, C.; Wang, C.; Biddle, S. & Chatzisarantis, N. (2006) Understanding Motivation in Sport: An Experimental Test of Achievement Goal and Self-determination Theories, *European Journal of Sport Science*, 6 (1), 43–51.

Steinberg, C.; Singer, R. & Murphey, M. (2000) The Benefits to Sport Achievement When a Multiple Goal Orientation is Emphasized, *Journal of Sport Behavior*, 23 (4), 407–423.

Stenseng, F. & Dalskau, L. (2010) Passion, Self-esteem, and the Role of Comparative Performance Evaluation, *Journal of Sport and Exercise Psychology*, 32 (6), 881–894.

Thill, E. & Cury, F. (2000) Learning to Play Golf Under Different Goal Conditions: Their Effects on Irrelevant Thoughts and on Subsequent Control Strategies, *European Journal of Social Psychology*, 30 (1), 101–122.

Treasure, D. & Roberts, G. (1994) Cognitive and Affective Concomitants of Task and Ego Goal Orientations During the Middle School Years, *Journal of Sport and Exercise Psychology*, 16 (1), 15–28.

Vallerand, R. & Houlfort, N. (2003) Passion at Work: Toward a New Conceptualization, In: S. Gilliland; D. Steiner, & D. Skarlicki (Eds.) *Emerging Perspectives on Values in Organizations*, Greenwich, CT: Information Age Publishing, pp. 175–204.

Vallerand, R.; Mageau, G.; Elliot, A.; Dumais, A.; Demers, M. & Rousseau, F. (2003) Passion and Performance Attainment in Sport, *Psychology of Sport and Exercise*, 9 (3), 373–392.

Vallerand, R.; Salvy, S.; Mageau, G.; Elliot, A.; Denis, P.; Grouzet, F. & Blanchard, C. (2007) On the Role of Passion in Performance, *Journal of Personality*, 75 (3), 505–534.

Vandewalle, D. & Cummings, L. (1997) A Test of the Influence of Goal Orientation on the Feedback Seeking Process, *Journal of Applied Psychology*, 82 (3), 390–400.

24

INDIVIDUAL DIFFERENCES IN COGNITIVE PROCESSES AND GOLF PERFORMANCE

Patrick R. Thomas, Andrea J. Furst and Gerard J. Fogarty

Introduction

Individual differences in cognitive processes have long been of interest to psychologists and educators and are crucial for understanding and improving golf performance. Paivio (1971) proposed that we have one system for coding and processing verbal information and another for coding and processing nonverbal information. In his Dual Coding Theory (DCT), the structures and processes of verbal and imaginal systems are independent of each other. Both systems can be used to code information, but one code tends to be emphasised more than the other. Paivio (1971) thus developed an Individual Differences Questionnaire (IDQ) to assess tendencies or preferences for processing information either verbally or imaginally.

Both verbal and imaginal systems process information in different modalities, but this multisensory assumption of DCT was often overlooked, perhaps because research on the theory emphasised visual imagery more than other modalities (Paivio, 1991). Many studies investigating individual differences in cognitive styles have been based on self-report instruments such as Richardson's (1977) Verbalizer-Visualizer Questionnaire (VVQ). Although much of that research has been conducted in classrooms, some studies have examined cognitive styles and preferences in athletes, including golfers.

Many psychological skills training (PST) programmes are designed to develop golfers' cognitive processes such as self-talk, imagery and attentional control skills. Confidence and optimistic thinking are also crucial. Is it correct to assume that the same PST programme or approach will be equally effective for all clients, or should the intervention be tailored to the needs and preferences of each individual? If golfers prefer to process information verbally or visually, will they benefit more from developing their self-talk or imagery skills respectively? Are preferences for other modalities (e.g., kinaesthesis) important in learning and performing golf skills? These questions are examined in this chapter to inform the professional practice of coaches and sport psychologists in golf.

Cognitive processes in golf

This section examines how specific cognitive processes optimise golf performance, reviews the evidence from sport and other contexts for individual differences in cognitive processes, and considers the implications of the findings for tailoring PST programmes in golf.

Self-talk

Athletes readily acknowledge the importance of thinking positively if they are to perform well. Nevertheless, some golfers repeatedly apologise to their playing partners for the poor state of their game, commenting how badly they are driving or chipping, how difficult it is to read breaks on the greens, and so on. These negative statements are public, but the player's internal self-talk may also be negative and adversely affecting performance. Ravizza (2010) argues that awareness is the first step in gaining control of this situation, changing self-talk from negative to positive. Some practitioners have gone to great lengths to develop athletes' awareness of their negative self-talk. Owens and Bunker (1989), for example, asked a professional golfer to transfer a paper clip between pockets every time she thought negatively while playing. After one round of 84 shots, she had transferred 87 paper clips. Self-talk training activities are needed once the athlete's awareness is heightened.

Before any intervention is attempted, the factors that shape athletes' self-talk need to be understood. Research identifies personal, situational and social-environmental factors as significant antecedents (Theodorakis et al., 2012). For example, athletes with high task and moderate ego orientations are more inclined to set self-referenced process goals that focus attention on task mastery and make significantly more use of self-talk in competitions and at practice than those with other combinations of these goal orientations (Harwood et al., 2004). Negative self-talk is more likely when pre-competition cognitive anxiety is high and when a discrepancy arises between goals and performance during a game (Hatzigeorgiadis & Biddle, 2008). Significant others, particularly coaches, play an important role in shaping athletes' self-talk (Zourbanos et al., 2010).

The where, when, what, why and how athletes use self-talk have been investigated by Hardy et al. (2001, 2009). Athletes report using self-talk at home and in their sporting environment, particularly before and during competition and during practice. They report positive self-talk more frequently than negative self-talk, but also give themselves task instructions (Van Raalte et al., 1994). Athletes use self-talk for various cognitive and motivational functions: to develop and execute skills and strategies; improve performance; remain focused; increase self-confidence; ensure mental readiness; cope with difficult situations; regulate arousal (psych themselves up, relax); and to maintain and increase motivation, determination and effort. Athletes increase their use of self-talk in later stages of the competitive season, with highly skilled athletes in individual sports using self-talk more frequently and consistently than less skilled athletes and those in team sports (Hardy et al., 2004).

Many studies have examined relationships between self-talk and performance. Evidence of the effectiveness of self-talk began with findings that those who qualified for elite competition reported more frequent self-talk in training and competition than those who did not qualify. Later evidence emerged that positive and instructional self-talk tended to improve sport performance, whereas negative self-talk was associated with worse performance (Theodorakis et al., 2012). A meta-analysis of the effectiveness of self-talk interventions revealed a moderately positive effect size, $d = .48$ (Hatzigeorgiadis et al., 2011). Interventions that included training were more effective ($d = .80$) than those that did not ($d = .37$); self-talk was more effective for novel tasks ($d = .73$) than well learned tasks ($d = .41$), and for fine motor skills requiring precision and coordination ($d = .67$) than tasks requiring strength and endurance ($d = .26$).

Useful guidelines for conducting self-talk interventions are provided by Zinsser et al. (2010). Thought-stopping techniques are often used, but sometimes golfers need to change negative thoughts into positive thoughts. After identifying when their self-talk is negative and what causes these statements, they learn to substitute positive affirmations that bring them back to the present and in control of the situation. Negative self-statements may need to be countered – using facts and reasons to refute underlying beliefs that are counterproductive. Concern about the negative impact of a swing change can be countered by reference to how others have made that change successfully. Another form of cognitive restructuring – reframing – transforms what appears to be a problem, weakness or difficulty into an opportunity, strength or possibility. Reframing can help golfers focus on the advantages of drawing a strong opponent in the initial round of a match-play competition, or interpret prematch butterflies in the stomach as a sign their body is ready to perform.

Imagery

Golfers are often quick to acknowledge the potential benefits of using imagery to improve performance, perhaps after reading how Jack Nicklaus never hit a shot in competition or at practice without first having a sharp picture of that shot in his head, or watching Jason Day's preshot routine. Athletes may be aware they can improve their verbal processes by thinking positively, but often need help learning how to use imagery in sport. As is the case for self-talk, research shows that imagery ability can improve with training and have substantial benefits. We will not provide a comprehensive review of the research – that has been done by Cumming and colleagues in Chapter 19 of this book and elsewhere (e.g., Murphy et al., 2008; Cumming & Williams, 2012). Rather, we will consider some similarities and differences in research findings on self-talk and imagery, and focus particularly on individual differences.

Substantial research has investigated where, when, what, why and how athletes use imagery. Cumming and Williams (2012) summarise those research findings in their revised applied model of deliberate imagery use. Situational factors (where, when) are significant antecedents of athletes' imagery use, as are personal factors (who), which include age, experience, gender, goal orientation and other dispositions, and the person's imagery ability. Paivio's (1985) proposal that imagery has both cognitive and motivational functions led to the content or type of imagery (what) being inherently linked to its function (why). Correct execution of the golf swing would be imagined if the function was to optimise skill performance, whereas imagining a successful competition outcome would serve a motivational function. Cumming and Williams (2012) introduced a conceptual distinction between the type/content and function of imagery, reflecting evidence that some athletes prefer to use technical and tactical images rather than affective or mastery-based content to improve confidence, control anxiety, and prepare effectively for competition. The personal meaning of imagery differs between individuals and forms a crucial bridge between content and function in their model.

Those conducting imagery interventions with golfers need to take such individual differences into account. They also need to consider differences between individuals in imagery ability, as well as differences within individuals in their ability to generate various types of images associated with performance such as the feelings (affect), skills, strategies, goals, and mastery of adversity (Williams & Cumming, 2011). Interventions are more effective when imagery rehearsals match crucial aspects of physical performance. Holmes and Collins (2001) drew attention to Physical, Environmental, Task, Timing, Learning, Emotion, and Perspective factors in their PETTLEP model. There is good support for this model in sport, and it should prove useful in guiding further research on the development of imagery ability.

It is clear that interventions should be tailored to the specific needs of the performer (Cumming & Williams, 2012). Differences between and within individuals in imagery ability, the vividness and controllability of various types of images and their personal meaning highlight the importance of working closely with the athlete in selecting images and planning how they will be used. Individuals who find it easier to imagine some aspects of performance (e.g., feelings) make more use of that type of imagery (Williams & Cumming, 2011). In a similar way, they may be more inclined to form images using a particular perspective (first-person, third-person), angle, or modality. Imagery is a multisensory construct although visual and kinaesthetic modalities are prominent in sport. We examine such individual differences in cognitive preferences in the next section.

Cognitive preferences

An understanding of athletes' verbal and visual information processing preferences could help coaches introduce new motor skills or refine existing skills more effectively, improving learning outcomes and athletes' performance (Fuelscher et al., 2012). Substantial classroom research has focused not only on the differences between verbalisers and visualisers (e.g., Riding & Rayner, 1998), but also on students' preferences for processing visual, auditory, and kinaesthetic information (e.g., Dunn et al., 1984). Those preferences formed the basis of learning style theories, which emphasise the need for teaching or coaching method to match students' learning style. Howard-Jones (2014) reported that more than 90% of primary and secondary school teachers sampled in five countries agree that individuals learn better when they receive information in their preferred learning style (e.g., visual, auditory or kinaesthetic). He acknowledged that cognitive preferences may exist but questioned the neuroscientific assumptions underlying the matching hypothesis, and others have questioned the validity of the learning styles construct (e.g., Pashler et al., 2008; Willingham et al., 2015). This discrepancy between science and practice indicates the need for a better appreciation of the complex nature of cognitive preferences and how knowledge of such preferences can be used in golf coaching and other instructional settings.

Some studies have demonstrated that individuals learn best when instructional material matches their cognitive style. Thomas and McKay (2010) measured university students' cognitive styles on three dimensions: verbal, object visual, and spatial visual, following evidence for two types of visualisers (Kozhevnikov et al., 2002, 2005). Participants' memory and comprehension of three personality theories were assessed when the information was presented as text only (verbal); text + picture (object visual); or text + schematic diagram (spatial visual). Students had better recall and comprehension when the presentation format matched their cognitive styles. Augmenting verbal information with different types of images helped many students learn more effectively.

It has also been argued (e.g., Kozhevnikov et al., 2014) that studies of cognitive styles in psychology, learning styles in education, and decision-making styles in business and management address the same phenomena. All of these individual differences in cognition represent patterns of adaptation to the environment. The authors acknowledged the limited utility of the matching hypothesis, focusing instead on the need to develop cognitive flexibility so individuals can respond appropriately to the demands of the task or situation. Kozhevnikov et al. (2014) proposed a matrix framework that attempted to synthesise research on styles across different domains, but their review did not include research on cognitive styles in sport, which we consider next.

Most cognitive psychology texts, even applied cognitive psychology publications, contain few if any references to sport or athletes, despite the opportunities provided in this domain to study basic cognitive processes (Moran, 2009). There have been studies on the learning styles of athletes in different sports. Gonzalez-Haro et al. (2010), for example, measured the learning styles of professional, amateur and recreational athletes in basketball, soccer and cycling using an instrument derived from Kolb's (1984) experiential learning model. They found that athletes have different learning styles rather than a predominant style; similar styles were reported by athletes at different levels of expertise; and the styles were not related to years of experience.

Do athletes benefit from instruction congruent with their learning style? Thomas and Fogarty (1997) hypothesised that individuals with high verbalising tendencies would respond better to self-talk training techniques, whereas high visualisers would favour imagery training. Baseline measures on psychological and psychomotor skills were obtained from 32 amateur golfers, who then responded to the 30-item Your Information Processing Preferences Scale (YIPPS) to indicate their use of verbal (e.g., 'When preparing for a shot, I tell myself how I will play it') and visual information (e.g., 'When preparing for a shot, I form a mental image of how it will be played'). After two self-talk and two imagery training workshops, which were counterbalanced across two research sites, the golfers' skills were re-assessed and they completed an evaluation questionnaire. The self-talk and imagery training resulted in significant improvements in psychological and psychomotor skills. Performance on a Golf Skills Test improved significantly after training, and participants' handicaps decreased significantly over time. There were also significant increases in the vividness and controllability of images, as well as participants' knowledge and application of self-talk and imagery techniques. However, there was no evidence that the self-talk and imagery training benefits were linked to the golfers' cognitive preferences. The YIPPS subscale scores were significantly correlated at the start of the program. High use of verbal information was thus associated with high use of visual information – very few individuals had a strong preference for one type of information rather than the other (cf. Fogarty & Burton, 1996).

This research was extended by (Furst, 2010) using the Your Information Processing Preferences Scale-Revised (YIPPS-R), in which 15 items were added to measure golfers' use of kinaesthetic information (e.g., 'When preparing for a shot, I have a practice swing to feel how it will be played'). She administered the YIPPS-R, together with measures of dispositional optimism and sport confidence (Fogarty et al., 2016), to 95 professional golfers aged 22–54 years playing in major PGA Tour of Australasia events, some co-sanctioned by the PGA European Tour. Players' responses indicated the verbal, visual, and kinaesthetic subscales had satisfactory internal consistency, so subscale totals were calculated. There were significant group differences in the use of verbal, visual, and kinaesthetic information. These professional golfers made significantly more use of kinaesthetic information than both verbal and visual information; they also used visual information more than verbal information. Significant correlations were found between preferences for verbal and visual, verbal and kinaesthetic, and visual and kinaesthetic information, indicating that professional golfers who made high use of one type of information were also likely to make high use of other information. Table 24.1 shows the number of professional golfers in the sample reporting low, medium, and high use of verbal, visual, and kinaesthetic information. The first three rows in Table 24.1 reveal that none of the professional golfers had a distinct preference for just one type of information (e.g., High, Low, Low). Half of the sample ($n = 48$) had balanced profiles such as low ($n = 1$), medium ($n = 38$), or high ($n = 9$) scores on all subscales. Relatively few professional golfers reported low use of a specific type of information, particularly kinaesthetic information ($n = 4$). These elite golfers clearly tended to combine information in the different modalities when thinking about their shots.

Cognitive neuroscience provides support for such cross-modal information processing. Brain mapping using functional magnetic resonance imaging (fMRI) during motor skill execution has shown that visual and kinaesthetic imagery activate different neural processes. When forming general representations of skilled movement, individuals with good motor imagery abilities are able to favour one sensory modality or select between visual and kinaesthetic imagery depending on the characteristics of the skill (Guillot et al., 2009). The evidence also indicates that

Table 24.1 Touring golf professionals' (N = 95) cognitive preferences for verbal, visual, and kinaesthetic information

Verbal	Visual	Kinaesthetic	n
High	Low	Low	0
Low	High	Low	0
Low	Low	High	0
Low	Low	Low	1
Low	Low	Medium	4
Low	Medium	Medium	10
Medium	Low	Medium	5
Medium	Medium	Medium	38
Medium	Medium	High	13
Medium	High	High	6
High	High	High	9
Medium	Low	Low	1
Low	Medium	Low	1
Medium	Medium	Low	1
High	Medium	Low	0
Medium	High	Low	0
High	High	Low	0
High	Low	Medium	0
High	Medium	Medium	1
Low	High	Medium	0
Medium	High	Medium	1
High	High	Medium	0
Medium	Low	High	1
High	Low	High	0
Low	Medium	High	1
High	Medium	High	1
Low	High	High	1

Source: Adapted from Furst (2010).

athletes can distinguish visual and kinaesthetic processes when using imagery, often use more than one modality when reporting their imagery, and are able to switch between modalities either voluntarily or when instructed to do so (Munzert et al., 2009).

Attentional control

Research in sport has also contributed significantly to understanding cognitive processes in areas such as attention, anticipation, decision making, and expertise (Abernethy et al., 2007; Moran, 2009, 2012). Concentration, the ability to focus attention on the task and deal with distractions, is a crucial skill in golf. A detailed review of the substantial research on concentration in golf and other sports is beyond the scope of this chapter. Instead, this section concludes with a consideration of relationships between self-talk, imagery, and concentration, and how these cognitive processes can be combined to optimise performance in golf.

Sport psychologists often help athletes use self-talk to draw attention to key aspects of movement, ensure mental readiness, focus on the present rather than past or future, and prevent distractions from internal or external stimuli (see Zinsser et al., 2010). Care is needed, however, in the selection of verbal cues. Phrases may act as reminders and help novices consciously learn and perform motor skills. A coach's verbal instructions to focus attention internally on body movement or externally on the target also influence movement kinematics and performance accuracy when novices are learning golf skills (Munzert et al., 2014). Elite athletes, however, perform better when skills are executed automatically (see other chapters in this book). Experienced golfers can use holistic process goals involving swing thoughts such as 'smooth' or 'tempo' to improve concentration, the allocation of attentional resources, and golf performance (Kingston & Hardy, 1997). Focusing on holistic movement cues such as the rhythm of the golf swing has also been found to benefit elite performers (Winter et al., 2014).

Athletes use imagery to learn and improve the performance of skills and strategies, modify cognitions, and regulate arousal and competitive anxiety (Martin et al., 1999). Imagery training improved the selective attention of elite softball players, helping them focus more on task-relevant stimuli and ignore distracters such as crowd noise (Calmels et al., 2004). Bernier and Fournier (2010) noted that one of the main functions of mental imagery used by nine elite amateur and 12 professional golfers was to 'get focused'. The main focus of attention in their imagery was on ball trajectory/flight in the air or roll on the ground, but they modified the imagery content (e.g., speed of the ball) to select more relevant information and achieve optimal concentration on the shot to be played. These golfers used imagery to collect information, analyse different trajectory options, and choose either the more efficient trajectory or the one they were more confident about in executing the shot. They also reported using imagery several times and generating different kinds of imagery content (e.g., line of the putt, ball falling into the hole) as they prepared to play a shot.

An understanding of how athletes use self-talk, imagery and concentration, and the relationships between these cognitive processes, enhances the development of effective preshot routines in golf. Some sport psychologists have urged athletes to use their dominant perceptual learning

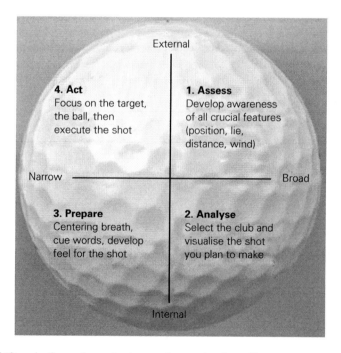

Figure 24.1 Shifting the focus of attention in a preshot routine for golf.

Source: Adapted from Thomas (2001).

Photo credit: Robert Weismantel.

style in preshot routines (Cohn, 1990), but it is now clear that these routines should enable athletes to combine self-talk and imagery processes in ways that accommodate individual differences. As shown in Figure 24.1, Nideffer's (1985) dimensions of attention provide a useful framework for developing an effective preshot routine in golf.

Initially the focus is broad and external as the golfer assesses the situation by processing task-relevant information such as ball position, lie of the ball, distance from the target, and wind. The focus of attention remains broad but shifts internally as the golfer analyses this information, selects an appropriate club, and visualises the planned shot, particularly the ball trajectory (Bernier & Fournier, 2010). Attentional focus remains internal but narrows as the golfer prepares for the shot. Elite and experienced golfers putt when their heart rate is low and they have exhaled, whereas novices tend to hold their breath (Neumann & Thomas, 2009, 2011), so centring techniques can be effective as the golfer prepares to address the ball (Nideffer, 1985). The golfer can select an effective holistic verbal cue (e.g., 'smooth'), and incorporate a waggle of the club, practice swing or kinaesthetic image to develop feel for the shot. Finally, attention should be narrow and external as the golfer focuses on the target, the ball, and executes the shot. Research by Wulf (2007) and colleagues (see Chapter 8 of this book) demonstrates the benefits of an external focus of attention in the learning and performance of motor skills. Like other skills in golf, the preshot routine needs to be practised so it becomes automatic.

Implications for the game

Research on individual differences in cognitive processes has a number of implications for those working with golfers. Sport psychologists and coaches conducting PST interventions should not assume that the programme has to match players' processing preferences as if verbalisers benefit more from self-talk and visualisers from imagery. Instead they should ensure their presentation format facilitates cross-modal information processing to enhance learning and performance. Psychologists have an important role in helping players monitor and self-regulate their cognitive processes, developing their skills through self-talk and imagery training, as well as their cognitive flexibility in switching modalities as the task or situation demands. Kinaesthetic information is important and should be utilised with verbal and visual information in PST interventions. When giving lessons coaches should use videotaped examples and modelling to augment their verbal instructions, and help players feel the correct body position, swing plane, or movement pattern. Physiotherapists play an important role working with coaches in developing players' kinaesthetic proficiency, but can also help players use self-talk and imagery strategies for injury prevention, rehabilitation and pain relief. Although they recognise the importance of psychological skills, physiotherapists underutilise them in their professional practice; their understanding of self-talk and imagery strategies is often inadequate; and they would benefit from further training on a range of psychological techniques (Arvinen-Barrow et al., 2010; Alexanders et al., 2015).

Differences in cognitive processes between and within individuals can be addressed by personalising interventions rather than assuming the same information benefits all golfers. Cumming and Williams (2012) emphasised the personal meaning of imagery, but the same applies in the player's selection and use of verbal cues. They recommend partially individualised interventions in which participants provide stimuli information based on their past experiences that is integrated with response information provided by the consultant. Psychologists and coaches need to work closely with golfers in personalising the preshot routine shown in Figure 24.1.

Summary and future directions

Golfers may prefer particular types of information and make more use of that information when thinking about their shot. A group of professional golfers was found to favour kinaesthetic information. However, golfers also process task-relevant information in other modalities and switch their attention between modalities as the task demands. Interventions aimed at optimising performance in golf need to accommodate significant differences between and within individuals in cognitive processes.

Verbal and imagery processes have been extensively researched, but that research is ongoing (see the planned 2018 special issue of *The Sport Psychologist* on self-talk). Research has tended to focus on visual imagery, but more work is needed on kinaesthetic imagery, which is particularly important in golf and other sports. The vividness of kinaesthetic imagery plays an important role when golfers rehearse physical skills to correct swing techniques (Parker et al., 2015), yet there is evidence that amateur golfers underutilise kinaesthetic imagery (Bernier & Fournier, 2010). Cognitive neuroscience will continue to contribute significantly to our understanding of the mechanisms underlying self-talk, imagery and attentional control, and their relationship to learning and performance in golf.

The psychometric properties of the instruments used by researchers and practitioners need to be verified with golfers. The YIPPS-R has ecological validity and its subscales demonstrate internal consistency, but some other instruments have been adapted from classroom contexts and have questionable validity (Leite et al., 2009; Fuelscher et al., 2012). Sport psychology research is often conducted with novice golfers who are undergraduate students. More research is needed with experienced and elite golfers. Although laboratory-based research will significantly advance understanding of cognitive processes in golf, there is also a need for field-based studies and interventions.

Sport confidence and dispositional optimism are distinct but related constructs (Fogarty et al., 2016). Although both are characteristic of elite athletes (Gould et al., 2002), sport confidence has been more thoroughly investigated than optimism. Both are important in golf, as are other characteristics like mental toughness and resilience. More research is needed on how these characteristics can be developed in golfers through interventions targeting cognitive processes. Most applied sport psychologists currently adopt a cognitive-behavioural framework in PST programmes, but mindfulness offers an alternative approach emphasising acceptance rather than control (Birrer et al., 2012). Mindfulness is particularly concerned with the awareness that emerges through purposeful attention. There is increasing interest in applying mindfulness training in golf and other sports (e.g., Bernier et al., 2009; Mardon et al., 2016), and this approach is expected to play a prominent role in guiding and informing interventions aimed at improving golfers' well-being and performance in the years ahead.

References

Abernethy, B.; Maxwell, J.; Jackson, R. & Masters, R. (2007) Skill in Sport, In: F. Durso (Ed.) *Handbook of Applied Cognition* (2nd Ed.), Chichester, UK: Wiley, pp. 333–359.

Alexanders, J.; Anderson, A. & Henderson, S. (2015) Musculoskeletal Physiotherapists' Use of Psychological Interventions: A Systematic Review of Therapists' Perceptions and Practice, *Physiotherapy*, 101 (2), 95–102.

Arvinen-Barrow, M.; Penny, G.; Hemmings, B. & Corr, S. (2010) UK Chartered Physiotherapists' Personal Experiences in Using Psychological Interventions with Injured Athletes: An Interpretive Phenomenological Analysis, *Psychology of Sport and Exercise*, 11 (1), 58–66.

Bernier, M. & Fournier, J. (2010) Functions of Mental Imagery in Expert Golfers, *Psychology of Sport and Exercise*, 11 (6), 444–452.

Bernier, M.; Thienot, E.; Codron, R. & Fournier, J. (2009) Mindfulness and Acceptance Approaches in Sports Performance, *Journal of Clinical Sport Psychology*, 25 (4), 320–333.

Birrer, D.; Röthlin, P. & Morgan, G. (2012) Mindfulness to Enhance Athletic Performance: Theoretical Considerations and Possible Impact Mechanisms, *Mindfulness*, 3 (3), 235–246.

Calmels, C.; Berthoumieux, C. & d'Arripe-Longueville, F. (2004) Effects of an Imagery Training Program on Selective Attention of National Softball Players, *The Sport Psychologist*, 18 (3), 272–296.

Cohn, P. (1990) Preperformance Routines in Sport: Theoretical Support and Practical Applications, *The Sport Psychologist*, 4 (3), 301–312.

Cumming, J. & Williams, S. (2012) The Role of Imagery in Performance, In: S. Murphy (Ed.) *Oxford Handbook of Sport and Performance Psychology*, New York, NY: Oxford University Press, pp. 213–232.

Dunn, R.; Dunn, K. & Price, G. (1984) *Learning Style Inventory*, Lawrence, KS: Price Systems.

Fogarty, G. & Burton, L. (1996) A Comparison of Measures of Preferred Processing Style: Method or Trait Variance? *Journal of Mental Imagery*, 20 (3&4), 87–112.

Fogarty, G.; Perera, H.; Furst, A. & Thomas, P. (2016) Evaluating Measures of Optimism and Sport Confidence, *Measurement in Physical Education and Exercise Science*, 20 (2), 81–92.

Fuelscher, I.; Ball, K. & MacMahon, C. (2012) Perspectives on Learning Styles in Motor and Sport Skills, *Frontiers in Psychology*, 3, Article 69.

Furst, A. (2010) *Dispositional Optimism, Sport Confidence, and Golf Performance*, Unpublished PhD Thesis, Brisbane, Australia: Griffith University.

Gonzalez–Haro, C.; Calleja-Gonzalez, J. & Escanero, J. (2010) Learning Styles Favoured by Professional, Amateur, and Recreational Athletes in Different Sports, *Journal of Sports Sciences*, 28 (8), 859–866.

Gould, D.; Dieffenbach, K. & Moffett, A. (2002) Psychological Characteristics and Their Development in Olympic Champions, *Journal of Applied Sport Psychology*, 14 (3), 172–204.

Guillot, A.; Collet, C.; Nguyen, V.; Malouin, F.; Richards, C. & Doyon, J. (2009) Brain Activity During Visual Versus Kinaesthetic Imagery: An fMRI Study, *Human Brain Mapping*, 30 (7), 2157–2172.

Hardy, J.; Gammage, K. & Hall, C. (2001) A Descriptive Study of Athlete Self-talk, *The Sport Psychologist*, 15 (3), 306–318.

Hardy, J.; Hall, C. & Hardy, L. (2004) A Note on Athletes' Use of Self-talk, *Journal of Applied Sport Psychology*, 16 (3), 251–257.

Hardy, J.; Oliver, E. & Tod, D. (2009) A Framework for the Study and Application of Self-talk Within Sport, In: S. Mellalieu & S. Hanton (Eds.) *Advances in Applied Sport Psychology: A Review* (2nd Ed.), London: Routledge, pp. 37–74.

Harwood, C.; Cumming, J. & Fletcher, D. (2004) Motivational Profiles and Psychological Skills Use Within Elite Youth Sport, *Journal of Applied Sport Psychology*, 16 (4), 318–332.

Hatzigeorgiadis, A. & Biddle, S. (2008) Negative Self-talk During Sport Performance: Relationships with Pre-competition Anxiety and Goal-performance Discrepancies, *Journal of Sport Behavior*, 31 (3), 237–253.

Hatzigeorgiadis, A.; Zourbanos, N.; Galanis, E. & Theodorakis, Y. (2011) Self-talk and Sports Performance: A Meta-analysis, *Perspectives on Psychological Science*, 6 (4), 348–356.

Holmes, P. & Collins, D. (2001) The PETTLEP Approach to Motor Imagery: A Functional Equivalence Model for Sport Psychologists, *Journal of Applied Sport Psychology*, 13 (1), 60–83.

Howard-Jones, P. (2014) Neuroscience and Education: Myths and Messages, *Nature Reviews, Neuroscience*, 15 (12), 817–824.

Kingston, K. & Hardy, L. (1997) Effects of Different Types of Goals on Processes That Support Performance, *The Sport Psychologist*, 11 (3), 277–293.

Kolb, D. (1984) *Experiential Learning: Experience as a Source of Learning and Development*, Englewood Cliffs, NJ: Prentice Hall.

Kozhevnikov, M.; Evans, C. & Kosslyn, S. (2014) Cognitive Style as Environmentally Sensitive Individual Differences in Cognition: A Modern Synthesis and Applications in Education, Business, and Management, *Psychological Science in the Public Interest*, 15 (1), 3–33.

Kozhevnikov, M.; Hegarty, M. & Mayer, R. (2002) Revising the Verbalizer-visualizer Dimension: Evidence for Two Types of Visualizers, *Cognition and Instruction*, 20 (1), 47–77.

Kozhevnikov, M.; Kosslyn, S. & Shephard, J. (2005) Spatial Versus Object Visualizers: A New Characterization of Visual Cognitive Style, *Memory & Cognition*, 33 (4), 710–726.

Leite, W.; Svinicki, M. & Shi, Y. (2009) Attempted Validation of the Scores of the VARK: Learning Styles Inventory with Multitrait-Multimethod Confirmatory Factor Analysis Models, *Educational and Psychological Measurement*, 70 (2), 323–339.

Mardon, N.; Richards, H. & Martindale, A. (2016) The Effect of Mindfulness Training on Attention and Performance in National-level Swimmers: An Exploratory Investigation, *The Sport Psychologist*, 30 (2), 131–140.

Martin, K.; Moritz, S. & Hall, C. (1999) Imagery Use in Sport: A Literature Review and Applied Model, *The Sport Psychologist*, 13 (3), 245–268.

Moran, A. (2009) Cognitive Psychology in Sport: Progress and Prospects, *Psychology of Sport and Exercise*, 10 (4), 420–426.

Moran, A. (2012) Thinking in Action: Some Insights From Cognitive Sport Psychology, *Thinking Skills and Creativity*, 7 (2), 85–92.

Munzert, J.; Lorey, B. & Zentgraf, K. (2009) Cognitive Motor Processes: The Role of Motor Imagery in the Study of Motor Representations, *Brain Research Reviews*, 60 (2), 306–326.

Munzert, J.; Maurer, H. & Reiser, M. (2014) Verbal-motor Attention-focusing Instructions Influence Kinematics and Performance on a Golf-putting Task, *Journal of Motor Behavior*, 46 (5), 309–318.

Murphy, S.; Nordin, S. & Cumming, J. (2008) Imagery in Sport, Exercise, and Dance, In: T. Horn (Ed.) *Advances in Sport Psychology* (3rd Ed.), Champaign, IL: Human Kinetics, pp. 298–324.

Neumann, D. & Thomas, P. (2009) The Relationship Between Skill Level and Patterns in Cardiac and Respiratory Activity During Golf Putting, *International Journal of Psychophysiology*, 72 (3), 276–282.

Neumann, D. & Thomas, P. (2011) Cardiac and Respiratory Activity and Golf Putting Performance Under Attentional Focus Instructions, *Psychology of Sport and Exercise*, 12 (4), 451–459.

Nideffer, R. (1985) *Athletes' Guide to Mental Training*, Champaign, IL: Human Kinetics.

Owens, D. & Bunker, L. (1989) *Golf: Steps to Success*, Champaign, IL: Human Kinetics.

Paivio, A. (1971) *Imagery and Verbal Processes*. New York, NY: Holt, Rinehart and Winston.

Paivio, A. (1985) Cognitive and Motivational Functions of Imagery in Human Performance, *Canadian Journal of Applied Sport Sciences*, 10 (4), 22S–28S.

Paivio, A. (1991) Dual Coding Theory: Retrospect and Current Status, *Canadian Journal of Psychology*, 45 (3), 255–287.

Parker, J.; Thompson, L.; Jones, M. & Lovell, G. (2015) Imagery Vividness as a Predictor of Imagery Use in Highly Skilled Golfers, *Journal of Sports Sciences*, 33 (Supplement 1), 34.

Pashler, H.; McDaniel, M.; Rohrer, D. & Bjork, R. (2008) Learning Styles: Concepts and Evidence, *Psychological Science in the Public Interest*, 9 (3), 105–119.

Ravizza, K. (2010) Increasing Awareness for Sport Performance, In: J. Williams (Ed.) *Applied Sport Psychology* (6th Ed.), Boston, MA: McGraw-Hill, pp. 189–200.

Richardson, A. (1977) Verbalizer-visualizer: A Cognitive Style Dimension, *Journal of Mental Imagery*, 1 (1), 109–125.

Riding, R. & Rayner, S. (1998) *Cognitive Styles and Learning Strategies. Understanding Style Differences in Learning and Behaviour*, London: David Fulton.

Theodorakis, Y.; Hatzigeorgiadis, A. & Zourbanos, N. (2012) Cognitions: Self-talk and Performance, In: S. Murphy (Ed.) *Oxford Handbook of Sport and Performance Psychology*, New York, NY: Oxford University Press, pp. 191–212.

Thomas, P. (2001) Cognitions, Emotions and Golf Performance, In: P. Thomas (Ed.) *Optimising Performance in Golf*, Brisbane, Australia: Australian Academic Press, pp. 337–353.

Thomas, P. & Fogarty, G. (1997) Psychological Skills Training in Golf: The Role of Individual Differences in Cognitive Preferences, *The Sport Psychologist*, 11 (1), 86–106.

Thomas, P. & McKay, J. (2010) Cognitive Styles and Instructional Design in University Learning, *Learning and Individual Differences*, 20 (3), 197–202.

Van Raalte, J.; Brewer, B.; Rivera, P. & Petitpas, A. (1994) The Relationship Between Observable Self-talk and Competitive Junior Tennis Players' Performances, *Journal of Sport & Exercise Psychology*, 16 (4), 400–415.

Williams, S. & Cumming, J. (2011) Measuring Athlete Imagery Ability: The Sport Imagery Ability Questionnaire, *Journal of Sport & Exercise Psychology*, 33 (3), 416–440.

Willingham, D.; Hughes, E. & Dobolyi, D. (2015) The Scientific Status of Learning Styles Theories, *Teaching of Psychology*, 42 (3), 266–271.

Winter, S.; MacPherson, A. & Collins, D. (2014) To Think, or Not to Think, That is the Question, *Sport, Exercise, and Performance Psychology*, 3 (2), 102–115.

Wulf, G. (2007) *Attention and Motor Skill Learning*, Champaign, IL: Human Kinetics.

Zinsser, N.; Bunker, L. & Williams, J. (2010) Cognitive Techniques for Building Confidence and Enhancing Performance, In: J. Williams (Ed.) *Applied Sport Psychology* (6th Ed.), Boston, MA: McGraw-Hill, pp. 305–335.

Zourbanos, N.; Hatzigeorgiadis, A.; Tsiakaras, N.; Chroni, S. & Theodorakis, Y. (2010) A Multi-method Examination of the Relationship Between Coaching Behavior and Athletes' Self-talk, *Journal of Sport & Exercise Psychology*, 32 (6), 764–785.

25

GOLF AND THE PROMISE OF MENTAL HEALTH AND WELL-BEING FOR THE ELITE AND PROFESSIONAL PLAYER

Kitrina Douglas and David Carless

Introduction

Participation in sport is often promoted on the basis of the physical and mental health benefits that it provides (Paluska & Schwenk, 2000). Such reasoning, Bär and Markser (2013) suggest, may underlie an assumption that individuals who compete at the highest levels in sport will be immune to mental illnesses. The suicides of German national goal-keeper Robert Enke in 2009 and Wales' most capped footballer and national team manager Gary Speed in 2011 are two incidents which reveal this assumption to be flawed. Enke's death was followed by news that for some time he had been receiving treatment for depression. That few people knew about this is an illustration of how mental illness within sport is shrouded in silence.

Silence around mental illness is just one of the challenges likely to face an athlete struggling with mental health difficulties. Others include clinicians who may not understand diagnostic and therapeutic issues unique to sport (Reardon & Factor, 2010), lack of interest, care, provision and support from governing organisations and stigma and discrimination (Schwenk, 2000). Further, stress and anxiety surrounding competition, a loss of autonomy due to the typical policing policies associated with contemporary high-performance sport, as well as lifestyle challenges unique to sport may increase athletes' susceptibility to mental illnesses (Reardon & Factor, 2010). Reflecting on these issues, Schwenk (2000, p. 4) notes:

> The current conceptualisation of, and approach to mental illness in athletes is fraught with stigmatisation, denial, and dichotomous paradigms of 'psychological' versus 'physical' disease, which are inaccurate, unhelpful, and deprive the athlete of effective care.

A number of high-profile sports people have recently began to talk publically about their experiences of serious mental illnesses (e.g., boxer Frank Bruno, New York Jets receiver Brandon Marshall, gymnast Gloria Viseras and golfer David Feherty). It seems timely, therefore, that in golf, like other sports, we begin to become more educated and aware about mental illness, understand the risks to mental health in high-performance sport, and begin to challenge stigma and discrimination in our 'backyard'.

In this chapter, therefore, we would like to draw attention to how mental health and well-being can be compromised in pursuit of sporting excellence. With a better understanding, we hope it becomes possible to identify and adopt strategies that support the positive mental health and well-being of golfers.

Mental health, mental illness and well-being

A number of contrasting perspectives and definitions exist within the literature concerning mental health, mental illness and well-being. *Mental illness* is a serious health condition commonly studied within the discipline of psychiatry and refers to a range of disorders that include bipolar disorder, schizophrenia, attention-deficit hyperactivity disorder (ADHD), post-traumatic stress disorder (PTSD) and clinical depression (Dodge et al., 2012)[1]. Mental health and illness have traditionally been portrayed as existing along a continuum with mental health referring to an absence of illness, as illustrated below:

Mental health  Mental illness

More recently, it has been suggested that an individual who has been diagnosed with a mental illness (e.g., clinical depression, a mood disorder or schizophrenia) can also, at the same time, experience positive well-being (Davidson & Roe, 2007). This understanding has given rise to mental health and illness, and mental well-being and loss of well-being existing on different continuums, as illustrated below:

Mental health　Mental illness

Positive well-being　Negative well-being

This conceptualisation allows for the possibility that a person can *live with* or *manage* a mental illness and achieve or maintain positive levels of well-being despite their diagnosis. This fits with definitions of mental health which we have found helpful in our own work, such as the following:

> the emotional and spiritual resilience which enables us to enjoy life and to survive pain, disappointment and sadness. It is a positive sense of well-being and an underlying belief in our own and others' dignity and worth.
>
> (Department of Health, 2003, p. 8)

Well-being, for Pollard and Lee (2003, p. 60), is "a complex, multi-faceted construct that has continued to elude researchers". In part, this is down to 'wellness', 'well-being' and 'health' being used interchangeably and, secondly, that "what it means to be mentally healthy is subject to many different interpretations that are rooted in value judgements that may vary across cultures" (USDHS, 1999, p. 5). Definitions of well-being include:

> a global assessment of a person's quality of life according to his own chosen criteria.
>
> (Shin & Johnson, 1978, p. 478)

> A measure of life satisfaction consisting of three interrelated components 'life satisfaction' (a cognitive awareness of satisfaction with life) along with, 'pleasant' and 'unpleasant' affect (meaning moods and emotions).
>
> (Diener & Suh, 1997, p. 200)

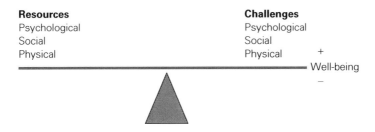

Resources
Psychological
Social
Physical

Challenges
Psychological
Social
Physical

+

Well-being

−

Figure 25.1 See-saw analogy.
Source: Adapted from Dodge et al. (2012, p. 230).

In the development of more accurate terminology, well-being has, in different eras, included the ability to fulfil goals and experience life satisfaction (Foresight Mental Capital and Wellbeing Project, 2008) and to maintain homeostasis while responding to challenges (Cummins, 2010). Recently, Dodge et al. (2012) described well-being as a state where an individual has the psychological, social and physical resources to meet the challenges. Using the analogy of a see-saw, if an individual has the resources to meet psychological, physical or social demands, then the individual's well-being is in a state of equilibrium. However, when demands (or challenges) outstrip resources, well-being dips.

An additional important consideration is the distress that can be experienced due to stigma that is associated with mental illnesses. Critically, stigma and discrimination are sociocultural forms of oppression, located in *others* rather than the person diagnosed with a mental illness. Thus, no medical 'treatment' can eradicate stigma or discrimination – the required change is societal. In recognition of this, the mental health charity MIND has called on sport organisations to instigate policies and practices to challenge stigma and discrimination more vociferously, as these issues lie beyond the control of the individual athlete.

Mental illness in sport

In their review of mental illness and diagnosis among athletes, Reardon and Factor (2010) note that the most frequently diagnosed mental illnesses among athletes are clinical depression, over-training syndrome, and eating and mood disorders. We provide an overview of these below.

Clinical depression (also referred to as major mood disorder) refers to depressed mood and loss of interest or pleasure in daily activities that occurs for more than two consecutive weeks (American Psychiatric Association, 2013). In current times, clinical depression is typically treated with medication, yet there are increasing concerns over the dominance of pharmacological interventions. The 'biopsychosocial model' (Engel, 1978) makes the case that because biological, psychological and social factors can all contribute to the development of a mental illness, an interdisciplinary approach is required to support recovery. A less expected depressive disorder found among athletes is *grief*, experienced by up to 10–20% of athletes, which mirrors the response to bereavement, and has resulted in attempted suicide and warranted clinical intervention (Walker et al., 2007). As with overtraining, grief has been linked to the experience of losing, deselection and the transitional phase out of high-level sport (Carless & Douglas, 2009).

Overtraining syndrome describes an imbalance between the stress and recovery pathways effecting neurohormonal changes, the central nervous system, and mood (Lehmann et al.,1999) and is often linked with injury, losing, ageing, retirement from sport and increased training loads (Reardon & Factor, 2010). A challenge for practitioners is the difficulty of distinguishing overtraining syndrome from other mood disorders (such as depression and bipolar disorder) due to the many similarities. The lack of differentiation, Schwenk (2000) notes, can lead to an increased risk of misdiagnosis:

> the stigmatisation of and denial by athletes with OT, similar to the behaviour of patients with clinical depression, are preventing sports doctors and scientists from a proper study and treatment of overtrained athletes.
>
> (Schwenk, 2000, p. 4)

Diagnostic challenges also exist in distinguishing overtraining syndrome from *burnout*. Research into burnout in sport has been heavily influenced by research within occupational settings where Schaufeli and Enzmann (1998, p. 36) defined burnout syndrome as:

> a persistent, negative, work-related state of mind in 'normal' individuals that is primarily characterised by exhaustion, which is accompanied by distress, a sense of reduced accomplishment, decreased motivation and the development of dysfunctional attitudes and behaviors at work.

In sport, burnout is regarded as a multidimensional syndrome incorporating energy depletion, depressed mood, and exhaustion, yet, unlike overtraining syndrome the symptoms usually include a devaluation of sport and a sense of reduced accomplishment (Gufstaffson, 2007).

To our minds, the symptoms and experiences of overtraining and burnout are very similar. It seems the main difference between the two is the types of research they produce. For example, research exploring overtraining syndrome has tended to focus on symptoms of maladaptive physiological training responses, whereas research exploring burnout has focused more on the psychosocial precursors of exhaustion and depressed mood which include loss of agency, and social and familial pressure to excel (Gufstaffson, 2007). Coakley (1992), for example, theorised from his research that coupled with competitive stress, burnout is in part due to the way sport is socially organised resulting in the individual losing agency.

Given that many athletes treat their sport as 'work' and are often encouraged to respond to setbacks, poor performance or deselection by increasing training and commitment, it is unsurprising that researchers in the areas of both overtraining and burnout report athletes to be affected. Peluso and de Andrade (2005) reported that overtraining affects between 20 and 60% of athletes, with distance runners being most affected, while Cresswell and Eklund (2007) suggested 10% of athletes to be affected by burnout.

Eating disorders refer to a range of pathologies that include anorexia (refusal to maintain minimal body weight) and bulimia (episodes of binge eating followed by compensatory behaviours such as fasting, self-induced vomiting or excessive exercise). While some research suggests eating disorders affect 10% of elite athletes – and in high intensity sports up to 17.2% for males and 32% for females (Sundgot-Borgen & Torstveit, 2010) – other research among male rowers and wrestlers has reported much lower levels (Hausenblas & McNally, 2004), with prevalence similar between males and females (Thiel et al., 1993).

In sports where weight, aesthetic appearance, and/or a lean body mass are considered important (such as women's gymnastics, swimming and distance running), Smolak et al. (2000) suggests there is an elevated risk of developing an eating disorder. Elevated risks of eating disorders have also been linked with the intense scrutiny that athletes' bodies receive (Anderson et al., 2012; Papathomas & Lavallee, 2012).

Mental health and well-being in sport

Moving beyond the most frequently diagnosed mental *illnesses* among athletes identified by Reardon and Factor, mental *health* and *well-being* are also issues of considerable importance. For example, athletes who create and sustain a strong or exclusive athletic identity (Brewer et al., 1993) appear to be at greater risk of mental health problems. Although developing an athletic identity can result in greater adherence to training, improved motivation and expanded social networks (Horton & Mack, 2000), research suggests a strong and exclusive athletic identity frequently leads to under-developed career and lifestyle planning, and emotional and psychological distress upon withdrawal from sport (Murphy et al., 1996; Stephan et al., 2003; Douglas & Carless, 2015).

Understanding identity development and mental health: The role of narrative theory

Narrative theory has made an important contribution to better understanding the links between identity development and mental health illustrating how the process is sociocultural as well as individual (Crossley, 2000). Narrative theory shows how creating and sharing stories about one's life and self makes it possible not only to create and develop an identity, but also for others to recognise and validate that identity. Validation brings acceptance, and an opportunity to become a valued member of one's community (Bruner, 1986; McLeod, 1997; Crossley, 2000).

This being the case the opposite can also occur – that is, some stories may be rejected, disbelieved, or devalued, and the individual silenced, shamed and/or stigmatised. In narrative terms risks to mental health are most likely when (a) stories and actions do not align, (b) when a story cannot be told or shared for fear it would bring shame, (c) when the individual's story runs counter to what is expected and valued and, (d) when the individual has no means to communicate their experiences.

These processes have been illuminated through an analysis of narratives (Douglas & Carless, 2006a, 2015; Carless & Douglas, 2013a, 2013b) which showed there to be three different narratives in elite sport: the *performance, discovery* and *relational* narrative types. The first-*the performance narrative*-is a story of single-minded dedication to sport performance where winning is valued above all other aspects of sport and life. The second-*the discovery narrative*-is the antithesis to the performance narrative revealing it is possible to reach the very top of sport without sacrificing interests, relationships or a multidimensional identity and sense of self. The third type-*the relational narrative*-has as its axis the people who the individual makes the journey with, and the special bonds that are possible through sport.

For athletes whose lives align with the performance narrative, life is commonly described as a '*rollercoaster*' as self-worth and mental well-being rise and fall with success and failure. For these athletes, who tell a 'winning is everything' story, emotional trauma ensues when they are no longer able to sustain their winning identity and story (such as after injury, deselection and retirement). In longitudinal research (Douglas & Carless, 2015) participants whose lives aligned with the performance narrative all experienced a loss of mental health following retirement from sport, which included feeling worthless, depression, emotional and psychological trauma, and in one case attempted suicide.

The dominance of performance stories has consequences for athletes whose lives align with the discovery or relational narrative. Within sport contexts these individuals have their lives, values and actions judged from the perspective of the performance narrative where they are expected to change their stories (and the actions that go with them) to performance outcomes – i.e., winning – as their priority. The process of denying what is valued (such as a relationship, faith or desire to explore) is likely to elicit emotional distress, risks mental health and well-being (see Carless & Douglas, 2015). However, for these individuals no transitional difficulties were observed during retirement or withdrawal from sport.

Mental illness among golfers

> There are advantages to having a mental illness. You know, I tell people I don't suffer from bipolar disorder, I live with it.
>
> (golfer David Feherty, cited in Bonner, 2015)

Having outlined some of the ways mental health and well-being have been conceptualised in sport, we now turn to research among elite and professional golfers. It is difficult to gain an accurate picture regarding the prevalence of mental illnesses given there have been no scoping studies to establish pervasiveness. Further, given that stigma and discrimination act to silence those who develop a mental illness, seldom do people talk about it publically. An exception is former European tour golfer David Feherty (cited above), who has spoken about his alcohol and pain-killer addictions, and about his depression and bipolar disorder. In the course of doing so he also hints that 'others' frequently 'story' mental illness as something that is 'suffered'. This is likely to invite negative responses or even pity, as opposed to the less stigmatising way David Feherty states that he 'lives' with it.

While research among golfers is necessary to gain a better understating about both prevalence and support strategies, research among elite and professional female tour golfers has provided some insights into the links between playing golf at the highest level and the onset and development of depression and bipolar disorder. This research also documents attempted suicide and self-harming, and some of the contributing factors to these behaviours, which include sexual abuse and rape, sexual bullying, and the negative and traumatic aspects of motherhood (Carless & Douglas, 2009; Douglas & Carless, 2009b; Douglas & Carless, 2015).

Alongside the above, the longitudinal methodology made it possible to document the recovery processes using the examples of two tour players, Bernie and Debbie (Douglas & Carless, 2009a, 2015). These cases illustrate a point Schwenk (2000) made regarding the difficulty of gaining an accurate diagnosis when 'mood swings' (joy to sadness) are common and expected responses to winning and losing and the expectations within sport culture where requires an athlete needs to 'look' 'hurt', 'shameful' or 'devastated' after losing, or risk being accused of 'not caring enough' (Douglas & Carless, 2015). Such was the case for Debbie, who was diagnosed initially with post-natal depression by her general practitioner. Later, and only after she had tried to commit suicide, was she diagnosed with bipolar disorder which required psychiatric intervention and sectioning (under the United Kingdom 1983 Mental Health Act), followed by medication and counselling support. Bernie, the second female tour player, successfully negotiated a return to mental health without clinical intervention, but before leaving the tour disclosed feelings of worthlessness and unexplained physical health issues (Douglas & Carless, 2009a, 2015).

A number of factors were essential for recovery. Firstly, each woman needed protection (in the form of asylum) from the expectations and values of those in golf culture (where what is valued is winning and being competitive). Secondly, each required a significant period of time away from this culture, along with access to alternative activities in order to develop a different life story. Through taking on different (non-golf related) roles and activities each woman was able to rebuild a different yet valued identity and a sense of hope about the future (Douglas & Carless, 2009a, 2015).

These studies reveal that through 'doing' and 'talking about' non-golf related activities, and having them validated by others, an individual has the potential to expand their identity repertoire in ways that maintain mental health.

Given most practitioners in sport are very positive about the benefits of sport participation Reardon and Factor (2010) ask us to hold in mind that the development of a mental illness may come about, or be exacerbated by, participation in high performance sport. We see this evidenced in several of the women in the above research where playing golf was implicated in self-harming, cheating, or the onset of depression and bipolar disorder. Alongside this, Reardon and Factor (2010) also make the point that performing at this level may have nothing to do with the development of a particular mental illness and, further, that playing golf at a high level may be a way to cope with a mental illness.

Mental health and well-being among elite and professional golfers

The majority of research in golf has, as its focus, some aspect of performance enhancement – such as peak performance (Cohn, 1991), athlete development, or factors leading to performance decrement (Hill et al., 2010). Thus, mental health and well-being are typically only considered in terms of their effect on performance. For example, Cotterill et al. (2010) note that stress has a potentially debilitating effect upon preparation and performance which is perhaps why a great deal of golf research investigates some dimension of stress. Examples include choking (Hill et al., 2011), the use of pre-shot routines (Cotterill et al., 2010), effective and ineffective coping strategies (Nicholls et al., 2010) and perfectionism (Kang et al., 2016). These studies reveal stressors in golf, like other sports, are complex and multifaceted, but mental health and well-being beyond the performance environment has not been addressed.

Other areas of research that have explored dimensions of mental health or well-being in elite golf include research into transitions and burnout. Factors that facilitate successful transition among tour players include the ability to meet financial challenges and having the motivation and desire to be successful (Douglas, 2004; Pitkänen & Toms, 2016). A common theme among both tour players and amateur elite golfers is receiving psychological and emotional support from family, friends and coaches (Hayman et al., 2014). Important as it may be to have parental support, few studies have examined tensions or problems within these parent/athlete relationships. For example, when parents 'take-over' roles and responsibilities from young people (to allow a young person to dedicate their time to sport) it can result in the young person failing to develop important life skills. When family, officials or coaches rigorously police behaviour and training, it can reduce opportunities for self-discovery and self-direction. Other problems arise when family members place undue expectations on the golfer. Hayman et al.'s (2014) research illustrates that despite these threats to well-being, parents and youth golfers had no understanding or awareness about the risks to mental health associated with an exclusive athletic identity and performance narrative. Without recognition and awareness of these potential hazards young golfers remain at risk.

Research has documented both supportive and problematic aspects of relationships. For example, when expectations of close relatives exert extreme pressure it can lead to the individual attempting to remove themselves from the competitive environment by whatever means possible, including cheating by purposefully playing badly. These types of actions have been illustrated in two multiple-winning female tour golfers. The first, during the World Amateur Team Championships, and the second, in an important season ending professional tournament (see Douglas, 2004; Douglas & Carless, 2015). In both cases, cheating brought a degree of agency. In one case, the golfer had self-harmed for several years, yet this was undetected by family members, coaches or other officials.

The above research also showed different ways governing organisations can respond (see Douglas & Carless, 2015). Schwenk (2000) suggested governing organisations often show a lack of care and support for athletes. When the above research was presented at a conference representatives from the English Golf Union (EGU) and English Ladies Golf Association (ELGA) wanted to identify the young golfer, yet showed no interest in her well-being, or what may have caused her to self-harm and cheat, thereby avoiding interrogating the potential role of golf culture. In contrast, when the research was presented in Holland, Dutch Golf Federation officials wanted to explore ways to change the culture within golf in their country to minimise the risks of self-harming and cheating.

Along with stress, burnout (as defined earlier) has been examined amongst women golfers of the Korean Ladies Professional Association (KLPGA), non-tour members (Kang et al., 2016) and among college students (Cohn, 1990). These studies suggest pre-cursers of burnout were anxiety and self-doubt, and associated with the demands of competition and relationship. Like the research above, a common source of stress for all participants was striving to meet self-expectations, and those of parents and coaches.

Loss of well-being, exhaustion and burnout, emotional and psychological stress (such as sexist behaviour) have been explored through a number of autoethnographies (Douglas, 2009, 2014a, 2014b, 2014c). Here, the aim was to take the reader behind the scenes of high performance golf using a storytelling methodology, thus providing unique insights into the 'lived experience' of an elite amateur and tour professional. These stories at times run counter to what is expected in high performance sport. For example, preparation for competition is typically storied as 'training', repetitive, demanding, arduous 'hard work' that often increases stress (e.g., Therberge, 1980; Cohn, 1991; Crosset, 1995). In contrast, these studies show it possibly for preparation to be storied as 'play' even at the professional level– and as something that can be joyous, fun, and creative, when an individual has agency and autonomy (Douglas, 2009, 2012).

Implications for the game

In the previous sections we identified some of the risks and threats to mental health and well-being for golfers. One of the risks identified was developing an exclusive athletic identity or performance narrative. In this regard the research made the case that others (parents, coaches, relatives, performance directors and fans) play an important role in either contributing to the development of a performance narrative or equally can contribute to the development of a discovery or relationship narrative type. One implication of this relates to the responsibility 'others' have to invite conversations and stories about non-golf related activities, as these legitimise and value alternative actions, behaviours and stories upon which the building blocks of a multidimensional identity are established. That is, if we ask questions about non-performance related things (such as the countries visited, people, politics, food, fashion, or wine) it demonstrates these 'other things' are important, of interest to us, valuable activities, and that time invested in them is well spent. Over time, it is these types of actions (and the opportunity to have them validated through sharing stories) that helps develop 'the person' as opposed to 'the golfer' and makes the telling of discovery stories possible. Those golfers who had a multidimensional identity were less effected by poor performances, losses and transition, yet performed equally well. In contrast, if members of golf clubs, journalists, researchers, coaches, and relatives only ever ask the golfer about performance related issues (such as *how did you do, what's the next event, how did you play that shot*) it demonstrates that *these* things are only what is valued and of worth.

It is likely in doing so the golfer will continue to feel their self is on the line every time he or she steps on the golf course, and that during performance dips it is the whole 'self' that is failing and losing and not just one aspect of life, and that the self that is valued is lost at retirement.

A second implication of the research cited above relates to the limited awareness about mental health, mental illness and mental well-being within golf culture, and the recognition that stigma silences people. In this regard governing organisations might play a more central and active role in informing and educating the golfing community (and especially performers, parents, selectors, and coaches) about what mental illness is and the different ways it can develop. Education of this this type can pave the way for golfers who are experience a loss of mental health to begin to share their concerns or/and feel able to ask for help when facing difficulties. We would like to conclude with some suggestions to give impetus to these developments.

Summary and future directions

Taken together the research presented above shows that mental illness is something any of us might experience. It also showed that should we become unwell, we will cope more effectively if others around us are informed and supportive. When others are informed and educated it opens the way to talk more candidly without fear of oppression and stigma. The research presented also revealed the fragile nature of mental well being and the many factors that threaten positive mental health. In light of these severe consequences of mental health problems for individuals and their families outlined above, it seems greater attention needs to be paid to 'early warning' signs of mental health problems among golfers of all ages and abilities. We would advocate that in the future increased specialist support (from mental health professionals such as counsellors, psychotherapists, and clinical psychologists) should be made available.

As mentioned above, stigma and discrimination can be traced to fear and ignorance of mental health and illness. Both are associated with an assumption that mental health problems are down to the individual, rather than being a collective responsibility we all share. Overcoming stigma and discrimination will necessitate greater awareness, understanding, sensitivity, care and empathy for those who are, or may be experiencing mental distress.

A third area for future research relates to the absence of research which reveals how male golfer's might experiences the development of a mental illness, or recovery, or symptoms of self-harming or cheating. By presenting only stories about female golfers it may misleadingly appear that it is only women who experience problems such as cheating, self-harming, heterosexism or homophobia, or abuse. Is it the case that male golfers do not share these experiences? Or is it the case that the research community has thus far been unable to support the telling and sharing of these types of stories among male cohorts? Recent studies (Douglas & Carless, 2012a, 2012b) show how researching taboo issues requires not only long term investments and close trusting relationships, but a different researcher/participant dynamic than is often the case in sport research. The use of innovative research methodologies may help overcome this hurdle.

Finally, too often, in our view, the horizon of interest amongst the research community is limited to performance enhancement. Under these conditions, 'taboo' issues – such as mental health and illness – will be unlikely to be voiced or witnessed. Broadening our horizon of interest in future research will move underexplored issues higher up the agenda.

Note

1 This is not an exhaustive list; further information can be found in the American Psychiatric Association. 2013. *Diagnostic and statistical manual of mental disorders.* 5th ed. Arlington: American Psychiatric Publishing, 160–168.

References

American Psychiatric Association (2013) *Diagnostic and Statistical Manual of Mental Disorders* (5th Ed.), Arlington, VA: American Psychiatric Publishing.

Anderson, C. & Petrie, T. (2012) Prevalence of Disordered Eating and Pathogenic Weight Control Behaviors among NCAA Division I Female Collegiate Gymnasts and Swimmers, *Research Quarterly for Exercise and Sport*, 83 (1), 120–124.

Bär, K.-J. & Markser, V.Z. (2013) Sport Specificity of Mental Disorders: The Issue of Sport Psychiatry, *European Archives Psychiatry Clinical Neuroscience*, 263 (Suppl 2), S205–S210, DOI: 10.1007/s00406-013-0458-4.

Brewer, B.; Van Raalte, J. & Linder, D. (1993) Athletic Identity: Hercules' Muscle or Achilles Heel? *International Journal of Sport Psychology*, 24 (2), 237–254.

Bonner, S. (2015, December 9) *Rolling Stone*, Available at www.Rollingstone.Com/Sports/Features/David-Fehertys-Charmed-Life-Golfs-Iconoclast-Comes-Clean-20151209 (Accessed March 3, 2016).

Bruner J. (1986) *Actual Minds, Possible Worlds*, Cambridge, MA: Harvard University Press.

Carless, D. & Douglas, K. (2009) "We Haven't Got a Seat on the Bus for You" or "All the Seats Are Mine": Narratives and Career Transition in Professional Golf, *Qualitative Research in Sport and Exercise*, 1 (1), 51–66.

Carless, D. & Douglas, K. (2013a) Living, Resisting, and Playing the Part of Athlete: Narrative Tensions in Elite Sport, *Psychology of Sport and Exercise*, 14 (5), 701–708.

Carless, D. & Douglas, K. (2013b) "In the Boat" but "Selling Myself Short": Stories, Narratives, and Identity Development in Elite Sport, *The Sport Psychologist*, 27 (1), 27–39.

Coakley, J. (1992) Burnout among Adolescent Athletes: A Personal Failure or Social Problem? *Sociology of Sport Journal*, 9 (4), 271–285.

Cohn, P. (1991) An Exploratory Study of Peak Performance in Golf, *The Sport Psychologist*, 5 (1), 1–14.

Cohn, P.; Rotella, R. & Lloyd, J. (1990) Effects of a Cognitive-behavioural Intervention on the Pre-shot Routine and Performance in Golf, *The Sport Psychologist*, 4 (1), 33–42.

Cotterill, S.; Sanders, R. & Collins, D. (2010) Developing Effective Pre-performance Routines in Golf: Why Don't We Ask the Golfer? *Journal of Applied Sport Psychology*, 22 (1), 51–64.

Cresswell, S. & Eklund, R. (2007) Athlete Burnout: A Longitudinal Qualitative Investigation, *Sport Psychology*, 21 (1), 1–20.

Crosset, T. (1995) *Outsiders in the Clubhouse: The World of Women's Professional Golf*, New York, NY: Suny.

Crossley, M. (2000) *Introducing Narrative Psychology: Self, Trauma and the Construction of Meaning*, Milton Keynes, UK: Open University Press.

Cummins, R. (2010) Subjective Wellbeing, Homeostatically Protected Mood and Depression: A Synthesis, *Journal of Happiness Studies*, 11 (1), 1–17.

Davidson, L. & Roe, D. (2007) Recovery From Versus Recovery in Serious Mental Illness: One Strategy for Lessening Confusion Plaguing Recovery, *Journal of Mental Health*, 16 (4), 459–470.

Department of Health (2003) *Promoting Mental Health: Strategy and Action Plan 2003–2008*, Belfast: Department of Health, Social Services and Public Safety.

Diener, E. & Suh, E. (1997) Measuring Quality of Life: Economic, Social, and Subjective Indicators, *Social Indicators Research*, 40 (1–2), 189–216.

Dodge, R.; Daly, A.; Huyton, J. & Sanders, L. (2012) The Challenge of Defining Wellbeing, *International Journal of Wellbeing*, 2 (3), 222–235.

Douglas, K. (2004) *What's the Drive in Golf: Motivation and Persistence in Women Professional Tournament Golfers*, Unpublished Doctoral Thesis, Bristol, UK: University of Bristol.

Douglas, K. (2009) Storying My Self: Negotiating a Relational Identity in Professional Sport, *Qualitative Research in Sport, Exercise & Health*, 1 (2), 176–190.

Douglas, K. (2012) Signals and Signs, *Qualitative Inquiry*, 18 (6), 525–532.

Douglas, K. (2014a) A Truth Waiting for a Telling, In: N. Short N; L. Turner, & A. Grant (Eds.) *Contemporary British Autoethnography: A Handbook for Postgraduate Qualitative Researchers*, Rotterdam, The Netherlands: Sense Publishers, pp. 79–95.

Douglas, K. (2014b) Going Home, In: T. Adams & J. Wyatt, J. (Eds.) *Stories of Presence and Loss*, Rotterdam, The Netherlands: Sense Publishers, pp. 103–114.

Douglas, K. (2014c) Challenging Interpretive Privilege in Elite and Professional Sport: One [Athlete's] Story, Revised, Reshaped, Reclaimed, *Qualitative Research in Sport, Exercise and Health*, 6 (2), 220–243.

Douglas, K. & Carless, D. (2009a) Abandoning the Performance Narrative: Two Women's Stories of Transition From Professional Golf, *Journal of Applied Sport Psychology*, 21 (2), 213–230.

Douglas, K. & Carless, D. (2009b) Exploring Taboo Issues in High Performance Sport Through a Fictional Approach, *Reflective Practice*, 10 (3), 311–323.

Douglas, K. & Carless, D. (2012a) Membership, Golf and a Story about Anna and Me: Reflections on Research in Elite Sport, *Qualitative Methods in Psychology Bulletin*, 13 (1), 27–33.

Douglas, K. & Carless, D. (2012b) Taboo Tales in Elite Sport: Relationships, Ethics, and Witnessing, *Psychology of Women Section Review*, 14 (2), 50–56.

Douglas, K. & Carless, D. (2015) *Life Story Research in Sport: A Narrative Approach to Understanding the Experiences of Elite and Professional Athletes*, London: Routledge.

Engel, G. (1978) The Biopsychosocial Model and the Education of Health Professionals, *Annals of the New York Academy of Sciences*, 310 (1), 169–187.

Foresight Mental Capital and Wellbeing Project (2008) *Final Project Report*, London: The Government Office for Science.

Gufstaffson, H. (2007) *Burnout in Competitive and Elite Athletes*, Unpublished PhD Thesis, Sweden: Örebro Universitetbiblioteket.

Hausenblas, H.A. & McNally, K.D. (2004) Eating Disorder Prevalence and Symptoms for Track and Field Athletes and Non-athletes, *Journal of Applied Sport Psychology*, 16, 274–286, Doi: 10.1080/10413200490485630.

Hayman, R.; Borkoles, E.; Taylor, J.; Hemmings, B. & Polman, R. (2014) From Pre-Elite to Elite: The Pathway Travelled by Adolescent Golfers, *International, Journal of Sports Science & Coaching*, 9 (4), 959–973.

Hill, D.; Hanton, S.; Matthews, N. & Fleming, S. (2010) A Qualitative Exploration of Choking in Elite Golf, *Journal of Clinical Sport Psychology*, 4 (3), 221–240.

Hill, D.; Hanton, S.; Matthews, N. & Fleming, S. (2011) Alleviation of Choking Under Pressure in Elite Golf: An Action Research Study, *The Sport Psychologist*, 25 (4), 465–488.

Horton, R. & Mack, D. (2000) Athletic Identity in Marathon Runners: Functional Focus or Dysfunctional Commitment? *Journal of Sport Behavior*, 23 (2), 101–119.

Kang, K.; Hannon, J.; Harveson, A.; Lee, J.; Nam, J. & Han, D. (2016) Perfectionism and Burnout in Women Professional Golfers, *The Journal of Sports Medicine and Physical Fitness*, 56 (9), 1077–1085.

Lehmann, M.; Foster, C.; Gastmann, U.; Keizer, H. & Steinacker, J. (1999) Definitions, Types, Symptoms, Findings, Underlying Mechanisms, and Frequency of Overtraining and Overtraining Syndrome, In: M. Lehmann; C. Foster; U. Gastmann; H. Keizer & J. Steinacker (Eds.) *Overload, Performance Incompetence, and Regeneration in Sport*, New York, NY: Plenum, pp. 1–6.

McLeod, J. (1997) *Narrative and Psychotherapy*, London: Sage.

Murphy, G.; Petitpas, A. & Brewer, B. (1996) Identity Foreclosure, Athletic Identity and Career Maturity in Intercollegiate Athletes, *The Sport Psychologist*, 10 (3), 239–246.

Nicholls, A.; Hemmings, B. & Clough, P. (2010) Stressors, Coping, and Emotion among International Adolescent Golfers, *Scandinavian Journal of Medicine & Science in Sports*, 20 (2), 346–355.

Paluska, S. & Schwenk, T. (2000) Physical Activity and Mental Health: Current Concepts, *Sports Medicine*, 29 (3), 167–180.

Papathomas, A. & Lavallee, D. (2006) A Life History Analysis of a Male Athlete with an Eating Disorder, *Journal of Loss and Trauma*, 11 (2), 143–179.

Peluso, M. & Deandrade, L. (2005) Physical Activity and Mental Health: The Association Between Exercise and Mood, *Clinics*, 60 (1), 61–70.

Pitkänen, J. & Toms, M. (2016) Elite Irish Golfer's Experiences of Transition From Amateur to Professional, *International Journal of Golf Science*, 5 (Supplement), S59–S60.

Pollard, E. & Lee, P. (2003) Child Well-being: A Systematic Review of the Literature, *Social Indicators Research*, 61 (1), 9–78.

Reardon, C. & Factor, R. (2010) Sport Psychiatry: A Systematic Review of Diagnosis and Medical Treatment of Mental Illness in Athletes, *Sports Medicine*, 40 (11), 961–980.

Schaufeli, W. & Enzmann, D. (1998) *The Burnout Companion to Study Research and Practice: A Critical Analysis*, London: Taylor & Francis.

Schwenk, T. (2000) The Stigmatisation and Denial of Mental Illness in Athletes, *British Journal of Sports Medicine*, 34 (1), 3–6.

Shin, D. & Johnson, D. (1978) Avowed Happiness as an Overall Assessment of the Quality of Life, *Social Indicators Research*, 5 (1), 475–492.

Smolak, L.; Murnen, S. & Ruble, A. (2000) Female Athletes and Eating Problems: A Meta-analysis, *International Journal of Eating Disorders*, 27 (4), 371–380.

Stephan, Y.; Bilard, J.; Ninot, G. & Deligniéres, D. (2003) Repercussions on Transition Out of Elite Sport on Subjective Well-being: A One-year Study, *Journal of Applied Sport Psychology*, 15 (4), 353–371.

Sundgot-Borgen, J. & Torstveit, M. (2010) Aspects of Disordered Eating Continuum in Elite High-Intensity Sports, *Scandinavian Journal of Medicine & Science in Sports*, 20 (2), 112–121.

Therberge, N. (1980) The Systems of Rewards in Women's Professional Golf, *International Review of Sport Sociology*, 15 (2), 387–393.

Thiel, A.; Gottfried, H. & Hesse, F. (1993) Subclinical Eating Disorders in Male Athletes: A Study of the Low Weight Category in Rowers and Wrestler, *Acta Psychiatiatrica Scandinavica*, 88 (4), 259–265.

United States Department of Health and Human Services (1999) *Mental Health: A Report of the Surgeon General*, Rockville, MD: U.S. DHHS.

Walker, N.; Thatcher, J. & Lavallee, D. (2007) Psychological Responses to Injury in Competitive Sport: A Critical Review, *Journal of Royal Society for the Promotion of Health*, 127 (4), 174–180.

26

THE PSYCHOPHYSIOLOGY OF GOLF PERFORMANCE

Debbie J. Crews and Amanda Cheetham

Introduction

Psychophysiology is the study of the physiological representation of the psychological state. In golf and sport it allows for data to be collected just prior to performing motion as an indicator of preparation for performance. Typical measures recorded during golf and sport performance include electroencephalography (EEG), heart rate (HR) and electrodermal responses (EDR) of the skin. These data are often compared among elite and novice golfers (inter-golfer comparisons) and between best and worst performances (intra-golfer comparisons). In addition, different experimental conditions (i.e., increased stress) may be compared to baseline measures of performance and to rest conditions. Psychophysiological measures can also be used in a feedback paradigm. Auditory or visual feedback provides the golfer with real-time indicators of their psychophysiological state and can be used to train the golfer to optimize this. Lastly, electrical stimulation (i.e., brain) provides frequency stimulation to enhance learning and performance. This chapter will provide a basic description of the psychophysiological measures used in golf and sport. Golf research results will be discussed along with applicable research from similar sports such as archery and marksmanship. A research summary, future directions and application of these findings will be presented.

Review of current research

Brain measures

EEG is a representation of the electrical activity in the brain. The number of sensor locations recorded in golf and sport has varied from 1 to 56 (typically 19 or less). The most common locations used in golf and sport are displayed in Figure 26.1 (prefrontal, frontal, central, temporal, parietal and occipital).

Measures of EEG used in golf and sport include amplitude, evoked potentials, contingent negative variation (CNV), coherence and power at each sensor location. Amplitude is a measure of the size of the wave form; average and peak amplitude are most often reported. Evoked potentials, also known as event-related potentials, are recorded and have meaning relative to a specified event. These are the average of multiple trials that then form a wave in response to the stimulus (i.e., the start of the motion). The components of the averaged wave

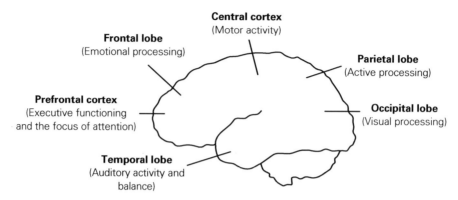

Figure 26.1   Cerebral cortex lobes.

represent different aspects of cognitive processing and decision making (i.e., N1 or matching to previous stimulus, P3 or stimulus classification/discrimination). CNV, also known as slow potential shift, is a readiness potential that occurs in anticipation of an event (motion in golf). CNVs are a slow negative shift in the baseline of the EEG that occurs before the stimulus, while evoked potentials occur in response to the event (after the stimulus). Coherence represents the functional coupling (relationship) of typically two areas of the brain (Figure 26.2). However, multiple pairs of electrodes can be compared for coherence values across the brain (synchrony). In order to measure power in the brain, the raw data is organized into frequency bands using a fast Fourier analysis.

Power represents the contribution of each frequency band for a given period of time. Figure 26.2 illustrates the most common frequency bands: delta (0–3 Hz), theta (4–7 Hz), alpha (8–12 Hz), beta (13–30 Hz) and gamma (31–44 Hz). Alpha and beta bands can be organized into low (8–10 Hz) and high (11–12 Hz) alpha and low (13–20 Hz) and high (21–30 Hz) beta bands. Each frequency band represents levels of processing. Delta is sleep and mostly irrelevant for golf performance. Theta is a meditative state and can be pleasure/displeasure. Alpha is a relaxed learning state; beta represents active processing; and gamma is the harmonizing frequency that unifies incoming information. There can exist a general level of activation in the brain and, at the same time, differential activation in various regions and frequencies specific to the task (phasic activation). For example, increased slow wave power (theta and alpha) represents reduced cognitive processing, while increased fast wave power (beta and gamma) represents increased cognitive activity. In general, the optimal brain patterns have been defined and are presented in this chapter.

Data is collected for a given period of time (epoch) relative to an event (the start of motion or impact). These data are either averaged over the timeframe selected (usually a measure of rest) or compared as epochs (often 1 s intervals) showing change over time as the golfer approaches the start of the motion. The interpretation of the power data can be confusing. If alpha increases in power, then brain processing is reduced because there is more slow activity. Remember, alpha wave refers to a relaxed learning state, and if there is an increase in alpha, the brain activity is slower. If beta (active processing) increases in power, then brain processing increases because there is faster activity. However, if all frequency bands (theta, alpha, beta, gamma) decrease power, then brain processing is also reduced (increased efficiency). If all frequency bands increase power, then brain activity is higher (adrenaline engagement). Therefore, it is most helpful to know the activity in all the frequency bands when interpreting power results.

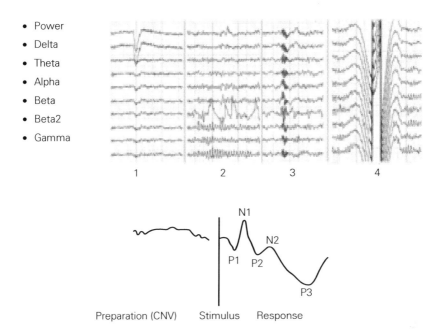

- Power
- Delta
- Theta
- Alpha
- Beta
- Beta2
- Gamma

Figure 26.2   EEG measures of power, CNV and evoked potentials.

EEG in golf and sport

Several measures of EEG have been used in golf and sport research in an acute (descriptive) paradigm. The exception is training studies that either measure EEG pre- and post-*skill* training or the neurofeedback studies that measure EEG pre- and post-*brain* training. One concept that has emerged to explain changes in neural processing is hemispheric differentiation, suggesting that one hemisphere of the brain is active (right side) while the other is quiet (left side) immediately prior to initiating motion (Hatfield et al., 1984; Crews & Landers, 1993). A second hypothesis is neural efficiency, or a reduction in activity across the brain due to the increase in automatic processing (marksmen: Haufler et al., 2000; golf: Babiloni et al., 2010).

EEG research results for golf show that the left hemisphere quiets during the final 3 s before motion, while the right hemisphere becomes slightly more active (nonsignificant) during the final 1 s before motion begins. This pattern creates balance or synchrony between the two hemispheres in the final 1 s before motion begins (Crews & Landers, 1993). Higher right hemisphere alpha during the final second before motion correlated with and predicted 24% less error in putting among 34 skilled golfers (handicap = 3.64). The left hemisphere of the brain includes analytical, logical, sequential processing and is very important during preparation of the shot, but not immediately before the motion. The right hemisphere of the brain is intuitive, imaginative, creative and responsible for automatic functions in the body (heart rate, breathing, etc.). Thus, being in balance between the two hemispheres or slightly right-sided just prior to starting the motion is an advantage for best performance.

Experts tend to have lower overall hemispheric activity than novice golfers, and this is most often referred to as efficiency in the brain. Experts 'best' performance often has higher activity than their 'poor' performance (Crews, 1994). The activity patterns may be influenced by the complexity of the putt (Cremades, 2014). Known outcomes (knowing the ball is going in the hole before you putt it) elicit low activity probably since the processing is complete (Crews et al., 1999). More recently, Muangjaroen and Wongsawat (2012) confirmed that high theta and alpha power in three different brain regions (C4 right side motor area, FZ central emotion area, and PZ central processing area) could predict successful golf putting among skilled right-handed golfers.

EEG signals that represent visual processing are important in many aiming tasks. Aiming while shooting is similar to aim in golf. However, it is also important in both sports to let go of the aim and shoot or hit. EEG was recorded from the visual processing area of the brain (occipital region) in the 1–3 seconds before air-pistol experts fired the pistol (Loze et al., 2001). In best shots left hemisphere alpha increased prior to firing the shot (indicating a quieter left side) and in worst shots it decreased (more activity), indicating continual visual processing. They concluded that suppression of visual attention during the final seconds of the pre-shot period is necessary for automatic shot execution.

The coherence measure between visual and spatial areas of the brain for elite athletes was compared to non-athletes during pistol shooting (Del Percio et al., 2011). They measured coherence (synchrony) both intra and inter hemisphere (between the two hemispheres) in the final seconds before the shot for theta, alpha, beta and gamma frequencies. As hypothesized, coherence was stable among elite athletes and not among non-athletes indicating the importance of functional coupling in the brain for best performance.

Coherence in the brain suggests that the areas being measured are synchronized. Intra-hemispheric functional coupling (within the same hemisphere) of alpha rhythms was related to more successful putting among 12 expert golfers (Babiloni et al., 2011). Both low frequency and high frequency alpha coherence increased with successful putting performance at P3-F3, P4-F4, P3-C3 and P4-C4. Deeny et al. (2001) used coherence measures to examine the cognitive involvement (coherence) between the left hemisphere (T3) and the motor region of the brain (FZ). Results for the 10 skilled marksmen compared to the 9 less skilled shooters demonstrated less coherence, confirming less involvement of cognition as they prepared to perform a motor skill. If the measure of coherence is monitored over time, as in a pre-performance routine of the marksmen, the reduction of coherence can be an indication of the reduction of cortical involvement. At the same time, increased coherence during the final second before performance represents balance across the brain and reduced cognitive involvement because the conscious brain completed its task and the skill can now be performed automatically by the subconscious mind.

Neurofeedback

Neurofeedback is the technique of making brain activity perceptible to the senses (as by recording brain waves with an EEG) and presenting them visually or audibly in order to consciously alter such activity. It is a form of self-regulation that can be used by athletes to enhance sport performance. There are two EEG training paradigms typically used. One paradigm attempts to quiet the mind and reduce stress to enhance performance (football and basketball: De Witt, 1980; skiing: Pop-Jordanove & Demerdzieva, 2010). This approach often uses only one EEG location. In other words, there is only one sensor on one part of the brain that is being fed back to the performer. A more representative approach uses more than one location in the brain and trains a signal suggested to elicit a brain state conducive with best performance (Landers et al., 1991). Archers were trained to increase or decrease low frequency alpha. Increasing left hemisphere alpha improved performance (quieting the left side), and increasing low frequency right hemisphere alpha (quieting the right side) inhibited performance in elite archers.

Neurofeedback (NFB) studies of EEG demonstrate the efficacy of training the brain to enhance performance. Two golf studies used NFB training of different EEG signals and influenced performance. NFB of slow potential shift during golf putting (20 golfers putting 40, 12 ft. putts per condition) showed improved performance (+2.6 putts made) compared to a relaxation and control reading condition. NFB was equivalent to an imagery training condition (+2.6 putts for improving putts made) (Crews et al., 1991). Interestingly, relaxation training elicited the poorest performance (−1.6 putts) of the four interventions compared to the control reading condition. Arns et al. (2008) used an ABAB design to feedback a brain signal unique to the individual from two locations FZ and PZ, while 6 amateur golfers, with an average handicap of 12.3, performed 80 putts in each condition. A tone was emitted until the golfer was able to reach their own personal optimal EEG profile. The golfers were instructed to putt when the tone subsided. During feedback conditions, putting performance improved by an average of 25 percent.

NFB and quiet eye training

Quiet eye refers to the gaze behavior seen immediately prior to an aiming task such as shooting or golfing. Quiet eye and left-right hemisphere EEG measures were examined among expert and nonexpert rifle shooters (Janelle et al., 2000). Experts exhibited superior performance, a longer quiet eye period preceding the shot, increased left hemisphere alpha power and reduced right hemisphere beta power over time in preparation for the shot. This means that as the shooter approached firing the shot, the left hemisphere quieted (logical, analytical side) and the right hemisphere became more active (creative, imaginative, intuitive).

NFB and motor learning

Two studies have examined EEG and performance over an extended period of time in archery. Landers et al. (1994) trained college students over a 14-week beginning archery class and measured EEG and performance. Students developed EEG asymmetry in the left and right hemispheres, heart rate deceleration and a 62% improvement in performance. Asymmetry for the novice performer is important as the student learns the task. It is an indication that only the needed areas of the brain are firing instead of all areas of the brain. This is similar to the fact the novice performers use more muscles than they need when they start a new motion. Then as they become more skilled they use only the required muscles. Since the brain is running the selection of muscles, it makes sense that the same feature (efficiency) is occurring in the brain. Then as the golfer becomes skilled, synchrony occurs during the final second of performance since all the processing in the various areas of the brain is complete. The second study, Kerick et al. (2004) trained novice pistol shooters to quiet the left hemisphere (i.e., increase left hemisphere alpha II) over a 12–14 week program. Results showed an improvement in shooting percentage which was associated with an increase in alpha II (11–13 Hz) power in the left hemisphere (decreased cortical activity). The magnitude of increase in alpha II during the 5s aiming period was also increased following 12–14 weeks of training. The authors suggested that this reduction in cortical activation is indicative of enhanced sensory integration and reduced cognitive effort associated with automaticity of shot execution.

Two studies examining EEG co-activation (coherence) between the verbal-analytical (T3) and motor planning (FZ) regions were conducted during a golf putting task (Zhu et al., 2011). This combination of locations in the brain (T3 and FZ) represents more (coherence) or less (non coherence) conscious interference with performing the motor task. Thus, when the task is learned, less T3 involvement with FZ would be preferred, meaning that it becomes less of a conscious motion. In Study 1, participants with a strong propensity to consciously monitor and control their movements, displayed more alpha II T3-FZ co-activation than participants with a weak propensity. In Study 2, participants who practiced a golf putting task implicitly (via an errorless learning protocol) displayed less alpha II T3-FZ co-activation than those who practiced explicitly (by errorful learning). In addition, explicit but not implicit motor learners displayed more T3–FZ co-activation during golf putting under pressure, implying that verbal-analytical processing of putting movements increased under pressure. These findings provide neuropsychological evidence that supports claims that implicit motor learning can be used to limit movement specific reinvestment.

Thus far the studies presented have been looking at the activity in various parts of the brain and relating the activity with performance, or they have been training the brain using NFB. A more recent approach to influencing learning and performance has been through neuromodulation. This involves stimulating specific regions of the brain to enhance the learning process or enhance performance of skilled performers.

Electrical stimulation

The goal of electrical stimulation when used in sport research is to elicit a frequency change in the brain that will enhance implicit motor learning. Transcranial direct current stimulation (tDCS) refers to excitability changes induced in the brain (cortex) by weak tDCS. Excitability changes tend to last several minutes after current stimulation, and is a noninvasive, painless stimulation of the selected area of the brain. Stimulation of the left dorsolateral prefrontal cortex during motor learning is hypothesized to suppress working memory activity and explicit verbal-analytical involvement in motor control. Zhu et al. (2015) tested 27 individuals who putted with real tDCS or with sham (fake) stimulation. Performance was measured during and a day after the training. Real tDCS training suppressed verbal working memory after training and putting performance improved both during and after training and also continued to show improvement on a later day.

Transcranial random noise stimulation (tRNS) is another type of transcranial stimulation where the stimulation current is varied randomly. The main effects are excitatory and thus, may have merit for motor learning. A study utilizing (tRNS) to the motor area of the brain during golf putting was compared with a sham stimulation condition (Lima De Albuquerque, 2015). Pre, post and retention testing was completed, along with 60 training putts among 24 male participants. It appears that the training influenced the execution of the motor skill by enhancing the endpoint error and variability of the putter face angle relative to ball path at impact during training; however, this did not result in differences in pre, post and retention tests. Thus, motor skill learning was not improved with tRNS.

Clearly additional research is needed in this new area of brain training for golf. It is questionable whether exciting some areas of the brain may be inhibiting other areas, and whether the short term benefits will enhance the long term learning of the skill. Studies examining different types of stimulation, location, duration and retention would contribute to understanding the mechanisms of change. Influences in golf might include: golf learning, golf performance, and potential benefits for golfers suffering from the yips (focal dystonia). Thus, it may be possible for golfers to learn the skills faster by using brain stimulation before they take a lesson. Perhaps under pressure golfers perform poorly and electrical stimulation may be able to inhibit the stress response before the tournament and thus, enhance performance. Clearly yips affected golfers (uncontrollable spasm or jerking motion) may benefit from inhibition of both the stress response and the exaggerated muscle activation associated with the condition.

Heart measures

Heart activity can be examined using several specific measures that contribute to performance (Figure 26.3). Tonic heart rate is the most common and is a general measure of the heart's electrical activity. It is measured in beats per minute (bpm). Tonic heart rate often changes as a function of arousal state in the body. Phasic heart rate is the change in electrical activity in the heart over a very short period of time (seconds) and is most often measured as inter beat interval (IBI), or the distance between R spikes in milliseconds. Phasic IBI can be representative of changes in attentional focus in the brain. Heart rate deceleration facilitates sensorimotor efficiency by increasing sensitivity of the central nervous system to environmental stimuli and thus, represents the intake of external stimuli. Heart rate acceleration represents rejection of the environment and internal cognitive elaboration (Lacey & Lacey, 1978).

Heart measures in golf and sport

Heart rate drops an average of 6 bpm in the final 3s before motion begins during the golf putt and this is purely a function of attention (phasic HR) (Molander & Backman, 1989; Boutcher & Zinsser, 1990; Crews, 1994). During best performance the pattern of HR deceleration takes longer to return to baseline (pistol shooting, Tremayne & Barry, 2001). Older individuals (over 60 years) show the opposite pattern during best performance, meaning HR acceleration occurs instead of deceleration prior to motion (Molander & Backman, 1989, 1994; Crews, 1994). It has been suggested that perhaps different attentional strategies are required of older individuals to perform successfully. Molander and Backman (1994) also reported that older individuals exhibit greater distractibility to self-perceived external and internal stimuli, thus lowering their ability to manage stress. Thus, heart rate acceleration patterns may actually be increasing their active focus on relevant performance strategies.

Heart measures and biofeedback

While heart rate biofeedback has been used to manage anxiety in sport, these studies did not determine whether this change improved performance. One heart rate deceleration biofeedback training study (tonic or phasic heart patterns) in golf did not elicit changes in golf putting performance (Damarjian, 1992). An interesting study (Berka et al., 2010) combined EEG and heart rate feedback among golfers, archers and marksman. The feedback program was developed from the patterns of expert performers in each sport. Feedback training of novice trainees showed improved performance for marksmanship but not for archery and golf. Clearly additional IBI feedback studies are needed in sport to determine the efficacy of this intervention to influence performance.

Heart rate variability is defined as the variation in the time interval between heartbeats or variation of IBIs. Research has linked higher amounts of HRV to good health and decreased levels of stress. In other words, it is the ability to react to changes (internal and external stimuli) quickly and spend less time in stress. HRV is controlled by the two pathways of the autonomic nervous system: The sympathetic nervous system, 'fight, flight or freeze' and the parasympathetic nervous system, 'rest and digest'. In psychophysiology, HRV is considered to be the balance between the two pathways and this influences heart rate.

Two studies in golf have used HRV biofeedback to reduce anxiety (Lagos et al., 2008) and to enhance golf performance in a virtual reality golf game (Lagos et al., 2011). A case study of an anxious golfer training once a week for 10 weeks resulted in a personal record of reducing his 18-hole score by 15 shots. The virtual reality study of HRV training while playing 9 holes of virtual reality golf showed increased HRV, a decrease in stress and anxiety, and an increase in virtual golf scores. HRV potentially enhances general states of arousal in our system and our preparation to hit a golf shot. HRV is not the same HR pattern immediately preceding the motion in a preshot routine, but it can certainly prepare the golfer for their preshot routine.

Between shots HR variability will serve to keep the golfers in a good state and help them prepare for their preshot routine. In addition, HRV may increase resiliency or the 'bounce back' after each shot in golf.

Skin measures

The skin is the largest organ of the body and it is what separates the inside world from the outside world. Electrodermal (EDR) is unique because it is very responsive (1–3 s) to changes in our mental state and emotional response. It represents changes in the sympathetic and parasympathetic nervous system. Sweat glands are used to maintain the body's temperature. The more aroused the sympathetic nervous system (i.e., stress), the more sweat is created and skin conductance increases.

Specific research examining EDR in golf was not found; however, results for pistol shooting differentiated elite and novice shooters and, the best and worst shots from the elite shooters (Tremayne & Barry, 2001). EDR showed a slow reduction prior to the shot and a rebound increase immediately following the shot among the experts. The EDR values were also lower among the experts' best shots compared with their worst shots. The results were indicative of performance states prior to and following the shot. EDR holds promise for evaluation and training among golfers of all skill levels. For example, a golf glove with sensors added that detect EDR could measure when a golfer is approaching stress levels that could interfere with their performance. The golfer could then use EDR feedback (from the glove) to learn to lower these levels for best performance results.

Implications for the game

Thought precedes motion. Therefore, where our consciousness is, prior to motion, dictates which swing will be created and where the ball will go. For learning the skills of golf or making subtle adjustments to the swing, the student can use brain maps to identify swing cues that elicit the desired swing outcome. For performing the skills of golf the participant can test different focus of attention that elicit the desired outcomes. All of these thoughts can be mapped and compared. Wearable sensing devices (with adequate signal detection and processing) make it possible to record and train the best states for performance more easily. Brain-mapping can provide a visual representation of what the brain looks like using different focus strategies. Once the skills are learned and performed automatically by the subconscious, the focus of the conscious (cortical activity) will either enhance or interfere with the programming of the subconscious. Figure 26.3 shows brain maps illustrating the states in the brain during the 1s preceding motion. A novice golfer, made and missed putt, is displayed along with a yipped putt (darker shade is more activity). The made putt for the novice golfer has more synchrony (4 maps are very similar in pattern) compared to the missed putt. The yips golfer shows the strong left sidedness in alpha activity (darker color) that interferes with performance. When skilled golfers perform best they typically report focusing on the 'target' or 'feel' in the final second before putting. When golfers are not performing well they typically report thinking about mechanics and positions. This may be important for learning (motor learning), but not for performing (motor control).

Brain maps can also be used to compare best and worst shots, favorite and least favorite clubs, putting vs. driving, to understand the differences in the brain during the preshot routine. Lastly, neurofeedback is used to train individuals to create the brain patterns that create best performance. Auditory feedback allows the golfer to hear what is going on in their brain while actually performing the motion and thus, train their focus of attention to elicit the desired response.

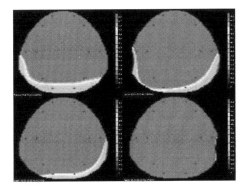 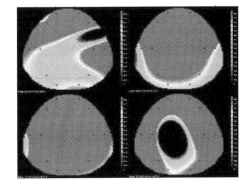

Theta (top left), Alpha (top right), Beta (bottom left), Beta2 (bottom right).

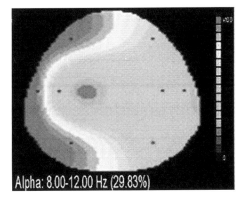

Alpha activity of yips golfer.

Figure 26.3 Brain maps for a novice golfer made and missed putts, and for a yips golfer.

Traditionally visual and auditory feedback provide the training so the golfer learns to adjust the signal of choice. While performing a golf shot, auditory feedback in the form of beeps, etc. can be used to train the desired responses.

Heart rate patterns can also be trained using biofeedback. Patterns of heart rate acceleration (older golfers, over 60 years of age) and deceleration (young golfers) train focus of attention just prior to initiating the motion. Heart rate variability can train post shot and between shot patterns that keep the golfer in the best performance state and help prepare for the next shot. For example, a golfer walking down the fairway could be listening to beeps that indicate their level of HRV. They would learn to manage their heart patterns to be in the best state for the upcoming shot.

EDR biofeedback will train emotional preparation and response to golf shots. Resiliency is an important skill for lower scores. Learning to manage emotions in practice and on the golf course are key to managing attentional focus and performance outcomes. When it feels like our emotions are running us, we have a difficult time focusing attention, and then performance is less than desirable. However, with feedback training we learn that we can manage our emotions and the result is that we can think clearly and perform optimally.

At the present time coaches and instructors find out about the mental side of their players by asking them questions. This is valuable to understand the golfer's perceptions regarding their own decision making, intentions and focus of attention. However, it is not practical to ask the golfers these questions in the midst of their shot. Brain maps provide a tool to visually see differences related to mental states in the brain. Neurofeedback and biofeedback training teach the brain and body to be in a state for best performance. There are so few tools that currently exist for the mental game; thus, brain training is a welcome addition to potentially enhance performance.

Summary and future directions

The majority of research examining the psychophysiological measures associated with golf and sport, learning and performance are acute, descriptive studies. Many of the studies compare expert and novice golfers and also the best and worst performance of experts. While these studies provide a glimpse of signal patterns, they must be interpreted with caution. Factors that influence the interpretation of the results include the time period over which the signals were recorded (seconds prior to motion or the final second before motion), location of the sensors, the number of sensors, the frequency bands examined, the sampling rate of recording, the management of artifact and noise in the signals. Training studies are needed to verify the patterns related to best performance.

The main findings from 30+ years of recording psychophysiological measures suggests that experts are more efficient in their brain and they tend to be either balanced or slightly right sided during best performance (not left sided). These brain states can be trained using neurofeedback. Heart rate patterns for best performance exist. While these patterns can also be trained, more research is needed to verify the efficacy of the patterns to influence performance. Additional research is required for EDR recordings and training. Future directions are exciting with the refinement of wearable sensing devices. Recording and training golfers on the golf course (Figure 26.4) and during competition (recording only is now legal during tournaments) can provide insights into the mysteries of highly successful and less successful performance.

Figure 26.4 A tour player wearing a portable headset to record and to feedback brain signals.

Photo credit: Debbie J. Crews.

References

Arns, M.; Kleinnijenhuis, M.; Fallahpour, K. & Breteler, R. (2008) Golf Performance Enhancement and Real-life Neurofeedback Training Using Personalized Event-locked EEG Profiles, *Journal of Neurotherapy*, 11 (4), 11–18.

Babiloni, C.; Infarinato, F.; Marzano, N.; Iacoboni, M.; Dassà, F.; Soricelli, A.; Rossini, P.; Limatola, C. & Del Percio, C. (2011) Intra-Hemispheric Functional Coupling of Alpha Rhythms Is Related to Golfer's Performance: A Coherence EEG Study, *International Journal of Psychophysiology*, 82 (3), 260–268.

Babiloni, C.; Marzano, N.; Infarinato, F.; Iacoboni, M.; Rizza, G.; Aschieri, P.; Cibelli, G.; Soricelli, A.; Eusebi, F. & Del Percio, C. (2010) Neural Efficiency of Experts' Brain During Judgment of Actions: A High-resolution EEG Study in Elite and Amateur Karate Athletes, *Behavioural Brain Research*, 207 (2), 466–475.

Berka, C.; Behneman, A.; Kintz, N.; Johnson, R. & Raphael, G. (2010) Accelerated Training Using Interactive Neuro-educational Technologies: Applications to Archery, Golf and Rifle Marksmanship, *International Journal of Sport and Society*, 1 (4), 87–104.

Boutcher, S. & Zinsser, N. (1990) Cardiac Deceleration of Elite and Beginning Golfers During Putting, *Journal of Sport & Exercise Psychology*, 12 (1), 37–47.

Cremades, J. (2014) EEG Measures Prior to Successful and Unsuccessful Golf Putting Expert Performance, *Athletic Insight*, 6 (1), 81–92.

Crews, D. (1994) Research Based Golf: From the Laboratory to the Course, In: A. Cochran & M. Farrally (Eds.) *Golf and Science II* (1st Ed.), London: E & FN Spon, pp.127–137.

Crews, D. & Landers, D. (1993) Electroencephalographic Measures of Attentional Patterns Prior to the Golf Putt, *Medicine & Science in Sports & Exercise*, 25 (1), 116–126.

Crews, D.; Lutz, R.; Nilsson, P. & Marriott, L. (1999) Psychophysiological Indicators of Confidence and Habituation During Golf Putting, In: M. Farrally & A. Cochran (Eds.) *Science and Golf III* (1st Ed.), Leeds, UK: Human Kinetics, pp.158–165.

Crews, D.; Martin, J.; Hart, E., & Piparo, A. (1991, June) The Effectiveness of EEG Biofeedback, Relaxation, and Imagery Training on Golf Putting Performance, *North American Society for the Psychology of Sport and Physical Activity Conference*, Monterey, CA.

Damarjian, N. (1992) *Effect of Heart Rate Deceleration Biofeedback Training on Golf Putting Performance*, Unpublished M.S. Thesis, Greensboro, NC: University of North Carolina at Greensboro.

De Witt, D. (1980) Cognitive and Biofeedback Training for Stress Reduction with University Athletes, *Journal of Sport Psychology*, 2 (4), 288–294.

Deeny, S.; Hillman, C.; Janelle, C. & Hatfield, B. (2001) EEG Coherence and Neural Efficiency in Expert and Non-expert Marksmen, *Medicine & Science in Sports & Exercise*, 33 (5), S177.

Del Percio, C.; Iacoboni, M.; Lizio, R.; Marzano, N.; Infarinato, F.; Vecchio, F.; Bertollo, M.; Robazza, C.; Comani, S.; Limatola, C. & Babiloni, C. (2011) Functional Coupling of Parietal Alpha Rhythms Is Enhanced in Athletes Before Visuomotor Performance: A Coherence Electroencephalographic Study, *Neuroscience*, 175, 198–211.

Hatfield, B.; Landers, D. & Ray, W. (1984) Cognitive Processes During Self-paced Motor Performance, *Journal of Sports Psychology*, 6 (1), 42–59.

Haufler, A.; Spalding, T.; Santa Maria, D. & Hatfield, B. (2000) Neuro-cognitive Activity During a Self-paced Visuospatial Task: Comparative EEG Profiles in Marksmen and Novice Shooters, *Biological Psychology*, 53 (2–3), 131–160.

Janelle, C.; Hillman, C.; Apparies, R.; Murray, N.; Meili, L.; Fallon, E. & Hatfield, B. (2000) Expertise Differences in Cortical Activation and Gaze Behavior During Rifle Shooting, *Journal of Sports & Exercise Psychology*, 22 (2), 167–182.

Kerick, S.; Douglass, L. & Hatfield, B. (2004) Cerebral Cortical Adaptations Associated with Visuomotor Practice, *Medicine and Science in Sports and Exercise*, 36 (1), 118–129.

Lacey, B. & Lacey, J. (1978) Two-way Communication Between the Heart and the Brain: Significance of Time Within the Cardiac Cycle, *American Psychologist*, 33 (2), 99–113.

Lagos, L.; Vaschillo, E.; Vaschillo, B.; Lehrer, P.; Bates, M. & Pandina, R. (2008) Heart Rate Variability Biofeedback as a Strategy for Dealing with Competitive Anxiety: A Case Study, *Biofeedback*, 36 (3), 109–115.

Lagos, L.; Vaschillo, E.; Vaschillo, B.; Lehrer, P.; Bates, M. & Pandina, R. (2011) Virtual Reality Assisted Heart Rate Variability Biofeedback as a Strategy to Improve Golf Performance: A Case Study, *Biofeedback*, 39 (1), 15–20.

Landers, D.; Han, M.; Salazar, W.; Petruzzello, S.; Kubitz, K. & Gannon, T. (1994) Effect of Learning on Electroencephalographic and Electrocardiographic Patterns in Novice Archers, *International Journal of Sports Psychology*, 25 (3), 313–330.

Landers, D.; Petruzzello, S.; Salazar, W.; Crews, D.; Kubitz, K.; Gannon, T. & Han, M. (1991) The Influence of Electrocortical Biofeedback on Performance in Pre-elite Archers, *Medicine & Science in Sports & Exercise*, 23 (1), 123–129.

Lima De Albuquerque, L. (2015) *The Influence of Transcranial Random Noise Stimulation on Motor Skill Acquisition and Learning in a Modified Golf Putting Task*, Unpublished M.S. Thesis, Las Vegas, NV: University of Nevada, Las Vegas.

Loze, G.; Collins, D. & Holmes, P. (2001) Pre-Shot EEG Alpha-power Reactivity During Expert Air-pistol Shooting: A Comparison of Best and Worst Shots, *Journal of Sports Sciences*, 19 (9), 727–733.

Molander, B. & Backman, L. (1989) Age Differences in Heart Rate Patterns During Concentration in a Precision Sport: Implication for Attentional Functioning, *The Journal of Gerontology: Psychological Sciences*, 44, 80–87.

Molander, B. & Backman, L. (1994) Attention and Performance in Miniature Golf Across the Life Span, *Journal of Gerontology*, 49 (2), 35–41.

Muangjaroen, P. & Wongsawat, Y. (2012) Real-time Index for Predicting Successful Golf Putting Motion Using Multichannel EEG, *2012 Annual International Conference of the IEEE Engineering in Medicine and Biology Society*, pp. 4796–4799.

Pop-Jordanova, N. & Demerdzieva, A. (2010). Biofeedback Training for Peak Performance in Sport-case Study, *Macedonian Journal of Medical Sciences*, 3 (2), 113–118.

Tremayne, P. & Barry, R. (2001) Elite Pistol Shooters: Physiological Patterning of Best vs. Worst Shots, *International Journal of Psychophysiology*, 41 (1), 19–29.

Zhu, F.; Poolton, J.; Wilson, M.; Maxwell, J. & Masters, R. (2011) Neural Co-activation as a Yardstick of Implicit Motor Learning and the Propensity for Conscious Control of Movement, *Biological Psychology*, 87 (1), 66–73.

Zhu, F.; Yeung, A.; Poolton, J.; Lee, T.; Leung, G. & Masters, R. (2015) Transcranial Direct Current Stimulation Over Left Dorsolateral Prefrontal Cortex Area Promotes Implicit Motor Learning in a Golf Putt, *Brain Stimulation*, 8 (4), 784–786.

PART V

The golfing body

Introduction

Golf is a complex, technical sport with millions of enthusiasts worldwide. This could be because golf has no age or gender limits associated with it, and it can be played as competitively as one would like, making it an ideal activity for all people. Golf also has many health benefits associated with it. The American Heart Association classifies golf as a low-intensity sport, and a moderate-intensity sport if executed without an electric cart. Further, golfers who walk the course weekly demonstrate health-related training effects comparable to those established after walking programmes. Thus, it is well established that regular involvement in golf can help improve the health and fitness of individuals, including both physical and mental health.

Although it may seem like a simple activity, the game of golf is quite multi-dimensional. Once a sport where successful performance was almost exclusively linked to technique, golf has evolved to also include preparation of the mind and body before, during, and after golf participation. This includes attention to factors such as athleticism and physicality, cognizance of one's limitations based on age, injury history, and physique, and physical and mental preparation of the mind and body.

It is well known that golfers will do just about anything to enhance their performance on the course – nothing seems so extravagant or silly when in pursuit of a few extra yards, or dropping a few extra strokes from one's game. As you continue reading through this part, it is my hope that you will find numerous scientifically sound suggestions that can easily be incorporated into a golfer's routine to not only improve their on-course performance, but also sustain longevity in the game. The following part describes some of the most up-to-date scientific research on areas relating to the golfing body.

The chapter by Horan focuses on the physiological and musculoskeletal characteristics of the golfer, more specifically breaking down how six key physical attributes of a golfer relate to the golf swing. This chapter describes how each of these attributes has been tested and measured in golfers, and concludes with the best, or 'gold standard', measurement method for each. This is then followed by a review of the most germane golf studies utilising these key elements, focusing only on those studies which have been deemed methodologically sound in terms of the validity and reliability of the measurement approaches. Horan concludes this chapter by highlighting that there is no 'one size fits all' approach for the optimal combination of these physical characteristics, and furthermore, even the measurement and evaluation of these elements and their direct link to golf performance is fluid and challenging.

This premise leads directly into the chapter by Evans that describes the importance of individualising exercise testing and prescription for golfers. Evans argues that while there is good evidence that exercise programmes for golfers can result in positive physiological and golf performance outcomes, individualising exercise testing and prescription may offer superior results for golfers of all ages and abilities. The need for the application of individual, evidence-informed exercise programmes for golfers that incorporate the well-established three pillars of evidence informed medicine is stressed. This chapter concludes that irrespective of the type of exercise undertaken, it is better that a golfer do some form of exercise rather than no exercise at all.

Strength and conditioning for golf is the focus of the chapter by Hellström, and it emphasises many of the same facets as the previous two chapters. Namely that undertaking strength and conditioning exercises is an important piece in the training puzzle for golfers; however, the exercises should be specific to the individual players' needs as well as to the demands of the golf game. Performing an appropriate strength and conditioning routine has the potential to alter the structure of one's body in a number of different ways, many of which are beneficial for golfers. Hellström details out specific ways that these changes might be achieved, including the principles of specificity, progression, and overload, and links all this back to how this relates to golf performance and different genres of golfers.

Vandervoort and colleagues explore many of the same topics as the preceding chapters, but they focus these matters strictly on older golfers. This chapter describes the age-related musculoskeletal changes in older adults, and highlights how this may directly influence golf participation and performance. This chapter emphasises that golf is particularly appealing for older adults because they can continue to perform well if they maintain their conditioning and participation level. Nonetheless, there are also associated health risks influenced by the fact that older adults' musculoskeletal systems may not be as efficient at withstanding the strain and stress of the ballistic type of repetitive movement found in a golf swing, and thus, special attention is warranted in this population.

Another potential barrier to golf participation and successful golf performance is presented in the chapter by Fradkin on golf injuries. There is currently a paucity of scientific research that adequately describes the epidemiology of golfing injuries, and there is even less information pertaining to appropriate preventive strategies. In this chapter Fradkin summarises the existing golf injury literature, providing information on the injuries sustained by both recreational and professional golfers, how this information is collected, and potential preventive measures that may help reduce the injury risk. Further, the importance of proper mechanics in each phase of the golf swing, along with the common injuries sustained and how they can be prevented is also discussed. Although injuries are an inevitable part of golf participation, they are occurring at a greater rate than they should be, and as such, understanding the epidemiology of these injuries is simply the first step in combating the injury problem. Once this is achieved, studies on appropriate preventive measures will be the next logical step to begin reducing the overall injury risk to golfers.

As mentioned previously, nowadays, successful golf performance incorporates more than simply practice and good technique. The chapter by Close et al. describes one of those other aspects deemed essential for optimal golf performance – nutrition. Nutrition is an important component that needs to be considered by golfers since it can affect body composition, game day performance, recovery from training and competition, immune function, adaptations to training, and general health. Close and colleagues relied heavily on studies performed in sports other than golf for this information, as there is a paucity of golf-specific research in this area.

This chapter discusses the current research into sport nutrition and offers practical recommendations for golfers based on all the major nutrients. Finally, practical suggestions that can be incorporated by golfers of all levels are provided including the timing of food and fluid ingestion, and strategies to help golfers who may need to travel to play golf.

The chapter by Wharen and colleagues discusses perhaps the most common golf psychological affliction – the yips. Based on the incidence of the yips in golfers, it is clear that there are a substantial number of golfers affected by this phenomenon. Unfortunately, this phenomenon is not well understood, and as such, there are very few management and treatment options that have been shown to be effective. In this chapter, Wharen et al., explore the science of the yips in golf, define the current state of understanding of this phenomenon, delineate the controversies of what is known or not known, and attempt to describe the implications for the game of golf. Further, information on how the yips can be detected, measured, and treated are also discussed.

There are multitudes of factors that golfers, and those health-care professionals that work with golfers, need to consider to produce optimal golf performance as well as maintaining overall health. No longer is golf a sport whereby players can dash from their cars to the pro shop to check-in, then run to the tee-off area seconds before their tee-off time and expect to play to a great round. Not only is this scenario likely to result in very unsteady play, it is also likely to result in damage to the body which may end up causing an injury and limiting, or even ending, the golfers playing career. By understanding and incorporating the suggestions from the various topics presented in this part, golfers will be fully prepared to make their best swings from the opening tee shot all the way through their final putt on the 18th hole.

Although there is more scientifically rigorous golf research being undertaken than ever before, there is still much to understand about how to assist golfers in improving their game and avoiding injury. A lot more research is needed in this area, and the concluding remarks in all the following chapters highlight the need for more scientific research, and include some of the more crucial areas of focus. The topics presented in this part are by no means the only areas of importance in relation to the golfing body. Instead, this part highlights seven very important aspects relating to the golfing body, with the hopes that golfers and golf enthusiasts alike can garner a better understanding of some of the many factors that may contribute to successful golf performance and longevity in the game we all love.

Dr. Andrea Fradkin, FACSM
Bloomsburg University, USA

27

PHYSIOLOGICAL AND MUSCULOSKELETAL CHARACTERISTICS OF THE MODERN GOLFER

Sean A. Horan

Introduction

The game of golf has changed. Once a sport where successful performance was almost exclusively linked to technique, golf has evolved to include a heavy emphasis on the physicality and athleticism of the player. Rhetoric around the successful modern-day 'golf athlete' often includes reference to Tiger Woods training with Navy Seals, Rory McIlroy performing Olympic lifts in the gym, or Jason Day using his 'muscular physique' to launch driver shots well over 300 yards. Professional golfers now employ not only golf coaches to work with them on their technique, but also physiotherapists and trainers to help them optimise their body for golf. In general, the modern-day golfer is stronger and more athletic than his predecessor. This is probably in part due to a more concerted effort to improve their physical preparation, and in part due to advances in sports science and athletic training approaches. While corollary improvements in on-course performance are difficult to tease out due to continued advancements in equipment and changes in golf course design, there is no denying that modern-day professional golfers hit the ball further and average less strokes per round (USGA & R&A, 2016).

Relationship between golf swing biomechanics and physical attributes

The biomechanics of the full golf swing has been studied extensively in recent times (e.g., Horan et al., 2010; Kwon et al., 2012). While such studies have not always led to agreement on what might be considered 'optimal' golf swing biomechanics, they have, to some extent, helped focus the areas deemed important for hitting high-quality golf shots. Even among skilled golfers, there is considerable variation in the kinematics, kinetics and neuromuscular control of movement during the swing (Horan et al., 2011; Tucker et al., 2013). The many degrees of freedom within the golfer-club system mean countless different movement control strategies can be used to achieve the same outcome of hitting the golf ball (Glazier, 2011). The strong association between hitting the ball long distances accurately and success, however, has led to the emergence of a number of well-accepted principles relevant to the execution of the golf swing. Biomechanical principles commonly acknowledged as being central to a successful golf swing and the associated implications on player physical development include:

- A proximal-to-distal pattern of movement that utilises the summation of speed principle (Putnam, 1993; Hume et al., 2005) >> *Emphasizing the importance of the larger, more proximal body segments and timing and/or coordination of movement of those segments.*
- Stretch-shorten cycles, where a muscle is lengthened prior to contracting, allowing for potentiation and thus a more powerful contraction (Ingen Schenau et al., 1997; Hume et al., 2005) >> *Emphasising the importance of adequate range-of-motion and flexibility particularly of the larger muscle groups of the pelvis, trunk and shoulder, and the importance of timing and coordination of movement.*
- Utilisation of ground reaction forces to enhance the generation of torque and consequently speed in the golf swing. The interaction of the feet and lower limbs with the ground is a fundamental component of this principle (Lynn et al., 2012; Kwon & Han, 2016) >> *Emphasising the important contribution of the lower body (legs and pelvis) and need for a strong supportive base.*
- Adoption of movement patterns that allow for an accurate and repeatable golf swing >> *While not strictly a principle, this notion highlights the need for simple, 'efficient' and coordinated movements, all of which are influenced by adequate range-of-motion, strength, proprioception and neuromuscular control.*

Measuring the physical attributes of a golfer

In order to determine and document the key physical attributes of golfers, clinicians and researchers have utilised and developed a range of testing protocols (Smith, 2010). While this has enabled the examination of many different physical performance domains, it is important to consider the reliability and validity of the testing protocol used and, perhaps more importantly, the relevance of the resultant outcome measure to on-course performance. For example, when assessing lung function of a golfer, the use of spirometry may be a very reliable and valid measure of total lung capacity, but the measure itself may have little or no influence on overall golf performance. Historically, the relevance of a physical attribute or skill has typically been verified by either collecting data from golfers across a range of performance levels (e.g., high *vs* low handicap) and investigating the relationship between that attribute and some golf performance indicator (e.g., driving distance or handicap), or implementing some intervention aimed at improving a physical attribute and examining whether there are concomitant improvements in golf performance (Hume et al., 2005; Smith, 2010). While this approach has yielded important information about the most influential physical traits of golfers, limitations in research methodologies (e.g., the heavy reliance on cross-sectional designs and correlation analyses), and inconsistency of findings, have meant there is still a lack of consensus regarding which physical traits and associated testing protocols are most useful. Physical measures with an obvious link to the execution of the golf swing and some evidence to support their use are briefly outlined below.

(i) *Body composition:* Golfers, and the fitness professionals they work with, have become increasingly interested in measuring and monitoring body composition (Dorado et al., 2002; Kawashima et al., 2003). Measures of interest have included total and regional areas of muscle mass, fat mass and, to a lesser extent, bone mass. While it does not directly influence golf swing performance, muscle mass is a useful measure due to its very strong positive relationship with the force output of a muscle (Lieber et al., 2000; Weeks et al., 2016). It is also frequently measured in an effort to evaluate the effectiveness of strength-based training programs elite golfers frequently engage in. Common methods used to measure body composition include skin-fold measurements, underwater weighing, and bioelectrical impedance; however, owing to its established reliability and validity, dual-energy x-ray absorptiometry is considered the gold standard.

(ii) *Range of motion (ROM)/flexibility:* While both terms are used interchangeably, ROM is often referred to as the amount of movement of a joint in a specific direction (e.g., hip joint internal rotation), while flexibility is typically referred to as the extensibility of a muscle or muscle group (e.g., hamstring length) (Kendall et al., 1993). The general consensus among health and fitness professionals is that it is more advantageous for golfers to have greater levels of flexibility so they can perform a swing exploiting the biomechanical principles outlined previously (Hume et al., 2005). Furthermore, the joints and regions where adequate ROM and/or flexibility is deemed most critical to the golf swing varies among different professionals, but generally includes the lumbar, thoracic and cervical joints of the spine; the hip and shoulder joints; the iliopsoas, gluteal, hamstring and gastrocnemius muscle groups; and the pectoral and latissimus muscle groups (Chettle & Neal, 2001; Smith, 2010). ROM and flexibility are typically measured during a musculoskeletal or general movement screening. Goniometry is the most common measurement method; however, other less common methods include electro-goniometers, tape measures and 2D and 3D videography.

(iii) *Strength/power:* A central focus of golf-specific training programs has been the assessment and development of strength and power. While it is beyond the scope of this chapter to detail all the different aspects of strength and the training of it, a number of important points warrant acknowledgement. Isolated strength at the single joint level is relatively simple and reliable to measure (Lieber et al., 2000). However, its relevance needs to be considered carefully given the complexity of movement and the differing roles of muscles (e.g., eccentric vs concentric) during the golf swing. Potentially in response to these limitations, the emergence of more global or 'functional' measures of strength and power (e.g., lateral jump distance or medicine ball throw distance) relevant to the golf swing has occurred. Like ROM, the muscle groups in which strength and/or power are thought to be most critical to the golf swing are often debated. Based on electromyography studies of the golf swing (McHardy et al., 2005); however, the most common groups measured and targeted in training programs include the major muscle groups of the legs, in particular the gluteals; the abdominals and other major muscles of the lumbar spine; the major muscles of the shoulder girdle and chest such as the trapezius, rhomboids, latissimus, triceps, deltoids, and pectorals; and the muscles of the forearm and wrist (Doan et al., 2006; Lephart et al., 2007). Assessment of strength involves the measurement of force and torque, or impulse in the case of power. Isokinetic dynamometry is considered the gold standard for measuring such parameters; however, it is best suited to single joint movements and some controlled multi-joint movements. Another common method of quantifying strength includes the displacement of a given load; examples include the number of repetition maximums for a given free weight, medicine ball toss distance, vertical jump height, and number of chin ups.

(iv) *Balance/control of centre of mass (COM):* Effectively controlling balance during the golf swing is touted as a key hallmark of skilled golfers (Adams et al., 2001; Smith, 2010). With the advent of user friendly, economical measurement tools such as portable force plates and pressure mats, the objective assessment of balance is becoming increasingly common. Researchers typically focus on the examination of parameters such as ground reaction force (GRF), COM, and centre of pressure (COP) during the swing, or alternatively use more 'clinically' oriented assessments that include functional postures such as standing with feet together, standing on one leg or walking on unstable surfaces. Examples of clinical based tests with known reliability and validity, include the Single Leg Stance Test with eyes open or closed, the Functional Reach Test, and the Star Excursion Balance Test. While many clinical tests have been found to be predictive of adverse balance events such as falls, their relevance to the execution of the golf swing and overall performance is yet to be fully established.

(v) *Posture:* Golf coaches and trainers frequently advocate the importance of maintaining 'good posture' throughout the golf swing (Adams et al., 2001; Chettle & Neal, 2001). Static posture is typically referred to as the position of the body at rest (typically in sitting or standing), and is generally attributed to the habitual positions individuals adopt throughout everyday life (Chek, 2001). Assessing and measuring posture is more challenging than one might expect. In elite golfers, static posture is most often assessed as part of a musculoskeletal screening conducted by a physiotherapist, and is typically measured according to some subjective, checklist type format (Chek, 2001; Chettle & Neal, 2001). Common postural traits assessed include head position relative to the trunk, shoulder symmetry, primary spinal curvature (cervical, thoracic, lumbar), scapulae position, pelvis rotation and tilt, and lower limb and feet alignment (Chettle & Neal, 2001).

(vi) *Neuromuscular control of movement:* The precision and speed at which skilled golfers are able to perform the full swing is a remarkable motor control feat. To achieve this, golfers need to be able to coordinate the movement of a large number of body segments with accuracy, timing, and speed (Glazier, 2011; Horan et al., 2011; Horan & Kavanagh, 2012). Accordingly, there is interest in assessing a golfers' ability to control movement during not only the golf swing, but other functionally relevant tasks, with the overarching aim of identifying regions or patterns of movement where control issues exist. Neuromuscular control of movement has not always been clearly defined, with other terms being used interchangeably to represent the same, or a similar concept such as dynamic postural control, movement patterning, and movement quality. Like posture, the objective measurement of neuromuscular control is a difficult undertaking. During the golf swing, objective measurement using 3D motion analysis and electromyography can be illuminating, although their cost and unwieldiness negate their uptake more widely. A more convenient approach is to examine movement control during other functionally relevant tasks such as the overhead squat, the lateral hop, and trunk and pelvis rotational movement tasks. The obvious limitation of this approach, however, is the subjective and qualitative nature of the assessment. Attempts have been made to minimise these limitations, namely the use of video and criterion based reference scales (Dalgleish et al., 2011; Olivier et al., 2016).

Physiological and musculoskeletal characteristics of the modern-day golfer

Other than a number of strength based studies, there are relatively few methodologically robust studies that have clearly documented the physiological and musculoskeletal characteristics of the successful modern-day golfer. The following section provides a review of the most pertinent studies, with a particular emphasis on studies that have utilised sufficiently valid and reliable measurement methods in accordance with the discussion in the previous section.

(i) *Body composition:* To date, only a modicum of scientific attention has focussed on the physical makeup of the modern-day golfer. A group of Japanese researchers compared the somatotypes and body composition of six different groups of males, including four golfer groups ($n = 63$) and two control groups ($n = 65$) (Kawashima et al., 2003). The well accepted 'Health-Carter' anthropometric method was utilised, where skin-fold and anthropometric measurements were used in conjunction with standardised equations to calculate body composition. Results revealed that professional and collegiate golfer groups were more mesomorphic (i.e., muscular or athletic) in appearance than their respective non-golfer control groups, and that professional golfers had larger biceps and calf girths, greater body mass index (BMI) percentages, and greater fat free mass than the non-golfer control group. In a similar cross-sectional type investigation of Caucasian individuals (Dorado et al., 2002), professional golfers ($n = 15$) were found to have a similar overall body mass and body fat percentage compared to age matched sedentary controls ($n = 18$), although dominant arm muscle mass was significantly greater in the professional golfers (9%, $p < 0.05$). Likewise, Keogh and colleagues (2009), found no difference in BMI, body fat percentage, and fat-free mass in a group of high handicap (20.3 ± 2.4) and low handicap (0.3 ± 0.5) golfers who were matched for age and height.

(ii) *ROM/flexibility:* Possessing or attaining adequate ROM and flexibility has long been promoted as important for golf success. Professionals frequently incorporate 'stretching' into their fitness regimes. Even coaching vernacular references the importance of flexibility, with common instructional cues such as 'create a good turn', 'develop separation at the top', and 'stay loose and relaxed during the backswing' (Adams et al., 2001). Despite the importance bestowed upon flexibility, there is a dearth of high quality evidence supporting such assertions. Of the investigations undertaken to date, Sell et al. (2007) conducted one of the largest and most methodologically sound investigations of the physical characteristics (including flexibility) of skilled golfers. The golfers examined ($n = 257$) were separated into one of three groups based on playing ability (handicap < 0; handicap = 1–9; handicap = 10–20), with a range of flexibility, strength and balance measures investigated. Hip and shoulder joint ROM, as well as general trunk ROM, and hamstring muscle flexibility were assessed using standard goniometry techniques. Overall the handicap < 0 group possessed the greatest ROM, followed by the 1–9 handicap group, and finally the 10–20 handicap group. The most highly skilled golfers (handicap < 0) displayed the greatest shoulder extension and external rotation ROM, greatest hip extension and flexion ROM, and greatest torso rotation ROM in the backswing direction. It is important to acknowledge, however, that absolute differences in degrees between groups ranged on average between 2-6 degrees, and that the average age of the groups was significantly different (handicap < 0: 39 years; handicap = 1–9: 44 years; and handicap = 10–20: 51 years; $p < 0.001$). This inverse relationship between age and ability, may in part explain the observed differences in ROM between the groups.

Others have in part corroborated the findings of Sell and colleagues (2007), with a modestly sized cohort study ($n = 20$) reporting low handicap golfers ($n = 10$; handicap = 0) tending to have greater trunk rotation ROM, but conversely lesser hip internal and external rotation ROM than high handicap golfers ($n = 10$; handicap = 20) (Keogh et al., 2009). Interestingly, absolute values for hip internal and external rotation ROM reported by Sell et al. (2007) were very similar to those reported for a group of elite tennis players ($n = 147$) and professional baseball pitchers ($n = 101$) (Ellenbecker et al., 2007). Golfers, baseball pitchers, and tennis players all undertake loaded hip rotation on a planted foot, and consequently are likely to require similar amounts of hip ROM in their respective sports. Moreover, in a correlational investigation by Gordon et al. (2009), trunk rotation ROM was found not to be related to clubhead speed (a surrogate measure of skill level) in a small group of low handicap male golfers ($n = 15$; handicap = 5). These findings were not unexpected given the low subject numbers, and the homogeneity (from a skill perspective) of the group examined. Sex comparisons in ROM and flexibility have also been conducted in collegiate level golfers (Doan et al., 2006). Although the premise of the study was to examine the effect of a golf conditioning program, baseline data revealed that males (n = 10; handicap = 0) and females (n = 6; handicap = 5–10) had comparable amounts of trunk rotation ROM in both directions (72–76°), which compared favourably to other investigations of similar level golfers (Sell et al., 2007; Gordon et al., 2009; Keogh et al., 2009).

(iii) *Strength/power:* Of all the physical characteristics examined in golfers, strength and power has received the most attention. Most studies have either been modestly powered cross-sectional investigations, or uncontrolled training interventions that incorporate some form of strength training. Parameters evaluated in both skilled and unskilled golfers have included single joint expressions of strength or power, or functional, multi-joint expressions of strength or power (e.g., medicine ball toss distance). For the upper body, both bench press strength (i.e., one repetition maximum – 1RM) and shoulder internal and external rotation strength (% body weight) have been reported to be greater in lower handicap golfers than higher handicap golfers (Sell et al., 2007; Keogh et al., 2009). Doan and colleagues (2006) examined sex differences in upper body strength in collegiate golfers, and predictably, found shoulder overhead press strength (1RM) and lat pull down strength (1RM) to be greater in males (handicap = 0) compared to females (handicap = 5–10).

Another key area of focus has been trunk strength and power in golfers. The trunk is often considered the hub or focal point of the golf swing, and is frequently examined by researchers. An investigation by Bae et al. (2012), examined isokinetic trunk rotation strength (30, 60, and 120 deg/s) using a gold standard Biodex isokinetic dynamometer in a large group of Korean male professional golfers (n = 51). The study was strengthened by the addition of a closely matched (age, height, and body mass) non-golfing control group (n = 50). Results demonstrated that professionals were significantly stronger (i.e., peak torque at 60 deg/s) than controls when rotating toward the target side (Professionals = 140.6 ± 30.9 Nm; Controls = 132 ± 28.7 Nm; p = 0.012), however no differences were evident when rotating toward the non-target side. Interestingly, professionals exhibited asymmetry in trunk rotation strength (i.e., toward target side was stronger) at all three speeds of movement, while the control group was symmetrical for two of the three speeds tested. The observed asymmetry in trunk rotation strength in professionals was very likely an adaptive response to hitting many thousands of shots toward the target side, and although potentially advantageous from a performance perspective, may increase the risk of injury if excessively large. Others have found similar positive relationships between trunk rotation strength and golf playing ability. Using the same method of assessment (Biodex III, 60 deg/s), Sell et al. (2007) found trunk rotation strength in both directions to be significantly greater in < 0 handicap players, when compared to both 0–9 and 10–20 handicap players (handicap < 0: right = 157.3 ± 31.3%; Left = 154.9 ± 31.5 %; handicap 0–9: right = 136.9 ± 36.7%; left = 138.8 ± 34.9%; handicap 10–20: right = 122.7 ± 33.4%; left = 125.2 ± 34.1%; p < 0.05). Furthermore, trunk rotation strength was significantly greater in the 0–9 handicap players compared to the 10–20 handicap players (p < 0.05).

Lower limb strength has been examined in low and high handicap golfers by a number of different research groups. Sell et al. (2007) found significantly greater isometric hip abduction and adduction strength (% body weight; p < 0.001 – p = 0.014) in low handicap golfers (handicap < 0) compared to high handicap golfers (handicap = 0–9 and 10–20), while Keogh et al. (2009) reported a tendency toward greater lower limb strength (1RM) in low handicap players (low handicap = 96 ± 26 kg; high handicap = 83 ± 13 kg) based on hack squat performance. In the same cohort of golfers, hack squat performance was positively correlated (r = 0.533, p < 0.05) with clubhead speed. Others have confirmed similar positive relationships, with

Lewis (2016) reporting a strong positive relationship between squat jump performance (jump height) and clubhead speed in a modest sized group of PGA professionals ($n = 20$; age $= 32 \pm 7$ years).

The golf swing is a dynamic, powerful, multi-planar movement. Consequently, a large focus of modern training methods has been on functional, or 'golf specific' movements. This has been verified in part by a number of cross-sectional and training studies that have demonstrated positive relationships between golf performance and functional measures of strength. For example, Keogh et al. (2009) reported a significant between group difference ($p < 0.01$, effect size $= 1.88$) in cable woodchop rotational strength in a group of low and high handicap golfers (low handicap $= 69 \pm 9$ kg; high handicap $= 54 \pm 7$ kg). When grouped together ($n = 20$), there was a significant and strong positive relationship ($r = 0.706$, $p < 0.001$) between cable woodchop rotational strength and clubhead speed. Lewis and colleagues (2016) also reported a positive relationship ($r = 0.706$, $p < 0.01$) between sitting medicine ball throw distance and clubhead speed in professional golfers, further verifying the importance of 'golf specific' strength to the modern-day golfer.

(v) *Balance/control of COM:* Somewhat surprisingly, only a handful of investigations have examined the balance of golfers. This is despite many anecdotal claims that golfers have better balance than the general population. Using a rigorous methodological approach, Stemm et al. (2006) examined measures of static stability and dynamic weight shift in a relatively large group of golfers ($n = 51$) varying in skill level. For the assessment of static balance, postural sway velocity (using a force plate) was examined during bilateral stance and unilateral stance on the right and left legs, while the assessment of dynamic balance included examination of the speed and accuracy at which golfers could displace their COP by leaning forward and backward and side to side (without losing their balance or stepping). Analysis of static and dynamic data grouped by skill level (low handicap $= 0$–9, $n = 17$; medium handicap $= 10$–16, $n = 16$; and high handicap > 17, $n = 19$), revealed no significant differences, indicating similar levels of balance between all three groups. Contrasting these findings, Sell et al. (2007) reported lower handicap golfers (handicap < 0) had greater balance during right single leg standing with their eyes open in both the anterior-posterior and medial-lateral direction compared to higher handicap golfers (handicap $= 10$–20). In light of the contrasting findings and the scarcity of balance related research, it is obvious that further examination of the balance of golfers is required, particularly given the rapid and multiple weight shifts encountered during the swing.

(iv) *Posture:* Posture is perhaps the most difficult of all physical characteristics to examine in golfers owing to a lack of consensus on what is 'good' and what is 'poor' posture, as well as the difficulty in measuring it. Formal investigations of posture in golfers is almost non-existent, with only a few anecdotal accounts of postural observations in golfers. Chettle and Neal (2001) and Booth (2005), have both described a number of common postural abnormalities in golfers including excessive thoracic spine kyphosis, asymmetry in shoulder height, and spinal scoliosis (resulting in asymmetry of trunk rotation). These descriptions however, are based on experiential accounts of working with golfers, rather than formal scientific investigation.

The relationship between spinal posture and trunk rotation is particularly important to golfers given the motion that occurs during the swing. Montgomery et al. (2011) examined how different spinal postures affected trunk rotation in a group of non-golfing adult males ($n = 20$, age $= 31 \pm 8$ years). Using gold standard 3D motion analysis technology, Montgomery et al. (2011) revealed that when standing in 45° of trunk inclination there was a significant reduction in trunk rotation when subjects adopted a flexed (i.e., kyphotic; 5% decrease, $p < 0.01$) and extended (i.e., lordotic; 4% decrease, $p < 0.05$) spinal posture compared to a neutral spinal posture. While the results are not representative of a golfing population, they do highlight the importance of examining spinal posture in golfers during physical assessments and screenings.

(vi) *Neuromuscular control of movement:* Like posture, the examination of neuromuscular control of movement in golfers is a difficult undertaking. The general approach by previous researchers has been to investigate movement control during the golf swing rather than during some other functional task performed during a physical assessment. A recent study by Olivier et al. (2016), however, investigated movement control during a number of functional movement tasks in a group of collegiate level golfers before and after a 2-month training intervention ($n = 43$, age = 24 ± 9 years; handicap = 8.6 ± 8.3). Specific functional movements examined included the overhead squat (i.e., hands overhead), single-leg squat, and single-leg bridging. Each movement was scored using a 1–5 criterion based reference scale, with different qualitative descriptions of movement control provided for each of the possible scores. Although no comparisons were made between golfers of different skill levels, pre/post-intervention comparisons revealed significant improvements in movement control for the single-leg squat (pre = 2.4/5; post = 3.0/5; $p < 0.001$) and single-leg bridge (pre = 4.5/5; post = 4.8/5; $p = 0.024$) movements.

Using a different approach, Gulgin et al. (2014) examined the relationship between movement control assessed using a range of commonly prescribed functional movement tests (based on the Titleist Performance Institute protocol) and golf swing faults in a group of mid-level handicap golfers ($n = 36$; handicap = 14 ± 10). Of the movement control tests performed (i.e., isolated pelvic rotation and tilt, isolated trunk rotation, overhead squat, and single-leg bridge), a deficit or limitation in single leg bridging was found to be significantly associated with 'early hip extension' ($p = 0.050$) and 'loss of posture' ($p = 0.028$) swing faults. Although the testing procedures and scoring criteria were not fully described, the preliminary findings of Gulgin et al. (2014) support further examination of the relationship between movement control and golf swing technique and/or performance.

Implications for the game

There is no denying that being physically fit and athletically competent is strongly correlated with improved golf performance (Lephart et al., 2007; Sell et al., 2007; Smith, 2010). While the musculoskeletal, biomechanical, and overall task-related requirements of the swing dictate that certain attributes will always be more influential, individual variation amongst golfers is inevitable. Like a deterministic model, golfers likely utilise unique combinations of physical attributes, each 'weighted' differently to achieve the end outcome of hitting the golf ball. It is essential, therefore, that golfers have truly individualised training programs.

Not all physical attributes are easily modifiable, with some considered non-modifiable such as height and limb length. Furthermore, some attributes are challenging to objectively measure, making it difficult to accurately assess their change over time, and if they are truly related to golf performance. Such challenges have also led to ambiguity in defining different physical characteristics by not only researchers, but also health and fitness professionals. To overcome this issue, consensus must be reached on what the key physical characteristics (physiological and musculoskeletal) for the modern golfer are, and what the most practical and scientifically valid and reliable methods of measuring such characteristics include.

Importantly, the consequences of the increasing physicality of professional golf should not be overlooked. Golfers who choose not to improve physical performance are likely to find it progressively more difficult to compete on the major tours around the world. Conversely, for golfers who do choose to engage in physical training, the development of individually relevant and targeted training programs will become more important in their quest for success. While the human body is incredibly adaptable and resilient, there is also a physical limit for all individuals. Consequently, golfers and health and fitness professionals need to be cognizant of the risks of overtraining, and the potential of suffering a career ending injury when training and playing too close to one's physical capacity.

Summary and future directions

The modern-day golfer has evolved in a way that places great importance on hitting the ball long distances. Data supports this, with analysis of PGA Tour results demonstrating that the long game is a crucial determinant of success on tour (Broadie, 2012, 2014). It is therefore unsurprising that empirical data from investigations of physical characteristics of golfers has included predominantly measures of strength and power, and to a lesser extent ROM, body composition, and balance. Critical review of those investigations suggests that trunk strength and ROM have the greatest influence on golf performance. While some evidence exists to support other physical characteristics, the lack of consensus between researchers, and the preliminary nature of many of the investigations, makes it difficult to draw any firm conclusions on the value of other characteristics. Researchers and health and fitness professionals must attempt to reach agreement on the fundamental physical characteristics of the modern golfer, and how to best measure them if the field of physical performance and golf is to continue to evolve.

References

Adams, M. & Tomasi, T. (2001) *The Complete Golf Manual*, Singapore: Carlton Books Ltd.

Bae, J.; Kim, D.; Seo, K.; Kang, S. & Hwang, J. (2012) Asymmetry of the Isokinetic Trunk Rotation Strength of Korean Male Professional Golf Players, *Annals of Rehabilitation Medicine*, 36 (6), 821–827.

Booth, L. (2005) A Physiotherapy Perspective on Improving Swing Technique in a Professional Golfer: A Case Study, *Physical Therapy in Sport*, 6 (2), 97–102.

Broadie, M. (2012) Assessing Golfer Performance on the PGA TOUR, *Interfaces*, 42 (2), 146–165.

Broadie, M. (2014) *Every Shot Counts: Using the Revolutionary Strokes Gained Approach to Improve Your Golf Performance and Strategy*, New York, NY: Gotham.

Chek, P. (2001) *The Golf Biomechanics Manual* (2nd Ed.), San Diego, CA: CHEK Institute Llc.

Chettle, D. & Neal, R. (2001) Strength and Conditioning for Golf, In: P. Thomas (Ed.) *Optimising Performance in Golf*, Brisbane, Australia: Australian Academic Press Ltd, pp. 192–199.

Dalgleish, M.; Corso, B.; Mctigue, B.; Green, M.; Ajzenmann, S. & Neal, R. (2011) *The Golf Athlete: Ten Test-on Range Golf Screening Protocol*, Brisbane, Australia: The Golf Athlete.

Doan, B.; Newton, R.; Kwon, Y. & Kraemer, W. (2006) Effects of Physical Conditioning on Intercollegiate Golfer Performance, *Journal of Strength & Conditioning Research*, 20 (1), 62–72.

Dorado, C.; Sanchis Moysi, J.; Vicente, G.; Serrano, J.; Rodriguez, L. & Calbet, J. (2002) Bone Mass, Bone Mineral Density and Muscle Mass in Professional Golfers, *Journal of Sports Sciences*, 20 (8), 591–597.

Ellenbecker, T.; Ellenbecker, G.; Roetert, E.; Silva, R.; Keuter, G. & Sperling, F. (2007) Descriptive Profile of Hip Rotation Range of Motion in Elite Tennis Players and Professional Baseball Pitchers, *The American Journal of Sports Medicine*, 35 (8), 1371–1376.

Glazier, P. (2011) Movement Variability in the Golf Swing: Theoretical, Methodological, and Practical Issues, *Research Quarterly for Exercise & Sport*, 82 (2), 157–161.

Gordon, B.; Moir, G.; Davis, S.; Witmer, C. & Cummings, D. (2009) An Investigation into the Relationship of Flexibility, Power, and Strength to Club Head Speed in Male Golfers, *Journal of Strength & Conditioning Research*, 23 (5), 1606–1610.

Gulgin, H.; Schulte, B. & Crawley, A. (2014) Correlation of Titleist Performance Institute (TPI) Level 1 Movement Screens and Golf Swing Faults, *Journal of Strength & Conditioning Research*, 28 (2), 534–539.

Horan, S.; Evans, K. & Kavanagh, J. (2011) Movement Variability in the Golf Swing of Male and Female Skilled Golfers, *Medicine & Science in Sports & Exercise*, 43 (8), 1474–1483.

Horan, S.; Evans, K.; Morris, N. & Kavanagh, J. (2010) Thorax and Pelvis Kinematics During the Downswing of Male and Female Skilled Golfers, *Journal of Biomechanics*, 43 (8), 1456–1462.

Horan, S. & Kavanagh, J. (2012) The Control of Upper Body Segment Speed and Velocity During the Golf Swing, *Sports Biomechanics*, 11 (2), 165–174.

Hume, P.; Keogh, J. & Reid, D. (2005) The Role of Biomechanics in Maximising Distance and Accuracy of Golf Shots, *Sports Medicine*, 35 (5), 429–449.

Ingen Schenau, G.; Bobbert, M. & Haan, A. (1997) Does Elastic Energy Enhance Work and Efficiency in the Stretch-shortening Cycle? *Journal of Applied Biomechanics*, 13, 389–415.

Kawashima, K.; Kat, K. & Miyazaki, M. (2003) Body Size and Somatotype Characteristics of Male Golfers in Japan, *Journal of Sports Medicine & Physical Fitness*, 43 (3), 334–341.

Kendall, F.; McCreary, E. & Provance, P. (1993) *Muscles: Testing and Function* (4th Ed.), Baltimore, MD: Williams & Wilkins.

Keogh, J.; Marnewick, M.; Maulder, P.; Nortje, J.; Hume, P. & Bradshaw, E. (2009) Are Anthropometric, Flexibility, Muscular Strength, and Endurance Variables Related to Clubhead Velocity in Low- and High-Handicap Golfers? *Journal of Strength & Conditioning Research*, 23 (6), 1841–1850.

Kwon, Y.; Como, C.; Singhal, K.; Lee, S. & Han, K. (2012) Assessment of Planarity of the Golf Swing Based on the Functional Swing Plane of the Clubhead and Motion Planes of the Body Points, *Sports Biomechanics*, 11 (2), 127–148.

Kwon, Y. & Han, K. (2016) *Bridging The Gap: Key Principles in Biomechanically Good Golf Swings*, Paper Presented at the 34th International Conference on Biomechanics in Sport, Tsukuba, Japan, July 18–22.

Lephart, S.; Smoliga, J.; Myers, J.; Sell, T. & Tsai, Y. (2007) An Eight-week Golf-specific Exercise Program Improves Physical Characteristics, Swing Mechanics, and Golf Performance in Recreational Golfers, *Journal of Strength & Conditioning Research*, 21 (3), 860–869.

Lewis, A.; Ward, N.; Bishop, C.; Maloney, S. & Turner, A. (2016) Determinants of Club Head Speed in PGA Professional Golfers, *Journal of Strength & Conditioning Research*, 30 (8), 2266–2270.

Lieber, R. & Fridén, J. (2000) Functional and Clinical Significance of Skeletal Muscle Architecture, *Muscle & Nerve*, 23 (11), 1647–1666.

Lynn, S.; Noffal, G.; Wu, W. & Vandervoort, A. (2012) Using Principal Components Analysis to Determine Differences in 3D Loading Patterns Between Beginner and Collegiate Level Golfers, *International Journal of Golf Science*, 1 (1), 25–41.

McHardy, A. & Pollard, H. (2005) Muscle Activity During the Golf Swing, *British Journal of Sports Medicine*, 39 (11), 799–804.

Montgomery, T.; Boocock, M. & Hing, W. (2011) The Effects of Spinal Posture and Pelvic Fixation on Trunk Rotation Range of Motion, *Clinical Biomechanics*, 26 (7), 707–712.

Olivier, M.; Horan, S.; Evans, K. & Keogh, J. (2016) The Effect of a Seven-week Exercise Program on Golf Swing Performance and Musculoskeletal Measures, *International Journal of Sports Science & Coaching*, 11 (4), 610–618.

Putnam, C. (1993) Sequential Motions of Body Segments in Striking and Throwing Skills: Descriptions and Explanations, *Journal of Biomechanics*, 26 (Supplement 1), 125–135.

Sell, T.; Tsai, Y.; Smoliga, J.; Myers, J. & Lephart, S. (2007) Strength, Flexibility, and Balance Characteristics of Highly Proficient Golfers, *Journal of Strength & Conditioning Research*, 21 (4), 1166–1171.

Smith, M. (2010) The Role of Physiology in the Development of Golf Performance, *Sports Medicine*, 40 (8), 635–655.

Stemm, J.; Jacobson, B. & Royer, T. (2006) Comparison of Stability and Weight Shift among Golfers Grouped by Skill Level, *Perceptual & Motor Skills*, 103 (3), 685–692.

Tucker, C.; Anderson, R. & Kenny, I. (2013) Is Outcome Related to Movement Variability in Golf? *Sports Biomechanics*, 12 (4), 343–354.

USGA & R&A. (2016) *Joint Statement of Principles. A Review of Driving Distance – 2015*, Far Hills, NJ, Available at www.Usga.Org/Content/Dam/Usga/Pdf/Equipment/Distance-Study.Pdf (Accessed November 10, 2016).

Weeks, B.; Gerrits, T.; Horan, S. & Beck, B. (2016) Muscle Size Not Density Predicts Variance in Muscle Strength and Neuromuscular Performance in Healthy Adult Men and Women, *Journal of Strength & Conditioning Research*, 30 (6), 1577–1584.

28

THE IMPORTANCE OF INDIVIDUALISING EXERCISE TESTING AND PRESCRIPTION FOR GOLFERS

Kerrie Evans

Introduction

The importance of exercise as an essential component of an individual's health is well accepted (Buford et al., 2013). Many studies have outlined the benefits of exercise for a wide range of populations and conditions. However, whether comparing one form of exercise to another, or comparing an exercise intervention to a control group, the majority of studies have tended to report main effects and group differences with few evaluating individual responses to the intervention (Buford et al., 2013; Hecksteden et al., 2015). The studies that have investigated the effects of exercise for improving performance and preventing injury in golfers fall into the category of group data evaluation. More recently, however, the concept of exercise as 'personalised medicine' has gained more attention, with several studies in non-golfing populations demonstrating that exercise programs that are tailored to an individual's attributes are more effective than generic exercise programs. While there is good evidence that exercise programs for golfers can result in positive physiological and golf performance outcomes, individualising exercise testing and prescription may offer superior results for golfers of all ages and abilities. There is also a need for application of individual, evidence-informed exercise programs for golfers that incorporate the well-established three pillars of evidence-informed medicine: (1) the best available evidence from scientific studies; (2) the expertise, experience and judgement of the practitioner or coach; and (3) the values and preferences of the golfer/s.

Evidence of the efficacy of exercise programs for golfers

Several review papers have emphasised the important role physiological factors play in optimising performance in golf (Hume et al., 2005; Hellström, 2009; Smith, 2010) and, therefore, the need for golfers to undertake physical preparation programs if they want to improve performance (Fradkin et al., 2004), prevent injury (Grimshaw et al., 2002; Lindsay & Vandervoort, 2014), or maintain or improve health-related outcomes (Broman et al., 2004; Jackson et al., 2009). The studies that have evaluated exercise interventions aimed at improving either physiological attributes (e.g., muscular strength, range of movement) or golf-related performance variables (e.g., clubhead speed, driving distance) have been diverse in terms of the exercises prescribed, the frequency and duration of the program and the age and skill level of the golfers. Older male golfers have benefitted, both in terms of physiological changes and increased clubhead speed, from programs that combine progressive resistance training and flexibility (Thompson & Osness, 2004) as well as more multimodal exercise programs incorporating resistance, balance, flexibility and spinal stabilisation exercises (Thompson et al., 2007). Favourable outcomes have been reported for junior golfers following programs that involve 9-weeks of sling exercise training (Seiler et al., 2006), 12-weeks of resistance band exercises (Smith et al., 2014), or an 8-week resistance and flexibility program (Lennon, 1999). Plyometric exercises, used in isolation (Bull & Bridge, 2012) and combined with strength and flexibility exercises (Fletcher & Hartwell, 2004) have been found to influence swing kinematics and clubhead speed respectively, in good amateur golfers. Different warm-up programs have been shown to have positive effects on golf performance measures (Fradkin et al., 2004) with, for example, a warm-up program focussing on dynamic rotation stretches being equally effective as a warm-up program involving more sagittal plane movements (Tilley & Macfarlane, 2012). Overall, the findings supporting exercise programs for golfers are promising, yet it appears that it is more important that a golfer do some form of exercise rather than no exercise, irrespective of the particular type of exercise undertaken (Evans & Tuttle, 2015).

Golf-specific vs. *generic exercise programs*

It has been argued that the majority of the studies investigating the effectiveness of exercise programs for golfers have predominately evaluated generic exercise programs for middle- to older-aged male recreational golfers, where any training stimulus would likely elicit positive adaptations (Smith et al., 2011). Smith et al. (2011) argued that skilled golfers would likely achieve greater benefits from undertaking golf-specific exercises, i.e., those that mimic comparable patterns of motor coordination, in similar planes and ranges of movements, and with similar speeds, compared to generic exercise programs. The concept of golf-specific exercise is not new, but to date, very few high-quality studies have compared the effectiveness of golf-specific exercises to generic exercises in skilled golfers, and fewer still have utilised exercises that would comply with the definition of 'golf-specific' as described by Smith and colleagues (2011). For example, it was reported that the addition of non-dominant (lead) arm strength training to five 'core' exercises produced superior improvement in driving distance compared to core exercises alone in a group of elite (handicap <3) male golfers (Sung et al., 2016). The additional arm strengthening exercises were designed to target muscles active during the golf swing, but lacked exercises that involved comparable motor patterns to the golf swing. An earlier study by Alvarez et al. (2012) compared the effects of an 18-week general exercise and stretching program to a three-phase exercise program that incorporated 6 weeks of maximal strength training, 6 weeks of explosive strength training (combined weights and plyometric exercises), and 6 weeks of two golf-swing-specific exercises (golf drives with weighted clubs and with resistance tubing) in 10 skilled male golfers (handicap <5). The results suggested that the golfers in the three-phase exercise group achieved greater improvement in ball speed and club mean acceleration, but not until after 12 weeks of training. There were several good design features of this study (e.g., both groups participated in 2 months of regular training before data commencement, exercises were supervised, and measurements were taken at several time points during the study), but the small sample size (*n* = 5 in each group) necessarily limited the generalisability of the findings.

Interestingly, and supporting the statement by Smith et al. (2011) that recreational golfers are likely to achieve positive adaptations with any training stimulus, golf-specific exercises and generic exercises seem to produce similar results in less proficient golfers. In a group of 15 male golfers (mean ± SD: age, 47.2 ± 11.4 years; handicap, 12.1 ± 6.4), an 8-week unsupervised golf-specific exercise program performed three to four times per week resulted in increased upper torso axial rotation velocity (+7%), club head velocity (+5.2%), ball velocity (+5%) and total driving distance (+6.8%) (Lephart et al., 2007). The program consisted of a series of stretching, strengthening and balance exercises designed to improve lower limb stability, both lower limb and upper limb mobility, and included golf-swing exercises with resistance bands. In a later study, with a similar population (male golfers; age, 47 ± 12 years; handicap, 11.2 ± 6.1), Weston et al. (2013) reported that an 8-week unsupervised exercise program that incorporated 'isolated core training' (squats, bent-leg curl up, lunge, side bridge, prone bridge, superman, quadruped, and supine bridge), three times per week with progressions made at 4 weeks, also resulted in improvements in clubhead speed (+3.6%) and a decrease in variability for clubhead speed and backspin compared to the control group. While the previous studies measured different golf performance parameters, it would be difficult to argue that one form of exercise approach produced significantly superior results compared to the other for this demographic of golfers.

Golf-specific exercise programs are not golf-specific individualised exercise programs

Although the concept of a golfer undertaking a golf-specific exercise program is popular, golf-specific exercise programs are not synonymous with golf-specific individualised exercise programs. Given differences between individuals, it is unlikely that a group of golfers, even those grouped together based on attributes such as handicap, gender, age, or injury-status, will have the same magnitude of response to the same exercise stimulus, golf-specific or otherwise. That is, even in well controlled studies using homogenous populations, there may be significant heterogeneity in training responses due to the complex interaction of factors such as an individual's genetics, anthropometrics, previous history of injury, disease, lifestyle, psychological state, goals, beliefs, and environment (Mann et al., 2014). For example, significant heterogeneity in response to an exercise intervention has been reported in studies investigating resistance training (Churchward-Venne et al., 2015), aerobic training (Legaz-Arrese et al., 2015), and those investigating exercise for weight loss (King et al., 2008), and osteoarthritis (Kobsar et al., 2015). From a search of the literature, all of the studies that have evaluated exercise programs for improving physiological and performance variables in golfers have reported main effects and group differences, with little attention paid to an individual golfer's response to a specific exercise intervention.

The quantification and prediction of individual responses to an exercise intervention is associated with specific study design considerations and statistical challenges, compared with the investigation of main effects. Review papers such as those by Hopkins (2015) and Hecksteden et al. (2015) have outlined procedures for quantifying and reporting individual responses to an intervention over and above the group's response. For example, in golf research where examining large sample sizes of a specific group of golfers can be challenging, averaging repeated measures to compensate for a large error measurement may be an option (Hopkins, 2015). Pre-post (or change) scores for each study participant, including those in the control group/comparator arm, should be represented visually to highlight the variability in a golfer's response for a given outcome variable, and the means and standard deviations of the change scores should be included (Buford et al., 2013; Hopkins, 2015). Even if there was a significant group effect for an intervention, reporting pre-post scores for individuals in the above manner would assist in identifying characteristics of responders *vs* non-responders to the particular intervention, and could therefore help tailor more effective, individualised exercise programs.

Other than statistical challenges, it has proven challenging in other areas of research to develop theoretical and practical frameworks that consider enough of a person's biological, as well as psychological characteristics to develop effective, more tailored treatment strategies (Huijnen et al., 2015). For example, and perhaps most notably in low back pain (LBP) research, attempts have been made to individualise exercise programs based on sub-grouping patients and developing clinical prediction rules, in order to more specifically tailor interventions based on a set of patient characteristics. Sub-grouping is an approach that recognises that not all patients with LBP are the same, and that experienced clinicians make treatment decisions based on an individual's patho-anatomical, psychosocial, and neurophysiological presentation (Ford et al., 2016). Preliminary evidence supports the notion that patients with LBP who receive a more individualised treatment approach based on sub-grouping achieve better outcomes (Asenlof et al., 2005; Ford et al., 2016). Experienced coaches and health practitioners working with golfers will observe that not all golfers they work with need to undertake the same type of exercise, or respond to the same exercise program in the same way. For example, young, skilled, lean, hypermobile golfers are not likely to need the same exercises as young, skilled, stocky, less flexible golfers. Similarly, not all golfers are likely to enjoy, and therefore, adhere to the same type of exercise program. Thus, it may be that in order to compare the effectiveness of different exercise approaches, researchers, with expert input from skilled coaches and health practitioners, need to first consider developing more detailed sub-groups of golfers, based on attributes such as the golfer's anatomy and structure, functional capabilities, cardiovascular capacity, history of injury and illness, technical skills, psychosocial parameters, and so on. It seems that only then, will the evidence be able to answer the question often posed by coaches and health practitioners working with golfers – what exercises are going to offer the greatest benefits to the individual golfer with whom I am working?

Designing individualised golf-specific exercise programs

The first step in developing an individualised exercise program for a golfer is to understand the physiological requirements of golf, and then whether or not the golfer's structure and function is likely to meet the demands of those requirements. Different approaches have been used to evaluate the physiological demands of golf including muscle activity measured during the golf swing (see review papers by McHardy and Pollard (2005) and Cole and Grimshaw (2016) for example), the metabolic demands of playing rounds of golf (Broman et al., 2004), the kinetics and kinematics of the golf swing (Nesbit, 2005; Nesbit & Serrano, 2005; Lim et al., 2012), physiological differences between skilled and less-skilled golfers (Dorado et al., 2002; Hellström, 2009), and differences in swing kinematics between golfers with different attributes such as female and male golfers (Zheng et al., 2008; Horan et al., 2014), younger and older golfers (Foxworth et al., 2013), and golfers with and without injury (Lindsay & Horton, 2002; Tsai et al., 2010). These studies provide comprehensive information regarding the physiological complexity of the golf swing, and highlight the significant impact different attributes (e.g., gender or injury) can have on the outcomes measured. Nevertheless the majority of authors emphasise the importance of a golfer having optimal muscle strength, endurance, and activation patterns; joint and muscle flexibility; balance and stability; and cardiovascular fitness to reduce the likelihood of injury and optimise performance. Consequently, there has been increasing interest in developing golf-specific physical performance tests (PPTs) to help identify physical limitations, or areas to target to reduce the likelihood of a golfer experiencing an injury, or to improve performance. Despite this increased interest, there remains controversy as to what specific tests to include in a golf screening, and the relationship between performances on these tests, risk for injury, and relationship to golf performance.

Physical performance tests for golfers

Numerous tests have been proposed to measure physiological attributes thought to be important for preventing injury and achieving optimal golf performance. While some of these tests require specialised expensive equipment, many physical performance tests can be conducted in the field with relatively simple equipment, and with little training. Perhaps this is one reason why functional movement screening became so popular – the functional movement screen (FMS), as it was originally described (Cook et al., 2014), involves a series of seven tests designed to assess and rank movement patterns based on a 0–3 point scoring system, and is simple to perform in a clinical environment. The movement screen/tests developed by groups such as the Titleist Performance Institute are based on a similar concept – global movement tests designed to assess a golfer's flexibility, balance, and strength (Gulgin et al., 2014). However, there is little evidence that performance on these global movement tests can be used to identify golfers at risk of injury, or identify areas to target in a golf-specific exercise program to improve performance (Parchmann & McBride, 2011; Olivier et al., 2016). Certainly, in other areas of sport research, there appears to be a limited relationship between the FMS and sport-specific performance (Kraus et al., 2014; Lockie et al., 2015). The complexity of many sporting tasks, the influence of speed and load on movement behaviour (Frost et al., 2015a), and the influence of a participant's awareness of the scoring criteria (Frost et al., 2015b), have together called into question the value of PPTs. Nevertheless, the utility of whole-body movement evaluations may be in assisting in identifying areas that need further evaluation in an individual golfer. For example, determining the physiological mechanisms underpinning the inability of a golfer to perform an overhead deep squat with good technique. Conducting simple tests on-course has distinct advantages, but to develop an individualised program that considers all of a player's biological as well as psychological characteristics, together with information provided by the player and coach, requires a more comprehensive assessment than whole-body-movement screens can provide.

Relationship between physical performance tests, risk of injury, and golf performance

To date, very few prospective studies investigating the relationship between performance on physical tests and risk of injury in golfers have been conducted. An early study in a group of young, trainee professional golfers found that those with a body mass index <25.7 kg/m2, and a right side deficit of 12.5 seconds on the side bridge endurance test were more likely to report moderate-severe episodes of low back pain during the subsequent 10-month period, but this was a small study ($n = 14$), in a reasonably specific group of golfers (Evans et al., 2005). That is, while incorporating a side bridge endurance test in a golf-specific screening may be relevant for young, trainee golfers, performance on this test may be irrelevant for identifying risk for LBP in a senior golfer.

Other studies have compared performance on physical tests in golfers with and without injury. For example, professional golfers with a history of LBP were found to have limited lumbar extension and lead hip internal and external range of motion (ROM), compared to golfers without a history of LBP (Vad et al., 2004). In a group of older male golfers, those with a history of LBP were found to have less trunk extension strength at 60 deg/s, less left hip adduction strength, and less trunk rotation ROM to the non-lead side compared to those golfers without a history of LBP (Tsai et al., 2010). Interestingly, golfers with limited hip internal rotation ROM have been shown to have different kinematic characteristics compared to golfers with normal hip ROM (Kim et al., 2015), and golfers with LBP have different neuromuscular co-ordination strategies to golfers without LBP (Silva et al., 2015). However, these studies cannot determine cause and effect, and further studies are warranted to determine whether these parameters increase the risk for injury.

Several studies have found correlations between performance on physical tests and golf-performance variables such as handicap, clubhead speed, and driving distance (e.g., Dorado et al., 2002; Keogh et al., 2009), but very few studies have examined the relationship between physical parameters and other aspects of golf performance such as accuracy, performance under pressure/tournament conditions, prevention of the deleterious effects of fatigue associated with practice and playing (Evans et al., 2008; Horan et al., 2014), and so on. Additionally, increased awareness of both between-individual and within-individual movement variability in the golf swing, even in low-handicap golfers (Brown et al., 2011; Glazier, 2011; Horan et al., 2011; Tucker et al., 2013), suggests that while there may be key elements worth assessing in the majority of golfers, assuming that all golfers need to undertake the same physical performance tests is too simplistic.

Several published case studies have examined the ability of exercise and/or technical training to reduce pain and improve golf performance (Grimshaw & Burden, 2000; Lejkowski & Poulsen, 2013). To be considered together, articulation of the underlying principles to the approach is needed through n-of-1 trials. As more is understood about individual variation and the importance of evaluating individual response to an intervention, golf researchers may benefit from the use of n-of-1 studies (Senn, 2001). The n-of-1 trial is a randomised controlled trial in an individual patient, characterised by periodic switching from one active treatment to placebo, or between active treatments. While study designs employed to date have provided a wealth of information about exercise and golf performance, in the current era of personalised medicine, when exercise is considered medicine, n-of-1 trials may help design optimal, individualised, golf-specific screening and exercise programs.

Implications for the game

True evidence based practice involves combining the best available evidence with professional expertise, experience, and judgement (Greenhalgh et al., 2014). To date, evidence supports the notion that exercise can have positive effects on physiological and performance variables for golfers, but there is little evidence that one form of exercise is superior to another for any group of golfers. Given the likelihood of individual golfers responding differently to a particular exercise intervention, health practitioners and coaches working with golfers are encouraged to consider each golfer's individual physiological and psychosocial attributes when conducting physical performance testing, and devising exercise programs.

Summary and future directions

Exercise programs designed to improve performance and prevent injury in golfers have been encouraged for many years, and a wide range of exercise approaches have been evaluated in the scientific literature. The majority of studies support the idea that it is more important that a golfer do some form of exercise rather than no exercise, irrespective of the type of exercise undertaken. While golf-specific exercises have been advocated, particularly for skilled golfers, there is currently little evidence that golf-specific exercises offer greater benefit over generic exercise programs. However, the lack of difference in outcomes between exercise approaches may be a function of the more common study design which compares two (or more) groups, where every member of the group receives the same intervention. As in other areas of research, it is highly unlikely that an individual golfer will respond to the same exercise intervention in the same way. Researchers need to consider statistical and methodological designs that will allow the evaluation of individual responses to an exercise intervention. In the meantime, health practitioners and coaches working with golfers are encouraged to combine the best available evidence with the values and preferences of the golfer with whom they are working. Only a truly collaborative approach is likely to result in optimal golf performance.

References

Alvarez, M.; Sedano, S.; Cuadrado, G. & Redondo, J. (2012) Effects of an 18-Week Strength Training Program on Low-Handicap Golfers' Performance, *Journal of Strength and Conditioning Research*, 26 (4), 1110–1121.

Asenlof, P.; Denison, E. & Lindberg, P. (2005) Individually Tailored Treatment Targeting Motor Behavior, Cognition, and Disability: 2 Experimental Single-case Studies of Patients with Recurrent and Persistent Musculoskeletal Pain in Primary Health Care, *Physical Therapy*, 85 (10), 1061–1077.

Broman, G.; Johnsson, L. & Kaijser, L. (2004) Golf: A High Intensity Interval Activity for Elderly Men, *Aging Clinical and Experimental Research*, 16 (5), 375–381.

Brown, S.; Nevill, A.; Monk, S.; Otto, S.; Selbie, W. & Wallace, E. (2011) Determination of the Swing Technique Characteristics and Performance Outcome Relationship in Golf Driving for Low Handicap Female Golfers, *Journal of Sports Sciences*, 29 (14), 1483–1491.

Buford, T.; Roberts, M. & Church, T. (2013) Toward Exercise as Personalized Medicine, *Sports Medicine*, 43 (3), 157–165.

Bull, M. & Bridge, M. (2012) The Effect of an 8-Week Plyometric Exercise Program on Golf Swing Kinematics, *International Journal of Golf Science*, 1 (1), 42–53.

Churchward-Venne, T.; Tieland, M.; Verdijk, L.; Leenders, M.; Dirks, M.; De Groot, L. & Van Loon, L. (2015) There Are No Nonresponders to Resistance-type Exercise Training in Older Men and Women, *Journal of the American Medical Directors Association*, 16 (5), 400–411.

Cole, M. & Grimshaw, P. (2016) The Biomechanics of the Modern Golf Swing: Implications for Lower Back Injuries, *Sports Medicine*, 46 (3), 339–351.

Cook, G.; Burton, L.; Hoogenboom, B. & Voight, M. (2014) Functional Movement Screening: The Use of Fundamental Movements as an Assessment of Function-Part 2, *International Journal of Sports Physical Therapy*, 9 (4), 549–563.

Dorado, C.; Sanchis Moysi, J.; Vicente, G.; Serrano, J.; Rodriguez, L. & Calbet, J. (2002) Bone Mass, Bone Mineral Density and Muscle Mass in Professional Golfers, *Journal of Sports Science*, 20 (8), 591–597.

Evans, K.; Refshauge, K.; Adams, R. & Aliprandi, L. (2005) Predictors of Low Back Pain in Young Elite Golfers: A Preliminary Study, *Physical Therapy in Sport*, 6 (3), 122–130.

Evans, K.; Refshauge, K.; Adams, R. & Barrett, R. (2008) Swing Kinematics in Skilled Male Golfers Following Putting Practice, *Journal of Orthopaedic and Sports Physical Therapy*, 38 (7), 425–433.

Evans, K. & Tuttle, N. (2015) Improving Performance in Golf: Current Research and Implications from a Clinical Perspective, *Brazilian Journal of Physical Therapy*, 19 (5), 381–389.

Fletcher, I. & Hartwell, M. (2004) Effect of an 8-Week Combined Weights and Plyometrics Training Program on Golf Drive Performance, *Journal of Strength and Conditioning Research*, 18 (1), 59–62.

Ford, J.; Hahne, A.; Surkitt, L.; Chan, A.; Richards, M.; Slater, S.; Hinman, R.; Pizzari, T.; Davidson, M. & Taylor, N. (2016) Individualised Physiotherapy as an Adjunct to Guideline-based Advice for Low Back Disorders in Primary Care: A Randomised Controlled Trial, *British Journal of Sports Medicine*, 50 (4), 237–245.

Foxworth, J.; Millar, A.; Long, B.; Way, M.; Vellucci, M. & Vogler, J. (2013) Hip Joint Torques During the Golf Swing of Young and Senior Healthy Males, *Journal of Orthopaedic and Sports Physical Therapy*, 43 (9), 660–665.

Fradkin, A.; Sherman, C. & Finch, C. (2004) Improving Golf Performance with a Warm Up Conditioning Programme, *British Journal of Sports Medicine*, 38 (6), 762–765.

Frost, D.; Beach, T.; Callaghan, J. & McGill, S. (2015a) The Influence of Load and Speed on Individuals' Movement Behavior, *Journal of Strength and Conditioning Research*, 29 (9), 2417–2425.

Frost, D.; Beach, T.; Callaghan, J. & McGill, S. (2015b) FMS Scores Change with Performers' Knowledge of the Grading Criteria-Are General Whole-Body Movement Screens Capturing "Dysfunction"? *Journal of Strength and Conditioning Research*, 29 (11), 3037–3044.

Glazier, P. (2011) Movement Variability in the Golf Swing: Theoretical, Methodological, and Practical Issues, *Research Quarterly for Exercise and Sport*, 82 (2), 157–161.

Greenhalgh, T.; Howick, J. & Maskrey, N. (2014) Evidence Based Medicine: A Movement in Crisis? *British Medical Journal*, 13 (348), G3725.

Grimshaw, P.; Giles, A.; Tong, R. & Grimmer, K. (2002) Lower Back and Elbow Injuries in Golf, *Sports Medicine*, 32 (10), 655–666.

Grimshaw, P. & Burden, A. (2000) Case Report: Reduction of Low Back Pain in a Professional Golfer, *Medicine and Science in Sports and Exercise*, 32 (10), 1667–1673.

Gulgin, H.; Schulte, B. & Crawley, A. (2014) Correlation of Titleist Performance Institute (TPI) Level 1 Movement Screens and Golf Swing Faults, *Journal of Strength and Conditioning Research*, 28 (2), 534–539.

Hecksteden, A.; Kraushaar, J.; Scharhag-Rosenberger, F.; Theisen, D.; Senn, S. & Meyer, T. (2015) Individual Response to Exercise Training – A Statistical Perspective, *Journal of Applied Physiology*, 118 (12), 1450–1459.

Hellström, J. (2009) Competitive Elite Golf: A Review of the Relationships Between Playing Results, Technique and Physique, *Sports Medicine*, 39 (9), 723–741.

Hopkins, W. (2015) Individual Responses Made Easy, *Journal of Applied Physiology*, 118 (12), 1444–1446.

Horan, S.; Evans, K. & Kavanagh, J. (2011) Movement Variability in the Golf Swing of Male and Female Skilled Golfers, *Medicine and Science in Sports and Exercise*, 43 (8), 1474–1483.

Horan, S.; Evans, K.; Morris, N. & Kavanagh, J. (2014) Swing Kinematics of Male and Female Skilled Golfers Following Prolonged Putting Practice, *Journal of Sports Science*, 32 (9), 810–816.

Huijnen, I.; Rusu, A.; Scholich, S.; Meloto, C. & Diatchenko, L. (2015) Subgrouping of Low Back Pain Patients for Targeting Treatments Evidence from Genetic, Psychological, and Activity-Related Behavioral Approaches, *Clinical Journal of Pain*, 31 (2), 123–132.

Hume, P.; Keogh, J. & Reid, D. (2005) The Role of Biomechanics in Maximising Distance and Accuracy of Golf Shots, *Sports Medicine*, 35 (5), 429–449.

Jackson, J.; Smith, J.; Shah, J.; Wisniewski, S. & Dahm, D. (2009) Golf After Total Knee Arthroplasty: Do Patients Return to Walking the Course? *The American Journal of Sports Medicine*, 37 (11), 2201–2204.

Keogh, J.; Marnewick, M.; Maulder, P.; Nortje, J.; Hume, P. & Bradshaw, E. (2009) Are Anthropometric, Flexibility, Muscular Strength, and Endurance Variables Related to Clubhead Velocity in Low- and High-Handicap Golfers? *Journal of Strength and Conditioning Research*, 23 (6), 1841–1850.

Kim, S.; You, J.; Kwon, O. & Yi, C. (2015) Lumbopelvic Kinematic Characteristics of Golfers with Limited Hip Rotation, *American Journal of Sports Medicine*, 43 (1), 113–120.

King, N.; Hopkins, M.; Caudwell, P.; Stubbs, R. & Blundell, J. (2008) Individual Variability Following 12 Weeks of Supervised Exercise: Identification and Characterization of Compensation for Exercise-Induced Weight Loss, *International Journal of Obesity*, 32 (1), 177–184.

Kobsar, D.; Osis, S.; Hettinga, B. & Ferber, R. (2015) Gait Biomechanics and Patient-Reported Function as Predictors of Response to a Hip Strengthening Exercise Intervention in Patients with Knee Osteoarthritis, *Plos One*, 10 (10), E0139923.

Kraus, K.; Schutz, E.; Taylor, W. & Doyscher, R. (2014) Efficacy of the Functional Movement Screen: A Review, *Journal of Strength and Conditioning Research*, 28 (12), 3571–3584.

Legaz-Arrese, A.; Lopez-Laval, I.; George, K.; Puente-Lanzarote, J.; Moliner-Urdiales, D.; Ayala-Tajuelo, V.; Mayolas-Pi, C. & Reverter-Masia, J. (2015) Individual Variability in Cardiac Biomarker Release After 30 min of High-Intensity Rowing in Elite and Amateur Athletes, *Applied Physiology, Nutrition, and Metabolism*, 40 (9), 951–958.

Lejkowski, P. & Poulsen, E. (2013) Elimination of Intermittent Chronic Low Back Pain in a Recreational Golfer Following Improvement of Hip Range of Motion Impairments, *Journal of Bodywork and Movement Therapies*, 17 (4), 448–452.

Lennon, H. (1999) *Physiological Profiling and Physical Conditioning for Elite Golfers,* Paper Presented at the Science and Golf III, World Scientific Congress of Golf, St. Andrews, UK.

Lephart, S.; Smoliga, J.; Myers, J.; Sell, T. & Tsai, Y. (2007) An Eight-Week Golf-Specific Exercise Program Improves Physical Characteristics, Swing Mechanics, and Golf Performance in Recreational Golfers, *Journal of Strength and Conditioning Research*, 21 (3), 860–869.

Lim, Y.; Chow, J. & Chae, W. (2012) Lumbar Spinal Loads and Muscle Activity During a Golf Swing, *Sports Biomechanics*, 11 (2), 197–211.

Lindsay, D. & Horton, J. (2002) Comparison of Spine Motion in Elite Golfers with and Without Low Back Pain, *Journal of Sports Sciences*, 20 (8), 599–605.

Lindsay, D. & Vandervoort, A. (2014) Golf-Related Low Back Pain: A Review of Causative Factors and Prevention Strategies, *Asian Journal of Sports Medicine*, 5 (4), E24289.

Lockie, R.; Schultz, A.; Jordan, C.; Callaghan, S.; Jeffriess, M. & Luczo, T. (2015) Can Selected Functional Movement Screen Assessments Be Used to Identify Movement Deficiencies that Could Affect Multidirectional Speed and Jump Performance? *Journal of Strength and Conditioning Research*, 29 (1), 195–205.

Mann, T.; Lamberts, R. & Lambert, M. (2014). High Responders and Low Responders: Factors Associated with Individual Variation in Response to Standardized Training, *Sports Medicine*, 44 (8), 1113–1124.

McHardy, A. & Pollard, H. (2005) Muscle Activity During the Golf Swing, *British Journal of Sports Medicine*, 39 (11), 799–804.

Nesbit, S. (2005) A Three Dimensional Kinematic and Kinetic Study of the Golf Swing, *Journal of Sports Science and Medicine*, 4 (4), 499–519.

Nesbit, S. & Serrano, M. (2005) Work and Power Analysis of the Golf Swing, *Journal of Sports Science and Medicine*, 4 (4), 520–533.

Olivier, M.; Horan, S.; Evans, K. & Keogh, J. (2016) The Effect of a Seven Week Long, One Session Per Week Exercise Program on Golf Swing Performance and Musculoskeletal Measures, *Journal of Strength & Conditioning Research*, 11 (4), 610–618.

Parchmann, C. & McBride, J. (2011) Relationship Between Functional Movement Screen and Athletic Performance, *Journal of Strength and Conditioning Research*, 25 (12), 3378–3384.

Seiler, S.; Skaanes, P.; Kirkesola, G. & Katch, F. (2006) Effects of Sling Exercise Training on Maximal Clubhead Velocity in Junior Golfers, *Medicine & Science in Sports & Exercise*, 38 (5), S286.

Senn, S. (2001) Individual Therapy: New Dawn or False Dawn? *Drug Information Journal*, 35 (4), 1479–1494.

Silva, L.; Vaz, J.; Castro, M.; Serranho, P.; Cabri, J. & Pezarat-Correia, P. (2015) Recurrence Quantification Analysis and Support Vector Machines for Golf Handicap and Low Back Pain EMG Classification, *Journal of Electromyography and Kinesiology*, 25 (4), 637–647.

Smith, C.; Callister, R. & Lubans, D. (2011) A Systematic Review of Strength and Conditioning Programmes Designed to Improve Fitness Characteristics in Golfers, *Journal of Sports Sciences*, 29 (9), 933–943.

Smith, C.; Lubans, D. & Callister, R. (2014) The Effects of Resistance Training on Junior Golfers' Strength and On-Course Performance, *International Journal of Golf Science*, 3 (2), 128–144.

Smith, M. (2010) The Role of Physiology in the Development of Golf Performance, *Sports Medicine*, 40 (8), 635–655.

Sung, D.; Park, S.; Kim, S.; Kwon, M. & Lim, Y. (2016) Effects of Core and Non-Dominant Arm Strength Training on Drive Distance in Elite Golfers, *Journal of Sport and Health Science*, 5 (2), 219–225.

Thompson, C.; Cobb, K. & Blackwell, J. (2007) Functional Training Improves Club Head Speed and Functional Fitness in Older Golfers, *Journal of Strength and Conditioning Research*, 21 (1), 131–137.

Thompson, C. & Osness, W. (2004) Effects of an 8-Week Multimodal Exercise Program on Strength, Flexibility, and Golf Performance in 55- to 79-Year-Old Men, *Journal of Aging And Physical Activity*, 12 (2), 144–156.

Tilley, N. & Macfarlane, A. (2012) Effects of Different Warm-Up Programs on Golf Performance in Elite Male Golfers, *International Journal of Sports Physical Therapy*, 7 (4), 388–395.

Tsai, Y.; Sell, T.; Smoliga, J.; Myers, J.; Learman, K. & Lephart, S. (2010) A Comparison of Physical Characteristics and Swing Mechanics Between Golfers with and Without a History of Low Back Pain, *Journal of Orthopaedic and Sports Physical Therapy*, 40 (7), 430–438.

Tucker, C.; Anderson, R. & Kenny, I. (2013) Is Outcome Related to Movement Variability in Golf? *Sports Biomechanics*, 12 (4), 343–354.

Vad, V.; Bhat, A.; Basrai, D.; Gebeh, A.; Aspergren, D. & Andrews, J. (2004) Low Back Pain in Professional Golfers: The Role of Associated Hip and Low Back Range-of-Motion Deficits, *American Journal of Sports Medicine*, 32 (2), 494–497.

Weston, M.; Coleman, N. & Spears, I. (2013) The Effect of Isolated Core Training on Selected Measures of Golf Swing Performance, *Medicine and Science in Sports and Exercise*, 45 (12), 2292–2297.

Zheng, N.; Barrentine, S.; Fleisig, G. & Andrews, J. (2008) Swing Kinematics for Male and Female Pro Golfers, *International Journal of Sports Medicine*, 29 (12), 965–970.

29

STRENGTH AND CONDITIONING FOR GOLF

John Hellström

Introduction

Strength and conditioning (S&C) training is a critical component of most athletes' training programmes. With S&C training, it is possible to change the body structure (decrease fat, increase muscle mass and strengthen bones and connective tissues), improve the neuromuscular capacity (strength, power, balance and coordination), increase energy-giving capacities (anaerobic/muscular endurance and aerobic/cardiovascular endurance) and increase range of motion (ROM). However, as late as the mid-1980s, physical conditioning was not a priority among golf professionals (Jobe et al., 1994). S&C training became more popular when the number 1 ranked players Annika Sörenstam and Tiger Woods used it as a key part of their training. Visible evidence of the need for S&C training in golf is the presence of fitness trailers on the professional tours today. Many elite players use physical training as a complement to golf training to stay injury-free and to improve their performance on the course (McMaster et al., 2001). Experts around them have different approaches. Physiotherapists often focus on slow movements with low loads, and athletic trainers may emphasise faster movements with higher loads (Chettle & Neal, 2001). There can also be a progression if the training is periodised (Ratamess et al., 2009). Furthermore, golf instructors check players' technical shortcomings and thus need to understand what techniques a player's physique allows them to do before giving them training advice. Therefore, S&C training is nowadays one important piece in the training puzzle for golfers (Hellström, 2009).

Review of current research

Swinging the club

The whole body needs to be considered when doing S&C training for golf, as it is activated from the feet to the hands when swinging. Larger muscles around the legs and torso create forces and torques against the ground and rotate the pelvis in the downswing. Fitness test results where gluteus muscle groups are highly activated, such as squat jump (SJ) height (30.3 ± 4.9 cm) and one-repetition maximum (1RM) squat (112 ± 25 kg), have shown significant correlations ($r = 0.45$, $p < 0.01$ and $r = 0.54$, $p < 0.01$) to clubhead speed (179.3 ± 9.7 km/h) (Hellström, 2008). Elite players have also shown larger pelvic rotation speed in the downswing using 3D equipment, compared to less skilled players (Callaway et al., 2012), and maximal voluntary activation via electromyography (EMG) measurements on the trailing gluteus maximus when starting the downswing (Watkins et al., 1996). This is the muscle group that in general has the highest activation in the average professional golf swing according to EMG studies (McHardy & Pollard, 2005). Exercises that allow players to create and control forces towards the ground should, therefore, be included in golf fitness programmes.

Torso strength and flexibility is also important for clubhead speed and control. Ballistic tests, such as 3 kg medicine ball rotational throws towards the target (9.6 ± 1.7 m), have shown a moderate correlation ($r = 0.63$, $p < 0.01$) to clubhead speed (Read et al., 2013). Parts of the lower body and torso musculature are eccentrically activated before the direction changes in the downswing (Bechler et al., 1995). The increase in striking distance associated with X-factor stretch is likely due to the increased force attained through the early eccentric action and the increased time over which the force can be applied, compared to a static start of the downswing (Newton et al., 1997). Sitting rotation flexibility tests around the spine in both directions have also shown positive correlations (clockwise: $r = 0.52$, $p < 0.05$; counterclockwise: $r = 0.71$, $p < 0.01$) to clubhead speed (Brown et al., 2011) and skill level (Sell et al., 2007). Thus, strength and range of motion (ROM) in spinal axial rotation is important to consider when striving for longer striking distances.

The arms and hands transfer energy from the body and create a force couple on the shaft by activating muscles around the shoulders, elbows and wrists. EMG studies indicate high levels of activation on both sides' pectoralis major muscles after gluteus maximus reaches its maximum activation, immediately prior to impact (Okuda et al., 2002). Such activation may at least partly explain why seated 4 kg medicine ball push throws (5.81 ± 4.94 m) have shown a significant correlation to clubhead speed (168.7 ± 10.5 km/h, $r = 0.71$, $p < 0.05$) for professionals (Lewis et al., 2016), and why better golfers have shown higher cable woodshop chest strength (68.9 ± 9.2 kg) compared to less skilled golfers (53.7 ± 7.0 kg) ($r = 0.71$, $p < 0.01$) (Keogh et al., 2009). When male professional golfers' body compositions were compared to sedentary subjects, the only significant ($p < 0.05$) difference between the groups was a 9% increase in muscle mass in the dominant arm of the professional golfers (Dorado et al., 2002). This may be caused by actively extending the trailing elbow through impact. Grip strengths have also shown positive correlations to driver distance (dominant grip: $r = 0.77$, $p < 0.05$; non-dominant grip: $r = 0.81$, $p < 0.05$) (Wells et al., 2009). It may be difficult to time the use of the wrists in the release phase (Sprigings & Neal, 2000), but strong fingers may control the club through thick grass, sand and when decelerating the club. Thus, the ability of the arms and hands to transfer and generate forces at high speeds is important for golf.

Training goals

Different goals require different training programmes. Injury rehabilitation, preparation, and endurance training usually consist of many repetitions (>12) with light loads, and a rather slow speed of performance. It is common for many golfers who want to work out to join a local gym and use traditional hypertrophy (or so-called bodybuilding) training methods. Gym training usually means repeating the movement around 6–12 times each set, with heavier loads than endurance training (>60% of 1RM), and a slow speed of performance (Hackett et al., 2013). It is a common belief amongst 'bodybuilders' that muscle failure should occur at the end of each set, and they should have a short rest interval between sets (1–2 minutes). For those whose aim it is to increase maximal strength, like Olympic weight lifters, the repetitions are often few, between 1–5 with very heavy loads, and the speed of performance is often as high as possible (Swinton et al., 2009). The rest interval is usually longer (4–5 minutes) than that of the hypertrophy training, which could help the central nervous system (CNS) to recover better. Strength training for explosive events is often performed with comparatively light loads (Cormie et al., 2011). The repetitions do not exceed the number beyond which the athlete can perform the movement at near maximum speed, and the rest interval is similar to that of those who train to increase their maximal strength (4–5 minutes). Changing training programmes over different periods makes it possible to combine these goals over time. In general, golfers first need to prioritise training to be injury free, then finding the ball, and lastly hitting it further. Striking distance may be of higher importance than precision in some training periods, but never at the cost of becoming injured.

S&C training may prevent some athletic injuries because of its favourable effect on the physical strength and function of the various musculo-skeletal tissues (Evans & Tuttle, 2015). It may also aid in the ability to swing consistently, which can reduce the probability of injuries (Cole & Grimshaw, 2016), and improve the club-to-ball delivery and the following ball displacement. A case study of a professional golfer with low back pain who was coached over three months to increase his range of hip turn and decrease the amount of upper torso turn, attempted to decrease the loads acting on his spine (Grimshaw & Burden, 2000). He also performed a lying spinal stretch and seated spinal stretch twice a day, 3–4 times per week. The player decreased his spinal rotation (X-factor) from a very large 90°, to 68° at the top of backswing, as measured with 3D equipment, and his lower back pain ceased. In a different training study, fifteen recreational golfers with performance goals trained a combination of strength, flexibility, and balance training over 8 weeks (Lephart et al., 2007). They significantly ($p < 0.05$) decreased pelvis axial rotation in the backswing (13.4%) and upper torso rotational velocity (7.0%), and increased X-factor velocity (14.0%), with subsequent significant increases of clubhead speed (5.2%), initial ball speed (5.5%), and carry distance (7.7%). Thus, the goals of injury prevention and performance improvement need to be carefully considered as they may require different training programmes.

Training for precision

A player's flexibility can affect the swing and the resulting ball flight precision. A group of 20 amateur golfers who did static and proprioceptive neuromuscular facilitation (PNF) stretching for 15–30 seconds, 3–5 times, over 12 weeks improved their golf performance (Lee et al., 2015). Agonistic and antagonistic muscles were stretched in turn. The flexibility training group improved their hit-ball direction deviation compared to the control group (3.0° ± 1.2° *vs.* 3.6° ± 1.9° before; 2.3° ± 1.4° *vs.* 3.5° ± 1.3° after). However, the segments that were stretched and the exact definitions of the measured ball flight parameters were not revealed. Also, dynamic stretching movements have been shown to improve performance (Fradkin et al., 2004a) and decrease the risk of golf-related injuries (Fradkin et al., 2007). General stretching studies indicate that dynamic stretching may be used during the warm-up before performing sports, and static flexibility training used after strength and sport-specific training when needing to change ROM long term (Behm & Chaouachi, 2011). It is therefore important to consider flexibility training methods when making training programmes for golf.

Precision of ball flight does not need to decrease when undertaking strength training to improve driving distance (Lanford, 1976). Eleven weeks of strength, power and flexibility training was shown to increase clubhead speed (from 170.3 ± 13.7 km/h to 172.3 ± 10.8 km/h, $p < 0.05$) without a negative effect on driving and putting precision in intercollegiate men and women golfers (Doan et al., 2006). Fifteen swings with the driver were measured with a laser-based GolfAchiever (Focaltron Corp., Sunnyvale, CA). There were no significant changes in driver face angle (2.2° ± 0.8° before, 2.2° ± 0.4° after), or golf ball launch angle (2.3° ± 0.5° before, 2.0° ± 0.7° after) measured. Although the reliability of the GolfAchiever was not revealed, the results indicated that it was possible to maintain or increase the precision of the club-to-ball deliveries and ball flights, as a consequence of conditioning training.

Core stability is often considered an important physical attribute for both injury prevention and performance enhancement (Booth, 2005). Stability is achieved by both passive (through the osseous and ligamentous structures), and active (through the muscles) stiffness (Panjabi, 1992). Stability training is believed to enhance the neuro-muscular system's ability to control the joints (Bliss & Teeple, 2005). Worse scores in physiotherapist stability tests have shown significant correlations to larger upper body sway (Prone bridge: $r = 0.64$, $p < 0.01$; One-legged squat: $r = 0.53$, $p < 0.05$) and pelvic rotation (Supine hip extension: $r = -0.51$, $p < 0.05$; One-legged squat: $r = -0.67$, $p < 0.01$) in the backswing for skilled golfers (Hellström & Tinmark, 2008). As the player creates higher forces on the club in the forward swing, the club in turn creates higher reaction forces on the player. Strength in the lower part of the back (measured with a dynamometer: 144 ± 39 kg), has shown a positive correlation to clubhead speed (95.2 ± 12.0 km/h, $r = 0.56$, $p < 0.05$) and driver carry distance (167 ± 40 m, $r = 0.47$, $p < 0.05$) for male amateur golfers (Loock et al., 2013), as a higher clubhead speed may require a stronger and heavier body to control the club from swing to swing when driving close to maximal speed. Core strength and flexibility training have also improved driving distance for professional players compared to a control group (Sung et al., 2015). Thus, when a muscle pulls a distal body segment, it is beneficial for its precision and acceleration if the proximal pulling base is stable (Kreighbaum & Barthels, 1996).

If players have a stable base to pull distal segments from, they may benefit from increasing their maximal strength and power too. A smooth, constant torque on the club in the downswing was recommended based on computer modelling to achieve high clubhead speed (Nesbit & Serrano, 2005). Smooth accelerations and decelerations of the lower body joints are related to the smoothness of clubhead trajectory (Choi et al., 2014). Stability, balance, coordination, and flexibility should therefore be a general focus area in the beginning of a periodised training programme, before starting with heavier loads or faster movements. Future studies should investigate the effect of S&C training on the kinematic and kinetic sequence in general, and in particular, the smoothness of changes in velocities.

Elite golfers have shown a decrease in putting performance when fatigued (Mathers & Grealy, 2014). The six tested players holed fewer putts (from $91.7 \pm 2.8\%$ to $82.3 \pm 4.9\%$, $p < 0.01$) after 1 hour of treadmill walking at 6.5 km/h at about 70% of maximum heart rate. However, only elderly play golf with such a high cardiovascular demand during a round (Broman et al., 2004). Middle aged men have shown a mean exercise intensity of only 35–41% (Murase et al., 1989), and 43–55% (Magnusson, 1999) of VO_{2max} when playing golf, which indicated a low aerobic requirement. Hence, it is probably less effective for younger players compared to older players to improve golf performance by doing cardiovascular training.

Training for clubhead speed

Higher clubhead speed has shown to be strongly associated ($r = 0.95$, $p < 0.001$) with better golf handicap for amateur players (Fradkin et al., 2004b). Several S&C training studies have also reported increased clubhead speed or striking distance after a period of strength and/or flexibility training (Smith et al., 2011). Recreational players with low fitness levels were shown to improve their game by starting S&C training (Evans & Tuttle, 2015). Middle aged (52.4 ± 6.7 years) to older (70.7 ± 7.1 years) male amateur players also had increased clubhead speed and/or striking distance after generic fitness programmes (Hetu et al., 1998; Thompson et al., 2007). Clubhead speed increased 6.3% from 126.2 to 134.1 km/h (Hetu et al., 1998), and 4.9% from 127.3 ± 13.4 to 133.6 ± 14.2 km/h (Thompson et al., 2007) after 8 weeks of training. Skilled college golfers have also shown significant, but lower, increases (1.5–1.6%) in clubhead speed after 8–11 weeks of training (Fletcher & Hartwell, 2004; Doan et al., 2006). Thus, less improvement can be expected when using generic conditioning programmes on skilled players with better physiques.

The duration of training that is used in studies can also affect the results. Neuronal adaptation predominates during the first weeks of strength training. Subsequently, muscular adaptation in form of hypertrophy may occur as well. Training studies in golf have commonly been done over 8 weeks (Read & Lloyd, 2014). Alvarez et al. (2012) made a longer training study over 18 weeks, with ten male players with similar skill level and age. They were randomly grouped into a training or control group (mean handicap: 2, and mean age: 24 years in both groups), and were not allowed to participate in any other exercise programme during this training period. The training group showed significant improvements in maximal and explosive strength after the first 6 weeks of maximal strength training, but ball speed did not increase significantly until 12 weeks of training (from 226.0 ± 12.2 to 249.6 ± 6.9 km/h, $p < 0.05$). This indicated that fit, low handicap players need individualised conditioning programmes and longer physical training time than 8 weeks to transfer significant gains from strength training to golf performance. However, a smaller relative increase in clubhead speed for skilled players versus recreational players may also be explained by the relative smaller room for improvement that skilled players have.

The effect of strength training on the rate of force development (RFD) depends on how the strength training is performed and the subject's fitness status (Wilson et al., 1993). When a bodybuilding-training method was compared with maximum and explosive strength training, it was found that bodybuilding resulted in the largest hypertrophic increase (Hakkinen et al., 1985). A higher body mass may be helpful to counteract the momentum of the golf club in the swing. Maximal strength training however, is more effective than explosive strength training in gaining absolute strength and to increase muscle mass (Hakkinen et al., 1985). Bodybuilding can also be an effective way of improving maximal strength (Schmidtbleicher & Buehrle, 1987), which may explain why striking distance can be improved by this training method for some players (Lanford, 1976; Pinter, 1992). Bodybuilding, however, has shown to only increase RFD slightly as opposed to the significantly higher increase of RFD of groups who perform maximal and explosive strength training (Schmidtbleicher & Buehrle, 1987). It might even be possible that well trained athletes can decrease their swing speed when bodybuilding, and non-trained golfers increase their swing speed with the same strength training methods, depending on their RFD capacity when they start bodybuilding.

The athletes' initial RFD (iRFD) and maximum RFD (mRFD) are more important in increasing the equipment's speed than the maximal strength factor when the equipment is light (<25% of 1RM), and the time to affect it is short (<0.25 sec) (Schmidtbleicher & Buehrle, 1987). The downswing takes about 0.2 to 0.3 seconds for the average tour player and the club is light. Well-trained, top-class players with high clubhead speeds may therefore not succeed in increasing clubhead speed after a period of slow velocity strength training, due to the difference in neural activity and RFD compared to explosive training. Maximum and explosive strength training, where the participants moved the load as fast as possible and had larger rest intervals, showed the largest increase in mRFD, but explosive strength training was shown to improve iRFD and mRFD more than maximum strength training (Hakkinen et al., 1985).

Test methods

Test instructions and statistical methods are important to consider when interpreting the training results. Pinter (1992) and Reyes et al. (2002) did not find significant correlations between strength and/or flexibility training, and clubhead speed or striking distance. The lack of significant correlations between S&C training and clubhead speed may be explained by the instructions to 'swing as in competition' as opposed to 'swing for maximum distance' in the tests (Pinter, 1992), and the use of isometric training (Reyes et al., 2002) that is less specific to the dynamics of the golf swing, than for example, ballistic training. There were also few players in their training groups ($n = 6$ and $n = 11$), which gave a low statistical power to detect significant changes. When using a traditional significance level ($p < 0.05$) with a low sample size, the statistical power may not be high enough to differentiate true changes in golf performance parameters, such as ball speed. A number of 50 participants over at least 3 trials have been suggested to have enough precision for estimates of reliability (Hopkins, 2000). Scientists may also consider the use of more finely graded magnitudes (such as trivial, small, moderate, and large) instead of only a binary significance level, to support decisions about the practical use of training results (Batterham & Hopkins, 2006).

The test designs are important to consider when investigating golfers' physical capacities and training results. The associative strength between the same physical tests and performance variables can vary depending on how the tests are measured. When investigating 33 elite players' physique and clubhead speed, it was found that the same tests could have weak or strong correlations to clubhead speed depending on how the results were presented (Hellström, 2008). For example, bar-dips and pull-ups were significantly ($p < 0.05$) related to clubhead speed when measuring total mass lifted (repetitions x body mass) ($r = 0.35$ and $r = 0.42$, respectively), but not when measured with repetitions only ($r = 0.21$ and $r = 0.29$, respectively). Squat strength was related to clubhead speed when measured as absolute mass lifted (112 ± 25 kg, $r = 0.54$, $p < 0.01$) but not when using mass lifted relative to body mass ($149 \pm 28\%$, $r = 0.33$, $p > 0.05$). Thus, when the aim of the tests is to give feedback associated with clubhead speed, the strength test should be measured in absolute values. There are no 'weight-classes' when comparing driving distances, so the strength tests should be presented in mass lifted, not in repetitions only or as percentage of body mass lifted.

Playing the game

Elite golfers, in general, have better physiques than average golfers. Female Korean professional ($n = 40$) and national team players ($n = 30$) were shown to be significantly stronger and more flexible than general golf players ($n = 30$) (Kim & Park, 2015). Also, fitness tests of maximal strength, muscle endurance, isokinetic trunk strength, and peak power were strongly correlated for these players with driver distance and average scores. This indicates that modern elite players probably do more deliberate conditioning training compared to general golf players, although genetic factors may have an effect too.

S&C training studies have shown positive effects on end results such as scoring and handicap index (Van Der Ryst et al., 2010; Smith et al., 2015). Thirty-eight junior amateur players (16–19 years, handicap 5.1 ± 4.5) were placed into a conditioning training group ($n = 31$) or control group ($n = 7$). The conditioning group exercised 1 hour, 3 times per week, for 14 weeks (48 sessions with 100% compliance) (Van Der Ryst et al., 2010). The conditioning group improved their golf handicap (from 7.0 to 4.7), as well as cardiovascular fitness, and several strength and flexibility measurements. The control group did not improve significantly in golf handicap or in any fitness tests. Smith et al. (2015) also investigated the fitness training effect on golf performance. Junior players (12–18 years) were divided into an experimental group ($n = 20$, handicap 15.20 ± 9.51) or a control group ($n = 10$, handicap 15.26 ± 8.86). The experimental group did a strength and flexibility programme for 12 weeks. Both groups practiced and played golf as they normally would, and golf performance was measured via monitoring golf handicap change. The experimental group made moderate to large improvements in upper body, core, and lower body strength, and trivial to small increases in flexibility. The experimental group improved their handicap by 2.9 strokes compared to the control group's 1.6 strokes, which was a non-significant difference between the groups. The relationships between improvements in fitness tests (side bridge endurance strength, modified push-ups, and shoulder mobility) and handicaps were significant ($p < 0.05$). Thus, S&C training has in general shown to be positive for the golf game.

Implications for the game

S&C training for golfers should be specific to the individual players' needs and to the demands of the golf game. Thus, it can be beneficial if the player sets goals and makes training programmes together with both the S&C professional and the golf coach. Cardiovascular training may have a positive effect on golf performance for elderly players, but possibly not on young players. There should thus be more focus on increasing aerobic capacity for older golfers compared to younger golfers. Further, an improved physique may decrease the risk of injuries, which should be prioritised before golf performance improvements. The progression of training may be to first learn to perform exercises safely, with slower movements and lighter loads in the beginning, compared to a later stage of training. The training should progressively overload the current capacities in a safe way, and include sufficient recovery so that an adaptation occurs toward the set goals.

A good long game is important to achieve a low score. A higher control of the clubhead velocity, clubface angle, and impact location on the clubface is critical to hit the ball closer to the target. The ability to hit fairways instead of roughs would on average lower a PGA Tour player by 0.3 strokes per improved par-4s and par-5s (Hellström et al., 2014). Although there is a need for more research regarding the effect of S&C training on golf swing and ball flight precision, it is likely that some flexibility and neuro-muscular training should be specific to the golf swing to have a better effect on the golf performance. That means standing up, using multi-joint exercises that coordinate the whole body in a down-to-up kinematic sequence, and including horizontal plane movements. The training also needs to be varied over time, to achieve both injury prevention and performance goals. If the players are prepared and have the goal to increase clubhead speed and striking distance, then they may include some training with heavy loads to improve maximal strength, and ballistic exercises with lighter loads to increase speed. An increase in clubhead speed after S&C training can lead to lower scores. A 1.6% increase in clubhead speed and 5 m increase in driving distance as a result from S&C training (results from Doan et al., 2006) would result in a reduction of about 0.02 strokes per hole on the PGA Tour (Hellström et al., 2014). The interpretation of these recommendations needs to be applied in context, depending on the player's individual goals, physical and technical capacities, and training history.

Summary and future directions

The literature shows that the best players differ from less skilled players in physique, technique, and playing results. These variables are interrelated and can be improved with training. Range of motion and neuromuscular capacities are associated with clubhead speed and skill level. Generic S&C training can improve golf performance on unfit golfers. If players are skilled and fit, then training programmes need to be more individualised, and it may take longer time to achieve beneficial effects on golf performance. Research is needed on how physical training can affect swing technical precision to achieve higher control of ball displacements. Future studies should further investigate how players' physique and swing technique are related on individual levels, to reveal causalities that are otherwise hidden in group studies. In summary, S&C training can be helpful for golfers to be able to play, to hit the ball further with higher precision, and to score lower.

References

Alvarez, M.; Sedano, S.; Cuadrado, G. & Redondo, J. (2012) Effects of an 18-Week Strength Training Program on Low-Handicap Golfers' Performance, *Journal of Strength and Conditioning Research*, 26 (4), 1110–1121.

Batterham, A. & Hopkins, W. (2006) Making Meaningful Inferences about Magnitudes, *International Journal of Sports Physiology and Performance*, 1 (1), 50–57.

Bechler, J.; Jobe, F.; Pink, M.; Perry, J. & Ruwe, P. (1995) Electromyographic Analysis of the Hip and Knee During the Golf Swing, *Clinical Journal of Sport Medicine*, 5 (3), 162–166.

Behm, D. & Chaouachi, A. (2011) A Review of the Acute Effects of Static and Dynamic Stretching on Performance, *European Journal of Applied Physiology and Occupational Physiology*, 111 (11), 2633–2651.

Bliss, L. & Teeple, P. (2005) Core Stability: The Centerpiece of Any Training Program, *Current Sports Medicine Reports*, 4 (3), 179–183.

Booth, L. (2005) A Physiotherapy Perspective on Improving Swing Technique in a Professional Golfer: A Case Study, *Physical Therapy in Sport*, 6 (2), 97–102.

Broman, G.; Johnsson, L. & Kaijser, L. (2004) Golf: A High Intensity Interval Activity for Elderly Men, *Aging Clinical and Experimental Research*, 16 (5), 375–381.

Brown, S.; Nevill, A.; Monk, S.; Otto, S.; Selbie, W. & Wallace, E. (2011) Determination of the Swing Technique Characteristics and Performance Outcome Relationship in Golf Driving for Low Handicap Female Golfers, *Journal of Sports Sciences*, 29 (14), 1483–1491.

Callaway, S.; Glaws, K.; Mitchell, M.; Scerbo, H.; Voight, M. & Sells, P. (2012) An Analysis of Peak Pelvis Rotation Speed, Gluteus Maximus and Medius Strength in High Versus Low Handicap Golfers During the Golf Swing, *International Journal of Sports Physical Therapy*, 7 (3), 288–295.

Chettle, D. & Neal, R. (2001) Strength and Conditioning for Golf, In: P. Thomas (Ed.) *Optimising Performance in Golf*, Brisbane, Australia: Australian Academic Press Ltd, pp. 207–223.

Choi, A.; Joo, S.; Oh, E. & Mun, J. (2014) Kinematic Evaluation of Movement Smoothness in Golf: Relationship Between the Normalized Jerk Cost of Body Joints and the Clubhead, *Biomedical Engineering online*, 13 (1), 1–18.

Cole, M. & Grimshaw, P. (2016) The Biomechanics of the Modern Golf Swing: Implications for Lower Back Injuries, *Sports Medicine*, 46 (3), 339–351.

Cormie, P.; Mcguigan, M. & Newton, R. (2011) Developing Maximal Neuromuscular Power: Part 2 – Training Considerations for Improving Maximal Power Production, *Sports Medicine*, 41 (2), 125–146.

Doan, B.; Newton, R.; Kwon, Y. & Kraemer, W. (2006) Effects of Physical Conditioning on Intercollegiate Golfer Performance, *Journal of Strength and Conditioning Research*, 20 (1), 62–72.

Dorado, C.; Moysi, S.; Vicente, G.; Serrano, J.; Rodriguez, L. & Calbet, J. (2002) Bone Mass, Bone Mineral Density and Muscle Mass in Professional Golfers, *Journal of Sports Sciences*, 20 (8), 591–597.

Evans, K. & Tuttle, N. (2015) Improving Performance in Golf: Current Research and Implications from a Clinical Perspective, *Brazilian Journal of Physical Therapy*, 19 (5), 381–389.

Fletcher, I. & Hartwell, M. (2004) Effect of an 8-Week Combined Weights and Plyometrics Training Program on Golf Drive Performance, *Journal of Strength and Conditioning Research*, 18 (1), 59–62.

Fradkin, A.; Cameron, P. & Gabbe, B. (2007) Is There an Association Between Self-reported Warm-up Behaviour and Golf Related Injury in Female Golfers? *Journal of Science and Medicine in Sport*, 10 (1), 66–71.

Fradkin, A.; Sherman, C. & Finch, C. (2004a) Improving Golf Performance with a Warm Up Conditioning Programme, *British Journal of Sports Medicine*, 38 (6), 762–765.

Fradkin, A.; Sherman, C. & Finch, C. (2004b) How Well Does Club Head Speed Correlate with Golf Handicaps? *Journal of Science and Medicine in Sport*, 7 (4), 465–472.

Grimshaw, P. & Burden, A. (2000) Case Report: Reduction of Low Back Pain in a Professional Golfer, *Medicine and Science in Sports and Excercise*, 32 (10), 1667–1673.

Hackett, D.; Johnson, N. & Chow, C. (2013) Training Practices and Ergogenic Aids Used by Male Bodybuilders, *Journal of Strength and Conditioning Research*, 27 (6), 1609–1617.

Hakkinen, K.; Komi, P. & Alen, M. (1985) Effect of Explosive Type Strength Training on Isometric Force- and Relaxation-time, Electromyographic and Muscle Fibre Characteristics of Leg Extensor Muscles, *Acta Physiologica Scandinavica*, 125 (4), 587–600.

Hellström, J. (2008) The Relation Between Physical Tests, Measures, and Clubhead Speed in Elite Golfers, *Annual Review of Golf Coaching*, 3 (1), 85–92.

Hellström, J. (2009) Competitive Elite Golf: A Review of the Relationships Between Playing Results, Technique and Physique, *Sports Medicine*, 39 (9), 723–741.

Hellström, J. & Tinmark, F. (2008) The Association Between Stability and Swing Kinematics of Skilled High School Golfers, In: D. Crews, & R. Lutz (Eds.) *Science and Golf V. Proceedings of the World Scientific Congress of Golf*, Mesa, Arizona: Energy in Motion Inc, pp. 37–43.

Hellström, J.; Nilsson, J. & Isberg, L. (2014) Drive for Dough. PGA Tour Golfers' Tee Shot Functional Accuracy, Distance and Hole Score, *Journal of Sports Sciences*, 32 (5), 462–469.

Hetu, F.; Christie, C. & Faigenbaum, A. (1998) Effects of Conditioning on Physical Fitness and Club Head Speed in Mature Golfers, *Perceptual and Motor Skills*, 86 (3 Pt 1), 811–815.

Hopkins, W. (2000) Measures of Reliability in Sports Medicine and Science, *Sports Medicine*, 30 (1), 1–15.

Jobe, F.; Yocum, L.; Mottram, R. & Pink, M. (1994) *Exercise Guide to Better Golf*, Arizona: Human Kinetics.

Keogh, J.; Marnewick, M.; Maulder, P.; Nortje, J.; Hume, P. & Bradshaw, E. (2009) Are Anthropometric, Flexibility, Muscular Strength, and Endurance Variables Related to Clubhead Velocity in Low- and High-Handicap Golfers? *Journal of Strength and Conditioning Research*, 23 (6), 1841–1850.

Kim, K.-J. & Park, D.-H. (2015) Comparative Analysis of Physical Fitness and Relationship of Driver Distance and Average Score in General, National and Pro Female Golf Players, *Exercise Science*, 24 (3), 305–313.

Kreighbaum, E. & Barthels, K. (1996) *Biomechanics: A Qualitative Approach for Studying Human Movement* (4th Ed.), New Jersey, NJ: Allyn & Bacon.

Lanford, E. (1976) *Effect of Strength Training on Distance and Accuracy in Golf*, Unpublished Ed.D Thesis, Oregon, US: University of Oregon.

Lee, J.; Lee, S.; Yeo, Y. & Park, G. (2015) Effects of Special Composite Stretching on the Swing of Amateur Golf Players, *Journal of Physical Therapy Science*, 27 (4), 1049–1051.

Lephart, S.; Smoliga, J.; Myers, J.; Sell, T. & Tsai, Y.-S. (2007) An Eight-Week Golf-Specific Exercise Program Improves Physical Characteristics, Swing Mechanics, and Golf Performance in Recreational Golfers, *The Journal of Strength and Conditioning Research*, 21 (3), 860–869.

Lewis, A.; Ward, N.; Bishop, C.; Maloney, S. & Turner, A. (2016) Determinants of Club Head Speed in PGA Professional Golfers, *Journal of Strength and Conditioning Research*, 30 (8), 2266–2270.

Loock, H.; Grace, J. & Semple, S. (2013) Association of Selected Physical Fitness Parameters with Club Head Speed and Carry Distance in Recreational Golf Players, *International Journal of Sports Science & Coaching*, 8 (4), 769–777.

Magnusson, G. (1999) Golf: Exercise for Fitness and Health, In: A. Cochran (Ed.) *Heart Rate and Metabolic Responses to Participation in Golf*, London: E & FN Spon, pp. 51–57.

Mathers, J. & Grealy, M. (2014) Motor Control Strategies and the Effects of Fatigue on Golf Putting Performance, *Frontiers in Psychology*, 13; 4, 1–10.

McHardy, A. & Pollard, H. (2005) Muscle Activity During the Golf Swing, *British Journal of Sports Medicine*, 39 (11), 799–804; Discussion 799.

McMaster, R.; Herbert, R.; Jamieson, S. & Thomas, P. (2001) An Integrated Approach to the Golfer's Physical and Technical Development, In: P. Thomas (Ed.) *Optimising Performance in Golf*, Brisbane: Australian Academic Press Ltd, Brisbane, pp. 231–244.

Murase, Y.; Kamei, S. & Hoshikawa, T. (1989) Heart Rate and Metabolic Responses to Participation in Golf, *The Journal of Sports Medicine and Physical Fitness*, 29 (3), 269–272.

Nesbit, S. M. & Serrano, M. (2005) Work and Power Analysis of the Golf Swing, *Journal of Sports Science and Medicine*, 4 (4), 520–533.

Newton, R.; Murphy, A.; Humphries, B.; Wilson, G.; Kraemer, W. & Hakkinen, K. (1997) Influence of Load and Stretch Shortening Cycle on the Kinematics, Kinetics and Muscle Activation that Occurs During Explosive Upper-Body Movements, *European Journal of Applied Physiology and Occupational Physiology*, 75 (4), 333–342.

Okuda, I.; Armstrong, C.; Tsunezumi, H. & Yoshiike, H. (2002) Biomechanical Analysis of Professional Golfer's Swing: Hidemichi Tanaka, In: E. Thain (Ed.) *Science and Golf IV. Proceedings of the World Scientific Congress of Golf*, London: Routledge, pp. 19–27.

Panjabi, M. (1992) The Stabilizing System of the Spine. Part I. Function, Dysfunction, Adaptation, and Enhancement, *Journal of Spinal Disorders*, 5 (4), 383–9; Discussion 397.

Pinter, M. (1992) *Effect of Strength Training and Flexibility on Club Head Speed and Accuracy in the Golf Drive*, Unpublished PhD Thesis, Mississippi, US: Mississippi State University.

Ratamess, R.; Alvar, B.; Evetoch, T.; Housh, T.; Kibler, B.; Kraemer, W. & Triplett, T. (2009) American College of Sports Medicine Position Stand. Progression Models in Resistance Training for Healthy Adults, *Medicine and Science in Sports and Excercise*, 41 (3), 687–708.

Read, P. & Lloyd, R. (2014) Strength and Conditioning Considerations for Golf, *Strength & Conditioning Journal*, 36 (5), 24–33.

Read, P.; Lloyd, R.; De Ste Croix, M. & Oliver, J. (2013) Relationships Between Field-based Measures of Strength and Power, and Golf Club Head Speed, *Journal of Strength and Conditioning Research*, 27 (10), 2708–2713.

Reyes, M.; Munro, M.; Held, B. & Gebhardt, W. (2002) Maximal Static Contraction Strengthening Exercises and Driving Distance, In: E. Thain (Ed.) *Science and Golf IV. Proceedings of the World Scientific Congress of Golf*, London: Routledge, pp. 45–53.

Schmidtbleicher, D. & Buehrle, M. (1987) Neural Adaptation and Increase of Cross-Sectional Area Studying Different Strength Training Methods, *Biomechanics X-B*, 615–620.

Sell, T.; Tsai, Y.; Smoliga, J.; Myers, J. & Lephart, S. (2007) Strength, Flexibility, and Balance Characteristics of Highly Proficient Golfers, *Journal of Strength and Conditioning Research*, 21 (4), 1166–1171.

Smith, C.; Callister, R. & Lubans, D. (2011) A Systematic Review of Strength and Conditioning Programmes Designed to Improve Fitness Characteristics in Golfers, *Journal of Sports Sciences*, 29 (9), 933–943.

Smith, C.; Lubans, D. & Callister, R. (2015) The Effects of Resistance Training on Junior Golfers' Strength and On-course Performance, *International Journal of Golf Science*, 3 (2), 128–144.

Sprigings, E. & Neal, R. (2000) An Insight into the Importance of Wrist Torque in Driving the Golfball: A Simulation Study, *Journal of Applied Biomechanics*, 16 (4), 356–367.

Sung, D.; Park, S.; Kim, S.; Kwon, M. & Lim, Y.-T. (2015) Effects of Core and Non-Dominant Arm Strength Training on Drive Distance in Elite Golfers, *Journal of Sport and Health Science*, 5 (2), 219–225.

Swinton, P.; Lloyd, R.; Agouris, I. & Stewart, A. (2009) Contemporary Training Practices in Elite British Powerlifters: Survey Results from an International Competition, *Journal of Strength and Conditioning Research*, 23 (2), 380–384.

Thompson, C.; Cobb, K. & Blackwell, J. (2007) Functional Training Improves Club Head Speed and Functional Fitness in Older Golfers, *Journal of Strength and Conditioning Research*, 21 (1), 131–137.

Van Der Ryst, R.; Cilliers, J.; Shaw, I.; Shaw, B.; Toriola, A. & Pieterse, J. (2010) Can a Conditioning Programme Improve Handicap Index in Adolescent Amateur Golfers? *African Journal for Physical, Health Education, Recreation and Dance*, 16 (4), 605–615.

Watkins, R.; Uppal, G.; Perry, J.; Pink, M. & Dinsay, J. (1996) Dynamic Electromyographic Analysis of Trunk Musculature in Professional Golfers, *The American Journal of Sports Medicine*, 24 (4), 535–538.

Wells, G.; Elmi, M. & Thomas, S. (2009) Physiological Correlates of Golf Performance, *Journal of Strength and Conditioning Research*, 23 (3), 741–750.

Wilson, G.; Newton, R.; Murphy, A. & Humphries, B. (1993) The Optimal Training Load for the Development of Dynamic Athletic Performance, *Medicine and Science in Sports and Excercise*, 25 (11), 1279–1286.

30

THE OLDER GOLFER

Anthony A. Vandervoort, David M. Lindsay and Scott K. Lynn

Introduction

Golf can be enjoyed by people of all ages. Toddlers with toy clubs eagerly attempt to imitate a golf swing they have observed, while, at the other end of the age spectrum, there are examples of nonagenarian golfers with amazing skill (Morehouse, 1990; Baker et al., 2007). The focus of this chapter is to demonstrate that, regardless of whether one is a life-long participant for many decades, or just taking up the sport in their retirement years, golf can be both an enjoyable leisure time pursuit and a valuable exercise option for the older adult population (Farahmand et al., 2009; Lindsay & Vandervoort, 2014). Walking generates a moderate exercise intensity for most seniors, and regular golf participation can provide the motivation to get active at the recommended level several times per week (American College of Sports Medicine, 2014).

Current demographic trends in developed countries (e.g., in Europe, North America, and parts of Asia, such as Japan) indicate potential growth for large numbers of senior golfers due to the aging of the large 'baby-boomer' cohort born shortly after World War II, who are now entering the last third of their lifespan (World Health Organization, 2015). Indeed, it has also been observed that there is a core group of senior male golfers who play a higher-than-average number of rounds per year, thereby making this age group a particularly important component of the golf community, numbers that could expand even more if greater participation by females can be encouraged (World Golf Foundation, 2016). This overrepresentation by seniors is not surprising when one considers that golf can usually be performed at a comfortable pace, inducing a relatively moderate exercise intensity level (Broman et al., 2004). Knowledge of the body's limitations is also important too, because a full and powerful golf swing will take some joints near the limit of their range of motion, and so there can be some possible injury risks and potential barriers to life-long participation (Lindsay et al., 2000). In addition, while old age is a time when chronic diseases such as arthritis, cardiovascular problems, balance disorders, breathing limitations and type II late-onset diabetes may appear (World Health Organization, 2015), golf can still be part of an active lifestyle for people with disabilities. Modifications to swing biomechanics, mobility aids and other similar interventions can be implemented when necessary to prolong participation.

Review of current research

Most tissues and functional systems of the body have some level of age-related loss of physiological capacity during the lifespan, with these affecting performance of the senior golfer to varying extents. A brief summary of key alterations in the musculoskeletal system is provided in Table 30.1. It should also be noted that even middle-aged golfers may thus start to experience physical limitations in their ability to move the clubhead rapidly into desirable positions for optimal biomechanics of control and speed generation (e.g., Brown et al., 2002; Lindsay & Vandervoort, 2010; Gulgin et al., 2014). For example, a well-known effect of the aging process is generalized stiffness in the joints (Stathokostas & Vandervoort, 2016). From a physiological standpoint, much of the reduced flexibility relates to connective tissue changes within the body, due to the significant water loss with age that contributes to a reduction in this tissue's plasticity. These age-related changes in connective tissue and joint structure are manifested by losses in maximal range of joint movement. One study comparing spinal motion during the golf swings of recreational, low-handicap players (aged 18–21 years) and senior players (aged 50+ years) showed that maximum trunk side bending range of motion was 25% less in the older group (Morgan et al., 1999). Another investigation by this group compared maximal golf swing shoulder ranges of motion between golfers aged 18–24 years and those aged 50–86 years and found that the older players used about 15% less shoulder elevation and 30% less shoulder external rotation when swinging the club (Mitchell et al., 2003).

The reported rate of change in flexibility in physical function surveys is dependent on the aging body part measured, the training status of the sample and population being studied. After middle age, the rate of decline in a generally healthy sample has been shown to be 0.5 degree per year in males and 0.6 degree per year in females in upper body flexibility (shoulder abduction), and declines in hip flexion of 0.6 degree per year in males and 0.7 degree per year in females (Stathokostas et al., 2013). An even greater loss of 1% per year in shoulder abduction range of motion was observed in a sample of older men and women reporting high disability (Bassey et al., 1989), and 1.5 degrees per year for lower back flexion (Einkauf et al., 1987). When considering the population of very old golfers (70–92 years), James and Parker (1989) noted decreases in active

Table 30.1 Brief summary of age-related musculoskeletal changes in the older golfer

Connective tissue and cartilage	– altered proportions and properties of connective tissue components
	– ↑ stability of cross-links in collagen, ↑ resistance to lengthening
	– becomes non-pliable, brittle and weak due to ↓ water and ↓ plasticity
	– predisposition occurs for tendon and ligament injury
Muscular	– after growth and maturation, muscle strength is stable across middle age, then a pattern of about 1.5% loss yearly from age 60 onwards due to:
	– ↓ number of motor units
	– ↓ number of muscle fibres and ↓ size of type II fibres
	– some lean muscle replaced with fat and connective tissue
Nervous system	– muscle atrophy is compounded by neurological changes
	– one-third loss of spinal cord axons in old age
	– 10% ↓ of nerve conduction velocity and ↑ in time for reflex responses
	– ↓ sensory, visual and proprioceptive function
Skeletal	– after third and fourth decade, ↓ bone mineralization of 0.3–0.5% per year
	– over full lifetime: 35% of cortical and 50% of trabecular bone can be lost
	– older women are particularly susceptible to osteoporosis following menopause

and passive motion in lower limb joints, with the aging effect becoming more pronounced during the ninth decade. Similarly, Chakravarty and Webley (1993) reported a greater decrease in shoulder flexibility in those aged over 75 years versus those aged 65–74 years.

Muscular strength is also one of the more obvious physical parameters influenced by age: the ability to generate force increases via growth and maturation up to one's early 20's, has a plateau phase until the fifth decade, and then decreases by about 15% per decade thereafter, albeit retaining plasticity for training effects into very old age (Vandervoort, 2002; Borde et al., 2015). The decline in simple isometric strength measures are primarily the result of decreased muscle mass (age-related sarcopenia), although coordination can also be a factor in complex rapid movements. Total muscle cross sectional area declines by 10% between the ages of 24–50 years, then drops another 30% between 50–80 years and beyond (Lexell et al., 1988). Equal amounts of both type 1 (slow twitch) and type 2 (fast twitch) muscle fiber numbers are thought to be lost with old age. However, in addition to overall fiber loss, type 2 fibers also undergo a much greater decrease in size compared to their type 1 counterparts (Power et al., 2013).

The existence of a curvilinear relationship between age and strength implies that a middle-aged golfer would not be expected to have any large decrease in maximum torque generation compared to a young player, but an 80-year old would have only about half the overall strength level of the young adult. It is quite interesting to note that golf performance tends to follow the same pattern, as evidenced by comparisons of average golf handicaps versus age. Recreational golfers tend to reach their prime in the third decade, and then begin to experience some loss of performance in their forties. However, they can still continue to play well, and even compete with other age groups via the handicap system, for the rest of their lives. For example, Lockwood (1999) observed in his survey that the average handicap of recreational golfers in England was about 19 for adolescents, dropped to 13 for young adults aged 20–39 years, and then increased by about one stroke per decade thereafter to again reach 19 for players in the 70–79 year age range. Thus, the older golfer's net score can be adjusted statistically to compare expected performance on a more equal basis, especially if players are willing to use an appropriate tee box for their typical skill level.

There are definite benefits for senior golfers who decide to take up a properly designed, periodized, resistance training program that can help optimize the motor system's ability to generate effective muscle forces for the golf swing. Some older individuals can also take advantage of the muscle strengthening benefits of eccentric plyometric resistance training principles, given that this mode of exercise also causes less cardiovascular stress compared to concentric exercises (Bellew et al., 2005). Finally, it is useful to optimize any motor learning associated with the training exercises, especially those involving coordinated ballistic movements among several muscles that directly simulate motions of the golf swing in which rapid acceleration is needed (Gabriel et al., 2006).

Activated muscles that are used to walk the golf course and swing clubs need a steady supply of oxygen and nutrients via the cardiorespiratory system, but cardiac output decreases by about 30% between the ages of 30–70 years (Bellew et al., 2005; Taylor & Johnson, 2008). Indeed, when heart rates were monitored in a study of adult recreational golfers, the female participants tended to reach a peak of about 80% of their maximum heart rate while walking some of the uphill fairways (Broman et al., 2004). For the men in this sample, the peak intensity reached was about 70% of their maximum heart rate, depending on whether the terrain was level or uphill, and also the age of the golfer. Another investigation by Dobrosielski et al. (2002) confirmed that the metabolic demand during nine-holes of golf for 20 male golfers aged 49–78 years was on average about four times the resting metabolic rate. Interestingly, these golfers all had a previous history of heart disease, and the recorded exercise intensity of approximately 57% of their peak functional capacity was indicative that they were performing adequate amounts and intensity of exercise for improving cardiovascular fitness (Nelson et al., 2007). Notable then was that Parkkari et al. (2000) found increased aerobic performance (measured during a walking treadmill test), as well as improved body composition and high density lipoprotein serum cholesterol levels in a previously sedentary group of 55 healthy Finnish male subjects aged 48 to 64 years who participated in a golf program 2–3 times per week over a 20 week season. Finally with regard to implications for body weight management, it has also been calculated that the average male golfer burnt about 900 calories per typical round of walking an 18-hole course, whilst females metabolized about 700 calories. And carrying clubs with shoulder straps added approximately 10–15% to these numbers (Wallace & Reilly, 1993). Studies have shown walking during a round of golf consistently provided over 11,000–12,000 steps of exercise (Kobriger et al., 2006; Peterson, 2012), which surpasses common healthy living guidelines of attempting to achieve at least 10,000 steps per day. Furthermore, playing golf also has the potential to improve knee joint proprioception and the limits of postural stability in older people, both important components of balance that have been shown to help reduce the risk of falls in this age group (Tsang & Hui-Chan, 2004).

Given that the overall ability of older adults to carry an absolute load over time is reduced compared to younger adults, this change can create fatigue-related problems with muscle coordination and subsequent injuries. However, it is possible to increase fatigue resistance with appropriate exercise strategies. Senior golfers can thus be encouraged to participate in continuing training programs throughout the year that include cardiovascular endurance, if additional physiological stimulation is necessary beyond the effects of walking the course. Physiological reductions in the body's ability to maintain cardiovascular and muscular homeostasis in stressful environmental conditions also indicate that older players need to pay close attention to maintaining adequate hydration, nutritional supplementation, and blood electrolytes during their round, particularly in hotter climates (Smith, 2007).

Golf swing and musculoskeletal injuries

Unlike contact sports, the large majority of injuries for golfers are in effect, self-induced, because they occur at some point in their own golf swing (Fradkin et al., 2007a; Lindsay & Vandervoort, 2014). The motions that allow elite players to generate hand movements and clubhead speeds in excess of 200 km/hr are highly ballistic in some parts of the swing, because the club acceleration phase before striking the ball can be as brief as 0.2 seconds (Lindsay & Vandervoort, 2010). Unskilled recreational golfers attempting to imitate professionals may induce muscle strains because their less efficient swing styles are typically compensated for by greater muscular exertions, and poor postures. For example, both the spine and the shoulder are typically taken near, but not quite to, the maximum range of all available joint motion by skilled golfers in a full swing with the driver, and slightly less with a more controlled 7-iron swing (Lindsay et al., 2002; Mitchell et al., 2003). Given the large momentum developed at the point of ball impact by the various body segments' rotational patterns, it can be a challenge for the player to have a smooth follow-through, while still maintaining postural stability. Indeed golf teaching and rehabilitation professionals pay close attention to where the final positions and weight transfer end up, due to the implications for both efficiency, and musculoskeletal damage.

Epidemiological surveys have indicated some trends that older golfers may be more prone to injury than young adults, but the etiological picture involves a complex mix of player characteristics, frequency of participation, and environmental conditions (Sugaya et al., 1999; Gosheger et al., 2003; Palmer et al., 2003; Fradkin et al., 2007a). For example, Palmer and colleagues' survey of injuries and orthopaedic problems amongst senior recreational players found that half of the 100 respondents reported having musculoskeletal conditions in the last three years that affected their golf game, with 46% of these conditions affecting the upper extremity, and 34% involving the spine (Palmer et al., 2003). Furthermore, approximately one-third of this sample had, on occasion, experienced notable discomfort in the lumbar region after playing. Low back pain can be an ongoing concern for both older and young professional golfers too, evidenced in the survey results of Sugaya et al. (1999), plus examples of current top-level Tour players such as Fred Couples, Jason Day, Rory McIlroy, Inbee Park, and Tiger Woods (the latter athlete returning to tour competition in early 2017 following several disc surgeries).

Shoulder joints are susceptible to injury because their complex anatomical structures allow flexibility in multiple directions, but at the expense of strong stability. Shoulder problems among golfers typically take place in the lead side of their swing, via the high eccentric load that is applied to the shoulder muscles during the transition between the back- and down-swing. Another mechanism of injury identified was taking an excessively deep divot, or inadvertently striking a buried object such as a tree root (Kim et al., 2004). The vulnerability of the shoulder to injury in aging athletic populations has been reported by other authors too, and may lead to long-term rotator cuff problems that are a challenge for rehabilitation (Lewis et al., 2015), as well as chronic arthritis of the glenohumeral joint. Many older golfers with joint problems are determined to keep playing and adopt technique modifications that can include: shortening the back-swing, keeping the elbows in-close to the trunk during the back-swing, and finishing with the hands low and the club shaft horizontal on the follow-through. Keeping the elbows in and hands low helps promote a slightly flatter swing plane, and reduces the chance of impinging the rotator cuff. It is thus recommended that rotator cuff and scapular stabilizer strengthening programs should be a regular component of any senior golfer's rehabilitation or training program.

Osteoarthritis (OA) is more prevalent with age, and areas of special concern in golfers include the first metacarpal phalangeal joint of the top hand, the facets of the lumbar and cervical spines, and the hip and knee joints. Those with significant foot pain or deformities will also experience limitations in completing the arching motion onto the ball of the foot during the follow-through phase of the swing. However, it is encouraging to note that having to resort to arthoplastic procedures for treating these joints does not preclude future participation in golf, and can indeed lead to substantial improvement in performance when range of motion and strength are restored (Mallon, 1994). The orthopaedic history of well-known professional golfers such as Jack Nicklaus and Tom Watson, who returned to successful competitive golf after a hip joint replacement, serves as inspiration for those players with advanced osteoarthritic degeneration. The latter player gave much inspiration to older golfers around the globe in 2009 when he came within one shot of winning The Open major championship in Turnberry, Scotland – at the amazing age of 59 years.

Implications for the game

Swing accommodation can also involve the angle of the foot at set-up. It has been recommended by Ben Hogan, in his famous golf instruction book (Hogan & Wind, 1957), that the optimal golf set-up places the lead foot into a toe-out position (although a clear biomechanical rationale remains to be provided for why this is a desirable technique). Of related interest however, is the observation that people with symptomatic knee osteoarthritis tend to adopt a toe-out style gait pattern, and this strategy has been shown to help in unloading the diseased medial compartment of the knee – where most knee arthritis occurs (Lynn & Noffal, 2010). Further research with golfers who continue to play with chronic osteoarthritis will help to illuminate the possible application of this finding to their particular situation. Some other general recommendations can also be offered. First, it has been reported that golfers who perform a pre-game warm up routine greater than 10 minutes experienced less than half the injuries per player than those who warm up for 10 minutes or less (Gosheger et al., 2003). Therefore, a substantial warm-up period appears to be good advice for incorporation into the golfer's normal pre-game routine. Secondly, a proper athletic setup needs to be achieved with the spine in a straight position (e.g., reminding recreational players to flex at the hips, rather than the low back). Thirdly, use of a shorter backswing has been shown to reduce muscle activation in the trunk muscles while maintaining clubhead speed (Bulbulian et al., 2001). This modification would indicate that using an abbreviated backswing has the potential to reduce the chance of back and shoulder injury or pain while maintaining performance, a strategy which can be optimal for the senior golfer. In another study, players who had a history of low back pain demonstrated approximately 30% restriction of lead side hip internal hip rotation, as well as a similar limitation to lumbar extension compared to the asymptomatic golfers (Vad et al., 2004). The authors speculated that as the body pivoted onto the lead leg during the swing, the decreased amount of hip rotation might have caused an increased force to be transmitted to the lumbar spine, resulting in low back pain. By changing the lead foot's starting position to a more open stance (i.e., toed out towards the target), this adaptation should reduce the internal rotation force translating up into the spine. Furthermore, avoiding an excessive posture of extension (inverted C position) on follow-through will help to reduce excessive forces on the lumbar spine at the end of the swing.

A positive study for older golfers was conducted by Thompson and Osness (2004) who examined muscle strength and flexibility in male recreational players (mean age = 65.1 years), and determined that both resistance training and flexibility exercises emphasizing trunk rotation generated improvements in clubhead speed. Similar findings came from Hetu et al. (1998) in their study of fitness and performance measures that improved amongst mature golfers (average age 52.4 years) after an 8-week conditioning program that increased trunk rotation flexibility by 47%, and also produced a 6% gain in maximum clubhead speed. For golfers looking for an alternative to heavy weight-lifting, Jones (1999) has also shown that using an 8-week Proprioceptive Neuromuscular Facilitation (PNF) program of stretching agonist muscles against their opposite (antagonist) group also had a positive impact on increasing clubhead speed. The PNF stretches were aimed at improving the flexibility of hip flexion and extension, shoulder abduction and external rotation, and trunk rotation. In summary, the older golfer can utilize various training approaches to optimize their existing physical capacity, and thus attempt to maintain performance as much as possible (Newton, 2007; Reid & Fielding, 2012).

Useful advice, but often ignored due to haste, is to follow a proper warm-up routine before taking full golf swings with maximal effort (Gosheger et al., 2003; McCrary et al., 2015). Given the age-related changes in the motor and skeletal systems that tend to inhibit the ability of senior golfers to make a full, repeatable swing with optimal tempo and rhythm, such warm-up seems particularly valuable for this age group. However, the need for warm-up is often ignored by recreational golfers who proceed to the first tee with just a few minutes of quick stretches and ineffective practice swings (Palmer et al., 2003). Similar observations were reported by Fradkin et al. (2007b) in their study of Australian amateur golfers, and this lack of preparation before playing is rather perplexing when one realizes that both performance and injury prevention strategies are easily enhanced by an adequate warm-up prior to commencing the round of golf.

Additional motivation to take the extra time for a warm-up comes from another study by Fradkin et al. (2004) who demonstrated that performing a brief warm-up routine of approximately 10 minutes duration prior to swinging a 5-iron improved clubhead speed of a group of male recreational golfers (mean age of 39.6 years) by 3–6m/s (12.8% change). They also found that performing this warm-up routine for five weeks, five times per week either before practice, before an actual round, or even at home, improved clubhead speed by 7–10 m/s (24% difference) compared to the control group. The warm-up routine consisted of three parts: first were windmill and trunk rotations along with two other vigorous exercises performed for 15 seconds each. These were utilized in an effort to increase body temperature. Secondly, stretches were performed with the main golf muscles, including three shoulder stretches, lateral trunk/torso, hamstring/lower back, two for the wrist, and one for the forearm. Each of these stretches were held at the end range of the stretch for duration of at least twelve seconds and repeated twice on each side. Finally 30 seconds of air swings with a golf club were performed with gradual increasing range of motion and vigour. Subsequently, Versteegh et al. (2011) demonstrated that senior recreational golfers over the age of 65 years can also benefit from this type of brief warm-up strategy. It should be motivating for older players to realize they can take advantage of the simple fact that an increase of just a few percentage points in swing speed will translate into several more yards of distance on long golf shots.

Summary and future directions

In summary, we advocate golf for its clear value as a healthy physical activity that can provide much enjoyment for all ages and skill levels. It is particularly appealing for older adults because they can continue to perform well if they maintain their conditioning and participation level. Nonetheless, there are also associated health risks influenced by the fact that older adults' musculoskeletal systems may not be as efficient at withstanding the strain and stress of the ballistic type of repetitive movement found in a golf swing. Following a moderate approach to playing pace and swing speed is therefore advisable, as well as preparing well for participation.

Older golfers who choose to access professional teaching and coaching provided by knowledgeable personnel can be proactive with regard to injuries resulting from poor swing mechanics or improper equipment. More golfers need to be made aware too of the benefits of adequate warm up practices and key principles of healthy exercise practices (e.g., hydration, skin protection, non-slip footwear). For dedicated older players, the utilization of a targeted conditioning program for golf, emphasizing the key body structures involved, also helps to optimize performance and prevent further injury. Sedentary lifestyle patterns create health risks, and future research is needed regarding how to best promote golf as a valuable physical activity for older people. Then these health promotion strategies can be combined with effective educational programs for management of injuries and chronic diseases so that this segment of the golf population can keep playing into very old age.

References

American College of Sports Medicine (2014) *ACSM's Guidelines for Exercise Testing and Prescription* (9th Ed.), Philadelphia, PA: Wolters Kluwer/Lippincott Williams & Wilkins.

Baker, J.; Deakin, J.; Horton, S. & Pearce, G. (2007) Maintenance of Skilled Performance with Age: A Descriptive Examination of Professional Golfers, *Journal of Aging and Physical Activity*, 15 (3), 300–317.

Bassey, E.; Morgan, K.; Dallosso, H. & Ebrahim, S. (1989) Flexibility of the Shoulder Joint Measured as Range of Abduction in a Large Representative Sample of Men and Women Over 65 Years of Age, *European Journal of Applied Physiology and Occupational Physiology*, 58 (4), 353–360.

Bellew, J.; Symons, T. & Vandervoort, A. (2005) Geriatric Fitness: Effects of Aging and Recommendations for Exercise in Older Adults, *Cardiopulmonary Physical Therapy Journal*, 16 (1), 21–32.

Borde, R.; Hortobágyi, T. & Granacher, U. (2015) Dose-Response Relationships of Resistance Training in Healthy Old Adults: A Systematic Review and Meta-analysis, *Sports Medicine*, 45 (12), 1693–1697.

Broman, G.; Johnsson, L. & Kaijser, L. (2004) Golf: A High Intensity Interval Activity for Elderly Men, *Aging, Clinical and Experimental Research*, 16 (5), 375–381.

Brown, D.; Best, R.; Ball, K. & Dowlan, S. (2002) Age, Center of Pressure and Clubhead Speed in Golf. Biomechanical Analysis of Professional Golfer's Swing, In: E. Thain (Ed.) *Science and Golf IV: Proceedings of the World Scientific Congress of Golf*, London: Routledge, pp. 28–34.

Bulbulian, R.; Ball, K. & Seaman, D. (2001) The Short Golf Backswing: Effects on Performance and Spinal Health Implications, *Journal of Manipulative and Physiological Therapeutics*, 24 (9), 569–575.

Chakravarty, K. & Webley, M. (1993) Shoulder Joint Movement and Its Relationship to Disability in the Elderly, *Journal of Rheumatology*, 20 (8), 1359–1361.

Dobrosielski, D.; Brubaker, P.; Berry, M.; Ayabe, M. & Miller, H. (2002) The Metabolic Demand of Golf in Patients with Heart Disease and in Healthy Adults, *Journal of Cardiopulmonary Rehabilitation*, 22 (2), 96–104.

Einkauf, D.; Gohdes, M.; Jensen, G. & Jewell, M. (1987) Changes in Spinal Mobility with Increasing Age in Women, *Physical Therapy*, 67 (3), 370–375.

Farahmand, B.; Broman, G.; De Faire, U.; Vågerö, D. & Ahlbom, A. (2009) Golf: A Game of Life and Death – Reduced Mortality in Swedish Golf Players, *Scandinavian Journal of Medicine and Science in Sports*, 19 (3), 419–424.

Fradkin, A.; Cameron, P. & Gabbe, B. (2007b) Is There an Association Between Self-reported Warm-up Behaviour and Golf Related Injury in Female Golfers? *Journal of Science and Medicine in Sport*, 10 (1), 66–71.

Fradkin, A.; Sherman, C. & Finch, C. (2004) Improving Golf Performance with a Warm Up Conditioning Programme, *British Journal of Sport Medicine*, 38 (6), 762–765.

Fradkin, A.; Windley, T.; Myers, J.; Sell, T. & Lephart, S. (2007a) Describing the Epidemiology and Associated Age, Gender and Handicap Comparisons among Golfing Injuries, *International Journal of Injury Control and Safety Promotion*, 14 (4), 264–266.

Gabriel, D.; Kamen, G. & Frost, G. (2006) Neural Adaptations to Resistive Exercise: Mechanisms and Recommendations for Training Practices, *Sports Medicine*, 36 (2), 133–149.

Gosheger, G.; Liem, D.; Ludwig, K.; Greshake, O. & Winkelmann, W. (2003) Injuries and Overuse Syndromes in Golf, *American Journal of Sports Medicine*, 31 (3), 438–443.

Gulgin, H.; Schulte, B. & Crawley, A. (2014) Correlation of Titleist Performance Institute (TPI) Level 1 Movement Screens and Golf Swing Faults, *Journal of Strength and Conditioning Research*, 28 (2), 534–539.

Hetu, F.; Christie, C. & Faigenbaum, A. (1998) Effects of Conditioning on Physical Fitness and Club Head Speed in Mature Golfers, *Perceptual and Motor Skills*, 86 (3), 811–815.

Hogan, B. & Wind, H. (1957) *The Modern Fundamentals of Golf*, London: Kaye and Ward.

James, B. & Parker, A. (1989) Active and Passive Mobility of Lower Limb Joints in Elderly Men and Women, *American Journal of Physical Medicine and Rehabilitation*, 68 (4), 162–167.

Jones, D. (1999) The Effects of Proprioceptive Neuromuscular Facilitation Flexibility Training on the Clubhead Speed of Recreational Golfers, In: M. Farrally & A. Cochran (Eds.) *Science and Golf III: Proceedings of the World Scientific Congress of Golf*, Champaign, IL: Human Kinetics, pp. 46–50.

Kim, D.; Millett, P.; Warner, J. & Jobe, F. (2004) Shoulder Injuries in Golf, *American Journal of Sports Medicine*, 32 (5), 1324–1330.

Kobriger, S.; Smith, J.; Hollman, J. & Smith, A. (2006) The Contribution of Golf to Daily Physical Activity Recommendations: How Many Steps Does It Take to Complete a Round of Golf? *Mayo Clinic Proceedings*, 81 (8), 1041–1043.

Lewis, J.; Mccreesh, K.; Roy, J. & Ginn, K. (2015) Rotator Cuff Tendinopathy: Navigating the Diagnosis–Management Conundrum, *Journal of Orthopaedic and Sports Physical Therapy*, 45 (11), 923–937.

Lexell, J.; Taylor, C. & Sjostrom, M. (1988) What Is the Cause of the Ageing Atrophy? *Journal of Neurological Sciences*, 84 (2), 275–294.

Lindsay, D.; Horton, J. & Paley, R. (2002) Trunk Motion of Male Professional Golfers Using Two Different Golf Clubs, *Journal of Applied Biomechanics*, 18 (4), 366–373.

Lindsay, D.; Horton, J. & Vandervoort, A. (2000) A Review of Injury Characteristics, Aging Factors and Prevention Programs for the Older Golfer, *Sports Medicine*, 30 (2), 89–103.

Lindsay, D. & Vandervoort, A. (2010) Applied Biomechanics of Golf, In: D. Magee; R. Manske; J. Zachazewski & W. Quillen (Eds.) *Athletic and Sport Issues in Musculoskeletal Rehabilitation*, Philadelphia, PA: Elsevier, pp. 217–233.

Lindsay, D. & Vandervoort, A. (2014) Golf and Low Back Pain: A Review of Causative Factors and Prevention Strategies, *Asian Journal of Sports Medicine*, 5 (4), 1–8.

Lockwood, J. (1999) A Small Scale Local Survey of Age-Related Male Golfing Ability, In: M. Farrally & A. Cochran (Eds.) *Science and Golf III: Proceedings of the World Scientific Congress of Golf*, Champaign, IL: Human Kinetics, pp. 112–119.

Lynn, S. & Noffal, G. (2010) Frontal Plane Knee Moments in Golf: Effect of Target Side Foot Position at Address, *Journal of Sports Science and Medicine*, 9 (2), 275–281.

Mallon, W. (1994) The Golfer with a Total Joint Replacement, In: C. Stover; J. McCarroll & W. Mallon (Eds.) *Feeling Up to Par: Medicine from Tee to Green*, Philadelphia, PA: FA Davis, pp. 85–92.

McCrary, J.; Ackermann, B. & Halaki, M. (2015) A Systematic Review of the Effects of Upper Body Warm–Up on Performance and Injury, *British Journal of Sports Medicine*, 49 (14), 935–942.

Mitchell, K.; Banks, S.; Morgan, D. & Sugaya, H. (2003) Shoulder Motions During the Golf Swing in Male Amateur Golfers, *Journal of Orthopaedic and Sports Physical Therapy*, 33 (4), 196–203.

Morehouse, C. (1990) The Super Senior Golfer, In: A. Cochran (Ed.) *Science and Golf: Proceedings of the World Scientific Congress of Golf*, London: Chapman and Hall, pp. 14–23.

Morgan, D.; Cook, F.; Banks, S.; Sugaya, H. & Moriya, H. (1999) The Influence of Age on Lumbar Mechanics During the Golf Swing, In: M. Farrally & A. Cochran (Eds.) *Science and Golf III: Proceedings of the World Scientific Congress of Golf*, Champaign, IL: Human Kinetics, pp. 120–126.

Nelson, M.; Rejeski, W.; Blair, S.; Duncan, P.; Judge, J.; King, A.; Macera, C. & Castaneda-Sceppa, C. (2007) Physical Activity and Public Health in Older Adults: Recommendation from the American College of Sports Medicine and the American Heart Association, *Medicine and Science in Sports and Exercise*, 39 (8), 1435–1445.

Newton, H. (2007) Effective Strength Training for Golf: What's the Right Approach? *Annual Review of Golf Coaching*, 2 (1), 135–140.

Palmer, J.; Young, S.; Fox, E.; Lindsay, D. & Vandervoort, A. (2003) Senior Recreational Golfers: A Survey of Musculoskeletal Conditions, Playing Characteristics and Warm Up Patterns, *Physiotherapy Canada*, 55 (2), 79–86.

Parkkari, J.; Natri, A.; Kannus, P.; Mänttäri, A.; Laukkanen, R.; Haapasalo, H.; Nenonen, A.; Pasanen, M.; Oja, P. & Vuori, I. (2000) A Controlled Trial of the Health Benefits of Regular Walking on a Golf Course, *American Journal of Medicine*, 109 (2), 102–108.

Peterson, M. (2012) *Physical Activity Parameters for Walking Golf Participation: An Analysis of Volume and Intensity*, Available at www.Golf2020.Com/Reports/Walking.Pdf (Accessed May 21, 2012).

Power, G.; Dalton B. & Rice, C. (2013) Human Neuromuscular Structure and Function in Old Age: A Brief Review, *Journal of Sport and Health Science*, 2 (4), 215–226.

Reid, K. & Fielding, R. (2012) Skeletal Muscle Power: A Critical Determinant of Physical Functioning in Older Adults, *Exercise and Sports Science Reviews*, 40 (1), 4–12.

Smith, M. (2007) Physical Preparation for Golf: Strategies for Optimising Movement Potential, *Annual Review of Golf Coaching*, 2 (1), 151–164.

Stathokostas, L.; McDonald, M.; Little, R. & Paterson, D. (2013) Flexibility of Older Adults Aged 55–86 Years and the Influence of Physical Activity, *Journal of Aging Research*, Article: 743843.

Stathokostas, L. & Vandervoort, A. (2016) The Flexibility Debate. Implications for Health and Function as We Age, *Annual Review of Gerontology and Geriatrics*, 35, 169–192.

Sugaya, H.; Tsuchiya, A.; Moriya, H.; Morgan, D. & Banks, S. (1999) Low Back Injury in Elite and Professional Golfers: An Epidemiologic and Radiographic Study, In: M. Farrally & A. Cochran (Eds.) *Science and Golf III: Proceedings of the World Scientific Congress of Golf*, Champaign, IL: Human Kinetics, pp. 83–91.

Taylor, A. & Johnson, M. (2008) *Physiology of Exercise and Healthy Aging*, Champaign, IL: Human Kinetics.

Thompson, C. & Osness, W. (2004) Effects of an 8-Week Multimodal Exercise Program on Strength, Flexibility, and Golf Performance in 55- to 79-Year-Old Men, *Journal of Aging and Physical Activity*, 12 (2), 144–156.

Tsang, W. & Hui-Chan, C. (2004) Effects of Exercise on Joint Sense and Balance in Elderly Men: Tai Chi Versus Golf, *Medicine and Science in Sports and Exercise*, 36 (4), 658–676.

Vad, V.; Bhat, A.; Basrai, D.; Gebeh, A.; Aspergren, D. & Andrews, J. (2004) Low Back Pain in Professional Golfers: The Role of Associated Hip and Low Back Range-of-Motion Deficits, *American Journal of Sports Medicine*, 32 (2), 494–497.

Vandervoort, A. (2002) Aging of the Human Neuromuscular System, *Muscle and Nerve*, 25 (1), 17–25.

Versteegh, T.; Vandervoort, A.; Overend, T.; Birmingham, T. & Jones, I. (2011) Effect of a Dynamic Warm-Up on Clubhead Velocity in Senior Golfers, *Proceedings of 16th Annual Confederation of World Congress for Physical Therapy*, Amsterdam, June 22–23, 2011.

Wallace, P. & Reilly, T. (1993) Spinal and Metabolic Loading During Simulations of Golf Play, *Journal of Sport Science*, 11 (6), 511–515.

World Golf Foundation (2016) *The Global Economic Value of Increased Female Participation in Golf*, Available at www.Golf2020.Com (Accessed January 25, 2017).

World Health Organization (WHO) (2015) *World Report on Ageing and Health*, Available at www.Who. Int/Ageing/Events/World-Report-2015-Launch/En/ (Accessed January 25, 2017).

31

GOLF INJURIES

Andrea Fradkin

Introduction

Injuries can be an unfortunate consequence of sports participation. As the number of individuals who participate in physical activity increases, so too will the number of injuries occurring due to exercise (van Mechelen, 1997). In addition to being an enormous public health issue, injuries continue to usurp limited financial healthcare resources (Finch, 2012).

Recognising that an injury is exclusively caused by golf is the most important aspect of defining a golf injury. This is not a straightforward task considering golfers may have physically challenging occupations, or may participate in other sports that could contribute to the injury. The occurrence of golf injuries has received little attention in the literature, and many of the reported studies have focussed on unusual case reports. Although informative, it does not provide details of cases occurring at high frequencies, or those that preventive strategies may help avoid, and therefore, these reports are not useful for prevention purposes. Even though golf is generally considered to be a gentle activity, it has been recognised that golfers play in spite of many minor and major ailments.

Review of current research

Emergency department presentations

Injury surveillance is the first phase of sports injury prevention research (van Mechelen et al., 1992). To describe the more severe injuries sustained during sporting activities, emergency department presentation data are useful and effective (Finch et al., 1998). Only four studies have described golf injuries presenting to hospital emergency departments. The main limitation in this type of surveillance is that a substantial number of injuries are not treated at hospitals, and as such, only a small percentage of the actual injuries sustained are captured. Further, although the injury may have been coded as a golf injury, based on this type of surveillance, it cannot be determined whether golf was the primary cause of injury, or merely a contributing factor that exacerbated an unknown pre-existing condition.

A report on 300 patients attending emergency departments over a six-and-a-half-year period found that accidental injuries caused by being struck by a club or ball were the most common factor leading to presentation (Wilks & Jones, 1996). They also found that children were at particular risk when playing with golf clubs in unsupervised settings, and for adult players, they found the greatest risk was being hit by a ball on the fairway. Finch et al. (1998) investigated emergency department visits over a one-and-a-half-year period and found 61 persons aged at least 15 years presented for treatment of a golf injury. They also found that being hit by a golf ball was the most frequent cause of presentation for adults, and being hit by a golf club was the main reason for children's presentations. These studies provided a broad overview of golfing-related injuries requiring presentation to hospital emergency departments; however, the information reported was insufficient for guiding injury prevention research due to combining mechanisms and the nature of injury data.

When investigating emergency department presentations by children, Fradkin et al. (2005a) highlighted that these injuries occurred away from a registered golf course, being more likely to happen while children were at play. Children aged 5–9 years most commonly presented for treatment at an emergency department with injuries caused by golfing equipment, with head and face injuries being the most common. The main limitation of this study was that not all children who were injured with golfing equipment would be treated at an emergency department; therefore, less serious injuries may have been missed, and the extent of the injury problem was underestimated through this surveillance method.

In 2006, Fradkin et al. reported on 547 presentations to an emergency department for treatment of a golf injury extracted over a 5-year period. Males outnumbered females 3:1, and the proportions of participants in each age group were similar. The majority of injuries were sustained by being struck by a ball or club, through a collision with another person, or falls. Head injury was the most common reason for presentation, accounting for over one-third of all cases, and this study found open wounds to be the major injury type, followed by strains/sprains, and fractures. Both the cause of injury and body regions injured showed a significant association with age. Golfers older than 65 years sustained a higher proportion of injuries related to falls, and a higher than expected proportion of lower extremity injuries. Golfers younger than 15 years had more head, neck, and face injuries due to being struck by an object. Compared with previous studies, a significantly higher proportion of eye injuries were identified which could reflect a change in injury mechanisms over time, or the pattern of presentation for treatment whereby patients sought treatment from alternative sources.

Retrospective questionnaires

Retrospective studies have been conducted since the early 1980s examining the injury profile in golf, with all suggesting the need for injury prevention. The literature contains very little research about golf injuries, and 6 of the 11 prior studies have looked at career incidence, a methodology likely to result in considerable recall bias.

Investigations into 226 professional golfers showed the incidence of injury to be 89% during their playing career (McCarroll & Gioe, 1982). The study's validity can be questioned with a non-respondent rate of almost 55%, and this should be considered when evaluating the results. Nonetheless, this study highlighted that the lifetime incidence of injuries was 88% for women and 81% for men, with an average of two injuries during their career. Lower back injuries were the most widespread among professional male golfers (25%), followed by wrist (16%) and shoulder injuries (11%), whereas female professional golfers most frequently injured the wrist (24%) and lower back (24%). Finally, the leading self-reported mechanisms of injury were too much play or practise (69%), followed by contact with a static object (20%) (McCarroll & Gioe, 1982).

Eighty-eight professional male golfers who sought treatment from the medical team over a 7-year period at the British Open (1984–1990) were studied (Hadden et al., 1991). During the

7-year period, approximately 1 in every 200 golfers required treatment. Musculoskeletal problems accounted for 98% of the injuries, with 65% of the golfers' problems originating in the axial skeleton – especially the lower back. This study also reported that 57% of the complaints were an exacerbation of chronic conditions, suggesting that the majority of the injuries were not 'new' (Hadden et al., 1991).

The high career incidence of injury to professional golfers can be attributed to the fact that they often play for up to 10 hours per day, 6 days per week (McCarroll & Gioe, 1982). Compared to professionals, recreational golfers do not place equivalent physical loads upon their bodies in terms of frequency of play and practice, yet those lesser loads are placed upon bodies not as well conditioned to the task as those of the professionals (Mallon & Hawkins, 1994). In addition, it is well established that the techniques practiced by recreational golfers are less refined and may place greater strain upon the musculoskeletal system during any individual swing (Hosea et al., 1990).

Although not studied in detail, injuries to recreational golfers have been shown to occur. With a response rate of only 28%, the lifetime incidence of injury was 62% for men and 61% for women, with a mean of 1.3 injuries per golfer (McCarroll et al., 1990). The most commonly injured body region among male golfers was the lower back (36%), followed by the elbow (33%), whereas female golfers tended to injure the elbow (36%), followed by the lower back (27%). The most frequently reported mechanisms of injury were excessive play (23%), poor swing mechanics (17%), and hitting the ground (13%). This study also showed that golfers with low handicaps (1–9) and those aged over 50 years had a higher incidence of injury (McCarroll et al., 1990).

The lifetime incidence of injury was found to be 57% in another study on recreational golfers with a low response rate (42%) (Batt, 1992). The wrist was the most commonly injured region among men (28%), followed closely by the back (25%). Among females, the elbow was the most commonly injured body region (50%). Wrist and elbow injuries were more common in younger players (<37.5 years), and shoulder injuries more common in older players (average 63.5 years). The main mechanism of injury was a miss-hit (41%), followed by overuse (26%), and failure to warm-up (9%) (Batt, 1992).

A questionnaire administered to 368 recreational golfers showed half of the respondents had been struck by a golf ball on at least one occasion (47.6%), and 23% of the injuries were to the head or neck (Nicholas et al., 1998). Male golfers were 2.66 times more likely to be struck by a golf ball than females, while women, and golfers with a higher handicap, were at increased risk for upper extremity problems. Further, Nicholas et al. (1998) showed younger and overweight golfers were more likely to have golf-related back problems.

A retrospective cohort study investigating injuries to 703 golfers showed professional golfers were most likely to injure their back, wrist, and shoulder, whereas recreational golfers reported mainly elbow, back, and shoulder injuries (Gosheger et al., 2003). Overall, 83% of the injuries were overuse injuries, while the remaining 17% were caused by single trauma events. The severity of the injuries was also reported, with over half of all injuries being minor (52%), approximately a quarter being moderate (26%), and the remaining 22% of cases being major (Gosheger et al., 2003).

All the aforementioned golf injury studies have used career incidence, a methodology likely to result in considerable recall bias. They also had broad or undefined injury definitions which may have been unlikely to trigger complete recall, and the questionnaires were only completed by interested golfers, leading to the potential for selection bias. However, five studies by Fradkin determined the injuries sustained by golfers in the previous 12-months, and attempted to overcome many of the previous studies' limitations.

With a response rate of 76%, Fradkin et al. (2005b) determined the injuries sustained by 522 female pennant golfers (golfers who competed on a weekly basis). Over one-third of golfers (35.2%) reported having sustained an injury within the previous 12 months, with strains being the most frequent type (67.9%). There was a trend showing pelvic and wrist injuries occurred in younger (40.0 and 44.5 years, respectively), more able players (handicap averages 8.0 and 11.0, respectively). The small number of neck injuries occurred in middle-aged (52.0 years), higher handicap golfers (mean 22.5). Better players (in terms of handicap) sustained more thorax and forearm injuries (median handicaps 10.0 and 11.0, respectively). Older golfers sustained more knee and ankle injuries (median ages 62.0 and 61.5 years, respectively). The most common mechanism of injury (excluding unsure) was overuse (43.6%), followed by a technical error (18.0%), contact with a static object (11.3%), and a sudden or rapid change of club speed (9.8%) (Fradkin et al., 2005b).

Whilst this study managed to overcome the limitations of the previous retrospective studies, it still had its own set of limitations that could affect the generalisability of the results. This group of golfers would probably play and practice more frequently than most golfers, thus it is possible the incidence of injury in this group may not be representative of other female golfers. As golfers playing pennant must have a registered handicap, it is possible the skill level of these golfers would be higher than the average golfer, and that skill level could relate to injury incidence. Finally, as in all the previous golf injury studies, the data in this study were all self-reported and validation was not undertaken.

Another study by Fradkin et al. (2007) consisted of 304 golfers with a median age of 53 years, with the majority of golfers being male (71.4%). There were 111 golf injuries reported, equating to 36.5% of golfers with an injury history. Strains were the most frequent type of injury (37.8%), followed by stiffness and inflammation (9.9% each). The most common mechanisms of injury (excluding unsure) were overuse (29.7%) and overexertion (26.1%). The most common injury sequelae were an inability to play (47.4%) and an altered swing (21.1%). Statistical analyses showed that golfers' handicaps, hours of play, and hours of practice were significantly associated with their injury status. Younger golfers and highly skilled golfers were more likely to report sustaining a golf injury. Less skilled players sustained more hip, elbow, and knee injuries, while older golfers sustained more knee, groin, and foot injuries (Fradkin et al., 2007). The results of this study add further weight to the evidence that golf injuries are a common occurrence and impact golfers' lives.

Other retrospective 12-month injury studies undertaken by Fradkin in 2010 and 2012, and by Fradkin and Eisenhart in 2011, also found injury incidences consistent with these studies and ranged between 31.7–38.2%. These studies incorporated both genders and a wide age range, and also showed agreement with the injury locations, types, and mechanisms of the aforementioned studies. A summary of the sites of injury for previously conducted studies is shown in Table 31.1. This table shows that although the most frequently injured body regions change with different studies, the lower back, shoulder, wrist, and elbow are always among the most commonly injured sites.

Prospective injury data

To date, there has only been one published prospective golf injury study, however, these were just preliminary results of an on-going study. Fradkin (2016) followed 268 golfers and found 26.2% reported having sustained a golf injury over the nine-month period. The majority (75.7%) of injuries were sustained during play as opposed to practice. Strains were the most frequent type of injury (41.8%), followed by stiffness, and inflammation. The most common

Table 31.1 Injury locations in previous golf studies (%)

	Head/neck	Shoulder	Back	Elbow	Wrist	Hand/fingers	Hip	Knee	Ankle	Foot/toes	Other
Professional golfers											
McCarroll and Gioe, 1982 (n = 226)	0.5	9.4	28.7	6.6	27.0	10.4	1.0	6.6	2.0	3.3	4.3
Hadden et al., 1991 (n = 88)	22.0	–	43.0	1.0	6.0	9.0	1.0	5.0	6.0	1.0	6.0
Recreational golfers											
McCarroll et al., 1990 (n = 1144)	5.7	11.7	34.5	33.1	20.1	Inc. with wrist	3.1	9.3	2.5	1.7	6.3
Batt, 1992 (n = 193)	–	6.6	24.6	13.1	26.2	3.3	–	6.6	4.9	3.3	9.8
Theriault et al., 1996 (n = 528)	–	10.6	36.4	19.2	18.2	Inc. with wrist	4.0	4.0	4.6	3.0	–
Fradkin et al., 2003 (n = 1040)	9.3	22.3	42.9	7.0	7.7	–	–	5.4	5.4	–	–
Gosheger et al., 2003 (n = 703)	6.8	17.6	26.4	22.3	14.1	Inc. with wrist	2.8	3.6	4.6	Inc. with ankle	1.9
Fradkin et al., 2005b (n = 522)	1.1	17.8	32.4	11.3	5.2	3.2	4.8	7.0	3.2	7.0	7.0
Fradkin et al., 2007 (n = 304)	1.8	13.4	37.5	11.6	5.3	5.3	1.8	7.1	5.4	2.7	8.1
Fradkin, 2010 (n = 501)	1.3	17.4	42.3	12.0	5.4	2.8	1.3	7.3	3.1	4.9	2.2
Fradkin and Eisenhart, 2011 (n = 478)	–	17.1	52.9	12.8	7.1	–	–	4.3	2.9	2.9	–
Fradkin, 2012 (n = 886)	1.8	15.9	46.8	12.9	6.3	2.3	1.8	5.6	4.0	2.6	–
Fradkin, 2016 (n = 268)	–	17.7	48.6	14.7	8.8	–	–	4.4	2.9	2.9	–

mechanisms of injury (excluding unsure) were overuse, followed by a technical error, overexertion, and contact with a static object (e.g., the ground).

The importance of proper mechanics and the stages of the golf swing

Due to the biomechanical complexity of the golf swing, golf injuries and the athletic demands of the game are becoming more recognised. An inapt blend of flexibility, co-ordination, strength, and balance, along with inappropriate swing mechanics can cause atypical stresses on the body that end in injury (Hosea & Gatt, 1996). To evaluate, treat, and prevent golf injuries, the biomechanics of the golf swing need to be understood.

Takeaway comprises the setup and movement to the top of the backswing. Fewer than 25% of all golf injuries occur during this swing phase, with the back and wrist comprising most of the injuries. The set-up is composed of the correct grip and body arrangement. A proper grip allows the hands to function together. A golfer who does not allow their wrists to work through their full range of motion (ROM) will most likely compensate by involving excessive motion from other joints. This may lead to inconsistent performances, as well as an increased injury possibility. Body position also can also have an effect on injury. Too wide of a stance puts greater strain on the vertebral column as it diminishes the ease of trunk rotation which may lead to injury (Theriault & Lachance, 1998).

The function of the backswing is to position the golfer and club in the most favourable position from which to commence the downswing. The backswing begins with the golfer addressing the ball, and the golfer swivels in order, the knees, hips, and lumbar and cervical spine, while the head remains reasonably motionless (McCarroll, 1996). Less than one-quarter of all golf injuries take place during this stage. Impact consists of the downswing and the impact of the club with the ball. More than twice as many injuries occur during impact than during takeaway. This is easy to believe as during the downswing the club covers the same ROM as the backswing but moves three times as fast. The wrist, hand, and elbow are often hurt during the compression of impact, however, the back still sustains the most injuries in this phase.

A study by McCarroll and Gioe (1982) showed there were more than twice as many downswing as backswing injuries. The energy attained at impact is transmitted up the club to the golfer which contributes to injury. The downswing phase ends with impact. The head of the club and the ball are in contact for approximately half a millisecond. From a performance aspect, the idea of impact is to hit the ball as far as possible in the correct direction. From a safety aspect, the purpose of impact is to have an even shift from acceleration to deceleration, even though contact is made with an object (usually the ball, but occasionally the ground). About 25% of all golf injuries take place during follow-through. The function of follow-through is to decelerate the body without unnecessary effort from the muscles. Most injuries in this segment occur to the back (particularly lower back), due to hyperextension.

How does the golf swing affect different body regions?

Bearing in mind the different stages of the golf swing, the loads placed on different regions of the body at each point in the swing can result in different injury types and natures. Injuries occurring to the lower back, shoulder, and lower and upper extremities have previously been shown to occur at a high incidence, and these injuries may be prevented by better preparing the regions of the body involved in the swing for the activity to be undertaken.

Lower back

When attempting to identify injuries associated with golf, epidemiologic studies have acknowledged low back pain as the most common complaint (McCarroll, 1996), with incidences ranging from 25–36%. There has only been one scientific trial published which showed that golf did not cause lower back pain (Burdoff et al., 1996). This study was performed on 196 men beginning golf who were given a questionnaire when they started playing, and a follow-up questionnaire 12 months later. The results showed over the 12-month period, the incidence of first-time back pain was 8%, and the authors concluded there was no significant outcome of golf being accountable for back pain, however, the analysis had limited power due to the small number of participants.

Injuries to the lower back are most likely caused by a combination of factors, including faulty swing mechanics, overuse, inadequate core strength, and flexibility limitations. Significant rotary torque is placed upon the spinal column when swinging a golf club. This is only one type of force encountered during the golf swing. Other forces occurring during the swing include lateral bending, compression, and shearing. All four components of force occur at the same time in the downswing and follow-through, with each force vector producing unique stress to the lumbar spine. In a standard round of golf, a golfer swings the club more than 100 times, including practice swings. The repetitive action of the swing predisposes golfers to muscle strains, herniated discs, and other injuries if they are not appropriately conditioned.

Sub-optimal physical fitness levels and inappropriate swing mechanics have been identified as risk factors for lower back injuries in golfers (Watkins et al., 1996). These factors can increase spinal loads during the golf swing, which in turn, may negatively impact a golfer's back. Direct evidence for the role of poor swing mechanics in low back pain for golfers is non-existent because the lower back is susceptible to injury from a number of different and varied sources. Medical and golf experts have long suspected that back pain in the game of golf is as much related to swing-imposed axial torques on the spine as it is to poor swing mechanics.

It has been shown that the lower back is the most frequently injured site for golfers, however, there are many probable reasons and confounders that may contribute to lower back pain in golfers. Electromyography (EMG) studies have demonstrated all the major back muscles are active at several phases during the golf swing, however, certain muscles are only active during parts of the swing. Future work needs to focus upon pinpointing when these muscles are being overloaded, thus determining when they are most vulnerable to injury. This will then allow prevention strategies to be developed that are targeted at the muscles most likely to be overloaded.

Shoulder

Another body region reported in the golf literature to have a high prevalence of injury is the shoulder. Shoulder injuries are related to the biomechanics of the golf swing (Pink et al., 1990), and problems occur most often at the top of the backswing, and less often, at the end of the follow-through. The shoulder is affected in multiple ways by the golf swing during each of the phases (Mallon & Colosimo, 1995). A professional golfer might execute over 2000 shoulder revolutions each week, and with this quantity of repetition, the tissues can break down faster than they can be repaired causing overuse injuries to develop (Pink et al., 1985; Jobe & Pink, 1996). The incidence of shoulder injuries range from 8–21% in all the previous studies.

Shoulder problems habitually occur amongst older players and on the non-dominant side (left shoulder in right-handed golfers). The deterioration of the rotator cuff in elderly people may be the basis for the higher occurrence of shoulder injuries amongst older golfers. Although not strictly an overhead sport, golf still entails a component of humeral elevation and rotation to execute a mechanically sound swing (Jobe et al., 1989). The literature shows shoulder flexibility is highly correlated to the subject's age. Studies investigating shoulder injuries in golf also highlight the effects of aging, including the relationship between degenerative changes and rotator cuff tears (Theriault & Lachance, 1998). Therefore, stretching and strengthening the shoulder joint and the surrounding muscles may help reduce the number of shoulder injuries.

Most golf-related shoulder injuries are associated with overuse or poor swing mechanics. The literature has also shown that as a golfer ages, they are more at risk of sustaining a shoulder injury due to the degeneration of the shoulder. EMG studies have shown the active shoulder muscles during certain portions of the golf swing, which should lead to further research investigating preventive strategies for different muscles during different phases of the swing. Also, further research should focus on being able to identify changes to the golf swing as a golfer ages which may help protect the shoulder complex.

Lower extremity

The lower extremity consists of the hips, legs, knees, ankles, and feet. In golf, the lower extremity has been virtually ignored in terms of preventive strategies, injury incidences, and causes of injury. There have been no scientific studies focusing on the ankle in the golf swing, with most studies focusing on ground reaction forces of the feet, and EMG activity of the hip and knee. The knee is the only lower extremity body location that consistently features in the golf injury literature, with approximately 10% of all golf injuries being to the knees.

Over the last 20 years, an increase in the overall rate of frequency of knee injuries from golf has been seen. Gutin (1996) suggested four likely reasons for this increase. First he noted there are probably more injuries as a result of a larger number of people participating in golf. Second, there have been more people who have had knee injuries and surgery in the last 20 years with the introduction of knee arthroscopy, and as such, these people may be turning to an apparently less demanding sport in golf, and unknowingly aggravating their previous knee injuries. Third, an escalating number of golfers are altering their swing to manage their back pain which may in turn be aggravating their knees. Finally, Gutin (1996) suggested current equipment that permits golfers to hit the ball further applies more pressure to the body, including the lower extremities. This suggests that golfers need to be aware of the strain they are placing upon their knees, and take care to ensure that they learn the correct mechanics of the golf swing to help protect their knees.

The lack of studies investigating the lower extremities in the golf swing may be because these areas are not as frequently injured in golf as other regions. While foot injuries are not often reported in the golfing literature, most of the biomechanical work conducted on the lower limbs has focussed on the foot. Recent studies have shown that proper biomechanics of the foot are necessary for the proper transference of weight and an efficient swing. Therefore, alterations in foot biomechanics, structure, and function may adversely affect the swing. More research needs to be conducted into the lower extremity region if these injuries are to be prevented.

Upper extremity

The upper extremity consists of the arm, elbow, forearm, wrist, and hand. There are some very specific injuries associated with the upper extremity including medial and lateral epicondylitis, De Quervain's Disease, and fractures to the hook of hamate. McCarroll et al. (1990) found lateral elbow pain to be more widespread than medial pain by a 5:1 ratio. Other investigators have found the incidence to be roughly equal (Shiri et al., 2006). Overall, the incidence of either is reported between 0.4–2.3%. The elbow and the wrist are the two areas that have been most extensively studied in this region, whilst the hand and forearm have been virtually ignored. The incidence of golf injuries to the wrist range from 16–24%, and from 11–33% in the elbow.

Once again, there has been very little information presented in the scientific literature regarding the potential causes of upper extremity injuries. Most of the injuries sustained to this area are related to overuse, miss-hits (such as striking the ground), or poor technique (gripping too tightly on the club). Possible preventive measures include having golf lessons with a golf professional so that correct technique can be taught and learnt. This might help reduce the number of miss-hits and correct over-gripping on the club which may in turn reduce the number of injuries.

Most of the injury mechanisms and preventive plans for upper extremity injuries in golf are based on racquet sport related injuries. Research focusing on the mechanics of the upper extremity and related musculature would allow for the accurate aetiology of golf-related upper extremity injuries to be determined. Understanding how these injuries occur in golfers would ensure the development of appropriate management strategies targeting golf specific injury mechanisms.

There is a severe lack of research investigating the upper extremity region in golf. The research that has been performed has looked at very specific injuries that occur to the wrist, hand, and elbow, however there have been minimal studies conducted investigating when the muscles are active and for how long they remain active. Future research needs to focus upon this aspect of upper extremity injuries.

Implications for the game

The golf swing is a very unusual high speed motion which may place considerable stress on the body. The body's motion during the golf swing can produce club head speeds over 160 kilometres per hour in less than a fifth of a second (McCarroll, 1996). Recreational golfers are anxious to emulate the techniques of professionals, but to achieve their proficiency requires extensive training and proper physical conditioning. These golfers' bodies are not prepared to receive equivalent stresses upon their bodies as those of professionals, and their performance is less efficient. This combination can result in golfing-related injury, and suitable countermeasures need to be investigated to help reduce the risk of injury to golfers.

With increased accessibility and participation, an increase in golf injuries is to be expected. Additionally, in golf, high performance and skill have limited ageing effects, and a player's career can span more than 50 years, resulting in a wide variety of player profiles with diverse physical, psychological, socioeconomic, nutritional, and functional conditions. While enjoying the game for decades, golfers show tremendous variations in practice level, competitive experience, intensity, and frequency of practice. This helps to explain why golf is one of the most diverse sports activities, and may also reflect the diversity of musculoskeletal problems encountered in the game.

There is still much to understand about how to assist golfers improve their game and avoid injury. Despite the growing body of research investigating golf injuries, much remains unknown, and translating the findings from the biomechanical, physiological, motor learning, and motor control research into injury prevention strategies, remains challenging. Diversity of ages and abilities among golfers leads to a wide spectra of injuries. Studies performed in recreational golfers have shown a lifetime injury incidence ranging from 57–62%, and a 12-month injury incidence ranging from 31.7–38.2%.

Summary and future directions

The golf swing is a complex movement that utilises the whole body in a coordinated fashion, and when repeated frequently, can result in injury. Injuries can be overuse or traumatic in nature, with overuse injuries predominating in professional golfers. Recreational golfers' injuries tend to occur secondarily to an incorrect golf swing. Fortunately, injury from a club or ball strike is rare in adults, however this is a serious issue in children. Most golf injury data have been collected retrospectively and further epidemiological study of a prospective nature is required to determine injury incidence and factors relating to the onset of injury.

In conclusion, the literature on golf injuries is mostly descriptive. The mechanisms of golf injuries and the factors that may place golfers at risk are poorly understood or controversial because of the many factors (age range, level of skill, conditions of play, cultural aspects) affect both the internal and external validity of the published studies. The treatment of sports injuries can be time consuming, difficult, and expensive, making preventive strategies justified, not just from a medical perspective, but also an economic one. Golf is also one of a few activities that people of all ages and skill level can play, however, injuries can have participation-ending consequences. As such, preventive measures need to be researched to determine the best way to keep golfers healthy and able to continue their golf participation.

References

Batt, M. (1992) A Survey of Golf Injuries in Amateur Golfers, *British Journal of Sports Medicine*, 26 (1), 63–65.

Burdoff, A.; Van Der Steenhoven, G. & Tromp-Klaren, E. (1996) A One-year Prospective Study on Back Pain among Novice Golfers, *The American Journal of Sports Medicine*, 24 (5), 659–664.

Finch, C. (2012) Getting Sports Injury Prevention on to Public Health Agendas – Addressing the Shortfalls in Current Information Sources, *British Journal of Sports Medicine*, 46 (1), 70–74.

Finch, C.; Valuri, G. & Ozanne-Smith, J. (1998) Sport and Active Recreation Injuries in Australia: Evidence from Emergency Department Presentations, *British Journal of Sports Medicine*, 32 (3), 220–225.

Fradkin, A. (2010) Golf Injuries: Par for the Course? *Medicine and Science in Sports and Exercise*, 42 (5 Supplement), 30.

Fradkin, A. (2012) Describing the Epidemiology of Female Golfing Injuries, *International Journal of Golf Science*, 1 (Supplement), S19–S20.

Fradkin, A. (2016) Does Warming-up Reduce the Risk of Injury to Golfers? A Cluster Randomized Controlled Trial, *Presentation to the World Scientific Congress on Golf VII*, St. Andrews, Scotland.

Fradkin, A.; Cameron, P. & Gabbe, B. (2005a) Children's Misadventures with Golfing Equipment, *International Journal of Injury Control and Safety Promotion*, 12 (3), 201–203.

Fradkin, A.; Cameron, P. & Gabbe, B. (2005b) Golf Injuries – Common and Potentially Avoidable, *Journal of Science and Medicine in Sport*, 8 (2), 163–170.

Fradkin, A.; Cameron, P. & Gabbe, B. (2006) Opportunities for Prevention of Golfing Injuries, *International Journal of Injury Control and Safety Promotion*, 13 (1), 46–48.

Fradkin, A. & Eisenhart, C. (2011) To Practice or to Play: Is Golf Participation Associated with an Increased Risk of Injury? *Medicine and Science in Sports and Exercise*, 43 (5 Supplement), 357.

Fradkin, A.; Finch, C. & Sherman, C. (2003) Warm-up Attitudes and Behaviours of Amateur Golfers, *Journal of Science and Medicine in Sport*, 6 (2), 210–215.

Fradkin, A.; Windley, T.; Myers, J.; Sell, T. & Lephart, S. (2007) Describing the Epidemiology and Associated Age, Gender and Handicap Comparisons of Golfing Injuries, *International Journal of Injury Control and Safety Promotion*, 14 (4), 264–266.

Gosheger, G.; Liem, D.; Ludwig, K.; Greshake, O. & Winkelmann, W. (2003) Injuries and Overuse Syndromes in Golf, *The American Journal of Sports Medicine*, 31 (3), 438–443.

Gutin, G. (1996) Knee Injuries in Golf, *Clinics in Sports Medicine*, 15 (1), 111–128.

Hadden, W.; Kelly, S. & Pumford, N. (1991) Medical Cover for "The Open" Golf Championship, *British Journal of Sports Medicine*, 26 (3), 125–127.

Hosea, T. & Gatt, C. (1996) Back Pain in Golf, *Clinics in Sportsmedicine*, 15 (1), 37–53.

Hosea, T.; Gatt, C.; Galli, K.; Langrana, N. & Zawadsky, J. (1990) Biomechanical Analysis of the Golfer's Back, In: A. Cochran (Ed.) *Science and Golf: Proceedings of the First Scientific Congress of Golf*, London: E & FN Spon, pp. 43–48.

Jobe, F.; Perry, J. & Pink, M. (1989) Electromyographic Shoulder Activity in Men and Women Professional Golfers, *The American Journal of Sports Medicine*, 17 (6), 782–789.

Jobe, F. & Pink, M. (1996) Shoulder Pain in Golf, *Clinics in Sportsmedicine*, 15 (1), 55–63.

Mallon, W. & Colosimo, A. (1995) Acromioclavicular Joint Injury in Competitive Golfers, *Journal of the Southern Orthopaedic Association*, 4 (4), 277–282.

Mallon, W. & Hawkins, R. (1994) Injuries in Golf, In: P. Renstrom (Ed.) *Clinical Practice of Sports Injury Prevention and Care*, Oxford, UK: Blackwell Scientific Publications, pp. 495–506.

McCarroll, J. (1996) The Frequency of Golf Injuries, *Clinics in Sports Medicine*, 15 (1), 1–7.

McCarroll, J. & Gioe, T. (1982) Professional Golfers and the Price They Pay, *The Physician and Sportsmedicine*, 10 (7), 64–70.

McCarroll, J.; Rettig, A. & Shelbourne, K. (1990) Injuries in the Amateur Golfer, *The Physician and Sportsmedicine*, 18 (3), 122–126.

Nicholas, J.; Reidy, M. & Oleske, D. (1998) An Epidemiologic Survey of Injury in Golfers, *Journal of Sport Rehabilitation*, 7(2), 112–121.

Pink, M.; Jobe, F. & Perry, J. (1985) Electromyographic Analysis of the Shoulder During the Golf Swing, *International Journal of Sports Biomechanics*, 1 (3), 221–232.

Pink, M.; Jobe, F. & Perry, J. (1990) Electromyographic Analysis of the Shoulder During the Golf Swing, *American Journal of Sports Medicine*, 18 (2), 137–140.

Shiri, R.; Viikari-Juntura, E.; Varonen, H. & Heliovaara, M. (2006) Prevalence and Determinants of Lateral and Medial Epicondylitis: A Population Study, *American Journal of Epidemiology*, 164 (11), 1065–1074.

Thériault, G. & Lachance, P. (1998) Golf Injuries – An Overview, *Sports Medicine*, 26 (1), 43–57.

Thériault, G.; Lacoste, E. & Gaboury, M. (1996) Golf Injury Characteristics: A Survey from 528 Golfers, *Medicine and Science in Sports and Exercise*, 28 (5), 65.

van Mechelen, W. (1997) The Severity of Sports Injuries, *Sports Medicine*, 24 (3), 176–180.

van Mechelen, W.; Hlobil, H. & Kemper, H. (1992) Incidence, Severity, Aetiology and Prevention of Sports Injuries. A Review of Concepts, *Sports Medicine*, 14 (2), 82–99.

Watkins, R.; Uppal, G.; Perry, J.; Pink, M. & Dinsay, J. (1996) Dynamic Electromyographic Analysis of Trunk Musculature in Professional Golfers, *American Journal of Sports Medicine*, 24 (4), 535–538.

Wilks, J. & Jones, D. (1996) Golf-related Injuries Seen at Hospital Emergency Departments, *The Australian Journal of Science and Medicine in Sport*, 28 (2), 43–45.

32

NUTRITION FOR GOLF

Graeme L. Close, Jamie Pugh and James P. Morton

Introduction

Sport nutrition is becoming increasingly recognised as one of the most important subdisciplines of sports science, with the sports nutritionist now becoming an integral part of the support team for elite golfers. Nutrition is an important component that needs to be considered by golfers since it can impact body composition, game day performance, recovery from training and competition, immune function, adaptations to training and general health. Despite the increased awareness of the importance of sport nutrition, athletes across a multitude of sports demonstrate a lack of nutritional knowledge (Alaunyte et al., 2015; Devlin & Belski, 2015), and professional golfers are certainly no exception. This chapter will discuss some of the current research into sport nutrition, the limited golf-specific research, as well as offer practical recommendations for the golfer.

Review of the current literature

Unlike endurance and team sports, research into nutrition in golf is limited, with only a handful of papers found on the topic (Smith, 2010). Given the lack of golf-specific research, much of the following information were drawn and modified from the most relevant literature available across other sports, as well as personal reflections and observations from the authors' own experiences from working with elite-level golfers.

Carbohydrates

Given that the body's storage capacity for carbohydrates (CHO) is limited (~500 g), but that muscle glycogen (the body's main store of CHO) is the main fuel source for moderate to high-intensity exercise, an adequate dietary intake of CHO has traditionally been the focus for many athletes. However, there has been a great deal of debate regarding the role of CHO in an athlete's diet, especially for sports like golf, given the low-intensity nature of the game. With this in mind, it is probably important to consider the CHO requirements of golf competition and training separately.

CHO and golf performance

It is now well recognised that both endogenous and exogenous CHO can improve competition performance in a variety of endurance and team sports. Such sports are typically characterised by 90 minutes of high-intensity activity that is dependent on CHO metabolism (Krustrup et al., 2006; Leckey et al., 2016). Given the lower overall intensity of golf, and the reduced rate of CHO oxidation, such research does not directly translate to the elite golfer. It is noteworthy, however, that elite players can take over 2,000 swings (Pink et al., 1993), with up to 300 powerful movements per practice (Theriault & Lachance, 1998), and cover in excess of 10 km during the course of play (Smith, 2010). As such, many golfers perceive fatigue in the latter stages of play and show increased signs of both mental and physical fatigue as play duration increases (Doan et al., 2007). This may in part be due to the fall in blood glucose that has been observed following an 18-hole round. For example, it has been shown that blood glucose can fall by as much as 10–30% during a round (Broman et al., 2004). Both low-level fatigue and reductions in blood glucose have been related to a lack of focus and poor decision making (Brooks et al., 2000), which could impair performance, especially towards the end of a round. While the provision of high CHO diets and glycogen-loading strategies may not be required for golfers, the provision of CHO-containing foods 'during' play would still seem advisable in order to potentially offset any manifestation of fatigue.

CHO and golf training

Many golfers now include some form of non-golf training, such as aerobic exercise, high-intensity intermittent training or resistance training into their everyday training programmes. The focus of this structured exercise can either be to manipulate body composition (including reducing fat mass or gaining lean muscle mass) or to improve physical strength and fitness, with the intention that this will then translate into improved on-course performance. It is now well known that nutrition (especially CHO) is able to regulate adaptions to exercise training (Bartlett et al., 2015), and therefore, golfers should be knowledgeable on how to fuel these training sessions to ensure maximum benefit. Given the potential for individual differences in training load and daily routines, elite golfers should seek professional advice in tailoring their individual CHO requirements. Nonetheless, if it is assumed that the modern-day golfer incorporates a daily training session into their practice routines, a general CHO intake of 4–5 g.kg^{-1} body mass per day would be recommended. Such recommendations are based on the most recent guidelines from the International Olympic Committee (IOC) (Burke et al., 2011). It should be stressed that flexibility in CHO requirements is advisable; for example, lower intakes could be recommended when trying to reduce body fat loss (e.g., <3 g.kg^{-1} body mass), while higher intakes (>5 g.kg^{-1} body mass) may be helpful when trying to increase lean muscle mass. The type of CHO is also important, with research suggesting that lower glycaemic index (GI) CHO offers a metabolic advantage. Some common foods typically eaten by golfers include:

* high GI – boiled potato, whole-meal bread, boiled white rice
* medium GI – boiled brown rice, sweet potato, oat porridge
* low GI – banana, whole meal spaghetti, carrots

Proteins

Proteins are essential for life and are crucial for a variety of key functions in the human body. The body contains structural proteins, contractile proteins, immunoproteins and regulatory proteins. It is crucial to recognise that proteins are continually broken down and remade throughout the day.

This constant turnover allows for damaged proteins to be removed and replaced and new proteins to be formed in response to exercise training. Given this continual turnover of proteins, athletes should consume protein regularly, and in sufficient quantities throughout the day, to allow adaptations to exercise training to occur. This does not necessarily require large doses of protein, with approximately 20–30 g of high-quality protein being sufficient per meal (Phillips, 2011), or approximately 0.3 g of protein per kg body mass per meal (Moore et al., 2015). To put this in context, one large chicken fillet contains approximately 30 g of protein.

Protein requirements of golfers

There is a growing appreciation that strength is essential for optimal golf performance, with lower handicap players possessing greater strength in movements that mimic the golf swing compared to higher handicap players (Sell et al., 2007). An effective strategy to increase both muscle mass and strength is to combine resistance-type exercise with an adequate dietary protein intake (Kerksick et al., 2006; Willoughby et al., 2007). As such, across all sports, protein supplements have become the most widely used of all sports supplements. There is a great deal of debate with regard to the protein needs of golfers, and hence, athletes are often confused with regard to their daily needs. Some researchers believe that athletes in general do not require additional protein intake (Rodriguez et al., 2009), while others suggest that the protein needs of athletes are significantly higher than that recommended for sedentary individuals (Lemon, 1995; Phillips, 2004). There is also considerable debate as to whether protein supplements are required, or if the protein needs of athletes can be achieved from diet alone. With specific reference to golfers, this debate is heavily influenced by the size of the golfer in question and their training demands. For example, an appropriate daily protein intake has been suggested to be approximately 2 g.kg^{-1} body mass per day for athletes engaged in resistance training, which is easily achieved for a 75 kg golfer (150 g per day of protein, equivalent to approximately five chicken breasts). However, this dose of protein is much harder to achieve in a 100 kg golfer (200 g per day of protein, equivalent to approximately seven chicken breasts).

When working with elite golfers, a general recommendation is to distribute protein intake evenly throughout the day starting at breakfast, with a final feed prior to bedtime. Typically, golfers backload their protein intake with inadequate protein at breakfast, and then face large gaps during the day during practice or game play that is not optimal for muscle recovery and growth. It is, therefore, crucial that golfers plan their day effectively and take food with them to be consumed during their rounds or during long practice sessions.

Fats

Fat has historically been viewed in a negative light, and as such, many golfers attempting to reduce fat mass believe that they should eliminate all fats from their diets. Over the last decade, a number of studies have challenged this belief, even questioning the assumption that all saturated fats are problematic (Hu, 2010). Although an excessive intake of fat is a problem for general health and weight control (as is over-consumption of any macronutrient), too little dietary fat is also a problem for health. The body needs a good supply of essential fatty acids (omega 3 and omega 6 fatty acids), as well as the fat-soluble vitamins A, D, E, and K. Finally, it should also be noted that fats are required during exercise as an energy store, especially when the exercise is greater than 90 minutes, which is therefore important in 4–5 hour rounds of golf. In terms of reducing fat mass, rather than demonise one particular macronutrient, i.e., fat or CHO, golfers should develop strategies to ensure that their energy intake is less than expenditure, ensuring this still contains healthy fats.

Types of dietary fat

Fats are generally classified as saturated or unsaturated based on their chemical structure. Despite some foods being described as saturated or unsaturated fats, all fats contain a mixture of fatty acids, and they are simply classified according to the majority fat source they contain. Therefore, it may be unwise to advise golfers regarding the types of fats they should be consuming, and better advice may simply be based on recognising the best types of food to eat (Astrup et al., 2011). Traditionally, saturated fats have been classed as 'bad fats', and have been advised to be consumed in moderation, whereas unsaturated fats have been classed as 'good fats'. A major problem with the notion of removing saturated fats from the diet is the issue of what to replace them with. Studies have clearly demonstrated that reducing saturated fat intake will be of no benefit, and can even cause more harm, if the saturated fats are replaced with refined CHO (Hu, 2010). In contrast, replacing some saturated fats with unsaturated fats including foods such as salmon, nuts, avocadoes, and seeds, has been shown to improve health. The simple message is to choose 'natural' fats and avoid processed ones, especially trans fats that should, without question, be eliminated from a golfer's diet. Typically, trans fats are found in some margarines and some deep fried foods. Conversely, fats found in foods such as oily fish, nuts, avocado, and olive oil play a crucial role in an athlete's diet, and should be encouraged.

Hydration

The main biological mechanism for losing heat during exercise is through evaporation of sweat. Dehydration due to sweat loss has been shown to reduce cognitive function and alertness in a number of athletic populations (Grandjean & Grandjean, 2007). In golfers, mild dehydration has been shown to reduce shot distance and shot accuracy, and impair players' distance judgement (Smith et al., 2012), which could have significant implications, especially when competing in hot conditions, or in countries with high humidity. Given that rounds of golf are now often in excess of 5 hours, even walking for this length of time, especially on warm days, is likely to result in dehydration. In addition to fluid loss *per se*, sweat also contains electrolytes such as sodium, chloride, potassium, calcium, and magnesium, and it is important that these are replaced, as well as water. Simple monitoring strategies such as examining clothing post-exercise for salt stains may help identify golfers with increased electrolyte loss through sweat, though sweat patch testing is the preferred objective method for assessing this.

Fluid requirements for golfers

In an attempt to ensure pre-exercise euhydration, it is recommended that 5–7 ml.kg^{-1} of fluid (approximately 0.5 L for a 75 kg golfer) is consumed at least 4 hours prior to exercise (Sawka et al., 2007). Additionally, if the individual does not produce urine, or the urine remains dark coloured, a further 3–5 ml.kg^{-1} should be consumed about 2 hours before exercise. Drinking within this time schedule should allow for fluid absorption, and enable urine output to return to normal levels (Sawka et al., 2007). Consumption of low calorie sports drinks at this time, as opposed to water, may also be beneficial given that they also contain electrolytes, and cold beverages (10° C) are beneficial to reduce the rise in body temperature during exercise (Lee & Shirreffs, 2007). Further, many companies now produce tubes of low calorie electrolyte tablets that are ideal for golfers to keep in their golf bag during a round to make their own sports drinks, without the need to carry multiple bottles, or pre made sports drink.

After training or competition, the goal is to replace any fluid and electrolyte loss incurred by the exercise sessions. The extent of the drinking strategy is dependent on the time-scale with which re-hydration must occur. Current guidelines recommend 1.5 L of fluid for every 1 kg body mass loss induced by exercise (Sawka et al., 2007). This suggests that where possible, it is beneficial for golfers to monitor their weight prior to, and following, a round of golf to assess the extent of the dehydration that may have occurred. Furthermore, fluids should be consumed (with electrolytes) over time as opposed to large boluses (Kovacs et al., 2002), to maximise fluid retention. Golfers should be aware of their hydration status when they have double rounds, or even during 4 day competition, as a poor rehydration strategy over 4 days could lead to impaired performance towards the end of the tournament.

Micronutrients

Micronutrients are compounds that are required in small quantities (<1 g) to maintain normal physiological function. Broadly speaking, micronutrients can be divided into vitamins and minerals. While it is accepted that deficiency in most micronutrients could adversely affect health and performance, it is also known that some micronutrients taken in excess could be equally harmful to health. A full review of the different vitamins and minerals is beyond the scope of this text, but there are many comprehensive reviews for those interested (Serra & Beavers, 2015).

Assessing if a golfer is deficient in micronutrients

It is important to identify factors that may increase the chances of a golfer suffering from deficiencies in micro-nutrients. Some major factors that could contribute to micronutrient deficiencies include:

- eliminating food groups from diets, either due to food dislikes, allergies, modern dietary trends, or moral reasons;
- low-calorie diets often utilised when attempting to reduce body fat;
- very low fat diets, which could affect the fat-soluble vitamins;
- a lack of variety in the diet;
- lack of sunlight exposure (including constant use of sunscreen or protective clothing).

Micronutrients that athletes are most likely to be deficient in include: vitamin D, iron (particularly in female athletes), zinc, magnesium, and calcium (Misner, 2006). However, in practice, unless golfers fit into one of the categories described above, it is highly unlikely they will be deficient in micronutrients, with the exception of vitamin D, given that this vitamin is mainly obtained from sunlight rather than diet (Owens et al., 2015).

Sports supplements and ergogenic aids

A recent systematic review suggested that around 60% of all athletes regularly use dietary sport supplements (Knapik et al., 2016), with a higher prevalence in elite athletes compared with non-elite athletes. Once an athlete's diet has initially been addressed, there may be some instances where a targeted supplement plan may be of use, but this should only be prescribed by qualified individuals (such as those on the Sport and Exercise Nutrition Register (SENr)) who are up-to-date with current golf-specific anti-doping regulations.

It is crucial that golfers considering using supplements only obtain them from companies that have their products independently batch tested. Golfers should also be aware that although a product may have been tested, this does not guarantee that the supplement is drug free, with testing of products best described as 'risk-minimisation'. It is not possible within this chapter to cover all supplements available to golfers, thus the reader is referred to a book by Castell et al. (2015) as well as collection of review articles entitled the A–Z of sports supplements published in The British Journal of Sports Medicine over a period of years. Some supplements that may be applicable to golf and their ergogenic claims include:

Creatine has been shown to improve speed, strength, and power, although supplementation can increase body mass, which may not be desirable by all golfers.

Caffeine – benefits include increased lipid oxidation, increased mental alertness, and improved performance during prolonged exercise. However, high doses can cause side effects such as nausea and tremors, which may be detrimental during putting. Moreover, if golfers take this late in the day, it could also affect sleep. A typical performance enhancing dose of caffeine is approximately 2 mg.kg^{-1} body mass. So, for a 75 kg golfer this would be 150 mg, the equivalent to a strong filter coffee, or 3 pro plus tablets. Recently, research has suggested that this dose of caffeine (155 mg) consumed before and after 9 holes, improved golf-specific markers of performance including total score, iron club accuracy, greens in regulation, and driving distance in skilled golfers, likely due to offsetting the reduced energy levels experienced during a competitive round of golf.

Fish oil – claimed to improve heart and brain health, as well as promoting muscle protein synthesis, and improving immune function. Also claims that it may reduce inflammation, which could be useful during tournament situations. Research is still limited so it is difficult to recommend a strategy, although the most recent suggestions indicate approximately 1 g of high-quality eicosapentaenoic acid (EPA)/docosahexaenoic acid (DHA) per day.

Probiotics – helps to support normal functioning of the digestive tract as well as improve general immune function. Important that a broad-spectrum probiotic is taken with >10 billion live cultures.

Vitamin D – many golfers are deficient in vitamin D due to the use of high-factor sun creams and lack of sunlight exposure. Low vitamin D can be detrimental to bone health, immune function, and muscle recovery. Supplementation with 2000 IU of vitamin D$_3$ per day during the winter months will help deficient golfers.

Implications for the game of golf

As the cardiorespiratory demands of golf are not considered intense, the resultant energy demands are relatively low compared to other sports (Smith, 2010). However, given that an elite player can cover in excess of 10 km during the course of play, with a single round taking between 3 and 6 hours, effective nutrition strategies both before, and during match play, can help prevent the onset of mental or physical fatigue. Moreover, it is important to remember that including a one hour warm up, post-game recovery, and a 5 hour round, this could take up 7 hours of the golfer's day, and therefore, it is also important to consider the long term effects of poor eating during the vast majority of the day. A simple strategy for elite golfers can be seen in Table 32.1.

Table 32.1 Timing of game day food intake in relation to tee off time

Tee time Food and timings

Tee time			GAME				
7 am	5 am **Breakfast** Muesli with Greek yoghurt	6.30 am **Snack** Muesli bar or banana	GAME See following section	12 noon **Lunch** Protein (meat, fish) with colourful vegetables and CHO (i.e., rice, potatoes)	3 pm **Snack** Greek yoghurt and fresh berries	6 pm **Dinner** Chicken and vegetable stir fry with small portion of rice	9 pm **Snack** Glass of milk
11 am	9 am **Breakfast** 2–3 poached eggs on 2 wholegrain slices of toast and a banana	10.30 am **Snack** Muesli bar or banana	GAME See following section	4 pm **Snack** Greek yoghurt and fresh berries	6.30 pm **Dinner** Chicken and vegetable stir fry with rice	9 pm **Snack** Glass of milk	
1 pm	9 am **Breakfast** 3 poached eggs on 3 wholegrain slices of toast with baked beans and a banana with yoghurt	11.30 am **Snack** Muesli bar or banana	GAME See following section	6.00 pm **Dinner** Chicken and vegetable stir fry with rice	9 pm **Snack** Glass of milk with Greek yoghurt and berries		

These are suggestions to highlight the timing of food intake, and the actual choices of the food can be changed to suit the player's personal preferences.

In-game nutrition strategy

During match-play, golfers should consume food every 60–90 minutes. Convenient snacks such as nuts and seeds, or muesli bars are easy to carry on course, pack during international travel, and can again provide a more sustained release of energy. Players should also ensure adequate hydration, especially in warmer, more humid climates. Taking a 'little and often' approach is often advised, but rarely implemented in practice. Carrying a water bottle and a tube of electrolyte tablets out on the course, and taking a mouthful of fluid at the end of each hole, is a simple way to try to maintain hydration status. It is important to stress though that golfers should not force fluid into themselves, and thirst should also be used to help dictate how much to drink. A practical feeding strategy during a round may be to consume food at holes 5, 10, and 15. Holes 5 and 15 should generally be snack-based foods such as muesli bars, while hole 10 should contain protein as well as CHO, such as a chicken wrap. Practically, many courses do not provide the quality of food recommended, or it may be hard to get a chicken wrap at 9 am ready to be consumed at hole 10, therefore golfers are strongly advised to be prepared and bring their own food with them. Golfers could also implement a check-list system including what foods and drinks to pack in their golf bag, as well as timings that the items should be consumed. Simply putting a circle around holes 5, 10, and 15 on the scorecard can remind the golfer to eat at the correct times.

Weight gain for golfers

There are two key nutritional considerations when it comes to increasing lean muscle mass: (1) the golfer must consume sufficient calories on a daily basis, and (2) protein intake must be sufficient to allow for maximum rates of muscle protein synthesis. Golfers often fail on both of these, hence their struggle to gain lean muscle mass. The 2 major components of total energy expenditure are the resting metabolic rate (RMR) (energy used at rest and everyday living), and the thermic effects of exercise (energy used playing golf and in the gym). There are equations available to estimate RMR, and one that is commonly used with athletes (since it is based upon lean muscle mass) is the Cunningham equation:

RMR = 500 + (22 × lean body mass in kg) (Cunningham, 1991).

For a 75 kg golfer with 12% body fat, this predicts a RMR of 1952 Kcal. Energy expenditure during golf has been estimated (Murase et al., 1989), with data suggesting that the rate is approximately 6 Kcal per minute of golf, (i.e., 1440 Kcal for a typical 4 hour round). Therefore, in a typical day, if a 75 kg golfer engages in one game of golf (1440 Kcal), and one hour in the gym (estimating 500 Kcal), accounting for their RMR (1952 Kcal), their minimum energy requirement would be around 3892 Kcal. If golfers desire to gain lean mass, a daily energy surplus of 500 Kcal is recommended, and so a daily food intake could equate to 4392 Kcal, almost double that of a non-athlete. It is therefore not surprising that the biggest mistake made by young golfers trying to gain lean muscle mass is they simply do not eat enough food. From this daily food intake, golfers should consume sufficient protein to gain lean muscle mass (see protein requirement section).

Weight loss for golfers

Another common nutritional service requested by the modern professional golfer is for diets to be prescribed to assist in reductions in fat mass. To achieve a reduction in body mass, it is necessary to induce a daily calorie deficit, not just a low CHO diet. It is important that this energy deficit does not come from protein, as this has been shown to result in a loss of lean muscle mass, with evidence beginning to emerge that protein should actually increase when athletes are in a calorie deficit to preserve their lean mass. Intakes of approximately 2.5 g kg^{-1} have been effective for athletes trying to preserve lean mass while in a calorie deficit (Mettler et al., 2010).

The major change in this diet compared to that of a weight maintenance, or weight gain diet, is a reduction in CHO and fat intake to facilitate the reduced energy intake. It is important to stress that this is not a zero CHO diet, and that CHO are still included, often around training sessions to fuel maximum performance. Contrary to popular belief, fat loss is not as simple as just reducing CHO intake. A total energy deficit is paramount, and the reduced CHO intake is just one practical method to achieve this.

Nutrition for the travelling golfer

With major championships and Opens taking place all over the world, international travel offers a unique challenge to the elite golfer. During long haul flights, dry air is circulated throughout the plane through air conditioning units. This dry air can cause gradual and unperceived dehydration. Therefore, athletes are advised to consume small amounts of fluid regularly throughout the flight. The electrolyte tablets golfers keep in their golf bag are ideal to bring onto a plane to make electrolyte drinks. Athletes may also need to plan to bring their own food supplies, as on-board options from airlines can often fail to meet the nutritional needs of the elite athlete.

Making prior contact with any agencies or accommodation venues can afford athletes or coaches the opportunity to request particular menu plans, or make alternate arrangements if these cannot be met. Where this is the case, it may be possible to bring or send non-perishable foods, although this will be subject to any customs laws in force within each country. As well as ensuring availability of well-accustomed food, this will also offer the benefit of reducing the risk of gastrointestinal illness that is often associated with unaccustomed foods.

Travel-related gastrointestinal disturbances are common occurrences for athletes, and will have negative effects on athletes' well-being and performance. As many as 60% of athletes travelling for international training or competition experience 'travellers' diarrhoea' (Reilly et al., 2007), often caused by pathogens within food or water (Boggess, 2007). Therefore, it is important for athletes to be vigilant in their food choices, and avoid foods such as raw or unpeeled fruits and vegetables, uncooked meats, and unpasteurised dairy products (Young et al., 2006). Athletes should also practice good personal hygiene including washing their hands thoroughly before meals.

Summary and future directions

This chapter has (unfortunately) had to rely on many studies performed in sports other than golf. As a consequence, there are still many fundamental nutritional questions that remain unanswered within the sport. However, a number of key suggestions and recommendations, which if implemented correctly, could improve the health and performance of many golfers include:

1   While CHO may not be as important in golf as others sports, research has suggested that maintenance of blood glucose during the round could improve performance, and therefore, strategies should be put in place to provide foods containing CHO regularly during the game.
2   Protein is an essential nutrient for all athletes, including golfers. Golfers should aim for approximately 2 g of protein per kg of body mass per day, and this should be split evenly across 4-5 meals, including eating some protein during the round.

3 Fats are an integral part of every golfer's diet, with natural sources such as nuts, dairy, meats, and olive oil preferred. Golfers trying to drop body fat should be aware that fats are energy dense, so caution should be taken not to overeat them.

4 Dehydration prior to, and during the round, can negatively affect game-day performance. Golfers should implement a structured hydration plan at all times, and self-monitor their hydration status.

5 Unless golfers fall into a specific category (eliminating food groups, trying to drop body fat etc.), it is unlikely that they will need specific vitamin or mineral supplements. An exception to this could be vitamin D, and where possible, players should get their vitamin D concentrations checked.

6 There are few sports supplements that have golf-specific ergogenic effects. If supplements are to be used, it is vital that they are tested for prohibited substances. Before taking any sports supplement, golfers should check them with a qualified sport nutritionist, ideally someone on the SENr or equivalent. Things like caffeine and creatine, if taken correctly, could offer some benefit.

7 During a round of golf it is crucial that players are organised and bring food with them. Players should establish consistent eating patterns during the game, and use a checklist to help to facilitate this. The food available in the golf shop may not be sufficient, so bringing their own food is often advisable.

8 Travel presents a particular problem for many golfers. It is crucial that golfers consider the travel related nutritional problems, and plan ahead to counteract many of these issues. With careful planning, and the provision of their own food, it is possible to deal with all of the travel related nutritional problems.

References

Alaunyte, I.; Perry, J. & Aubrey, T. (2015) Nutritional Knowledge and Eating Habits of Professional Rugby League Players: Does Knowledge Translate into Practice? *Journal of the International Society of Sports Nutrition*, 12 (1), 18–27.

Astrup, A.; Dyerberg, J.; Elwood, P.; Hermansen, K.; Hu, F.; Jakobsen, M.; Kok, F.; Krauss, R.; Lecerf, J.; Legrand, P.; Nestel, P.; Riserus, U.; Sanders, T.; Sinclair, A.; Stender, S.; Tholstrup, T. & Willett, W. (2011) The Role of Reducing Intakes of Saturated Fat in the Prevention of Cardiovascular Disease: Where Does the Evidence Stand in 2010? *American Journal of Clinical Nutrition*, 93 (4), 684–688.

Bartlett, J.; Hawley, J. & Morton, J. (2015) Carbohydrate Availability and Exercise Training Adaptation: Too Much of a Good Thing? *European Journal of Sport Science*, 15 (1), 3–12.

Boggess, B. (2007) Gastrointestinal Infections in the Traveling Athlete, *Current Sports Medicine Reports*, 6 (2), 125–129.

Broman, G.; Johnsson, L. & Kaijser, L. (2004) Golf: A High Intensity Interval Activity for Elderly Men, *Aging Clinical and Experimental Research*, 16 (5), 375–381.

Brooks, G.; Fahey, T.; White, T. & Baldwin, K. (2000) *Exercise Physiology: Human Bioenergetics and Its Applications*, Mountain view, CA: Mayfield Press.

Burke, L.; Hawley, J.; Wong, S. & Jeukendrup, A. (2011) Carbohydrates for Training and Competition, *Journal of Sports Sciences*, 29 (Supplement 1), S17–S27.

Castell, L.; Stear, S. & Burke, L. M. (Eds.) (2015) *Nutritional Supplements in Sport, Exercise and Health: An AZ Guide*, London: Routledge.

Cunningham, J. (1991) Body Composition as a Determinant of Energy Expenditure: A Synthetic Review and a Proposed General Prediction Equation, *American Journal of Clinical Nutrition*, 54 (6), 963–969.

Devlin, B. & Belski, R. (2015) Exploring General and Sports Nutrition and Food Knowledge in Elite Male Australian Athletes, *International Journal of Sport Nutrition and Exercise Metabolism*, 25 (3), 225–232.

Doan, B.; Newton, R.; Kraemer, W.; Kwon, Y. & Scheet, T. (2007) Salivary Cortisol, Testosterone, and T/C Ratio Responses During a 36-Hole Golf Competition, *International Journal of Sports Medicine*, 28 (6), 470–479.

Grandjean, A. & Grandjean, N. (2007) Dehydration and Cognitive Performance, *Journal of the American College of Nutrition*, 26 (Supplement 5), 549S–554S.

Hu, F. (2010) Are Refined Carbohydrates Worse than Saturated Fat? *American Journal of Clinical Nutrition*, 91 (6), 1541–1542.

Kerksick, C.; Rasmussen, C.; Lancaster, S.; Magu, B.; Smith, P.; Melton, C.; Greenwood, M.; Almada, A.; Earnest, C. & Kreider, R. (2006) The Effects of Protein and Amino Acid Supplementation on Performance and Training Adaptations During Ten Weeks of Resistance Training, *Journal of Strength and Conditioning Research*, 20 (3), 643–653.

Knapik, J.; Steelman, R.; Hoedebecke, S.; Austin, K.; Farina, E. & Lieberman, H. (2016) Prevalence of Dietary Supplement Use by Athletes: Systematic Review and Meta-analysis, *Sports Medicine*, 46 (1), 103–123.

Kovacs, E.; Schmahl, R.; Senden, J. & Brouns, F. (2002) Effect of High and Low Rates of Fluid Intake on Post-exercise Rehydration, *International Journal of Sport Nutrition and Exercise Metabolism*, 12 (1), 14–23.

Krustrup, P.; Mohr, M.; Steensberg, A.; Bencke, J.; Kjaer, M. & Bangsbo, J. (2006) Muscle and Blood Metabolites During a Soccer Game: Implications for Sprint Performance, *Medicine and Science in Sports and Exercise*, 38 (6), 1165–1174.

Leckey, J.; Burke, L.; Morton, J. & Hawley, J. (2016) Altering Fatty Acid Availability Does Not Impair Prolonged, Continuous Running to Fatigue: Evidence for Carbohydrate Dependence, *Journal of Applied Physiololgy*, 120 (2), 107–113.

Lee, J. & Shirreffs, S. (2007) The Influence of Drink Temperature on Thermoregulatory Responses During Prolonged Exercise in a Moderate Environment, *Journal of Sports Science*, 25 (9), 975–985.

Lemon, P. (1995) Do Athletes Need More Dietary Protein and Amino Acids? *International Journal of Sport Nutrition*, 5 (Supplement 1), 39–61.

Mettler, S.; Mitchell, N. & Tipton, K. (2010) Increased Protein Intake Reduces Lean Body Mass Loss During Weight Loss in Athletes, *Medicine and Science in Sports and Exercise*, 42 (2), 326–337.

Misner, B. (2006) Food Alone May Not Provide Sufficient Micronutrients for Preventing Deficiency, *Journal of the International Society of Sports Nutrition*, 3 (1), 51–56.

Moore, D.; Churchward-Venne, T.; Witard, O.; Breen, L.; Burd, N.; Tipton, K. & Phillips, S. M. (2015) Protein Ingestion to Stimulate Myofibrillar Protein Synthesis Requires Greater Relative Protein Intakes in Healthy Older Versus Younger Men, *Journal Gerontology a Biological Science Medical Science*, 70 (1), 57–62.

Murase, Y.; Kamei, S. & Hoshikawa, T. (1989) Heart Rate and Metabolic Responses to Participation in Golf, *Journal of Sports Medicine and Physical Fitness*, 29 (3), 269–272.

Owens, D.; Fraser, W. & Close, G. (2015) Vitamin D and the Athlete: Emerging Insights, *European Journal of Sport Science*, 15 (1), 73–84.

Phillips, S. (2004) Protein Requirements and Supplementation in Strength Sports, *Nutrition*, 20 (7–8), 689–695.

Phillips, S. (2011) The Science of Muscle Hypertrophy: Making Dietary Protein Count, *Proceedings of the Nutrition Society*, 70 (1), 100–103.

Pink, M.; Perry, J. & Jobe, F. (1993) Electromyographic Analysis of the Trunk in Golfers, *American Journal of Sports Medicine*, 21 (3), 385–388.

Reilly, T;, Waterhouse, J.; Burke, L. & Alonso, J. M. (2007) Nutrition for Travel, *Journal of Sports Sciences*, 25 (S1), S125–S134.

Rodriguez, N.; Dimarco, N. & Langley, S. (2009) Position of the American Dietetic Association, Dietitians of Canada, and the American College of Sports Medicine: Nutrition and Athletic Performance, *Journal of the American Dietetic Association*, 109 (3), 509–527.

Sawka, M.; Burke, L.; Eichner, E.; Maughan, R.; Montain, S. & Stachenfeld, N. (2007) American College of Sports Medicine Position Stand. Exercise and Fluid Replacement, *Medicine in Science of Sports and Exercise*, 39 (2), 377–390.

Sell, T.; Tsai, Y.; Smoliga, J.; Myers, J. & Lephart, S. (2007) Strength, Flexibility, and Balance Characteristics of Highly Proficient Golfers, *Journal of Strength and Conditioning Research*, 21 (4), 1166–1171.

Serra, M. & Beavers, K. (2015) Essential and Nonessential Micronutrients in Sport, In: M. Greenwood; M. Cooke; T. Ziegenfuss; D, Kalman & J. Antonio (Eds.) *Nutritional Supplements in Sports and Exercise*, Switzerland: Springer, pp. 77–103.

Smith, M. (2010) The Role of Physiology in the Development of Golf Performance, *Sports Medicine*, 40 (8), 635–655.

Smith, M.; Newell, A. & Baker, M. (2012) Effect of Acute Mild Dehydration on Cognitive-Motor Performance in Golf, *Journal of Strength and Conditioning Research*, 26 (11), 3075–3080.

Theriault, G. & Lachance, P. (1998) Golf Injuries. An Overview, *Sports Medicine*, 26 (1), 43–57.

Willoughby, D.; Stout, J. & Wilborn, C. (2007) Effects of Resistance Training and Protein Plus Amino Acid Supplementation on Muscle Anabolism, Mass, and Strength, *Amino Acids*, 32 (4), 467–477.

Young, M.; Fricker, P.; Burke, L. & Deakin, V. (2006) Medical and Nutritional Issues for the Travelling Athlete, In: L. Burke & V. Deakin (Eds.) *Clinical Sports Nutrition* (3rd Ed.), Sydney, NSW: McGraw-Hill, pp. 755–764.

33

THE SCIENCE OF THE YIPS

Robert E. Wharen, Jr., Debbie J. Crews and Charles H. Adler

Introduction

The 'yips' is a phenomenon in which there is a loss of fine motor skills, without apparent explanation, that can occur in a number of different sporting activities, including darts, cricket, snooker, baseball, rugby, tennis, archery, rifle shooting and particularly golf. A similar phenomenon occurs in musicians (violinists, guitarists, pianists, woodwind players) and in others performing specific activities, including telegraph operators, seamstresses, knitters, masons, painters, enamellers, cigarette makers or those with writer's cramp. Athletes affected by the yips demonstrate an unexplained deterioration or loss of previous skills, and in golf, the yips most commonly involves putting, short putts in particular. Athletes affected by the yips may sometimes recover their ability, sometimes compensate by changing technique, or may be forced to abandon their sport often at a high level. Currently, science cannot completely explain why someone with a highly refined motor skill (putting) should lose that ability.

Review of current research

Defining the yips

The question of what are the yips is both important and complex. Hypotheses (Table 33.1) have been proposed suggesting that the yips may be a psychological problem, a mechanical flaw, a focal dystonia, a combination or continuum of a neurological problem and performance anxiety, or a dysfunction of a motor-neural network.

The yips can have different meanings dependent upon how one approaches or examines the phenomenon. Overall, the yips is a colloquial term that is often thought to have been coined by the Scottish golfer Tommy Armour, who defined it as "a brain spasm that impairs the short game" (Owen, 2014, p. 30). Although well known to golfers, the yips first entered the medical literature in 1977 (Foster, 1977) when it was considered akin to the occupational neuroses. Sir William Gowers, an articulate and revered 19th-century neurologist, described the occupational neuroses as a

> group of maladies in which certain symptoms are excited by the attempt to perform some often-repeated muscular action, commonly one that is involved in the occupation of the sufferer ... Other acts do not excite the symptom and are not interfered

with. The most frequent symptom is spasm in the part, which disturbs or prevents the due performance of the intended action.

(Gowers, 1886, pp. 656–657)

Writer's cramp, one of the more common of the occupational neuroses, was first described by Bell (1833) as an epidemic among clerks of the British Civil Service and attributed to the new steel pen nib. Our understanding of the pathophysiology of these 'occupational neuroses' remains, at best, incompletely understood. Critchley (1977, p. 368) reviewed the topic of occupational palsies in musicians and described the 'violinist's cancer', an occupational cramp involving the bowing hand "causing an audible and offensive extension of the note". Lees (1985) described that a person with these disorders is not usually overtly neurotic, with none of the accepted accompaniments of hysteria, and the problem is a rogue conditioned reflex. The affected movements are skilled, and he proposed that the yips were a form of an occupational cramp akin to the craft palsies previously described by Gowers and others.

Expanding on the concept of occupational neuroses, McDaniel et al. (1989) proposed that the yips represented a form of focal dystonia that shares many features with other occupational dystonias or cramps. The study consisted of a 69-item questionnaire mailed to 1,050 golfers that included 500 Professional Golfers' Association (PGA) club members from the United States (300 regular tour members and 200 senior tour members), 300 United States Golf Association (USGA) members and 250 Ladies Professional Golf Association (LPGA) members. Of the 360 golfers who returned the questionnaires, 28% reported suffering from the yips, described as freezing (61%), jerks (49%), jerks and tremors (9%), tremors (8%), jerks and spams (7%), spasms (4%) or a combination (23%). All golfers were affected during tournaments, and 77% reported intensification with anxiety. Interestingly, 24% reported involvement in activities other than golfing such as writing, billiards and playing a musical instrument. There was no difference in performance anxiety between yips-affected and non-affected golfers. One demographic feature and one psychiatric question statistically differentiated between the two groups: the number of years of golf played was greater, and obsessional thinking more common, in the yips affected golfers.

Although early investigators emphasized the organic basis for occupational cramps (Poore, 1878; Gowers, 1886), others (Pai, 1947; Crisp & Moldofsky, 1965; Bindman & Tibbetts, 1977) shifted the emphasis to psychological causes such as anxiety, phobia, hysteria, obsessionality, and personality disorder considered as possible explanations (Sachdev, 1992). Some authors took a dual view (Adler et al., 2005) suggesting that a subgroup of those with occupational cramps had dystonia, while others probably were psychogenically determined. Sachdev (1992) recruited 20 golfers suffering the yips and 20 controls from various golf clubs who completed a plethora

Table 33.1 Hypotheses regarding the cause of the yips

Task-specific dystonia	Foster, 1977; McDaniel et al. 1989; Sachdev, 1992; Smith et al. 2000; Candia et al. 2002; Altenmuller, 2003; Smith et al. 2003; Rosted, 2005; Adler et al. 2005; Stinear et al. 2006; Ringman, 2007; Rosenkranz et al. 2008; Adler et al. 2011; Dhungana and Jankovic, 2013; Klampfl et al. 2013a; Klampfl et al. 2013b; Owen, 2014; Klampfl et al. 2015
Reinvestment	Masters, 1992; Masters and Maxwell, 2008
Chronic and severe form of choking under pressure	Bawden and Maynard, 2001; Klampfl et al. 2013a; Klampfl et al. 2013b
Neurophysiological–psychological interaction	Smith et al. 2000; Adler et al. 2005
Learned or conditioned response	Marquardt, 2009a; Lobinger et al. 2014

of psychological tests measuring anxiety, phobia, psychopathology, mental and motor speed, and visuomotor coordination. There were no significant differences between the two groups, and the more severely affected golfers did not differ from the mildly affected ones. This study concluded that the yips was not an anxiety disorder or a neurosis, but the role of anxiety in the manifestation of the yips was recognized.

A multidisciplinary study of the yips (Smith et al., 2000) concluded that the yips represented a continuum on which choking (anxiety-related) and dystonia symptoms anchored the extremes, and that the etiology may have been an interaction of psychoneuromuscular influences. In the first part of this study, a yips questionnaire was mailed to 2,630 tournament-playing golfers (handicap <12) registered with the Minnesota Golf Association, and 1,031 questionnaires (39%) were returned. From these returned questionnaires, the authors selected a subgroup of responses from men (handicap 10 or less) and women (handicap 12 or less) resulting in 453 yips-affected (53.5% of responders in this subgroup) and 393 non-affected golfers entered into a database. From this selected subgroup of golfers with the defined handicaps who returned questionnaires, 359 yips-affected and 278 non-affected golfers agreed to participate in the study (75%). Inclusion criteria suggested for a diagnosis of the yips were that most golfers (mean handicap 4.5) were excellent putters before the onset of the yips, most experienced symptoms episodically, changes in mechanics such as a different grip resulted in temporary improvement, and stressful situations enhanced the symptoms. Based on this survey, the authors perpetuated a prevalence rate of yips-affected golfers between 32.5% and 47.7% depending upon assumptions that 25% and 50% of the non-respondents, respectively, were affected by the yips. However, the documented prevalence rate would actually be 44% of the questionnaires returned, or as low as 17% of those mailed. Phase II of this study measured putting behavior, including heart rate, grip force, electromyography (EMG) and relative putting performance using a standard grip in four yips-affected and three non-affected golfers. Golfers affected by the yips had a faster mean heart rate, increased EMG patterns, exerted more grip force and had a poorer putting performance.

Another study by Smith et al. (2003) reported the subjective experience of 72 yips-affected golfers and differentiated the yips into a type I (dystonia) and type II (choking), both of which could be exacerbated by performance anxiety. The yips was defined as a motor phenomenon of involuntary movement affecting golfers, with multiple possible etiologies spanning the continuum from the neurologic disorder of dystonia to the psychological disorder of choking. In many golfers, the pathophysiology of the yips was postulated to be an acquired deterioration in the function of motor pathways that were exacerbated when a threshold of high stress and physiologic arousal was exceeded. In other golfers, the yips was postulated to result from severe performance anxiety. Yips (type I) symptoms were frequently described as jerks, tremors, or freezing in the hands and forearms, resulting in a deterioration of golf performance (added 4.9 strokes per 18 holes), and causing some golfers to pursue the frequent use of alcohol or beta-blockers, or to quit the game entirely.

In an attempt to better define the yips, Adler et al. (2005) studied surface EMG activity in an indoor putting laboratory in 10 yips-affected and 10 non-affected golfers matched for age and handicap. They observed that 200 ms before impact, 50% yips-affected and 0% non-affected golfers had co-contraction of wrist flexors/extensors ($p = 0.06$). Adler et al. (2011) expanded this research by increasing the number of golfers, moving the research outdoors to a real putting green, and adding measurements of finger and wrist joint movements. Fifty golfers (25 with, and 25 without complaints of the yips) were studied using videotape, surface EMG, and a CyberGlove II (Immersion Technologies, Palo Alto, CA). All golfers were right–handed with handicaps <16, had no examination finding of a movement disorder other than while putting, and all performed 70 putts of different lengths and breaks. When grouped by subjective complaints, there were no differences in any movement parameter. When grouped by video evidence of an involuntary movement, yips cases had more ($p < 0.001$) angular movement in wrist pronation/supination and a trend ($p = 0.08$) for wrist flexor/extensor co-contraction (yips: 41%; no yips: 18%). These data suggested that a subset of golfers had a task-specific dystonia or golfer's cramp, although further studies are needed. The occurrence and movement characteristics observed in this study may be underestimated because the study was not done under tournament or stressful conditions. The authors opined that it remained unclear what the hallmark of the dystonic yips should be, and it was unlikely that a single finding or diagnostic test could be used for the diagnosis of any focal dystonia. Co-contraction alone did not appear to be diagnostic of golfer's cramp, while pronation/supination measures may best identity this phenomenon.

The concept of two subtypes of yips proposed by Smith et al. (2000, 2003) was further explored by Stinear et al. (2006). They hypothesized that: 1) Type I golfers would exhibit greater levels of upper-limb muscle activation during putting than type II and control golfers, 2) Type II golfer's performance would be impaired to a greater extent under high-pressure conditions than would putting performance of type I and control golfers, and 3) Type II golfers would have higher cognitive-state anxiety than type I or control golfers. Twenty-four golfers (15 with, and 9 without yips symptoms) were recruited and completed a golf history questionnaire and a Competitive State Anxiety Inventory (CSAI-2). In the first experiment EMG data was obtained during putting under low-pressure and high-pressure conditions, with high pressure intended to increase anxiety through a monetary reward, videotaping of performance, and the presence of a confederate who provided negative feedback. In a second experiment the same golfers completed a task that required the inhibition of an anticipated response, and the accuracy and ability to inhibit their response was determined. The results demonstrated that golfers with the yips could be categorized as type I (movement-related symptoms) or type II (anxiety related symptoms). Type I yips-affected golfers exhibited greater muscle activity during putting, and greater errors and less inhibition of the anticipated response task. Type II yips-affected golfers exhibited greater changes in cognitive anxiety and normal performance of the anticipated response task. This study supported the model proposed by Smith et al. (2000, 2003) and was proposed as a useful framework for the management of yips symptoms.

A systematic review (Dhungana & Jankovic, 2013) provided further evidence that the yips, at least in some players, could be a form of a task-specific dystonia. One illustrative case was presented in which the yips were successfully treated by selective botulinum toxin injections after examination by a movement disorder neurologist. This case represented the only case in the literature of the yips in golf actually treated by selective botulinum toxin injections. However, there have been reports of other focal dystonias such as writer's cramp successfully treated by botulinum toxin injections (Kruisdijk et al., 2007).

The relative frequency of the various types of the yips remains poorly understood. The prevalence rate of task-specific dystonia in the general population is estimated between 0.01% and 0.03% (Nutt et al., 1988; Fukuda et al., 2006) and in the specific population of musicians at 1% (Altenmuller, 2003). The reported prevalence rates of the yips of 25–48% (McDaniel et al., 1989; Smith et al., 2000; Smith et al., 2003) is considerably higher. However, Smith et al., (2003) emphasized that we do not have a denominator necessary to calculate the true incidence, as these studies were based on questionnaire surveys with methodological flaws. Klampfl et al. (2015) estimated the prevalence of the putting yips across the entire skill range of golfers using self-reports (on-line surveys) in one study, and kinematic and performance measures in a second study. The prevalence of yips-affected golfers was 22.4% in the first study and 16.7% in the second study. In both studies, more yips-affected than unaffected golfers had experience in playing other racket sports. The inclusion of golfers at lower skill levels, or even novices, however, represented a different definition of the yips compared to loss of a highly refined fine motor skill used in other studies. As emphasized by Klampfl et al. (2015), the current knowledge of the epidemiology indicated that there were clearly other causes of the yips besides task-specific dystonia.

The psychological etiology of the yips has been described as a severe form of choking (Masters, 1992; Bawden & Maynard, 2001), and the yips may represent a chronic form of choking in golf (Gucciardi et al., 2010). The mechanisms of choking under pressure can be placed into two categories: drive theories or attentional theories (Hill et al., 2010). Drive theories (Spence & Spence, 1966; Beilock & Gray, 2007) espouse that an increased level of arousal/drive produced by the desire to perform well under pressure detrimentally affects performance. This concept has been challenged for its inability to account for all cases of choking, as many athletes have performed well while experiencing high levels of drive (Baumeister & Showers, 1986; Vickers & Williams, 2007). Because of the limitations of drive theories, attentional theories have been proposed as a more likely explanation of choking under pressure, and are divided into distraction (Eysenck & Calvo, 1992) and self-focus (Baumeister, 1984) theories. Distraction theories suggest that pressure-induced anxiety produces a shift of attention away from task-relevant information, while self-focus theories propose that performance anxiety shifts the focus of attention inward, producing a conscious monitoring of the activity negatively impacting a well-learned, automated action.

Attempting to unite the many different views of conscious control, Masters (1992) and Masters and Maxwell (2008) assimilated ideas under the term 'reinvestment', a term first used by Deikman (1969) who argued that automatization can be undone by "reinvesting actions and percepts with attention" (p. 31). However, Klampfl et al. (2013b) subsequently conducted a study designed to evaluate whether reinvestment caused the yips and if the tendency to reinvest could explain yips behavior. Nineteen yips-affected golfers, defined by the observation of involuntary movements during the execution of one-handed putts (Klampfl et al., 2013a), putted with the dominant arm in a skill-focused and an extraneous condition, performing different dual tasks designed either to direct their focus on their own skill, or to distract then from it. Yips behavior was assessed by putting performance and movement variability, and reinvestment was estimated via the Movement-Specific Reinvestment Scale. The yips-affected golfers showed no difference in yips behavior between the skill-focus and the extraneous condition, and the study conclusion was that the data did not support a link between the yips and reinvestment.

The studies examined thus far have predominantly examined the concept of a task specific focal dystonia (type I yips) and choking (type II yips) as the extremes of a continuum on which the yips are viewed. Lobinger et al. (2014) explored the gray zone between these extremes and extended this continuum model of Smith et al. (2003) suggesting that the yips was a movement stereotype, or learned or conditioned response. Marquardt (2009a) proposed that the yips was a contextual movement disorder influenced by anxiety, overcontrol, interference, and awareness of the problem. He observed that for some golfers, the yips may disappear if the putting context is changed, such as if the ball is removed. In this study the yips was defined using a SAM PuttLab system (Science & Motion GmbH, Munich, Germany) which is a measurement tool capable of producing a plethora of variables related to the 3-D motion of the putter. Golfers with an average handicap of 16.6 putted a straight putt from 4 meters. The main findings were that golfers who had the yips tended to exhibit greater error and variability in their putting strokes for a number of key variables compared to golfers who did not have the yips, and that this error and variability apparently increased with the severity of the yips. Glazier (2009) however, opined in his commentary of this study that although the golfers studied by Marquardt exhibited yip-like symptoms, it did not necessarily mean that they had the yips. He recommended that to make substantive progress regarding the yips, product-related research designs needed to be superseded by process-oriented research designs so that the physical mechanisms causing the yips might be revealed, and the underlying neurophysiological processes better understood.

He suggested that dynamical systems theory might be a useful framework for further studies. Marquardt (2009b) retorted that the research defining the yips as a continuum from choking to focal dystonia introduced more confusion than clarification, and proposed that the yips be defined on objective measurement of disturbed movements. An objective measurement like this, however, results in a definition of the yips that includes golfers who do not meet the initial description of the yips, namely a skilled and accomplished golfer that loses the ability to putt for reasons most frequently described by the involvement of freezing, jerking, tremors, and spasms exacerbated in tournaments and by anxiety.

In a more recent study, Klampfl et al. (2013a) attempted to develop a standardized method for diagnosing the yips, which were defined as a multi-aetiological phenomenon characterized by an involuntary movement affecting a golfer's putting performance. In this study of 20 yips-affected and 20 non-affected golfers, yips-affected golfers were defined, not based upon self-reports as in previous studies, but by a pre-test observation of twisting of the wrist while putting up to five times from 1 meter with only the dominant right arm. Although an objective measure, the authors proposed that this pre-test criteria for defining the yips was not an optimal solution.

A renowned teaching professional, Hank Haney (2006) in his book *Fix the Yips Forever* defined the yips as an involuntary movement in the hands or wrists (or both) during a stroke, almost always at impact. Kinematic data using SuperSam (Science & Motion GmbH, Munich, Germany) were used to subdivide the yips into directional and acceleration, with directional yips coming from the hands and wrists trying to overcontrol the alignment of the clubface through impact, and acceleration yips coming from the hands and wrists applying a burst of speed through impact.

In summary, the studies in this review clearly elucidate that the yips can have different meanings dependent upon how one approaches or examines these phenomena. The research studies cited include case studies, descriptive studies (self-report and performance), and quasi-experimental designs. They each contribute a piece to the puzzle of the yips. While our understanding of the yips has clearly evolved, it remains far from complete.

How the yips can be detected and measured

As H. James Harrington (1999, p. 19) so eloquently stated "measurement is the first step that leads to control and eventually to improvement. If you can't measure something, you can't understand it. If you can't understand it, you can't control it. If you can't control it, you can't improve it". A standardized method to identify and measure the yips independent of etiology is therefore, an important goal to further our understanding of the yips. So far such a method does not exist, but progress has been made. The yips has been measured using many different methods: examination, videotape review, psychometric measures, behavioral measures, muscle activity by surface EMG, grip force, finger and wrist joint movement, heart rate, putting performance, kinematic measures, 3-D motion analysis, and electroencephalography (EEG).

Attempting to find an objective hallmark of the dystonic yips, Adler et al. (2005, 2011) evaluated the measurement of surface EMG and the observation of cocontraction of the extensor/flexor muscles and pronation/supination muscles of the forearm combined with video analysis and measurement of hand movement measured by 18 sensors embedded in a flexible glove (CyberGlove II; Immersion technologies, Palo Alto, CA) with wireless data transmission. When grouped by evidence of an involuntary movement, yips cases had more angular movement in wrist pronation/supination ($p < 0.001$), and a trend for wrist flexor/extensor cocontraction. While a combination of these parameters were helpful, cocontraction by itself was not a definitive measure for the dystonic yips.

The Sam Putt Lab (Science & Motion GmbH, Munich, Germany) and its various versions utilized ultrasound technology to obtain 3-D motion data during a putting stroke. Marquardt and Fisher (2008) and Marquardt (2009a), utilizing this technology, reported that kinematic parameters such as rotation standard deviation (SD), face angle SD, impact velocity SD, and acceleration SD were able to separate yips-affected from non-affected golfers. This technology was also utilized by Klampfl et al. (2013a) who performed measurements of putting performance, situational anxiety, EMG, electrocardiogram (EKG), and kinematic parameters of the putter in 20 yips-affected and 20 non-affected golfers. Putting performance was measured in five different conditions: a control condition using a normal putting stroke, a pressure condition (with monetary incentive, videotaping, and extraneous noise distraction), using only the dominant arm, with a unihockey racket, and with latex gloves on both hands. All golfers also completed standardized questionnaires measuring trait anxiety, perfectionism, stress-coping strategies, somatic complaints, and movement and decision reinvestment. The findings were that the groups were separated only by putting performance and kinematic parameters, and the recommendation was made to use kinematics to further investigate the aetiology of the yips and possible interventions.

Mayo Clinic researchers (Associated Press, 2003; Mell, 2003) studied the yips in a four hole putting tournament (putts 4–10 feet) in three conditions (baseline, placebo, beta-blocker) on an outdoor green with a gallery, media, caddies, and prize money, and all recorded on video. Sixteen international golfers participated. Seven had type I (dystonia) yips, and nine had type II (choking) determined by an enrollment questionnaire and a pre-tournament interview. Participants putted the baseline condition before being randomized to double-blind placebo and beta blocker (40 mg oral Propranolol™) conditions. Psychometrics (Marlowe-Crowne Social Desirability scale, Spielberger Inventorories (STAI)), physiological (EMG, EEG, salivary cortisol, heart rate, blood pressure, electrocardiogram, grip force) and performance variables were measured. Golfers with type I yips had less state anxiety ($p = 0.05$) and less trait anxiety ($p = 0.006$) than golfers with type II yips. Heart rate, blood pressure, and cortisol decreased significantly ($p = 0.01$) after the placebo and beta blocker conditions, but beta blockers did not improve performance. The EEG and EMG results suggested that golfers with type I yips had quiescent EEG and co-contraction on EMG, while those with type II yips had high beta on EEG and no co-contraction on EMG, although the numbers were small and not statistically significant. Crews and Landers (1993), Crews (1998), and Crews et al. (1998) have evaluated the EEG of golfers at various skill levels. Positive performance correlated with an increase in right hemisphere alpha activity during the last second preceding a putt, and negative performance correlated with increases in left hemisphere alpha and beta activity as they approached the start of the motion. EEG evaluation of one golfer with type I yips in the Mayo Clinic putting tournament exhibited hyperactivity in the left hemisphere at baseline and following administration of placebo, a slight decrease in activity following a beta blocker, and improvement in EEG symmetry and reduction in hyperactivity of the left hemisphere following changes in putting mechanics such as left hand low, change in grip, and putting left handed. Further evaluation of EEG findings in golfers with the yips are needed to better determine if EEG could be a method to differentiate golfers with the yips and perhaps assist in determining the best treatment for an individual.

How the yips can be treated

Based upon our current understanding of the yips, a golfer whose putting performance has consistently declined, or is concerned about the possibility of the yips, should start with an assessment by a golf professional who can assess the mechanics of the putting stroke. After issues related to putting mechanics have been addressed with a golf professional, a kinematic evaluation can be done for additional information, and an evaluation with a sports psychologist may be helpful for some golfers. For golfers that may have a neurologic cause, or focal dystonia, a more comprehensive evaluation with a movement disorder neurologist should be considered. Although treatments have not been studied in a systematic manner, focal hand dystonia (writer's cramp and musician's cramp), and a few golfers, have been successfully treated with botulinum toxin injections (Rivest et al., 1991; Dhungana & Jankovic, 2013). The selection of the appropriate dosage and site of injection to involve only the overactive muscles is crucial. The main side effect of botulinum toxin injections is weakness, so dosage and muscle placement are key, as if over-weakness of the hand or wrist occurs, other activities may be affected. Single case reports have indicated some benefit from the use of memantine (Ringman, 2007) and acupuncture (Rosted, 2005) for yips-affected golfers. Several studies in musicians (Candia et al., 2002; Byl et al., 2003; Rosenkranz et al., 2008; Berque et al., 2010) involving sensory and motor interventions have also been reported, but it is unknown whether such therapies that propose to restore sensorimotor organization could be effective in yips-affected golfers. A plethora of other strategies have been recommended by golf professionals, coaches, and psychologists such as changing the gripping technique, putting mechanics, or putting routine, hypnosis, psychotherapy, or cognitive-behavioral interventions (Murphy & Woolfolk, 1987; Beauchamp et al., 1996; Thomas & Fogarty, 1997), however, none of these have been subjected to well-designed controlled trials.

Implications for the game of golf

Given the current information on the incidence of the yips in golfers, it is clear that there are a substantial number of golfers at various skill levels affected by this phenomenon in some manner that may result in ruining a golf career, reducing performance, negatively impacting one's enjoyment of the game, or quitting the game altogether. The yips phenomenon is almost surely multifactorial, and a better understanding of the etiology of the yips in each golfer is necessary for effective treatments to be evaluated and developed.

Summary and future directions

This chapter has explored the science of the yips in golf, defined the current state of our understanding of this phenomenon, delineated the controversies of what is known or not known, and attempted to describe the implications for the game of golf. In the future, a combination of tools such as 3-D motion analysis, EEG, EMG, and functional magnetic resonance imaging could be helpful in developing objective measures that help determine the best options for the management or treatment of each individual with the yips. Once our understanding and ability to measure this phenomenon improves, we may then begin to explore the neurophysiology associated with the yips that currently we really know very little about.

References

Adler, C.; Crews, D.; Hentz, J.; Smith, A. & Caviness, J. (2005) Abnormal Co-contraction in Yips-affected but Not Unaffected Golfers: Evidence for Focal Dystonia, *Neurology*, 64 (10), 1813–1814.

Adler, C.; Crews, D.; Kahol, K.; Santello, M.; Noble, B.; Hentz, J. & Caviness, J. (2011) Are the Yips a Task-specific Dystonia or "Golfer's Cramp"? *Movement Disorders*, 26 (11), 1993–1996.

Altenmuller, E. (2003) Focal Dystonia: Advances in Brain Imaging and Understanding of Fine Motor Control in Musicians, *Hand Clinics*, 19 (3), 523–538.

Associated Press (2003) *Mayo Clinic Trying to Determine What Causes the Yips* [Online], Available at www. Espn.Com/Golf/Story?Id=1584090 (Accessed January 4, 2016).

Baumeister, R. (1984) Choking Under Pressure: Self-consciousness and Paradoxical Effects of Incentives on Skillful Performance, *Journal of Personality and Social Psychology*, 46 (3), 610–620.

Baumeister, R. & Showers, C. (1986) A Review of Paradoxical Performance Effects: Choking Uner Pressure in Sports and Mental Tests, *European Journal of Social Psychology*, 16 (4), 361–383.

Bawden, M. & Maynard, I. (2001) Towards an Understanding of the Personal Experience of The "Yips" in Cricketers, *Journal of Sports Sciences*, 19 (12), 937–953.

Beauchamp, P.; Halliwell, W.; Fournier, J. & Koestner, R. (1996) Effects of Cognitive-Behavioral Psychological Skills Training on the Motivation, Preparation, and Putting Performance of Novice Golfers, *The Sport Psychologist*, 10 (2), 157–170.

Beilock, S. & Gray, R. (2007) Why Do Athletes Choke Under Pressure? In: G. Tenenbaum & R. Eklund (Eds.) *Handbook of Sports Psychology* (3rd Ed.), Hoboken, NJ: Wiley & Sons, pp. 425–444.

Bell, C. (1833) *Partial Paralyses of the Muscles of the Extremities: The Nervous System of the Human Body*, London: Taylor and Francis.

Berque, P.; Gray, H.; Harkness, C. & Mcfadyen, A. (2010) A Combination of Constraint-Induced Therapy and Motor Control Retraining in the Treatment of Focal Hand Dystonia in Musicians, *Medical Problems of Performing Artists*, 25 (4), 149–161.

Bindman, E. & Tibbetts, R. (1977) Writer's Cramp—A Rational Approach to Treatment? *The British Journal of Psychiatry*, 131 (2), 143–148.

Byl, N.; Nagajaran, S. & Mckenzie, A. (2003) Effect of Sensory Discrimination Training on Structure and Function in Patients with Focal Hand Dystonia: A Case Series, *Archives of Physical Medicine and Rehabilitation*, 84 (10), 1505–1514.

Candia, V.; Schafer, T.; Taub, E.; Rau, H.; Altenmuller, E.; Rockstroh, B. & Elbert, T. (2002) Sensory Motor Retuning: A Behavioral Treatment for Focal Hand Dystonia of Pianists and Guitarists, *Archives of Physical Medicine and Rehabilitation*, 83 (10), 1342–1348.

Crews, D. (1998) *EEG Insights into Attentional Patterns Associated with Stress and Golf Putting*, Association for the Advancement of Applied Sport Psychology (AAASP), Cape Cod, MA.

Crews, D. & Landers, D. (1993) Electroencephalographic Measures of Attentional Patterns Prior to the Golf Putt, *Medicine and Science in Sports and Exercise*, 25 (1), 116–126.

Crews, D.; Lutz, R. & Nilsson, P. (1998) Psychological Indicators of Confidence and Habituation During Golf Putting, In: M. Farrally & A. Cochran (Eds.) *World Scientific Congress for Golf III*, Champaign, IL: Human Kinetics, pp. 158–165.

Crisp, A. & Moldofsky, H. (1965) A Psychosomatic Study of Writer's Cramp, *The British Journal of Psychiatry*, 111 (478), 841–858.

Critchley, M. (1977) Occupational Palsies in Musical Performers, In: M. Critchley & R. Henson (Eds.) *Music and the Brain: Studies in the Neurology of Music*, Springfield, IL: C. C. Thomas, pp. 365–377.

Deikman, A. (1969) Deautomatization and the Mystic Experience, In: C. Tart (Ed.) *Altered States of Consciousness*, New York, NY: Wiley, pp. 23–48.

Dhungana, S. & Jankovic, J. (2013) Yips and Other Movement Disorders in Golfers, *Movement Disorders*, 28 (5), 576–581.

Eysenck, M. & Calvo, M. (1992) Anxiety and Performance: The Processing Efficiency Theory, *Cognition and Emotion*, 6 (6), 409–434.

Foster, J. (1977, June 29) Putting on the Agony, *World Medicine*, 12 (19), 26–27.

Fukuda, H.; Kusumi, M. & Nakashima, K. (2006) Epidemiology of Primary Focal Dystonias in the Western Area of Tottori Prefecture in Japan: Comparison with Prevalence Evaluated in 1993, *Movement Disorders*, 21 (9), 1503–1506.

Glazier, P. (2009) The Vicious Circle Involved in the Development of the Yips: A Commentary, *Journal of Sports Science and Coaching*, 4 (Supplement 1), 79–82.

Gowers, W. (1886) *A Manual of Diseases of the Nervous System*, Vol. II, London: J & A Churchill.

Gucciardi, D.; Longbottom, J.; Jackson, B. & Dimmock, J. (2010) Experienced Golfers' Perspectives on Choking Under Pressure, *Journal of Sport & Exercise Psychology*, 32 (1), 61–83.

Haney, H. (2006) *Fix the Yips Forever: The First and Only Guide You Need to Solve the Game's Worst Curse*, London: Gotham.

Harrington, H. (1999) In My Opinion, *CIO*, 10 (Section 2), 19.

Hill, D.; Hanton, S.; Matthews, N. & Fleming, S. (2010) Choking in Sport: A Review, *International Review of Sport and Exercise Psychology*, 3 (1), 24–39.

Klampfl, M.; Lobinger, B. & Raab, M. (2013a) How to Detect the Yips in Golf, *Human Movement Science*, 32 (6), 1270–1287.

Klampfl, M.; Lobinger, B. & Raab, M. (2013b) Reinvestment—The Cause of the Yips? *PLoS One*, 8 (12), E82470.

Klampfl, M.; Philippen, P. & Lobinger, B. (2015) Self-report vs. Kinematic Screening Test: Prevalence, Demographics, and Sports Biography of Yips-affected Golfers, *Journal of Sports Sciences*, 33 (7), 655–664.

Kruisdijk, J.; Koelman, J.; Ongerboer De Visser, B.; De Haan, R. & Speelman, J. (2007) Botulinum Toxin for Writer's Cramp: A Randomised, Placebo-Controlled Trial and 1-year Follow-up, *Journal of Neurology, Neurosurgery, and Psychiatry*, 78 (3), 264–270.

Lees, A. (1985) *Tics and Related Disorders*, Edinburgh, UK: Churchill Livingstone.

Lobinger, B.; Klampfl, M. & Altenmuller, E. (2014) We Are Able, We Intend, We Act—But We Do Not Succeed: A Theoretical Framework for a Better Understanding of Paradoxical Performance in Sports, *Journal of Clinical Sport Psychology*, 8 (4), 357–377.

Marquardt, C. (2009a) The Vicious Circle Involved in the Development of the Yips, *Journal of Sports Science and Coaching*, 4 (Supplement 1), 67–78.

Marquardt, C. (2009b) The Vicious Circle Involved in the Development of the Yips: A Response to Commentary, *Journal of Sports Science and Coaching*, 4 (Supplement 1), 83–88.

Marquardt, C. & Fisher, M. (2008) Movement Kinematics of the Golfers' Yips, In: D. Crews & R. Lutz (Eds.) *Science & Golf V. Proceedings of the World Scientific Congress of Golf*, Mesa: Energy in Motion, pp. 216–223.

Masters, R. (1992) Knowledge, Nerves, and Know-how: The Role of Explicit Versus Implicit Knowledge in the Breakdown of a Complex Motor Skill Under Pressure, *British Journal of Psychology*, 83 (3), 343–358.

Masters, R. & Maxwell, J. (2008) The Theory of Reinvestment. *International Review of Sport and Exercise Psychology*, 1 (2), 160–183.

McDaniel, K.; Cummings, J. & Shain, S. (1989) The "Yips": A Focal Dystonia of Golfers, *Neurology*, 39 (2 Pt 1), 192–195.

Mell, R. (2003) *A Twitch, a Flinch, and Suddenly a Golfer Feels Like a Jerk. Scientists Are Working to Help Sufferers Shake the Yips* [Online]. Available at Http://Articles.Sun-Sentinel.Com/2003-08-11/Sports/0308100308_1_Yips-Thompson-Mayo-Clinic (Accessed January 4, 2016).

Murphy, S. & Woolfolk, R. (1987) The Effects of Cognitive Interventions on Competitive Anxiety and Performance on a Fine Motor Skill Accuracy Task, *International Journal of Sport Psychology*, 18 (2), 152–166.

Nutt, J.; Muenter, M.; Aronson, A.; Kurland, L. & Melton, L., 3rd. (1988) Epidemiology of Focal and Generalized Dystonia in Rochester, Minnesota. *Movement Disorders*, 3 (3), 188–194.

Owen, D. (2014) *The Yips: What's Behind the Condition That Every Golfer Dreads?* [Online]. Available at www.Newyorker.Com/Magazine/2014/05/26/The-Yips (Accessed March 31, 2015).

Pai, M. (1947) The Nature and Treatment of Writer's Cramp, *The Journal of Mental Science*, 93, 68–81.

Poore, G. (1878) Analysis of Seventy-five Cases of "Writer's Cramp" and Impaired Writing Power, *Medico-Chirurgical Transactions*, 61, 111–146.

Ringman, J. (2007) Serendipitous Improvement in the Yips Associated with Memantine Use, *Movement Disorders*, 22 (4), 598–599.

Rivest, J.; Lees, A. & Marsden, C. (1991) Writer's Cramp: Treatment with Botulinum Toxin Injections, *Movement Disorders*, 6 (1), 55–59.

Rosenkranz, K.; Butler, K.; Williamon, A.; Cordivari, C.; Lees, A. & Rothwell, J. (2008) Sensorimotor Reorganization by Proprioceptive Training in Musician's Dystonia and Writer's Cramp, *Neurology*, 70 (4), 304–315.

Rosted, P. (2005) Acupuncture for Treatment of the Yips?—A Case Report, *Acupuncture in Medicine*, 23 (4),188–189.

Sachdev, P. (1992) Golfers' Cramp: Clinical Characteristics and Evidence Against It Being an Anxiety Disorder, *Movement Disorders*, 7 (4), 326–332.

Smith, A.; Adler, C.; Crews, D.; Wharen, R.; Laskowski, E.; Barnes, K.; Valone Bell, C.; Pelz, D.; Brennan, R.; Smith, J.; Sorenson, M. & Kaufman, K. (2003) The "Yips" in Golf: A Continuum Between a Focal Dystonia and Choking, *Sports Medicine*, 33 (1), 13–31.

Smith, A.; Malo, S.; Laskowski, E.; Sabick, M.; Cooney, W., 3rd; Finnie, S.; Crews, D.; Eischen, J.; Hay, I.; Detling, N. & Kaufman, K. (2000) A Multidisciplinary Study of the "Yips" Phenomenon in Golf: An Exploratory Analysis, *Sports Medicine*, 30 (6), 423–437.

Spence, J. & Spence, K. (1966) The Motivational Component of Manifest Anxiety: Drive and Drive Stimuli, In: C. Spielberger (Ed.) *Anxiety and Behavior*, New York, NY: Academic Press, pp. 291–326.

Stinear, C.; Coxon, J.; Fleming, M.; Lim, V.; Prapavessis, H. & Byblow, W. (2006) The Yips in Golf: Multimodal Evidence for Two Subtypes, *Medicine and Science in Sports and Exercise*, 38 (11), 1980–1989.

Thomas, P. & Fogarty, G. (1997) Psychological Skills Training in Golf: The Role of Individual Differences in Cognitive Preferences, *The Sport Psychologist*, 11 (1), 86–106.

Vickers, J. & Williams, A. (2007) Performing Under Pressure: The Effects of Physiological Arousal, Cognitive Anxiety, and Gaze Control in Biathlon, *Journal of Motor Behavior*, 39 (5), 381–394.

PART VI

The golfer in context

Introduction

The social and cultural context of the game is central to those who play it. This can differ significantly between the person playing it and those involved in delivering it (often coaches – although they may also be called instructors or teachers depending upon the cultural context they inhabit). As such, any engagement in the game at all carries with it not just a social experience, it also contains a set of 'rules' and conventions with it. At the same time, any engagement with the game also means that there is always a context, be that a game against others, yourself or just as a means of physical activity – let alone the involvement of others in the process. This part contains six chapters dedicated to the player within the social context of golf and also raises some significant questions about how well these are understood by those involved in the game and what impact this understanding can have on participation moving forwards.

The first chapter by Murray and colleagues highlights a key aspect of the game that is becoming more prevalent in the minds of governments and other health organisations – the role golf plays in maintaining physical, social and mental health. Their exhaustive systematic review identifies the research evidence (from within and beyond the game) that golf can play in the health of the participant. Their review of the research suggests that not only does physical activity through golf increase life expectancy, but that it can support the reduction of a plethora of other health problems as well, although, as with any physical activity, there is an increased risk of injury through physical participation. However, the evident health benefits of playing golf are certainly food for thought for participants (linked also to the chapter by Close and colleagues on nutrition for golf in Part V of this book). This then has significant implications for policy makers, health organisations and players alike.

Moving from a wider perspective to a more focussed one, Toms explores the sociological and social-psychology-based sources and research evidence around young people in golf and the role that the game can have in their lives. He acknowledges that there is limited research on young people and the grassroots level of the game and that the majority of work is focussed upon those young people of a high ability. While this is an important aspect of the game to understand and develop, the chapter also examines the work that has been undertaken (particularly in the United States) around the use of the game as a means of gaining social and developmental skills through programmes such as The First Tee project. In addition, the chapter goes on to explore some of the developing works that ground youth participation within social and cultural contexts. Finally, the chapter calls for more work on this area, and particularly at the initial stages of engagement to better understand the social contexts that can improve retention and participation within the young person's context.

The chapter on gender by Kitching provides a timely reminder that, while the game is open to everyone, there is still gender discrimination within it. As a sport that has historically and culturally been male-focussed, she explores the research evidence that suggests it is not just historical practice but also modern-day conventions that mean the game is still dominated by men. Such an important chapter cannot be ignored for anyone involved in the development of the game; so a better understanding of issues will allow for appropriate policies and the creation of opportunity for women of all ages. This is something that a number of initiatives have recently been trying to address, but is, as Kitching points out, an area of normative masculine practice that needs challenging in many contexts. While there are clearly cultural and political aspects to the way women are treated in both sport and society, it cannot be forgotten that these contexts will dictate opportunities to engage in the game.

The importance of understanding the individual in the process of participation is important, and in coaching is even more so. Wright and Toms next explore the developing notion that coaches and golf educators/policy makers are beginning to move beyond the focus of the coach telling the students what to do, towards a more holistic and player centred approach. Using the concepts of social interactionism and the need to further develop the 'how' rather than the 'what' of coaching to each individual, and the importance of this within coach education. Since research on this area of the game is limited, the chapter also draws on work beyond golf, and explores the importance of understanding the needs of the individual in order to provide them with the best experience possible. While this is a key focus within formal coaching/instruction, the same can apply to anyone who has involvement with players in the game.

In a relatively similar vein, Fitzsimmons explores the role of humour within coaching as being central to the relationship between coach and learner. The chapter explores the developing area of humour as a social tool and identifies ways in which it can be used within both informal and formal social interaction and coaching settings. An important aspect of communication that we all use, the deliberate and subtle use of humour can be used to strengthen the coach-athlete relationship as well as help improve the practical way coaching is delivered in practice – it is a social experience after all. When taken with the work of other chapters (and that of Schempp in this part) it is clear that there are a number of vitally important communication skills that need development – of which humour is one – when engaged in coaching.

In the final chapter of this part and the book, Schempp and colleagues explore their previous work on Golf Expertise and Instruction and provide a summary of the broader research on the area. From the empirical work already undertaken they explore and expand upon the key skills required to become an expert coach/instructor/teacher (note the cultural context and interchangeable use of these words) and the additional skills and technologies that are available to help further explore and develop learning opportunities. The key areas the chapters cover include the role of formal education and development; the skills required, and the communication skills necessary for the development of players. While the concept of expertise is often seen as emotive and subjective, the chapter uses clear definitions and theoretical concepts in order to help the reader understand not just how these occur, but how these are socially constructed and developed as a set of criteria – important points for the development of the game.

This part of the book deliberately begins to put into context the importance of the social and cultural contexts to the way that golf is experienced. From the broad angle of health and well-being through the game, to the engagement of young people and women and the importance of understanding them all by adopting a player centred approach to coaching. Within these, the importance of humour as a tool and the skills required to achieve expertise as a coach also become apparent as we continue to build up the understanding that individual players of all abilities are 'people' and not just 'bodies', and it is an understanding and appreciation of this that makes the context that they are in so important. Thus, it is the context of the individual that becomes central to the way that they need to be treated as golfers, and within each chapter the recommendations and implications of these points are given in context to the reader. After all, the game is learned, experienced and played within macro and micro socio-cultural contexts, and it is these that dictate the engagement or attrition of the player. To better understand these contexts allows those involved in the game to better engage with players and to produce an environment that can nurture and encourage golfers from an holistic perspective.

Martin Toms
University of Birmingham, England

34

UNDERSTANDING GOLF AND HEALTH

Andrew Murray, Evan Jenkins and Roger Hawkes

Introduction

Health has been defined on page one of the constitution of the 1946 World Health Organization as 'a state of complete physical, mental and social well-being and not merely the absence of disease or infirmity' (World Health Organization, 1946). Reviews have highlighted that evidence is consistent and growing that golf is associated with overall positive effects on physical health and mental well-being and likely has a positive impact on longevity, principally through the physical activity that golfers accrue while out on the course (Walker Research Group, 2011; Murray et al., 2016). While golf has been associated with extra years of life (Farahmand et al., 2009; Coate & Schwenkenberg, 2013), improved lipid profiles (Palank & Hargreaves, 1990; Parkkari et al., 2000) and better cardiovascular and respiratory health (Hoberty & Craig, 1983; Weisgerber et al., 2008; Murray et al., 2016), health problems can occur. These include an increased susceptibility to skin cancer and a moderate risk of musculoskeletal injury (Cabri et al., 2009).

Review of current research

There are a number of studies that assessed golf and its associations with health, allowing the relationships between golf and health to be better understood. A 2016 review included 301 studies pertaining to golf and health, noting this chronological increase, and that North America, Europe and Australasia are the regions most prolific in producing health-related golf literature. Principal thematic areas included (a) golf and physical activity, (b) golf and physical health, (c) golf and mental health, and (d) golf and injury/illness (Murray et al., 2016). This study outlined findings, which are described and developed in this chapter.

Golfers live longer

The most recent Global Burden of Disease study found physical inactivity to be one of the ten leading causes of death worldwide, causing 3.2 million preventable deaths annually (Lim et al., 2013). This study guides policy-makers worldwide and clearly highlights that the impact of physical inactivity is relatively greater (being in the top four leading causes of death) in North America, Western

Europe, Oceania and other areas that golf is commonly played. Golf can provide health-enhancing physical activity, although the relative intensity of exercise varies while playing golf. Factors including the age, gender and baseline fitness of the participant, the length and topography of the course, and whether participants ride a golf-cart or walk the course while playing influence the exercise intensity (Ainsworth et al., 2011; Murray et al., 2016).

There are a few studies that have focussed on associations between golf and life expectancy. These reports have agreed that, on average, people who play golf live longer than those who do not. A study that looked at 313 ex-US Champions tour players (Coate & Schwenkenberg, 2013), and research that assessed a cohort of over 300,000 Swedish players (Farahmand et al., 2009) estimated that, on average, people who play golf lived 5 years longer than non-golfers. This was thought, at least in part, to be due to the playing of golf providing valuable physical activity.

In the Swedish study, the calculated overall Standardised Mortality Ratio was 0.6 (compared to 1.0 for the general population), and 95% confidence intervals were 0.41–0.67 (Farahmand et al., 2009). The authors described improved life expectancy for golfers regardless of gender, age or socio-economic status, with lower handicap golfers having the highest life expectancy, inferring that playing more frequently may deliver greater benefits than playing less often. However, golfers may be different to non-golfers in many ways, so differences seen could potentially be related to playing golf, but could also be explained by other lifestyle factors. While this study adjusted for socio-economic status, there was no description of dietary, smoking or alcohol habits among the golfers or non-golfers. A cross-sectional study assessing longevity in Champions Tour players ($n = 313$) found life expectancy in golfers to compare favourably to elite sportsmen from other sports, as well as to the general US male population, with a median survival of 89 years and mean of 85 years (Coate & Schwenkenberg, 2013). This study could not adequately control for confounding factors, so while this longevity advantage may in part be due to the playing of golf, it may reflect that golfers as a group have different characteristics compared to non-golfers.

A longitudinal prospective cohort study tracking over 8,000 Harvard alumni showed that those who met the minimum energy expenditure recommendations and those who participated in sport on more than 1–2 days per week achieved a larger reduction in mortality (Lee et al., 2004). For golfers, this means that playing more frequently likely benefits health more than playing 1–2 times per week, and participating in additional activities on days that golf is not played may bring further benefits. Taken as a whole, the evidence available suggested that golfers do live longer compared to non-golfers, and that playing golf may contribute to increased longevity, although further research is required to demonstrate a cause-and-effect relationship between golf and longevity.

Effects on physical health

As a moderate-intensity physical activity, golf could be expected to have significant beneficial effects on rates of heart disease, type 2 diabetes, stroke, colon and breast cancer, hip fractures, and overall function (Four Home Countries' Chief Medical Officers, 2011). While the evidence of physical health benefits for those who are active is compelling, the evidence for golf is more modest, but growing. A non-systematic review commissioned by the World Golf Foundation found that participating in golf can be associated with a number of positive health effects (Walker Research Group, 2011). Conversely, a systematic review of a variety of sports found sufficient evidence of health benefits only in football and running when assessing observational and interventional studies (Oja et al., 2015).

Cardiovascular system

Data has highlighted that cardiovascular responses to exercise varies and is greater in older adults (Broman et al., 2004), females, those with pre-existing cardiorespiratory illness (Unverdorben et al., 2000; Dobrosielski et al., 2002), and those with a low baseline level of fitness. Golf, in most people, can help maintain or improve aerobic fitness (Parkkari et al., 2000; Dobrosielski et al., 2002), although golfers can improve their fitness further by taking part in higher-intensity exercise, for example, running or fitness classes. This may positively impact golfing performance as well as health.

The leading risk factor for global disease burden and premature mortality is high blood pressure (Lim et al., 2013). Although regular physical activity (including walking) is known to have a beneficial effect on blood pressure in the medium and long term, the effects of a season of golf on blood pressure have been studied, with no significant difference in systolic blood pressure found in a controlled trial of 55 golfers and 55 non-golfers in Finland (Parkkari et al., 2000). A trend, but no significant difference, was noted in diastolic blood pressure. Thus, longitudinal studies investigating the effects of golf on blood pressure are merited.

Heart disease

Golf as a moderate-intensity aerobic physical activity can be expected to reduce the risk of coronary artery disease, with a clear inverse relationship between physical activity and cardiovascular risk established (Wen et al., 2011; Lee et al., 2012). Lee et al. (2012), in their meta-analysis of global disease burden, estimated that 6% of coronary heart disease was attributable to physical inactivity.

Direct evidence assessing the medium- and long-term impact of golf on coronary heart disease via prospective longitudinal research is lacking. The available evidence does report that playing golf may improve risk factors for heart disease (and stroke), notably aerobic fitness (Parkkari et al., 2000), lipid and cholesterol levels (Palank & Hargreaves, 1990; Parkkari et al., 2000), insulin-glucose metabolism (Broman et al., 2004) and body composition (Palank & Hargreaves, 1990; Parkkari et al., 2000). These studies are more fully discussed in the section looking at golf and metabolic health.

Cardiac events

A number of cross-sectional studies have assessed the occurrence of acute cardiac events and cardiac arrest during sport, with golf reported to have an incidence of sudden death higher than other sports (Murray et al., 2016). This increased incidence of sudden death relative to other sports likely reflects the demographics of those taking part. Golf is played by a cohort that may well have underlying cardiovascular risk factors, being particularly popular in middle and older age. In one study, 80% of persons suffering cardiac arrest during sport had known risk factors for coronary artery disease, which included 60% of these patients being smokers (Fujiwara et al., 1995). The rate of cardiac arrest per person attending golf facilities is high relative to other community locations. However, the low density of persons relative to, for example an airport or shopping centre, means the frequency of cardiac arrest per facility is low to moderate (Reed et al., 2009). There has been disagreement in the literature on the cost effectiveness of ensuring Automatic External Defibrillators and whether they should be provided, or even mandated at each facility.

Recommendations to reduce the risk for individuals include seeking medical input when symptoms occur, using a golf cart if cardiovascular limitations deem this prudent, and taking medications as prescribed (Fujiwara et al., 1995; Dobrosielski et al., 2002). Studies have also highlighted golf as a useful activity for cardiac rehabilitation, providing an adequate and appropriate cardiovascular stimulus. Overall, the best available evidence suggests that playing golf regularly may reduce cardiovascular risk for participants, although risk is temporarily elevated while in the act of playing.

Stroke

A 'clear inverse relationship' (US Department of Health and Human Services, 2008) between physical activity and stroke has been well demonstrated. While playing golf likely decreases the medium and long terms risk of stroke, a Korean study reported that seven out of 5,469 patients suffering a stroke at their facility had a stroke the authors felt related to the biomechanics of golf (Choi et al., 2014), specifically compressive forces in the neck from a repetitive swinging motion. The authors reviewed the literature, finding 14 cases worldwide.

There have been no published studies that specifically assess effects or relationships between golf and the incidence of stroke, so although a reduction in incidence can be extrapolated for golf from physical activity in general, it cannot be directly shown. Overall, physical activities including golf are generally recommended for primary prevention of strokes, and offer potential physical and social benefits post-stroke within a rehabilitation program.

Respiratory system

Playing golf may have a general beneficial effect on lung function (Getchell, 1965; Brown et al., 2016), helping increase aerobic capacity and respiratory reserve, and maintaining function with ageing. While these studies were of modest size, lung function in a cohort of older golfers was equal to younger controls, although confounding factors had not been eliminated (Brown et al., 2016). In relation to asthma, experimental research which compared the impact of swimming or golf on 7–14-year-old children with asthma, showed both interventions decreased emergency visits to hospitals and the severity of asthma symptoms, and increased parental confidence and quality of life for participants (Weisgerber et al., 2008). Ninety-two percent of participants reported being 'extremely' or 'very' happy with the programs.

Golf has been used as a part of numerous pulmonary rehabilitation programmes, with a methodologically limited study noting improvements in function and self-confidence after an intervention of 20 weeks (Hoberty & Craig, 1983). This intervention included both golf and educational sessions, without featuring a control group receiving only the educational sessions. Thus, it is not possible to know whether the golf, the education, or both, contributed to the improvements.

Golf and metabolic health

Guidelines and reviews cite a clear inverse relationship between physical activity and both type 2 diabetes and metabolic syndrome (US Department of Health and Human Services, 2008; Four Home Countries' Chief Medical Officers, 2011). Therefore, it can be expected that people who participate in golf regularly will gain the benefits that physical activity brings, and there are a few studies that have looked in detail at this area. Broman and colleagues assessed blood glucose levels in young, middle aged, and older male golfers (Broman et al., 2004). This study had participants play 18 holes of golf, eating a sandwich and a banana after nine holes. Blood glucose levels decreased by 33% in the older golfers, 10% in the middle aged, and 20% in the young. Further, a 17% overall decrease in blood glucose levels was seen in a study of five middle aged males (Murase et al., 1989). However, both studies lacked a control group, and no longitudinal research has been identified specifically assessing the effects of golf on blood glucose levels, or of golf on the incidence of type 2 diabetes.

Experimental studies have assessed the associations of golf on short and medium term cholesterol and lipid profile. These studies (Murase et al., 1989; Palank & Hargreaves, 1990; Stauch et al., 1999; Parkkari et al., 2000) all showed positive associations with overall lipid and cholesterol profile. Stauch et al. (1999), in a mixed cohort with respect to age and gender, assessed relationships between playing golf and short term lipid levels. Following play, an 18% decrease in triglycerides, and a beneficial 8% increase in High Density Lipoprotein (HDL) cholesterol ('good cholesterol') was demonstrated, both of which improve lipid profile and potentially can decrease cardiovascular risk. There was however, no statistically significant difference in Low Density Lipoprotein (LDL), or total cholesterol seen. A further small study involving five subjects also claimed short term improvement in lipid parameters (Murase et al., 1989). The authors claimed the mean 47% increase in plasma Free Fatty Acids reflected an increase in fat metabolism, causing the release of free fatty acids into the bloodstream. Both these studies analysed only the short-term effects of golf, not assessing the effects and relationships of golf on lipid metabolism in the medium and long term.

By contrast, Palank and Hargreaves (1990) followed golfers and controls over the course of a golfing season, having noted both groups to be sedentary before. Their conclusion was that golf lowered TC (total cholesterol), and LDL cholesterol levels, and improved risk ratios, quoting 'very significant' statistical reductions for these parameters. They could not however, demonstrate an increase in HDL cholesterol. This study looked at middle aged men who played on average 3 times per week, a frequency of play greater than the general golfing population. A non-randomised controlled trial of 55 middle aged male golfers who had not played over the winter months were compared to a sedentary group (Parkkari et al., 2000). The golfers had improved lipid profiles, including HDL to total cholesterol ratio, and an increase in HDL cholesterol.

Statistically significant improvements for the golfers compared to controls were found for body composition parameters. When compared with controls, golfers demonstrated a 1.4 kg greater weight loss (95% CI: 0.6 to 2.1 kg, $P < 0.001$), a 0.4 kg.m^2 reduction of Body Mass Index (95% CI: -0.2 to -0.7 kg/m^2, $P < 0.001$), 1.3% reduction in waist to hip ratio (95% CI: -0.5 to -2.1%, $P < 0.002$), a 2.2 cm reduction in skin fold thicknesses of the abdomen (95% CI: 0.9 to 3.4 cm, $P < 0.001$) and a 2.2 cm reduction of waist circumference (95% CI: 1.0 to 3.3 cm, $P < 0.001$) (Parkkari et al., 2000). A US study found a mean 1.4 kg decrease in the weight of golfers compared to a 1.6 kg weight gain in sedentary controls (Palank & Hargreaves, 1990). The golfers in this study played on average three times per week, and the weight loss was reported to be due to an increase in physical activity as opposed to a change in dietary habit. By contrast, Getchell (1965) did not show any objective difference in body composition, or any statistically significant weight loss when studying a smaller cohort of golfers and comparing them to non-golfers before, and after, the golfing season.

In summary, the best available evidence suggests that golf can have a positive effect on lipid profile and body composition, and is associated with a decrease in blood sugar while playing. However, much of this research has been conducted on golfers who walk the course, and play 18 holes three times per week. Less is known about golfers who play less (or more) frequently, and those that ride a golf cart when they play, which is known to decrease energy expenditure compared with walking the course.

Golf and cancer

Regular physical activity has been associated with a reduction in the incidence of breast and colon cancer (Lee et al., 2012). In addition, a systematic review and meta-analysis concluded that following the diagnosis of cancer, physical activity has a positive effect on fitness, strength, quality of life, anxiety, and self-esteem, with exercise generally very well tolerated (Speck et al., 2010).

Sports participation was associated with improved wellness measures including quality of life and self-esteem, and lower levels of affective disorders including stress and depression (Belanger et al., 2013), with golf being the most commonly played sport in this cohort of 78 golfers. In a cohort of 600 respondents to a survey of colorectal cancer survivors in Canada, golf was by far the most frequently played sport in terms of number of participants, with cited reasons for participation including increasing fitness (45.4%), and better health (22.5%) (McGowan et al., 2013). In summary, there are no studies that show a reduction in cancer specifically attributable to golf, but as golf can provide moderate physical activity, which more widely has been shown to reduce breast and colon cancer, it is biologically plausible that golf can positively influence the incidence of these diseases.

Golf and musculoskeletal health

There is no evidence that regular, moderate physical activity increases the incidence of osteo-arthritis, presuming that there is no major structural joint injury. Donaldson quoted a risk reduction of osteoarthritis of 22–83% through walking programs in his Chief Medical Officer report (Department of Health, 2004). Studies specific to golf that assessed the effects on osteo-arthritis and osteoporosis would be of importance to golfers, as these are common conditions suffered by middle aged and older adults.

Studies have noted improved balance and proprioception in older adults that regularly golf compared to non-golfing controls (Tsang & Hui-Chan, 2010; Gao et al., 2011), which Gao and colleagues attributed to both psychological and physical aspects of controlling balance. However, a cross sectional study that assessed bone mineral density in post-menopausal women golfers versus non-golfers found no statistical difference in cross sectional muscle area between these groups (Eser et al., 2008). These studies all suffered from failing to control confounding lifestyle and health related factors.

There is no consistent and reliable evidence to show an increase in bone mineral density in golf players. A study of professionals showed no significant difference, particularly in areas of interest (those areas that are most vulnerable to fracture with increasing age) (Dorado et al., 2002). However, caddies may benefit from muscular and bone strengthening associated with walking and carrying the load of the golf bag (Goto et al., 2001). Overall, musculoskeletal benefits can be observed in terms of strength and balance specific to golf, while regular physi-cal activity has been shown to have wider musculoskeletal benefits that may apply to golf and merit further study. This chapter has not examined musculoskeletal injuries in golfers, as this is covered elsewhere in this book.

Sun exposure

Ultraviolet radiation exposures for golfers are larger when conditions are sunny compared to cloudy, when the sun is higher in the sky, during summer compared to winter, and at lower latitudes, particularly in high ambient ultraviolet climates (Downs et al., 2009, 2011). The top and back of the head is the area of maximum exposure, which is typically covered by hair or a hat, while the back of the shoulders, neck, and back also receive large doses of sun exposure, particularly during summer conditions (Downs et al., 2009). These areas receive more exposure than the front of the body due to golfing posture. A cross-sectional study of 51 professional and 142 amateur golfers showed that professionals on the Ladies Professional Golf Association (LPGA) tour were exposed to over six hours of exposure per day, while female amateurs from Indiana averaged over two hours of golf-related exposure per day (Hanke et al., 1985).

Of the 51 professional LPGA players assessed in a cross-sectional study, four golfers had developed Basal Cell Carcinoma at an average age of 25.5 years, and seven pre-malignant conditions were found, which although numbers were small, was a cause for alarm (Hanke et al., 1985). Of the 142 amateurs, 11 had developed Basal Cell Carcinomas at an average age of 51.4 years, with a further 20 having pre-malignant conditions. Ultraviolet Radiation (UVR) can also cause painful sunburn reactions, skin pigment changes, accelerated skin ageing, and eye disorders such as cataracts. Sunlight, particularly in the winter months, is beneficial in moderation, with exposure to sunshine and UVR having important health benefits related to adequate vitamin D stores.

It is difficult to provide 'one size fits all' advice regarding amount and timings of sun exposure due to varying environmental conditions, skin types, and ethnicity of participants. The literature has generally recommended that golfers play out-with times that the sun is strongest (avoiding mid-morning tee-off times (Downs et al., 2011), use chemical sunscreens, and wear clothing (particularly headwear, and collared shirts) that provide protection, particularly for vulnerable areas. In summary, the best evidence suggests that golfers may be exposed to high levels of UVR which may predispose one to skin damage and skin cancers, although longitudinal studies assessing the incidence of skin cancer compared to the general population are required.

Golf carts and health

Golf carts offer some benefits including allowing some with medical limitations to participate. Riding a golf cart while playing golf is currently categorised by the compendium of physical activity as a moderate physical activity, with a Metabolic Equivalent of Task (MET) value of 3.5 (Ainsworth et al., 2011). Persons utilising a cart can be expected to walk around 4 miles, or 6000 steps, and expend 600 K/Cals when playing 18 holes (Murray et al., 2016), which corresponds to useful physical activity. However, the benefits are significantly less than if players were to golf while walking and carrying their clubs, or walking and using a pull or push cart, where up to 8 miles, or 11,000–17,000 steps are walked, and around 1200 K/Cals are expended (Murray et al., 2016). Overall, participants should be encouraged to walk when playing golf rather than riding in a cart, however, using a cart to play golf is better for health than not playing at all. A worrying trend is private and public clubs mandating the use of a golf cart – this should be strongly discouraged.

Golf spectating and health

Golf spectators often walk the course to see the arena and follow favourite players (Hansen & Gauthier, 1994). Unpublished data from the 2014 Ryder Cup, the 2015 Alfred Links Championship, and 2016 Shenzhen Open, indicated health enhancing physical activity accrued by spectators. Studies from the USA and South Korea have identified that spectators frequently highlight 'exercise' as a reason for attending a golfing event (Hansen & Gauthier, 1993; Lyu & Lee, 2013). However, robust research is required to accurately characterise the type, intensity, and duration of physical activity associated with spectating at a golf event, which may offer benefits to the spectators, and could result in an attractive marketing angle for organisers.

Table 34.1 Health implications for golfers

The evidence suggests	Implication for players	Implications for golf facilities and industry
Golfers live longer, and have better health.	Continue participation.	Communicate health benefits clearly to players and decision makers to increase participation.
A minimum of 150 mins a week of physical activity is recommended.	Play golf at least 150 mins per week, or engage in other physical activities additional to golf.	Communicate health benefits of at least weekly play to players.
Playing more than minimum recommendations brings further benefits.	Play frequently.	Communicate health benefits of frequent play to players.
Walking the course has greater health benefits than riding a golf-cart.	Walk the course if able.	Encourage players to walk the course if able. Avoid mandatory riding of golf carts. Consider legislation in the rules of the game to avoid mandatory cart use.
Spectators can accrue useful physical activity by walking.	Spend time walking when spectating.	Advertise benefits of walking to spectators.
Golfers are likely at increased risk of skin damage and skin cancer.	Moderate exposure to sunlight. Plan tee times, utilise sun-screen and appropriate clothing (collared shirt, hat etc).	Educate players. Facilities should stock sun-screen, hats, and collared shirts.
Those with cardiac risk factors are at higher risk of a cardiac event while playing.	Recognise that golf is beneficial for overall heart health. Players should report concerning symptoms to a doctor, and take medication as prescribed.	Consider providing Automatic External Defibrillators at facilities. Consider emergency situation training for staff.

Implications for players and the golf industry

The literature has suggested actions that can be taken by players, golf facilities, and by the golf industry that can positively influence the health of golfers. Table 34.1 highlights implications and potential actions for players based on the available evidence.

Summary and future directions

Evidence is consistent and growing that playing golf is associated with better physical health, and improved wellness. Golf has been shown to be a moderate intensity physical activity, which is important as health professionals, policy makers, and researchers are clear that being physically active for 150 minutes per week can help prevent and treat many chronic diseases such as heart attacks, strokes, type 2 diabetes, and depression. The best evidence we have suggests that playing golf has longevity benefits, probably due to the health enhancing physical activity accrued while playing.

While over 300 studies were identified by a scoping review that directly pertained to golf and health (Murray et al., 2016), there are clear research priorities that need to be addressed. Much of the current literature has focused on specific injuries and musculoskeletal complaints suffered by golfers, while there is little quality research assessing golf and mental health, looking at how health behaviours amongst golfers can be influenced to benefit health, and demonstrating cause and effect relationships specific to golf. Due to the various study designs employed, much of the evidence highlights associations, but could not confidently demonstrate causation.

References

Ainsworth, B.; Haskell, W.; Herrmann, S.; Meckes, N.; Bassett, D.; Tudor-Locke, C.; Greer, J.; Vezina, J.; Whitt-Glover, M. & Leon, A. (2011) 2011 Compendium of Physical Activities: A Second Update of Codes and MET Values, *Medicine and Science in Sports and Exercise*, 43 (8), 1575–1581.

Belanger, L.; Plotnikoff, R.; Clark, A. & Courneya, K. (2013) Prevalence, Correlates, and Psychosocial Outcomes of Sport Participation in Young Adult Cancer Survivors, *Psychology of Sport and Exercise*, 14 (2), 298–304.

Broman, G.; Johnsson, L. & Kaijser, L. (2004) Golf: A High Intensity Interval Activity for Elderly Men, *Aging Clinical and Experimental Research*, 16 (5), 375–381.

Brown, S.; Samuel, D.; Agyapong-Badu, S.; Herrick, I.; Murray, A. & Stokes, M. (2016) Age Related Differences in Lung Function Between Female Recreational Golfers and Less Active, *International Journal of Golf Science*, 5 (Supplement), 10.

Cabri, J.; Sousa, J.; Kots, M. & Barreiros, J. (2009) Golf-related Injuries: A Systematic Review, *European Journal of Sport Science*, 9 (6), 353–366.

Choi, M.; Hong, J.; Lee, J.; Shin, D.; Choi, H. & Lee, K. (2014) Preferential Location for Arterial Dissection Presenting as Golf-related Stroke, *American Journal of Neuroradiology*, 35 (2), 323–326.

Coate, D. & Schwenkenberg, J. (2013) Survival Function Estimates for Champions Tour Golfers, *Journal of Sports Economics*, 14 (6), 656–663.

Department of Health, Physical Activity, Health Improvement and Prevention (2004) *At Least Five a Week: Evidence on the Impact of Physical Activity and Its Relationship to Health*, London: Department of Health.

Dobrosielski, D.; Brubaker, P.; Berry, M.; Ayabe, M. & Miller, H. (2002) The Metabolic Demand of Golf in Patients with Heart Disease and in Healthy Adults, *Journal of Cardiopulmonary Rehabilitation and Prevention*, 22 (2), 96–104.

Dorado, C.; Moysi, J.; Vicente, G.; Serrano, J.; Rodriguez, L. & Calbet, J. (2002) Bone Mass, Bone Mineral Density and Muscle Mass in Professional Golfers, *Journal of Sports Sciences*, 20 (8), 591–597.

Downs, N.; Parisi, A. & Schouten, P. (2011) Basal and Squamous Cell Carcinoma Risks for Golfers: An Assessment of the Influence of Tee Time for Latitudes in the Northern and Southern Hemispheres, *Journal of Photochemistry and Photobiology B: Biology*, 105 (1), 98–105.

Downs, N.; Schouten, P.; Parisi, A. & Turner, J. (2009) Measurements of the Upper Body Ultraviolet Exposure to Golfers: Non-Melanoma Skin Cancer Risk, and the Potential Benefits of Exposure to Sunlight, *Photodermatology, Photoimmunology & Photomedicine*, 25 (6), 317–324.

Eser, P.; Cook, J.; Black, J.; Iles, R.; Daly, R.; Ptasznik, R. & Bass, S. (2008) Interaction Between Playing Golf and HRT on Vertebral Bone Properties in Post-Menopausal Women Measured by QCT, *Osteoporosis International*, 19 (3), 311–319.

Farahmand, B.; Broman, G.; De Faire, U.; Vågerö, D. & Ahlbom, A. (2009) Golf: A Game of Life and Death–Reduced Mortality in Swedish Golf Players, *Scandinavian Journal of Medicine & Science in Sports*, 19 (3), 419–424.

Four Home Countries' Chief Medical Officers (2011) *Start Active, Stay Active. A Report on Physical Activity for Health From the Four Home Countries' Chief Medical Officers*, London: Department of Health.

Fujiwara, M.; Asakuma, S.; Nakamura, K.; Nakamura, T.; Yasutomi, N. & Iwasaki, T. (1995) Acute Myocardial Infarction During Sport, *Journal of Cardiology*, 26 (4), 213–217.

Gao, K.; Hui-Chan, C. & Tsang, W. (2011) Golfers Have Better Balance Control and Confidence than Healthy Controls, *European Journal of Applied Physiology*, 111 (11), 2805–2812.

Getchell, L. (1965) *An Analysis of the Effects of a Season of Golf on Selected Cardiovascular, Metabolic, and Muscular Fitness Measures on Middle-Aged Men; And the Caloric Cost of Golf*, Unpublished PhD Thesis, Oregon: University of Oregon.

Goto, S.; Ishima, M.; Shimizu, M.; Kobayashi, Y. & Moriya, H. (2001) A Longitudinal Study for Femoral Neck Bone Mineral Density Increases in Premenopausal Caddies Using Dual-Energy X-Ray Absorptiometry, *Journal of Bone and Mineral Metabolism*, 19 (2), 125–130.

Hanke, C.; Zollinger, T.; O'Brian, J. & Bianco, L. (1985) Skin Cancer in Professional and Amateur Female Golfers, *Physician and Sportsmedicine*, 13 (8), 51–68.

Hansen, H. & Gauthier, R. (1993) Spectators' Views of LPGA Golf Events, *Sport Marketing Quarterly*, 2 (1), 17–25.

Hansen, H. & Gauthier, R. (1994) The Professional Golf Product: Spectators' Views, *Sport Marketing Quarterly*, 3 (4), 9–16.

Hoberty, R. & Craig, M. (1983) "Living Up to Par" – A Golf Tournament for Persons with COPD, *Respiratory Care*, 28 (11), 1480–1483.

Lee, I.; Sesso, H.; Oguma, Y. & Paffenbarger, R. (2004) The "Weekend Warrior" and Risk of Mortality, *American Journal of Epidemiology*, 160 (7), 636–641.

Lee, I.; Shiroma, E.; Lobelo, F.; Puska, P.; Blair, S.; Katzmarzyk, P. & Lancet Physical Activity Series Working Group (2012) Effect of Physical Inactivity on Major Non-communicable Diseases Worldwide: An Analysis of Burden of Disease and Life Expectancy, *The Lancet*, 380 (9838), 219–229.

Lim, S.; Vos, T.; Flaxman, A.; Danaei, G.; Shibuya, K.; Adair-Rohani, H.; Almazroa, M.; Amann, M.; Anderson, H.; Andrews, K. & Aryee, M. (2013) A Comparative Risk Assessment of Burden of Disease and Injury Attributable to 67 Risk Factors and Risk Factor Clusters in 21 Regions, 1990–2010: A Systematic Analysis for the Global Burden of Disease Study 2010, *The Lancet*, 380 (9859), 2224–2260.

Lyu, S. & Lee, H. (2013) Market Segmentation of Golf Event Spectators Using Leisure Benefits, *Journal of Travel & Tourism Marketing*, 30 (3), 186–200.

McGowan, E.; Speed-Andrews, A.; Rhodes, R.; Blanchard, C.; Culos-Reed, S.; Friedenreich, C. & Courneya, K. (2013) Sport Participation in Colorectal Cancer Survivors: An Unexplored Approach to Promoting Physical Activity, *Supportive Care in Cancer*, 21 (1), 139–147.

Murase, Y.; Kamei, S. & Hoshikawa, T. (1989) Heart Rate and Metabolic Responses to Participation in Golf, *The Journal of Sports Medicine and Physical Fitness*, 29 (3), 269–272.

Murray, A.; Daines, L.; Archibald, D.; Hawkes, R.; Schiphorst, C.; Kelly, P.; Grant, L. & Mutrie, N. (2016) The Relationships Between Golf and Health: A Scoping Review, *British Journal of Sports Medicine*, 51 (1), 12–19.

Oja, P.; Titze, S.; Kokko, S.; Kujala, U.; Heinonen, A.; Kelly, P.; Koski, P. & Foster, C. (2015) Health Benefits of Different Sport Disciplines for Adults: Systematic Review of Observational and Intervention Studies with Meta-analysis, *British Journal of Sports Medicine*, 49 (7), 434–440.

Palank, E. & Hargreaves, E. (1990) The Benefits of Walking the Golf Course: Effects on Lipoprotein Levels and Risk Ratios, *Physician and Sportsmedicine*, 18 (10), 77–80.

Parkkari, J.; Natri, A.; Kannus, P.; Mänttäri, A.; Laukkanen, R.; Haapasalo, H.; Nenonen, A.; Pasanen, M.; Oja, P. & Vuori, I. (2000) A Controlled Trial of the Health Benefits of Regular Walking on a Golf Course, *The American Journal of Medicine*, 109 (2), 102–108.

Reed, D.; Birnbaum, A.; Brown, L.; O'Connor, R.; Fleg, J.; Peberdy, M.; Van Ottingham, L.; Hallstrom, A. & PAD Trial Investigators (2009) Location of Cardiac Arrests in the Public Access Defibrillation Trial, *Prehospital Emergency Care*, 10 (1), 61–67.

Speck, R.; Courneya, K.; Mâsse, L.; Duval, S. & Schmitz, K. (2010) An Update of Controlled Physical Activity Trials in Cancer Survivors: A Systematic Review and Meta-analysis, *Journal of Cancer Survivorship*, 4 (2), 87–100.

Stauch, M.; Liu, Y.; Giesler, M. & Lehmann, M. (1999) Physical Activity Level During a Round of Golf on a Hilly Course, *Journal of Sports Medicine and Physical Fitness*, 39 (4), 321–327.

Tsang, W. & Hui-Chan, C. (2010) Static and Dynamic Balance Control in Older Golfers, *Journal of Aging and Physical Activity*, 18 (1), 1–13.

Unverdorben, M.; Kolb, M.; Bauer, I.; Bauer, U.; Brune, M.; Benes, K.; Nowacki, P. & Vallbracht, C. (2000) Cardiovascular Load of Competitive Golf in Cardiac Patients and Healthy Controls, *Medicine and Science in Sports and Exercise*, 32 (10), 1674–1678.

US Department of Health and Human Services and Office of Disease Prevention and Health Promotion (2008) *Physical Activity Guidelines for Americans*, Washington, DC: US Department of Health and Human Services.

Walker Research Group (2011) *The Health & Wellness Benefits of Golf Participation & Involvement*, Scotland: Golf 20/20 and World Golf Foundation.

Weisgerber, M.; Webber, K.; Meurer, J.; Danduran, M.; Berger, S. & Flores, G. (2008) Moderate and Vigorous Exercise Programs in Children with Asthma: Safety, Parental Satisfaction, and Asthma Outcomes, *Pediatric Pulmonology*, 43 (12), 1175–1182.

Wen, C.; Wai, J.; Tsai, M.; Yang, Y.; Cheng, T.; Lee, M.; Chan, H.; Tsao, C.; Tsai, S. & Wu, X. (2011) Minimum Amount of Physical Activity for Reduced Mortality and Extended Life Expectancy: A Prospective Cohort Study, *The Lancet*, 378 (9798), 1244–1253.

World Health Organization (1946) *Official Records of the World Health Organization: 2*, London: WHO.

35

YOUNG PEOPLE AND GOLF

Martin Toms

Introduction

The study of youth engagement and young people in golf is very much a marginalised (yet developing) one. With the focus on adult participation and engagement, equipment technology and other participation aids (such as those highlighted within this book), the focus on young people is most evidently missing. While there are plenty of studies emerging within the sport science literature on young people exploring things, such as talent and football at both grassroots (e.g., O'Gorman & Greenough, 2015) and elite (e.g., Clarke et al., 2016) levels, as well as tennis (e.g., Knight & Holt, 2013), these tend to come from a psychosocial perspective. In contrast to many other sports, research in golf is limited, and where it does exist, it is mainly focussed upon performance measurement and training.

This chapter aims to explore the developing area of work (and understanding) of young people's engagement in golf from a sociological and psychosocial perspective, as well as beginning to highlight the important area of talent development in the game (an area mentioned elsewhere in the book – cf. the chapter by Robertson in Part II). Taking the viewpoint of research in the psychosocial domain, this chapter will review the most recent perspectives of the game and offer an insight into the way the game is changing for young people and the challenges that it now faces in the 21st century.

This chapter intends to focus upon the empirical work on golf that emphasises involvement rather than performance and will explore some of the key works from a multidisciplinary perspective while calling for more research to be undertaken in the game to better understand the importance and impact of the game. After all, young people are the future of the sport, and an understanding of the cultural and social context they inhabit is important at both micro and macro levels. Certainly, policy-makers and coaches need to appreciate the differences within cultures and countries, as much as between individuals, as they plan strategies for engagement moving forwards.

It must be said that relative to performance and the science of the game, there is a dearth of research into the experiences of young people in golf, and this is something that needs to be rectified for the future development of the game. Importantly, this also needs to be undertaken within the cultural and historical context of the country of origin. In other words, countries with an established history and tradition of golf (such as the United Kingdom, the United States and parts or Europe) will require different approaches than countries newer to the game.

Review of current research

The study of young people in sport is a relatively new phenomenon (since the 1970s), where the 'leisure' field first engaged with it (e.g., Witt, 1971) in broad concepts as a part of lifestyle research. It is only since the 1990s that these have become more focussed on sport-specific development, as the growth of sport pedagogy research (and the growth of sports science more broadly as a discipline) has led to a more intensive focus on young people from multiple perspectives. While the generic research data still looks at sport from a health and participation angle, there is a growing focus on the young person from an applied perspective and a stronger understanding of their participation within sport from biopsychosocial perspectives (Bailey et al., 2010).

Focussing on the key empirical research in golf, this chapter will explore the development of this thinking from a psychosocial perspective. The chapter acknowledges that studies currently exist investigating young people in golf from multiple angles (e.g., in physiology – heart rate and pre-shot routine: Zienius et al., 2015; and in skill learning – study of golf swing and putting assessments: Barnett et al., 2015), but will focus more on the developing area of the sociological and psychosocial studies, underpinned by the key point that participation and development of young golfers must be culturally contextual.

A key starting point, and one of the few in-depth studies on young people in golf, is that of Zevenbergen et al. (2002). Their study of 'cadet' golfer's in a New Zealand golf club is framed using Bourdieu and his concepts of Capital (cf. Bourdieu, 1988; Field, 2003). While this is just a case study of one club and sixteen 8–14-year-old golfers, the data very strongly highlights the importance of the young players ascribing to, and assimilating, the culture of the golf club in order to achieve both recognition and success. This, they found, was central to the whole golf experience, and thus is an important consideration into how we offer golf club experiences to young people in order for them to engage (as Toms et al., 2008 has noted for junior cricket). This suggests that social and cultural capital in the golf club is directly related to participation and attrition, and that conformity to club norms is essential for continued engagement and participation.

While this finding may not be unusual, the implications of the need to reflect the image of the game and the club highlight the profound importance for young people on taking on the habitus of a golfer and thus the rules of the game. It is this conformity and control that is often seen to dominate the game; young people perceive the sport to be old-fashioned and lacking modern conveniences (e.g., in the United Kingdom, this is highlighted by both Sports Marketing Surveys, 2013, and Syngenta, 2013), and this creates a challenge to youth participation. However, the challenge of creating ways of engaging young people into the culture of conformity and rules has been explored in more detail in the United States. There, *The First Tee* project runs as a way of engaging young people with the concept of positive youth development, using golf as a medium and identifying how the sport can transfer into life skills (Weiss et al., 2013, 2014, 2016). Reviews of the project highlighted that the use of a positive youth development framework showed that the game helped improve the self-reported life skills and developmental outcomes for the young people.

Indeed, such approaches and strategies for social engagement are also found at university level in the United States, such as the review of 20 university golf programmes in the United States and engagement of minority groups through PGA education initiatives and their relative success (Fjelstul et al., 2011). Further, the role of golf for young people in the United States within minority communities has some historical context. Some African-American young people became involved in golf initially through caddying and then graduated to academies set up for underprivileged children (Usher, 2010). More recently, Anderson-Butcher et al. (2013) explored the importance of youth-based sports programmes for the development of social and life skills and also developing athletic competence. Their sample of 193 students aged between 9 and 16 years linked to the First Tee programme highlighted a culturally based summer sports programme/camp that may have had social benefits to those involved. This model could perhaps be further explored in other countries during summer vacations. So the game (particularly in the United States) has been used as a vehicle for engagement and social change, although the relative success of these broader strategies needs more investigation since it is not yet clear whether those who engage in the project become life-long participants or indeed join clubs as regular members.

Within the participation literature, the seminal piece of work on young people and club golf at a grassroots level is clearly that of Zevenbergen et al. (2002), but a number of other studies have been emerging in the United Kingdom exploring the developmental experiences of young golfers. Hayman et al. (2011, 2012, 2014) explored the experiences of 11 late adolescent 'elite' (national amateur) golfers and their engagement in the game. This study of UK golfers provided some valuable insight into their developmental journeys, practice routines and engagement in the game at a competitive level, although it focussed solely on golfers clearly at a high ability level. Further, Wright and Toms (2015) and Wright (2016) spent 2 years exploring the relationship of twenty-four 16–18-year-old players with the game, within a golf academy in the United Kingdom. This longitudinal study noted that the lack of success and engagement of those involved and the shattering of (what were) unrealistic dreams lead to significant levels of attrition from the group and drew into question the talent development pathways that were not focussed upon the individual, but the performance outcome. While both studies used predominantly young male players, further work in Ireland by Kitching highlighted the context of gender differences (see also Chapter 36 in this book).

There is also the context of age which has an impact upon engagement and participation in the sport. Kitching's 2011 doctoral thesis and her 2015 paper explore some of the issues around social and gendered space in a golf club and the hierarchical nature of the clubhouse, which would clearly have an impact on the way the club is socially constructed (and understood) by the juniors. So, while the participants in these studies were individuals who had already overcome barriers to play the game at a good level, the lack of research focussing upon beginner golfers and their experiences (beyond Zevenbergen et al., 2002) is an area for future work.

Thus, while golf can be restricting in terms of conformity, there are other areas where it can be used as a means of creating capital, and as a means of socialising young people into society through the game. A similar approach to the use of golf as a means of a socially inclusive activity had been explored by Carless and Douglas (2004) for adults with mental health issues with some success. Thus, the game of golf has some considerable context as an avenue for the development of young people's social norms and their role and position within society (MacPhail & Kirk, 2006), and more broadly, an as area that programmes like The First Tee Project (see Weiss et al., 2013, 2014, 2016) have contributed to in the United States. Yet understanding these experiences is an important aspect of the development of the game.

A systematic review for the PGA (GB&I) on golf and youth sports participation (Bailey & Cope, 2016) identified that there was a lack of research on junior coaching in golf, and that there was a need to further research this area, especially around the attitudes, behaviours, and experiences of young people in the game. They highlighted that there were clearly stages that needed to be considered when young people engaged with the game, not just based upon age, but also ability and gender. So, while we can apply the generic principles of sports participation and coaching experiences, this neglects the particular tradition and context that golf has in, and of, itself.

An area that does engender some study with young people is the psychological aspects of the game and the perception that this is central to performance. A brief review of this area highlighted a number of studies exploring the psychology and social psychology of the game for young people. In a small-scale survey of five, 16–18 year-old male, Scottish elite amateur golfers, Nicholls et al. (2005) and Nicholls (2007) explored their coping strategies in competition over a 28 day competition period, using diaries to identify the issues within competition and practice, and their strategies to overcome issues. This provided a limited, but useful, approach to the importance of working with applied practitioners in the field. Similarly, Majzub and Muhammad (2010) undertook a study of 80 young Malaysian golfers aged 16 to 18 years (the majority being male) who played on the national junior golf circuit, to explore their Task and Ego orientations. Unsurprisingly, the study highlighted the need for more sport psychology training, as well as the weaknesses of mental training of athletes in the country. Further work has been undertaken on the psychology of junior golfers in Norway, with Nordbotten (2011) studying 22 junior golfers (aged 16–18 years) from golf high schools, and identified that self-handicapping did not affect the motivational climate of performance. Indeed, the development of these psychological studies with young athletes appears to be on the increase (particularly it seems in Europe).

A case study by Henriksen et al. (2014), explored the talent development golf environment of a group of eleven young golfers (aged 16–19 years) in Denmark and their experiences of a boarding style talent development environment. Their exploration of the athletic talent development environments (ATDEs) highlighted that there was a need to engage in more dialogue between all involved; that elite and recreational environments needed to be made distinct; and that coach led group culture was essential for integrating the participants in the game. The underlying assumption being made was of the importance of engagement with others, and also an understanding of the social context in which they experienced the game – something particularly highlighted by Henriksen et al. (2014). But it is not just the experience of the game that was highlighted as being important here, Slater et al. (2012) found that adult gofers' perception of their own ability was inherently built up from their experiences as young players, from improving through solitary practice and playing against others (something identified in the work of Cafaro & Toms, 2015). In this way, they were able to construct their own perceptions that were moulded through the experiences of the club and also ability (Zevenbergen et al., 2002). Finally, when considering the importance of the social and cultural context, the work of Bum and Shin (2015) explored the experiences of 216 South Korean middle and high school golfers (aged 12–18 years) with their coach, and how leadership style and relationships impacted the psychological state and performance of the young golfers. They identified that, in a Korean context, social support and training decreased cognitive anxiety prior to competition, but that autocratic coach behaviour increased it, and called for more training for Korean golf coaches in the broader psycho-social skills of coaching juniors.

What cannot be ignored however, is the relative social impacts that the likes of socio-economics, family involvement, geographical location, and broader cultural context, young people have access to in order to support their participation and development (for a review of these in sport see Bailey et al., 2010; Bailey and Cope, 2016). It is quite clear that the perception and reality of the cost (and time it takes) to play golf has a negative impact upon participation, and thus, is more likely to only impact those who are not in a position to pay. The perception of golf being seen as an exclusive and elitist sport by some young people (and their parents) is clearly an issue for the game in countries with a long tradition of the sport. Yet these images also link to the wider contexts of the game, for example, work undertaken by the PGA (GB&I). Toms and Colclough (2012), highlighted that of a sample of 590 PGA assistant professionals (in training), there was a significant over-representation of those from biological two parent families compared to the national average, and that almost 70% of the sample had parents who also played the game (not unusual in junior sport as Kay, 2009 pointed out). In addition, virtually all of the sample had at least one parent employed full time (similar to Hayman et al., 2011). Thus, the importance of family support and engagement 'with' young people in the game is crucial.

Another example of this was seen by Stoszkowski and Collins (2011) who undertook a study of 8 English County Academy coaches, and highlighted that the coaches' view was that the emergence of young golfing talent was based upon their ability to overcome numerous socio-contextual barriers to ability around family, access, socio-economics, and physical ability. This was further explored by Branton and Toms (2015) in the study of 5 young golfers and their experience of the parent-coach-athlete triad in golf development in the UK. They found that the incidental social interaction between coach and parent was a stumbling block to success, and that parents would feel isolated as the young players became more reliant and aligned with the coach. Further, Jenkins et al. (2015) in their retrospective study of 125 Tour players and their developmental journeys, identified the importance of young people simply playing the game with friends at local facilities, and thus learning in context.

The issue of geography and access to facilities is also an area of consideration when it comes to engagement and involvement of young people in the game. Quite clearly, an individual who lives in an urban or very rural environment may have trouble accessing a club due to their location. Yet even where this is possible, Côté et al. (2006) noted that in the United States, one was most likely to become a golfer if they came from a city with a population between 50,000 and 100,000. While this was quite clearly culturally appropriate to the United States (not every country will be the same), it did highlight the role that location has in the context of access, competition, and the opportunity to engage with a nurturing environment. Thus, the 'accident' and luck of geography can have an impact upon engagement and sustained participation (Bailey & Toms, 2010).

However, the importance of the social environment and context of the club is paramount, with both family involvement and club environment being crucial to socialisation experiences in the game (Toms et al., 2008). While there is a need for coaching and involvement at a grass roots level, where most of that coaching is based at club level, the vicious circle of engagement becomes very apparent here. It is difficult for a young person to engage in the game (if they have no family members who do), if the only way they can achieve this is at a club. The strategies that have been implemented within junior school-club programmes and the work in communities across the world by the R&A are an example of this, but the need for golf as part of a Physical Education curriculum subject is one that needs socio-political consideration across many countries. Indeed, a novel way of providing children with the skills of golf has been explored in the US PE system by using croquet as a medium (Brusseau & Scheer, 2013), although perhaps the socio-economic connotations of this need further context. The work of Piggott et al. (2011) exploring the impact of initiatives in the UK also highlights many of these socio-cultural and socio-historical factors that impact the participation of young people, and the multiple barriers young people can face to even engage with a club in the first instance.

Additional concerns for the game of golf in England is that there appears to be relatively low levels of participation of juniors in the game, with only 7% of new members being boys and 1% girls (England Golf, 2014). Problematically, it is not easy to identify the precise number of junior players in many other countries (particularly where golf is in its infancy), and while the R&A (2015) have attempted to identify the number of golfers globally, that level of demographic detail is understandably out of reach. There are a few exceptions (although methodologically these tend to be simply survey data based upon overall memberships, which do not allow simple comparisons where previous data is unavailable) that do bring a broader perspective to the engagement of juniors as club members, but these still need more detailed interrogation to identify the state of participation for juniors. For example, in the United States, The National Golf Foundation (2017) consider that at 12.4% of the playing membership, there are roughly the same number of young players as there have been since 2013 (although there are slightly more boys than girls playing). In Australia, Golf Australia (2015) suggest that 3.6% of their registered playing members are also under 18 years of age (again higher for males than females). Further, the European Golf Course Owners Association (2016) suggest that junior golf members across Europe are in fact in decline, with only Belgium, the Czech Republic, Poland, and Spain noting any increase in registered junior players between 2010 and 2015.

In a report for Golf 2020 (HSBC, 2012), they consider that golf is moving fastest in Asia, and predict that there will be more juniors (as well as tour winners) coming from that continent in the future. While these are only illustrative examples of survey data, they do suggest that perhaps in some newer golf countries, junior membership has increased. However, such inferences need further contextual exploration and consideration, but do suggest that there is a level of socio-political and socio-cultural context that needs to be taken into account. It will be very interesting to see how these participation rates develop over the next decade, and even more importantly the studies that will follow them.

Thus, it is clear that there are a plethora of socio-cultural factors that have an impact upon the engagement and socialisation of young people in the game, which are mediated by the cultural context of the country in which the game is played. The evidence presented begins to explore the impacts of a number of key socio-cultural factors on participation – that of parents, family, socio-economics, geography, and the context of coaching. As Bailey et al. (2010) highlighted, the way that young people engage in sport from a biopsychosocial perspective was important for policy makers, coaches, and parents to understand. The sources used in this chapter begin to highlight that underpinning much of the participation in golf are key socio-cultural factors that need more research and contextual understanding. For example, when developing active young sports people, should golf be a part of the broader diet of physical activity?

While this chapter does not intend to focus upon the issues of talent identification and selection in golf (despite this being a pertinent problem at this time), it is important to note that there is currently a plethora of schemes across the world that focus upon the perceived benefit of early specialisation in golf (where young people are encouraged to focus on just golf from a young age). The vast quantity of literature that argues against this approach in sport for medical, social, and psychological related reasons is quite clear (cf. Russell & Limle, 2013; Bergeron et al., 2015), yet golf still tends to suffer from this. Many junior championships seemingly push young children towards the need to specialise in the game, because it appears others did so in order to achieve success (for example Myer et al., 2016 discussed the example and 'myth' of Tiger Woods solely playing golf from a young age). Jenkins et al. (2015) further explored the experiences of a number of tour pros and identified that they were predominantly late specialisers in the game. However, as Wright (2016) also identified in his work, the commercialisation of selling the dream of becoming a professional player versus the statistical reality, has become an industry in itself in many parts of the world – arguably to the detriment of the game and young people.

Implications for the game

The future of the game of golf relies significantly on the impact of junior development, and at the earliest of stages, basic golfing engagement. As this chapter shows, there is a significant lack of detailed and in-depth research on youth participation in the game (and this is not just related to golf). Even where research has been undertaken, it is clear that the environment and culture of the club/facility, as well as the attitudes of coaches and adults who engage with them in the game, is crucial. The studies summarised here clearly show that there are a number of implications that can be taken from the research. In order to develop the next generation of golfers, it is important to create a supportive and nurturing environment for them to play in; that opportunities for them to engage in the game away from the formal club structure (such as at school, with peers, and at other venues) is an important place to learn skills in a non-threatening environment; and that the value of parents/family and important others is essential in the creation of an environment in which golf can be experienced in a positive way as part of a healthy sporting diet. Ultimately, these are essential characteristics for the future of the game that need to be employed by policy makers, clubs, coaches, and other adult players alike. To turn a blind eye to the needs of these young performers will have significant consequences for the game, so appropriate strategies (such as cultural contextual approaches similar to the *First Tee* programme) should be introduced and further developed.

Summary and future directions

This chapter highlights the available research literature around young people and golf, and highlights that there is a dearth of work in this area at every level. Beyond the in-depth work of Zevenbergen et al. (2002), the majority of available research has been based on those who already play the game at a good level, and the majority of this work is based in Europe. While a number of studies use golf as a medium to explore other factors, the lack of understanding of the game from the perspective of the young players themselves is clear (cf. Bailey & Cope, 2016). Thus, while there are still multiple agendas around participation for young people in sport, the undoubted health and social benefits of golf as a form of physical activity are clear (see Murray et al. in this section). However, there are still social, historical, and cultural hurdles to get over in order to ensure the game is open to young people (across all cultural contexts and countries). The need for further (longitudinal) research on young people engaging with and participating from a grass roots level onwards is important, making Zevenbergen et al. (2002) instrumental in this understanding.

What cannot be underestimated is the impact of the history and tradition of the game within the culture of the country that the young person inhabits. Since this is the context in which they are socialised and experience the game, this will have a direct impact upon the opportunities they have to play it. As such, future research needs to take these golfing contexts into account when exploring young people's participation in the game, from both established and new golfing nations.

References

Anderson-Butcher, D.; Iachini, A.; Riley, A.; Wade-Mdivanian, R.; Davis, J. & Amorose, A. (2013) Exploring the Impact of a Summer Sport-Based Youth Development Program, *Evaluation and Program Planning*, 37, 46–49.

Bailey, R.; Collins, D.; Ford, P.; MacNamara, A.; Toms, M. & Pearce, G. (2010) *Participant Development in Sport: An Academic Review*, Leeds, UK: Sportscoach UK.

Bailey, R. & Cope, E. (2016) *A Review of Research and Evidence on Factors That Impact on Young People's Behaviours and Attitudes to Golf Coaching: Report for the PGA(GB&I)*, West Midlands, UK: PGA.

Bailey, R. & Toms, M. (2010) Youth Talent Development in Sport – Rethinking Luck and Justice, In: A. Hardman & R. Jones (Eds.) *The Ethics of Sports Coaching*, London: Routledge, pp. 149–164.

Barnett, L.; Hardy, L.; Brian, A. & Robertson, S. (2015) The Development and Validation of a Golf Swing and Putt Skill Assessment for Children, *Journal of Sports Science & Medicine*, 14 (1), 147–154.

Bergeron, M.; Mountjoy, M.; Armstrong, N.; Chia, M.; Côté, J.; Emery, C.; Faigenbauam, A.; Hall, G.; Kriemler, S.; Léglise, M.; Malina, R.; Pensgarrd, A.; Sanchez, A.; Soligard, T.; Sundgot-Borgen, J.; van Mechelen, W.; Weissensteiner, J. & Engebretsen, L. (2015) International Olympic Committee Consensus Statement on Youth Athletic Development, *British Journal of Sports Medicine*, 49 (13), 843–851.

Bourdieu, P. (1988) Program for a Sociology of Sport, *Sociology of Sport Journal*, 5 (2), 153–161.

Branton, B. & Toms, M. (2015) Understanding the Relationships Between Parents, Coach and Golfer and Their Role in Talent Development, *International Journal of Golf Science*, 3 (Supplement), S102–S103.

Brusseau, T. & Scheer, D. (2013) Using Croquet to Teach Golf in Physical Education, *Strategies*, 26 (4), 12–17.

Bum, C. & Shin, S. (2015) The Relationships Between Coaches' Leadership Styles, Competitive State Anxiety, and Golf Performance in Korean Junior Golfers, *Sport Science Review*, 24 (5–6), 371–386.

Cafaro, V. & Toms, M. (2015) Early Developmental Experiences of Elite Golfers: A Case Study from the UK, *International Journal of Golf Science*, 3 (Supplement), S105–S107.

Carless, D. & Douglas, K. (2004) A Golf Programme for People with Severe and Enduring Mental Health Problems, *Journal of Public Mental Health*, 3 (4), 26–39.

Clarke, N.; Harwood, C. & Cushion, C. (2016) A Phenomenological Interpretation of the Parent-Child Relationship in Elite Youth Football, *Sport, Exercise, and Performance Psychology*, 5 (2), 125–143.

Côté, J.; Macdonald, D.; Baker, J. & Abernethy, B. (2006) When "Where" Is More Important than "When": Birthplace and Birthdate Effects on the Achievement of Sporting Expertise, *Journal of Sports Sciences*, 24 (10), 1065–1073.

England Golf (2014) *England Golf Membership Survey*, Surrey: Sports Marketing Surveys, Inc.

European Golf Course Owners Association (2016) European Player Participation Rates 2014–15, Available at www.egcoa.eu/statistic-central/ (Accessed April 20, 2017).

Field, J. (2003) *Social Capital*, London: Routledge.

Fjelstul, J.; Jackson, L. & Tesone, V. (2011) Increasing Minority Golf Participation Through PGA Education Initiatives, *Sage Open*, 1–5, Doi: 10.1177/2158244011416009.

Golf Australia (2015) *Golf Participation Report 2015*, Melbourne, Australia: Golf Australia

Hayman, R.; Borkoles, E.; Taylor, J.; Hemmings, B. & Polman, R. (2014) From Pre-elite to Elite: The Pathway Travelled by Adolescent Golfers, *International Journal of Sports Science & Coaching*, 9 (4), 959–974.

Hayman, R.; Polman, R. & Taylor, J. (2012) The Validity of Retrospective Recall in Assessing Practice Regimes in Golf, *International Journal of Sport and Exercise Psychology*, 10 (4), 329–337.

Hayman, R.; Polman, R.; Taylor, J.; Hemmings, B. & Borkoles, E. (2011) Development of Elite Adolescent Golfers, *Talent Development and Excellence*, 3 (2), 249–261.

Henriksen, K.; Larsen, C. & Christensen, M. (2014) Looking at Success from Its Opposite Pole: The Case of a Talent Development Golf Environment in Denmark, *International Journal of Sport and Exercise Psychology*, 12 (2), 134–149.

HSBC (2012) *Golf's 2020 Vision: The HSBC Report*, London: The Future's Company.

Jenkins, J.; Bridge, M. & Toms, M. (2015) The Critical Parameters to Elite Performance in Golf: The Modern Need to Specialise? *International Journal of Golf Science*, 3 (Supplement), S7–S8.

Kay, T. (2009) *Fathering Through Sport and Leisure*, New York, NY: Routledge.

Kitching, N. (2011) *'Practice' Makes Perfect: Locating Young People in Golf Club Culture*, Unpublished PhD Thesis, Ireland, Europe: University of Limerick.

Knight, C. & Holt, N. (2013) Factors that Influence Parents' Experiences at Junior Tennis Tournaments and Suggestions for Improvement, *Sport, Exercise, and Performance Psychology*, 2 (3), 173–189.

MacPhail, A. & Kirk, D. (2006) Young People's Socialisation into Sport: Experiencing the Specialising Phase, *Leisure Studies*, 25 (1), 57–74.

Majzub, R. & Muhammad, T. (2010) Goal Orientation and Achievement of Junior Golfers in Malaysia, *Procedia Social and Behavioral Sciences*, 9, 583–588.

Myer, G.; Jayanathi, N.; DiFiori, J.; Faigenbaum, A.; Kiefer, A.; Logerstedt, D. & Micheli, L. (2016) Sports Specialisation, Part II: Alternative Solutions to Early Sport Specialization in Youth Athletes, *Sports Health*, 8 (1), 65–73.

National Golf Foundation (2017) *Golf Participation in the U.S. – 2017 Edition*, Florida, USA: National Golf Foundation.

Nicholls, A. (2007) A Longitudinal Phenomenological Analysis of Coping Effectiveness Among Scottish International Adolescent Golfers, *European Journal of Sport Science*, 7 (3), 169–178.

Nicholls, A.; Holt, N.; Polman, R. & James, D. (2005) Stress and Coping Amongst International Adolescent Golfers, *Journal of Applied Sport Psychology*, 17 (4), 333–340.

Nordbotten, T. (2011) *Motivational Climate and Self-Handicapping in Elite Junior Golf*, Unpublished Msc Thesis, Oslo, Norway: Norwegian School of Sport Sciences.

O'Gorman, J. & Greenough, K. (2015) Children's Voices in Mini Soccer: An Exploration of Critical Incidents, *Soccer & Society*, 17 (6), 810–826.

Piggott, D.; Leslie, G. & Poller, G. (2011) *Widening Participation in Golf: Barriers to Participation and Golfmark*, Lincoln, UK: University of Lincoln.

R&A (2015) *Golf Around the World 2015*, St Andrews, Scotland, UK: R&A.

Russell, W. & Limle, A. (2013) The Relationship Between Youth Sport Specialization and Involvement in Sport and Physical Activity in Young Adulthood, *Journal of Sport Behavior*, 36 (1), 82–98.

Slater, M.; Spray, C. & Smith, B. (2012) "You're Only as Good as Your Weakest Link": Implicit Theories of Golf Ability, *Psychology of Sport and Exercise*, 13 (3), 280–290.

Sports Marketing Surveys (2013) *Membership Recruitment & Retention: Key Themes for Implementation*, Surrey: Sports Marketing Surveys Inc.

Stoszkowski, J. & Collins, D. (2011) Money, Money, Money? An Investigation of the Mediators of Talent Development in Golf, *Journal of Qualitative Research in Sports Studies*, 5 (1), 39–54.

Syngenta (2013) *Growing Golf in the UK*, Cambridge, UK: Syngenta.

Toms, M.; Kirk, D. & Juntumaa, B. (2008) "It's Like a Family Here..." the 'Family Club' in Junior Sport: A Case Study Analysis, In: J. Quinn & I. Zambini (Eds.) *Family Relations: 21st Century Issues and Challenges*, New York, NY: Nova Publishers, pp. 169–185.

Toms, M. & Colclough, D. (2012) Developing Elite Performers: Participant Profiling PGA Assistants Pros in the UK, *International Journal of Golf Science*, 1 (Supplement): S69–S70.

Usher, J. (2010) "The Golfers": African American Golfers of the North Carolina Piedmont and the Struggle for Access, *The North Carolina Historical Review*, 87 (2), 158–193.

Weiss, M.; Bolter, N. & Kipp, L. (2014) Assessing Impact of Physical Activity-Based Youth Development Programs: Validation of the Life Skills Transfer Survey (LSTS), *Research Quarterly for Exercise and Sport*, 85, 263–278.

Weiss, M.; Bolter, N. & Kipp, L. (2016) Evaluation of the First Tee in Promoting Positive Youth Development: Group Comparisons and Longitudinal Trends, *Research Quarterly for Exercise and Sport*, Doi: 10.1080/02701367.2016.1172698.

Weiss, M.; Stuntz, C.; Bhalla, J.; Bolter, N. & Price, M. (2013) 'More than a Game': Impact of the First Tee Life Skills Programme on Positive Youth Development: Project Introduction and Year 1 Findings, *Qualitative Research in Sport, Exercise and Health*, 5 (2), 214–244.

Witt, P. (1971) Factor Structure of Leisure Behavior for High School Age Youth in Three Communities, *Journal of Leisure Research*, 3 (4), 213–220.

Wright, J. (2016) *Dazzling Dreams and Dawning Reality: The Unholy Alliance of Sports Performance and Education for Apprentice Golfers in an Academy Structure*, Unpublished PhD Thesis, Birmingham, UK: University of Birmingham.

Wright, J. & Toms, M. (2015) Dazzling Dreams and Dawning Reality: The Unholy Alliance of Sports Performance and Education for Apprentice Golfers Within an Academy Structure, *International Journal of Golf Science*, 3 (Supplement), S104–S105.

Zevenbergen, R.; Edwards, A. & Skinner, J. (2002) Junior Golf Club Culture: A Bourdieuian Analysis, SOSOL: *Sociology of Sport Online*, 5 (1), 1–11.

Zienius, M.; Skarbalius, A.; Zuoza, A. & Pukenas, K. (2015) Total Time Taken and Heart Rate Changes of Youth Golfers During Pre-shot Routines in On-Course Conditions, *International Journal of Performance Analysis in Sport*, 15 (2), 560–571.

36

WOMEN IN GOLF

A critical reflection

Niamh Kitching

Introduction

The culture of golf and its environment is widely regarded as male-dominated and exclusionary. Historical accounts dating to 16th-century Scotland detail instances where females were shunned from the golf course and restricted to secret games involving little more than putting (George, 2009). Exclusionary practices continue to impact the modern game, where females still struggle for equality of access, participation, employment and decision making in golf (Kitching et al., 2017). Global golf participation figures indicate the low visibility of female participants, and some golf club institutions still preclude female members. It is not just on the fairways that female participants are less evident, but governance, administration and service provision in the golf industry is largely male-dominated, making it difficult for females to gain employment and forge careers (MacKinnon, 2013). The earnings of female professional golfers pale in comparison to those of their male counterparts (Saffer, 2016). Research has confirmed the discriminatory environment in which golf takes place for females of all ability levels both on and off the golf course; some of this is consented exclusion (McGinnis & Gentry, 2006; Mitchell et al., 2016). Prevailing perceptions of female golfers reduce them to less able, slower players, while the marketing of golf merchandise and products and the presentation of golf settings is normatively male (Hundley, 2004; McGinnis et al., 2005). This chapter reviews research on women in golf, both from historical and modern-day contexts, and concludes with some thoughts for the future. While efforts were made to include evidence from a range of international contexts, much of the research cited in this chapter emanates from the traditional golfing nations of Australia, Great Britain, Ireland and the United States.

Review of current research

Perspectives

The social history of golf is significant in understanding females' positioning in golf environments. Historical golf traditions and gendered institutionalised practices contribute to a culture that inhibits involvement and legitimises inequality, thus negatively influencing female engagement in golf. Taking this into account, this chapter is framed by critical feminism, a perspective that acknowledges the broad socio-historical context. Derived from critical theory, feminist perspectives begin with the assumption that sporting practices are historically produced, socially constructed and culturally defined to serve the needs and interests of powerful groups in society (Dewar, 1991). Critical feminists write in relation to power, where gender relations are often defined by hegemonic masculinity and supported by cultural norms of male domination and female subordination. Thus, the framework presented here acknowledges the oppression of minority participants and the normalisation of patriarchal power relations. The literature reviewed in this chapter is derived from a combination of sources, e.g., journal articles on the history and sociology of sport, golf governing body reports and legislative evidence. Given the global and economic significance of golf, some of the included sources are derived from business perspectives.

A short history of women's golf in Britain

During the nineteenth and twentieth centuries, the popularity of golf grew exponentially both in Britain and beyond. This period represents a significant time in the international development of golf, through a combination of industrialisation and the migration of golf to the commonwealth by the British monarchy and British workers (Concannon, 1995). Exploration of golf practices from this period is important, where the rapid spread of golf globally was accompanied by the spread of exclusionary golf practices, some of which prevailed in other countries (see Haig-Muir, 1998). This section summarises the contested terrain on which women participated in golf in Britain in the nineteenth and twentieth centuries.

Female golfers were not well received in nineteenth- and twentieth-century Britain, when the first accounts of women's golf were recorded. Up until the mid-1800s in Britain, women were often not tolerated in golf settings, and it was seldom that a female golfer would be seen on the golf course. For years, women were confined to secret games or putting activities, away from the 'real' golf played by male members (George, 2009). Writing on the acceptance of females in British golf clubs prior to 1914, Vamplew (2010) states that golf clubs were homosocial spaces for males of similar social backgrounds, where men could dine, drink, play cards, read papers all free from female involvement. While the rapid rise in popularity of golf at the time allowed women to develop a presence, their involvement was not taken seriously, where exclusion and discrimination was normalised and their play was ridiculed. Further, women generally accepted their subordinate and inferior roles in golf settings.

Women's access to golf was limited by golf club regulations, where female golfers were restricted to particular tee times, expected to give way to men on the course and confined to separate spaces in golf clubhouses. While male members were afforded full membership and uncontested playing rights in golf clubs, women formed 'ladies' sections where in many clubs they became known as associate members. Gender-segregated golf governing bodies formed and women's golf developed independently from the men's game (George, 2007; Vamplew, 2010). Discrimination of women in golf was generally consented and women appeared to accept their subordinate role in golf clubs (George, 2007). Further, George (2010) found that tension prevailed not only between women and men but also between different groups of women.

With the rapid spread of golf during this time, the game became an acceptable activity for well-to-do women, for whom it was a form of moderate exercise which allowed opportunities for social contact, did not threaten male players and helped to develop socially desirable attributes such as self-control (George, 2009). It also offered these women an opportunity to emphasise femininity and fashion, particularly where the majority of women who participated in golf viewed the game as a social activity (Cashmore, 2010). While shorter, less challenging courses facilitated these players, they did not appeal to the better, more competitive golfers, who were also aware that they could be derided if they displayed overly flamboyant playing styles and dress sense (George, 2007, 2009; Vamplew, 2010). Female golfers were widely perceived as inferior to their male counterparts, particularly given the higher number of shots they took and their 'inadequacy' in dealing with bunkers and other hazards (Vamplew, 2010). Around this time, as recorded by Haig-Muir (1998), women were perceived as emotionally unstable and incompetent in sport. While some aspects of golf such as equipment, technology and facilities have radically changed since the 1800s, the following sections detail how golf culture and practices have altered very little.

Visibility of females in golf

Golf participation figures in the period 2010–2016 indicate the low visibility of females in the game worldwide. In Great Britain and Ireland, female golfers typically comprise less than a fifth of participants, compared with a quarter or even a third in other European countries (KPMG, 2013; European Golf Association, 2016). The 2014 England Golf membership survey states that females account for 15% of members in England, with junior girls comprising a tiny 1% of members (England Golf, 2014). In contrast, some European countries have much higher ratios of adult female golfers, with Germany and Austria (35%), Switzerland (33%), the Netherlands (32%) and Belgium (31%) recording the highest rates (KPMG, 2013). In Australia, female participants account for 21% of the total golf club membership (Golf Australia, 2015). While female participation in golf is gradually increasing, it appears that women leave golf almost as quickly as they enter. In America, female golfer drop-out is almost double that of males; golf declined by 14% between 2005 and 2011, but the decrease in female golf participation in the same period was 27% (National Golf Foundation, 2012). Golf club membership attrition rates are higher than attraction rates in Australia, where membership declined by 21% from 1998 to 2014, with comparatively more females leaving the game (Golf Australia, 2015). In New Zealand, women's membership dropped by 17% between 2010 and 2015 (New Zealand Golf, 2015). The recent global decline in golf participation appears to have greatly impacted women's golf.

Not only are the fairways void of female participants, but golf industry governance, administration, and service provision could be largely homogeneous, making it more difficult for females to forge employment and progression opportunities. A report instructed by the Australian Sports Commission found that women were underrepresented in all facets of leadership and management in Australian golf (Sheppard, 2008). Female PGA golf professionals make up less than 3% of all PGA Professionals in Britain and Ireland (Kitching et al., 2017). This figure is less than 4% in America, where female PGA of America members are twice as likely as male members to become inactive. MacKinnon (2013) identified family and personal commitments, unsociable working hours and the lack of schedule flexibility as the primary reasons for this attrition. For the minority of females in the golf industry, there is some evidence of unpleasant working conditions. A study on female professionals' employment in the golf industry in Great Britain and Ireland found that both trainee and fully qualified female PGA professionals experienced access and rights discrimination both on and off the golf course, while the low expectations of male members, employers and club committees compromised their career progression opportunities (Kitching et al., 2017). Respondents to an LGU survey identified the male dominated industry (27%) as the biggest barrier to a career in golf for women (Ladies Golf Union, 2005). As will be considered in later sections, the under representation of females in golf can imply that their mere presence presents a challenge to the status quo.

It is important to acknowledge the significant roles that male family members play as gate-keepers to golf participation for females. Similar to the nineteenth and twentieth centuries, when young girls' motivation to play golf was triggered by fathers, brothers and uncles (George, 2009), male family members are key influencers and socialising agents (Shin & Nam, 2004; Reis & Correia, 2013). In one of the most comprehensive surveys on female involvement in golf in Great Britain and Ireland (*n* = 1,500), 65% of respondents identified their husbands, partners, parents and other family members as the primary reasons why they took up golf, with almost 9 of every 10 golfers surveyed having another member of the household that participated (Ladies Golf Union, 2005). A 2014 study in the UK identified the participation of fathers, partners and children as key reasons for taking up golf (Syngenta, 2014). Thus, female participation is positively influenced by male family members.

Golf club regulations

Golf club rules, regulations and constitutions still limit female members, where both associate membership and male-only clubs remain in existence, particularly in the USA, Great Britain and Ireland. Contentious legislation in some jurisdictions upholds the right of clubs to pursue all male memberships, as long as it is written into the club's legal constitution (Song, 2007; Lenkiewicz, 2011). A number of high profile clubs, tournament venues and governing bodies have been caught out in the debate on female membership. Following media scrutiny and the objections of equality campaigners, the annual US Masters venue Augusta National admitted their first female members in 2012. The Royal and Ancient (R&A) golf club at St. Andrews admitted its first female members in 2015. However, all male memberships exist in other well-known clubs such as the Australian Club in Sydney, Muirfield in Scotland, Pine Valley in New Jersey, USA and Portmarnock in Ireland. In their examination of the daily presentation of gender issues in a private golf club in England, Shotton et al. (1998) suggest that gender discrimination does not end once women gain access to golf club membership.

Women's golf – what is 'acceptable'?

Women's golf is becoming more reflective of female's multiple and varied femininities and ethnicities, something which has not been widely welcomed. A strong competitiveness and will to win – traits that have often been associated with masculine performance – have been encouraged by male family members and coaches in their socialisation of girls into golf (Reis & Correia, 2013). In contrast, a study in Midwest America found that women golfers embraced stereotypical roles where their emphasis on the femininity of golf was an important factor in their continued participation; McGinnis et al. (2005) termed this 'role entrapment'. Contrasting assumptions about the appropriateness of golf as a female activity can be problematic for some female participants. In conducting an ethnography on the American LPGA (Ladies' Professional Golf Association) tour, Crosset (1995) detected that LPGA tour players experienced tensions between their roles as athletes and societal expectations of them as females. These expectations about femininity are not limited to professional athletes; McGinnis and Gentry (2006) discuss the peer, spouse and family expectations that are placed on women, including the 'ethic of care', and embracing gender appropriate roles.

Like other female sports, golf has often been closely associated with lesbian and tomboy identities, and women's golf has been characterised as attractive to lesbian followers. Referring specifically to an ongoing preoccupation with lesbianism among professional ranks, Haig-Muir (1998) even referenced the 'image problem' permeating western media coverage of women's professional golf. In writing about gender differences in perceptions and attitudes toward the LPGA and its tour professionals, Dixon (2002) found that almost all survey respondents were aware of sexual orientation 'issues' in the LPGA tour. The LPGA itself has even been criticised for a controversial 2002 marketing plan, which along with appearing as homophobic, encouraged golfers to display femininity to compensate for the traditional masculine characteristics associated with sport (Wolter, 2010). While modern golf is more accepting of female players, it appears that traditional notions of fixed femininities are preferred.

The growth of golf in Asia has resulted in an influx of female professionals on the LPGA tour, particularly from South Korea. Korean fathers have identified professional golf as a respected and appropriate career for their daughters where it serves as a way to gain advantage in education settings (Shin & Nam, 2004). Korean females have been characterised as disciplined and hardworking, and from 1998 to 2011 Korean women won one hundred tour titles (Yoo, 2012). The growth of influence of Asian players on the LPGA tour wasn't initially celebrated; in 2008 the tour imposed a regulation requiring international players to pass an oral test to demonstrate proficiency in English (Claussen, 2010). Choi (2010) found that ethnic diversity and the dramatic increase of Asian players on the LPGA tour influenced the sponsorship decisions of a brewing company. In a study examining newspaper coverage on the three top women golfers at the time, Kim et al. (2006) found that South Korean golfer Se Ri Pak received less coverage than Annika Sorenstam and Karrie Webb, while more negative characteristics were used to describe Pak. It appears that professional women's golf has yet to fully welcome participants from varied backgrounds and ethnicities.

The portrayal of female professional golfers in television coverage and print media in the USA has been widely researched, much of which depicts females as less important and less able. In examining over 200 hours of nationally televised PGA and LPGA golf across eight US television networks, Billings et al. (2005) found that women golfers were more likely to be described in terms of why they succeeded or failed, whereas men were more likely to be described in terms of their personality or physicality. An examination of hidden media biases surrounding Annika Sorenstam's involvement in the 2003 PGA Colonial Tournament showed that commentators were more likely to highlight Sorenstam's emotions and outside pressures (Billings et al., 2006). In both of these studies, women golfers were more likely to be depicted as succeeding because of their intelligence, composure, and even luck, and failing because they lacked athletic ability. Two studies of golf magazines revealed how women were underrepresented, and deemed inferior athletes and spectators of golf who lived conventionally feminine, heteronormative lifestyles (Maas & Hasbrook, 2001; Apostolis & Giles, 2011). An examination of the portrayal of LPGA player Nancy Lopez during her final professional tournaments outlined how magazines represented her as a heterosexual, married mother, thereby perpetuating a model of family life and divisions of labour that benefits white men and subordinates women (Douglas & Jamieson, 2006). Overall, these studies show how media reproduce images about white, wealthy, able-bodied golfers, and reinforce dominant ideologies in golf culture. The acceptability of women in golf is often influenced by the social or competitive motivations of the golfers themselves. This will be considered in later sections.

Assumptions and perceptions

Female golfers are widely perceived as inferior to their male counterparts. Driving distance has frequently been used to frame women as less able golfers, and in a study on golfers from Midwest America, McGinnis et al. (2005) reported women feeling singled out when it came to slow play. Female participants in the McGinnis and Gentry (2006) study expressed frustration in relation to their golfing ability, where they were less assured than male golfers and admitted a knowledge deficit about golf, all of which contributed to anxiety and a lack of confidence on the golf course. In writing about gender differences in perceptions and attitudes toward the

LPGA and its tour professionals, Dixon (2002) found that women had much higher perceptions of female golfers' skill levels than men, and were much more likely to regard negative comments made about female golfers as being inappropriate. Women enter golf aware of gender stereotypes and perceived ability limitations, and can pressurise themselves to perform. In gathering the views of golf professionals, McGinnis and Gentry (2002, p. 7) comment in relation to female golfers "to excel or be noticed, they have to try harder than men, and if they do succeed, they often have to suffer the consequences of not doing gender appropriately". This has been confirmed in relation to Portuguese elite female golfers (Reis & Correia, 2013) and female golf professionals (Kitching et al., 2017). Coupled with negative ability perceptions, these performance role expectations contribute to female golfers' feelings of inferiority in golf settings, and particularly on the golf course itself.

Linked to the inferiority element of female participation in golf, there is some evidence of golf clubs and golf courses making assumptions about the social or competitive intentions of female golfers. While some studies have indicated how female participants placed more value on the social rather than competitive elements of golf (Shotton et al., 1998; Wright, 2008; Danylchuk et al., 2015), there is also evidence of a lack of competitive options for female players. In their interviews with golf professionals in Midwest and West USA, McGinnis and Gentry (2002) found professionals promoted their women's programmes around meeting groups, wine-tastings and themed events, with less focus on competitive golf. Female participants in the McGinnis et al. (2005) study suggested that the emphasis on mixed, social events indicated to female golfers that the serious play was left for the men.

Similar to women in predominantly male occupations, recreational female golfers have identified how they experienced heightened visibility and typecasting on the golf course, where they reported feeling ignored, overlooked or unimportant, particularly in their on course interactions with males (McGinnis et al., 2005; McGinnis & Gentry, 2006). According to golf professionals, male golfers use body language such as folded arms, sending unwelcoming signals in order to hurry female golfers on the course; while male professionals commented that they often fielded complaints and questions from male patrons about women's slow play (McGinnis & Gentry, 2006). In their study of female recreational golfers in an English golf club, (Mitchell et al., 2016) found that female members recounted feeling under surveillance when both out on the course and in the clubhouse; they described themselves as being objectified, 'othered' and highly visible as women, and uncomfortable that their appearance and social behaviour were being subjected to scrutiny and critique. The inferiority experienced in women's engagement with golf environments is likely influenced by these assumptions about ability, heightened visibility, performance role expectations and negative on-course interactions. When these gendered expectations become hegemonic, and 'the way things are supposed to be', females are further marginalised from golf settings and the gender divide in golf is reinforced.

The presentation of golf

A wealth of evidence from the American golf industry confirms how the presentation and marketing of golf can isolate female participants. In examining the language used in scorecards from 85 golf courses in 12 states, Hundley (2004) found that gendered tee boxes related to skill level served as hegemonic signs of the value placed on male and female golfers. Looking at approximately 500 golf courses in the USA, Arthur et al. (2011) found that highly gendered golf courses may result in women teeing off from separate parts of the course, and taking separate golf carts. Thus women who use golf for networking can be omitted from valuable conversations about business and career opportunities. Hundley (2004) suggests that tee box locations (where men have freedom of choice) imply that men are always stronger, more skilled and more qualified than women, regardless of their golfing ability. Haig-Muir (1998) suggests that this gender-marking separates women's golf from 'real' golf, where the men's game becomes the benchmark against which all else is measured. Kitching et al. (2017) found that by denying women access to tee times and parts of the golf course and clubhouse, male members and patrons sometimes deliberately suppressed female golfers' participation. Further, a number of studies have shown how the golf industry does not take female customers seriously, through marketing practices and strategies, the presentation of merchandise, lack of gender specific equipment and products, inadequate on–course restroom facilities and the overall prioritisation of male customers (McGinnis et al., 2005; MacKinnon, 2011). In what they termed 'sensible business practice' and the 'good old boy network', McGinnis and Gentry (2002, 2006) found that some professionals demonstrated their need to appease the male golfing population by rationalising male exclusivity, devaluing the female golfer and succumbing to sexist commentary.

The presentation of golf as normatively male means that the mere presence or involvement of women can be viewed as different or unexpected. Female golfers are sometimes presented and positioned as the 'other' in contrast to the dominant male position, as exemplified in the use of language such as 'ladies' rather than 'golfers' (Haig-Muir, 1998). Hundley's (2004) study of golf scorecards demonstrated how language illuminates sexism in golf, where gender is represented and reproduced in a way that preserves difference. While McGinnis and Gentry (2002) found that the term 'lady' was widely used by golf professionals as a label of respect, in other contexts the term 'lady' can be seen as archaic, patronising, derogatory or demeaning. McGinnis and Gentry (2006) also cited examples of how golf personnel and professionals use condescending language and actions that create an unwelcoming environment for women. They termed this 'traditional politeness', where using the term 'lady' prolongs the female stereotype that confines and limits women's performance and participation. Collectively, this evidence can enhance feelings of gender segregation and exclusion, and may also portray negative assumptions about women's positioning and abilities, all of which serves to perpetuate the gender gap in golf.

Female complicity?

The evidence presented thus far indicates how discrimination has been experienced in golf settings by females of all ability levels, while prevailing patriarchal practices are maintained and reproduced in golf club institutions. Hegemony works when the practices of dominant groups become normalised and privileged, and often goes unquestioned. While the interests of dominant groups are furthered, the preferences of marginalised groups become less significant, particularly when they themselves consent to or comply with the existing order. Where they seek out fellow females as playing partners, female cohesion in golf club settings has been shown to be an important strategy in their continued participation (McGinnis & Gentry, 2002). However, at times it appears that women golfers often fail to support each other and are complicit with marginalisation. McGinnis and Gentry (2006) noted that much of the insensitivity and hostility that female golfers experience actually comes from other female golfers. The exclusion of women in golf settings is sometimes supported by females themselves, who even perpetuate the status quo by accommodating to and playing by men's rules (Reis & Correia, 2013). Following in–depth interviews with 22 women golfers, McGinnis et al. (2009) found that 'accommodating' golfers tolerated rather than challenged golf rituals that privileged men; some of these women felt more intimated by other female golfers. Where male hegemonic discourses were consistently encountered by female professionals in golf settings, experienced professionals resorted to passive acceptance; 'it's better not to say anything' (Kitching et al., 2017). Kitching (2011) also found that girl golfers' adoption of peer group hierarchy based on ability meant that they complied with the prevailing power relations in the golf club, potentially reinforcing rather than challenging gender relations. This complicity can also be seen in the way the LPGA has dealt with ethnicity and difference amongst its tour players. McGinnis et al. (2005) suggest that when individuals find ways to accommodate gender inequity, the system remains unchanged. By placing more value on what is male, these strategies can reinforce the masculine hierarchy in and of golf, deeming it more difficult to interrupt conventional order and elicit change. The prevailing male hegemony, coupled with this evidence of female complicity and acceptance ensures that gender gaps prevail.

Summary and future directions

Acknowledging the critical outlook framing this chapter, and granted that much of the evidence emanates from the traditional golfing nations, the position of women in golf as presented here offers little optimism for the image and future advancement of the game. Patriarchy is a strong force in reproducing a culture in which male preferences are valued and female participants are less visible, perceived as inferior and marginalised from decision making. Golf remains a homogenous, linear and exclusionary sport for many cohorts, including lower social classes, disability groups and non-whites. The regressive image of golf hampers the game; the majority of respondents in the LGU research (65%) believed that single sex/gender segregated golf clubs damage the image of golf, while the intimidating atmosphere and male pervasiveness deem the sport unwelcoming for newcomers (Ladies Golf Union, 2005; Syngenta, 2014). While there is evidence of a lack of strategic leadership to address the low participation of women in golf (Sheppard, 2008), a milestone was reached in Scotland in January 2017 when the R&A merged with the LGU. While the introduction of novel participation initiatives (e.g., LPGA/USGA Girls Golf), the merging of male/female golf governing bodies in Great Britain, and the recent admission of female members to heretofore male only clubs may be perceived as progressive, there is a view that these moves are tokenistic, triggered by the threat of losing endorsements and state sport funding. Forced moves and empty gestures will do little to change attitudes, affect female participation and initiate real change in the game at grassroots or club level.

Golf has social, cultural and economic significance globally; from the playing population it reaches, to the celebrated icons and the industry, tourism and employment generated. With the growth of world tours, television exposure and the emergence of Tiger Woods some commentators anticipated that golf would reach a new diverse audience. While there is increasing interest in junior golf, golf participation declined particularly during the global economic recession, and aside from the re-introduction of golf into the 2016 Olympics, and the European Tour's proposal of alternative golf formats in 2017, there is little reason to expect a revolution in the game. The prevalence of younger players on professional tours could present an opportunity; in spite of the complicity of older professionals in the Kitching et al. (2017) study, younger professionals appeared more willing to challenge, discuss and confront the underlying discrimination, thereby marking a shift across the generations. Nonetheless, the evidence gathered to date on junior golf also points to stagnation and a reproduction of culture, where young golfers have to assimilate to learn the cultural system of golf or face marginalisation (Zevenbergen et al., 2002), while golf clubs use rules, restrictions and other symbolic practices to classify and reproduce cultural capital among young golfers (Kitching, 2011). Haig-Muir (1998) suggests that the socialisation of young males into golf from a young age is a strong force in maintaining and legitimating existing patriarchal practices and hierarchies.

Attempts at making golf more inclusive must go beyond growing the professional women's game, merging of golf governing bodies and the promotion of novel participation initiatives. Many of these moves address women as the 'problem', where they are perceived as lacking the interest, time and ability to persist at golf, while some participation strategies superficially focus on females socialising together or playing on women friendly courses. McGinnis et al. (2005) call for systematic changes in golf institutions including challenging the prevailing stereotypes of women golfers and providing support for working mothers to play. MacKinnon (2011) suggests that golf coaches should modify their traditional instructional techniques that were developed by men for men, and also acknowledge the anxiety facing women golfers in a male dominating environment. McGinnis and Gentry (2006) suggest treating female customers as equals and as serious golfers, creating a sense of belongingness and avoiding gender segmentation (i.e., separate competitions, equipment and teeing grounds), deference and archaic 'lady' language. Changing the culture of golf requires a fundamental shift in assumptions, attitudes and policies within golf club settings, otherwise as Crosset (1995) posits, females will continue to remain outsiders in the masculine world of golf.

References

Apostolis, N. & Giles, A. (2011) Portrayals of Women Golfers in the 2008 Issues of Golf Digest, *Sociology of Sport Journal*, 28 (2), 226–238.

Arthur, M.; Del Campo, R. & Van Buren III, H. (2011) The Impact of Gender-Differentiated Golf Course Features on Women's Networking, *Gender in Management: An International Journal*, 26 (1), 37–56.

Billings, A.; Angelini, J. & Tyler Eastman, S. (2005) Diverging Discourses: Gender Differences in Televised Golf Announcing, *Mass Communication and Society*, 8 (2), 155–171.

Billings, A.; Craig, C.; Croce, R.; Cross, K.; Moore, K.; Vigodsky, W. & Watson, V. (2006) "Just One of the Guys?" Network Depictions of Annika Sorenstam in the 2003 PGA Colonial Tournament, *Journal of Sport & Social Issues*, 30 (1), 107–114.

Cashmore, E. (2010) *Making Sense of Sports* (5th Ed.), London: Routledge.

Choi, J. (2010) The Impact of Ethnic Diversity on the Ladies Professional Golf Association: A Case Study of Anheuser-Busch and Its Sponsorship Objectives and Strategies, *Sport Marketing Quarterly*, 19 (1), 51–57.

Claussen, C. (2010) The LPGA's English Proficiency Rule: An-E-Yo, Kamsa-Hamnida, *Journal of Legal Aspects of Sport*, 20 (2), 135–150.

Concannon, D. (1995) *Golf: The Early Days*, London: Salamander.

Crosset, T. (1995) *Outsiders in the Clubhouse: The World of Women's Professional Golf*, Albany, NY: State University of New York Press.

Danylchuk, K.; Snelgrove, R. & Wood, L. (2015) Managing Women's Participation in Golf: A Case Study of Organizational Change, *Leisure/Loisir*, 39 (1), 61–80.

Dewar, A. (1991) Feminist Pedagogy in Physical Education: Promises, Possibilities and Pitfalls, *Journal of Physical Education, Recreation and Dance*, 62 (6), 68–77.

Dixon, M. (2002) Gender Differences in Perceptions and Attitudes Toward the LPGA and Its Tour Professionals: An Empirical Investigation, *Sport Marketing Quarterly*, 11 (1), 44–54.

Douglas, D. & Jamieson, K. (2006) A Farewell to Remember: Interrogating the Nancy Lopez Farewell Tour, *Sociology of Sport Journal*, 23 (2), 117–141.

England Golf (2014) *Golf Club Membership Questionnaire 2014 Results Book*, Woodhall Spa, UK: England Golf.

European Golf Association (2016) *Member Federations* [Online], Available at www.Ega-Golf.Ch/Federations (Accessed August 3, 2016).

George, J. (2007) Women to the Fore: Gender Accommodation and Resistance at the British Golf Club Before 1914', *Sporting Traditions*, 23 (2), 79–98.

George, J. (2009) An Excellent Means of Combining Fresh Air, Exercise and Society: Females on the Fairways, 1890–1914, *Sport in History*, 29 (3), 333–352.

George, J. (2010) "Ladies First?": Establishing a Place for Women Golfers in British Golf Clubs, 1867–1914, *Sport in History*, 30 (2), 288–308.

Golf Australia, (2015) *2014 Golf Participation Report*, Melbourne, Australia: Golf Australia.

Haig-Muir, M. (1998) Qualified Success? Gender, Sexuality and Women's Golf, *Sporting Traditions*, 14 (2), 37–52.

Hundley, H. (2004) Keeping the Score: The Hegemonic Everyday Practices in Golf, *Communication Reports*, 17 (1), 39–48.

Kim, E.; Walkosz, B. & Iverson, J. (2006) USA Today's Coverage of the Top Women Golfers, 1998–2001, *Howard Journal Communications*, 17 (4), 307–321.

Kitching, N. (2011) *Practice' Makes Perfect: Locating Young People in Golf Club Culture*, Unpublished PhD Thesis, Limerick: University of Limerick.

Kitching, N.; Grix, J. & Philpotts, L. (2017) Shifting Hegemony in "A Man's World": Incremental Change for Female Golf Professional Employment, *Sport in Society*, 1–18.

KPMG (2013) *Golf Participation in Europe 2013*, Budapest, Hungary: KPMG.

Ladies Golf Union (2005) *Research 2005*, St. Andrews, Fife: Comperio/Ladies Golf Union.

Lenkiewicz, T. (2011) Green Jackets in Men's Sizes Only: Gender Discrimination at Private Country Clubs, *Vanderbilt Journal of Transnational Law*, 44 (3), 777–818.

Maas, K. & Hasbrook, C. (2001) Media Promotion of the Paradigm Citizen/Golfer: An Analysis of Golf Magazines' Representations of Disability, Gender and Age, *Sociology of Sport Journal*, 18, 21–36.

Mackinnon, V. (2011) Techniques for Instructing Female Athletes in Traditionally Male Sports: A Case Study of LPGA Teaching Professionals, *International Journal of Sport & Society*, 2 (1), 75–87.

Mackinnon, V. (2013) Golf Industry Attrition: Challenges to Retaining Qualified Golf Professionals, Particularly Women, *Sport & EU Review*, 5 (2), 9–29.

McGinnis, L. & Gentry, J. (2002) The Masculine Hegemony in Sports: Is Golf for 'Ladies'? *Advances in Consumer Research*, 29, 19–24.

McGinnis, L. & Gentry, J. (2006) Getting Past the Red Tees: Constraints Women Face in Golf and Strategies to Help Them Stay, *Journal of Sport Management*, 20 (2), 218–247.

McGinnis, L.; Gentry, J. & McQuillan, J. (2009) Ritual-based Behavior that Reinforces Hegemonic Masculinity in Golf: Variations in Women Golfers' Responses, *Leisure Sciences*, 31 (1), 19–36.

McGinnis, L.; McQuillan, J. & Chapple, C. (2005) 'I Just Want to Play': Women, Sexism, and Persistence in Golf, *Journal of Sport & Social Issues*, 29 (3), 313–337.

Mitchell, S.; Allen-Collinson, J. & Evans, A. (2016) "Ladies Present!": An Auto/Ethnographic Study of Women Amateur Golfers at an English Provincial Golf Club, *Qualitative Research in Sport, Exercise & Health*, 8 (3), 273–286.

National Golf Foundation (2012) *Golf Participation in the U.S: 2012 Edition*, Jupiter, FL: National Golf Foundation.

New Zealand Golf (2015) *New Zealand Golf: Annual Report and Statement of Accounts*, Auckland, New Zealand: New Zealand Golf.

Reis, H. & Correia, A. (2013) Gender Inequalities in Golf: A Consented Exclusion? *International Journal of Culture, Tourism and Hospitality Research*, 7 (4), 324–339.

Saffer, M. (2016) *Dollars but No Sense: Golf's Long History of Shortchanging Women* [Online], Available at www.Espn.Com/Espnw/Sports/Article/15160220/Big-Gap-Earnings-Men-Women-Professional-Golfers (Accessed January 24, 2017).

Sheppard, M. (2008) *Women's Involvement in Golf: Understanding the Industry for the Next Generation of Golf*, Melbourne, Australia: Smart Connection Company.

Shin, E. & Nam, E. (2004) Culture, Gender Roles and Sport: The Case of Korean Players on the LPGA Tour, *Journal of Sport & Social Issues*, 28 (3), 223–244.

Shotton, P.; Armour, K. & Potrac, P. (1998) An Ethnographic Study of Gender Influences on Social Behaviour of Members at a Private Golf Club, *SOSOL: Sociology of Sport Online*, 1 (2).

Song, E. (2007) No Women (And Dogs) Allowed: A Comparative Analysis of Discriminating Private Golf Clubs in the United States, Ireland and England, *Washington University Global Studies Law Review*, 6 (1), 181–203.

Syngenta (2014) *The Opportunity to Grow Golf: Female Participation*, Cambridge, UK: Syngenta.

Vamplew, W. (2010) Sharing Space: Inclusion, Exclusion, and Accommodation at the British Golf Club Before 1914, *Journal of Sport & Social Issues*, 34 (3), 359–375.

Wolter, S. (2010) The LPGA's Five Points of Celebrity: 'Driving' the Organization 'Fore-Ward' or a Snap-Hook into the Next Fairway? *International Journal of Sport Communication*, 3 (1), 31–48.

Wright, J. (2008) *Coffee and Golf: A Monday Night Ritual*, Unpublished MRes Thesis, Birmingham, UK: University of Birmingham.

Yoo, S. (2012) The Impact of Global Sport on Local Media: A Case Study of Korean Newspaper Coverage of Women's Golf, *International Journal of Sport Communication*, 5 (3), 403–412.

Zevenbergen, R.; Edwards, A. & Skinner, J. (2002) Junior Golf Club Culture: A Bourdieuian Analysis, *SOSOL: Sociology of Sport Online*, 5 (1).

37

THE MOVE FROM COACH-CENTRED TO PARTICIPANT-CENTRED GOLF COACHING

Jonathan Wright and Martin Toms

Introduction

Historically within golf education programmes (as in many other sports coaching programmes), coaches have been trained and educated along bioscientific lines – a focus on the 'what' of coaching. Coaching has been represented as "an apolitical, unemotional and rationalistic activity underpinned by technical, tactical and bio-scientific knowledge and methods" (Toner et al., 2012, p. 67). This overfocus on technical issues has relegated other important areas of coach development and under-standing – the 'how' of coaching – to a much smaller, subsidiary role (Jones, 2011). It could be argued that this focus has led to a coaching culture that is predominantly technical and coach-centred, rather than one that is flexible, meeting the wants and needs of the individual golfer. However, while programmes are still inherently bioscientific in nature, there is an increasing realisa-tion of the need to focus upon the individual and the skills of social engagement. After all, coaching does not happen in a social vacuum; rather, it is a humanistic pursuit, one that is above all "an interactive, communal endeavour: a social practice" (Jones, 2011, p. 3). This chapter will explore the research evidence that suggests that golf coaching per se needs to move from a coach–centred model to a participant-centred approach, one that could be described as being 'socially constructed'.

Within golf coaching there are a plethora of technical models of instruction that treat the participant as almost incidental. Indeed, there has been an assumed belief that only science can hold the answer to improvement, as Bailey et al. (2010) critique, and that applying technical modification is the answer to all coaching challenges. However, it is this culture that often drives the self-directed learning of golf coaches – as well as the sales of particular technologies. In sharp contrast, there are few models for understanding the 'wants and needs' of participants within a coaching context. An understanding of the person being instructed, and his or her own personal goals and objectives, must be an essential element of the coach–athlete relationship (Bailey et al., 2010). As such, a holistic approach to participant learning and development must then be adopted (North, 2007). Participants' journeys in sport and golf are non-linear (Collins & MacNamara, 2012), and there is a growing awareness among coaches and coach educators that, in order to be successful, coaches need to understand why people take up a sport and what motivates them to stay – more than just having an understanding of the execution of the 'correct' technique to improve that person's performance.

This chapter explores these issues from a sociocultural perspective. Moreover, using the empirical evidence, it suggests that engagement with, understanding of and adaptation to the golfer should be the mainstay of any coaching relationship and, as such, must be central to the business of golf coaching at all levels. Good coaching requires that the coach must engage with the participant as an individual, such that they must be able to understand them in a holistic manner and deliver in a fashion to best aid learning and development *of that person*. In this way, the coach is in a position to meet the golfers' unique requirements, thereby securing their own future as well as that of the game. With limited published research within golf coaching, this chapter explores the wider coaching research and looks to apply this to a golf-specific context.

Review of current research

Coach education and development has often been theoretical in nature, not practical and as such has led to the production of two-dimensional coaches, who are concerned with technical matters and have had little opportunity to develop skills in the area of human interaction (Cushion et al., 2010). While technical understanding and excellence is undoubtedly of great importance to effective coaching, how this is delivered, allied to a deep understanding of the participants' 'wants and needs', is equally important if coaching is to be effective and sustained over a period of time.

Coaching theory has often relied on a prescriptive approach, in which direct instruction is used that has no benefit to cognitive athlete development (Potrac & Jones, 1999), where the 'coach is king', the sole source of knowledge. Investigation into the coaching process has failed to fully explore and understand the "essential humanistic, social nature of the process" (Jones, 2000, p. 34). In one of the few studies that focussed upon young golfers, Zevenbergen et al. (2002) describe how the coach undertook golf lessons in a technical, non-thinking way. Indeed, they noted that knowledge was handed down from the coach in such a way that the young (8–14 years old) "Cadets came to construct golf as a form of skilled knowledge that was transmitted from one who knew to those who didn't know" (Zevenbergen et al., 2002, p. 11). This approach may suggest that coaches may choose to simply take a 'mindless' approach to their practice (Cassidy et al., 2006), simply reeling off technical models/demonstrations again and again (i.e., reinforcing coach-centred practice). In sharp contrast, Dismore and Bailey (2011), in their longitudinal study of young peoples (aged 7–14 years) and their attitude to physical education, found that fun and enjoyment (not technical drills) were what participants valued. Fun was the single most important factor in retaining positive attitudes to physical activity although the constituents of 'fun' changed over time (the hedonistic enjoyment of play was replaced with the desire to engage with learning opportunities). In a doctoral study of a British college golf academy, Wright (2016) found that coaching was delivered in a bioscientific, coach-centred approach. The 24 golfers in this study were all taught one particular way to execute golf skills, giving no account of their technical needs, personal outlook or individual circumstance. The coach, who often acts as the facilitator of activity, should understand participant needs and shape their delivery around this rather than simply reeling off technical information. Understanding participants and delivering in an engaging way, while drawing out knowledge and understanding from them, is desirable and could legitimately be described as having a participant-centred approach (Wikeley & Bullock, 2006).

Academic research into the area of sports coaching has increased since 2000; however, an understanding and exploration of the complex, humanistic dimension of the endeavour remains relatively low. The social interaction of coach and players(s) within the coaching environment is acknowledged to be a complex pedagogical process (e.g., Armour & Griffiths, 2012). Learning takes place within situational constraints, and this suggests that the situated learning of each individual is set against the backdrop of their relationship with the coach (Jones, 2006a).

Coaching practice should include the coach reflecting on their own delivery so as to better understand him/herself as well as the participant. In their study of 31 expert golf instructors from the United States, Schempp et al. (2007) found that superior teaching and 'expert coaches' used reflection to improve their insight and awareness of the teaching and learning process. Expert coaches were found to set goals and take actions, both in areas of perceived strength and weakness, following their reflections. With this in mind, it has been recommended that the training and development of coaches needs to be upgraded and incorporated into a life-long continuous professional development culture that incudes areas such as reflection and reflective skill development (Davies & Grecic, 2012; Gilbourne et al., 2013). The deeper understanding that reflection allows could lead to more sophisticated insight into interpersonal relationships and coaching practice, thereby enhancing the personal development and expertise of coaches (Lyle, 2002).

The role of the coach in athlete performance is key. For example, in their Korean study of 12–18-year-old golfers ($n = 232$) taking part in a national schools championship, Bum and Shin (2015) found that training, instruction and social support from the coach decreased performance anxiety and increased confidence, whereas autocratic behaviour from the coach decreased golf performance. However, in this context, it is important to take account of the personal preferences of coach and player and the social interaction and relationship they have – direct autocratic coaching styles might not be universally successful, but there are occasions (and even cultures) when they might be. This research is symptomatic of a wider problem in the research of coaching and coaches – it is simply not appropriate to generalise regarding styles of delivery. Coaching is a social, humanistic pursuit undertaken with groups, teams or individuals, and this human dimension must be taken into account so as to make interactions as successful as they can be. Coaches should, therefore, explore and understand their delivery from the point of view of the athlete and ask questions, such as has the athlete understood their instruction, how does the athlete learn best, how can coaching be best delivered to ensure performance is optimised?

It would seem that the quality of the coach-participant relationship is critical to positive outcomes, and is mutually beneficial (Occhino et al., 2013), with the coach acting as a powerful socialising agent. This is especially pertinent regarding coaches' work with children and young people (Smith & Smoll, 2002). The coach finds himself or herself in a unique position regarding the development of the young person; areas such as co-operation, assertion, responsibility, empathy and self-control can be positively affected (Côté, 2002). The human interaction involved is the very essence of coaching, and athlete learning and development is dependent upon it. Effective coaching facilitated through successful interpersonal relationships is beneficial in two specific ways. Firstly, a significant influence on continued participation and development is associated with how comfortable the athlete feels in the environment created and managed by the coach (Woods, 2011). Indeed, the interaction of coach and athlete defines the quality of the relationship and is a major predictor of the quality of coaching and participation (Jowett & Poczwardowski, 2007). Secondly, successful interpersonal relationships would seem to make it more likely that athletes reach their potential. Toner et al. (2012) suggests that in the autoethnographic study of his own golf coaching engagement, his stubbornness to provide the coach with some critical pieces of information, ultimately led to frustration and poor performance resulting in a dysfunctional relationship with the coach and eventually a breakdown of the relationship entirely. Toner also points out that the lack of a quality relationship between athlete and coach was the critical factor in this poor performance (Toner et al., 2012) – clearly this is a single case example but is indicative of the crucial nature of relationship between coach and athlete.

The essence of coaching can said to be the interaction between coach and athlete. The interpersonal nature of coaching means that the process can have a myriad of effects on participants and hence participation. Holistic, 'good' coaching can lead to enjoyment, the maximisation of personal potential and life-long participation whereas 'poor' coaching can lead to dropout and damage participation and engagement in sport and physical activity, such as the example described by Toner et al. (2012). A positive personal relationship between athlete and coach does seem to be a reasonable standpoint and may be operationalised through different strategies, one of which could be the development of rapport between the two. In their study of 198 university and club-level athletes, Baker et al. (2003) found seven coaching behaviours that were significant in terms of coaching satisfaction, one of which was 'personal rapport'. More recent research has also indicated that relational factors between coach and athlete are critical; Boyce et al. (2010) in their study of 74 client-coach relationships found that rapport, trust and commitment were indicators of positive coaching outcomes – both of these projects were undertaken from a North American perspective so their generalisability to other cultures and contexts would need some further consideration.

The effective interrelationship between coach and player enables the coach to have a complete picture, and understanding of, the player and therefore allow a truly 'holistic' approach to be adopted; the coach attending to the athlete as a whole with all the complexity and sophistication this brings and needs. According to Douglas and Carless (2008) coaching holistically means that the coach adopts an approach where knowledge from numerous (and possibly innumerable) areas are integrated and not compartmentalised. The approach of 'coaching the whole', being cognizant of and playing a part in social construction, may therefore be at odds with historic coaching culture in golf where the technical side of the pursuit has been overemphasised. It may well therefore be challenging to shift this culture given that the coaching workforce are well educated in technical, technological and biomechanical matters but are likely to have received little formal education concerning athletes' broader developmental needs (Douglas & Carless, 2008).

One strategy for helping coaches to understand and better relate to participants is to ensure that during training and education they better understand their own socialisation into the game. A coaches' own journey can be explored and deconstructed and in so doing becoming a "base for which to critically evaluate social situations and the behaviour of others" (Jones, 2000, p. 40). It could be argued that coaches therefore need enlightenment and educating within the social milieu in which they operate; this would result in more socially informed decision-making and improved social relations and could lead to a better understanding of interpersonal relationships, development of reflexive practitioners, and enhanced personal development (Lyle, 2002). Indeed, Armour and Jones (2000, p. 76) suggest that "putting the person before the body" is essential to fully realising an athlete's potential and is therefore of paramount importance because only the coach can completely understand the social context in which they work. Grecic and Collins (Grecic & Collins, 2012, 2013; Collins et al., 2015) have explored 'Epistemological Chains' (EC) in order to investigate coach learning and behaviour. The EC of eight high level golf coaches (qualified in GB&I) were explored, and it was found that there were very strong linkages between coaches' own sources of knowledge and experience and the learning episodes they sought to facilitate. It was found that coaches' interpersonal, intrapersonal and contextual factors were high; they valued relationship management, fostered high levels of player autonomy and were person-centred. Furthermore, coaches recognised the initial benefit of their formal training (that was characterised by a technical focus) but then pro-actively sought to widen their knowledge base by means of more informal and non-formal learning. What remains unclear from this work is whether the EC is a causal or correlative factor in the development of coaches' expertise. That is, did the EC play a significant part in developing their expertise, or did their EC become significant as they were operating at a high level? Grecic and Collins (2012) suggest that coaches at elite levels could be compared in terms of the prevalence of EC and factors such as 'growth mindset' and experimentation/reflection (both of these elements were evident within the sample of golf coaches) so as to better understand elite coaching development.

Coaching is much more than an information transfer function. Indeed, the interpersonal nature of coaching is the critical feature of coaching practice that needs attending to if coaching is to be successful (Potrac & Purdy, 2004), however this is an area that has been under-researched (Jones et al., 2002). The continuing prevalence of bio-scientific subject matter and content in coach education and the self-directed education of golf coaches has perhaps something to do with the difficulty of selling the benefits of social and interpersonal education (Matthews et al., 2013), and hence the case needs to be made for this area of work.

A person-centred approach to coaching should, according to Douglas and Carless (2008), consider an individual's social, psychological, spiritual, emotional, and cultural development. It should also be non-prescriptive in nature even when dealing with technical issues and areas (Kidman, 2005). Indeed, the coach's approach must surely be directed by the wants and needs of the participant. Allender et al. (2006) undertook a meta-analysis of reasons for participation and non-participation in sport and physical activity of children and adults in the UK. The review covered the period 1990–2004 and twenty-four papers met all search criteria. The majority of these papers related to young people in community settings where weight management, social interaction and enjoyment were, in the main, reasons for participation. Adults cited participation motivations based on staving off the effects of aging as well as providing social support, where factors creating barriers to participation included having to show an unfit body to others, lacking confidence and competence. A person-centred approach to coaching should focus on motivations for participation while trying to mitigate these types of barrier.

An advantage of positive engagement in the coaching context is that personal issues and concerns that may hinder progression can be addressed (Joseph, 2010). These non-technical factors and roles, the interpersonal element of coaching, make it a complex pursuit undertaken with, and between, athlete and coach together. To date, however, there is little informing research that presents the humanistic approach to coaching with the associated implications for coaching and coach education (Nelson et al., 2012). That said, in a UK based study, Vinson et al. (2016) examined non-linear approaches to youth sports (including golf) in three detailed case studies and found that coaches had an advanced understanding of pedagogical principles and had spent a significant time developing and constructing their own individual approach. In their practice, there was a reduced emphasis on technical instruction and centrality of the coach in participant learning. Three key core themes emerged from this work that enabled this approach: (1) creating an environment of participant centredness, (2) holistic development and (3) authentically situated learning. Within this research, coaches used strategies such as additional questioning and use of silence while reducing direct instruction. The case study of the golf coach did reveal a non-traditional approach, based on 'mindset', movement skills and life skills where a child-centred approach was the stated goal. There was however, no evidence reported that this approach was received positively by the young people or that it led to greater engagement, retention or learning.

To help depict the role and function of a coach, the metaphor of 'orchestration' could be useful; decisions are constantly being made within the realms of the personal interaction of coach and athlete and this could result in a lack of clarity and therefore makes the pursuit less than straightforward (Wallace, 2003). There is a delicate balance to be sought where over-control may lead to 'squashing of talent', whereas a more laissez-faire approach may risk talent being dissipated unproductively (Jones & Wallace, 2005). Rather than ignore such problems, Jones and Wallace (2005) believe that they should be acknowledged, reflected upon and dealt with, although they recognise that the culture of coaching is not changing to take account of these factors and the coach is still considered to have control over everything. To deal with this, coaches should perhaps seek out solutions and approaches that can mitigate the 'social vagaries' that coaching presents. These solutions should be actively managed by the coach, taking account of their personality and approach. The approach adopted may be explained by the coaches' own experiences as a player and may affect their outlook and this will impact on the relationship with the athlete and how the coaching process proceeds. The operationalised actions of the coach can be linked to the coaches personal beliefs and their knowledge and learning and these become apparent through the planning, learning environments, operational actions and reviews of performance that coaches undertake (Grecic & Collins, 2012).

The nature of coaching as a social venture does inevitably mean that the coaching process will be unpredictable. Coaching cannot be a wholly managed concern – the inherent dilemmas that exist are endemic to the nature of coaching, but coaches could use encouragement, incentives, open-handedness, sincerity, understanding and sensitivity to draw the best from their athletes (Jones & Wallace, 2005). In addition, coaches should perhaps also seek to understand themselves on a deeper level and continue to develop their expertise throughout their careers, although that comes with both practice and experience.

Implications for the game

Although the current model of largely technical coaching could be said to be meeting the wants and needs of those who are taking part, there is the danger that prescriptive methods of coaching may result in attrition rather than sustained participation (Foster et al., 2005). This situation could perhaps explain why there is not a 'culture' of coaching within the sport. Excellent coaching practice does exist but often this is in isolated instances and may not be the result of the system of coach education and instead having been developed by individuals in a rather ad hoc fashion (Taylor & Garratt, 2010). Jones (2011) suggests that coaching has becoming increasingly acknowledged as a social activity but that the application of social theory to sports coaching has not been forthcoming and this leads him to suggest that coach educators and scholars may not value its relevance. However, there is a significant opportunity for coach educators, coaches and the business of golf coaching to positively impact the sport. This requires a workforce that understands, and can interact with, people more effectively and thoughtfully by being truly participant-centred.

Coaches need to be better educated and supported to be able to develop and refine their philosophy. Vinson et al. (2016) found that, by and large, coaches are unaware of coaching theory and that pedagogies are ill-defined and under developed – as such coaches do not have anything other to 'go on' apart from the technical models that they experienced in initial training. Perhaps the implication here is for coach education where a better-informed educational pathway is needed for golf (Davies & Grecic, 2012). However, even where coaches have been educated in this area there may be problems with application. In their study of top-level youth soccer coaches, Partington and Cushion (2011) found that there was an epistemological gap between understanding and practice, with statements of intent not being matched by practice. There may also be the 'theory to practice' lag (Jones, 2011) that may be due, in part, to a disconnect between academia and coaches on the ground – academics being more concerned with theory development, coaches more concerned with practice and coach educators being slow to respond. Coach educators resistance to change may be possible because it challenges known practice and prompts something that is messy and is full of "problems, tensions and dilemmas" (Jones, 2011, p. 8). To remedy this situation coach education should be more agile and be able to feed up-to-date material into education programmes in a more timely fashion.

Certainly, the 'social skills' of coaches need to be developed. Social bonds between players and coaches can lead to increased levels of satisfaction and therefore increased participation. However, coach educators and coaches do not always recognise the role of social skills as a coaching tool or participation tool (North, 2007). The use of humour in golf coaching (for example) is evaluated and discussed by Fitzsimmons (Chapter 38 in this book) as an important aspect of social skills that are important in any coach-athlete relationship.

The overall quality and impact of coaching are certainly aided by practitioners who are open-minded and have the capability to develop themselves over time, a process that is greatly aided and enabled by self-reflection (Potrac & Cassidy, 2006). As such coaches can be more aware of and sensitive to the wants and needs of the participant that should in turn "result in better and more inclusive coaching, leading to enhanced athlete learning and therefore performance" (Cassidy et al., 2006, p. 18). Gilbourne et al. (2013) suggest that within modern coaching environments where coaches and sport are increasingly being used as agents of positive societal change, the reflective practices of the coach become even more powerful and important. However, there is no evidence that this has been embraced in golf coach education to any great degree.

Coaching has a direct impact on the sporting experiences of participants to a great extent (Bailey et al., 2010) and therefore coaches need to attend to the needs of the individual in a holistic way. This should lead to greater player satisfaction as well as improved performance and enjoyment; securing participation and benefits for all. The coaching process should be both conceptualised and recognised as being multi-faceted, non-linear and in reality 'messy' in nature. A paradigm shift is therefore needed away from technical, coach-centred models towards a more interactive and engaging player-centred model. If this holistic coaching is going to happen, coach educators and coaches alike need to develop their own awareness and understanding. If coaching can help secure future participation (North, 2007), then a coaching culture is desirable, not only for the individual golfers benefit but for the health of the game in addition but this culture must be based on the wants and needs of the individual golfer.

Summary and future directions

Historically, knowledge and the timely delivery of this knowledge in a formulaic sequence, has been thought of as all-important for effective coaching (Jones, 2006b). This of course suggests that the knowledge is more important than interpretation and indeed than understanding the participant. In golf coaching, there is plenty of available evidence reviewing technical content: the 'what' of coaching. However, there is much less that addresses the 'how' of coaching. It is these 'hows' of coaching that relate much more to participants; how you communicate with participants, how you understand them as an individual, how you assess their wants and needs, how you deliver a coaching offer that is enjoyable and effective.

Technical expertise and knowledge have certainly been regarded as the most important factor for coaches for many years and have formed the mainstay of coach education. This has led to a culture in golf where many practitioners remain committed to technically led pedagogies – there are pockets of good practice but that these have been developed by individuals and not as the result of a robust coach education system (Vinson et al., 2016). The constituent elements of 'coaching' are challenging to classify given its humanistic dimension. Good golf coaching is vital to the sport as it can provide participants with quality experiences, meeting their wants and needs and enabling them to play and enjoy the game more. It is therefore imperative that coaches are able to offer more than 'standard' technical coaching.

Coaching experiences that are characterised by participants' active involvement, where learning is facilitated with the aid of self-development and problem solving are beneficial. This process is aided by creating authentic practice environments within which effective social relationship between player and coach can take place.

It is clear that investigation of new approaches that embrace a more participant-centred, holistic approach are inadequate. If this area of work is to be taken forward, challenged, developed and refined, then this research is vital. The endless possibilities that revolve around a humanistic pursuit make it a never-ending journey of learning and development for coaches and this needs to be supported by effective coach education. The difficulties of researching, writing and assessing these humanistic dimensions are a possible contributing factor in the slow progress of development. However, there are a few examples from golf of where this approach has been researched and positive results have been achieved. The benefits need to be documented; information and learning should be fed into coach education as the case is strengthened and this process should continue and evolving on an ongoing basis.

References

Allender, S.; Cowburn, G. & Foster, C. (2006) Understanding Participation in Sport and Physical Activity among Children and Adults: A Review of Qualitative Studies, *Health Education Research*, 21 (6), 826–835.

Armour, K. & Griffiths, M. (2012) Case Study Research, In: Armour, K. & McDonald, D. (Eds.) *Research Methods in Physical Education*, London: Routledge, pp. 204–216.

Armour, K. & Jones, R. (2000) The Practical Heart Within: The Value of a Sociology of Sport, In: R. Jones & K. Armour (Eds.) *Sociology of Sport, Theory and Practice*, London: Pearson, pp. 1–12.

Bailey, R.; Collins, D.; Ford, P.; MacNamara, A.; Toms, M. & Pearce, G. (2010) *Participant Development in Sport: An Academic Review*, Leeds, UK: Sports Coach UK.

Baker, J.; Yardley, J. & Côté, J. (2003) Coach Behaviours and Athlete Satisfaction in Team and Individual Sports, *International Journal of Sports Psychology*, 34 (3), 226–239.

Boyce, L.; Jeffrey Jackson, R. & Neal, L. (2010) Building Successful Leadership Coaching Relationships: Examining Impact of Matching Criteria in a Leadership Coaching Program, *Journal of Management Development*, 29 (10), 914–931.

Bum, C. & Shin, S. (2015) The Relationships Between Coaches' Leadership Styles, Competitive State Anxiety, and Golf Performance in Korean Junior Golfers, *Sport Science Review*, 24 (5–6), 371–386.

Cassidy, T.; Jones, R. & Potrac, P. (2006) *Understanding Sports Coaching*, London: Routledge.

Collins, D. & MacNamara, Á. (2012) The Rocky Road to the Top, *Sports Medicine*, 42 (11), 907–914.

Collins, L.; Collins, D. & Grecic, D. (2015) The Epistemological Chain in High-Level Adventure Sports Coaches, *Journal of Adventure Education and Outdoor Learning*, 15 (3), 224–238.

Côté, J. (2002) Coach and Peer Influence on Children's Development Through Sport, In: J. Silva & D. Stevens (Eds.) *Psychological Foundations of Sport*, Boston, MA: Allyn & Bacon, pp. 520–540.

Cushion, C.; Nelson, L.; Armour, K.; Lyle, J.; Jones, R.; Sandford, R. & O'Callaghan, C. (2010) *Coach Learning and Development: A Review of Literature*, Leeds, UK: Sports Coach UK.

Davies, T. & Grecic, D. (2012) An Investigation into Golf Coach Education and Its Ability to Meet the Needs of Student Coaches, *Journal of Qualitative Research in Sports Studies*, 6 (1), 13–34.

Dismore, H. & Bailey, R. (2011) Fun and Enjoyment in Physical Education: Young People's Attitudes, *Research Papers in Education*, 26 (4), 499–516.

Douglas, K. & Carless, D. (2008) Using Stories in Coach Education, *International Journal of Sports Science and Coaching*, 3 (1), 33–49.

Foster, C.; Hillsdon, M.; Cavill, N.; Allender, S. & Cowburn, G. (2005) *Understanding Participation in Sport*, London: Sport England.

Gilbourne, D.; Marshall, P. & Knowles, Z. (2013) Reflective Practice in Sports Coaching: Thoughts on Process, Pedagogy and Research, In: R. Jones & K. Kingston (Eds.) *An Introduction to Sports Coaching Connecting Theory to Practice*, Oxford, UK: Routledge, pp. 3–14.

Grecic, D. & Collins, D. (2012) A Qualitative Investigation of Elite Golf Coaches' Knowledge and the Epistemological Chain, *Journal of Qualitative Research in Sports Studies*, 6 (1), 49–70.

Grecic, D. & Collins, D. (2013) The Epistemological Chain: Practical Applications in Sports, *Quest*, 65 (2), 151–168.

Jones, R. (2000) Towards a Sociology of Coaching, In: R. Jones & K. Armour (Eds.) *Sociology of Sport: Theory and Practice*, London: Routledge, pp. 33–43.

Jones, R. (2006a) How Can Educational Concepts Inform Sports Coaching, In: R. L Jones (Ed.) *The Sports Coach as Educator: Reconceptualising Sports Coaching*, London: Routledge, pp. 3–13.

Jones, R. (2006b) Dilemmas, Maintaining "Face", and Paranoia, *Qualitative Inquiry*, 12 (5), 1012–1021.

Jones, R. (2011) Introduction, In: R. Jones; P. Potrac; C. Cushion, & L. Ronglan (Eds.) *The Sociology of Sports Coaching*, London: Routledge, pp. 3–11.

Jones, R.; Armour, K. & Potrac, P. (2002) Understanding the Coaching Process: A Framework for Social Analysis, *Quest*, 54 (1): 34–48.

Jones, R. & Wallace, M. (2005) Another Bad Day at the Training Ground: Coping with Ambiguity in the Coaching Context, *Sport, Education and Society*, 10 (1), 119–134.

Joseph, S. (2010) The Person-Centred Approach to Coaching, In: E. Cox, T. Bachkirova, & D. Clutterbuck (Eds.) *The Complete Handbook of Coaching*, London: Sage, pp. 68–79.

Jowett, S. & Poczwardowski, A. (2007) Understanding the Coach-Athlete Relationship, In: S. Jowett & D. Lavallee (Eds.) *Social Psychology in Sport*, Champaign, IL: Human Kinetics, pp. 153–170.

Kidman, L. (2005) *Athlete Centred Coaching: Delivering Inspired and Inspiring People*, Christchurch, New Zealand: IPA Print Resources.

Lyle, J. (2002) *Sports Coaching Concepts – A Framework for Coaches Behaviour*, London: Routledge.

Matthews, N.; Fleming, S. & Jones, R. L. (2013) Sociology for Coaches, In: R. Jones & K. Kingston (Eds.) *An Introduction to Sports Coaching Connecting Theory to Practice*, Oxford, UK: Routledge, pp. 69–82.

Nelson, L.; Cushion, C.; Potrac, P. & Groom, R. (2012) Carl Rodgers, Learning and Educational Practice: Critical Considerations and Applications in Sports Coaching, *Sport, Education and Society*, 19 (5), 513–531.

North, J. (2007) *Increasing Participation in Sport: The Role of the Coach*, Leeds, UK: Sports Coach UK.

Occhino, J.; Mallet, C. & Rynne, S. (2013) Dynamic Social Networks in High Performance Football Coaching, *Physical Education and Sport Pedagogy*, 18 (1), 90–102.

Partington, M. & Cushion, C. (2013) An Investigation of the Practice Activities and Coaching Behaviors of Professional Top-Level Youth Soccer Coaches, *Scandinavian Journal of Medicine & Science in Sports*, 23 (3), 374–382.

Potrac, P. & Cassidy, T. (2006) The Coach as More Capable Other, In: R. L. Jones (Ed.) *The Sports Coach as Educator*, London: Routledge, pp. 39–50.

Potrac, P. & Jones, R. (1999) The Invisible Ingredient in Coaching Knowledge; A Case for Recognising and Researching the Social Component, *Sociology of Sport Online* [online], 2 (1), Available at www.brunel.ac.uk/depts/sps/sosol/sosol.htm (Accessed June, 2007).

Potrac, P. & Purdy, L. (2004) Graham Taylor, In: R. Jones; K. Armour & P. Potrac (Eds.) *Sports Coaching Cultures: From Practice to Theory*, London: Routledge, pp. 21–31.

Schempp, P.; Mccullick, B.; St Pierre, P.; Woorons, S.; You, J. & Clark, B. (2007) How the Best Get Better: An Analysis of the Self-Monitoring Strategies Used by Expert Golf Instructors, *Sport Education and Society*, 12 (2), 175–192.

Smith, R. & Smoll, F. (2002) Coaching Behaviour Research and Intervention in Youth Sports, In: F. Smoll & R. Smith (Eds.) *Children and Youth in Sport: A Bio-Psychosocial Perspective*, Dubuque, IA: Kendall Hunt Publishing, pp. 211–234.

Taylor, B. & Garratt, D. (2010) The Professionalisation of Sports Coaching: Relations of Power, Resistance and Compliance, *Sport, Education and Society*, 15 (1), 121–139.

Toner, J.; Nelson, L.; Potrac, P.; Gilbourne, D. & Marshall, P. (2012) From "Blame" to "Shame" in a Coach-Athlete Relationship in Golf: A Tale of Shared Critical Reflection and the Re-Storying of a Narrative Experience, *Sports Coaching Review*, 1 (1), 67–78.

Vinson, D.; Brady, A.; Moreland, B. & Judge, N. (2016) Exploring Coach Behaviours, Session Contexts and Key Stakeholder Perceptions of Non-Linear Coaching Approaches in Youth Sport, *Sports Science and Coaching*, 11 (1), 54–68.

Wallace, M. (2003) Managing the Unmanageable? Coping with Complex Educational Change, *Educational Management Administration and Leadership*, 31 (1), 9–29.

Wikeley, F. & Bullock, K. (2006) Coaching as an Educational Relationship, In: R. L. Jones (Ed.) *The Sports Coach as Educator*, London: Routledge, pp. 14–24.

Woods, R. (2011) *Social Issues in Sport*, Champaign, IL: Human Kinetics.

Wright, J. (2016) *Dazzling Dreams, Dawning Reality: The Unholy Alliance of Sports Performance and Education for Apprentice Golfers in an Academy Structure*, Unpublished PhD Thesis, Birmingham, UK: University of Birmingham.

Zevenbergen, R.; Edwards, A. & Skinner, J. (2002) Junior Golf Club Culture: A Bourdieuian Analysis, *SOSOL: Sociology of Sport Online*, 5 (1).

38

SOCIAL INTERACTIONS BETWEEN COACHES AND PLAYERS

It really is a laughing matter

Charles Fitzsimmons

Introduction

Of all the potential social interactions in golf, those that occur between a player and a coach (i.e., anyone who formally instructs golfers) may be particularly critical. These interactions can bring new people to the game, positively influence the lives of young people and help to crown major champions. One area that perhaps deserved more attention is the use of humour and how it may be used in coaching to strengthen relationships, improve instruction and enhance coping strategies.

The context of humour

In his book on the psychology of humour, Martin (2007) asserts that it is a ubiquitous part of the human experience. Specifically, he suggests that there are cognitive, emotional and social components to the use of humour, which often work in concert and are related to a number of important outcomes (e.g., relationships, instruction and coping). The cognitive processes involve the interpretation of a stimulus, usually something incongruous, in a playful or non-serious way. An important part of this process is that humorous events can often have multiple interpretations, and it is the playful manipulation of these, often in comparison to one and other, that may cause something to be interpreted as funny (Martin, 2007). The emotional component of humour is what Martin identifies as the positive emotion of mirth which can be considered a result of cognitive processes discussed above – just as other emotions, such as pleasure or anger, are evoked from certain stimuli. The social component of humour is simply that people use it much more often when around others as compared to being alone (Provine & Fischer, 1989; Martin & Kuiper, 1999).

To distinguish between humour that may have beneficial and detrimental outcomes, Martin et al. (2003) created a classification of four distinct styles of humour based on whether the content was positive or negative and whether it was used to enhance the self or interpersonal relations (see Table 38.1).

As expected, Martin et al. (2003) found that these styles were related to different mental health outcomes. For example, self-defeating humour was negatively related to measures of psychological well-being, self-esteem, intimacy and social support satisfaction, and positively

Table 38.1 Styles of humour (definitions are taken from Martin et al., 2003, pp. 70–71)

	Positive	*Negative*
Self	Self-enhancing	Aggressive
	"tendency to maintain a humourous outlook on life … [and is used] in emotion regulation and coping"	"sarcasm, teasing … [and is used] to criticize or manipulate others … [or is the] compulsive expression of humour without regard for the effects on others"
Interpersonal	Affiliative	Self-defeating
	"tendency to joke around with others, say witty things, tell amusing stores, [and is used to] laugh with others and amuse others"	"excessively self-disparaging and ingratiating way, to allow oneself to be the butt of others' jokes and to use humour as a form of defensive denial to hide underlying negative feelings"

related to measures of depression, state/trait anxiety, hostility, aggression and psychiatric symptoms. Conversely, the adaptive styles of humour (i.e., self-enhancing and affiliative) were found to be positively related to measures of psychological well-being, optimism, intimacy and self-esteem, and negatively related to measures of depression and state/trait anxiety. It should be noted that aggressive humour was only positively related to aggression and hostility, and thus may only be tangentially connected to mental health outcomes. It should also be noted that, in the Martin et al. study, aggressive humour was positively correlated with all other styles of humour, suggesting it may have positive and negative components.

Despite there being a plethora of studies on a range of topics (e.g., relationships, instruction, education, coping) and an entire textbook on humour in traditional psychology (i.e., Martin, 2007), at the time of writing, only a small number of published studies (e.g., Burke et al., 1995; Gaudreau et al., 2002; Grisaffe et al., 2003; Giacobbi et al., 2004; Niefer et al., 2010; Ronglan & Aggerholm, 2014) and one doctoral dissertation (i.e., Hester, 2010) have discussed the use of humour in sport. Therefore, the aim of this chapter will be to review these studies as well as those from traditional psychology to illustrate how the use of humour in coaching may be able to strengthen relationships, improve instruction and enhance coping strategies for athletes and coaches alike. Perhaps the best way to frame this discussion is to think of humour use as a social skill, as Martin (2007) suggests. If a person uses certain styles of humour at the right times with specific people, it can have benefits for that individual, the people around them and the relationships between them. If not, there can be negative consequences of equal magnitude and breadth (Martin, 2007).

Strengthening relationships

Increasing initial attraction

There are two ways that humour could enhance initial attraction to a coach. The first is that humour is a valued social quality and thus someone who uses it will be more attractive to others (Martin, 2007). For example, Kuiper and Leite (2010) asked undergraduate students (*n* = 166, 61% female) to rate several personality attributes (e.g., pleasant, mean) for a hypothetical person described in a booklet who displayed one of the four styles of humour (e.g., affiliative, self-enhancing, aggressive and self-defeating). The results showed that in these hypothetical initial interactions between strangers, the use of adaptive styles, especially affiliative humour, had beneficial effects on personality impressions of others, whereas the maladaptive styles, especially aggressive humour, had detrimental effects (Kuiper & Leite, 2010). In a similar study of undergraduate students ($n = 176$, 72% female), Kuiper et al. (2014) found that the use of adaptive styles of humour by a casual acquaintance was related to more positive evaluations of that person, whereas the use of self-defeating humour, particularly by people who were considered socially anxious, was related to significantly less positive evaluations. Going even further, Cann and Matson (2014) studied three different samples – i.e., heterosexual romantic couples ($n = 164$), general undergraduate students ($n = 190$, females = 65%) and gender-balanced undergraduate students ($n = 100$) – in two different assessments and found that the adaptive styles, particularly affiliative humour, were related to judgements of a good sense of humour and increased social desirability, whereas the maladaptive styles were related to judgements of a bad sense of humour and decreased social desirability. Corroborating this idea is a study by Sprecher and Regan (2002) which found that humour was a preferred characteristic by university students ($n = 700$, 59% women) in a range of relationships (i.e., casual sex partner, dating partner, marriage partner, same-sex friend and opposite-sex friend). This may be especially true of female friends, as Hay (2000) in a study of conversations ($n = 18$) found that female friends appear to use more funny story-telling (i.e., affiliative humour) to cement relationships than do male friends. Taken together, these studies suggest that in an interaction with another person the use of adaptive styles of humour, particularly affiliative, will lead to more positive evaluations, impressions and social desirability.

The second way that humour could enhance initial interactions is by acting as a signal of interest. For example, Treger et al. (2013) conducted two experiments to explore how humour use by unacquainted participants would affect liking in a platonic and a romantic context. Experiment 1 ($n = 118$ undergraduate students, 81% female) was a self-disclosure social interaction task to test platonic liking. Experiment 2 ($n = 58$ undergraduate students) was a series of social interaction tasks, including one similar to experiment 1, that were manipulated to be either humorous or not to test for romantic liking. The results from both experiments supported the conclusion that in initial interactions the relationship between humour and liking, regardless of whether it was platonic or romantic, was found to be mediated by perceived reciprocal liking as well as enjoyment of the interaction (Treger et al., 2013). The authors concluded that in these types of social interactions humour is taken as a signal to show that the other person involved is enjoying themselves and likes the other person, which enhances liking for both.

All of this taken together suggests that a coach's use of humour in initial interactions with golfers can either be taken as a socially desirable trait or as a signal of mutual interest but either way, it should create a greater attraction which helps to form the basis of a strong and lasting relationship.

Maintaining liking

One way to measure the strength of a relationship is the extent to which a player likes a coach and one factor that may be particularly important is humour. For example, female high school volleyball athletes' ($n = 51$) perceptions of their coach's sense of humour were positively related to them liking the head coach (Burke et al., 1995). A similar relationship was found by Grisaffe et al. (2003) for head and assistant coaches in a study of university soccer players ($n = 33$, 60% male). It should be noted that the Grisaffe et al. (2003) study found that although the relationship was significant for both genders, female athletes had a significantly stronger relationship between perceived sense of humour and liking of head coaches than males. Although these studies were somewhat small and correlational in nature, they do demonstrate an underlying relationship between humour and liking of coaches.

An analogous scenario to golf coaching is education (i.e., there is a teacher trying to communicate knowledge to a student) where the equivalent of liking a coach is a high level of students' attendance to a teacher's class. One factor that is related to increased attendance is a teacher's ability to generate a sense of immediacy (i.e., an increased personal connection between student and teacher) through specific behaviours (Rocca, 2004). One such behaviour is the use of humour (Gorham & Christophel, 1990). In fact, Gorham and Christophel (1990) found that when university teachers ($n = 254$) used more positive (i.e., humorous anecdotes or verbal comedy, which could be akin to the affiliative style) than negative humour (i.e., tendentious or self-deprecating, which could be akin to the aggressive or self-defeating styles) it was positively related to their undergraduate students' ($n = 204$, 74 % males) feelings of immediacy. Corroborating this notion is a study by Rocca (2004) with university students ($n = 189$, 52% male) which found that teachers' use of verbal aggressive behaviours was negatively related to students' attendance whereas immediacy behaviours, which positive humour would be considered, was positively related. Indeed, a qualitative study of primary school teachers' (i.e., Kindergarten to Grade 12) ($n = 31$) perceptions of humour in the classroom revealed that it helped them to better connect with students (Lovorn & Holaway, 2015). Similarly, a doctoral dissertation involving a qualitative study of university professors ($n = 10$) who had a reputation for using humour found that teachers intentionally use it to forge closer bonds with students, understanding that it can have beneficial or detrimental outcomes (Buckman, 2010).

Ending conflicts

When determining how effective the use of humour will be in ending a conflict, Norrick and Spitz (2008) suggest that there are six factors that must be considered: 1) the seriousness, 2) the social power relationship between those involved, 3) the kind of humour, 4) the reactions of participants, and 5) who initiates the humour. Interestingly, managing a conflict may be one of the few times when a negative style of humour could be beneficial as self-deprecating humour (i.e., similar to self-defeating humour) may be more effective than humour aimed at the other person or some third party (Norrick & Spitz, 2008).

To understand possible gender differences in the use of humour to resolve conflicts between teenagers Connolly et al. (2015) examined female best friends ($n = 37$), male best friends ($n = 22$), and romantic couples ($n = 37$). The results showed that adolescent female best friends tend to use more affiliative behaviours (e.g., verbal humour) whereas adolescent male friends appear to use more aggressive behaviours, including aggressive humour such as teasing, to resolve conflicts (Connolly et al., 2015). This suggests that in addition to the six factors identified by Norrick and Spitz (2008), it may be important to consider the gender of those involved in the conflict so that the appropriate style of humour may be used to efficaciously resolve it.

Team cohesion

Although golf is usually played individually, there are times when it is a team game (e.g., The Ryder Cup, The Walker Cup). Given the important role of humour in forming and maintaining relationships its use should be associated with team cohesion. In sport, team cohesion is defined as "a dynamic process which is reflected in the tendency for a group to stick together and remain united in the pursuit of its instrumental objectives and/or for the satisfaction of member affective needs" (Carron et al., 1998, p. 213). It is an important variable to consider because it has a consistent and strong relationship with performance in sport (Carron et al., 2002). Unfortunately, the relationship between humour use and cohesion has never been tested in golf teams so we must look to research from other sports and areas. For example, a meta-analysis by Mesmer-Magnus et al. (2012) found that the use of positive humour by supervisors and subordinates in the workplace was related to increased workgroup cohesion. Similarly, the doctoral dissertation by Hester (2010) found a positive relationship between the use of adaptive styles of humour (e.g., affiliative and self-enhancing) and certain components of team cohesion in male collegiate basketball teams. As mentioned above, the use of self-defeating humour may help to resolve task conflicts (Norrick & Spitz, 2008), and so a coach's use of it may also increase cohesion.

Applied recommendations for golf coaches

It should be clear from the research discussed above that humour can play an important role in forming and maintaining successful relationships. As such, coaches should use affiliative humour to forge and strengthen bonds with golfers. This may be especially true of female golfers, whereas a very small amount of aggressive humour, in addition to affiliative humour, may be ok with males. A recommendation for an initial interaction between a coach and golfer would be to tell a humorous story, ideally related to golf, that the majority of people would enjoy. For those who feel they are not humorous or do not feel comfortable telling such a story, a funny video (e.g., a clip from a golf movie such as Happy Gilmore (Simonds & Dugan, 1996)) used at the right moment may still enhance golfers' perception of the meeting.

In the event of a conflict with a golfer, or between golfers on a team, as long as it is not an incredibly serious one, coaches should use adaptive styles of humour (i.e., self-enhancing and affiliative) as well as self-defeating humour to help resolve it, as per the framework by Norrick and Spitz (2008). A recommendation would be for the coach to tell a mildly embarrassing but humorous story from an analogous situation he or she was in previously.

Coaches of golf teams should use and encourage their golfers to use adaptive styles of humour whenever appropriate (i.e., as long as it does not distract from the task at hand) as it may enhance team cohesion. A hypothetical recommendation would be to take the golfers to a team building activity that they would not normally think of and will not only be humorous at the time but will also likely lead to humorous stories to be recounted in the future (e.g., taking a Ryder Cup team to an improvisation comedy class). Another recommendation would be to make a funny video involving the players from the team and possibly even the coaches. Real world examples include the 2012 US Olympic swimming team's parody video of the song "Call Me Maybe", the video of the Kansas University Men's basketball team doing the "Harlem shake", and the now infamous videos by the Golf Boys "team" of Bubba Watson, Ben Crane, Rickie Fowler, and Hunter Mahan in 2011 and 2013 (Dimengo, 2013).

Improving instruction

To be successful in their jobs expert golf teachers identified clear communication and instruction with students as critical skills (Schempp et al., 2006). Similarly, a golfers' recall of a lesson is related to the forms of communication used by the instructor (Webster, 2010). In a qualitative study of Scandinavian coaches ($n = 6$, 66% male) Ronglan and Aggerholm (2014) found that humour was used to help revitalise athletes during monotonous training sessions and as a tool to control athletes attention. There is also evidence from traditional educational settings that teachers use humour to communicate with and to instruct students (Banas et al., 2011).

Research into the use of humour in education has shown it to be beneficial in a range of settings including sex education (Buston & Wight, 2004), statistics (Zeedyk, 2006), nursing (Chauvet & Hofmeyer, 2007), accounting (Romal, 2008), and math (Matarazzo et al., 2010).

Indeed, students suggested that college teachers' use of humour as a form of instructional communication increased and maintained their attention as well as enhanced learning and understanding (Torok et al., 2004). Interestingly, college professors stated that humour was an important part of their teaching methods that helped to capture the attention of students (Buckman, 2010). The use of humour was also one of ten suggestions for enhancing teachers' lectures (Heitzmann, 2010).

To differentiate between forms of humour that increased student learning and those that did not, Wanzer et al. (2010) proposed the Instructional Humour Processing Theory (IHPT). In a preliminary test of IHPT with undergraduate students ($n = 378$, 64% female), the authors showed that appropriate forms of instructional humour, specifically what they titled related humour, was positively related with student learning. Conversely, they showed there was no correlation between student learning and offensive or disparaging and generally inappropriate forms of humour. One reason for this latter finding may be that observing another student being ridiculed with excessively aggressive humour caused students to be more conforming, have a greater fear of failure, and lower levels of creativity (Janes & Olsen, 2015). Although most teachers would not mind students being more conforming, it is the fear of failure and reduced creativity that may keep aggressive humour from being beneficial to student learning. It is interesting to note that that instructors' use of self-deprecating humour (i.e., akin to self-defeating humour) may actually increase creativity (Janes & Olsen, 2015). Although the use of aggressive humour appears not to have a positive relationship with learning, it should not be ruled out completely as 20% of students actually listed sarcasm (i.e., the prototypical type of aggressive humour) as appropriate in instruction (Torok et al., 2004).

Applied recommendations for golf coaches

Given the benefits of humour in the classroom noted above, coaches should use humorous stories (i.e., affiliative humour) to explain why certain lessons are important or to make drills novel and enjoyable. A recommendation would be to do an odd drill that still teaches an important lesson (e.g., practicing bunker shots with a long iron to learn proper hand position, or using a putter like a pool cue to see how a ball breaks on the green).

If an individual or team of golfers is not meeting a coach's expectations, especially if they are male, the infrequent use of mildly aggressive teasing (i.e., aggressive humour), may help them to conform. It is important to note that females may not respond as well to this type of humour and in general, it should be used very selectively as its overuse can quickly have detrimental consequences (e.g., damaged relationships).

Enhancing coping strategies

Coaches can directly and indirectly help athletes use humour to cope with challenges they face in four main areas, and coaches themselves may even benefit in one such area. The first area to consider is how athletes cope with poor performances. For example, Gaudreau et al. (2002) found that the continued use of humour throughout a tournament by male youth golfers ($n = 62$) who performed worse than expected helped to buffer them from the negative affect that would typically be expected after a poor performance. Coaches may be able to play an important role in helping golfers to cope with poor performances by encouraging them to be more optimistic (Wilson et al., 2015). Given the positive relationship between self-enhancing humour and optimism (Martin et al., 2003), coaches should not only use humour to improve golfers' mood but could also educate them about the positive effects it has and encourage them to use it when performing poorly. Indeed, a humour education program was shown to improve mental well-being outside of sport, presumably through enhanced coping (Crawford & Caltabiano, 2011). However, it is once again important to distinguish between adaptive and maladaptive styles as people who used more self-defeating humour in a conversation about their recovery from a divorce actually had more physical stress than those who used less or none (Frisby et al., 2016).

The second area that humour may be important to help athletes cope with is stress and/or anxiety within the context of their sport. At the time of writing this chapter, there appears to be only two studies conducted in sport which examined this possibility. The first was Giacobbi et al., (2004) which qualitatively examined the coping mechanisms used by female athletes ($n = 5$) in the transition to their first year of competition in university swimming. Amongst other mechanisms, the use of humour/fun was indicated as important during the beginning of the year to cope with sport challenges such as the intensity and frequency of training. The second was conducted by Niefer et al. (2010) and found that humour was cited, amongst other mechanisms, to help teenage female athletes ($n = 73$) cope with social physique anxiety. Outside of sport, there are multiple studies that have shown links between humour and coping with anxiety. For example, Colom et al. (2011) found that a humorous video helped to reduce university participants' ($n = 31$, 53% female) state-anxiety after a challenging task as well as from their baseline levels. Interestingly, the effect was stronger for optimistic participants, once again suggesting a connection between humour, coping, and optimism.

The third area to examine is the use of humour by athletes to cope with non-sport issues. In addition to the results mentioned above, Giacobbi et al. (2004) also showed that humour was mentioned as a coping mechanism to deal with non-sport (e.g., academic) challenges. Research from outside of sport corroborates the importance of humour in helping to cope with non-sport (i.e., everyday) challenges. For example, Martin et al. (2003) clearly shows that adaptive styles are positively related to psychological well-being and negatively related to outcomes such as depression whereas self-defeating humour (i.e., a maladaptive style) is negatively related to psychological well-being and positively related to depression. By encouraging the use of adaptive styles of humour by individual athletes, as well as within the player-coach relationship, and between teammates in a team setting, coaches can facilitate golfers coping with non-sport challenges.

The fourth area that is important to consider is that coaches and athletes are susceptible to burnout (Goodger et al., 2007) and thus both may benefit from using humour as a coping mechanism. Indeed, research from within sport suggests that certain coaching behaviours (e.g., showing empathy) are negatively related to athlete and coach burnout (Vealey et al., 1998). Further evidence comes from the workplace where the use of positive humour by supervisors and employees was related to reduced burnout and withdrawal from work (Mesmer-Magnus et al., 2012). Further to the point for coaches, humour has been indicated as important in reducing burnout in jobs where people have critical responsibilities for others including emergency service providers (Hageman, 2014), psychotherapists (Malinowski, 2013), and lecturers (Tumkaya, 2007). This suggests that not only can coaches' use of humour potentially reduce athletes' burnout but it may also reduce their own.

In each of the four areas discussed above, the use of humour may enhance coping in three ways: 1) the associated positive emotion of mirth can improve mood, 2) the cognitive processes can lead to reappraising situations as less threatening, and 3) it can enhance relationships which provide social support and a context for its use (Martin, 2007). Interestingly, the social component of humour use in coping also plays an important role in the emotional and cognitive areas. For example, there is a distinct kind of laughter that arises from social interactions that may be especially beneficial to coping (Scott et al., 2014). In a similar sense, the cognitions associated with humour that may aid in coping are almost always stimulated through social interactions. For example, Prisoners of War in Vietnam did not usually laugh or joke about their problems when alone but instead, humorous communications were used between individuals during or after a stressful experience to help cope with what happened (Henman, 2001). There is even evidence that the perceived availability of social support may mediate the positive relationship between adaptive styles of humour and coping (Dyck & Holtzman, 2013). There is also evidence of this in sport as the perceived availability of social support from teammates insulated athletes against burnout (DeFreese & Smith, 2013). This shows that the beneficial effects of humour in developing and maintaining relationships may be critical in enhancing a golfer's ability to cope.

Applied recommendations for golf coaches

Based on the research above, coaches should first and foremost use humour to initiate and maintain successful relationships with their golfers as this is a critical mediator in helping them to cope. Once a relationship is established, coaches should use and encourage their golfers to use adaptive styles of humour to enhance both of their abilities to cope with numerous challenges. For example, a well-timed humorous comment by a coach to a golfer, especially if he or she is optimistic, may help to reduce anxiety levels before a tournament. A coach's use of self-defeating humour may also help a golfer to cope but it should not be used by that coach to cope with their own challenges (e.g., burnout) as it may actually be detrimental. A recommendation for a coach who is helping a golfer to cope with a poor performance would be to make a joke about how "things can only get better from here" or about a humorous time when the coach performed poorly but recovered to be successful. Not only will these recommendations improve the golfer's positive affect but it may also help to inspire optimism.

Summary and future directions

Humour is a part of everyday life that often occurs spontaneously, however, people (e.g., coaches, athletes) can also strategically adapt their use of it to achieve desired outcomes. In essence, humour should be thought as a social skill that golf coaches can use to form and maintain strong relationships, improve their instruction, and enhance their own and their golfers' strategies to cope with challenges. To do this, a general rule is that golf coaches should use more adaptive styles of humour (i.e., self-enhancing and affiliative) and less maladaptive styles (i.e., self-defeating and aggressive). If coaches understand the beneficial as well as detrimental relationships that the use of humour has with important outcomes for golfers, they can use it to benefit themselves and their students, and maybe enjoy a laugh or two while doing so.

References

Banas, J. A.; Dunbar, N.; Rodrigues, D. & Liu, S-J. (2011) A Review of Humour in Educational Settings: Four Decades of Research, *Communication Education*, 60 (1), 115–144.

Buckman, K. (2010) *Why Did the Professor Cross the Road? How and Why College Professors Intentionally Use Humour in Their Teaching*, Unpublished PhD Thesis, Texas: Texas A&M University.

Burke, K.; Peterson, D. & Nix, C. (1995) The Effects of the Coaches Use of Humour on Female Volleyball Players Evaluation of Their Coaches, *Journal of Sport Behavior*, 18 (3), 83–91.

Buston, K. & Wight, D. (2004). Pupils Participation in Sex Education Lessons: Understanding Variation Across Classes, *Sex Education*, 4 (3), 285–301.

Cann, A. & Matson, C. (2014) Sense of Humour and Social Desirability: Understanding How Humour Styles Are Perceived, *Personality and Individual Differences*, 66, 176–180.

Carron, A.; Brawley, L. & Widmeyer, W. (1998) The Measurement of Cohesiveness in Sport Groups, In: J. Duda (Ed.) *Advances in Sport and Exercise Psychology Measurement*, Morgantown, WV: Fitness Information Technology, pp. 213–216.

Carron, A.; Colman, M.; Wheeler, J. & Stevens, D. (2002) Cohesion and Performance in Sport: A Meta-analysis, *Journal of Sport and Exercise Psychology*, 24 (2), 168–188.

Chauvet, S. & Hofmeyer, A. (2007) Humour as a Facilitative Style in Problem-based Learning Environments for Nursing Students, *Nurse Education Today*, 27 (4), 286–292.

Colom, G.; Alcover, C.; Sanchez-Curto, C. & Zararte-Osuna, J. (2011) Study of the Effect of Positive Humour as a Variable That Reduces Stress. Relationship of Humour with Personality and Performance Variables, *Psychology in Spain*, 15 (1), 9–21.

Connolly, J.; Baird, K.; Bravo, V.; Lovald, B.; Pepler, D. & Craig, W. (2015) Adolescents' Use of Affiliative and Aggressive Strategies During Conflict with Romantic Partners and Best-Friends, *European Journal of Developmental Psychology*, 12 (5), 549–564.

Crawford, S. & Caltabiano, N. (2011) Promoting Emotional Well-Being Through the Use of Humour, *The Journal of Positive Psychology*, 6 (3), 237–252.

DeFreese, J. & Smith, A. (2013) Teammate Social Support, Burnout, and Self-Determined Motivation in Collegiate Athletes, *Psychology of Sport and Exercise*, 14 (2), 258–265.

Dimengo, N. (2013) *20 Teams with a Great Sense of Humour*, Available at http://Bleacherreport.Com/Articles/1562803-20-Teams-With-A-Great-Sense-of-Humour (Accessed March 12, 2013).

Dyck, K. & Holtzman, S. (2013) Understanding Humour Styles and Well-being: The Importance of Social Relationships and Gender, *Personality and Individual Differences*, 55 (1), 53–58.

Frisby, B.; Horan, S. & Booth-Butterfield, M. (2016) The Role of Humour Styles and Shared Laughed in the Postdivorce Recovery Process, *Journal of Divorce and Remarriage*, 57 (1), 56–75.

Gaudreau, P.; Blondin, J.-P. & Lapierre, A.-M. (2002) Athletes' Coping During a Competition: Relationship of Coping Strategies with Positive Affect, Negative Affect and Performance-Goal Discrepancy, *Psychology of Sport and Exercise*, 3 (2), 125–150.

Giacobbi, P.; Lynn, T.; Wetherington, J.; Jenkins, J.; Bodendorf, M. & Langley, B. (2004) Stress and Coping During the Transition to University for First-Year Female Athletes, *The Sport Psychologist*, 18 (1), 1–20.

Goodger, K.; Gorley, T.; Lavallee, D. & Hardwood, C. (2007) Burnout in Sport: A Systematic Review, *The Sport Psychologist*, 21 (2), 127–151.

Gorham, J. & Christophel, D. (1990) The Relationship of Teachers Use of Humour in the Classroom to Immediacy and Student Learning, *Communication Education*, 37 (1), 40–53.

Grisaffe, C.; Blom, L. & Burke, K. (2003) The Effects of Head and Assistant Coaches' Uses of Humour on Collegiate Soccer Players' Evaluation of Their Coaches, *Journal of Sport Behavior*, 26 (2), 103–108.

Hageman, D. (2014) *The Efficacy of Positive Humour as a Coping Mechanism for Vicarious Occupational Stress Experienced by Emergency Service Provides*, Unpublished PhD Thesis, Minneapolis, MN: Walden University.

Hay, J. (2000) Functions of Humour in the Conversations of Men and Women, *Journal of Pragmatics*, 32 (6), 709–742.

Heitzmann, R. (2010) 10 Suggestions for Enhancing Lecturing, *The Education Digest*, 50–54.

Henman, L. (2001) Humour as a Coping Mechanism: Lessons From Pows, *Humour: International Journal of Humour Research*, 14 (1), 83–94.

Hester, N. (2010) *The Examination of Humour Usage and Its Relationship to Cohesion in Male Collegiate Basketball*, Unpublished PhD Thesis, Greensboro, NC: The University of North Carolina.

Janes, L. & Olson, J. (2015) Humour as an Abrasive or a Lubricant in Social Situations: Martineau Revisited, *Humour: International Journal of Humour Research*, 28 (2), 271–288.

Kuiper, N.; Aiken, A. & Pound, M. (2014) Humour Use, Reactions to Social Comments and Social Anxiety, *Humour: International Journal of Humour Research*, 27 (3), 423–439.

Kuiper, N. & Leite, C. (2010). Personality Impressions Associated with Four Distinct Humour Styles, *Scandinavian Journal of Psychology*, 51 (2), 115–122.

Lovorn, M. & Holaway, C. (2015) Teachers' Perceptions of Humour as a Classroom Teaching, Interaction, and Management Tool, *European Journal of Humour Research*, 3 (4), 24–35.

Malinowski, A. (2013) Characteristics of Job Burnout and Humour among Psychotherapists. *Humour: International Journal of Humour Research*, 26 (1), 117–133.

Martin, R. (2007) *The Psychology of Humour: An Integrative Approach*, Burlington, MA: Elsevier Academic Press.

Martin, R. & Kuiper, N. (1999) Daily Occurrence of Laughter: Relationships with Age, Gender and Type a Personality, *Humour: International Journal of Humour Research*, 12 (4), 355–384.

Martin, R.; Puhlik-Doris, P.; Larsen, G.; Gray, J. & Weir, K. (2003) Individual Differences in Uses of Humour and Their Relation to Psychological Well-being: Development of the Humour Styles Questionnaire, *Journal of Research in Personality*, 37 (1), 48–75.

Matarazzo, K.; Durik, A. & Delaney, M. (2010) The Effect of Humourous Instructional Materials on Interest in a Math Test, *Motivation and Emotion*, 34 (3), 293–305.

Mesmer-Magnus, J.; Glew, D. & Viswesvaran, C. (2012) A Meta-Analysis of Positive Humour in the Workplace, *Journal of Managerial Psychology*, 27 (2), 155–190.

Niefer, C.; McDonough, M. & Kowalski, K. (2010) Coping with Social Physique Anxiety among Adolescent Female Athletes, *International Journal of Sport Psychology*, 41, 369–386.

Norrick, N. & Spitz, A. (2008) Humour as a Resource for Mitigating Conflict in Interaction, *Journal of Pragmatics*, 40 (10), 1661–1686.

Provine, R. & Fischer, K. (1989) Laughing, Smiling and Talking: Relations to Sleeping and Social Contexts in Humans, *Ethology*, 83 (4), 295–305.

Rocca, K. (2004) College Student Attendance: Impact of Instructor Immediacy and Verbal Aggression, *Communication Education*, 53 (2), 185–195.

Romal, J. (2008) Use of Humour as a Pedagogical Tool for Accounting Education, *Academy of Educational Leadership Journal*, 12 (1), 83–106.

Ronglan, L. & Aggerholm, K. (2014) Humour Helps: Elite Sports Coaching as a Balancing Act, *Sports Coaching Review*, 3 (1), 33–45.

Schempp, P.; Mccullick, B.; Busch, C.; Webster, C. & Mason, I. (2006) The Self-Monitoring of Expert Sport Instructors, *International Journal of Sports Science and Coaching*, 1 (1), 25–35.

Scott, S.; Lavan, N.; Chen, S. & Mcgettigan, C. (2014) The Social Life of Laughter, *Trends in Cognitive Sciences*, 18 (12), 618–620.

Simonds, R. (Producer) & Dugan, D. (Director) (1996) *Happy Gilmore* [Motion Picture], United States: Universal Pictures.

Sprecher, S. & Regan, P. C. (2002) Liking Some Things (In Some People) More than Others: Partner Preferences in Romantic Relationships and Friendships, *Journal of Social and Personal Relationships*, 19 (4), 463–481.

Torok, S.; McMorris, R. & Lin, W. (2004) Is Humour an Appreciated Teaching Tool? Perceptions of Professors' Teaching Styles and Use of Humour, *College Teaching*, 52 (1), 14–20.

Treger, S.; Sprecher, S. & Erber, R. (2013) Laughing and Liking: Exploring the Interpersonal Effects of Humour Use in Initial Social Interactions, *European Journal of Social Psychology*, 43 (6), 532–543.

Tumkaya, S. (2007) Burnout and Humour Relationship among University Lecturers, *Humour: International Journal of Humour Research*, 20 (1), 73–92.

Vealey, R.; Armstrong, L.; Comar, W. & Greenleaf, C. A. (1998) Influence of Perceived Coaching Behaviors on Burnout and Competitive Anxiety in Female College Athletes, *Journal of Applied Sport Psychology*, 10 (2), 297–318.

Wanzer, M.B.; Frymier, A.B. & Irwin, J. (2010) An Explanation of the Relationship Between Instructor Humour and Student Learning: Instructional Humour Processing Theory, *Communication Education*, 59 (1), 1–18.

Webster, C. (2010) Relating Student Recall to Expert and Novice Teachers' Instructional Communication: An Investigation Using Receiver Selectivity Theory, *Physical Education and Sport Pedagogy*, 15 (4), 419–433.

Wilson, M.; Hawkins, B. & Joyner, B. (2015) An Investigation of Optimism Between Players and Coaches in NCAA Men's Division 1 Golf, *Journal of Sport Behavior*, 38 (1), 118–140.

Zeedyk, M. (2006) Detective Work on Statistics Street: Teaching Statistics Through Humourous Analogy, *Psychology Learning and Teaching*, 5 (2), 97–109.

39

RESEARCH ON GOLF INSTRUCTION AND COACHING

Paul G. Schempp, Bryan A. McCullick and Collin A. Webster

Introduction

This chapter reviews and summarizes research completed on golf instruction and coaching. The terms 'coach', 'instructor' and 'teacher' will be used interchangeably. The authors acknowledge that there are differences between the role of coach and the role of teacher or instructor. In many places throughout the world, however, those who teach golf also serve as coaches to elite players and golf teams. Mike Bender, for example, is the coach for Masters and Open Champion Zach Johnson, yet he teaches golf to hundreds of amateur golfers of all abilities and skill at his academy in Lake Mary, Florida. While there are professionals whose sole responsibilities are coaching (e.g., university and national team coaches), their work functions for the same primary purpose as teachers – improving player performance. Consequently, for the purposes of this chapter, research was reviewed that specifically addressed development and actions of those whose professional work is intended to improve the playing performance of golfers.

The chapter opens with a review of research pertaining to formal education and professional development of golf instructors and coaches. Next, a review of research on the skills and practices of golf instructors is presented followed by communication and additional skills necessary for effective golf instruction. The purpose of the chapter is to understand the research completed to date on golf instruction and those responsible for improving the playing performance of golfers. The authors were particularly interested in using this research to identify characteristics of exceptional or expert teachers and coaches of golf.

Before beginning the review, it would be imperative to understand the constitution of an expert coach or teacher. As Wharton et al. (2015) recognize, an expert is currently a contested term. For some, the definition is steeped in cognitive processes, experience and years of deliberate practice (Erickson et al., 2007; Ericsson & Pool, 2016). Expert coaches are perceived by some to be those who coach at the highest level of the sport (Horton et al., 2005). It is common to see a blend of characteristics such as a minimum number of years of professional experience, possessing the highest certification available, honors and recognitions, or working with elite athletes (Schempp, 2006; Greenwood et al., 2014). For the purposes of this chapter, we have included research and literature that engaged 'expert' golf instructors or coaches as participants, regardless of the selection criteria or definition. Also, included in the chapter are studies of golf instructors and coaches themselves or the practice of golf instruction, regardless of the level of instructional expertise. These studies were included to better understand the qualities necessary for one person to effectively teach another the skills and knowledge needed to play the sport of golf.

Golf teacher or coach education and development

A significant factor in a sport's perpetual growth is the quality of coaching within the sport (Cushion et al., 2003). The role of the coach has become almost unequivocally recognized as an occupation requiring extensive training and specialized knowledge, both of which are character-istics of a profession. Many professional golf associations (e.g., PGAs of America, Asia, Australia, Canada, Europe, Great Britain and Ireland; Ladies Professional Golf Association – LPGA) have established programs ensuring that coaches and instructors are certified and competent. Concurrently, as these programs were burgeoning, a handful of scholars recognized that the edu-cation of coaches was a fertile research area. Unfortunately, the majority of published scholarly work has been limited, with a few exceptions, to studies conducted in the United States, but appears to have implications for scholars and practitioners around the globe who have an interest in golf teacher or coach education (GTE) and development.

Golf teacher or coach education

While research on sport instructor and/or coach education has robustly increased since 1995 (McCullick et al., 2006), the study of GTE has not. An extensive literature review revealed that the first academic publication related to GTE programs was Hamilton's (1976) piece that was originally published in 1970 and reprinted 6 years later (Hamilton, 1976). Far from an empirical study, it is difficult to tell if Hamilton's essay about an aspiring golf teacher attending a "Golf Pro School" (p. 82) is a tongue-cheek allegory of GTE or a descriptive account of his time in a program. While an amusing read, the article lent little to what we know about GTE programs.

Conducted two decades later, the first study of golf instructors' professional knowledge investigated the sources of expert golf instructors' knowledge (Schempp et al., 1999). Although not a GTE study, it is noteworthy that GTE programs were found to be a less influential knowl-edge source than instructors' experiences as a student, player and teacher. These findings could be attributed to the teachers' expertise level or having participated in programs that had equal focus on being a club professional. Nonetheless, the findings indicated that formal GTE had little impact on the teachers' knowledge base.

It was not until 2002 that scholars began to take an interest in formal GTE programs. The first foray into this important and unstudied area emerged when McCullick et al. (2002) analyzed the LPGA's National Education Program (NEP). The researchers sought to analyze the program using the tenets of an existing theoretical framework outlining best practices for effective teacher education (Goodlad, 1990). The findings indicated the LPGA's NEP adhered to many presup-positions of effective teacher education. From the findings, a set of proposed guidelines emerged for developing effective GTE programs. Perhaps the most important findings from this study were that GTE faculty must: (a) be in consensus regarding the aims, standards and processes of the program, (b) care not only about teaching golf but also about GTE, and (c) model the pedagogical behaviors being promoted in the GTE. Data revealed two other inclusions essential to an effective GTE program surrounding assessment issues. The first imperative was that GTE programs should formally hold accountable those enrolled for competent instruction. The second was that the program had to be constantly assessed for its ability to meet its goals and the changing nature of golf instruction. While McCullick and colleagues' study provided a basis for future research on formal GTEs, the methodological rigor left something to be desired and thus the findings warranted caution.

Seeking a deeper analysis into the operations of GTE programs, McCullick et al. (2005) again analyzed the LPGA's NEP. In the second study, data were collected from those enrolled in the NEP. Using a more demanding, and perhaps more appropriate, qualitative research design, the findings shed light on what those learning to teach golf believed to be the most salient aspects of their formal education. One of the strongest themes to emerge was a GTE faculty possessing a high level of relevant content knowledge and pedagogical knowledge. The enrollees also lauded the introduction to and integration of contemporary research, especially if those who had conducted it were the ones presenting it. Perhaps the most encouraging aspect emerging from this study was that the field now had a reasonable association between GTEs and other teacher education programs as the findings paralleled those from the ample body of teacher education scholarship. As a result, GTE researchers were provided with a larger literature base to inform additional and more targeted studies on GTE programs. It should be noted however that, within the larger field of coach education, some scholars have critiqued these studies as being somewhat able to provide answers to a few critical questions but "quick (perhaps too quick) to offer solutions to problems that remain poorly understood" (Piggott, 2012, p. 6) and being conducted from only one perspective (Werthner & Trudel, 2006).

Unfortunately, this opportunity went nearly without capitalization. The next time GTE programs appear in the academic literature is Phillpots' (2007) narrative, which includes political implications for developing a coaching certificate program in the United Kingdom. He provides an account of the National Governing Board (NGB) entering the area of golf coach education that was previously the sole purview of the Professional Golfers' Association of Great Britain and Ireland (PGA GB&I). Golf instruction and coaching within the United Kingdom and Ireland was traditionally delivered by certified PGA Professionals. However, the desire of the governing bodies to standardize coaching and address a wider social agenda. The change led to an overhaul of coaching and coach education driven by recommendations from the Coaching Task Force. The development of a four-level structure for coaching and a formalized and standardized coach education programme known as the United Kingdom Coaching Certificate (UKCC) was the result of these recommendations. Within golf, this development was led by the PGA of GB & I in partnership with other governing bodies from the amateur game (Phillpots, 2007).

The narrative reveals the possibilities for GTEs when the focus is on teacher/coach competency. Comparing this to the recent trend of competing GTE programs that have little restriction on whom can become a golf instructor (e.g., The United States Golf Teachers Federation; World Golf Teachers' Federation) one can see that further study GTE programs is imperative for the future growth and expansion of the golf industry. If GTE programs continue without empirical study that is aimed at improving the process of becoming and learning to be a golf teacher/coach, there will remain little evidence to support the premise that these programs actually promote or improve the quality of golf instruction.

In a special issue dedicated to GTE in the *International Journal of Sports Science and Coaching*, Jenkins (2014) argued that golf instruction has a focus on professionalism or "matters of quality and standards" (p. 693). The conundrum, however, is that the preparation of golf instructors results in professionalization "which is concerned with occupational status" (p. 692). He further proposed that, as in the preparation of physicians and other professions, golf should have another layer of preparation that would "facilitate the development of professionalism in golf coaching" (p. 710) by systematically developing a graduate GTE degree. The 56 commentaries published in response to Jenkins' treatise from differing factions uniformly suggested that such a degree was not only needed but also important for the future of golf instruction and GTE. Less apparent, however, was an agreement on the content, eligibility, or the professional and ethical requirements of such a program.

Golf teacher/coach professional development

While the majority of GTE literature has analyzed formal certification and education programs, there have been two studies that analyzed self-monitoring and its role in the continuous professional development of expert golf instructors (Schempp et al., 2006; Schempp et al., 2007). While on the surface these studies are seemingly unrelated to GTE, exploring how golf teachers/instructors assess and maintain their own performance is of the utmost importance in understanding how other or aspiring teachers can be taught to do this in their careers.

Thirty-one of *GOLF Magazine*'s Top 100 Teachers in North America completed a written survey which asked them to list aspects of their teaching they considered strengths and aspects they considered weaknesses (Schempp et al., 2006). The findings from the first study found that the teachers identified both goals and actions in their self-monitoring and development strategies. Self-improvement goals included strengthening communication, adjusting personal lifestyle, examining teaching perspectives and increasing professional learning. In the second study (Schempp et al., 2007), teachers were requested to identify strategies they used to maintain their strengths and improve their weaknesses. The findings revealed that their most used strategies for self-improvement involved seeking help from others, reading, using technology, developing business strategies and adapting teaching practices.

Teaching skills and content

The science of teaching and instruction began to establish itself in the early 1970s largely due to the development of specific research instruments and the adoption of appropriate scientific protocols for analyzing and understanding the practices of sport and physical activity instruction (Locke, 1977). By the 1980s, 'sport pedagogy' was a recognized and robust field within the larger domain of sport science (Haag, 1989). The term retains its' currency today. This research has led to a robust supply of empirical information to help direct, guide, and stimulate player development and student learning in golf. This section summarizes the research on technology, teaching behavior, and instructional content that engaged golf instructors and coaches as the research participants.

Technology

The use of video/electronic recording has more recently become standard fare in many golf lessons, and one can even effectively use video for self-analysis (Breed & Midland, 2008; St. Pierre & Smith, 2012). An interesting study compared video instruction to verbal and self-guided instruction (Guadagnoli et al., 2002). The 30 participants were assigned to one of three groups: a) verbal instruction, b) video-assisted instruction, and c) self-guided instruction. Each group had four 90-minute practice sessions and 11 participants were required to strike 15 golf balls, with a 7-iron, from an artificial turf mat for distance and accuracy. The results showed that all groups were equal on the pre-test, but in the final assessment the two instruction groups performed better than the self-guided group, with the video-assisted group performing best. It appears, therefore, that video can significantly aid the instructional process.

A study comparing golf rules instruction using a computer-assisted instruction (CAI) module and a lecture method found no difference between the groups on a post-instruction test (Adams

& Kandt, 1991). It was, however, interesting to note that the students receiving CAI were able to complete the instruction in approximately half the time it took the traditional lecture method students to complete the course. The researchers consequently concluded that CAI can be an effective alternative for teaching the rules of golf.

Teaching behavior

Teaching and coaching sports have benefitted from an increasing prominence in recent research literature. In the past decade in particular, a considerable number of scholars have analyzed instructional behavior over a wide range of sports and consequently developed a body of knowledge based on pedagogic principles (Jones, 2006; Lyle & Cushion, 2010; Vinson et al., 2016). While limited in its' contribution, teaching behavior in golf has received some attention, with much of it focused on expert instructional practices.

A study by Schempp et al. (2004) identified the dominant instructional interaction patterns of 22 expert golf instructors. The study participants were selected by the LPGA as nationally recognized for their superior teaching skills. The instructors were videotaped teaching a 60-minute lesson to a novice college-age woman with no previous golf experience. The prevailing instructional interaction pattern of these expert teachers was comprised in extensive explanations and demonstrations followed by directions for student practice. The students followed the directions by practicing skills and received praise for their achievements from the instructor. The high rates of directions and praise from teachers prompted extensive student practice. Additionally, the teachers asked questions throughout the lesson, prompting student discussions of subject-related topics. The discussions revealed thoughtful analysis and skill-improvement related insights and questions by the students and indicated the expert teachers' students are more than passive participants in a golf lesson.

Instructional differences due to student gender were a topic of a study by MacKinnon (2011). A survey was administered to 100 female golf professionals with regard to their views on golf instruction for women. The results indicated that the majority of survey participants believe there are certain 'best practices' for teaching female golfers. Firstly, anatomical and physiological differences may influence both the substance and style of instruction. Secondly, because women often feel uncomfortable being new to a male dominated sport, they may need to be accompanied or given an orientation to the environment, the terminology, and the etiquette of the sport to help put them at ease. Thirdly, women often prefer to receive instruction away from the public eye where there is less pressure and less fear of embarrassment. Fourthly, when teaching women it is advisable to first tell them what they are doing right, and to use positive reinforcement throughout the lesson to build the critical confidence necessary for learning to take place. Finally, women appear to benefit from opportunities to learn the sport in a social environment (i.e., consider offering group instruction for players and their friends).

Instructional content

Research on golf instruction has focused on what teachers do (behavior) as well as what teachers say (content). The effectiveness of any golf lesson resides in the combination of an instructor's actions and information offered. Several completed studies have provided an informative picture on the instructional content of effective teachers.

An interesting insight into the instructional practices of expert teachers was found in a study examining metaphors used by expert golf instructors (St. Pierre & Smith, 2012). Fourteen individuals selected as Top 100 instructors by *GOLF Magazine* in North America participated in the study. The researchers found that not only was metaphor use pervasive in expert golf instruction, but that it resulted in immediate changes in student behavior and created memorable learning experiences. Further, when students were called several weeks after the lesson they could recall almost every metaphor used in the lesson and many reported that their performance continued to improve due to recollections of the metaphors during their practice and play.

It has been found that expert golf instructors do not, however, always agree on the content students should master. In a study examining content knowledge, major differences were found in how expert instructors conceived the 'fundamentals' of golf (Grant et al., 2012). Specifically, 50 of *GOLF Magazine's* Top 100 Teachers in North America answered the question: 'What are the fundamentals of golf that all students should learn?' Two groups of 'fundamentals' were identified. Based on the data analysis, teachers were either classified as *Element Instructors* or *Compound Instructors*. *Element Instructors* were characterized by agreement within their group that grip, posture, and alignment were the fundamental skills that all golfers should master. *Compound Instructors* had no set of agreed upon fundamentals as their topics included various combinations of *plane, contact, hand control, face, rhythm, speed,* and *rotation.* The take home lesson from this was that a student can expect to go to two or more golf instructors and hear very different information during the instruction.

Golfers are sometimes told by instructors to 'not think' about something. 'Don't think about hitting it in the water' and 'Don't think about mechanics during your swing' are two common examples. Despite it being an apparently common instructional occurrence, the impact of avoidant or negative instructions on skilled performance in sport has received little research attention. de la Pena et al. (2008) conducted one of the few studies in this area and reported that novice golfers who were instructed not to leave a putt short of a circle, overcompensated by leaving their putts significantly longer than they did prior to the instruction. In a more recent study, it was found that high-skilled golfers' overall putting proficiency was unaffected by avoidant instructions, while low-skilled golfers' performance was significantly degraded due to break downs in their putting stroke (Toner et al., 2013). Overcompensation appears more prevalent in low-skilled rather than high-skilled golfers. Consequently, a golf instructor may do well to closely monitor the degree of compensation students make as a result of instructor comments, particularly when teaching beginners to prevent specific actions or outcomes from occurring.

Another study comparing instructional content impact mediated by player expertise examined the influence of internal and external attention instructions on the performance of a pitch shot (Perkins-Ceccato et al., 2003). Under internal focus of attention instructions, the participants were told to concentrate on the form of the golf swing and to adjust the force of their swing depending on the distance of the shot. For the external focus of attention conditions, the participants were told to concentrate on hitting the ball as close to the target pylon as possible. The most intriguing finding was an interaction of skill with focus of attention instructions on performance variability. The highly skilled golfers performed better with external attention instructions and the low-skill golfers performed better with the internal focus of attention instructions.

A study by Shafizadeh et al. (2011) investigated the effect of different sources of external attentional focus on learning to putt. Thirty students (12 men, 18 women) were divided into three groups. The target group focused on the hole, the club swing group focused on executing the club swing, and the target-club swing group attended to both. All participants performed 50 trials in the acquisition phase and 10 trials in the 24-hr. delayed retention phase. Results revealed the target-club swing focus group had better scores in the acquisition and retention phases. The researchers concluded that external focus instruction that helped learners to integrate target cues with action cues was more effective in skill learning than external-focused only instructions.

The influence of varying the content of verbal-motor instructions with an internal versus external focus on the kinematics and outcome of a putting task was investigated by Munzert et al. (2014). Thirty novice golfers performed 120 trials with the instruction to focus their attention either on performing a pendulum-like movement (internal) or on the desired ball path (external). After 20 retention trials on Day 2, they performed 20 transfer trials with the opposite instruction. The results showed that the external instruction improved the performance outcome, while switching to an internal focus instruction resulted in a more pendulum-like putting stroke. It appears, therefore, that if the purpose of instruction for novices is technique improvement, internal cue instructions are more appropriate, and if the instructional goal is improved performance external cues are the better choice.

Three separate experiments were conducted with 168 college students to determine the acquisition, transfer, and retention of a putting task (Oliveira et al., 2013). The collective results of the experiments underscored previous research on the positive effects of instruction first focusing on internal attention followed by an external attentional focus when teaching beginners.

A similar series of studies were conducted by Christina and Alpenfels (2014) using 45 adult male, experienced golfers with a mean age of 65 years and an average handicap of 18.3. The golfers were randomly selected to the external cue group, internal cue group, or control group. In the first study, the golfers were instructed using the group-appropriate cues to make a swing path change using a 6-iron. In the second study, the golfers were also instructed to make a swing path change with group appropriate cues, but with a driver. Study 1 findings revealed that the instructor-selected external cue group learned and retained more of an inside-out swing path than either the instructor-selected internal cue group or participant-selected cue group. Study 2 results showed that both the instructor-selected external cue and participant selected cue groups learned and retained more of an inside-out swing path with a driver than the instructor-selected internal cue group. These findings provide two lines of evidence that reveal the benefit of using an instructor-selected, external focus of attention cue when teaching experienced players to learn to change (improve) their swing path.

Considering the combined findings of research on instructional content in golf, it appears that there is benefit from both internal and external attentional focus in golf instruction. Focusing instruction on internal cues appears particularly appropriate for beginners who are attempting to master golf skills, while external cues appear to provide greater benefit for more experienced players looking to improve performance.

Communication skills

Expert golf instructors closely monitor their instructional communication (Schempp et al., 2006), attend to both subject mastery and affective learning functions of their communication skills when teaching (Webster, 2009a), and use both direct and indirect teaching approaches (Webster et al., 2009). By way of their advanced cognitive attributes, these exceptional teachers localize learners' individual needs and custom fit communication to each student on a case-by-case basis.

This process begins with experts devoting several minutes at the start of their lessons to asking the student a series of questions designed with the dual purpose of communicating immediacy (i.e., approachability) and ascertaining a wealth of background information (Baker et al., 1998; Schempp et al., 2004; Webster, 2009a). For example, when working with a new student, experts asked questions about the student's golf experiences, other sport experiences, reasons for taking a golf lesson, hobbies, personal and professional goals, and physical limitations. Similar to other research findings (Gorham, 1988; Velez & Cano, 2008), the experts' questions served an affective learning function, as students indicated that the questions helped to create a comfortable learning environment, made them feel that the teacher cared about them and was easy to work with, and increased their motivation to learn (Webster, 2010). While interviewing the student, experts also harnessed their perceptual acuity and information processing skills to interpret student nonverbal communication behaviors.

After interviewing the student, expert golf instructors' communication behaviors continue to reflect prodigious cognitive skill. Webster (2009a) found that experts adapted their communication to the student in myriad ways throughout the remainder of the lesson. For instance, they matched their nonverbal behaviors to those of the student and made multiple connections between the lesson content and the student's other sport experiences, hobbies, and goals. Making the content personally relevant to students is an effective strategy for supporting affective learning outcomes (Webster et al., 2011). Additionally, students of expert golf instructors felt that this strategy helped them to recall the target information from the lesson (Webster, 2010), which can be viewed as an important step in mastering subject matter content. In another study, Webster and his colleagues (2009) found that expert golf instructors used a variety of strategies to close their lessons, including one in which the expert solicited questions from the student and then used the questions as bridges to review the target information from the lesson. These examples of communication adaptability and flexibility illustrate experts' abilities to rapidly access and retrieve from memory the student's verbal and nonverbal communication behavior from the lesson opening, as well as to quickly connect student questions to broad areas of focus from the entire lesson (Webster, 2009b).

Implications for the game

The review and summary of golf teaching research provided in this chapter offers both the scholar and practitioner useful information for understanding the practices and procedures necessary for meeting the instructional needs of golfers. The research to date on golf instructor education places a strong premium on the quality of the faculty conducting the program. This means that students appreciate and benefit most from faculty who share a wealth of knowledge of subject matter and the effective teaching of that subject matter. Education and professional development continues long after the certification program ends. Self-monitoring appears to be a method used by expert instructors to continually identify and improve their pedagogical practices (Schempp et al., 2006). Additionally, experts use a large variety of resources to continually pack their knowledge stores. Teaching experience, peers, students, and professional conferences top the list of knowledge sources for these excellent teachers (Schempp et al., 1999).

Research indicates that there are many effective skills and technologies available to assist a golf instructor in promoting student learning. Video and computer assisted instruction have both proven themselves in helping students learn golf (Guadagnoli et al., 2002). A teacher's behavior, however, remains the key tool at their disposal for prompting student learning. Expert teachers were found to ask many questions to which students would provide thoughtful, analytic responses that reinforced learning. They also provided extensive opportunities for students to engage in content focused discussions with teachers (Webster, 2009a). Due to the number of directions, amount of time allocated and reinforcing feedback by these teachers, students enjoyed a great deal of time to practice and master the skills being taught (Schempp et al., 2004).

During instruction, it appears that there is benefit from a teacher providing the student with both internally and externally focused cues when teaching swing skills. This, however, appears mediated by the experience and the level of golfing expertise of the student. Focusing instruction on internal cues seems particularly appropriate for beginners who are attempting to master golf skills, while external cues appear to provide greater benefit for more experienced players looking to improve performance (Christina & Alpenfels, 2014). But for a teacher to have information remembered and impact performance, using metaphors to explain golf concepts has proven to be a sound instructional strategy (St. Pierre & Smith, 2012).

Summary and future directions

The research on golf instruction, to date, provides useful and powerful information for both golf instructors and those conducting golf instruction education. There is, however, still a great many questions and insights left unstudied. Despite its' prominence in golf, there remains little empirical guidance in using technology to advance student learning. Golf instruction would also benefit from more in-depth analysis of the practices of expert and elite coaches, as well as the struggles and successes of novice teachers. Finally, experimenting with education and professional development strategies would also appear to pay dividends in improving golf instruction and coaching.

References

Adams, T. & Kandt, G. (1991) Computer-Assisted Instruction vs. Lecture Methods in Teaching the Rules of Golf, *Physical Educator*, 48 (3), 146–151.

Baker, K.; Schempp, P.; Hardin, B. & Clark, B. (1998) The Rituals and Routines of Expert Golf Instruction, In: M. Farrally & A. Cochran (Eds.) *Science and Golf III: Proceedings of the World Scientific Congress of Golf*, Champaign, IL: Human Kinetics, pp. 271–281.

Breed, M. & Midland, G. (2008) *The Picture-Perfect Golf Swing: The Complete Guide to Golf Swing Video Analysis*, New York, NY: Atria.

Christina, B. & Alpenfels, E. (2014) Influence of Attentional Focus on Learning a Swing Path Change, *International Journal of Golf Science*, 3 (1), 35–49.

Cushion, C.; Armour, K. & Jones, R. (2003) Coach Education a Continuing Professional Development: Experience and Learning to Coach, *Quest*, 55, 215–230.

de la Peña, D.; Murray, N. & Janelle, C. (2008) Implicit Overcompensation: The Influence of Negative Self-Instructions on Performance of a Self-Paced Motor Task, *Journal of Sports Sciences*, 26 (12), 1323–1331.

Erickson, K.; Côté, J. & Fraser-Thomas, J. (2007) Sport Experiences, Milestones, and Educational Activities Associated with High-Performance Coaches' Development, *The Sports Psychologist*, 21 (3), 302–316.

Ericsson, A. & Pool, R. (2016) *Peak: Secrets from the New Science of Expertise*, Boston, MA: Houghton, Mifflin, Harcourt.

Goodlad, J.I. (1990) *Teachers for Our Nation's Schools*, San Francisco, CA: Joessy-Bass.

Gorham, J. (1988) The Relationship Between Verbal Teacher Immediacy Behaviors and Student Learning, *Communication Education*, 37, 40–53.

Grant, M.; Mccullick, B.; Schempp, P. & Grant, J. (2012) 'Experts' Content Knowledge of Fundamentals, *International Journal of Sports Science & Coaching*, 7 (2), 399–410.

Greenwood, D.; Davids, K. & Renshaw, I. (2014) Experiential Knowledge of Expert Coaches Can Help Identify Informational Constraints on Performance of Dynamic Interceptive Actions, *Journal of Sports Sciences*, 32 (4), 328–335.

Guadagnoli, M.; Holcomb, W. & Davis, M. (2002) The Efficacy of Video Feedback for Learning the Golf Swing, *Journal of Sports Sciences*, 20 (8), 615–622.

Haag, H. (1989) Research in "Sport Pedagogy": One Field of Theoretical Study in the Science of Sport, *International Review of Education*, 35 (1), 5–16.

Hamilton, O. (1976) The Golf Pro School, *Quest*, 25 (1), 82–85.

Horton, S.; Baker, J. & Deakin, J. (2005) Experts in Action: A Systematic Observation of 5 National Team Coaches, *International Journal of Sport Psychology*, 36, 299–319.

Jenkins, S. (2014) Professionalism, Golf Coaching, and a Master of Science Degree, *International Journal of Sports Science & Coaching*, 9, 693–715.

Jones, R. (2006) How Can Educational Concepts Inform Sports Coaching? In: R. Jones (Ed.) *The Sports Coach as Educator: Re-Conceptualising Sports Coaching*, London: Routledge, pp. 3–13.

Locke, L. (1977) Research on Teaching Physical Education: New Hope for a Dismal Science, *Quest*, 27 (1), 2–16.

Lyle, J. & Cushion, C. (Eds.) (2010) *Sports Coaching: Professionalisation and Practice*, London: Churchill Livingstone.

MacKinnon, V. (2011) Techniques for Instructing Female Athletes in Traditionally Male Sports: A Case Study of LPGA Teaching Professionals, *The International Journal of Sport and Society*, 2, 75–86.

McCullick, B., Belcher, D. & Schempp, P. (2005) What Works in Coaching and Sport Instructor Certification Programs: The Participants' View, *Physical Education and Sport Pedagogy*, 10 (2), 121–137.

McCullick, B.; Schempp, P. & Clark, B. (2002) An Analysis of an Effective Golf Teacher Education Program: The LPGA National Education Program, In: E. Thain (Ed.) *Science and Golf IV: Proceedings of the World Scientific Congress of Golf*, London: Routledge, pp. 218–230.

McCullick, B.; Schempp, P.; Hsu, S.; Jung, J.; Vickers, B. & Schuknecht, G. (2006) An Analysis of the Working Memory of Expert Sport Instructors, *Journal of Teaching in Physical Education*, 25, 149–165.

Munzert, J.; Maurer, H. & Reiser, M. (2014) Verbal-Motor Attention-Focusing Instructions Influence Kinematics and Performance on a Golf-Putting Task, *Journal of Motor Behavior*, 46 (5), 309–318.

Oliveira, T.; Denardi, R.; Tani, G. & Corrêa, U. (2013) Effects of Internal and External Attentional Foci on Motor Skill Learning: Testing the Automation Hypothesis, *Human Movement*, 14 (3), 194–199.

Perkins-Ceccato, N.; Passmore, S. & Lee, T. (2003) Effects of Focus of Attention Depend on Golfers' Skill, *Journal of Sports Sciences*, 21 (8), 593–600.

Phillpots, K. (2007) The Development of the UK Coaching Certificate for Golf, *Annual Review of Golf Coaching*, 1, 167–179.

Piggott, D. (2012) Coaches' Experiences of Formal Coach Education: A Critical Sociological Investigation, *Sport, Education and Society*, 17 (4), 535–554.

Schempp, P. (2006) How Experts See What the Rest of Us Miss, *Development and Learning in Organizations*, 20 (4), 16–17.

Schempp, P.; McCullick, B.; Busch, C.; Webster, C. & Sannen-Mason, I. (2006) The Self-Monitoring of Expert Sport Instructors, *International Journal of Sports Science & Coaching*, 1 (1), 25–36.

Schempp, P.; McCullick, B.; St. Pierre, P.; Woorons, S.; You, J. & Clark, B. (2004) Expert Golf Instructors' Student-Teacher Interaction Patterns, *Research Quarterly for Exercise and Sport*, 75 (1), 60–70.

Schempp, P.; Templeton, C. & Clark, E. (1999) The Knowledge Acquisition of Expert Golf Instructors, In: M. Farrally & A. Cochran (Eds.) *Science and Golf III: Proceedings of the World Scientific Congress of Golf*, Champaign, IL: Human Kinetics, pp. 295–301.

Schempp, P.; Webster, C.; McCullick, B.; Busch, C. & Mason, I. (2007) How the Best Get Better: An Analysis of the Self-Monitoring Strategies Used by Expert Golf Instructors, *Sport, Education, & Society*, 12 (2), 175–192.

Shafizadeh, M.; McMorris, T. & Sproule, J. (2011) Effect of Different External Attention of Focus Instruction on Learning of Golf Putting Skill, *Perceptual & Motor Skills*, 113 (2), 622–670.

St. Pierre, P. & Smith, M. (2012) The Role of Metaphor in Sport Instruction: Insights from a Study of Expert Golf Instructors, *International Journal of Coaching Science*, 6 (1), 27–44.

Toner, J.; Moran, A. & Jackson, R. (2013) The Effects of Avoidant Instructions on Golf Putting Proficiency and Kinematics, *Psychology of Sport & Exercise*, 14 (4), 501–507.

Velez, J.J. & Cano, J. (2008) The Relationship Between Teacher Immediacy and Student Motivation, *Journal of Agricultural Education*, 49 (3), 76–86.

Vinson, D.; Brady, A.; Moreland, B. & Judge, N. (2016) Exploring Coach Behaviours, Session Contexts and Key Stakeholder Perceptions of Non-Linear Coaching Approaches in Youth Sport, *International Journal of Sports Science & Coaching*, 11 (1), 54–68.

Webster, C. (2009a) Expert Teachers' Instructional Communication in Golf, *International Journal of Sport Communication*, 2, 205–222.

Webster, C. (2009b) Found in Translation: How Expert Teachers Make Communication Work, In: L. Housner; M. Metzler; P. Schempp & T. Templin (Eds.) *Historic Traditions and Future Directions in Research on Teaching*, Morgantown, WV: Fitness Information Technology, pp. 105–110.

Webster, C. (2010) Relating Student Recall to Expert and Novice Teachers' Instructional Communication: An Investigation Using Receiver Selectivity Theory, *Physical Education and Sport Pedagogy*, 15 (4), 419–433.

Webster, C.; Connolly, G. & Schempp, P. (2009) The Finishing Touch: Anatomy of Expert Lesson Closures in Sport, *Physical Education and Sport Pedagogy*, 14 (1), 73–87.

Webster, C.; Mîndrilă, D. & Weaver, G. (2011) The Influence of State Motivation, Content Relevance and Affective Learning on High School Students' Intentions to Utilize Class Content Following Completion of Compulsory Physical Education, *Journal of Teaching in Physical Education*, 30 (3), 231–247.

Werthner, P. & Trudel, P. (2006) A New Theoretical Perspective for Understanding How Coaches Learn to Coach, *Sport Psychologist*, 20 (2), 198–212.

Wharton, L.; Rossi, T.; Nash, C. & Renshaw, I. (2015) How Would You Recognise an Expert Coach If You Saw One? *International Journal of Sports Science & Coaching*, 10 (2/3), 577–588.

INDEX

Printed in Great Britain
by Amazon